Contributions to Economics

The series *Contributions to Economics* provides an outlet for innovative research in all areas of economics. Books published in the series are primarily monographs and multiple author works that present new research results on a clearly defined topic, but contributed volumes and conference proceedings are also considered. All books are published in print and ebook and disseminated and promoted globally. The series and the volumes published in it are indexed by Scopus and ISI (selected volumes).

Mehmet Baha Karan

A History of Stock Exchanges

The Role of Institutions in Shaping Market Evolution

Springer

Mehmet Baha Karan
Department of Business Administration
Hacettepe University
Ankara, Türkiye

ISSN 1431-1933 ISSN 2197-7178 (electronic)
Contributions to Economics
ISBN 978-3-032-07787-5 ISBN 978-3-032-07788-2 (eBook)
https://doi.org/10.1007/978-3-032-07788-2

Translation from the Turkish language edition: "Tarihin İzinde Borsalar: Doğu Pazarlarından Wall Street'e Renkli Bir Hikaye" by Mehmet Baha Karan, © The author 2024. Published by Gazi Kitapevi. All Rights Reserved.

Previously published by Gazi Kitapevi

This Springer imprint is published by the registered company Springer Nature Switzerland AG
The registered company address is: Gewerbestrasse 11, 6330 Cham, Switzerland

Preface

This book was written to address financial markets and securities exchanges, which were not fully covered in our 2024 work, A History of Banks, published by Springer in collaboration with Prof. Jacob Wijngaard and Prof. Wim Westerman, from a similar historical and institutional perspective. The core content of the book is an expanded and updated version of the Turkish edition, "Tarihin İzinde Borsalar," published by Gazi Kitabevi in Ankara in 2024. The text has been developed through a peer review process conducted by Prof. Andre Dorsman, Prof. Jacob Wijngaard, and Prof. Wim Westerman, and enriched with sections, such as the Paris Stock Exchange. The English version was carefully revised by my former doctoral thesis students, Prof. Özgür Arslan-Ayaydın (University of Chicago, United States) and Prof. Yılmaz Yıldız (University of Kent, UK), of whom I am proud. I am grateful to them sincerely.

The book chronologically covers a broad period from the beginning of the first millennium to the Roman Empire, followed by the golden age of Islam, modern times, and up to 2025. Although page constraints prevented a detailed examination of every event, decisive historical developments are explained, and each chapter begins with a brief historical story to capture the reader's interest. This book also aims to highlight the knowledge and historical contributions of the East in the formation of Western markets.

Starting from the second chapter, meaningful stock exchanges or financial centers that emerged in each century are examined; the rise of centers such as Lyon, Antwerp, Bruges, Amsterdam, London, Paris, and Wall Street is evaluated in line with Andrew Lo's Adaptive Markets Hypothesis developed in 2004, along with their ability to adapt to changing environmental conditions. Although the title of the book refers to the history of stock exchanges, it also goes beyond stock exchanges to comment on the general development of financial markets. The Istanbul Stock Exchange, as one of the early financial institutions in the East, is also discussed in this context.

The book's central thesis is that inclusive institutions play a decisive role in the development of financial markets, as emphasized by Nobel Prize-winning economists Daron Acemoğlu and James Robinson. Historical examples are used to illustrate how these institutions emerged and expanded within "narrow corridors" where power was confined within certain limits.

This work primarily draws on secondary sources, presented in a narrative style enriched with historical anecdotes to make it more accessible to readers. In my book, I do not merely recount the history of financial institutions; I also question how these institutions have been intertwined with historical, cultural, and political contexts, under what conditions they developed, and why they grew stronger in some regions and weaker in others. In this sense, I believe that the book will be a valuable reference source not only for readers with an interest in history but also for academics and policymakers interested in institutional economics, political science, and finance.

I dedicate this book to my beloved wife, Birgül, who has shared the burdens of life with me for nearly 40 years, both in our academic pursuits and in our daily lives.

Ankara, Türkiye Mehmet Baha Karan

Competing Interests The author has no competing interests to declare that are relevant to the content of this manuscript.

Contents

Chapter 1
Introduction: The Development of Trade in the Mediterranean Basin and the Middle East (1st–13th Centuries)

1.1 Introduction

On a summer day in 301 AD, the city of Aizanoi, located in the west of the Roman Empire's Asia Minor region, within the borders of the Cavdarhisar District of Kütahya, was brimming with anticipation for an ordinary fair day (Fig. 1.1). The market was about to come to life. The city's inhabitants, eager for the day's activities, were chatting under the trees to shield themselves from the sun, while some sought refuge in the shade of the Macellum (food market). Children were bustling about selling food and drink. The building was surrounded by peasants carrying their goods from the villages to the Macellum, merchants, and locals. The fairs were the most essential entertainment for the people. Seeing their friends who came to the bazaar and watched the auctions added color to their lives by distracting them from the mundanity of daily life. A group of soldiers was in front of a large Temple of Zeus right next to the Macellum; they were assigned to guard the marketplace. Along the colonnaded road extending from the temple to the amphitheater, a crowd was walking toward the market; they were probably foreigners coming from the surrounding towns for trade. A few Roman aristocrats were chatting by the pool in the city's famous mosaic baths near the Macellum. They were engaged in a heated debate, speculating on how the emperor could solve the problem of skyrocketing prices. They and all the townspeople were discussing the rising food prices among themselves. For the last year, the prices of all goods, not just food, have risen rapidly. The Romans had met inflation.

Soon, the market would open its doors, and goods from the region, such as grain, wine, and wool, would be auctioned off. Since the third century BC, in Greek and Roman times, the auctioning of goods was commonplace in the Mediterranean region. In harbors, fairs, wholesale and retail markets, harvested crops, property, slaves, and all kinds of goods were sold by auction. An auction notice was an excellent way to advertise a sale. The official who presided over such auctions and sold the goods to the highest bidders was called Praeco. The other vital person was Coactores. Coactores

M. B. Karan, *A History of Stock Exchanges*, Contributions to Economics,
https://doi.org/10.1007/978-3-032-07788-2_1

Fig. 1.1 Macellum at the city of Aizanoi. https://commons.wikimedia.org/wiki/File:Aizanoi_Zeus_temple_2120.jpg

did not lend money at auctions but took a commission from the buyers to transfer the money to the sellers. The services of Coactores were indispensable and vital when both seller and buyer were absent from town. Coactores were responsible for keeping records of these auctions, noting dates, detailed descriptions of the objects sold, prices, and the names of sellers and buyers (Andreau, 1999).

The auction had begun; Praeco was standing on a stone and had just started to speak when the sound of hoofbeats suddenly appeared. Then, the clatter of swords and footsteps echoed through the building. A group of soldiers, led by a junior officer, had entered the Macellum. The officer came up to Praeco and stopped the auction. The officer had an inscription of the Emperor Diocletian in his hand and began to read it aloud. The writing was quite long, but in short, it said (İznik, 2011):

> It is a great pleasure to inform you that the wages in the list attached to the following plan will apply throughout our empire. We declare that anyone who defies the measures laid down by the law will be sentenced to death for their audacity. No one can think that this law is too harsh. We, therefore, expect everyone to abide by it. May the observance desired and the conscientious responsibility expected of the people, especially when a law has the force of law, be observed and carried forward in a single city or province and throughout our empire.

Under this inscription, a price list of the bazaar is displayed. In 301 AD, the emperor issued the famous "*Edictum de Maximis Pretiis*," which fixed prices and set maximum prices to prevent inflation, unfair profits, and buyer exploitation (Cousin, n.d.). The list included approximately 1,000 articles. Violation of the mandate was punishable by death; black marketeers were also to be severely punished. This document is the longest-surviving bureaucratic practice from that time (Cary & Scullard, 1975).

The events described above were essentially real, though somewhat dramatized. In 1971, tablets found during excavations in the region revealed a copy of the price adjustments made by Roman Emperor Diocletian in 301 AD to combat inflation. These were inscribed on stone blocks, and today, the selling prices of all goods in the imperial markets are still visible. Diocletian fixed the prices of traded goods and implemented nationwide measures to combat inflation. His "*Edict on Prices*" set tariffs for all commercial goods, ensuring consumers could buy products at the same price everywhere. From slaves to shoes, soldier wages to beer and wine prices, glass cups to ceramics, and teachers' salaries, all prices were listed. For instance, one strong slave equaled two donkeys, and one horse equaled three slaves.

However, such price-fixing policies were ineffective. Many merchants hoard goods and sell them at higher prices, creating a black market. Price fixing disrupted market dynamics, halting the signals between producers and consumers. Traders hoarded goods, collapsing markets until prices naturally restored themselves. This law was eventually repealed, teaching the Romans that non-market measures could not control market dynamics.

Trade had long flourished in the Mediterranean, even when Diocletian made economic missteps. When Alexander the Great united the Eastern Mediterranean under one kingdom, trade became simpler. Greek in the east and Latin in the west became the primary languages of international trade. Later, the Roman Empire's Pax Romana stability allowed trade to thrive, with Roman law governing the Mediterranean coast.

1.2 Development of Trade and the Silk Road

Regional trade markets emerged at the beginning of the first millennium, and economies became increasingly monetized. For trade to occur, money-clearing houses and credit mechanisms had to be established. In this context, interest-based banking had begun to emerge in Rome several centuries before Christ (Andreau, 1999). In the first century, trade with India started with Rome's acquisition of Egypt. According to the historian Strabo, 120 Roman ships traveled from Egypt to India every year. It is known that these ships reached Vietnam and Java. Silk from China could now also reach Europe. Seneca, the famous Roman philosopher of the first century, was appalled by the popularity of this thin and flowing silk fabric and argued that silk garments could not hide the curves of Roman ladies and protect their chastity. Silk cloth was costly and could even be used as money. In the second century AD, almost 10% of Rome's annual budget was spent buying silk. Besides silk, Rome also bought spices and dyes like indigo. In return, it received gold, wrought glass, silver, coral, and topaz from the Red Sea and white gold from Arabia. Meanwhile, the prosperity of the cities along the trade routes was rising. Communication and commercial networks were expanding, and settlements were becoming interconnected. Cities such as Palmmira on the edge of the Syrian Desert and Petra, connecting Arabia and the Mediterranean, were prospering. There were also fairs around the Euphrates, where merchants came from thousands of kilometers away. Trade with Persia also increased. Goods such as jade, onions, cucumbers, coriander, pistachios, and grapefruit were traded. Samarkand peaches from Central Asia were valuable (Frankopan, 2017).

The most essential element of trade in early medieval Europe was transportation. Goods had to be transported from the Wastern Mediterranean to the west and Northern Europe. The transportation of these goods was mostly done via rivers and waterways.

Under the Roman Empire, many waterways were developed, and roads were built. Road construction gradually increased, especially after the fourth century, giving rise to the expression "*All Roads Lead to Rome.*" However, trade along these developed routes declined after the fall of the Roman Empire. However, trade eventually resumed, using a wider range of trade routes that crossed multiple continents.

Credit and banking activity had to develop for trade in goods to function correctly. However, the growing church had started a significant debate on credit and interest. With the official adoption of Christianity by the Roman Empire in 379 AD, religious pressure on those who traded money for interest began. Although commodity markets flourished, financial activity became difficult due to religious pressure. In the eighth century, in the most critical state in Europe, under the rule of King Charlemagne of the Franks, they went even further and declared usury a general offense. This anti-usury movement would continue to gain momentum in the early Middle Ages and perhaps reached its peak in 1311 when Pope Clement V made the prohibition of usury absolute and declared all secular legislation in favor of usury null and void (Birnie, 1952). Since Christians were prohibited from usury during this period, Jews became indispensable in the credit and banking business. While Jews could not lend money at interest to other Jews because of their religion, they could lend money to Christians. They, therefore, filled a vital gap in the financial system. Jewish bankers provided much-needed capital for businesses and personal loans and contributed to developing commodity markets. They were not allowed to own land or belong to guilds, so they were pushed out of other fields. In addition, financial activities were more profitable (Botticini & Eckstein, 2003).

After the fall of the Western Roman Empire, several kingdoms were established in these regions, disrupting order in the area. The Eastern Roman Empire was still mighty and would remain so for a long time. The Silk Road was one of the most important trade routes during this period. This network of trade routes connected East Asia and Southeast Asia with South Asia, Iran, the Arabian Peninsula, East Africa, and Southern Europe. Camel caravans and ships to Northern Europe via Italy and Southern France transported goods and enslaved people from the East. The Silk Road got its name from the lucrative silk trade along the route during the Chinese Han Dynasty (207 BC–220 AD). The Han Dynasty expanded the Central Asian section of the trade routes through military conquests. The Chinese attached great importance to the security of their trade goods and expanded the Great Wall to protect the trade route. Syrian merchants, as well as Jews, filled the void left by the collapse of the Roman Empire until the seventh century AD; Syrian merchants traded from the Eastern Mediterranean Levant with the Maghrebis in North Africa and Spain. During this period, international trade was still the exclusive preserve of the elite aristocracy, supporting rather than driving economies.

From 700 BC to the first centuries AD, the Mediterranean experienced steady economic growth, especially in maritime trade. Economic activity during this period was so spectacular that this level of development would only be witnessed centuries later, in the early modern era. The trade in goods and money flourished, while the regions along this trade route linking East and West were inhabited by very different peoples of different religions, cultures, races, or tribes. Byzantine merchants began to play a more critical role in the economic life of Western Europe. The rebuilt Byzantine navy was firmly in control of the Mediterranean, and, as a direct consequence, trade in the West was considerably safer. The most important port in the region was Alexandria. During this period, trade northward from the Rhine basin also began. Nevertheless, Western Europe in the sixth and seventh centuries was at a low economic and cultural level; there was no taste and desire for exotic and refined luxury goods and large quantities of industrial products, but there was a surplus of raw materials that could be exported. Perhaps the most valuable of these exports from the West were slaves (Frankopan, 2017).

However, everything changed with the rise of Islam in the Middle East. Muslim conquests and migrations had cut the Byzantines off from sources of gold ore, and the value of Byzantine money could only be maintained with the strictest controls after the middle of the seventh century. Byzantine trade had to readjust itself to the new circumstances, which required favorable trade balancing in the West. Although steps in this direction were attempted as early as 650 AD, after the loss of territory in the west and the loss of direct contact with the sources of gold, there was a sharp decline in trade after Pirenne's closure of the Western Mediterranean by Muslim pirates (Adelson, 1960).

1.3 The Middle East and the Rise of Islam

The rise of Islam began in Mecca in the mid-seventh century with the Prophet Muhammad. His teachings, emphasizing monotheism and social justice, spread rapidly. After Muhammad died in 632, the Islamic world was ruled by Caliphs. During the Rashidun Caliphate (the first four caliphs, 632–661), Islamic rule expanded quickly, conquering much of the Middle East, including the Byzantine-controlled Levant, parts of Persia, Egypt, and North Africa. The Muslim army also advanced into Spain and India, spreading Islam. After the death of Ali, the fourth caliph, civil strife split the Muslim world into two groups: the Shi'ites, led by Hussein, who believed only Ali's descendants could lead, and the Sunnis, who thought any Muslim could lead. There are also hundreds of smaller Islamic sects. The Umayyads (661–750), a strict Sunni group, seized power, with Muawiya as their first leader. They moved the capital to Damascus and expanded the empire into Spain, North Africa, and Central Asia. During this period, cities like Damascus, Qurtuba, and Baghdad flourished.

The Abbasid Caliphate (750–1258), a Sunni polity, overthrew the Umayyads and moved the capital to Baghdad, a cultural and intellectual hub. The Abbasid era marked the golden age of Islam, with advances in science, mathematics, philosophy, and medicine. Baghdad became a learning center, attracting scholars from across the empire. Iranian poet Nasser Khosraw, who visited Basra in the eleventh century, reported that three bazaars were held daily in different parts of the city. Major cities like Baghdad, Kufa, Madinah, Damascus, Fustat, Jerusalem, and Tabriz (in modern Iran) exemplified medieval markets.

Despite the similarity of faith, there were many differences between the two dynasties that would lay the foundation for the future of Islam in the world. The Abbasids elevated Islam from an Arab religion to an international one. Although the principles of Islam took root under the Umayyads, it was under the Abbasids that Islam spread throughout the world. First, while the Umayyads were much more interested in the Mediterranean coast, the Abbasids focused on the plains of Iran and Iraq. This is why Syria, Israel, Lebanon, and Egypt were necessary under the Umayyad Dynasty, while under the Abbasids, the focus shifted to Iran and Iraq. An essential difference between the two dynasties lies in their attitude toward Muslims and non-Muslims. While the Umayyads did not increase the number of Muslims during their 100-year rule because they did not favor conversion, the Abbasids welcomed non-Muslims into their mid, leading to a massive increase in the number of Muslims worldwide. While the Umayyads focused on military expansion and territorial conquest, the Abbasids favored the spread of knowledge.

The Golden Age of Islam and Cultural Development in the 8th-10th Centuries. The Abbasids encouraged intellectual achievements, with scholars translating Greek, Persian, and Indian works into Arabic in institutions such as the House of Wisdom in Baghdad. Innovations in mathematics, astronomy, medicine, and engineering flourished. During this period, the preservation of classical Greek knowledge was also remarkable. However, from the ninth century onward, the Abbasid Caliphate began to weaken, and various regional powers emerged. In Egypt, the Fatimids (909–1171), a Shiite Dynasty, seized power, while in Iran and Iraq, the influence of the Buyids (Shiite) and Seljuk Turks (Sunni) increased. The Fatimids were exceptionally tolerant toward those of other religions and sects and paid attention to trade development in the Mediterranean. At that time, any disturbance in the market was the most feared event by the rulers. When disorder broke out, order and harmony in the markets would be replaced by stagnation, and the state would be deprived of essential tax revenues. The Fatimids developed a legal code to resolve court disputes, and the judiciary observed it throughout the Fatimid state. The Fatimids also held science in high esteem (Daftary, 2021).

This was a period of profound and lasting changes in the Mediterranean scene. On the African coast, the center of gravity shifted eastward toward Egypt from Tunisia, the core of Fatimid power throughout the tenth century. The commercial success of the Fatimids was due to relatively little government interference in the trade of their subjects and the generally favorable situation created by the growing needs of an economically emerging Europe, with Egypt and Syria serving as distribution centers and primarily as suppliers. The Italian republics were replacing Byzantium as the vanguard of Christendom. Throughout this period, neither the Mediterranean nor its western or eastern basins were ever under the sovereignty of a single state. Maritime supremacy gradually shifted from the Muslim south to the Christian north (Goitein, 1999).

At this time, the Mediterranean region was divided into three major regions. The "*East*," i.e., Egypt and the Muslim countries of southwest Asia; the "*Muslim West*," which included all of North Africa west of Egypt, including Muslim Sicily, and of which Andalusia or Spain formed a subdivision, the "*Maghreb*." Moreover, finally, the "*Land of the Romans*" originally referred to Byzantium. Until the twelfth century, it was used ambiguously for Christian Europe and its peoples in general. The term "*Franks*" was used for Western Europe. The Seljuks, a Turkic people, began migrating to the Middle East in the tenth century. By the eleventh century, the Seljuks dominated much of the region, including Iran and Iraq, and played an important role in defending the Islamic world against external threats. Under the Seljuks, the Sunni revival became prominent and helped organize an effective military force against external invaders. During this period, the Crusades also began. During the Crusades (1096–1291), Christians organized nine significant expeditions to the East. The desire for direct access to the riches of the East was the driving force behind Europeans' participation in the Crusades. The Mamluks in Egypt and Syria controlled the spice trade and imposed exorbitant taxes on European merchants. This restricted Europeans' access to valuable spices and increased their prices. Historians believe the desire for economic gain, including access to the spice trade, played an essential role in the Crusaders' decision to engage in these holy wars. Economic prospects were an attractive factor in recruiting troops and financing the Crusades. European merchants and powers wanted to expand their trade networks by capturing key ports and territories in the Eastern Mediterranean, and they planned to profit by controlling the spice trade. The Levant and the Eastern Mediterranean lands promised fertile farmland, abundant timber, precious metals, and other overstated riches. Although not as easy as they expected, these resources would fuel economic growth in Europe, stimulate trade, and increase the wealth and power of European states (Madden, 2005).

After the success of the First Crusade, Crusader states were established in the Levant, such as the Kingdom of Jerusalem. These states were in constant conflict with Muslim powers, especially the forces of the Muslim commander Saladin (Salah ad-Din al-Ayyubi; 1137–1193). Saladin became a hero of the Islamic world, uniting various Muslim groups and recapturing Jerusalem from the Crusaders in 1187. The Ayyubid Dynasty controlled most of the Levant and Egypt.

However, a new power had emerged in the East. The Mongols profoundly impacted the Middle East between the thirteenth and fifteenth centuries, reshaping the political, social, and cultural landscape. While their invasions caused widespread destruction, they also facilitated cultural exchange, trade, and the integration of Eurasian societies. The Mongol Empire was founded in 1206 by Genghis Khan (originally Temujin). By his death in 1227, Genghis Khan had united the Mongol tribes and built an empire that stretched across Asia from China to Iran. It included parts of Uzbekistan and Kazakhstan. The most important event for the Middle East during the Mongol invasions was the sack of Baghdad in 1258. This was a significant blow to Islamic civilization, as Baghdad had been a center of learning and culture during the Golden Age of Islam. The Mongols killed tens of thousands of people, including scholars, and destroyed libraries and essential infrastructure. The Mongols gradually adapted to the region's culture and Islam. By the late thirteenth century, many Mongol rulers, including Ghazan Khan (who was centered in what is today Iran and parts of Iraq, Turkey, and the Caucasus), converted to Islam, marking the beginning of the Islamization of the Mongol elite. Mongol rule brought significant economic integration and revitalized the Silk Road, allowing trade between East and West to flourish.

The Timurid Empire, founded by Timur (1336–1405) in the late fourteenth century, was one of the most powerful states in the Mongol succession. Its conquests covered Iran, the Caucasus, Mesopotamia, Anatolia, and parts of India. Timur's brutal military campaigns caused widespread destruction but also contributed to a cultural revival in the areas he conquered. The Timurid Empire was known for its patronage of art and architecture, especially in cities such as Samarkand, which became a center of learning and culture under Timur's rule. In Egypt, the Mamluks, a military class of Turkish-born enslaved people who rose to power, successfully repelled the Mongols at the Battle of Ayn Jalut in 1260. The Mamluks established their dynasty, which ruled Egypt and Syria and played an essential role in defending the region against further Mongol invasions.

The mostly Turkic peoples in the Mongol armies had gained power in the region. Genghis Khan, who founded the Mongol Empire, recognized the importance of trade from the early years of his reign and took measures to develop commercial activities. With the Mongols' entry into Eastern Europe after Central Asia, trade and economic relations in the region deteriorated for a while. Still, simultaneously, the unification of the Turkish tribes in the area under the rule of a centralized and powerful state led to the re-development of trade (Kalan, 2014). In the early fifteenth century, as the power of the Mongols waned, the Ottoman state, whose language was Turkish and whose religion was Islam, was established in Western Anatolia. They captured the Byzantine capital, Constantinople, in 1453 and then became the rulers of Egypt and Arabia in the sixteenth century.

1.4 Trade Routes and Markets

The Muslims had taken over a highly organized and taxable world. Thus, trade routes, oasis cities, and natural resources were in their possession. Ports linking trade between the Persian Gulf and China were also captured. The Islamic states dominated a vast network of trade and communication routes by linking the oases of Afghanistan and the Fergana valley with North Africa and the Atlantic Ocean. Thanks to this commercial power, as the amount of disposable income increased, so did the level of private enterprise. Partnership-type ventures became common (Frankopan, 2017). During this period, prices were set by auction or according to free market conditions.

Although Damascus was in a bright commercial position during the Umayyad period, the two main routes of international trade were the Tigris and the Euphrates. As a result of the Abbasid policy toward the East, Baghdad, where the Khorasan road passed and fairs were established as a region where caravan routes intersected, was chosen as the capital due to its favorable climatic conditions, economic opportunities, and military convenience. Basra, located south of Baghdad on the Gulf, gained importance as a market where everything could be found, including silk linen, pearls,

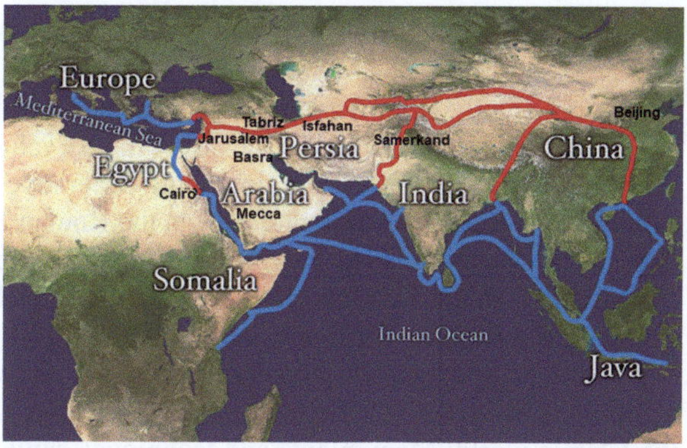

Fig. 1.2 Silk road at 9–12 centuries. https://en.wikipedia.org/wiki/Spice_trade#/media/File:Silk_route.jpg (This is a file from the Wikimedia Commons)

jewelry, henna, and rose water. As a result, two trade routes were used in this period. The first one was the route through the Indian Ocean. This route connected China with India, the Arabian Peninsula, the Persian Gulf, and Egypt. This road connected Alexandria and the Levant cities. The second road, strengthened during the Abbasid period, was the second road through China, Central Asia, Persia, and Anatolia. Especially Tabriz and Isfahan were critical commercial centers on this road. Since this road was also connected to Basra, the city of Basra was significant. However, the Tabriz road gained more importance when the Mongols destroyed Baghdad. In this period, cities such as Kufa, Mecca, Medina, Damascus, Fustat, and Jerusalem were prominent (Fig. 1.2).

The Arab world had a highly integrated urban system stretching from Qurtuba to Baghdad. Transaction costs were low because the region was politically united, shared a common language, and had an Islamic legal system that included several institutions that encouraged exchange (such as the rule of using written contracts). There was also efficient transportation through caravan routes between urban centers (Findlay & O'Rourke, 2008).

By the end of the first millennium, the major cities of the Middle East needed markets more than ever. While individual jewelers and bankers still carried out financial activities, commodity markets had begun to specialize east of the Mediterranean, and different markets for different types of goods had emerged in the major cities. Goods from the Middle East traveled through Italy to the north and west of Europe. In the tenth and eleventh centuries, regional markets and trade fairs were established in Europe as trade expanded between the West and the Byzantine and Islamic worlds (Mitchell, n.d.). In the eighth century, the Silk Road was a substantial network of trade routes linking the East (especially China, Central Asia, and India) to the West (the Middle East, Europe, and Africa). The goods exchanged along these routes were very diverse. Silk was the most important and highly valued commodity by elites in Europe, the Middle East, and Central Asia. Spices such as pepper, cinnamon, cloves, nutmeg, and cardamom were traded from India and Southeast Asia to the West. Gold, silver, and precious stones were frequently traded, especially between the Islamic world, Central Asia, and China. Jade was another highly valued material, especially in China. Tea began in China during this period, especially green tea. Ivory, usually from African elephants, was in demand in Asia and the Middle East. Wool, cotton, and linen textiles were highly valued in the West (Persia, Central Asia, and India), and glassware, including decorative items and vessels, was highly valued in the Roman Empire and later in the Roman Empire, and horses, especially those from Central Asia (such as the Arabian horse) were highly valued in other parts of Asia, the Middle East, and Europe. Paper was a Chinese invention that began to spread to the Islamic world and Europe in the eighth century. It became an important commodity, especially in administration, books, and religious texts. Medicinal plants and pharmaceutical knowledge were exchanged, especially between China and the Islamic world. Many plants and techniques came from these regions. Enslaved people, including those from Central Asia and Africa, were also part of the trade along the Silk Road. In addition to these material goods, the Silk Road facilitated the exchange of ideas, including technologies such as papermaking, gunpowder, and the compass, as well as religious and philosophical beliefs such as Buddhism, Islam, Christianity, and Manichaeism.

As gold and silver coins became more widely used, regional economies became more monetized, and debentures were introduced. Promissory notes originated in China during the Han Dynasty in 118 BC and were made of leather. Evidence suggests that the Romans may have used promissory notes as early as 57 AD as a durable medium. Historically, promissory notes served as a form of currency. Flying cash, or feiqian, was a promissory note used during the Tang Dynasty (618–907), often by tea merchants, and could be exchanged for hard currency in provincial capitals. Marco Polo introduced the Chinese concept of promissory notes to Europe (Promissory note, n.d.). Arab merchants used them by the twelfth century, and they helped merchants avoid carrying heavy coins over long distances (Barnard et al., n.d.). Various financial innovations were vital to trade growth in the Middle East, where a legal infrastructure was established, and the Islamic religion provided a favorable perspective. This led to more considerable capital and corporate structures, with partnerships and ventures into new markets. Merchants in the Middle East had established commercial ventures by the end of the first millennium. Complex institutions and accounting systems, including credit and partnerships, were developed to support long-distance trade and commerce. Some methods and institutions were exported to Italy in the 8th or ninth centuries, laying the foundation for European commercial organizations. These organizations contributed to the development of European business, trade, and financial institutions (Ashtor, 1976).

1.5 Legal Infrastructure of Trade in the Middle East

The legal system in Islamic countries differs significantly from that in many other countries. In Islam, the state is restricted from legislating, as Allah is the sole Lawgiver, leaving no room for legislative authority in Islamic political theory. Historical evidence suggests that Islam has benefited societies that have adopted it. Laws and legislation originated directly from God, and the ability to mix and choose qualities facilitated this initial phase. Political legitimization allowed Islamic leaders to promote cooperation and coordination on an unprecedented scale. The new states provided stability, security, and predictable dispute resolution across vast territories, fostering rapid trade growth within a framework established by Islamic law. The Islamic state imposed only small taxes, as noted by the scholar Ibn Khaldun, creating a favorable incentive environment. The state also provided public services, such as irrigation, which, along with expanding market opportunities, sparked significant agricultural investment and innovation (Acemoglu & Robinson, 2021).

Trade in Islamic states was based on Islamic law, with general principles shared across sects, although they were practiced differently. Islam's sensitivity to commerce is not surprising, as many religious scholars (ulema) were active in long-distance trade as investors and merchants. Cohen (1970) estimates that in the ninth and tenth centuries, 75% of religious scholars in the Arab region earned their living primarily from trade. Legal structures often reflected both practical and religious considerations. Our understanding of medieval Islamic trade mainly comes from the Cairo Geniza documents (found at the end of the nineteenth century), which offer valuable insights into North African social, commercial, and spiritual life from the eleventh century onward. These documents demonstrate that information about individuals and their connections was readily available in commercial exchanges based on trust, such as the "murabaha" method, which is rooted in Islamic finance principles (Udovitch, 1985). In this system, a sale is a bilateral transaction concluded through offer and acceptance, which becomes binding. For a sale to be permissible under Islamic law, it must be free from unjust enrichment, meaning neither party gains an advantage without providing counter value. This concept is central to Islamic usury (riba), which excludes any trace of it from transactions. Islamic law also insists on clarity regarding the contract's purpose and obligations and allows the right to terminate the transaction if defects in the merchandise are found. This discourages fraud (Udovitch, 1985). While each religion was judged under its own law, some non-Muslims chose to be judged under Islamic law (Kuran, 2003).

Medieval legal texts from Geniza show that these regulations were preventive, aiming to protect the innocent general consumer who lacked expertise in trade items from deceptive merchants. Customers were protected from unfair exploitation by basing the sale price on the initial cost. Open, honest, and transparent information about transactions was provided. The focus was on preventing fraud by setting detailed guidelines for determining commodity prices (Udovitch, 1985).

The Cairo Geniza documents show that commodity prices on trading days were periodically determined and announced in the market (Goitein, 1999). Commercial intelligence was a key concern, with merchants monitoring business volumes, capital availability, ship and caravan movements, and communications security. More than half of the business letters from Geniza contained commercial information and gossip, often unrelated to the specific transaction. Islamic commercial law highly values information about goods and the individuals involved in exchanges. Legal regulations require detailed type, quality, quantity, and price information. Many aspects were not defined, leaving merchants to rely on custom and practice for practical details (Udovitch, 1985).

1.6 Organization of Trade and Finance

Participants in the caravan trade of the pre-industrial Middle East were largely peddlers, buying and selling small quantities of goods as the convoy moved from market to market. Over time, large commercial investors diversified their risks by contracting with many merchants traveling in different directions. Apart from these, there were also merchants with much more valuable cargo. Many of these were financed by high-ranking officials. The pre-modern Middle East was never short of investors willing to risk their capital for financial gain. Nevertheless, there were no long-lasting organizations that could pool the resources of a large number of investors (Kuran, 2003).

1.6.1 Partnership

By the tenth century, the Middle East lacked modern commercial companies with legal personality. Instead, economic ventures relied on partnerships or family businesses, limited to the partners' lifespans or the venture's duration. Long-term trade prioritized family ties, though Islam allowed some flexibility in trading with outsiders. Nevertheless, the distinctive features of Islamic partnerships, particularly "*mudaraba*," contributed to the development of joint-stock companies. The venture aimed to build trust between unrelated individuals. Islamic law also permitted partnerships with non-Muslims, like Jews and Christians, though this structure remained unchanged for centuries (Kuran, 2003). The organization and technique of trade in Islamic countries have certainly impacted Europe's economic history. Accordingly, there were four types of cooperation: (a) friendship and informal cooperation; (b) partnership (Mudaraba or musharaka); (c) family partnership; (d) commission and agency (Goitein, 1999).

In this era, a typical enterprise involved a resident investor financing a merchant to run a business. Under Islamic law, this single-venture partnership was called mudaraba. If both parties contributed capital or labor, it was musharaka, with profits shared based on a pre-agreed formula. Merchants could negotiate a more considerable share based on skills like honesty and expertise. They bore no financial loss unless they invested capital, limiting their risk to labor. This practice resembled the "*Commenda*" system established in late medieval Europe. A commenda was a medieval contract between an investor partner and a traveling partner for conducting a commercial venture, typically overseas. It was an early and one-off form of limited partnership (Van Doosselaere, 2009). The investor partner would provide the capital and run a joint commercial enterprise (usually shipping), traveling to other localities to trade. At the end of the business, the initial capital would be returned to the investor partner, and the remaining profits would then be divided. The principle of commenda was that the partners in the commercial venture were equal, with one providing the capital and the other running the business. Some were family businesses where profits were transferred to a common fund without properly settling the accounts of the various partners. Risks and expected returns had to be distributed harmoniously. Remarkably, this exercise of commercial power occurred nearly two centuries before the commercial rules established by the European legal system took effect (Kuran, 2003). Islamic rules have undergone very little change since then. This is probably because there is a religious barrier to changing or reinterpreting Islamic law.

1.6.2 Mathematics and Early Accounting Practice

In the case of partnerships, income and expenses had to be calculated and shared. For this, accounting was needed. In commenda contracts, the initial capital invested was compared with the revenue to be generated, and the excess was marked as profit to be distributed. At the beginning of the ninth century, the Islamic mathematician Musa al-Khwarizmi introduced the numerals used today based on the Indo-Arabic system. People began to think in numbers, and the numerical system became a central part of the Islamic capitalist economy (Labib, 1969). This knowledge was not only necessary for merchants but was also part of the Ulama's education. Mathematics was part of trade at that time for at least three reasons: (1) astronomy was necessary for navigation on the seas. (2) Merchants needed to keep records of goods and money, mainly if their routes covered many countries and they financed their journeys with other people's money, such as families, trade agreements, or lenders. For this, they needed accounting or bookkeeping. (3) Another vital use of mathematics was in construction and engineering. Europeans did not have access to the mathematical knowledge found in Spain and North Africa until the twelfth and thirteenth centuries. Al-Khwarizmi's book was translated into Latin by Robert of Chester in 1145 and was used as the leading mathematics textbook in European universities until the sixteenth century. Mathematics entered Europe through translation and Italy's North African connections and trade (Hill & Awde, 2003).

Mathematics was crucial in accounting, especially for merchants managing partnerships. Fu (1971) noted that early accounting forms were advanced in China until the Chou Dynasty (1122–256 BC). The "*Four Pillar Balancing*" system, a precursor to double-entry bookkeeping, was used in government and private accounting during the Northern Song Dynasty in the eleventh century and possibly during the Tang Dynasty (900–950), as seen in 925 ledgers from Jingtu Temple (Guo, 1988). This more straightforward system resembled Italian accounting, categorizing activities into inflow, outflow, stocks, and claims. While Luca Pacioli (1447–1517) published his works centuries later, Chinese bankers and merchants may have developed double-entry bookkeeping independently, unlike in Europe, where it began in Italy (Lin, 1992).

The transmission of early accounting practices from the Chinese to the Arabs likely occurred through trade. Money traders accepted deposits that could be withdrawn via written orders, allowing for tracking individual values and capital circulation. This enabled merchants to record account movements and assess business success quantitatively. Typically, a merchant would finalize a sale and record the profit or loss in their ledger, making periodic account reporting unnecessary. Information on medieval Islamic accounting is scarce, as no commercial accounting books have been found; it is derived from law books, notarial records, and financial administration reports (Lieber, 1968).

In conclusion, the Islamic world's influence on mathematics and early Western accounting developments is apparent. Double-entry accounting features were utilized in the Muslim world before their adoption in the West. However, evidence does not support the idea that double-entry was first developed outside Italy. Italians appear to have created the earliest surviving complete double-entry systems and definitions, with the gradual evolution of double-entry elements evident in Italian records from the thirteenth and fourteenth centuries (Nobes et al., 2001).

1.6.3 Banking and Interest Practices

According to Geniza documents, selling on credit was a common practice, with loans often being deferred payments. Borrowing small or larger sums from friends or even those of another religion was typical. Merchants and artisans made interest-free loans, but by the eleventh century, Muslims lent money to Jews at fixed interest rates. At the same time, Jewish bankers offered secured and unsecured loans to Muslims, likely charging interest. Bankers' notes had significant economic importance, with loans often repaid in installments over several years. Collateral likely included hidden interest. Debt declarations, typically issued by a Muslim official, were endorsable and often validated by Jewish courts, reflecting their role in mutual aid and charity (Goitein, 1999).

While interest and usury were legally prohibited and religiously forbidden in the Islamic world, interest-based trade became a tradition. Many moneylenders operated secretly in the markets. All loans were made in gold dinars, while interest payments were made in dirhams. This practice was necessary to preserve the value of the lent capital, as the ratio of the dirham to the dinar fluctuated violently during those years.

Geniza documents show that by the tenth century, the interest rate in the Middle East was between 6 2/3% and 10%, while in Europe, it was 3%. By the twelfth century, the "Islamic" interest rate had risen to 10% and then to 15% in Egypt under Salah ad-Din al-Ayyubi, possibly due to the monetary crisis and the supply of precious metals (Shatzmiller, 2017). Even Caliphs, Sultans, and Emirs took out loans at high interest rates. These profit-driven loans granted lenders important trade, tariff, rent, and tax privileges. In 902, the Arab geographer al-Faqih al-Hamadan noted that the biggest moneylenders came from Basra and the Himyarites and could be found in far regions like Central Asia and Morocco. Ibn Battuta, the Berber scholar and explorer, described how merchants in Sindh and India would lend large sums to visitors of the Indian Sultan Muhammad Shah's court, knowing they would be repaid with gifts worth far more than the loan (Labib, 1969).

Banking activity during the Abbasid period was one of the era's significant economic developments. The Abbasid banking system evolved from the commercial practices of earlier caliphates, particularly the Umayyad period. Initially, banking focused on identifying and exchanging silver and gold coins. The government and the public gained expertise as the variety of coins and fluctuating exchange rates increased. A new class of specialists, known as "*Jihbadh*," emerged as bankers in the modern sense (Geva, 2017).

The position of the Jihbadhs evolved due to the distortions in the Abbasid political system. After the tenth century, the caliphs faded into the background, and the viziers increased in responsibility and power. However, once they gained great power, the viziers were undermined by the conspiracies of their political rivals and usually ended up in poverty. Therefore, top officials needed places to protect and hide their property. On the other hand, the empire had many coins of different denominations, which had to be converted into the same currency in centralized treasuries. Since the caliph's treasury was insufficient to cover expenses, the viziers obligated large sums of money to pay provincial rulers and organize military campaigns. These needs led to the emergence of the Jihbadh position in the Abbasids: Jihbadhs presided over a vast network of merchants and bankers, facilitating the movement of capital using letters of credit. They lent money to government officials; viziers would turn to a Jihbadh when the state needed an advance. Jihbadhs, according to Arab chroniclers, consisted of Muslims, Christians, and Jews, regardless of religion. Unlike in Fatimid Egypt or Umayyad Spain, Jews in Iraq never rose to important positions at the Abbasid court. The importance of bankers increased so much that the government established a special department, the Diwan-i Jihbadha, to regulate them (Bowden, 1977). The Jihbadhs were bound to the viziers mostly by ties of reciprocity: the Jihbadhs depended on the viziers to deposit money with them and repay their loans with interest, and the viziers depended on the Jihbadhs both to protect their assets from the state and to lend them large sums of money when the state needed them. Caliph Muqtedir changed fifteen viziers during his twenty-five-year reign, but his two Jewish jahābis, Yūsuf b. Fīnh¯ạs and Hārūn b. ʿAmrām "*were never dismissed until their death.*" According to Islamic sources, this was because their removal could have caused the caliphate's financial system to collapse (Grayson, 2017).

As bankers, Jihbadhs acted officially for the state and royal court, holding lifetime titles that could be inherited. Over time, they expanded from money changing to fundraising, money transfers, and loan liquidation. Their activities included depositing, advancing funds to the authorities, and remitting funds. Deposit-taking was not carried out by borrowing from depositors and accumulating funds to be lent. Instead, deposit taking was for safe custody purposes, pure and simple. Many were not properly recorded, as it was a way of concealing wealth with trusted individuals such as Jihbadhs. However, it is not sufficiently clear whether such deposits were utilized profitably by the Jihbadhs. Providing funds to public authorities was one of the main profitable activities of the Jihbadhs. However, this activity was not carried out through regular lending. However, in connection with tax farming, i.e., making advance payments for future or deferred tax collections, the Jihbadhs retained part of the income as profit (Geva, 2017). The remitting funds were done through "*suftaja (plural safajit)*" or "*sakk,*" which will be discussed in the next section.

In the tenth and eleventh centuries, a tax collector was essentially a concession granted by the state to a private or official tax contractor. These tax collectors were actively involved in trade and manufacturing and invested their earnings in these areas. Islamic capitalism was essentially commercial and consumer credit capitalism. However, the bad debts of sultans and viziers made their structure unstable. Sultans not only defaulted on their obligations but also confiscated the wealth of their creditors when they needed to (Ağır, 2017).

By the end of the Fatimid period, the provinces' most important Jewish merchant families in Egypt and outside Egypt (especially in Iraq and Iran) were mainly large merchants, bankers, and tax collectors. Whereas previously dyeing, tanning, and other handicrafts, especially those despised by the Arabs, were almost exclusively practiced by Jews in Muslim countries, as time passed, the social stratification changed, and a class of businessmen and bankers emerged among the Jews, thanks to their role as tax farming (Ashtor, 1956).

Government loan documents from bankers are primarily available from the tenth century onward. The apparent reason for this was that the Abbasid government faced frequent financial crises due to declining revenues and high expenditures. One way out of these crises was to take loans from bankers who worked as court bankers. To overcome frequent financial crises and maintain a transparent balance sheet, the Abbasid viziers sought the help of court bankers. This practice of the rulers gave great impetus to banking activities and elevated bankers to the position of providing or lending money to the state (Grayson, 2017).

10–11. It is unsurprising that 200 bankers (sarrafs) were in the Bankers' Bazaar in Isfahan in the tenth-eleventh centuries because they were needed and coexisted together. In Basra, about 400–1000 bankers had made themselves indispensable. The people of Basra, Iranians, and South Arabians were the best merchants among pious Muslims and had colonies wherever anything could be produced (Labib, 1969).

1.6.4 Fund Transferring and Other Islamic Finance Practices

Under the Abbasids, banking was limited to depositing, supplying, and transferring money to distant places. To avoid the risk and the burden of carrying heavy bags of cash, letters of credit (suftaja, plural safatij) were introduced. Suftaja has been known since the eighth century AD, long before the introduction of similar credit instruments in Europe (Lieber, 1968; Udovitch, 1979). Sufatij were written obligations issued by well-known merchants and drawn to be repaid in the same type of currency paid to the issuing agent (Ashtor, 1973; Udovitch, 1975).

The use of suftaja was quite common in trade. Small retailers operating in markets opened credit accounts with moneylenders. Through these accounts, retailers made non-cash payments to their wholesalers. With such deposit accounts, sarrafs provided overdraft facilities to retailers/account holders. Small retailers who did not have cash on hand could overdraw their deposit accounts with the sarrafs and pay their suppliers. In compliance with the prohibition on charging interest, sarrafs provided overdraft facilities on an interest-free basis. However, the moneylenders were able to profit from this practice by taking advantage of the bimetallic monetary system in place, whereby gold dinars deposited by retailers in silver dirhams were credited at a lower exchange rate than that applicable to the conversion (from silver to gold). In executing payment orders drawn on the accounts, the sarrafs thus provided a form of check services to the account holders (Geva, 2017). Suftaja (safatij) was often used in trade and for other purposes. For example, the Abbasid financial administration used suftaja to transfer money between provincial treasuries and Baghdad, bribes were paid in suftaja, and refugees used suftaja to pay royal treasuries (Ashtor, 1973; Lieber, 1968; Ray, 1997).

As with pre-sixteenth-century European bonds, suftaja could be neither transferred nor endorsed. When presented, the suftaja could be redeemed immediately (Goitein, 1967). If the suftaja was not paid or the drawer delayed payment, the suftaja was subject to a high penalty, which the holder could claim through a lawsuit in an Islamic court (Goitein, 1967). Like European bills of exchange, sufatij were written documents that provided credit and helped merchants avoid the risk of carrying money. However, unlike European bills of exchange, the suftaja did not involve an exchange of currency. The promissory note only allowed traders in one region to pay in the same currency in another area (Rubin, 2010). The differences between these two practices are given in Table 1.1.

During the Abbasid period, merchants and traders could only remit money through suftaja. At the beginning of the reign of Caliph Mansur (754–775), there are documents showing that a person (living in Kufa) purchased a house in Basra through a suftaja letter. While the Abbasid government suftaja was mainly used by the government to transfer revenues from the provinces to the capital, Baghdad, the commercial classes also used it for business transactions with different business centers. The payment against the suftaja was usually due in forty days. At the end of the term, the money could be cashed out in whole or installments. If payment was demanded

Table 1.1 Key differences between suftaja and bill of exchange

Aspect	Islamic tradition (Suftaja)	Western Christianity (bill of exchange)
Interest (Riba)	Guaranteed interest is explicitly prohibited (de jure)	Secular restrictions on interest gradually relaxed after the thirteenth century
Exchange rate profit	Profit from exchange rate differences is not permitted; only borrowers may benefit	Lenders are allowed to profit from differences in exchange rates
Institutional use	Suftaja is limited to trade facilitation within personal networks	Interregional, impersonal financial institutions support bills of exchange

Source Rubin (2010)

before the stipulated time, a discount was offered. The government usually commissioned special carriers, called faij, to bring the suftaja letters from the provinces to the capital (Islam, 1984).

Palace bankers were responsible for official payments. In this context, they accepted payment orders, called "*sakk*" in Persian, issued by their clients in favor of specified persons. These were an early implementation of today's checks. The tenth-century Arab geographer Ibn Hauqal, reporting his observations, states that in eastern Morocco, he saw a sakk of 42,000 dinars drawn by one person on another person in the same city. The use of checks had become very common in the tenth century (Chapra, 2014).

In the Middle East, finding the precursors of the forwards used in modern stock exchanges was possible. There were also trading activities typical of the contemporary commodity exchange, i.e., trading in goods that were not available in the marketplace but would be delivered later. Dates were legally sold at auction before they were ripe and harvested. Even the wholesale of many tuberous vegetables, such as onions, garlic, carrots, turnips, and radishes, occurred before the crops came out of the ground, i.e., before the merchant saw the harvested produce. Many Islamic jurists believe this is legal (Johansen, 2006).

There were various ways of charging interest without violating the spirit of Islamic law. This was done through "*Murabaha*," which we described earlier as a contract based on the principle of trust in Islamic finance. Later in Europe, this method was a double sale contract, where goods were sold when needed and resold at a higher price when the loan had to be repaid. Thus, without interest, the sales contracts were given a credit function, allowing the customer to be financed and to purchase the goods he demanded. In this practice, a compromise seems to have been reached between the needs of commerce and the just protection of the poor against the greedy hands of the usurer. Islamic law did not allow interest and usually insisted on repayment of the full value of the debt, i.e., in goods, not in money. In modern terms, loans were indexed to goods (El-Gamal, 2006).

1.7 Free Movement of Trade and the Merchants of the Silk Road

As the Andalusian philosopher and historian Ibn Hazm (994–1064) noted, in the tenth and eleventh centuries, merchants of various nationalities could travel the Mediterranean in ships of different origins, limited only by risk and opportunity. Ships were open to all paying passengers who could influence their routes without being bound by political distinctions. Goods changed hands regularly under the supervision of merchants or their representatives. There was no distinction between merchant ships, state-owned ships, passenger ships, or pirate ships. Merchants were less clearly defined and were individuals traveling with their goods. These characteristics were not prohibited by state policy, as in many European countries, nor restricted by monopolistic structures like the German Hanseatic League (Smith, 2015).

During the Crusades, trade increased as Europeans became more familiar with exotic goods. Increased contact and trade contributed to the rise of towns and cities in Western Europe, starting with Italy. Despite the wars, Italian merchant cities like Amalfi, Genoa, Venice, and Florence strengthened ties with ports in the Levant, allying with Crusader states such as Antioch, Edessa, and Jerusalem to access ports like Latakia, Tripoli, Acre, Alexandria, and Dimyat. As demand and production grew in Northern Europe, Atlantic and North Sea trade routes merged with Mediterranean ones. Trade influenced the wealthy, bringing new architectural, decorative, culinary, and musical styles.

A notable feature of the Crusader wars was merchants' immunity. Ibn Jubayr wrote that merchant caravans traveling between Muslim and Christian lands were unaffected by the war: "*We saw this when Salah al-Din was preparing for an expedition to Kerek… Caravans continuously passed through Frankish territory between Egypt and Damascus. Christians and Muslims paid a tax when passing through the other's land, and life continued in prosperity*" (Jubayr, 2019).

Customs stations were numerous, not only at borders but also at major cities. During the Umayyad and Abbasid periods, Muslims paid customs duties according to Sharia law, while non-Muslims paid double. This law was not strictly enforced under the Fatimids. Saladin Ayyubi tried to revive this old discrimination but abandoned it soon after (Goitein, 1999). During Egypt and Syria's Fatimid and Ayyubid periods, taxes were fair, and people generally did not complain about their governments except for legal protection and defense against enemies and pirates. Even during wars, Muslims and Christians could trade as long as they paid their taxes. As the Mongols took control of much of Asia, transportation and trade security increased, especially with rulers supporting long-distance trade and higher revenues. Significant developments in maritime transportation also occurred in the Persian Gulf during this time (Frankopan, 2017).

Meanwhile, Marco Polo (1254–1324), a Venetian traveler, took advantage of the free trade conditions and traveled to China. His book had a profound impact on Europe. Europeans were surprised to learn that there was a great civilization in the

East, which aroused a desire to interact with the East. So, their interest in eastern trade and the Silk Road grew.

Between the eleventh and thirteenth centuries, many communities or states carried on trade between the Middle East and Europe via the Mediterranean Sea. Still, four left a lasting mark on history as they became the key elements of the trade bridge between East and West. Thanks to free trade, these communities brought the goods of the East and their ideas and methods to Europe. These included the Karimis and the North African Moorish merchants as eastern merchants and the kingdoms of Genoa and Venice on the European side.

1.7.1 Karimi Traders

From the eleventh century onward, during the late Fatimid period, a unique group of capitalist entrepreneurs emerged in their relations with the West. These merchants, called Karimis, are believed to have arrived in Egypt in 1181 (Ashtor, 1956). The Karimis were significantly the most important merchants of the Mamluk State. It is believed that the Karimites were the most important players in the spice trade between Yemen and Egypt, and even monopolized it. This was probably the result of the economic policy of the Mamluk government, which oppressed small merchants through a system of taxation and monopoly (Ashtor, 1956). This group of large-scale merchants was distinguished by its entrepreneurship and competence, and it soon acquired wealth and influence in all the major markets of the East, thanks to its considerable financial activities and politics. Over time, they gradually dominated the important trade between East and West. Although they were a Muslim merchant group, according to historical records, they also included Jewish merchants (Ashtor, 1956). During the Crusades, Saladin Ayyubi's support for the Muslim Karimis had begun to diminish in favor of the Greek the Coptic and Jewish merchants in Egypt (Spuler, 1966). The main trade routes of the Karimites ran through the Red Sea and the Indian Ocean to China, and in times of peace, overland routes ran from Egypt to Syria, Iraq, and Persia. In the fifteenth century, as the Ottomans conquered significant parts of Asia Minor, the Karimis expanded their trade activities into this region (Vijayalekshmy, 2015). They controlled the trade routes between East and West, from China to the Eastern Mediterranean.

Karimi merchants were different from other entrepreneurs and prominent merchants. They were neither landlords nor tax collectors. They were also known as capitalists (Labīb, 1969). Venice had established a privileged trade relationship by buying a large part of the Asian spices that the Carimi merchants of Alexandria brought to Egypt from Asia via the Red Sea. In return, the Venetians sold metal, armor, woolen cloth, and slaves (Apellániz, 2013).

The education of the Karimis started when they were children. They were sent to various countries to gain the necessary experience and establish the family business more firmly. The Karimite merchants also had free and slave agents representing their commercial houses, importing and exporting goods. These houses played an important role in the history of Islamic capitalism, due to their considerable financial potential. These houses ran large projects and managed a banking institution, providing loans and deposit services. Their best customers were Western merchants and Sultans and Emirs, to whom they often extended loans and, when necessary, military aid. By the middle of the fourteenth century, their economic power had grown. They had a large international bank in Cairo that made large loans to a Yemeni king imprisoned by the Sultan of Egypt in 1351 (Ashtor, 1956). Detailed information on the fortunes of various Karimi merchants is available. 1394 Karimi merchants paid at least one million dirhams to fend off the Mongol invasion (Ashtor, 1956).

The general collapse of the Egyptian economy at the beginning of the fifteenth century probably also brought financial ruin to the Karimites. In Arabic sources, the leading Karimi merchants of the late fourteenth century are referred to as "*the last Karimis*" (Ashtor, 1956).

1.7.2 Maghrib Merchants

Another people that had relations with Europe in the Middle Ages was the Maghrebis. North Africa, where the Moors lived, was a "*crossroads region*" where "*Mediterranean, Atlantic, African, and European histories intersected*." The Maghrebis were an essential part of the trade between East and West and played an important role in transferring the knowledge of the East to the West. At the time, the Maghreb also included Spain under Islamic rule. The Maghreb people belonged to both Berber and Arab ethnic groups. Many other groups, including Phoenicians, Arabs, and the French, occupied the region and mixed ethnically. In the seventh and eighth centuries, the indigenous population converted to Islam. There were also many Jews and Christians among them (Maghreb, 2024).

The first appearance of the Maghreb on the stage of history was in the seventh–fourteenth centuries, when they traded gold for salt with the Wagadou Empire, which covered what is now southeastern Mauritania, western Mali, and eastern Senegal. While salt was in short supply in the region, the gold transported to the Mediterranean coast was purchased by merchants from Italian states, such as Genoa and Venice, and used in their trade with the Middle East to offset trade deficits (Green, 1998).

Trade with the West increased after the region was first Islamized, especially after it came under Fatimid rule. Spices, silk, and other goods from the East were reaching Western markets by land and sea, both through Sicily, Italy, and Spain. However, the Moorish merchants did not have an organized structure like the Karimis and Italians. Instead, they had developed a social norm. Commercial relations were conducted within the framework of these norms. Historians have particularly emphasized these social norms and have been the subject of serious debate in scientific circles in recent years. The commercial norms and relations established in the Moorish region had an impact not only on the balance of payments, the flow of precious metals, or production and demand but also on the institutional structure and, therefore, on the economic history of the Mediterranean.

To conduct long-distance trade, the Moors needed to be reliable, and their reputation ensured confidence in their trustworthiness. Maintaining this reputation was crucial for communities like the Radhanites and Moors. Economic sanctions were essential for this system. Avner Greif's work shows that complex social networks and diasporas can create reputation-based sanctioning mechanisms when formal rules are absent. These mechanisms replaced formal legal systems. Traders' shared religious and ethnic origins created natural boundaries, boosting credibility and motivating them to preserve their distinct identities (Greif, 1989).

The Moors, primarily through Spain, played a crucial role in transmitting the Enlightenment to the West. The Crusades and translation schools were critical tools that made Europeans aware of Moorish science. Andalusia became a center of art, medicine, science, music, literature, and philosophy. The work of the philosophers and scientists of the Andalusian state had a significant influence on the intellectual life of medieval Europe. Muslims and non-Muslims often came from abroad to the Iberian Peninsula to study in the libraries and universities of Andalusia. After the reconquest of Toledo, various translation institutions, such as the Toledo School of Translators, were established to translate books and texts from Arabic into Latin. In particular, Arabic letters and mathematics reached Europe in this way, contributing significantly to the development of accounting and joint ventures in commercial life (Essa & Ali, 2010).

1.7.3 Genoese Republic

The most important merchants of the eleventh–thirteenth centuries were the Genoese (Fig. 1.3). The Genoese State Archives reveal that direct trade between Genoese bases and the East was well established and regularly functioning in the second half of the thirteenth century (Piacentini, 2010). In medieval long-distance trade in the eleventh and twelfth centuries, armed Genoese merchants supplemented their early trade with aggression and piracy. Since Islamic states did not consider it a state obligation to protect commercial transport, the Italians had an advantage with their state organization behind them. The Italians were not only using military power, but they had also created an organizational structure in which this power could be used for trade and war and as part of their prestigious social position (Goldberg, 2012). Genoese large and well-equipped ships sailed east along the southern shores of the Black Sea to Kaffa and Tana, Genoese trading outposts on the Crimean Peninsula. The caravans traveled through the south of the valleys and mountains of the Taurus Mountains, through the vast steppes to the north, and on to the affluent markets of Central Asia.

The first Genoese merchants settled in Tabriz in 1280. From Tabriz, they could trade right into the heart of the Iranian plateau, from Lāristān to Hormuz, south of the Gulf. In the east, they could advance as far as Nīshāpur, Herat, Merv, Bukhārā, and Samarkand, the most important cities of the Silk Road. Under the Great Seljuks (1040–1157), the region was stabilized, and the Caspian provinces became a corridor

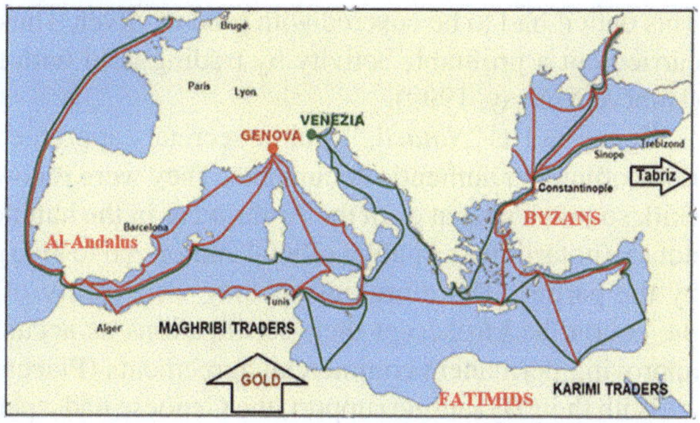

Fig. 1.3 Genoese and Venetian trade routes 12–14 centuries. https://en.wikipedia.org/wiki/Venetian_slave_trade#/media/File:Republik_Venedig_Handelswege01.png (public domain)

for the passage of nomads from Central Asia. The Genoese also benefited from their good relations with the Seljuks. The powerful Mongol state, later established in the region, attached importance to the safe operation of the Silk Road. In the early thirteenth century, the Islamic historian Ibn al-Asīr (1163–1239) wrote that the sense of security and prevailing justice at the time made people dare to display their wealth openly (Kamaruzaman et al., 2015).

By capturing Antalya, the Genoese could control the eastern waters of the Mediterranean and direct the flow of goods through the Red Sea. Despite competition from Venice, which sought to monopolize Euro-Asian trade, Genoa implemented a policy that suited its interests, enabling it to build the most comprehensive and impressive political-institutional and financial-commercial structure of the period. With their skilled maritime experience and technology, they introduced a series of innovations in both navigation and warfare. These innovations soon helped Genoa develop warfare methods that gave it unprecedented superiority at sea. They established important trade relations between the Turkic peoples of Central Asia and the "*city-states*" they established, such as Trabzon and Sinop. Genoese military and diplomatic initiatives were often carried out by individuals or groups of merchants acting independently rather than as the republic's representatives (Hunt & Murray, 1999). The Genoese had independent mercenary units in these regions. They used force when necessary. They acquired new skills and political responsibilities, adapting to some extent to local practices and to the established Iranian-Islamic models of sovereignty, authority, and power that were still very strong in some parts of Central Asia. Thus, they could advance eastward or southward through Tatar and Chinese territories, securing their maritime supremacy and political power. During the thirteenth and fourteenth centuries, the Mongol period, although Genoa, Venice, and Aragon were engaged in hostility and rivalry, which often escalated into naval conflicts, none could dominate the others in a specific trade area. In contrast, by the fourteenth century, a trade pattern had developed. The Genoese were the most critical traders in this trade, specializing in commodities such as "*gum*" (luban), silk, precious stones, horses, and furs. They sold these goods to Europe. In return, they gave enslaved people what they had bought from the Vikings. Trade with the East was based on barter, but since the value of the goods purchased from the East was high, the trade was in deficit.

This deficit had to be covered with gold or silver. Thus, to find precious metals, they carried out a profitable activity by trading gold with the Maghribs in North Africa (Hunt & Murray, 1999).

Genoa had its "*Notarii*," a public secretary appointed by the competent authority to issue official or authentic documents. They were renowned for their competence and skill, so much so that even the Arabs were in the habit of requesting their services. A notary (notarii) was a public official authorized to give public trust to the deeds issued by the parties. Therefore, unless they were guilty of forgery, everyone, including the courts, had to accept their certifications as accurate. They also contributed by approving permanent commercial agreements (Piacentini, 2010).

With their Byzantine support, the Genoese had a permanent base in Pera (Galata). For Genoa, the treaty laid the foundations of their commercial empire in the Near East and transformed it into the main commercial center of the region (Nicol, 1988). The Genoese would continue to use Galata (Pera) as a base after the Ottoman conquest of Constantinople in 1453.

1.7.4 Republic of Venice

The economic growth of the West and the Byzantine recapture of Crete in 961, which had been used as a hub by Arab pirates, reestablished maritime links between the Byzantine Empire and the West. Venice played an important role in this re-establishment and benefited from favorable trading conditions. Like their Genoese rivals, the Venetians were authorized to settle permanently in the neighborhoods and trade centers granted to them in Constantinople, where they established colonies with priests, notaries, and judges (Apellániz, 2013).

Venice was active in the Mediterranean even before the Crusades began. In the ninth and tenth centuries, it had commercial relations with Constantinople. Byzantium was under pressure from the Seljuk Turks, who had conquered Anatolia toward the end of the eleventh century. Venice obtained a series of commercial privileges from Byzantium in 1082 in exchange for help to strengthen its naval defenses. Their trade relations had improved after the Crusades. Venice then acquired bases in Dalmatia and a powerful position in the Aegean. It acquired the southern half of the Peloponnese, Corfu, and Crete, important bases in Constantinople, and access to trade in the Black Sea and the Sea of Azov (McNeill, 2009).

Venetian ships soon reached the Black Sea, where the Mongols revitalized trade by reopening the Silk Road through Central Asia through direct contact with Slavic and Asian merchants (Apellániz, 2013). Venice was as dedicated to trade and navigation as Genoa, but whereas in Genoa, competition and piracy were the norm, in Venice, cooperation and control prevailed (Hunt & Murray, 1999).

The goods brought by merchants from Venice (mainly salt, which was abundant in the Venetian lagoon) were of lesser value than those obtained from Eastern intermediaries, such as silk, spices, spice ointments, medicinal products, and dyes. As a result, the east–west trade established under Venetian control, like the Genoese trade, was structurally open. This imbalance needed to be offset by additional contributions of precious metals, primarily gold. Venetian merchants subsequently established a triangular trade system with North Africa. Through this trade network, they exchanged Western goods with the Maghreb for gold, which they used in Egypt to obtain valuable products such as spices. They then exchanged this gold in Istanbul markets for luxury goods (especially purple silk) and transported it to Italy for the wealthy Western aristocracy. Venice had important connections with both the East and Northern Europe. While it maintained close ties with Karimi merchants in the East, it also traded with the Low Countries. Italians showed great interest in the fairs of Bruges and Champagne, purchasing woolen goods and selling silk, spices, salt, sugar, and varnish. When a sea route opened between the Western Mediterranean and the Atlantic, trade with the Dutch began directly by ship. In this way, they began to manage a very extensive commercial network that could reach from the Black Sea and the Eastern Mediterranean to Western Europe (Norwich, 1982).

During the Mamluk period, Venetian merchants in Alexandria faced a bureaucratic, financial, and commercial system. This system was dominated by local elements represented by Alexandrian officials and merchants, as well as Venetian consulate officials and merchants. In 1490, the Venetian consul Ambrogio Contarini agreed with the Alexandria port and customs officials to determine the export expenses of merchants. After obtaining import permits, the Venetians would store, count, weigh, and seal their goods. Three main offices were involved in this process: the office that distributed the Sultan's spices, the customs inspector and his team, and the tax office. The Sultan's merchant was an important figure who was involved in political and commercial activities. The customs inspector oversaw commercial practices, while the tax office carried out final checks and sent the goods to Venetian ships (Sopracasa, 2016).

The Venetians had developed a highly sophisticated convoy system for trading large galleys in the East. Historians have described the ability to make such complex savings in shipping as a "*medieval maritime revolution.*" The convoy system of the Venetian Republic was designed to protect Venetian merchants, ships, and cargo from pirates, bandits, and rival states, ensuring safe and efficient trade routes. The convoy system allowed Venetian merchants to safely transport more significant quantities of goods across the Mediterranean and increase trade volume. By enabling reliable and predictable trade, the system encouraged merchants to invest in long-distance travel and further increased Venice's dominance in Mediterranean trade. Venice also controlled ports and key trading points, such as those in Dalmatia, the Levant, and North Africa, which gave them considerable economic power. The convoy system was not only about defense; it also facilitated alliances with other states and merchant groups. The convoy system contributed to Venice's economic growth and emphasized its commitment to maintaining order and security in the Mediterranean, making it a reliable partner for merchants and other states. The wealth generated from this trade allowed Venice to develop a sophisticated infrastructure, including banks, insurance systems, and advanced shipbuilding techniques, further strengthening its trading center position (Hunt & Murray, 1999).

1.8 Concluding Remarks and the Aim of the Book

The Middle East experienced a golden period called the Islamic Renaissance from the eighth century. This period lasted until the fifteenth century and even the sixteenth century. During this period, scientific studies were carried out in a vast geography from India to Andalusia, and essential developments in fields such as medicine, philosophy, theology, art, mathematics, astronomy, and Islamic law were made. The knowledge and ideas produced by past civilizations, including ancient Greece and famous philosophers, were transferred to the Islamic world through translations and to Europe through Andalusia (Kraemer, 1992).

During the Abbasids, there was a significant development in banking activities. Interestingly, the banking system under the Abbasids developed more rapidly during their decline and disintegration than during their heyday. This was due to the shortage of cash at that time, the lack of revenues, the debts of government officials, the development of the ikat system (giving the use of state property to individuals), especially the practice of rent (execution), and finally the unprecedented progress of trade and commerce, all factors that strengthened the banking system of the period (Islam, 1984). The profound impact of Muslim trade on the early medieval banks of the West is another question of historical importance. There is evidence that Florentine and Venetian bankers learned much from Muslim merchants (Bowden, 1977). In the Middle Ages, the riches of the East came to the West via the Mediterranean, not only trade goods but also accounting and financial methods, company structures, and even business sense. Almost all the technology used in Europe until the fourteenth century was inherited from Rome or borrowed from Chinese, Indian, or Arab sources. By the late Middle Ages, the major Greek and Arabic writings on physics, astronomy, mathematics, geometry, and geography had long been translated into Latin and widely disseminated (Hunt & Murray, 1999).

A large and powerful merchant class, rising from the tenth to the twelfth century, was the primary carrier of Muslim civilization, including in the Jewish and Christian enclaves in the East. At the same time, Italian and other Mediterranean merchants began to appear in Europe. The development of markets extended not only to Islamic countries but also to South India, a crucial hub on the Silk Road, situated between China and the Persian Gulf. Local guilds were established to ensure safety and quality control and prevent local competition. The high volume of business created a favorable environment for long-term trade. In his memoirs, the Chinese traveler Ma Huan wrote that "*Muslim merchants are extremely honest and trustworthy*" (Frankopan, 2017).

In the East, the country's rulers meticulously monitored the protection of the market and the orderly conduct of shopping activities. Although the narrow corridor where the state maintains order and its power is chained, as defined by Acemoğlu and Robinson (2019), is not fully formed, a channel has been created through which trade can be conducted freely. There was a unity of understanding between the merchant community and the state. This development was due to the moderate state administration approach of states such as the Abbasids and Fatimids. The highest priority of the rulers was to ensure that merchants' goods were not harmed, that trade was conducted honestly, and that incidents such as theft and extortion were prevented. The Islamic world experienced its most prosperous period, characterized by state administration and economic structure advancements. All evidence from the Geniza records suggests that in the eleventh-twelfth centuries, describing the Mediterranean region as a free trade zone was acceptable. Italian merchants traveled freely as far as Tabriz, where they established a trading base and reached Central Asia—despite being subjected to various external shocks such as the Crusades, Mongol invasions, and shifts in trade routes, the Middle Eastern region maintained its weight in world trade until the sixteenth century (Pamuk & Shatzmiller, 2014).

Islam's commercial heyday was underpinned by the concept that law was personal, not territorial. The individual was judged according to the law of their religious community, or even their religious "*school*" or sect, not the law of their region. Perhaps it would be more accurate to say that the states did not have any law, except for some local laws promulgated and repealed occasionally. They were under the protection of religions and their various subdivisions. It was expected and natural for Jews in Spain or France to seek "*Supreme Court decisions*" in Jerusalem, Baghdad, or later in Cairo, with Maimonides and his successors (Goitein, 1999).

In the eleventh century, despite the rise of European naval power and the encroachment of Italian cities, Mediterranean trade remained mainly in the hands of Islam. Over time, however, Eastern markets lost their supremacy, and by the twelfth century, Muslim merchants had lost their dominance in the Mediterranean to the Italians, who had better commercial organizations. Moreover, religious and socio-cultural factors, which could not keep pace with changing world conditions, slowed down the progress of the East. At the same time, the West gained supremacy that lasted for centuries.

1.8.1 The Rise of Italians in Mediterranean Trade

From the twelfth century onward, two factors contributed to the commercial superiority of the Genoese and Venetians over Muslim merchants. The first is that the Italians increased their credibility by making contracts under an official umbrella. While Maghreb merchants ensured their adherence to contracts through reputation-based sanctioning mechanisms, Italians ensured their adherence through the institution of notarization, which was inherited from Rome. From the twelfth century onward, as civil law grew in importance in the city-states of Italy, the notary began to play a central role in the administration of law. In his professional capacity as the bearer of publica fides, the notary represented the public face of authority and gave the documents he sealed or signed a specific, measurable evidential value (Peretz, 2006). Islamic countries also had officials called "*kātib or muhtesib.*" Both Islamic and Italian notaries were advanced in their respective legal systems. However, Italian notaries were perhaps more advanced in commercial law, commerce, and secular government, reflecting the expansion of Italy's merchant republics and legal infrastructure. On the other hand, Islamic notaries were deeply integrated into the religious and legal structures of the Islamic world and played an important role in certifying religious and personal matters, including marriage, inheritance, and other important legal transactions. Both systems were vital to their societies, but the Italian system was perhaps more specialized in the commercial and secular fields, giving it an advantage in overall development throughout the medieval period.

The second factor was the convoy system of maritime transportation. In particular, the Italian states used this system to control important trade routes between East and West and to consolidate their economic power through trade with Muslims. The convoys enabled merchants to trade in larger volumes with greater security, increasing the volume of trade and strengthening Western economic control. In addition, Venice and Genoa consolidated their power on the trade routes by forming strategic alliances with powerful states. In the East, on the other hand, merchants were unable to secure adequate protection for their merchant ships due to the lack of state power.

Venice was the most successful of the Northern Italian city-states in creating and maintaining a republic dominated by a merchant capitalist elite. Venetian merchants developed innovative business and banking techniques in their commercial activities in the Mediterranean basin. This transformation was mainly due to Venice's strategic position as a maritime republic and a dominant power on the East and West Mediterranean trade routes. They created political and legal institutions that guaranteed property rights and the enforceability of contracts and were pioneers in the development of foreign exchange and credit markets, banking, and accounting. An efficient government bond market was established in Venice, where interest was paid regularly. The ruling class and the religious leadership worked hard to create a tolerant environment where foreign merchants could operate with relative freedom. Although theoretically part of the Catholic world, it had privileged relations with the Byzantine Empire. Venetian diplomacy was highly professional, pragmatic, opportunistic, and dedicated to pursuing its commercial interests. They were also surprisingly adaptable to political change.

The shift of the Silk Road to the oceans due to geographical discoveries was a major factor in the strengthening of Western European trade and markets. However, there are religious and socio-cultural factors beyond this.

1.8.2 Institutional Divergence: The Evolution of Commerce in the East and West

Until the nineteenth century, Islamic partnership law formed the basis of commercial cooperation in the Islamic world. It changed little over time, developing an organizational structure conducive to commercial ventures established across familial and communal boundaries. It has not, however, given rise to radical and complex ventures capable of aggregating the people's savings, mobilizing their resources, and gaining the ability to survive for centuries. The structure of the partnerships did not lend itself to the model of a kind of joint-stock company with legal personality and longevity. The Western experience was completely different. From the tenth century onward, drawing on Eastern know-how, Europe developed increasingly long-lasting and complex commercial institutions, and the bourgeoisie gained political power. While the West developed increasingly powerful solutions to the problem of creating trust outside the family and commercial enterprise, Islamic countries failed to develop solutions to make commercial institutions work more effectively in the new era (Kuran, 2003). Although trade flourished in the cities of the Middle East, new institutions were created, and several innovations in finance and accounting emerged; neither Islamic law nor Islamic rulers allowed the city to develop new dynamics. Nor did the urban population demand autonomy or the ability to become a politically influential community through reconciliation with the rulers. This situation undoubtedly had economic repercussions. For example, although trade finance was flourishing, the Islamic States were unable to take steps to establish a national bank. As we have explained above, financial transactions were not new to the Islamic world. However, while banking activities began in Europe in the fifteenth century, in the East, neither the government nor the merchants were up to the task of establishing a state bank that could handle commercial transactions well and efficiently. While Islam's highly structured political system provided early benefits, it also constrained cultural adaptations in response to fundamental international and technological changes in later centuries. For example, prohibitions on interest are believed to have retarded financial development in the Islamic world (Acemoglu & Robinson, 2021). Moreover, such an institution could become a political force and assume an unusual position between the state economy and private enterprise, even becoming a threat to ruling elites (Taviani, 2022).

Although many institutional changes took place in the medieval and early modern Middle East, political power continued to be concentrated in the hands of the monarch and the state elites around him. Landowners, merchants, manufacturers, and moneylenders had considerable local control and autonomy but were not represented in centralized governments. Their influence on economic issues and, more generally, on the central government's policies remained limited. Although the Islamic ideology's legal infrastructure and understanding of sharing played an essential role in economic development, it was insufficient. The institutional change was thus not completely inclusive. There were laws and practices restricting individuals from owning land and property. Even at the end of the eighteenth century, as the Industrial Revolution began in Europe, local manufacturing in the Middle East was still largely intact. Still, the region could not carry out its own Industrial Revolution. With the economic rise of Europe, institutional changes in the region increasingly reflected the power of European states and corporations. In the East, on the other hand, rulers were never willing to share their power, and corrupt administrations never fully allowed the dynamics of society to work adequately (Pamuk, 2012). Moreover, cities in the Islamic world were, on average, much larger than those in Europe, indicative of a predatory state and low commercial openness. During this period, eastern cities were under the influence of powerful, predatory states that could and often did impose heavy tax and military burdens on the cities within their territory. Under these predatory regimes, usually, only the capital flourished (Bosker et al., 2013).

In conclusion, according to Robinson and Acemoglu (2012), the key to the success or failure of nations lies in their institutions. Inclusive institutions that provide secure property rights, fair legal systems, access to education, and broad political participation lead to prosperity and long-term growth. In contrast, extractive institutions that concentrate wealth and power in the hands of a few and limit the involvement of the broader population lead to stagnation, inequality, and failure. As Acemoğlu and Robinson (2019) argue, there is a need for a narrow corridor between the oppressive state and the society that wants liberty but cannot sustain order. Even if the state provides order, the power of the state must be shackled with inclusive institutions that offer a balance between the state and society. Robinson and Acemoğlu (2012) define inclusive institutions as protecting property rights, lowering market entry barriers, upholding the rule of law, and expanding economic opportunities (Fig. 1.4).

The presence or absence of inclusive institutions can often explain a society's historical trajectory. In the late Middle Ages, the Abbasid Caliphate, followed by the Fatimids, exhibited characteristics that could be considered relatively inclusive, including a thriving commercial economy, religious tolerance, and intellectual diversity, particularly from the 9th to the eleventh centuries. However, it also had significant limitations in political centralization, social stratification, gender inequality, and ethnic tensions, which prevented it from fully embodying inclusive institutions as the term is understood today. The success of the Abbasid period was primarily based on integrating diverse ethnic and religious groups into the empire's cultural

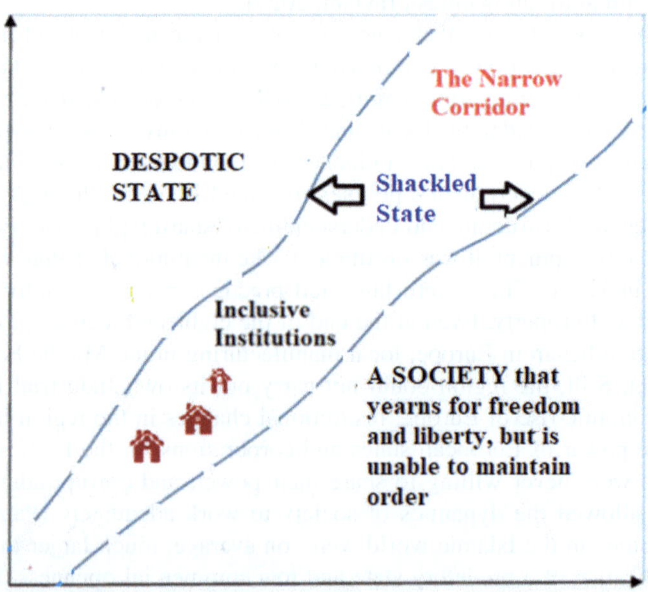

Fig. 1.4 The narrow corridor of Acemoglu and Robinson (2019)

and economic life. Nevertheless, its political system was not so inclusive, mainly as power was concentrated in the hands of the military elite. Therefore, although the Abbasid Caliphate had certain inclusive features, it did not fully meet the criteria for inclusive institutions, especially in the long term. In any case, it was impossible for the religious legal structure on which it was based to be stretched further. As we will see in the following chapters, from the fourteenth century onward, while commodity and financial centers were established in the West, the Ottoman Empire dominated the Middle East. They had no inclusive institutions. The Ottomans established an imperial order based on conquest, the acquisition of economic power, and territorial expansion. Although the Silk Road was weakening at the beginning of the New Age, the trade channels were still operational and partially under Islamic countries' control. It was thought that this would not change forever. While Western Europe entered a new era with the Renaissance and reforms, transforming its trade centers into financial centers and stock exchanges, Eastern states, which struggled to keep pace with this change, could not follow the dynamics in Europe and develop sufficiently. As Charles Darwin said, "It *is not the strongest of the species that survive, nor the most intelligent, but the one most responsive to change.*" Over time, this aphorism came to represent the increasing value of free competition in the West, whereas the East, which resisted change, could not grasp this understanding.

1.8.3 Aim and Scope of the Book

This book aims to explain how markets that were initially based solely on the trade of goods evolved into money markets, government bond markets, and stock markets. This long historical journey began in the Middle East during the Golden Age of Islam, as described in this section, and shifted toward the Western Mediterranean after the Crusades. The European chapter that benefited from the eastern experiences began with fairs and festivals in Champagne and Lyon. Permanent trade centers were later established in Bruges and Antwerp. In this way, commodity and money markets were integrated and structurally developed. The Amsterdam Stock Exchange, which fought for independence against Spain, became the world's first stock Exchange in the seventeenth century. Envious of the Amsterdam Stock Exchange, the English established the world's first global stock exchange in London after the glorious revolution. On the other hand, Paris emerged as the most important stock exchange in continental Europe after undergoing a different historical process marked by various wars and revolutions. However, after World War I, London lost its leadership to New York, the new center of capitalism, and the Paris Stock Exchange began to decline. Meanwhile, the Ottoman Stock Exchange has become an interesting and colorful example that inspires developing countries.

Undoubtedly, the development of financial markets has not followed a continuous, linear progression throughout history. On the contrary, this evolution has followed a fluctuating course, occasionally interrupted, and shifted direction depending on environmental conditions. As Andrew Lo (2004) argues in his Adaptive Markets Hypothesis, the evolution of financial markets has been influenced not only by rational decisions but also by dynamics such as cognitive biases in human behavior, institutional structures, and environmental variables. In his context, markets have evolved over time to adapt to these factors, and economic institutions and instruments have adapted accordingly, much like natural selection. In this book, the relationship between the formation of inclusive institutions and the development of financial markets will be examined first, drawing on the arguments of Acemoğlu and Robinson. We will also explain how financial market players, who gain power over time, challenge inclusive institutions such as strong legal systems, independent central banks, and regulatory institutions, as well as competitive elections and freedom of the press and civil society, which provide the foundation for their formation to achieve more significant benefits.

From Jonathan's and Garraway's coffeehouses in London to the sidewalk bankers of Paris and Wall Street, from the tulip speculators of Amsterdam to the air games of the Ottoman Stock Exchange and the stock barons of the Gilded Age, our book introduces the interesting venues where stocks were traded and the speculators, some dishonest, some skilled, who speculated there. By describing the glory days of capital markets and various crises, this book will assess developments in securities markets up to the first quarter of the twenty-first century and discuss the phases of capital markets, including institutional investor capitalism and digitalization. The role of inclusive institutions in this development will be explained. As the scope of the subject is vast, particular emphasis will be placed on the peak years of each market.

References

Acemoglu, D., & Robinson, J. A. (2019). The narrow corridor: How nations struggle for liberty. Penguin UK.

Acemoglu, D., & Robinson, J. A. (2021). Culture, institutions, and social equilibria: A framework (No. w28832). National Bureau of Economic Research.

Adelson, H. L. (1960). Early medieval trade routes. *The American Historical Review, 65*(2), 271–287.

Ağır, A. M. (2017). Al-Makrīzī's Khitat and the Markets in Cairo during the Mamlūks Era. *Belleten, 81*(291), 329–372.

Andreau, J. (1999). *Banking and business in the Roman world*. Cambridge University Press.

Apellániz, F. (2013). Venetian trading networks in the medieval Mediterranean. *Journal of Interdisciplinary History, 44*(2), 157–179.

Ashtor, E. (1956). The Kārimī merchants. *Journal of the Royal Asiatic Society, 88*(1–2), 45–56.

Ashtor, E. (1976). Spice prices in the Near East in the 15th century. *Journal of the Royal Asiatic Society, 108*(1), 26–41.

Ashtor, Eliahu. (1973). Banking instruments between the Muslim East and the Christian West. *Journal of European Economic History, 1*, 553–573.

Barnard, M., Angela, V., & Christine de Nobrega. (n.d.). Cambridge University Press 978-1-107-67342-7—Study & Master Economic and Management Sciences Learner's Book Grade 7. https://assets.cambridge.org/97811076/73427/excerpt/9781107673427_excerpt.pdf

Birnie, A. (1952). The history and ethics of interest. W. Hodge, Glasgow.
Bosker, M., Buringh, E., & Van Zanden, J. L. (2013). From Baghdad to London: Unraveling urban development in Europe, the Middle East, and North Africa, 800–1800. *Review of Economics and Statistics, 95*(4), 1418–1437.
Botticini, M., & Eckstein, Z. (2003). From farmers to merchants: A human capital interpretation of Jewish economic history.
Bowden, L. (1977). Finance in the medieval Muslim world. *British Journal of Middle Eastern Studies, 4*(1), 40–41.
Cary, M., Scullard, H. H. (1975). Diocletian and constantine. In *A history of Rome*. Palgrave Macmillan, London. https://doi.org/10.1007/978-1-349-02415-5_42
Chapra, M. U. (2014). *Morality and justice in Islamic economics and finance*. Edward Elgar Publishing.
Cohen, H. J. (1970). The economic background and the secular occupations of Muslim jurisprudents and traditionists in the classical period of Islam: (Until the Middle of the Eleventh Century). *Journal of the Economic and Social History of the Orient/Journal de l'histoire economique et sociale de l'Orient*, 16–61.
Cousin, J. (n.d.) Diocletian. Britannica. https://www.britannica.com/biography/Diocletian
Daftary, F. (2021). The Ismāʿīlīs and their traditions. In *Handbook of Islamic sects and movements* (pp. 235–254). Brill.
El-Gamal, M. A. (2006). *Islamic finance: Law, economics, and practice*. Cambridge University Press.
Essa, A., & Ali, O. (2010). Studies in Islamic civilization: The Muslim contribution to the Renaissance. International Institute of Islamic Thought (IIIT).
Findlay, R., & O'Rourke, K. H. (2008). Lessons from the history of trade and war. VoxEU. Org, Centre for Economic Policy Research, London.
Frankopan, P. (2017). *The silk roads: A new history of the world*. Vintage.
Fu, P. (1971). Governmental accounting in China during the Chou dynasty (1122BC-256BC). *Journal of Accounting Research, 9*, 40–51.
Geva, B. (2017). The medieval Hawale: The legal nature of the Suftaj and other Islamic payment instruments. Osgoode Legal Studies Research Paper, (42).
Goitein, S. D. (1999). A Mediterranean society. Univ of California Press.
Goitein, S. D. (1967). *A Mediterranean society: The Jewish communities of the Arab world as portrayed in the documents of the Cairo Geniza* (Vol. 1). University of California Press.
Goldberg, J. (2012). *Trade and institutions in the medieval Mediterranean: The Geniza merchants and their business world*. Cambridge University Press.
Grayson, J. R. (2017). Jews in the political life of Abbasid Baghdad, 908–1258 (Doctoral dissertation, Johns Hopkins University).
Green, R. (1998). The empire of Ghana. First book. New York. NY: Grolier Pub. ISBN 9780531202760.
Greif, A. (1989). Reputation and coalitions in medieval trade: evidence on the Maghribi traders. *The Journal of Economic History, 49*(4), 857–882. https://doi.org/10.1017/S0022050700009475
Guo, D. (1988). History of Chinese Accounting (Chinese Version) Vol. II, (1988), Beijing: Chinese Finance and Economics Publishing House.
Hill, F. J., & Awde, N. (2003). *A history of the Islamic world*. Princeton University Press.
Hunt, E. S., & James, M. M. (1999). *A history of business in medieval Europe, 1200–1550*. Cambridge University Press.
Islam, Z. (1984). Banking in the Abbasıd period: A special study of the tenth century AD. In *Proceedings of the Indian History Congress* (Vol. 45, pp. 780–789). Indian History Congress. 1984 January.
İznik, E. (2011). İmparator Diocletianus' un "Tavan (En Yüksek) Fiyatlar Fermanı""Edictum de pretiis Rerum Venalium." *Tarih Araştırmaları Dergisi, 30*(49), 97–130.

Johansen, B. (2006). The Salam contract: Law and Capital Formation in the Abbasid Empire (11th–12th Centuries). In *Annales. Histoire, Sciences Sociales* (Vol. 61, No. 4, pp. 863–899). Editions de l'EHESS.
Jubayr, I. (2019). The travels of Ibn Jubayr: A medieval journey from Cordoba to Jerusalem. Bloomsbury Publishing.
Kalan, E. (2014). XIII-XIV. yüzyıllarda kuzey ipek yolu ve altın orda hanları'nın ticaret politikaları. *Avrasya Etüdleri, 45*(1), 43–62.
Kamaruzaman, A. F., Jamaludin, N., & Fadzil, A. F. M. (2015). Ibn Al-Athir's Philosophy of History in Al-Kamil Fi Al-Tarikh. *Asian Social Science, 11*(23), 28.
Kraemer, J. L. (1992). *Humanism in the renaissance of Islam: The cultural revival during the Buyid age* (Vol. 7). Brill.
Kuran, T. (2003). The Islamic commercial crisis: Institutional roots of economic underdevelopment in the Middle East. *The Journal of Economic History, 63*(2), 414–446.
Labib, S. Y. (1969). Capitalism in medieval Islam. *The Journal of Economic History, 29*(1), 79–96.
Lieber, A. E. (1968). Eastern business practices and medieval European commerce. *Economic History Review, 21*(2).
Lin, Z. J. (1992). Chinese double-entry bookkeeping before the nineteenth century. *Accounting Historians Journal, 19*(2), 103–122.
Lo, A. W. (2004). The adaptive markets hypothesis: Market efficiency from an evolutionary perspective. *The Journal of Portfolio Management, 30*, 15–29.
Madden, T. F. (2005). *The new concise history of the Crusades.* Rowman & Littlefield.
Maghreb. (2024). Britannica. https://www.britannica.com/place/Maghreb
McNeill, W. H. (2009). *Venice.* University of Chicago Press.
Mitchell, P. I. (n.d.). Dallas Baptist Unıversity. Changes in Medieval Commerce and Production. https://www.dbu.edu/mitchell/medieval-resources/economicchangesmedieval.html
Nicol, D. M. (1988). *Byzantium and Venice: A study in diplomatic and cultural relations.* Cambridge University Press. ISBN 0-521-34157-4.
Nobes, C. W., & Zaid, O. A. (2001). Were Islamıc records precursors to accounting books based on the Italıan method? A comment [with Response]. *The Accounting Historians Journal, 28*(2), 207–218.
Norwich, J. J. (1982). *A history of Venice.* Alfred B. Knopf. ISBN 9780394524108. Retrieved 2020-12-06.
Pamuk, Ş. (2012). Political power and institutional change: Lessons from the Middle East. *Economic History of Developing Regions, 27*(sup1), S41–S56.
Pamuk, Ş, & Shatzmiller, M. (2014). Plagues, wages, and economic change in the Islamic Middle East, 700–1500. *The Journal of Economic History, 74*(1), 196–229.
Peretz, D. (2006). The Roman interpreter and his diplomatic and military roles. *Historia: Zeitschrift fur Alte Geschichte*, 451–470
Piacentini, V. F. (2010). The golden age of Genoa's eastwards trade (13th–15th Centurıes). *The Journal of Central Asian Studies, 19*(1), 25.
Promissory note. (n.d.). Wikipedia. https://en.wikipedia.org/wiki/Promissory_note
Ray, N. D. (1997). The medieval Islamic system of credit and banking: Legal and historical considerations. *Arab LQ, 12*, 43.
Robinson, J. A., & Acemoglu, D. (2012). *Why nations fail: The origins of power, prosperity, and poverty* (pp. 45–47). Profile.
Rubin, J. (2010). Bills of exchange, interest bans, and impersonal exchange in Islam and Christianity. *Explorations in Economic History, 47*(2), 213–227.
Sopracasa, A. (2016). Venetian merchants and Alexandrian officials (end of the fifteenth–beginning of the sixteenth century). *Mamlūk Studies Review, 19.*
Shatzmiller, M. (2017). Prices and price formation in the Islamic Middle East: The role of money supply and state policies. In I prezzi delle cose nell'età preindustriale: selezione di recherche (pp. 15–33). Firenze University Press.

Smith, R. D. (2015). Calamity and transition: Re-Imagining Italian trade in the eleventh-century Mediterranean. *Past & Present, 228*(1), 15–56.

Spuler, B. (1966). Geschichte Mittelasiens seit dem Auftreten der Türken. Handbuch der Orientalistik; Abt. 1, Bd. 5, 5: Abt. 1. Der Nahe und der Mittlere Osten: Bd. 5. Altaistik: Geschichte Mittelasiens, 123–310.

Taviani, C. (2022). *The making of the modern corporation: The Casa Di San Giorgio and its legacy (1446–1720).* Routledge.

Udovitch, A. L. (1979). Bankers without banks: Commerce, banking, and society in the Islamic world of the Middle Ages. In UCLA Center for Medieval.

Udovitch, A. L. (1975). Reflections on the institutions of credits and banking in the medieval Islamic near east. *Studia Islamica, 41*, 5–21.

Udovitch, A. (1985). Islamic law and the social context of exchange in the medieval middle east. *History and Anthropology, 1*(2), 445–465.

Van Doosselaere, Q. (2009). *Commercial agreements and social dynamics in medieval genoa.* Cambridge University Press.

Vijayalekshmy, M. (2015). From Egypt to India and Chına–The Karımımerchants in the Indian ocean trade of the medieval world. Twenty-First Issue, 112.

Chapter 2
Lyon Trade: From Fairs to Money Markets (13th–14th Centuries)

2.1 Introduction

On a sunny September day in 1180 AD, a caravan of merchants almost arrived at the fair of Troyes in the Champagne region. In front of the convoy was a yellow and red St. Mark's winged lion pennant, indicating that they had come from Venice. The convoy consisted of many horses and carts, all carefully loaded with valuable goods to be sold at the fair. Large horse-drawn carts carried wool, silk, glassware, spices, wine, and other luxury goods in high demand at the fair. They had bought most of these goods from the Venetian ships that had arrived from Alexandria a month earlier. The merchants were accompanied by servants, stewards, or assistants who managed the day-to-day running of the convoy. At the front of the convoy were the leading merchants, typically wealthy and well dressed in finely tailored clothes. These merchants wore long tunics or capes adorned in vibrant reds, blues, or purples and decorated with intricate embroidery or furs, symbolizing their wealth and status. As there was a risk of encountering bandits or enemies on the long journey to the Troyes Fair, merchants were accompanied by a small group of armed guards to protect their goods and ensure safe passage.

On both sides of the town's main road were narrow, Gothic-style buildings with multi-paned windows and overhanging upper floors. They could hear music coming from the marketplace next to the town. Pietro, one of the leading merchants of the caravan, estimated that the fun had already begun, his tired men in his entourage eager to taste the famous wines of Champagne as soon as possible. Many local merchants saw them approaching and rushed toward the caravan. It was vital for them that the Italians had come to the market; they knew that they usually brought highly sought-after goods. The fairgrounds were lined with tents and pavilions sewn with brightly colored fabrics. The tent fabrics, usually wool, linen, or silk, were dyed in rich hues of deep reds, blues, greens, and yellows. The tents were generally not luxurious, decorated with simple but functional details. Wooden poles supported the tent, some

M. B. Karan, *A History of Stock Exchanges*, Contributions to Economics,
https://doi.org/10.1007/978-3-032-07788-2_2

with decorative ropes or tassels hanging from the corners. Stalls were filled with goods.

Complete and neatly arranged to attract attention, the convoy headed toward the area where wealthier merchants or noble guests were staying. Apart from tents, elegant buildings were decorated with flags and symbols. Heraldic symbols hung in front of the buildings, fluttering to the rhythm of the gently blowing wind.

The street leading to the main square of the fair was decorated with greenery and garlands of flowers. On the one side of the road, stalls selling cloth, silk, and fine linen were draped with fabric. Rolls of brightly patterned cloth were neatly stacked and hung from high beams, creating a wave of colorful patterns that contrasted with the more mundane surroundings. On the other side of the road was the spice market. Spices, herbs, and perfumes were displayed in wooden crates or ceramic pots; some spices, such as saffron and cinnamon, were vividly colored. In the center of the square was a church. It was decorated with religious symbols and crosses. Since religious festivals were held, many religious people gathered here to pray. The smell of incense emanating from the church mingled with roasting meat.

As the caravan was heading east to the inn where they were to stay, Pietro separated from the caravan with one of his guards and walked toward the area where the moneychangers were. Pietro did not want to carry all his money in cash, so he would give the "*Lettres de foire*" (fair letter) he had received from a Venetian banker to David, a Jew he had known and trusted for a long time. David was like his personal banker at the fair. This time, he would pay some cash and the rest in letters. This letter showed that his money was blocked in an account. Three months ago, at the fair in Provins, he had borrowed money from him at interest to buy more goods, and he was going to pay it off. Since there was no prohibition on usury at fairs, they could freely trade money with the Jewish money changer. The money changer was significant in a busy medieval fair, providing essential services to international merchants and travelers who wanted to extend credit, exchange money, or buy or exchange fair letters. The décor was both practical and symbolic, reflecting the trust in and value placed on the role of the money changer.

The money changer's booth, made of a brown tent, was in the same area as the other money changers and close to the festival square. Guards could be seen stationed where the money changers were; this was supposed to be a safe area. On shelves or in small cabinets behind the money changer counter were coin scales, notebooks, and rolls of parchment. On the other side of the tent, David hung the emblem of his guild, embroidered in gold thread, indicating that the money changers worked under the guild's protection. There was also a delicate scale on the counter to measure the coins. Next to it was a set of weights, each carefully calibrated to show that the money changer dealt honestly in local and foreign currencies. The centerpiece of the stand was a variety of coins from all over Europe and beyond, carefully arranged in trays or wooden boxes. Gold, silver, and copper coins were categorized by size, type, and weight. On the one side of the table, letters of credit or promissory notes completed the décor of the sale. Attentive eyes could see a locked box behind the counter or fixed to the floor, used as a safe.

Pietro placed the "*Lettres de foire*" on the counter and the florins he had brought from the bag next to him in exchange for the debt. After carefully examining the lettres de foire, the assistant of the exchanger took the coins and carefully examined them with a magnifying glass. He also weighed the coins to check their authenticity and struck them against a stone to listen to the clang. He then converted them into Livre, the local currency. He recorded each transaction in a ledger written in Latin and stamped the documents to show that the debt had been paid. His account was closed for now, but he was not finished with David. At the end of the fair, when all the shopping was done, the merchants and the money exchangers would meet and settle accounts again.

Pietro left the money changer's booth and walked toward the inn where his caravan mates were. It was getting slightly dark. The market was illuminated by torches and oil lamps attached to poles on the sides of the tents. It cast a warm, flickering glow over the fairgrounds, creating a magical atmosphere in the twilight. Now, he could join them for the nightly entertainment and drink lots of wine.

The Fair of Troyes in the twelfth century, dramatized above, was the most important market of the late medieval period. By the mid-ninth century, a market had begun to develop between the Seine and Rhine Rivers in France, on Europe's trade routes from northern Italy. Here, surplus produce from early monastic farms was collected, and local markets were established where grain was exchanged for wine or other goods produced further afield. In England, markets were established in and around London in the eleventh century. By the time of the Norman Conquest, local markets had gained regional importance in Norwich, York, Winchester, and Lincoln. Most of Europe had a modest level of trade, but before the eleventh century, the European market structure was unstable and uncertain. Marketplaces and times were rarely fixed or permanent; laws governing market behavior were imprecise or non-existent; law and order on roads and waterways were uncertain. Here, too, landowner interference and claims of privilege determined the agreed terms, locations, rules, and security for buyers and sellers (Hunt & Murray, 1999).

In the tenth and eleventh centuries AD, Northern Europe also participated in international trade; goods from Venice began to reach the Dutch cities, and Vikings collected and sold large numbers of enslaved people from their raids. The buyers were Venice and Genoa. These slaves were highly valued in the Asian market. In return, they bought silk, spices, and various textiles from the East. Silver was exported from the mines in Saxony, while grain from England was exported to Norway. Scandinavian timber and fish were also imported. After the Norman conquest of Britain in 1066 AD, England expanded its trade to France and the Low Countries, importing cloth and wine. They exported grain and wool, from which Dutch weavers produced textiles. The Italian trio of Venice, Pisa, and Genoa became increasingly wealthy and expanded their trade network. Pisa was an Italian city-state that became especially powerful during the Crusades. Pisa was the historical rival of Genoa at sea and Florence and Lucca on land, but it declined in the thirteenth century. The strip from northern Italy through Lyon, Paris, and the Low Countries is still the most urbanized and economically powerful region of Europe, and it is known as the blue banana.

By the thirteenth century AD, as traders took advantage of better roads, canals, and, especially, more technologically advanced ships, longer-distance trade in less valuable, everyday goods became possible; factors that shortened transport time, increased capacity, reduced losses, and made costs more attractive. In addition, the growing urban population stimulated trade. Merchants were now more experienced and had learned to overcome difficulties. The growth of markets and trade in Europe from the tenth to the thirteenth century constituted a kind of economic renaissance. During this period, it became important what was bought and sold, how, and by whom. By now, market networks had grown to encompass regional and international spaces, and more distant market relationships brought more excellent transportation and payment problems, making the direct exchange of one commodity for another increasingly difficult. Trade in Europe was monetized, so the incentive for merchants to adopt coins as a medium of exchange became increasingly compelling. Merchants began to say, "*No mint, no market.*" From 730 to 849, the mints of the Carolingian Empire were concentrated precisely in the area of most significant economic expansion, in the region bordered by the Loire and Rhine rivers (Hunt & Murray, 1999).

International trade was booming as many cities established international trading posts where foreign merchants could live temporarily and trade their goods. As Fig. 2.1 shows, land trade routes between Italy and the Low Countries flourished in addition to maritime trade. At the beginning of the thirteenth century AD, Genoa had 198 resident merchants, 95 Dutch, and 51 French. There were German merchants in the Steelyard district of London, on Venice's famous Rialto Bridge, and in the Tyske Bryggen district of Bergen, Norway. Merchants from Marseille and Barcelona were permanently camped in North African ports. Economic migration had reached such a scale that these ports had to set up their consulates to protect the rights of their citizens. Along with trade came the exchange of money. With the experience and interaction they gained in the Italian and Asian markets, they developed practices such as bills of exchange and their commercial activities within the European continent (World History Encyclopedia, 2019).

With the growth of their economic activities, commercial relations between states and rulers became more complex with the addition of intermediaries and agents. Interregional commercial ventures were financed by wealthy investors who usually received 75% of the profits if they invested the entire initial capital. The rest of the money went to the merchants who collected the goods and shipped them to the requested destination. As we explained in Chapter 1, this commercial formation was called commenda and was an early and one-off form of limited partnership (Van Doosselaere, 2009). The investing partner would provide the capital, and the traveling partner would run a commercial enterprise (usually shipping); the initial capital would be returned to the investing partner; and the remaining profits would then be divided. An alternative arrangement, the Societas maris, was for the investor to provide two-thirds of the capital and the merchant the rest. Profits were then split 50–50 (Hawk, 2016). Merchant reputation and trust formed the basis of the commercial revolution in Western Europe. New accounting techniques in these

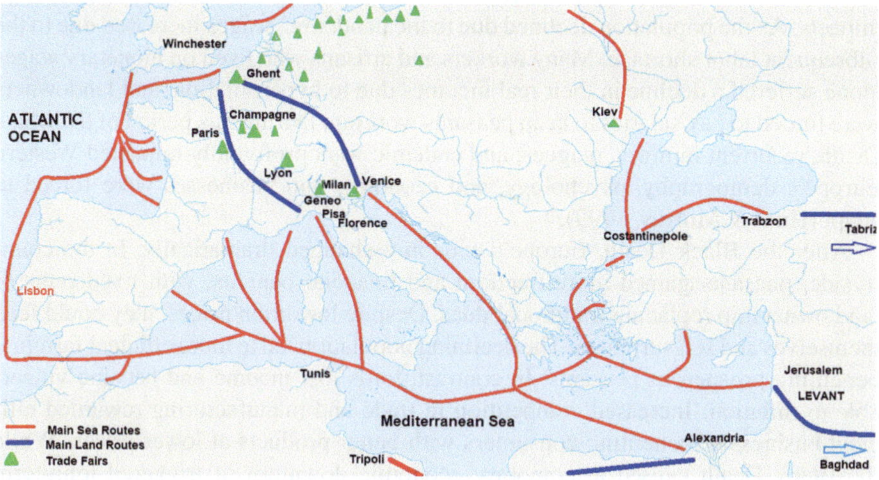

Fig. 2.1 Trade routes of Europe and Middle East in twelfth century. Drawn by the author

ventures provided additional security against fraud, while single-venture partnerships achieved excellent results (Hunt & Murray, 1999).

In most European cities of the twelfth century, schools were established to teach basic merchant education. City accounts and many commercial documents continued to be kept in Latin until the mid-thirteenth century, requiring either the employment of clerically trained scribes or at least some merchants to be educated in Latin. In southern Europe, this need for Latin documents was met mainly by civil or public notaries, who became the principal drafters of all kinds of commercial papers in twelfth-century Genoa and elsewhere. In the fourteenth and fifteenth centuries, most men and women of the European merchant class could read and write, often in more than one language. The successful merchants of the central Mediterranean trading ports enjoyed great prestige and formed the ruling elite. In the interior of Italy and Flanders, the landed nobility were initially somewhat disdainful of trade but soon overcame their dislike and successfully participated in it (Hunt & Murray, 1999).

For long-distance trade to flourish, there had to be a relationship of trust between the producer and the trader. As medieval businesspeople's surviving accounts and letters often show, business affairs and family relationships were intertwined. Italian merchant bankers can be an example (Hunt & Murray, 1999). In this context, two large companies emerged in the fourteenth century. These were the Bardi and Peruzzi companies. These merchant bankers established huge organizations throughout Europe and traded with England. However, they went bankrupt in 1343 due to Edward III, the king of England, failing to pay his debts.

In the fourteenth century, the plague epidemic called the "*Black Death*," which killed 30–50% of the European population, had just ended. This epidemic ravaged Europe from 1346 to 1353 (Hansen, 2012). It was one of the deadliest epidemics in human history. The Black Death had far-reaching population, economic, and cultural impacts. As the population declined due to the pandemic, wages increased due to the subsequent labor shortage. Many workers and artisans who lived on monetary wages alone suffered a decline in their real incomes due to hyperinflation, and landowners were forced to pay salaries to keep peasants working. During this period of the Black Death, recurrent famines, plagues, and endemic wars profoundly impacted Western Europe's demography, psychology, and economy, and businesses were forced to adapt (Hunt & Murray, 1999).

After the Black Death, Europe's economy changed dramatically. In the countryside, peasants gained more freedom and financial benefits, with fixed rents or land ownership replacing traditional dues. Despite low grain prices, they could feed themselves and sell surpluses. The declining population led to more efficient farming, benefiting prosperous peasants. In contrast, lords lost income and became vulnerable to inflation. Increased competition in trade and manufacturing rewarded efficient businesses, benefiting consumers with better products at lower prices. While the Black Death caused a temporary economic downturn, it triggered long-term changes in land distribution, wages, and technology, setting the stage for future growth. The population returned to 1100 levels, with more resources and improved skills, allowing survivors to seize new opportunities. The plague removed economic barriers and created new hope.

Freed from the Black Death, Europe moved from the Middle Ages into a new era, with trade and manufacturing flourishing by the fourteenth century. The Silk Road still ran through Arabia, the Middle East, Anatolia, and the Mediterranean. However, medieval businessmen still faced unreliable coinage, rulers confiscating goods, forced loans, monopolies, and other abuses from social superiors (Hunt & Murray, 1999).

Guild organizations developed under the law and public authority and became critical commercial entities. They increased the political power of merchants and artisans in city governments and contributed to the establishment of fairs, trade centers, and stock exchanges.

2.2 The Rise of Guilds

Guilds were groups of individuals with common goals. The guild was probably derived from the Anglo-Saxon root "*geld*," meaning "*to pay, to contribute*." The noun form of geld meant an association of people who contributed money for some common purpose, while the word's root also meant "*to sacrifice, to worship*." The dual definition probably reflected the origins of guilds as both secular and religious organizations (Richardson, 1961). For example, the archconfraternity is an example of a spiritual origin as a guild endowed with special powers by the Church authorities in Rome. The purpose of a professional guild was usually to maintain standards, provide apprenticeship training, pay for maintenance and health care, and offer financial assistance to widows and orphans of deceased members. Guilds could regulate the working hours and working conditions of guild members. However, more importantly, they were a form of social capital for their members. Guild affiliation brought together and protected business groups, giving them the prestige and confidence to pursue their professions. Typically, a guild creates a special relationship of trust among the members of its closed and multi-layered social network and with the groups it serves (Ogilvie, 2011).

The earliest documented example of a craft guild in medieval Europe dates from the twelfth century, but trade associations' emergence or re-emergence probably took place in the eleventh century. For example, craft guilds are mentioned in the Town Charter of 1156 in the German city of Augsburg. By the thirteenth century, such organizations were well established in cities and towns across Western Europe. They encompassed the artisanal trades discussed here and the "*industrial*" trades and merchants described later in this chapter. In general, craft guilds grew out of the need for merchants to band together to meet the pressures of increasing local and import competition. Guilds were associations of craftsmen, and although they tended to monopolize, they sought to regulate competition rather than eliminating it. They developed bylaws that set standards, apprenticeship requirements, and qualifications for admission as a member. They also set criteria for hiring journeymen and wage scales, established non-working holidays, and set quality standards. However, crafts and their guilds were often subject to municipal laws and regulations, especially in the food trade, where strict rules on quality, cleanliness, and sometimes pricing were applied (Hunt & Murray, 1999).

States immediately recognized their importance, and over time, a long historical interdependence between guilds and states and public economic and political institutions was established. Guilds could only maintain their members' collective monopoly over internal freedom and external competition with the support of political authorities in return for some form of taxation. Medieval cities and royal governments taxed guilds and demanded political support in return. By cooperating with the guilds, states could obtain information about markets and political affairs and benefit from the loans they could provide. Undoubtedly, for this wheel to function, there were mutually attractive bribes, gifts, loans, financial services, and offers of concessions. Thanks to this cooperation, guilds could survive for a long time in many places (Ogilvie, 2011). Guilds were politically crucial because, in most cities, guild leaders had a voice in municipal government and could influence public policy. Guilds' type, importance, and power varied greatly from city to city. In London, for example, the most influential guilds were those involved in the local distribution trade, while in Florence, the textile industry, long-distance trade, and finance dominated. In Paris, however, the monarchy controlled the guilds and forced them to submit to its bureaucracy (Hunt & Murray, 1999).

There were both craft and trade guilds. Trade guilds were organizations of merchants engaged in long-distance trade and local wholesale trade, and they could also be retail sellers of goods in their towns and distant places where they had the right to set up shops. The largest and most influential merchant guilds were involved in international trade and politics and established colonies in foreign cities. In many cases, they were inextricably intertwined with their governments, becoming representatives of their countries in distant lands. Although the term merchant guild is not used, Italian cities performed the same functions on behalf of their resident merchants. The city's role in coordinating embargo decisions is well reflected in the relations between Genoa and Tabriz, a vital city on the trade route to the Persian Gulf and the Far East. In 1340, when the ruler of Tabriz seized the goods of several Genoese merchants, Genoa responded by declaring a devoted commercial embargo against Tabriz. However, in 1344, the ruler of Tabriz sent envoys to Genoa and promised compensation for everything taken from the Genoese (Greif et al., 1994). Guilds had to control the behavior of their members. This was because medieval trade operated within the framework of community responsibility. If a merchant in a particular town failed to fulfill his part of the bargain or pay his debts, all his guild members could be held responsible. While in a foreign port, his goods could be seized and sold to collect the bad debt. Only in this way could they ensure security in long-distance trade. Without this relationship of trust in remote and isolated areas, where the law did not work so well, no manufacturer would have been able to give their goods to the merchants and expect to be sold or paid. The guarantee for this whole transaction was membership in a guild or a particular diaspora (Greif, 2008). While guilds enabled merchants to cooperate, they also reinforced a strong socio-economic structure. These structures enabled merchants to pursue their economic interests and influence politics and legal systems. Trade guilds created a structure based on written rules and traditional norms that regulated the relations of merchants. These systems complemented each other, leading to a more substantial trade network. Trade guilds in different regions have evolved according to their societies' cultural norms and historical conditions. In this context, Greif argues that an institution's success or longevity depends on the conditions of its environment (Greif, 2006).

There is no doubt that guilds in medieval and early modern cities were important in gaining political dominance or at least participating in decision-making processes. However, guilds were also political structures with different political affiliations and very heterogeneous social profiles. Guilds were also among the institutional bodies organizing cultural life in cities, and their public ceremonies were crucial for many urban performances, civic festivities, and religious practices. Rambrand's Syndics of the Drapers' Guild painting is shown in Fig. 2.2. This painting reveals the importance of guilds in that society and the rise of the merchant class during the Dutch Golden Age. The painting is a group portrait of five gentlemen from the Amsterdam cloth guild responsible for inspecting the cloth with their servants. They were not the guild regents but the wardens: two Catholics, a Mennonite, a Remonstrant, and a Reformed Protestant. Their one-year terms in office began on Good Friday, and they were expected to conduct their inspections thrice weekly. It was an unpaid honorary position.

The guilds were crucial for establishing and controlling social relations and social networks in cities, for group solidarity, and for developing collective identity (Stabel, 2004). For example, guilds played a central role in the governance of the Florentine Republic during the medieval period, with guild members forming the political and economic oligarchy of Florence (Brucker, 1998).

Fig. 2.2 Painting of syndics of the drapers' guild, 1662. https://upload.wikimedia.org/wikipedia/commons/9/95/Rembrandt_-_De_Staalmeesters-_het_college_van_staalmeesters_%28waardijns%29_van_het_Amsterdamse_lakenbereidersgilde_-_Google_Art_Project.jpg

Merchant guilds also protected their members against rulers' illegal and arbitrary decisions. Local rulers tended to confiscate money and goods from foreign merchants. Through the guilds, it was possible to boycott the rule of unruly rulers, a legal practice known in medieval England as Withernam. Since boycotts impoverished trade-dependent kingdoms or governments whose primary source of revenue was tariffs, the threat of retaliation deterred medieval rulers from confiscating merchants' goods (Richardson, 1961). For example, around 1050, the Muslim ruler of Sicily imposed a 10% tariff on goods imported into Sicily by Jewish merchants (instead of the 5% tariff prescribed by Islamic law). The merchants responded by imposing an embargo and sending their goods to Tunisia, a rival trading center. The embargo was effective, and a year later, the Sicilian ruler relented and abolished the tariff (Greif et al., 1994). Guild leaders often held privileged positions in religious and secular ceremonies and greatly influenced local government. Ogilvie (2014) has argued that guilds emerged and survived for centuries not because they were efficient but because they served the distributive interests of powerful groups.

Local guilds of large-scale merchants established branches abroad as "*merchant societies*" in foreign trading centers. As we will see later, Lyon and Bruges were organized this way. Some places, especially in Italy, also had "*sectoral*" guilds, uniting merchants and artisans in a particular industry. Sometimes, the merchant guilds of a group of towns formed a long-distance trade association called "*Universitas*" or "*Hansa.*" The most famous was the German Hansa, founded around 1300 under the leadership of a core group from 70 North German, Dutch, and Baltic cities (Ogilvie, 2011).

2.3 Hanseatic League

The Hanseatic League was a medieval trade and defense network of merchant guilds and market towns in Central and Northern Europe. Starting with a few North German towns in the late twelfth century, the league expanded between the thirteenth and fifteenth centuries, eventually including around 200 settlements across eight present-day countries, from Estonia to the Netherlands and inland to Cologne, Prussia, and Kraków, Poland. Initially, the Hansa was a loose association of German merchants and towns seeking to expand their commercial interests, protect against unfair taxation and harassment by northern princes, and secure trade privileges (Fig. 2.3). Over time, it evolved into a formal league, offering toll privileges and protection on trade routes. Economic interdependence and familial ties between merchant families led to deeper political integration and reduced trade barriers. This process included the standardization of trade arrangements among Hanseatic cities (Hunt & Murray, 1999).

As a 1469 document explained to the English Privy Council, the German Hanse was neither a corporation, partnership, nor guild, but a federation of cities, towns, and communities to ensure favorable commercial ventures and protection against pirates and bandits. The Hanseatic League dominated maritime trade in the North and Baltic Seas, establishing trading centers in towns like London (Steelyards), Bruges, Bergen, and Novgorod, which had considerable legal autonomy. Its economic power allowed it to impose blockades and even challenge kingdoms. Despite its influence, the league had a loose structure with no permanent administration, treasury, or military force. By the mid-sixteenth century, its weak links made it vulnerable, and it gradually dissolved as members merged with other kingdoms or seceded, disbanding in 1669 (Harreld, 2015).

The legal background of the Hanseatic League was complex and unique, reflecting the structure of the confederation as a network of independent cities and merchant

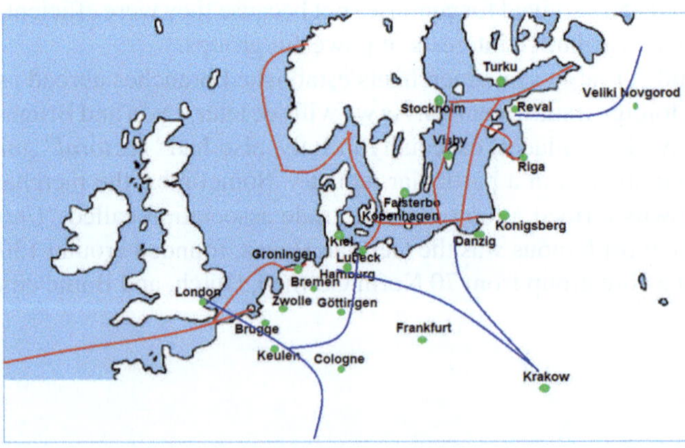

Fig. 2.3 Main Hansa trade centers and trade routes (fourteenth century). Drawn by the author

guilds rather than a centralized state. The League operated under its laws, treaties, and customs system to regulate trade, commerce, and internal relations. Each member city in the Hanseatic League maintained its own local laws and legal systems, which differed but were generally compatible with standard commercial interests. These cities were self-governing with their mayors, councils, and laws and were largely independent of external royal or feudal control. Despite the legal autonomy of each member city, the League developed a standard set of legal principles governing trade and commercial transactions. This was necessary to facilitate trade between the various towns and regions in the League (Harreld, 2015).

Over time, a body of legal principles known as "*Hanseatic Law*" emerged, consisting of a set of norms governing the conduct of trade and commerce in the territory of the Union. Although not written, the Hanseatic Law was a traditional legal system that developed over time. This legal system was based on justice and the mutual interests of merchants and cities, focusing on trade disputes, customs duties, and preventing unfair practices (Harreld, 2015). Arbitration played a central role in conflicts between merchants or cities. Disputes were usually resolved through negotiations or by neutral arbitrators who were respected members of the League. This helped to ensure that disputes did not disrupt trade (Dollinger, 1999).

There were also organizations called Kontors. These were trading centers or offices established by Hanseatic merchants in foreign cities. In these places, the League had its legal framework governing the activities of its merchants. For example, the Hanseatic Kontor in London, known as the Steelyard, had its own rules governing trade practices and arbitrating merchant disputes. The Kontors served as legal and commercial centers where disputes between merchants could be resolved according to Hanseatic law rather than the host country's laws (Dollinger, 1999).

The Hanseatic League was a politically important entity that negotiated treaties with various kingdoms and principalities, providing its members with exemptions from taxes, customs duties, and trade restrictions. These treaties, sometimes formalized through diplomatic missions, had legal weight. This made it possible to settle disputes, protect the interests of Hanseatic merchants, and secure favorable trading conditions. They were also used to create defense alliances between cities within the League.

The Union had a system for enforcing legal rules to ensure member cities and merchants followed them. This included economic sanctions such as trade restrictions or expulsion from the Union for violations. If a municipality obstructed trade or violated Union law, other members could impose sanctions like refusing business or declaring a trade embargo. This collective enforcement helped maintain order within the Union. In conflicts with foreign powers or rival trade groups, the League could use diplomatic negotiations or military action backed by powerful naval forces. As the League's power waned in the sixteenth and seventeenth centuries, its legal system weakened, and its ability to enforce trade laws declined. The rise of nation-states seeking control over trade and legal systems also contributed to the League's decline. The legacy of Hanseatic Law influenced the development of European trade laws and modern commercial legal practices (Dollinger, 1999).

For several reasons, the Hanseatic League holds a significant place in world history: It expanded economic influence and trade in Central Europe, dominating trade in the Baltic, North, and parts of Europe from the 13th to the seventeenth century. It also helped develop early capitalism by introducing banking systems and standardized accounting methods, with Hanseatic merchants shaping modern financial institutions. The League influenced European politics and diplomacy as a trade alliance and political entity. Its growth contributed to urbanization and cultural exchange in Northern Europe, with cities like Lübeck, Hamburg, and Riga becoming major trading centers and fostering a cosmopolitan, merchant-oriented culture. While the League declined due to rising national powers, it helped establish regional cooperation and formed stronger nation-states. It also weakened feudalism, encouraging towns and cities to become autonomous political and economic entities. The League's decentralized structure provided flexibility and resilience, offering lessons in cooperative governance that influenced future economic and political systems (Dollinger, 1999).

With the rise of guilds and trade organizations, efforts to standardize product quality, weights, measures, and coins across cultures increased, while state control over trade also grew. Trade fairs became a key commercial activity organized by guilds. The main driver of the Commercial Revolution during this period was the evolution of commercial and financial transaction systems.

2.4 Trade Fairs and Festivals

2.4.1 The Birth of Medieval Fairs

Religious and commercial organizations used spatial and temporal fairs in the Middle Ages. The terms in other European languages (English: fair, French: foire, Italian: fiera, Spanish: fiesta) derive from the Latin feria, feriae. However, this meant "*market*" and "*religious festivals,*" sometimes in separate periods. Medieval fairs started as religious ceremonies before they developed into a large commercial market. Later, local products were also sold at these fairs, and in time, fairs were formed. During the Roman Empire, the fair was used as a kind of vacation from labor and the work of the royal court. By the seventh century, the Carolingian Dynasty of the Frankish Kingdom organized a regular fair. The Carolingians, especially during the reign of Charlemagne (768–814), played a significant role in organizing and promoting markets and fairs to stimulate economic growth and trade within their empire. One of the most notable fairs organized during this time was the fairs of Saint-Denis, which were held near Paris and became prominent in medieval Europe. These events began to be held on Christian holy days throughout Europe, and merchants would gather in church courtyards to sell their wares. At annual intervals, fairs were moved to a day when the feast of a particular patron saint was celebrated. In the twelfth century, English towns received royal permission to organize a fair to serve residents. This fair usually lasted for several days. As well as being a significant way for people to buy and sell goods, fairs also had substantial social benefits. Medieval fairs were a source of entertainment for townspeople. They were entertained by jugglers, magicians, dancing bears, and mystery games. There was often music, drinking, and dancing. Mystery games were one of the types of entertainment offered at medieval fairs. Merchants and craft guilds also organized mystery plays. The plays were performed in the street and usually aimed to show a sense of dark humor by making fun of biblical characters (Richardson, 1961).

Fair and festival organizations had profound economic motivations. First, merchants sought to reduce costs. With fairs, they could reduce the cost of transporting products to customers. The second benefit was that princes could gain financial advantages by establishing and promoting fairs in their territories. Through fairs, local princes or counts could also generate significant income. Another factor was the spread of advanced road transportation technology. This made it easier for merchants to reach central markets. Finally, in centralized locations, it was easier for financial structures that supported trade to come together (Hunt & Murray, 1999). As a result, fairs and merchant guilds grew in strength. They found solutions to the three main problems affecting long-distance traders: (1) criminal attacks and arbitrary arrests, (2) dishonest behavior of intermediaries, and (3) uncertainty about the profitability of trade (Gelderblom, 2004a, 2004b).

From the twelfth century onward, fairs and regional markets grew in importance. In Europe, monarchs charged fees to the stallholders they licensed at markets and fairs, merchants earned money, and shoppers benefited from the services provided. As the local economy grew, large property owners, municipal councils, and some churches and monasteries contributed to the organization of these markets (Richardson, 1961). The number of weekly markets in England and Wales increased more than tenfold from the 1100 s to the 1300 s (Cucu, 2020). As historians say, no institution was more important in the early commercialization of the European economy than fairs (Munro, 2001). However, European fairs differed from fairs in Islamic countries of the same period due to some characteristics. Whereas in Europe, they were planned events, usually held in specific cities and often aligned with religious festivals, Islamic trade was characterized by year-round markets. There were bazaars and caravanserais in the Islamic world, always open and more integrated into urban economies. In Europe, Christianity played a central role in organizing fairs, including providing legal protections. In contrast, Islamic law, the Sharia, governed trading practices and provided ethical guidelines for merchants. The Islamic world had a more extensive network of global trade routes, including the Silk Road and the Indian Ocean, linking Islamic centers to China, India, and sub-Saharan Africa. This broad connectivity meant that Islamic trade depended less on specific fairs and relied more on ongoing commercial activity between cities. In contrast, European fairs were the center of early long-distance trade, especially as the economy became more market based during the Middle Ages.

In villages, towns, and large cities where rulers authorized them, markets were regularly held in public squares, wide streets, and specially built halls. They were also held outside castles and monasteries. Rulers profited from the market organization by charging fees, often renting buildings or plots of land. A fee was also charged for setting up stalls, and market professionals like brokers, notaries, innkeepers, and shopkeepers paid license fees. Tolls and transaction taxes were levied on goods brought to the market, and there were fees for services such as using official weights and measures and fines for market court violations (Kohn, 2003). Typically, large towns held fairs once or twice a week or daily markets in different parts of the city. Middlemen, known as regulators, bought goods from producers and sold them to stallholders, or producers paid vendors to sell on their behalf (World History Encyclopedia, 2019). Local merchants also bought products for resale in regional markets, while others acted as arbitrageurs, especially for grain, known as blatiers or bladers (Kohn, 2003).

In towns, shops selling similar goods were often clustered together to increase competition and make it easier for townspeople and guild inspectors. There were also banks and moneylenders, predominantly Jewish, since usury was forbidden to Christians by the Church. Jewish merchants enjoyed protection from princes in most of Western Europe until their expulsion from England in 1290 and France in the early 1300 s. Over time, trade fairs began to emerge in Europe, where merchants gathered periodically in active trade areas. In the twelfth and thirteenth centuries, fairs expanded in France, England, Holland, and Germany (Hunt & Murray, 1999).

In the Middle Ages, fairs stimulated growth in several ways, in both the short and long terms. First, fairs provided regular venues for local producers and consumers to meet, reducing transaction costs and increasing price transparency. For example, the early development of the market network in England led to less volatility in wheat prices and, thus, greater market integrity than its continental neighbors on the eve of industrialization. By the late medieval period, Britain had a relatively well-developed system of market towns, trade routes, and river routes that helped integrate regional markets. This network allowed grain to flow more efficiently across the country, preventing local shortages from causing widespread price spikes. In addition, medieval English markets were often governed by charters, which provided legal protections and regulations that helped maintain market integrity. Political stability in England, especially after the Norman Conquest (1066) and establishing a more centralized monarchy, helped create a relatively stable economic environment (Clark, 2010). Second, markets increased competition, encouraging improved practices and the adoption of cost-saving technologies. Third, markets quickly became public information centers, allowing information to circulate rapidly. Finally, medieval markets functioned as a coordination tool and likely positively influenced investment in the following centuries (Cucu, 2020). The opportunities offered by fairs enabled many more merchants to bring their goods to market, allowing for integration and specialization in Europe's more backward regions and innovation and economic rebirth in Europe's commercial centers (Hunt & Murray, 1999).

Fig. 2.4 Champagne fair, medieval period 13th century. https://commonser.wikimedia.org/wiki/File:Foire_de_Champagne_XIIIe.jpg

2.4.2 Champagne Fairs

One of the most famous regions for fairs was the Champagne region of France, 150 km east of Paris (Fig. 2.4). The fairs or fairs of Champagne are generally regarded as one of the most critical episodes in economic history, as it was the first major European-wide trading venue to emerge after at least the Dark Ages.

A semi-autonomous region in France, Champagne was located on the most critical land routes linking the Flanders/England axis in the north to the Italian/Mediterranean trade network in the south. In essence, the Champagne fairs acted as economic catalysts, fostering not just a local marketplace but helping to stimulate the development of more extensive commercial networks and trade routes across Europe. The fairs' role in connecting different parts of the continent, promoting financial innovations, and encouraging infrastructure development was a key factor that helped flourish long-distance trade. The legacy of the Champagne fairs lies in their contribution to the integration of European markets, which was essential for the subsequent rise of capitalism and the early stages of global trade. As part of the agricultural region of Paris, it had developed a crucial agrarian economy before the twelfth century. It had established urban markets, notably in Troyes, Provins, Lagny, and Bar-sur-Aube. These became venues for fairs, which were initially religious festivals. However, thanks to the attentive care of the counts of Champagne, who granted special privileges and safe passage to foreign merchants, the fairs of Champagne gained a European reputation as the preferred meeting place for southern and northern merchants and their goods. The Count of Champagne had an excellent aptitude for trade and was quick to recognize a lucrative commercial activity. By the end of the 1170 s, local counts had begun to appoint special "*fair guards*" to increase the attractiveness of the fairs. Their commercial institutions also greatly facilitated trade (Acemoglu & Robinson, 2019).

The social organization of the market was also strictly regulated. Merchants trading the same product had to set up shop in the same place, and those from the same city had to live together. Most were organized in consulates, interacting directly with the fair authorities and adjudicating disputes between their members. In the glory days of the fairs, Champagne had at least 22 Italian consulates and Spanish, Flemish, or Southern French consulates (Sgard, 2015).

There were six successive fairs in the towns of the Champagne region. Each fair lasted roughly two months, so in practice, the market operated all year round. The calendar of the fairs also had to follow the itineraries of the traveling merchants who visited them in turn. Goods, money, and credit were part of this circular movement. Money, of course, also provided energy for other, larger circuits, and usually headed toward a central point from which it would set off again (Braudel, 1992).

The Southerners who came to the fair brought a range of goods from the Western and Eastern Mediterranean valued by the increasingly wealthy elite of the north. In return, northern merchants offered a range of woolen textiles, from the simplest to the most luxurious, from wrought to unwrought. Still, their total value was insufficient to balance the demand for southern goods. This balance was primarily provided by the abundant bullion and coin silver supply from Freiberg's new and prosperous mines. The silver from Freiberg was transported mainly to Italy and the south of France, namely to the Champagne fairs. This transportation was mainly via trade and river routes (Hunt & Murray, 1999).

Interest was allowed on loans at fairs because fairs generally had a unique position in terms of rules. There was a kind of "*fair freedom*"; they were also exempted from the prohibition of usury. The Italian Lombard bankers, many of whom were Jewish, were the dominant and most innovative force in this market. Only a tiny fraction of promissory notes was paid in cash. Trading in promissory notes reduced the risk of loss or theft and was often more convenient. As long as the transactions were not too large, it was possible to adjust the maturity of the promissory notes to the date of the fairs. Commercial goods, currencies, real estate, insurance, lotteries, and financial instruments were traded at the Champagne fairs. Records from medieval fairs show that merchants traded only a small part of their trade in coins (Braudel, 1992).

The functioning of each of these fairs was also rigorously codified: merchants first had a few days to arrive and settle in. Different types of goods were successively exchanged, and a final period of two weeks was dedicated to the exchange of payments, followed by the signing and sealing of debt contracts that would extend the payment to one of the following fairs. At that moment, if any debt remained unpaid or unfunded, the debtor was declared in default, future access to the market was closed, his goods could be confiscated, and he could be arrested. There was also a prison at the fairs (Braudel, 1992). Champagne fairs did not only involve cash or barter transactions. As in the story in the introduction, Genoese merchants began to use the lettres de foire (fair letters) used by Genoese merchants in the twelfth and thirteenth centuries, introducing them at the Champagne fairs, gradually replacing the use of cash or precious metals. As they developed a payment system based on these credit instruments at the Champagne fairs, the fairs became even more famous. This instrument was the first form of the bills of exchange that would later be used, solving the problem of transporting large quantities of coins. It not only provided security benefits but also facilitated the exchange of money. Letters of exchange were a formal, written promise of payment certified by a notary. However, the most important innovation was the payment of each merchant's debts and credits through accounts at bankers. The currencies involved were converted using exchange rate tables. Therefore, the Champagne fairs were essential in developing European money markets. The methods applied here gradually spread throughout the continent. These documents recognized the sale of goods but usually stipulated that payment would be made at a later fair when the sum of debits and credits would be calculated over a season, and a final settlement between buyers and sellers would occur. Letters could not be endorsed, but could be transferred from one party to another. Sometimes, the payment could be denominated in a different coin from the original transaction, and as a result, the fair letter eliminated the need for large shipments of speculative money. Thus, the Champagne fairs increasingly became financial clearing houses for long-distance trade between the North and South. By the end of the twelfth century, debt securities were also being exchanged on a large scale, making the Champagne fairs Europe's first financial center (Hunt & Murray, 1999).

The fair authorities centralized the settlement process at fairs. The settlement procedure at medieval and early modern markets and fairs, such as Champagne, is known in the sources as "*rescontrire, rescontre, skontrieren or vivre compte/des parties*." The procedure worked as follows: all merchants gathered on certain days at the end of the market or fair, everyone declared their debts, and creditors had to confirm their debts. Then, traders tried to balance their receivables with their debts through a decentralized search and match procedure: in the first step, they canceled mutual debts; in the second step, they used swap loops; in the third and last steps, they used swap chains. Ultimately, the still unbalanced positions had to be paid in cash, or new promissory notes had to be drawn (Boerner & Hatfield, 2010).

Bills of exchange (letters of credit), developed in the thirteenth century, gradually replaced the "*Lettres de foire*." Bills of exchange were promises to pay a certain amount at a particular time and place. When a bill of exchange was due, it was usually determined by the distance to the place of payment. These became standardized over time. A payment between Genoa and Milan required only six days or between Genoa and Bruges, two months (De Roover, 1963). A Genoa-based merchant (middleman) planning to attend the fair in Champagne (France) to sell goods would eventually make a profit in France. Still, first, he needed money in Florence (Italy) to buy the goods he planned to sell in Champagne. To purchase this good, the merchant would ask his agent in Champagne to contact the buyer there to issue a bill of exchange, ordering him to pay later. This agent was the local correspondent in Champagne for his Florence-based merchant. By accepting this bill of exchange as a means of payment, the Florentine merchant was essentially financing the intermediary merchant. Merchants not only issued promissory notes for payment but also routinely accepted the promissory notes of others in their trade. The promissory notes circulated as money since they could be sold to third parties. Thus, if a merchant in Venice sold cloth in Bruges and received a promissory note payable in Bruges, he could sell it back home in Venice to a merchant in Bruges who needed cash to buy furs. This barter mechanism was developed in the late medieval fairs. It was perfected in the late sixteenth- and early seventeenth-century financial fairs, becoming a formal procedure with a legal framework. This was the dominant debt payment mechanism in Europe's most important trading centers (Boerner & Hatfield, 2010).

As a result, payment at fairs could be made in coins or, later, in fair letters or bills of exchange. Bills of exchange could also be issued to roll over any debt to the next fair. The resulting debts could be paid in cash (1), in whatever currency (due to the presence of bankers), or "*paid on account*" (2) if the merchants had an account with a local banker or moneylender, or new bills could be purchased (3), or an inter-fair loan could be arranged, formalized in a sealed letter (4). Fairs generally evolved to focus on credit rather than goods, on the tip of the pyramid rather than the base. In any case, this model emerges from the exemplary career of the old fairs of Champagne. In their heyday, around 1160, both goods and money traffic were brisk (Braudel, 1992).

Merchants and moneylenders facilitated trade by buying and selling promissory notes paid in different cities and currencies. These new merchant bankers essentially lent and exchanged money by purchasing a promissory note before its maturity. Sometimes, they profited by buying bills at a less favorable exchange rate than the market rate between the bill's currency and the seller's preferred currency (Boerner & Hatfield, 2010).

To encourage as many buyers and sellers as possible, local rulers took measures to ensure merchants' arrival, stay, and departure. Public order in the city was established through the courts. Although historians dispute the exact nature of this order, it functioned effectively and attracted merchants to the fair. Gelderblom (2004a, 2004b) argues that fairs like Champagne used courts and private judges to resolve commercial disputes swiftly. Greif (2004) said the judicial system was designed to prevent inter-city reprisals. The principle of collective responsibility meant municipal courts punished all guilty merchants similarly, regardless of nationality. Courts also allowed money exchangers to operate based on merchants' needs. Merchant guilds from the German and Dutch regions, or consuls of Italian and Spanish merchants, addressed key issues related to goods exchange. These guilds demanded security measures from foreign rulers and organized collective actions if rulers or merchants damaged or confiscated property. They also negotiated tax breaks, fee exemptions, or monopolies to maximize members' commercial and financial benefits. Institutional control and the threat of exclusion reduced the risk of default by guild members. Personal relationships among merchants helped share information about market conditions and business partners' creditworthiness (Gelderblom, 2004a, 2004b).

In contrast, Edwards and Ogilvie (2012) proposed a different thesis. They attribute the success of the Champagne fairs to the fact that they were supported by a rich array of public order institutions rather than private magistrates. He argued that there is no historical record of the existence of country (community) consulates with the practice of private magistrates. He noted the existence of a unique public law court operating during each fair and the princely officials who adjudicated cases in this court. According to them, international merchants also used other levels of the princely justice system to enforce their contracts. The towns where the fairs were held operated their municipal courts, while local monasteries also ran private courts at the fairs, and international merchants made use of both. The Champagne fairs had a public order that guaranteed property rights and the enforcement of contracts. Even municipal and monastic courts operated under delegated jurisdiction granted by the Champagne monarchs. Judgments rendered at the fairs were enforceable throughout the kingdom, regardless of local courts and seigneurial authorities. Courts worked according to specific rules. Speedy trials, demanding access to appellate procedures, and the significant role given to principles of equity, the possibility of playing for time and challenging jurisdiction was also clearly limited (Sgard, 2015).

According to Edwards and Ogilvie (2012), for the first 65 years (1180–1245), when fairs were centers of international trade, all visiting merchants were subject to the public law system applicable at fairs. No foreign group had a consul. In 1245, the Count of Champagne issued a charter exempting some of the visiting foreign merchants from the jurisdiction of his officials, but only by placing them under his direct jurisdiction as sovereign. Later, in Bruges and Antwerp, it was seen that foreign communities sought their rights through their consuls. From the beginning, merchants relied on the public legal system to enforce contracts between their members and merchants from different communities. The Champagne fairs developed as Europe's most important international trade center for 80 years, when no collective action (retaliation) against any community members was recorded. After 1260, during the last phase of the rise of the Champagne fairs, reprisals against merchants from some countries were used only in a limited way (Edwards & Ogilvie, 2012).

After long flourishing under the benevolent protection of the Count of Champagne, the annexation of this province to France in 1285 led to the sudden death of this market at the hands of a short-sighted and cash-strapped king. The French regime that took over the fairs did not maintain the general institutional mechanisms that attracted and sustained international trade. The security of property rights, the enforcement of contracts, and access to commercial infrastructure were no longer guaranteed as general services but became special "privileges" offered (and denied) to specific merchant communities to serve the short-term interests of French royal policy. Public authorities no longer offered a level playing field to all merchants but granted privileges that favored certain interest groups and discriminated against others. There is evidence of harassment, discrimination, or expulsion of Italian bankers, a sharp increase in tax rates, and the beginning of attacks on Jews (Sgard, 2015).

By the fourteenth century, trade fairs had begun to decline as people's ability to buy goods from anywhere and at any time significantly increased. Merchants moved more toward regions where they could trade, exchange money, and find credit facilities. Lyon, further south of Champagne, began to gain importance during this period (Edwards & Ogilvie, 2012). Nonetheless, the fairs of Champagne continued to function as payment clearinghouses for a long time, continuing an international exchange business until 1320 (Braudel, 1992), even long after they lost their importance as markets for authentic goods from the fourteenth century onward. By the fifteenth century, Champagne had primarily lost its status as a significant financial and commercial center. However, some smaller-scale fairs and markets continued in

Champagne, but they no longer had the considerable impact on European commerce and finance they once had. In medieval style, Champagne fairs managed to become something new in the guise of something old, fitting the role of a meeting point for merchants while at the same time becoming an international bridge between the major European economic regions to the north and south of the Mediterranean (Hunt & Murray, 1999).

2.5 Lyon: Fair and Money Exchange Center

Despite its distance from the sea, Lyon, located south of Paris on the Alpine slopes near Switzerland, was a key trade hub between Italy and Switzerland. This role persisted for centuries. In 1312, when King Philip IV annexed the city, its autonomy ended. Recognizing Lyon's commercial significance, Philip supported its trade by granting commercial privileges (Rau, 2024). By the early fifteenth century, foreign merchants had started using Geneva as a financial clearinghouse, where they settled accounts and traded bills of exchange. Lyon, at the confluence of two major rivers, controlled the north–south route between the French Mediterranean and the interior. Charles VII (1422–1462) granted fair visitors the same privileges as merchants at Champagne fairs and allowed up to 15% interest on deals, with no restrictions on money exchange or bills of exchange. Louis XI (1461–83), aiming to replace Geneva as a financial center, expanded the Lyon fair in 1463, directing subjects to attend instead of going to Geneva. The settlement of Italian merchants, who introduced banking and global trade, ensured Lyon's long-term success and global significance. After 1500, Lyon became synonymous with finance. Despite differences in size and function, fairs in the fifteenth and early sixteenth centuries were driven by a medieval need to reduce costs and streamline markets (Hunt & Murray, 1999). In 1420, two fairs were held annually, and by 1464, with Louis XI's support, this had increased to four.

The influence of religion was also evident in trade fairs such as those held in Lyon. The dates of these fairs were set according to the liturgical calendar: one began on Epiphany (January 6), another on Quasimodo Sunday (the first Sunday after Easter), and a third on August 4, a feast day. Payments were typically due around All Saints' Day. Each fair usually lasted fifteen days—the first week being devoted to the exchange of goods, and the second to financial settlements and barter. As a result, prices and payment terms were negotiable only during these specific periods (Bauer et al. 1998).

Until the fifteenth century, there was no fixed location for the Lyon fairs, where wholesalers and long-distance merchants gathered. This was only the case for smaller weekly markets: each category of goods was allocated a fixed public place where trading was allowed on a specific day. As early as 1420, soon after Lyon received the privilege of organizing two fairs, the consuls, representatives of foreign countries, designated the places where their merchants could exhibit their goods (Brésard, 1914). The first fair was held near the River Saône, in what is now Presqu'île; the second fair of the year was to be held on the other side of the River Saône, on the Royaume. Finally, it was decided that goods could be exhibited anywhere in the city, mainly on the left and right of the Saône River and wherever the merchants wished. For this purpose, exhibitions with wooden benches, which could be covered, were made available along the avenues, in the squares, on the bridge over the Saône, and everywhere near the city gates.

The temporal and spatial organization of the fairs, the large number of foreign merchants and bankers, and the diversity of products also created a city of its own. Council minutes and royal letters show that money exchanges took place only on the other side of the Saône River in the sixteenth century, which could only be crossed on the Pont du Change, the only stone bridge in the city (Allix, 1922).

Around the Pont du Change, the intermediary activities of money changers flourished, mainly due to the fair (Fig. 2.5). On Rue Porcherie, Jews played a key role as moneylenders until the twelfth century. However, as Northern Italian merchant bankers became more involved in the region, the power of local moneylenders declined (Bonnet, 1973). While never owning real estate in Lyon, the Medici family conducted business in a rented house on Rue de la Juiverie, near Place de la Draperie (later Place du Change), a popular spot for stockbrokers (De Roover, 1963). Italian bankers, benefiting from interest-free privileges, developed a robust commercial network from the twelfth century, undermining the local money changers. Meanwhile, the Lyon bourgeoisie, enriched by trade and money exchange, began challenging the Italian community from the fourteenth century onward.

Lyon was a fair for goods and a center for exchanging bills of exchange, conducting foreign currency transactions, and arranging loans with set repayment dates and locations. After the mid-fifteenth century, foreign merchants continued flocking to Lyon, gradually transforming it into a central communication hub (Bonnet, 1973). In 1557, the Venetian Ambassador reported that businessmen gathered at the Pont du Change to buy and sell money (Allen, 2004).

Information on the techniques of Lyon businessmen is partly available from municipal accounting books. The main task of the money changers was to exchange currencies prohibited in the kingdom for other officially valid currencies. In medieval Europe, metal coins were made of gold and silver; their value depended on their content. In Renaissance Europe, the city-states of Genoa, Hamburg, Venice, and the Netherlands, such as Venice, Hamburg, and Amsterdam, did not have their coins and had to use the coins of neighboring countries. Due to the variety and content of coins, disputes could arise between parties when exchanging in commercial centers (Karan et al., 2024).

The services of the Lyon money changer were also used by foreign merchants who had to obtain cash from the market to carry out their transactions in the city; in fact, royal decrees did not allow payment in "*foreign currencies*." More importantly, from the late thirteenth century onward, the official currencies used in France were frequently changed. Thus, categories of coins were replaced by a new type of money, requiring recourse to money changers to replace them with new ones, which now had legal status. The old types were then supposed to cease functioning, and the mints should turn to minting others based on the new rate. According to historical records,

Fig. 2.5 "View taken under the Pont du Change," drawing by Paulus Lauters (1806–1875), lithograph by Motte, plate 22 In Vues des rives de la Saône, drawn from nature by Nicolas Chapuy and lithographed by Paulus Lauters, Paris, Motte, 1835. https://fr.wikipedia.org/wiki/Pont_du_Change#/media/Fichier:Vue_prise_sous_le_pont_du_Change.jpg (Public Domain)

however, a few exchangers did not comply with these obligations and resold gold and silver when they found a sufficient profit. In this context, there are records of Lyon merchants-exchangers who were fined in 1334 by the bailiff of Mâcon, France, for carrying money in their coffers that the king forbade. This fine exemplifies the monetary regulations and efforts to control trade in France. In trade-intensive cities like Lyon, the carrying of foreign currency by merchants and moneylenders could often weaken centralized control over the economy. This shows how monetary and trade policies in France were intertwined with local economic activity and how there were sometimes conflicts between the central government and local commercial actors. The money changers gradually became the money changers, even bankers, of the Lyon bourgeoisie. It was not easy to do these jobs. While currency exchange required a great deal of working capital, it was necessary to have all kinds of cash from all countries at all times. For this reason, money changers, who were accustomed to keeping valuable materials in their shops, not only stored the unused wealth of the bourgeoisie but also lent them short-term loans. In this context, credit risk sometimes arose. In 1390, Rodrigue de Villandrando, a wealthy Lyons moneylender who had made a fortune through plunder and ransoms, deposited 1000 crowns with Eustache de Pompierre and never got his money back, despite written confirmation (Bonnet, 1973).

In markets like Lyon, where merchant bankers traded only with each other. Their purpose was mainly to exchange and pay for bills of exchange from elsewhere. Since the participants in such internal markets were few and well known, there was no need to use a bank for clearing: the participants could transfer their debts to others. The procedure at the Lyons fairs, for example, was as follows. At the beginning of each fair, merchant bankers gathered in the Florentine guild. Each banker prepared a "market book" in advance, listing the outstanding bills for which he would receive payment and those for which he would make payment. During the meeting, the bankers would compare the books. If the payer accepted a bill, he initialed the relevant entry in the creditor's ledger; if not, the creditor marked the "SP" entry for "protest." A few days later, the bankers would meet again to trade new bills, each new bill being recorded in the respective parties' market books. At the end of the fair, there would be a settlement period. Armed with their market books, the merchants would meet to settle the payments bilaterally. The remainder would be covered either by the assignment of third-party debts, which could then be netted in the process, or by drawing new bills of exchange payable at the next Lyons fair or other banking venues. Liquidity risk was addressed by participants providing each other with "overdrafts" on the market books (delaying payment) or by converting debt into new bills of exchange (Kohn, 2001). In Lyon, without any centralizing official institution, the deposit system allowed clearing mechanisms to function perfectly—a group of interrelated private banks organized the money market as efficiently as a central bank, as in Antwerp. Notably, despite such consensus, these banks did not form a homogeneous banking fabric (Matringe, 2017).

Various forms of credit were not alien to money changers. Interest rates were relatively high for the conditions of the time. In the tremendous fair centers of the sixteenth century, Lyon, Antwerp, Castile, and Besançon, Italian, German, and Spanish business people borrowed and lent from the deposit market at rates of 8–12% a year, or 2–3% from one fair to another (Matringe, 2017). The least risky money changers were pawnbrokers. Many moneychangers also lent against real estate, a form of mortgage financing. Large merchant moneychangers made business loans through promissory notes or term/demand debentures. It is necessary to see this transformation as part of the general evolution of activities that began with changing currencies, leading to the deposit bank. While this evolution was completed in Italy before the end of the thirteenth century, in Lyon, it was probably necessary to wait until the mid-fifteenth century to establish traditional banking operations (Bonnet, 1973). Nevertheless, the deposit process in Lyon banks did not align with today's understanding. In other words, there was no connection between the balances regularly calculated by the bank, the amount of loans, and the cash reserves held by banking institutions. At the Lyon fairs, the deposits of large-scale businessmen were used to close their current accounts at the end of each event. For example, at the August 1546 fair, the Lucchese bankers Jacopo Menochi and Martino Gigli—who had drawn on the Salviati bank abroad (Florence, Rome and Medina del Campo) and had Bartolini in Lyon make a payment in their name—balanced their accounts with promissory notes endorsed to Salviati from Paris and payments from other Lyon bankers (Antinori, Pecori, Montecatini & Malpigli, Passi). At the end of the fair, however, Menochi and Gigli's loans at the Salviati bank did not fully cover their debts. As a result, the overdraft was charged at the interest rate, and the remaining 2,500 écus (plus interest) was postponed until the next fair. Such transactions are repeated, especially among Lyon banks, showing that deposits often have a clearing function. Its origin seems to lie in the custom, already widespread at Champagne fairs, of postponing payments from one fair to another (Matringe, 2017).

Through their traditional and banking functions, money changers played an essential role in their relations with the municipality. They obtained some special privileges by having their monetary transactions recognized as an "*art*." Their activities, however, contradicted, on the one hand, the freedom of exchange granted to the city of Lyon by a privilege granted by the kings of France in 1312, and on the other hand, the strict regulation of money changers within the kingdom and abroad. While the privileges granted to the money changers allowed them a certain freedom, they were simultaneously limited by strict control and regulation in line with the economic interests of the kingdom. The privileged status of Lyon and the strict state control of the rules and regulations regarding the commercial activities of money changers indicated an attempt to strike a balance between private rights and public power. Unauthorized money exchange was forbidden in France, except in privileged places such as Lyon. On the other hand, the number of exchangers in Lyon was not theoretically limited. However, in the ordinance of July 5, 1373, on the moneychangers of the city of Lyon, Charles V ordered that "*henceforth there shall be only six moneychangers in the said city of Lyon.*" However, since currency trading did not require special skills and investments, it was always possible to overcome this numerical limitation. As in many other countries, barterers practiced their profession by hiding behind a grocery store, a texting shop, or another store. Indeed, in 1376, three years after the order limiting the number of barters to 6, the number was still over 19. From 1350 to 1450, merchants enrolled in the money-changing profession were considered to have a high art, in terms of both reputation and wealth, due to their practical skills. By the early fifteenth century, money changers exceeded 25 (Bonnet, 1973). From 1443 onward, professional moneylenders joined the City Council, the political embodiment of their newfound wealth. Accustomed to accounting techniques and experts handling money and currency fluctuations, Lyon's moneychangers were involved in the city's financial management very early and benefited in many ways (Bonnet, 1973).

Lyon's decline as a key financial and commercial center began in the late fifteenth century. It was fully felt by the sixteenth century due to factors such as the rise of maritime trade, the shift to other financial centers like Paris, political instability, and the loss of its key industries like silk. While still significant, the city was no longer the dominant commercial hub it had been in earlier centuries. In addition, merchants and money exchangers seeking to avoid the laws of the French kings set their sights on the city of Bruges, today a Belgian territory. This region, then known as the Low Countries, became increasingly important. A much more moderate government was much more attractive to merchants. Despite this, Paris could not pick up where Lyon, the famous international financial center, had left off in the sixteenth century (Braudel, 1992). Braudel said, "*The wealth of Paris was ill-intentioned, the propertied classes too absorbed in offices and estates, in socially rewarding, individually lucrative, economically parasitic activities.*"

2.6 Concluding Remarks

In the fourteenth and fifteenth centuries, markets in Western Europe grew rapidly. The Black Plague reshaped the economic structure, weakening feudalism, strengthening city governments, introducing wages, and revitalizing trade. This set the stage for capitalism. Major firms like the Italian Bardi and Peruzzi emerged, and commercial organizations, guilds, and merchant education flourished. Knowledge in mathematics and accounting gained importance, and legal infrastructure strengthened, with notaries playing a growing role in trade.

Medieval guilds were vital for maintaining order in trade and craft sectors, regulating labor markets, and fostering social solidarity by providing education, social security, and economic support. Guilds standardized production, supported local economies, and contributed to city development. Some even gained significant political power, influencing tax rates and city governments. Through guilds, European merchants developed political skills that Eastern merchants lacked, aiding the rise of capitalism.

During this period, governments in Italy, England, Germany, and the Low Countries adopted more participatory policies. The Hanseatic League, a mighty medieval trade confederation, is an example of inclusive institutions. It was based on collective action among cities and merchants, developed common legal frameworks, and ensured fairness in trade. The League was not centralized but a coalition of independent cities with regional autonomy, which allowed them to secure trade privileges and avoid military conflicts.

As city governments realized that markets could generate significant revenue for them, they began to support the organization of fairs and festivals. As the economy monetized and the importance of financial transactions increased, solutions were sought in credit and interest. One of these was easing the ban on interest at fairs and festivals. Medieval fairs became the center of great trade and economic activity in Europe, especially in regions such as France, Germany, and Italy, since the late twelfth century. These fairs were places of trade and large organizations where social and cultural interactions took place and legal and regulatory mechanisms functioned. The development of fairs in late medieval France did depend, to some extent, on the inclusive institutions that protected property rights, promoted trade, and encouraged broad economic participation. These features allowed fairs, especially in places like Lyon and Champagne, to become significant trade centers, financial exchange, and economic innovation. While parts of France remained under more extractive political systems, the areas where inclusive institutions were stronger saw more dynamic economic growth, supporting Acemoglu's argument about the importance of inclusive institutions for long-term prosperity.

One of the most essential lessons from medieval fairs is that the policies and actions undertaken by public authorities are crucial. The fair courts are a vivid example of the importance of well-functioning political authorities in ensuring the minimum requirements for market-based economic activity to flourish. They guaranteed security, property rights, and contract enforcement, built infrastructure, regulated weights and measures, supported foreign merchant lenders against politically powerful borrowers, and ensured equal treatment of foreign traders and locals (Edwards & Ogilvie, 2012). The second important lesson is that economic success is better guaranteed by "generalized" institutions accessible to all economic actors rather than by "specialized" institutions such as communities or guilds that guarantee property rights and contract enforcement only to members of privileged networks (Ogilvie, 2011; Ogilvie & Carus, 2014). The distinctive feature of all institutional services supporting international trade at the Champagne fairs was that the administrators provided them not as privileges granted to specific merchant guilds or communities but as generalized guarantees given to "*all merchants, goods, and persons of all kinds who came to the fair*" (Alengry, 1915).

For this reason, it was a vital necessity to establish a legal infrastructure in fairs and to conduct commercial activities on legal grounds. There were usually written and verbal agreements between merchants for trade in fairs. These agreements included specific rules about the buying and selling of goods between the parties, payment terms, delivery times, and other commercial issues. Local authorities in the area where the fair was held would supervise such contracts to ensure that trade could occur safely. Fairs provided specific legal protection so that merchants could defend their rights. Often, a local court was near the fairgrounds or in the city where the fair was held. If a trader faced a breach of contract or fraud, they could appeal to this court. This allowed trade to take place in a safe and orderly manner. In medieval fairs, public order and legal infrastructure were crucial for smooth and safe trade. These elements gained the trust of merchants, stimulated economic growth, and laid the foundations for the European trading system in the long run. Legal regulations ensured the efficient functioning of fairs, while security measures ensured trade continuity by protecting merchants' goods and capital.

In the Middle Ages, Lyon became one of Europe's most important commercial and financial centers, especially from the twelfth century onward, and served as a model for the economic centers to be established in the Low Countries years later. Throughout the Middle Ages, Lyon was strategically located on Europe's major trade routes. Lyon's money market was essential to local and international trade. The money market in Lyon facilitated merchant transactions in the city. Goods from different parts of Europe were collected in Lyon and sold in large markets here. This made the city's financial transactions and money exchange an important commercial activity. Banking activities began to develop rapidly in the city. This often included services such as lending, money transfer, currency exchange, and payment processing. The financial networks of merchants and bankers operating in Lyon supported the smooth functioning of trade across Europe. In the city, merchants and bankers from different parts of Europe exchanged different currencies. Bankers from the major trading cities of Italy ran operations in Lyon, further strengthening the city financially. These bankers were also involved in international payment transactions and long-term investments. The Lyon money market was one of the most critical milestones that led to the evolution of money exchange transactions into banking. Over time, the money market in Lyon became a center of financial innovation. New instruments were developed in the banking and financing systems during this period.

The economic historian Roberto Sabatino Lopez (1976) has argued that the most significant contribution of the medieval period to European history was the creation of a commercial economy between the eleventh and fourteenth centuries, initially centered on the Italo-Byzantine Eastern Mediterranean, but eventually spreading to the Italian city-states and the rest of Europe. According to Lopez, the growth of trade led to the rise of new towns and cities that became centers of trade and economic activity. These urban centers helped break down the traditional feudal structure and became focal points for markets, crafts, and trade. It was beginning to become clear how these metropolitan areas were becoming more prosperous and increasingly autonomous from the rural feudal economy. The growing importance of trade, banking, and money-based transactions created the conditions for the eventual rise of early capitalism.

The fairs and festivals established in Europe at this time were still not as spectacular as those in Baghdad, Cairo, or Tabriz. However, while the governance and legal infrastructure based on scripture remained static in the East, a crucial change occurred in the West. While in the East, the influence of religion increased and the rule of monarchs hardened, in the West, participatory institutions were developing, and the merchant class was rising. Moreover, this rise was not only economic; the legal infrastructure and the understanding of governance were also changing and investors adapt to environmental conditions. As the merchant class was gaining power in politics, the power of kings was eroding, creating a "narrow corridor," as the Acemoglu and Robinson described.

Fairs and festivals, such as those in Lyon and the Champagne region, no longer responded to the needs of the rising commercial formations. They needed centers where they could trade continuously. Moreover, the growing royal authority in France was making merchants uneasy. Entering the fifteenth century, there was a renewed interest in the Low Countries with moderate governments and free trade practices. Bruges would be the key stop for merchants.

References

Acemoglu, D., & Robinson, J. A. (2019). *The narrow corridor: How nations struggle for liberty*. Penguin UK.

Alengry, C. (1915). *Les foires de Champagne: étude d'histoire économique*.

Allen, L. (2004). *Global financial system 1750–2000*. Reaktion Books.

Allix, A. (1922). The geography of fairs: Illustrated by old-world examples. *Geographical Review, 12*(4), 532–569.

Bauer, H., Blackman, W. J., Bauer, H., & Blackman, W. J. (1998). *The medieval money economy*. Swiss Banking: An Analytical History, 3–19.

Boerner, L., & Hatfield, J. W. (2010). *The economics of debt clearing mechanisms.* Available at SSRN 1685149.
Bonnet, M. (1973). Les changeurs lyonnais au Moyen Age (1350–1450). *Revue historique, 249*(Fasc. 2 (506), 325–352.
Braudel, F. (1992). *Civilization and capitalism, 15th–18th century, vol. II: The wheels of commerce* (Vol. 2). University of California Press.
Brésard, M. (1914). Les foires de Lyon aux XVe et XVIe siècles. A. Picard.
Brucker, G. A. (1998). *Florence: The Golden Age 1138–1737* (pp. 116–121). University of California Press. ISBN 978-0-520-21522-1.
Clark, G. (2010). Industrial revolution. In *Economic growth* (pp. 148–160). Palgrave Macmillan UK.
Cucu, F. (2020). Markets and regional development in the long-run: Evidence from medieval England and Wales. Available at SSRN 3939018.
De Roover, R. (1963). *The rise and decline of the Medici bank: 1397–1494.* Harvard University Press.
Dollinger, P. (1999). *The German Hansa* (Vol. 1). Psychology Press.
Edwards, J., & Ogilvie, S. (2012). What lessons for economic development can we draw from the Champagne fairs? *Explorations in Economic History, 49*(2), 131–148.
Gelderblom, O. (2004). The decline of fairs and merchant guilds in the Low Countries. https://www.researchgate.net/profile/Oscar_Gelderblom/publication/253932534_The_Decline_of_Fairs_and_Merchant_Guilds_in_the_Low_Countries/links/54350a550cf294006f737de5.pdf. Et, 1, 2019.
Gelderblom, O. (2004). The decline of fairs and merchant guilds in the Low Countries. https://www.researchgate.
Greif, A., Milgrom, P., & Weingast, B. R. (1994). Coordination, commitment, and enforcement: The case of the merchant guild. *Journal of Political Economy, 102*(4), 745–776.
Greif, A. (2004). Impersonal exchange without impartial law: The community responsibility system. *Chicago Journal of International Law, 5*, 109.
Greif, A. (2006). *Institutions and the path to the modern economy: Lessons from medieval trade.* Cambridge University Press.
Greif, A. (2008). Contract enforcement and institutions among the Maghribi Traders: Refuting Edwards and Ogilvie. https://www.econstor.eu/bitstream/10419/26395/1/572272189.PDF
Hansen, V. (2012). *The silk road: A new history.* Oxford University Press.
Harreld, D. J. (2015). *A companion to the Hanseatic League* (Vol. 8). Brill.
Hawk, B. (2016). Business organizations: Families, partnerships, and companies. In *Law and commerce in pre-industrial societies* (pp. 206–262). Brill Nijhoff.
Hunt, E. S., & Murray, J. M. (1999). *A history of business in medieval Europe, 1200–1550.* Cambridge University Press.
Karan, M. B., Westerman, W., & Wijngaard, J. (2024). *A history of banks. Contributions to economics.*
Kohn, M. (2001). Payments and the development of finance in pre-industrial Europe. Dartmouth College Econ. Working Paper, (01–15).
Kohn, M. (2003). *Organized markets in pre-industrial Europe.* Available at SSRN 427764.
Lopez, R. S. (1976). *The commercial revolution of the Middle Ages, 950–1350.* Cambridge University Press.
Matringe, N. (2017). The fair deposit: credit reallocation and trade finance in the early modern period. *Annales. Histoire, Sciences Sociales-English Edition, 72*(2), 275–315.
Munro, J. H. (2001). The "New Institutional Economics" and the changing fortunes of fairs in medieval and early modern Europe: The textile trades, warfare, and transaction costs. *VSWG: Vierteljahrschrift Für Sozial- Und Wirtschaftsgeschichte, 88*(1), 1–47. http://www.jstor.org/stable/20740358
Ogilvie, S. (2011). *Institutions and European trade: Merchant guilds, 1000–1800.* Cambridge University Press.

Ogilvie, S., & Carus, A. W. (2014). Institutions and economic growth in historical perspective. *Handbook of economic development, 2*, 403–513.
Ogilvie, S. (2014). The economics of guilds. *Journal of Economic Perspectives, 28*(4), 169–192.
Rau, S. (2024). *At markets and fairs in Lyon.* https://urbrel.hypotheses.org/382
Richardson, H. (1961). *The medieval fairs and markets of York* (No. 20). Borthwick Publications.
Sgard, J. (2015). Global economic governance during the Middle Ages: The jurisdiction of the Champagne fairs. *International Review of Law and Economics, 42*, 174–184.
Stabel, P. (2004). Guilds in late medieval Flemenk: Myths and realities of guild life in an export-oriented environment. *Journal of Medieval History, 30*(2), 187–212.
Van Doosselaere, Q. (1961–2009). *Commercial agreements and social dynamics in medieval Genoa.* Cambridge University Press. ISBN 978-0-511-51790-7. OCLC 371197311.
World History Encyclopedia. (2019). https://www.worldhistory.org/article/1301/trade-in-medieval-europe/

Chapter 3
Bruges: The Cradle of Market Capitalism (13th–15th Centuries)

Abstract Bruges was a major economic and financial center in Europe in the fourteenth century. The establishment has done well, as it is in a good location and easily accessible. The city established rules that certain groups and courts had to follow to protect contracts and ensure fair trading. People might do business here easily. People generally believe that the Bourse, established in 1309, is the world's oldest stock exchange. The existence of well-known Italian banking families, such as the Medici, Bardi, and Peruzzi, made it easier to conduct complex financial operations, including letters of credit and bills of exchange. Bruges' inns did two important things. First, they rented out rooms to people so they could stay there. Second, they helped others by helping them with their work. Their help was crucial in facilitating trade deals and disseminating information more easily. Bruges became part of the larger European trade network because it had a lively network of enterprises and financial services that attracted many foreign traders. But Bruges was not as important as other cities at the end of the fifteenth century. The Zwin estuary became polluted, and there were also significant political issues, which were the primary reasons for this. As a result, Antwerp became the most important business center in Europe.

3.1 Introduction

Willem Ruwee, one of Bruges's most essential money changers, walked from his large house with elaborate stonework, pointed arches, or ornate stone reliefs on the canal bank to his workplace near the bridge. The weather was cool and chilly in March of 1368. He hurried along the stone-paved road in his leather shoes. He wore a brown wool doublet with a wide skirt that fit her upper body well. Over the doublet was a cloak made of bright green woolen cloth, indicating that he was wealthy. The cloak's collar was black, and the cuffs were lined with white fur. On his head, he wore a green hat. The street was quiet; the recent economic recession had reduced commercial activity. The lack of business had also taken its toll on his health, and occasionally, he felt a pain in his chest (Fig. 3.1).

M. B. Karan, *A History of Stock Exchanges*, Contributions to Economics,
https://doi.org/10.1007/978-3-032-07788-2_3

Fig. 3.1 Burges and waterways: A fascinating reflection of how geography, trade, and finance were intertwined in the late Middle Ages. https://upload.wikimedia.org/wikipedia/commons/e/ec/Bruges_Belgium_De-groote-Hollander-Huidenvettersplein-12-03.jpg

He followed the road beside the canal to the stone-built money exchange shop on St. Pieter's Bridge. The shop was a typical money changer's shop. Above the outer door was a symbol of his company, like a metal scale. The shop had a counter, a console with many drawers, and two large metal safes. Some symbols and writings on the wall were easy for illiterate people to understand. These symbols could give information about the value of a particular currency or product. He offered essential services in his shop, such as currency exchange, credit, and secure money transfer. When he entered the shop, his two sons and an employee converted the Livres of French merchants into Flanders florins. The French livre had a notable presence in Bruges in the fourteenth century, due to the city's trade ties with France. Still, it was less dominant than the Flemish and Florentine florin in international commerce. The most popular coin in Bruges in 1350 was the Florentine Florin with the lily symbol. On the other side was a picture of St. John the Baptist. This coin was made of 24-carat gold and weighed about 3.5 g. The Flanders florin was slightly lighter than the Florentine florin and typically weighed about 3.4 g. It featured the Flemish lion and cross or other local symbols. Because the Italian florin had a higher gold content, it was generally considered slightly more valuable or of higher quality than the Flanders florin. However, the Flanders florin was a reliable currency, especially in Flanders, where its minting and weight were carefully regulated. Both florins were circulated and accepted in Bruges, a major trading city and financial center in the fourteenth century. His wife, Margaret, also helped him sometimes. She had inherited the shop as a dowry from her father and was the official owner of the company.

On his desk, he saw some letters from the city administration. He realized the letters had come because of debts he could not pay. I hope they do not go to court right away, he muttered. The courts made decisions very quickly. He was in financial trouble because of the wine tax farmer business he had been in for the last three years. He had hoped to gain money and prestige by taking this job. Due to the nature of this business, he had initially paid a lump sum to the city government to get this job. He also recruited weekly paid agents and inspectors. They monitored all commercial activities in Bruges markets, ports, residential areas, and various trading points, recorded traders, made agreements with merchants or tradesmen, and inspected and collected taxes. Collecting taxes from the people was not easy, but it was too unpleasant. However, the income from this job was much lower than he had expected. He would not cover his losses by selling the properties he had bought because the housing market was in the doldrums due to the scarcity of money. He was very regretful that he had taken this job. To some extent, he began partnering with the innkeeper Jacob Sconeberghe to recover his financial situation and cover his losses. As the owner of one of the most essential inns in Bruges, Jacob, like other innkeepers, welcomed Italian merchants to his inn, stored their goods, and helped them sell them. He had given him a substantial amount of money as capital, but he had not been seen for a while. His wife said he was unwell, and he hoped there was nothing wrong with him.

Just then, he saw Father Ledenaert from the Church of the Virgin Mary enter his shop. He seemed very sad. Willem looked at him, sensing that something terrible had happened. The priest bowed respectfully and whispered that his partner, the innkeeper Jacob Sconeberghe, had died the night before. Suddenly, Willem felt a pain in his chest and sank into his chair. He was very sad; he had lost his partner, and he realized that he would have great difficulty in collecting his debts. After the priest left, he asked his friend, Advocati (Advocate), who Thymane was best. Maybe he could give some legal advice.

The above-dramatized story of Willem Ruwee is fictionalized based on the papers and findings of De Roover (1944) and Murray (1988). The information obtained about Willem Ruwee reveals how the moneylenders in Bruges worked at the time. We will see how Willem's story is finalized in Part Four of this chapter. However, it is necessary to go back to the early fourteenth century to see how the city of Bruges developed as a commodity and money exchange.

3.2 Decline of Fairs in Europe

In the late Middle Ages, fairs and merchant guilds were replaced by permanent markets and individual merchants with legal personalities. In the thirteenth century, the English, Dutch, and Rhineland fairs were superseded by the permanent open markets of London, Bruges, and Cologne. Champagne fairs declined rapidly after 1300 as Italian merchants began to turn to London and Bruges. Thus, after 1500, all the major commercial centers of Europe (Lyon, Venice, Antwerp, Genoa, Amsterdam, and London) became centers of goods and logistics, creating financial markets. A similar change was observed in the merchant guilds. In Florence in the fourteenth century and Augsburg and Nuremberg in the fifteenth century, merchants established multi-branch companies to organize trade with distant markets (Gelderblom, 2004).

In contrast, the northern Hanseatic League disbanded after 1550, while foreign merchants' associations in Venice, the Dutch Republic, and England disappeared in the sixteenth and seventeenth centuries. In cities where trade flourished, permanent commodity and money exchanges were established, thus creating a new commercial model (Liggio, 2007). Fairs and merchant guilds declined in some places, but they remained present in centers such as Lyon. This was likely due to the expansion of trade. As the volume of trade became extensive and valuable enough to necessitate the constant presence of merchants, certain cities emerged. Lyon's advantage was the trade volume and the development of financial transactions. At that time, agricultural production in the Italian city-states had increased significantly, and the supply and demand for manufacturing in the cities and goods from the Far East were so plentiful as to prevent the need for fairs. The local merchant guilds were also in decline. The rulers of countries and cities realized they could organize trade more efficiently and generate revenue when trade was concentrated in permanent markets. As a result, members of foreign merchant guilds were granted certain privileges in permanent trading centers, and these privileges were complemented and extended by legal, commercial, and financial institutions. Thus, the vacuum of local guilds was filled (Gelderblom, 2004). The importance of guilds gradually declined until the eighteenth century (Gelderblom & Grafe, 2010).

Central and regional states began to use law enforcement and diplomacy effectively and, if necessary, applied military intervention to protect established merchants from arbitrary confiscation or imprisonment. This proactive role of the state reassured merchants about the stability of the trade system. State formation also facilitated the creation of a legal system that treated all merchants equally, thus eliminating institutional jurisdictions. Moreover, local enforcement by central authorities regarding financial and commercial transactions became increasingly systematic. Finally, public finance reforms removed the obligation for merchants to make any financial contribution in exchange for trade privileges. Trade in Europe was now shifting north. The most important reason for this was that powerful states and the Church exerted pressure on merchants in the South. In contrast, in the North, moderate governments, relatively more secular practices, and better opportunities for merchants became the norm (Gelderblom & Grafe, 2010).

West European states began to protect resident merchants from arbitrary confiscation or imprisonment. State formation also facilitated the creation of a legal system that treated all merchants equally, thereby eliminating institutionalized jurisdictions. In addition, local practices of the central authorities regarding financial and commercial transactions were increasingly systematized. Finally, public finance reforms eliminated merchants' obligation to make any financial contribution in exchange for trade privileges. Trade in Europe was now shifting to the north. The primary reason for this was that powerful states and the Church exerted pressure on merchants in the South. In contrast, in the North, moderate governments, relatively more secular practices, and better opportunities for merchants emerged.

In the Dutch region of northern Europe, a series of extraordinarily talented ruling counts, notably the Count of Flanders, had managed to unite a group of territories throughout the eleventh and twelfth centuries. The Count of Flanders, in particular, retained his power and remained the head of an efficient bureaucracy—a testament to the impact of individual leadership on historical developments. Communes, which had originated in Italy and were spreading to the commercial cities of Europe, were also active in this region. Communes were formed by landowning aristocrats who saw opportunities in trade as a way to increase their incomes and banded together. They were sworn associations that negotiated with their overlords for contracts, establishing collective privileges for the communities. The chief negotiators were almost always businessmen, regardless of their social class, and they were responsible for establishing rules of behavior within the commune. Since much of the Dutch coast was marshy and prone to flooding, land reclamation owed much to a communal policy of excavation and drainage. The task of land reclamation was complemented by the creation of waterways linking the emerging urban centers. Almost all of West Flanders was navigable by the early twelfth century (Hunt & Murray, 1999).

In 1180, a monumental dam was built ten kilometers northeast of Bruges, providing access to the North Sea via the new port city of Damme. Trade policies also influenced the development of urban communities and local fairs in the country. Another significant incentive for urbanization was the establishment of five fairs in West Flanders in the early twelfth century. This was the oldest fair cycle in the northern European region. Each benefited from the support of the count, who was deeply committed to trade and growth, ensuring safe passage on Flemish roads and waterways and granting special privileges to foreign merchants. This fair cycle also stimulated trade and development in the rest of Flanders. Merchants from other Flemish communities could travel to the fairs and were either exempt from or subject to much lower tolls on their goods. By the thirteenth century, businessmen from the town's wealthiest and most powerful families had seized much of the economic initiative in the county, with the communes exercising considerable control over land reclamation, waterway construction, and agricultural investments. By the mid-fourteenth century, Bruges, Ghent, and Ypres, the "*three cities*" as they called themselves, were able to challenge the power of both the Count and the King of France when a conflict arose between communal politics and the economic interests of urban Flanders. Thus, Flanders' cooperation brought a sense of moderate governance in the region (Hunt & Murray, 1999).

3.3 The Rise of Bruges

Historian Murray (2005) has described medieval Bruges as a sketch of an early model of a large capitalist city, likening the community of merchants within the city walls to a nervous system in which each merchant acts as a node, providing access to new and ever-changing networks of people and goods. This city was the first cradle of market capitalism. Bruges was also the city where the name "*Bourse*" was first used, or more precisely, where the emerging financial market came to be known as the "*Bourse*." Since some Dutch settlements in present-day Belgium were located at the crossroads of international commodity flows between southern countries, such as Italy and France, and northern European states, including England and Sweden, this region began to play an essential role in the European economy from the thirteenth century. The most important city in this region, Bruges, would later become known as the Venice of the North. Bruges' economic rise, primarily driven by the vibrant commercial atmosphere fostered by its merchants, began with the floods caused by rain in 1134. This flood opened the city's access to the North Sea through the Scheldt estuary via the Zwin. This paved the way for the gradual increase of trade fairs in Bruges from 1200 onward. In the thirteenth century, Bruges had good access to the sea via the river, as seen from its geographical position (Fig. 3.2). Interestingly, however, at the beginning of the fourteenth century, a natural phenomenon severed the city's connection to the sea, and its heyday would be left behind (Murray, 2005).

The first urban concessions in Bruges and many other Flemish cities were granted in 1127 amid a civil war between two rivals vying for the throne. The inhabitants of Bruges took advantage of this situation to conclude a "*small contract*." It included clauses guaranteeing the city's exemption from customs duties, the security of the city's property, and the election of members to a governing council of the town. However, it is clear from the descriptions in the chronicles that Bruges had the character and functions of a commercial city long before it was granted urban privileges. It was already a market town with a population of merchants and artisans, a testament to its long-standing economic importance (Hunt & Murray, 1999).

An old fifteenth-century anonymous English poem, "*The Libelle of Englyshe Polycye*," enviously spoke of Dutch success. Bruges' role as a trans-regional market

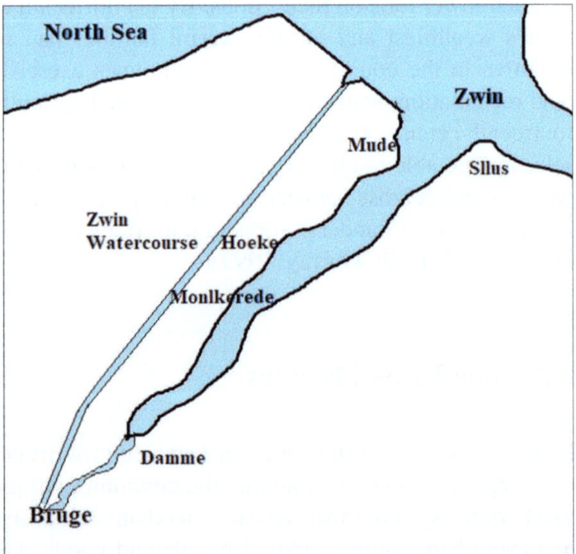

Fig. 3.2 Thirteenth-century Bruges and zwin watercourse. Drawn by the Author

was the secret of the city's economic development. It had a more comprehensive legal infrastructure and facilities than those in other international trading centers in Western Europe. Moreover, Bruges' laws stipulated that most goods entering Flanders via Zwin must be transported to and sold in the city (Lambert, 2016).

Through a series of regulations and concessions to merchants, the forward-thinking rulers of Bruges ensured their city a solid commercial position. By the end of the thirteenth century, Bruges had already become a necessary hub for goods traveling to or from the north. This was made possible by the privileges granted to foreign merchants by the Dutch counts and the privilege of collecting tolls enjoyed by the citizens of Bruges. In 1323, another, more far-reaching concession was granted, making the storage of staple food mandatory and privileged. Many of the settlements in the Zwin ports owed their development to their status as satellite towns of Bruges and, in keeping with their role, accepted a role in the staple food network (Lambert, 2016). In the mid-thirteenth century, English merchants began selling their wool in Bruges. In contrast, merchants and ship captains from Galicia, Castile, and Biscaye imported wool, iron, and wine from Bruges, and Biscaye imported wool and iron. By the end of the thirteenth century, merchant houses (companies) from Venice and Genoa had stopped going to the Champaign fairs, instead sending galleys full of silk, alum, dyes, fruit, and spices to Bruges, where they employed agents to supervise sales, organize exports, and sent money to Italy. Bruges continued to attract many foreign merchants during this period. Between the mid-fourteenth and late fifteenth centuries, more than a dozen foreign "nations" were officially represented in Bruges, with over 500 merchants. Among them were merchants from Venice, Genoa, Milan, Florence, Lucca, Piacenza, the German Hansa, and several firms from southern Germany, as well as merchants from Scotland, Portugal, Castile, Aragon, and Navarre (Gelderblom, 2004). Moreover, several firms from southern Germany and merchants from Scotland, Portugal, Castile, and Aragon established permanent agencies or branches in cities such as Bruges, Paris, and London, enabling them to conduct their business from their headquarters rather than transporting their goods north. Historians attribute this shift to the superior business organization made possible by new long-term partnership agreements, new accounting and control techniques, and new means of exchange. This transition was gradual and developed throughout the second half of the thirteenth century (Hunt & Murray, 1999).

In 1438, the Cordoban traveler Pero Tafur said this about Bruges (Bolton & Bruscoli, 2008): "*Anyone who wants to spend money can find everything the world produces in this city alone. There, I saw oranges from Castile that looked as if they had just been picked from the trees, fruit, and wine from Greece, which were as plentiful as in that country. I also saw confectionery and spices from Alexandria and all over the Levant, as if they had been produced there, and furs from the Black Sea, as if they had been harvested there. All of Italy was here, with its brocades, silks, armor, and everything that was made there, and indeed, there is no place in the world whose products are not found here at their best.*" Bruges' unique geographical location, the organization of trade in the city, the legal system, and the infrastructure attracted many merchants and businesspeople.

3.4 Legal System and Infrastructure of Trade in Bruges

The legal system governing markets in Bruges during the late medieval period was sophisticated and designed to support the city's role as a central hub for international trade. As part of the Hanseatic League and a center of European trade, Bruges established a legal framework that provided security, facilitated dispute resolution, and fostered economic activity. Here are the key features of this system. Bruges ensured the safety of merchants and goods through well-maintained public order and infrastructure, including warehouses and harbors. The city provided secure facilities for storing goods and employed officials to oversee fair transactions and prevent theft or fraud.

Undoubtedly, the presence of foreign merchants had a profound impact on the infrastructure of the Bruges market. Since local rulers at the time were hostile toward foreign merchants, these merchants required guarantees from the city administration to ensure their safety. They also needed a well-functioning judicial mechanism in case of disputes. Foreign merchants also attach great importance to promptly settling disputes and preserving their jurisdiction. They also wanted the Bruges administration to waive tolls and taxes and to facilitate transactions with the local population and between themselves. They expected a legal and commercial infrastructure to enable this. The demands of German, English, and Spanish merchants, who began trading with Bruges, were met by the legal and commercial institutions that managed the city's Annual Fair. In 1200, market rights granted by the Dutch Count would facilitate the arrival and departure of merchants. The local court also played an increasingly important role in settling commercial disputes. The Schepenbank, or alderman court, was the primary municipal court, adjudicating civil and criminal cases. It comprised elected officials who applied local customary law (Gelderblom, 2005).

In 1253, German merchants were represented by German officials. The merchants of Lübeck and Hamburg, under the guidance of the influential Dutch Countess, reached an agreement to reduce tolls, regulate the ownership of goods on sunken ships, prevent arrests for failure to pay debts on time, and even retaliate against the property of foreign merchants. For example, in 1434, the German Kontor banned all German merchant members from buying Spanish wool in retaliation for the seizure of 40 ships, primarily Hanseatic vessels, by Spanish pirates off La Rochelle (Dumolyn, 1997). In 1280, due to repeated treaty violations, they relocated to the neighboring port of Aardenburg for a time and only returned in 1282 after Bruges accepted the privileges they had demanded. Naturally, the city's administration did not want to be deprived of such income. One of the most critical new privileges was the permission to trade with other foreigners every day of the year.

The only condition for protecting the interests of the local business community was to require foreigners to use local brokers when trading among themselves and with foreigners. Once the organization of foreign merchants in Bruges was formalized, an increasing number of foreigners began to reside there in the first half of the fourteenth century. In the second half of the fourteenth and early fifteenth centuries, the Dutch Count granted most other nations corporate jurisdiction. The corporate jurisdiction of foreign nations in Bruges would allow their consuls to mediate or adjudicate commercial disputes between their members without the intervention of the Bruges government. By enforcing their own rules and regulations, the consuls effectively extended the jurisdiction of their hometown or country (De Roover, 1944). The rulers of Bruges understood that if the economy developed, they could quickly compensate for the tax exemptions granted to foreigners by taxing the expanding local economy. Merchants were often rightly concerned about the safety of banks. Therefore, some preferred to keep the money in their vaults with an innkeeper. To address such concerns, Bruges guaranteed bank deposits to members of some foreign merchants' associations (Kohn, 1999a).

However, the strengthening of Bruges' foreign national presence was not only due to its laws and rules. Social and religious ties between members were at least as important in creating a common identity and trust. The Italians had established large companies with numerous employees and apprentices, who used formal contracts, maintained double books, and kept information flowing through extensive correspondence, all while rigorously enforcing contracts. In addition, the local payment clearing system worked very well. Money exchangers were critical in the city. Foreign merchants used them to finance buyers and suppliers, while brokers used them to exchange foreign currencies, make deposits, transfer money between accounts, and take short-term loans (De Roover, 1944). Notary services in the city were initially limited. Notary services were introduced by Italian merchants (Stabel, 1997).

Most Italian, Castilian, or Portuguese merchants in Bruges had extensive commercial infrastructures and close and intimate relations with the city's commercial and political elite. On occasion, they relied on these relationships to circumvent the law. In addition to the experienced Portuguese sugar merchant Luís Martins, the Florentine Tommaso Portinari, the ambitious director of the Bruges branch of the Medici Bank, advisor to the Duke of Burgundy, and the Venetian Luigi Bembo, a usurer to the court, were caught trying to circumvent the tax laws. These cases appear in historical records, suggesting that influential smugglers were not immune to prosecution (Lambert, 2016).

3.4.1 Legal System

One of Bruges' greatest strengths was its solid legal infrastructure. Merchants who settled in Bruges brought a wide variety of goods and legal traditions—disputes needed to be settled relatively quickly in a city where representatives of many different nations traded extensively. The rulers of Bruges had a very pragmatic and flexible system in place.

Disputing merchants in Bruges had several options for reconciling with each other. Disputes could be settled amicably without resorting to the courts. If a merchant belonged to one of the foreign nations, which were associations of foreign merchants from the same city or region, disputes with members of other nations could be settled by the consul or president of the group. On the other hand, disputes with other foreign merchants or local citizens had to be brought before the city court, which was composed of municipal councilors. The central courts of the Dutch counts and later of the Burgundian dukes, such as the Dutch Council and the Grand Council, had jurisdiction over private cases and handled appeals against municipal fines (Lambert, 2019b).

The ways of settling commercial disputes that foreign merchants were most familiar with in their hometowns or regions fundamentally differed from those of other foreign visitors and hosts. Gelderblom (2013) has argued that the main force that attracted foreign merchants to Bruges over other markets was its developed institutional framework. Among these commercial institutions, the author most emphasized the city courts. As the jurisdiction of these courts was constantly and increasingly adapted to the needs of visiting merchants, they continued to trade in Bruges because they could settle their commercial disputes at lower transaction costs than elsewhere.

The jurisdiction of Bruges' city councilors was limited. Private cases involving, for example, the men of the Prince of Bruges were brought before the central courts. When a foreign merchant died in Bruges, the settlement of his estate fell under the jurisdiction of his home government; when merchants disagreed over the terms of bills of exchange, the municipal councilors would decide if the original contract had been drawn up in Bruges. The surviving normative texts agree on which law the councilors were to follow in these cases. For example, in 1410, the ducal decree on new money stipulated that merchants who issued bills of exchange in Bruges should pay half the amount in gold and half in Dutch silver. When the Italian nations complained that this was impossible, the city councilors postponed this measure. In 1467, Venetian merchants obtained an exemption from the common law. In cases involving Venetians, debtors could no longer swear that they owed nothing to their creditors, and creditors had no opportunity to present evidence of the debt. Since this exemption was granted by the duke and not by the city government, it could be revoked at any time. They strived for speedy legal and bureaucratic procedures. As early as 1304, when Bruges was emerging as a center of international trade, a decree issued by Philippe, son of the city's Dutch count, Guy of Dampierre, stated that if a merchant or foreigner came before the aldermen, he could expect "*justice to be done within three days, or at the latest eight days, according to the laws and customs of the city.*" A 1396 municipal ordinance stipulated that if a foreign merchant had his goods seized in a debt case, he must provide a surety and "*observe the laws, customs, and traditions of the city of Bruges.*" When John the Fearless, Duke of Burgundy, granted new commercial privileges to Venetian merchants operating in his territory in 1405, he made it clear that all disputes between these merchants and non-Venetians were to be "*tried according to the laws of our said territory and punished according to the laws and customs of the cities and places where they are found.*" John's grandson, Philip the Good, confirmed in a ducal decree of 1459 that all international commercial disputes in the Low Countries of Burgundy should be settled "*according to the local customs of the place where they occur*" and that no appeal against an interlocutory decision of a local court would be accepted. Therefore, the legislation on commercial litigation left little room for doubt (Lambert, 2019b).

If a nation member disagreed with the consul's ruling, he could appeal against the decision in the court of the members of the Bruges city council. In 1467, Alvaro Dyes appealed against the decision of the consul of the Portuguese nation in Bruges. The city council considered his case but upheld the consular decision, considering "*the custom of unloading goods from Portugal over the great sea and delivering them in the city of Bruges*" (Lambert, 2019b).

In 1449, Luciano Spinola of Genoa sued the English merchant Thomas Patrich on behalf of Loys Stoc and Anthoine Centurion, claiming that Patrich still owed them money. Patrich argued that he had paid his debts but was given two months to provide evidence. He then demanded more time, accusing Spinola of blocking access to his letters. The Genoese argued that the laws of Bruges prohibited further delay. The court ruled in Spinola's favor, ordering Patrich to pay £200 (Lambert, 2019b).

The late medieval Bruges commercial law was not a cosmopolitan blend of legal traditions. The influence of learned law in the central courts might have led to different practices. However, normative sources and legal practice indicate that most disputes brought before the Bruges city council were adjudicated according to Bruges customary law. The only exceptions were insurance disputes, which were resolved according to international rules, and cases concerning shipments and home country matters, which were determined according to the domestic law of foreign merchants. There is little evidence that Bruges customs, which also applied to the city's citizens, were constantly adapted to the needs of visiting international merchants. However, the city's customs showed adaptability, particularly in cases involving international merchants, demonstrating Bruges' openness to foreign trade and ability to accommodate diverse legal traditions (Lambert, 2019b).

3.4.2 Inns (Hostels) of Bruges

One of Bruges' most significant advantages was its warehouse and boarding house services to merchants. International trade depended on the use of inns (hostels) in various parts of the city and the services of the innkeeper. Historian Murray (2005) pointed out that the intense interest in the origins of bourses (stock exchanges) should not lead us to overlook the critical roles played by innkeepers and brokers in the history of trade in Bruges. During Bruges' economic heyday, in the fourteenth and fifteenth centuries, hostels functioned as guesthouses and places of entertainment, stables, warehouses, and trading centers. Goods were stored in the cellars of the lodgings or nearby store rooms. Foreign merchants did not own their buildings and warehouses in Bruges until the middle of the fourteenth century, when, realizing the importance of the institutional function of the hostels, they bought them. The innkeeper provided hotel and warehouse services and information to his guests. He acted as a business agent and was involved in commercial transactions and payments. If the merchant was absent, the innkeeper acted as their representative and sold the goods stored on the premises. The innkeepers were jointly responsible for the debts accrued by their guests. It was common for merchants to mention the inn's name where they stayed (Murray, 2005). Innkeepers and brokers often guaranteed settlement for the deals they brokered. Every sales contract involving deferred payment was guaranteed this way (Nicholas, 1992). In this context, it is believed that brokerage regulations in Bruges were drafted in the second half of the thirteenth century. Strong broker guilds had also developed in this city. In Bruges, rulers collaboratively regulated and directly organized broker behavior through brokerage regulations (Boerner, 2016).

Commercial transactions between merchants were concluded either through the services of the innkeeper and the broker employed by the innkeeper or through the services of an independent broker. Moreover, by the end of the thirteenth century, it had become compulsory for foreign merchants to utilize the services of a broker for all transactions exceeding five Dutch pounds. This close relationship between merchants and lodging houses and inns was quite common. It also allowed the seller and the buyer to inspect the goods on-site before signing the contract (Gelderblom, 2013). The innkeepers dominated the brokers' guild, and over time, they also became increasingly influential in local politics. Many of them were members of the municipal council (schepen). Hostelers, especially those who entertained Hanse merchants, were often employed in diplomatic posts. The degree of cooperation between the money exchange and the inns is critical to understanding the Northern European trading system through Bruges in the late Middle Ages. The two shared many banking functions in a cooperative and complementary manner, creating an exchange network whose reach extended far beyond Bruges. Through this network, commodities, gold, silver or small coins, foreign exchange and letters of credit, and "bank" money held on deposit were circulated according to customers' needs. Thus, innkeepers such as De Marke, about whom we know from historical records, delivered at least twelve types of gold coins from places such as Castile, Venice, and England to the inns of their customers as moneylenders, as well as "*black money*," the popular name for the mainly copper coins used for small purchases in the city. Payments for these coins and other transactions could be made through ledger transfers, as the moneychangers and innkeepers in Bruges had clearing accounts with each other. Such an intertwined local system, combined with connections abroad and the constant traveling to and from Bruges by foreign merchants, multiplied the possibilities for payment and credit. De Marke, for example, also made use of a dense network of regional moneylenders and innkeepers in Ghent, Leuven, Douai, Tournai, Geraardsbergen, Valenciennes, and Antwerp to offer financial services to its clients. Indeed, long-distance transactions were also possible, such as payments made in Prussia by Western knights on crusades, ransoms collected for prisoners in Spain, and, more typically, commercial payments made in Paris and London. What is clear is that merchants used their credit balances with the innkeepers and moneylenders of Bruges as currency, transferring their balances to a provincial traveling to Bruges or ordering payment by letter or messenger, thus avoiding the need to send coins or bullion (Hunt & Murray, 1999).

It is worth noting that after the heyday of Bruges, Antwerp, and Amsterdam, the importance of innkeepers as brokers gradually declined. Presumably, this decline was due to the availability of alternative accommodation for merchants. Sometimes, houses were rented or bought for groups of merchants in a town or region. Therefore, the need for innkeepers was decreasing. Furthermore, renting houses allowed the separation of innkeeper and brokerage services. The Bruges brokers were obliged to keep a linked ledger to present to the court if necessary in case of dispute; brokers were required to record the quantity, quality, and price of a deal and keep a sample of the product (Boerner, 2016).

The description of the daily routine of a German merchant in Bruges is quite revealing (Hapke, 1911): "*The working day starts early every morning; it is important to make use of daylight. Buying and selling require a lot of time and attention. People prefer to buy 'in person'. So the merchant appears in the salesroom or even goes down to the goods cellar. He tastes, tests, touches, and perhaps even exercises his sense of smell. Then comes the cumbersome weighing [...]. The most important thing yet to be done is to negotiate a price until, at the end of the deal, a small gift for charitable purposes, the 'God's penny' (Gottespfennig), is paid and celebrated together over wine.*"

Undoubtedly, the best-known boarding house in Bruges is Herberg ter Beurse on Vlamingstraat (Fig. 3.3). From the late thirteen to the late fifteenth century, this establishment was owned by boarders and brokers belonging to the Van der Beurse family and gave its name to the Bourse (Beursplein) square, which became the city's commodity and money exchange in the fifteenth century (Marechal, 1949).

The Van ter Beurse family was one of the city's most prominent and powerful elements; some of its members served as the mayor of the Dutch town or as an essential city administrator. The Ter Beurse Inn hosted foreign merchants who found its location on the Beursplein, a vital city square, convenient. In the fourteenth century,

Fig. 3.3 The main square in Bruges, painted c. 1691–1700 by Meunincxhove. https://en.wikipedia.org/wiki/Bruges#/media/File:Jan_Baptist_van_Meunincxhove_-_The_Burg_in_Bruges.jpg (public domain)

merchants gathered here to buy and sell bonds and bills of exchange, a money market instrument used in trade as a substitute for cash. In addition to bonds and bills of exchange, commodities and insurance were also traded here. The square was also close to the law courts and notaries, and the boarders acted as brokers, introducing merchants of different nationalities. This square was the commodity and money exchange. All vital services were nearby. When it rained, the trade in the square was moved inside the Ter Beurse Inn. The Ter Beurse Inn itself kept the guests' money. When one of the family lodgers, Laurens van der Beurse, died in 1351, a scandal had questioned the inn's future. The money entrusted to him was treated as his property and included in his estate. This incident alone is said to have damaged Bruges' image as a favored trading city and weakened the city's relationship with Hanseatic merchants (DeMatos, 2020).

The Beursplein, in essence, was a precursor to the modern bourse (stock exchange). It operated under the practices of the time, with limited public access, fixed trading hours, and the market's opening and closing signaled by a bell. The Beursplein's status as perhaps the most important financial market in Northern Europe also brought significant development to its surroundings. The nation houses serving the various trading nations were located near Beursplein Square. The street, protected on three sides by attractive houses, provided merchants from Europe with a permanent shopping center where they could meet daily and conduct their business. Beggars were not allowed to enter the city (Marechal, 1949).

3.5 Bruges Money Market

While commodities were traded around the boarding houses and warehouses, merchants met in various parts of Bruges, including Beursplein Square. According to Raymond de Roover (1963), Bruges was a "*money market*," and its meeting place was Beursplein Square, where Italians and Spaniards, if not Germans, who had no banking facilities east of the Rhine, had to be present. According to one of De Roover's sources from 1482, all merchants engaged in this activity were known as "*Marchans de la bourse*," the exchange merchants.

According to the original work of the Italian cartographer, writer, and merchant Lodovico Guicciardini (1521–1589), Bruges is believed to be the birthplace of the stock exchange in Europe. However, the idea that Bruges was the birthplace of the corporate structure is wrong. The Bruges Bourse was just the name of a square. There was never an Exchange (bourse) building in Bruges where financial securities were traded. In the first edition of his Descrittione di tutti i Paesi Bassi (Descrittione di tutti i Paesi Bassi) of 1567, Guicciardini describes the prevalence of the use of the name Borsa as follows: "*When we consider whence the name Borsa came and whence it is derived, let us say that it came into being in such an appropriate manner by chance. In Bruges, there is a square very suitable for any place in the world; at the head of this square, there is a large old house belonging to a noble family known as Borsa; the arms of this house are made of the same stone, and there are three bags over the door. This house, the family, and the arms take their name from this square. When the merchants of Bruges went to the Anuersa and Berga fairs, they chose this square or 'Borsa' as the basis for their trade, so they called the squares and places where they met in Anuersa and Berga Borsa. In Anuersa, this name became so widespread and accepted. It took on a different meaning that soon afterward, the French carried the same name, Borsa, to Roano and even to Toulouse and gave it to some of the commercial squares and trading houses organized for gathering merchants"* (Flume, 2021).

Cornelis Kiliaan (1528–1607), who translated Guicciardini's work into Dutch, describes it as follows in his Etymologicum Teutonicae Linguae of 1599: "*Bourse (borsa), in contemporary vernacular Bursa, derived from great house of the bursa, or purse, was the first to be thus designated in Bruges, Flanders."* While the name Borsa is not particularly original, it is certainly appropriate for a Bruges family. It goes back to the old Latin word byrsa, based on the Greek word for "Bursa" (coat, leather), the medieval word for leather wallet or pouch. It may not be coincidental that the expression Bursa like a purse gradually became a term for all economic activities. In medieval Europe, a bursa could also mean a common fund, a commercial corporation, or a student dormitory. An example of the latter use is the "*Bursagasse*" built at the University of Tübingen in the late fifteenth century. The "*rescontre,*" an important accounting practice in medieval bills of exchange, was also referred to as *"payment by closed purse (Zahlen mit geschlossenem Beutel)."* It is likely that medieval merchants memorized barter transactions as a square activity or that the exchange of goods evoked a square (Flume, 2021).

The name of this square in Bruges was so adopted that in Antwerp and Bergen, the places where they gathered to bargain were called bourses. This name was first adopted in Antwerp as well, and then the French began to give the same name to the bourse in Rouen and Toulouse, as well as to some trading places and houses where they exchanged goods (money) in the local area (Flume, 2021). The Bruges Guild was founded as early as 1303 by a Dutch count (Harreld, 2003). The presence of established international merchants and Bruges' position as a northern trade center made it one of the first banking centers in northern Europe. All banking services in medieval Europe were available in the only northwestern European city, namely Bruges.

Foreign exchange markets traded primarily in foreign exchange and were generally dominated by Italian merchant bankers, who had dominated the medieval money market. This traditional pattern began to change in the late fifteenth century in Antwerp, where many merchants of all nationalities joined the market as it expanded from commodities to financial instruments. During the Middle Ages, Bruges had three distinct classes of money traders: Italian merchant bankers, Lombards, and money changers. A closer examination of the activities of money traders provides a better understanding of how the Bruges money market functioned (De Roover, 1944).

3.5.1 Italian Merchant Bankers

In the late thirteenth century, advances in commercial practices and business management prompted the Italians to establish a permanent presence in Bruges. The Italians asked for a concession from the Dutch Count, demanding that their organization have "*nation houses*" run by a consul and that their trading colony be officially recognized. In Bruges, merchants from Genoa, Venice, Florence, Lucca, and Milan formed separate "*houses of nations*," but when it came to their shared interests, all the nations came together to create a united front. The commercial privileges granted to Italian merchants by the Dutch Count and the city of Bruges were often the subject of lengthy diplomatic negotiations, in which the protection of merchants against arbitrary actions by local authorities was discussed. They also solidified their privileges by discussing fundamental issues related to shipping, in addition to setting the tariffs for tolls and port charges. However, the commercial concessions contained no word on financial transactions. This is likely because these agreements covered the international transactions of Italian merchant bankers and fell outside the purview of local authorities. Italian merchants were considered foreigners due to their commercial privileges, and each Italian "house of the nation" was headed by a consul, typically assisted by two or more councilors. In Bruges, the Italian consular houses were located on the Bourse Square (Beursplein) in the heart of the business district (De Roover, 1944).

In the thirteenth century, the merchants of the cities of north-central Italy developed several new systems of risk management and capital allocation, establishing long-term business partnerships or companies that operated for several years, the duration of which was determined by the partners or shareholders. Sometimes, it was exclusively a family business; sometimes, it included non-family shareholders, but always bore the founding family's name. The division of risk and profit was similar to that of modern corporations. There were hundreds of such firms in every town in thirteenth-century Italy; most were small, but a few were of considerable size. The best-known management tool used by almost all essential organizations was bookkeeping, and the most widely used system was single-entry accounting. Feudal structures and governments recorded income, expenditure, and payment of obligations, sometimes in narrative form with figure references, sometimes on separate lines for each category, and sometimes on separate lines with figures in columns. This form of bookkeeping had the advantage of providing a rational basis for decision-making at a low cost. However, it had the disadvantage of not automatically measuring profit and could not distinguish between capital and income. Most importantly, it facilitated the concealment of fraud, leading to the need for frequent audits and other anti-fraud tools. In the late thirteenth century, as international merchants in Italy's ports and inland cities encountered more complex transactions in more and more places, they realized that they needed a system to improve control. Double-entry bookkeeping developed when accountants realized that a cash receipt contained two entries, a release in the debtor's account and a charge in the cashier's record, allowing cross-references. By 1300, trading prefixes distinguished positive entries (cash receipts) from negative entries (cash payments). The new system spread rapidly among Italian firms and reached a sophisticated level of development in large corporations by the early fourteenth century. This method was not "*true*" double-entry accounting as we define it today, but it largely met the immediate needs of international businesses. It generated data by creating a balance sheet, separating capital from revenue recognition, and introducing valuable concepts such as accruals and depreciation. Above all, it provided business owners with a much more advanced control system. Bardi and Peruzzi were the two most important Italian companies that emerged during this period. They were huge, and historians have called them "*super corporations*" (Hunt & Murray, 1999).

The sizeable Italian banking and trading companies had their headquarters in Italy but were represented by partners, agents, or correspondents based in Bruges and other commercial centers. From an administrative point of view, there were two different types of organizations: centralized and decentralized. The organization of the Peruzzi Company is an excellent example of the centralized type of organization. In the beginning, there was only one Peruzzi Company, and by 1331, the majority of the capital was owned by members of the Peruzzi family. The company had numerous agents abroad, including one in Bruges. A salaried representative always managed the Peruzzi bank. Occasionally, a partner would serve the company as a representative or manager of one of the branches. In such a case, he received a regular salary and the dividend to which he was entitled as a partner. The Peruzzi Company was the largest in Northern Italy until the fourteenth century. Still, in 1340, it suffered a significant financial crisis, sharing the same fate as the Bardi Company, as King Edward III of England defaulted on his debts (Karan et al., 2024). After this crisis, for a period, large companies in Europe, in general, began to decline. However, larger companies such as the Medici emerged in the fifteenth century (Hunt & Murray, 1999). One of the men who worked for the Peruzzi Company during this period was Giovanni Villani (1276–1348), who wrote the Nuova Cronica (New Chronicles) on the history of Florence. He was present in the Flemish region between 1302 and 1307. In 1306, he was involved in one of the first surviving barter contracts in Bruges, lending money to Tommaso Fini of the Gallerani Company on behalf of the Peruzzi Company. He has fascinating observations about human life. Villani's work is characterized by its focus on economic detail, statistical information, and the interplay of politics and psychology. He believed in the cyclical nature of fortune, likening it to economic cycles in which periods of prosperity are followed by periods of decline. He drew attention to recurring themes in history: "*Excess brings disaster*," "*Right and wrong are in constant struggle*," and "*God's will directly influences events.*" His views that markets move unpredictably reflect modern economic theory. Ironically, Villani's own life reflected his predictions. The Peruzzi bank, where he was a partner, went bankrupt in 1343, unable to pay its debts to King Edward II of England. Villani was subsequently imprisoned and became notorious (De Roover, 1963).

By the fifteenth century, the Medicis, forming a company that had risen to prominence as the most spectacular in Europe, showcased a different, yet equally effective, structure. The Medicis had several companies in common, each with its legal personality. Like today's conglomerates, the Medici family had a controlling stake in the capital of each subsidiary and could manage all the companies in this way. They created a separate partnership for each branch established abroad. The branches were handled not by representatives but by junior partners who were not paid a fixed salary but received a share of the profits of their branches. The manager carried the title of partner (De Roover, 1944).

Due to the slowness of communication, the Medicis had the advantage of giving branch managers freedom within the framework of the general policy set by the headquarters in Italy. This decentralized management strategy allowed for quicker decision-making and adaptation to local conditions. In the Medici firms, the senior partner took responsibility for all policy decisions. In contrast, in the Peruzzi Company, decisions were taken too late, as essential choices were submitted to a council of all partners residing in Florence. In both firms, the headquarters determined the policy outlines that branch managers, whether partners or representatives, were expected to follow in managing their branches (Karan et al., 2024).

The financial activity of the Italian merchant bankers in Bruges was mainly limited to transactions in bills of exchange and loans to the Dutch Count, the city of Bruges, the nobility, and the Church. Medieval bills of exchange were not negotiable and were not discounted. They were, therefore, purchased outright. Buying a foreign bill of exchange was the same as buying foreign currency. Such a transaction involved an extension of credit since the buyer of a bill of exchange had to advance money to the seller to be repaid later and in a different place (Karan et al., 2024).

Italian bankers used a new payment instrument called a "*bill of exchange*" to solve payment difficulties in such international trade. A bill of exchange is a payment order, typically issued by international trading company A in country X to correspondent trading company B in country Y (or an affiliate of trading company A in that country) to pay a specific party. For example, Alberto, a merchant in Florence, buys Dutch wool from Pierre in Bruges. Suppose he wants to pay Pierre for it. Alberto can buy such a bill of exchange from the Medici Bank in Florence and pay in local currency (florins). He sends a copy of the bill of exchange to the counterparty, Pierre, while the Medici Company sends a copy and instructions to pay it to its correspondent branch in Bruges (Fig. 3.4). To ensure that the merchant Pierre and the correspondent bank branch received copies of the invoice on time, the bill's due date was often pushed forward. This was because, at the time, it sometimes took up to a month for this to happen. Therefore, the bill would typically be presented before and executed on the due date. The correspondent Medici branch in Bruges would make the payment in Gulden. At this point, a foreign exchange commission would be deducted. The correspondent bank branch, which had to make the payment, would have refused if it had not received instructions from the Medici Company. The document of this refusal of payment could be used by the creditor (the merchant Pierre) to protest to the notary. The protest document would then be sent to the merchant Pietro, who could sue Alberto in Florence for default. However, if the paying correspondent, the Medici branch, had accepted the invoice, the creditor could sue him directly in case of problems. There was a commercial court for such cases (Kohn, 1999b). Using bills of exchange or forced letters reduced the transaction costs incurred in transporting large quantities of speculative goods. They were not affected by the restrictions of

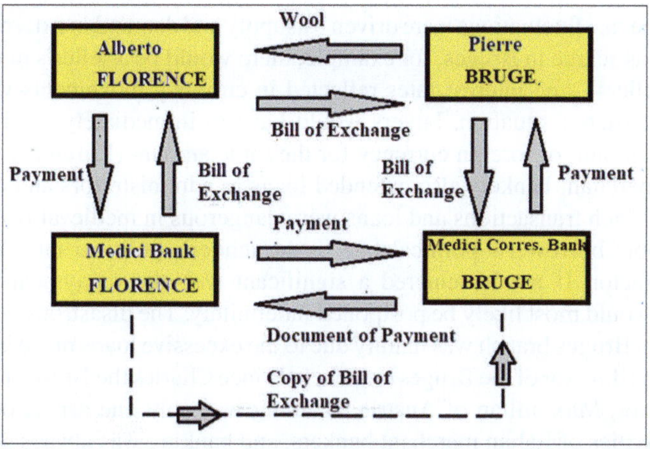

Fig. 3.4 Medicis payment system by bill of exchange-fourteenth century. Drawn by the Author

medieval governments on transporting precious metals. Every sensible merchant avoided carrying gold or silver from one place to another unless he had it in his possession and tried to use bills of exchange wherever possible (Spufford, 1988).

These transactions, facilitated by the bill of exchange system, were the main payment in international trade. The correspondent relationship was crucial in this model. In our example, the Alberto Company is the principal, and the Medici branch in Bruges is the correspondent. The model was flexible enough to organize all kinds of financial transactions. A bill of exchange was a way to postpone a payment and to combine it with a currency exchange. The prohibition of usury at the time, and the prohibition of interest, established and maintained by the Church, played a significant role in the development and use of this system. The interest was hidden in the exchange rate applied. The widespread use of bills of exchange was only made possible by developing a network of "*banking houses,*" i.e., places where the supply and demand for foreign exchange could be met. It spread first to the cities of northern Italy and Champagne, then to most of the commercial centers of Western Europe, the Levant, and Spain (Karan et al., 2024).

The transition from the bill of exchange to the letter of credit in the medieval period responded to the growing complexity and risk associated with long-distance trade. At the same time, both instruments facilitated commerce; the letter of credit provided greater security, maturity, and trust by involving a third-party guarantee. This made it increasingly attractive for merchants in the fourteenth and fifteenth centuries as international trade expanded. The development of these financial tools helped lay the groundwork for modern banking and international finance. Merchants and traders increasingly preferred letters of credit because they offered a more secure and reliable payment method in distant cities. This trend was significant as trade routes became more global, involving a diverse range of merchants who did not know each other personally.

Exchange rate fluctuations were driven by supply and demand in external balances. If money was scarce in Bruges, for example, there would be a seller's market (dominated by sellers), and interest rates reflected in currency movements would likely increase. In such a situation, buyers would have to immediately sacrifice a more significant amount of foreign currency for the same amount (Karan et al., 2024).

Italian merchant bankers also extended loans to administrators and other public authorities. Such transactions and loans were dangerous in medieval Bruges as they tied the noble borrower's political fate to the lender's political fate. War was an important factor. If a ruler entered a significant war, the repayment of loans to merchants would most likely be postponed indefinitely. The disastrous liquidation of the Medici's Bruges branch was mainly due to the excessive loans made by Tommaso Portinari, the director of the Bruges branch, to Prince Charles the Brave and his penniless successor, Maximilian of Austria. Banking was only one aspect of the multifaceted activities of Italian merchant bankers, and banking was always of secondary importance (De Roover, 1944).

In the second half of the fifteenth century, the Medici Company was very active in Bruges. It had developed into a full-fledged partnership under its branch manager, Angelo di Jacopo Tani (1415–1492). Tani's assistant was the ambitious Tommaso Portinari (1428–1501). He had had his eye on Tani's business for some time and was doing his best to discredit his chief. Finally, Tommaso Portinari was appointed head of the branch in April 1465. Tani, however, would continue as a senior partner. Initially, the London branch's business was conducted from Bruges. After March 25, 1451, the London and Bruges branches were separated. Both branches operated as separate partnerships. The London branch soon over-indebted the British Crown and could not collect its receivables. In 1467, the financial situation of the London branch of the Medici Bank was terrible. The Medicis sent Angelo Tani to London to straighten the mess and audit the accounts. Having completed his mission, Angelo Tani returned to Italy in the spring of 1469 and thought he had managed to save the London branch and get it back on its feet. However, the War of the Roses in England (1455–1487) disrupted these plans and worsened matters (De Roover, 1947). Ultimately, he agreed that the Bruges branch would take over the London branch with its assets and liabilities. When he learned of this, Tani wrote a strong protest in which he repeatedly emphasized that he was in no way responsible for the losses of the London branch. Thus, the Bruges branch also assumed interest burdens, severely reducing its earning capacity. Indeed, this was one of the reasons that led to the collapse of the Bruges branch in 1478 (De Roover, 1963).

3.5.2 Lombards (or Cahorsins)

Besides Italian merchants and merchant bankers, another class of Italian money traders lived in Bruges. These were commonly known as the Lombards or "*Cahorsins*." Cahors, as it was called, was located between Montpellier on the Mediterranean Sea and La Rochelle on the Atlantic coast. They specialized in lending money to pawns. The Cahorsins were initially known as merchants. Evidence of their long-distance merchant activity dates back to the late twelfth century, with their presence in Marseille and Saint-Gilles in 1178 and La Rochelle in 1194. The Cahorsins exported their local wines to England via the Lot and Garonne rivers and imported wool from there, while more valuable goods and spices imported from the Levant were transported to La Rochelle via land routes. Their presence at Champagne fairs is documented from 1216 onward (Renouard, 1961).

They were solitary bankers and began appearing in the Netherlands at the end of the thirteenth century with other Italians. Because of the prohibition of usury, the Lombard pawnshops, to disguise the interest, would sign a payment agreement with the debtor that did not contain the word interest or a repurchase agreement with the pawnbroker for a high amount (disguising the interest) to buy back the pledged property later on. Since the Church frowned upon lending, the Lombards were only tolerated out of necessity, as they were considered evil but necessary. Like Italian merchants, the Lombards were foreigners but were not protected by commercial privileges. Early fourteenth-century licenses, issued by authorities like the Count of Flanders and Bruges, placed them under princely protection and later granted certain privileges. Over time, the Lombards were also given certain privileges. Socially, the Lombards were ostracized and seen as flagrant sinners and open usurers, even though they were explicitly allowed to lend money at interest. In Canto XI of the Inferno, Dante denounced Cahors as a sinful place and associated it with sodomy and usury, respectively. Even in the seventeenth century, they were described as "*worse than the Jews*" (Renouard, 1961).

According to a map of the city of Bruges and other documents, the residence of the Cahorsins was quite large. They needed considerable space to store furniture and various pawned items, from jewelry to bulky utensils. The Cahorsins' specialization in personal loans was evident, with most of their loans secured by pledges of personal property. The Lombards lent to all classes, from the Dutch Count to humble weavers and journeymen, but most of their business came from small borrowers. Artisans sometimes pawned their tools in times of unemployment, which caused great hardship if debtors could not get their tools back when they found work again. Under the licenses, Lombards were allowed to charge interest at 2% per week, a high rate of 43% per pound per year. This rate, however, was necessary to cover all incidental costs, including storage costs, rent, fees, license fees, and other overhead expenses. When making loans, the Cahorsins used a type of receipt similar to the modern pawn ticket. Municipal officials only had to certify the transactions for essential loans. More formal contracts were, therefore, drawn up in the presence of at least two municipal council members. Property owners could not demand the return of their property unless the Cahorsins were paid in full. Fig. 3.5 shows a painting of a Lombard banker by the Dutch painter Rembrandt. Rembrandt used dramatic lighting and, in the spirit of the time, depicted the profession of money changer under an atmosphere of mystery and suspense (De Roover, 1944).

Fig. 3.5 Lombard Banker- Rembrandt, 1627. https://fr.wikipedia.org/wiki/Banquiers_lombards#/media/Fichier:Rembrandt_-_The_Parable_of_the_Rich_Fool.jpg (public domain)

3.5.3 Money Exchangers

Unlike Italian merchant bankers and Lombards, money exchangers had to be citizens. Women could also be employed, and money exchangers had to take an oath of office and promise to abide by monetary regulations. Accordingly, money exchangers face severe penalties if found guilty of collecting or destroying money, issuing coins, issuing gold bullion, or even putting banned coins into circulation. They fulfilled a quasi-public function, so the authorities had to rely on them to enforce monetary regulations. The number of money exchangers in Bruges was limited. There were fifteen or sixteen money exchangers in the fourteenth century, but there were down to four by the fifteenth century. Their Bruges offices were near the Wisselbrug (Bridge of Exchange), on the northeast corner of the Grote Markt (Great Place), in the city center, near the two clothing halls and the consular buildings.

In the fourteenth century, Bruges had a population of around forty thousand inhabitants, and probably one in forty or thirty-five people had a bank account. Having a bank account was more common than one might think. With the information that has survived, the account books of the money changers Collard de Marke and Willem Ruwee, it is clear that the money changers in Bruges in the fourteenth century were bankers who combined barter transactions (not bills of exchange) with deposit banking. Money changers' offices were commercial banks operating on fractional reserves, as cash reserves covered only part of the obligations to depositors (De Roover, 1944). In Northern Europe, Bruges was the first place money changers used a large part of their deposits for investment. Deposit banking in Bruges began in the early fourteenth century. However, this modern banking venture did not go beyond the mid-fifteenth century, as a series of failures led the Dutch counts to impose more and more restrictions on money-changing activities (Hunt & Murray, 1999).

The three primary functions performed by money changers were (1) the trading of money and bullion, (2) the deposit business, and (3) the lending or investment of accumulated deposits. The first of these three functions, money and bullion trading, was the link between the mint and the public. Such a link was vital for the proper functioning of the money market. In the Middle Ages, the Dutch currency was of the Groat standard. The Groat is an English silver coin of four old pence, minted between 1351 and 1662. The rates had to be adjusted according to a given coin's gold content, the base unit's Groat silver content, and the market ratio between gold and silver. In the event of a change in any of these three elements, the official valuation of gold coins had to be revised. The consequence of this system was that a fee had to be paid to the money exchanger for gold and silver to be put on the market. Otherwise, it could not be issued. If the depositor deposited silver, he could withdraw his deposit in the same currency, but if he wanted gold instead of silver, he had to pay an extra fee. According to the monetary laws, the exchangers were expected to deliver to the mint all the bullion they purchased from the public. The exchangers would only do so as long as the market price of the bullion did not exceed the mint price. When the market price of bullion exceeded the mint price due to an unfavorable balance of payments, the coin was sent abroad, and the system was disrupted. As a result, the flow of bullion to the mint would stop, and the mint would have to suspend its operations. The suspension of work at the mint by removing the medieval mint from production was one of the leading causes of impurity (the reduction of precious metals in money). Depreciation works like devaluation and reduces the currency's silver or gold content. When prices and wages were rigid, adulteration led to an artificial lowering of the price level. Therefore, the devaluation of the currency would mobilize forces that would ease the pressure on its conditions and stop the flow of bullion. In this case, the mint could also start operating again because adulteration would make it profitable to mint again. There is little doubt that frequent monetary tightness, rather than a long-term trend, was the leading cause of poverty in the Middle Ages. A significant problem of the period was that the quantity of precious metals, such as gold and silver, was insufficient when markets were buoyant (De Roover, 1944).

The Dukes of Burgundy raised the Groat standard two or three times and maintained it for several years. Such increases required a downward adjustment of prices and wages. However, deflationary reforms of the currency proved disastrous as prices influenced each other. In Bruges, the reform in 1390 led to riots, and the city treasurer was nearly lynched by an angry mob. If coins were needed to cover payments abroad, merchants were likely to withdraw them from their bank accounts, with the inevitable consequence that banks' reserve ratios would fall. Since medieval bankers could not easily contract their loans and investments, money naturally depreciated whenever tensions in the money market worsened.

In Bruges, bank deposits were widely used as a means of payment—payments by bank transfer far outnumbered cash payments. Since bank deposits were easily transferable, most payments between businessmen were made by "*assignment at the bank*." Account transfers were made by word of mouth with both the debtor and the creditor present.

Additional evidence for the existence of oral contracts is given in some paintings of the Dutch school. These are the works of a painter named Marinus van Reymerswael, who imitated Quinten Matsys' famous painting "*The Banker and His Wife*" in the Louvre, with some modifications. Several of Van Reymerswael's paintings represent a banker or a money changer sitting behind a desk with another man (apparently a customer). The money changer is writing something in a book. The act of dictating the writing is meaningfully depicted by the facial expression, the position of the hands, and the whole attitude of the man identified as the customer (Fig. 3.6). In Bruges, credit transfer was possible not only if the debtor and the creditor were clients of the same moneylender but also if the debtor was a client of one moneylender and the creditor was a client of another. In medieval Bruges, such a system worked effectively because all exchangers dealt with each other like a centralized clearing system (De Roover, 1944). The painting depicts a scene from the business life of a money changer, with coins prominently displayed. Moreover, the painter's portrayal of them as "*aggressively ugly*," satirical, and demeaning suggests that the profession of money changer at the time was evil and corrupting (Murray, 2016).

Money exchangers did not buy and discount bills of exchange. They were mainly merchants and other businessmen expanding the amount of credit in the market by allowing their clients to overdraw their accounts. This was an intermediate solution

Fig. 3.6 Painting by Marinus van Reymerswael, who imitated "*the banker and his wife*" by Quinten Matsys with some changes. https://commons.wikimedia.org/wiki/File:Marinus_van_Reymerswaele_%28Follower_of%29_-_The_Money_Changers_-_Google_Art_Project.jpg

to the shortage of precious metals that could be used as money in the market. They also invested money directly in commercial enterprises or business ventures, often in partnership with a merchant. Therefore, the assets of the Bruges banks were illiquid. It should be emphasized that there was a flaw in the system, as it was not a system based on central banks as it is today. Since no institution like a central bank could issue money to the market when needed, medieval banks had to rely solely on their cash reserves and could not contract when the money market was tight. When cash reserves were nearly exhausted, bankers inevitably wanted the currency to depreciate. According to Professor De Roover (1944), since medieval money exchangers operated on the fractional reserve principle and bank deposits are used today as a means of payment, there is little doubt that medieval banks effectively created money through their lending and investment activities. Although the banknote was not invented, transferable bank deposits served the same function. The non-invention of banknotes did not prevent capitalism's development in the Middle Ages.

3.6 The Story of Willem Ruweel, the Banker (Money Exchanger)

The historian Murray has described the intriguing life of the money changer Willem Ruweel, whose story was partly told in the introduction to this chapter. Murray (1988) presented it as a new documentary account of the family and business histories of some fourteenth-century Bruges' moneylenders documented by De Roover. In this context, he draws attention to how medieval traditions influenced bankers' business risk. Willem Ruweel, probably of French origin, settled in Bruges in the mid-fourteenth century after years of trading in Flanders. When he married, Ruweel was a skilled and knowledgeable merchant in Bruges and a favorite candidate in the marriage market. Around 1350, Ruweel married Margaret van Ruuslede, daughter of John van Ruuslede, a poor money exchanger. As a dowry, Margaret brought one of the five coin exchange shops in Bruges, located on St Pieter's bridge. It was in the city's center and dated back to her grandfather, who owned the exchange shop in 1316. Her father, John, died shortly afterward and left the shop to Ruweel and his wife.

Ruweel's marriage brought him two crucial advantages. One was his commercial interest. The location of the shop was perfect. It was a small place in the middle of the Bruges market, the trade and finance triangle formed by the Beurse square. He had easy access to the deposits of the people of Bruges. It was enough to accept deposits and perform simple coin exchanges. Few workers were needed to manage the shop, and few skills were required, such as speaking French, doing simple arithmetic, and entering accounts legibly in the ledger. All these skills were probably common in Bruges and, therefore, not too costly; Ruweel could further save on labor costs by employing family members in the business.

The second and vital advantage was his marriage to Margaret Ruweel. Their marriage created a kind of joint partnership in Dutch law in which all property was held in common under the husband's control. Still, in his death or business failure, half of the common property was guaranteed as the wife's share. Strict co-ownership partly eliminated the risk of bankruptcy, one of the greatest threats to medieval barter banking, which led to the wholesale withdrawal of deposits when investments failed or bank customers' confidence was shaken. Bank failures were expected in Europe, rife with war, weak kings, and inflexible debt instruments. Ruweel was probably acutely aware of the protection afforded to him by Flemish common law, which blunted the double-edged sword of banking. Thus, bank failure could protect half of the Ruweel family fortune from the claims of its creditors. Not surprisingly, in fourteenth- and fifteenth-century Bruges, the money change shop was an attractive dowry for the marriage of a poor man's daughter (De Roover, 1948).

According to the documents, Margaret Ruweel was probably the director of the Ruweel bank and the employees' supervisor. Women were managers and owners of money exchanges and other businesses, which was almost a common practice in Bruges (Maréchal, 1955). It was also customary for wives to continue their husbands' businesses in their absence or after their husbands' deaths. Independent businesswomen were among the depositors in the region. In Ghent, there is an example of an independent female moneylender named Celie Amelakens (Nicholas, 1992).

Many other moneylenders in Bruges continued their barter business as part of their trade or inn-keeping. Still, by the 1360s, the Ruweels concentrated their capital on banking and trade financing. Initially doing well, their business deteriorated, and the barter shop went bankrupt. The failure was probably due to three factors. The first was probably that his investments were not liquid enough. One of the most significant problems for a medieval banker was to find profitable investments that could be easily liquidated in the event of a run on the bank. Since there was no market for securities, this was a difficult task. Although real estate was a poor investment for the medieval banker because it could not be easily converted into speculative money, he inevitably directed a significant portion of his assets into real estate. Surviving documents show that Ruweel was too bold in this regard and invested excessively in real estate. A closer look at these investments reveals that Ruweel preferred to invest in commercial rather than residential ones and was particularly interested in properties around the Grote Market, the central market square of Bruges. However, these properties were not easy to sell in the face of a sudden demand for cash.

The second factor was his involvement in tax collection. For the medieval financier, the primary source of public revenue in Bruges was the excise tax collected by the tax farmer. This tax, paid by beer, mead, and wine consumers in the city, provided three-quarters of the city's revenue in the 1360s. Of these three taxes, the wine tax was by far the most significant revenue earner, as it was the drink of choice for the rich and was imported and consumed in large quantities by the city's wealthy bourgeoisie. The city sold the right to collect the tax to the highest bidder four times a year for thirteen weeks. The privilege of collecting the wine tax was the pinnacle of Bruges' high finance. At that time, bankers were rarely found on the list of successful bidders for the wine tax, and the very wealthy were the ones who took the plunge. It was probably Ruweel's most significant and riskiest investment, and it was probably partly responsible for the shake-up and collapse of the Ruweel bank. In his last three years in business, Ruweel entered the wine tax collection business three times, each paying an increasingly high price. Whatever his expectations from this business venture, Ruweel made minimal profits. If the administrative costs were considered, the Ruweel tax collection business would probably have been an apparent financial failure (De Roover, 1948).

Another area of Ruweel's investment was trade speculation, mainly through loans to the Bruges innkeeper Jacob Sconeberghe. However, this venture took a turn for the worse when Sconeberghe and his wife passed away suddenly in the summer of 1368, leading to the bankruptcy of their inn. The heirs refused to assume the debt, leaving many creditors, including Ruweel, who had to settle for only a quarter of the debt owed to him. This significant financial loss further contributed to Ruweel's decline.

Ruweel's business deteriorated in the spring and summer of 1370, but there is considerable evidence that the decline began much earlier. One indicator of Ruweel's decline in the 1360s is the relative size of the debts owed to the city government by all the moneylenders in Bruges in 1359 and 1362, the amount of which varied according to each moneylender's wealth. In 1359, out of fifteen moneylenders, Ruweel ranked fifth in the city in debt.

Various political and economic problems may also have accelerated Ruweel's bankruptcy. Another possibility is Willem Ruweel's death or illness during his bankruptcy. Whatever the reasons, the city authorities seized Willem's estate and sold it to pay off his debts. However, Margaret Ruweel was guaranteed half of the inheritance as her legal share by law. Margaret would be able to keep her property. Although we know little about Margaret's fate after 1370, she likely continued to run the bank and trained her sons in the family business. In the late 1390s, the estate was sold after her second son's death.

3.7 Declining Importance of Bruges

Bruges' importance declined at the beginning of the fifteenth century when the bay began to fill with mud. Nevertheless, the Dutch Revolt, which ravaged the county of Flanders between 1477 and 1492 and severely damaged Sluis, dealt a fatal blow to Bruges as a center of international trade. In an attempt to weaken his rivals economically, Maximilian, the archduke of Austria, ordered all foreign merchants to move to Antwerp in 1484. Although hostilities ended in 1485 and the trading communities returned, the internal unrest was not over. A new revolt broke out in 1487, and Maximilian again ordered foreign merchants to leave Bruges in 1488. Peace was finally concluded in 1492, and groups of foreign merchants partially returned. However, Bruges had lost much of its commercial appeal and could no longer adapt to the competitive conditions in Antwerp. The Portuguese consulate or official representation left Bruges in 1511. By 1516, the consulates of all the Italian merchant groups that had dominated the city's luxury trade for two centuries had followed suit. The last Portuguese and Italian merchants living in Bruges were recorded in 1518 and 1519. Although the German Hansa maintained a consulate in Bruges until 1553, Hanseatic trade in the Dutch city ceased in 1517 (Maréchal, 1951). The appearance of the famous German bankers Fuggers and their compatriots in Antwerp finance meant the end of the Bruges money market, and the Florentine firms, which nevertheless continued to operate to the end, were forced to move to Antwerp around 1516 (Bolton & Bruscoli, 2008).

Even though Bruges' star gradually faded from the 1460s, while Antwerp was on the rise, a specific volume of business remained. In the fifteenth century, Bruges' income was unquestionably higher. Over time, however, business would slow down, and the small-scale trading structure, which required limited investment, would force the merchants of Bruges to take their goods to markets in other cities. Moreover, Bruges forced them to bear the taxes and costs of services they did not use (Lambert, 2016). It is essential to underline that in the last decades of the fifteenth century and the first half of the sixteenth century, international trade in Bruges suffered a slow and gradual decline rather than a sharp and sudden one. The city continued to be a distribution point for the traditional cloth industries. International financial activity had an exceptionally long-lasting presence in Bruges, as the city continued to play an indispensable role in large money transfers and banking transactions and was often linked to the Antwerp market. The Bruges merchant community was still highly internationalized. Although many leading Florentine bankers moved their assets and activities to Antwerp, they continued their banking activities in this region. In the fifteenth century, the Dutch authorities became hostile to banking and tried to eradicate it. Finally, by the early 1540s, international financial services and most foreign merchants had disappeared. The Catholic mentality that dominated the region began to take strong measures against interest. From the Bruges Chamber of Commerce records, it is clear that by the early 1540s, Bruges had lost its role as an international financial center. Nevertheless, while Bruges continued to act as a center for Flemish textiles and became a gateway market for the surrounding regional economy, it maintained and even somewhat strengthened its position as the center of the Castilian wool trade in Northwestern Europe, continuing to attract specific groups of merchants and certain commercial and financial activities well into the sixteenth century (Lambert, 2019a).

3.8 Concluding Remarks

At the beginning of the fourteenth century, with the decline in the importance of fairs, Bruges could stand out in this region with the infrastructure it offered to merchants. The city's legal system and regulations were key to its success. While municipal courts enforced trade laws, resolved disputes, and protected contracts, guilds regulated trade practices, ensuring fair trade and protecting merchants. In addition,

Bruges had a dynamic money market with currency exchange and financial instruments that provided stability to local and international trade. These factors helped Bruges become an economic powerhouse, contributed to the growth of European trade networks, and laid the foundation for modern banking systems.

Bruges' other significant advantage was the support provided to merchants. Bruges Inns, adapted to the conditions of the period, served as housing and warehouses for merchants, allowing the boarding houses to represent them. It provided information to its guests and could act as a business agent. Bruges was undoubtedly not unique in its presence of innkeepers and moneylenders, as almost every medieval city had them, and some cooperated in commercial networks. For example, it has been suggested that innkeepers in Ghent in the 1360s and 1370s served as deposit bankers for their clients. Bruges' exceptionalism had less to do with a difference in type than with the density of its network. As Bruges' commercial infrastructure grew in size and scope, linking inns and exchanges in the densely urbanized hinterland of the Low Countries and northern France, it became a powerhouse. Bruges also had a strong money market. This market had very liberal rules. There was also a judicial system that functioned under the day's conditions. These rules, which many countries do not have even today, proved so valuable that Bruges became the first host of an actual money market (Hunt & Murray, 1999).

As a result, in the fourteenth century, Bruges was a significant financial and commercial center of Europe, playing an essential role in international trade and the money market. Its strategic location at the confluence of inland rivers and the North Sea made it a vital port for goods from all over Europe. The city's Bourse facilitated the exchange of goods, currencies, and financial instruments, encouraging efficient transactions. Bruges also became a center for banking, with leading Italian banks such as Medici, Bardi, and Peruzzi offering services such as bills of exchange and letters of credit to support long-distance trade. The inclusive institutions had emerged.

However, times were changing. Occasionally, the city's rulers ostracized the merchants, forcing them to leave. Religious and political conflicts had begun. Institutions were now in an extractive structure. While both internal turmoil and geographical events that made it difficult for Bruges to reach the sea decreased its importance, the city of Antwerp, with its unique seaside location about 90 km to the north, was becoming a candidate to become a new trade and financial center.

References

Boerner, L. (2016). Medieval market-making brokerage regulations in Central Western Europe, ca. 1250–1700

Bolton, J. L., & Bruscoli, F. G. (2008). When did Antwerp replace Bruges as the commercial and financial centre of north-Western Europe? The evidence of the Borromei ledger for 1438 1. *The Economic History Review, 61*(2), 360–379.

De Roover, R. (1944). *Money, banking, and credit in medieval Bruges; Italian merchant-bankers, Lombards, and money-chargers*. The University of Chicago.

De Roover, R. (1947). The decline of the Medici bank. *The Journal of Economic History, 7*(1), 69–82.
De Roover, R. (1948). *Money, banking, and credit in medieval Bruges*. Mass.
De Roover, R. (1963). *The Bruges money market around 1400.*
DeMatos, D. (2020). TCH: The original Bourse at Bruges. Retrieved from https://www.linkedin.com/pulse/tch-original-bourse-bruges-daniel-dematos/
Dumolyn, J. (1997). De Brugse opstand van 1436–1438.
Flume, J. W. (2021). Constructing the stock exchange. On the rise and fall of an iconic place of capitalism. In Legal history RG 29 (2021). pp. 412–430.
Gelderblom, O. (2004). The decline of fairs and merchant guilds in the low countries. Retrieved from https://www.researchgate.net/profile/Oscar_Gelderblom/publication/253932534_The_Decline_of_Fairs_and_Merchant_Guilds_in_the_Low_Countries/links/54350a550cf294006f737de5.pdf. Et, 1, 2019.
Gelderblom, O. (2005). The resolution of commercial conflicts in Bruges, Antwerp, and Amsterdam, 1250–1650. *Economy and society of the low countries working papers*, 2.
Gelderblom, O. (2013). Cities of commerce. The institutional foundations of international trade in the low Countries. pp. 1250–1650.
Gelderblom, O., & Grafe, R. (2010). The rise and fall of the merchant guilds: Re-thinking the comparative study of commercial institutions in premodern Europe. *Journal of Interdisciplinary History, 40*(4), 477–511.
Häpke, R. (1911). *Der deutsche Kaufmann in den Niederlanden.*
Harreld, D. J. (2003). Trading places: The public and private spaces of merchants in sixteenth-century Antwerp. *Journal of Urban History, 29*(6), 657–669.
Hunt, E. S., & Murray, J. S. M. (1999). *A history of business in medieval Europe, 1200–1550.* Cambridge University Press.
Karan, M. B., Westerman, W., & Wijngaard, J. (2024). A history of banks. Contributions to Economics.
Kohn, M. (1999a). Early deposit banking, Department of Economics. Dartmouth College
Kohn, M. (1999b). Bills of exchange and the money market to 1600, Department of Economics Working Paper, (99–04). Dartmouth College.
Lambert, B. (2016). Merchants on the margins: Fifteenth-century Bruges and the informal market. *Journal of Medieval History, 42*(2), 226–253.
Lambert, B. (2019a). Steep fall or gradual decline? International trade in sixteenth-century Bruges. In *Italien als vorbild? Ökonomische und kulturelle verflechtungen europäischer metropolen am vorabend der'ersten globalisierung'* (1300–1600) (pp. 153–162). Schnell und Steiner.
Lambert, B. (2019b). A legal world market?: The exchange of commercial law in fifteenth-century Bruges. In Migrating words, migrating merchants, migrating law (pp. 163–175). Brill Nijhoff.
Liggio, L. P. (2007). The hanseatic league and freedom of trade. *Journal of Private Enterprise, 23*(1).
Marechal, J. (1949) Geschiedenis van de Brugse beurs. Bruges: De Anjelier.
Maréchal, J. (1951). Le départ de Bruge des marchands étrangers. *Handelingen van het Genootschap voor Geschiedenis, 88*(1–2).
Maréchal, J. (1955). *Bijdrage tot de geschiedenis van het bankwezen te Bruge.* De Angelier.
Murray, J. M. (1988). Family, marriage and money changing in medieval Bruges. *Journal of Medieval History, 14*(2), 115–125.
Murray, J. M. (2005). *Bruges cradle of capitalism, 1280–1390.*
Murray, J. M. (2016). The devil's evangelists? Moneychangers in Flemish urban society. In *Money, morality, and culture in late medieval and early modern Europe* (pp. 69–84). Routledge.
Nicholas, D. (1992). *Medieval Flanders.* Longman.
Renouard, Y. (1961). Les Cahorsins, hommes d'affaires français du XIIIe siècle. *Transactions of the Royal Historical Society, 11*, 43–67.
Spufford, P. (1988). *Money and its use in medieval Europe (No. 1993).* Cambridge University Press.

Stabel, P. (1997). *Dwarf among giants: The flemish urban network in the late middle ages.* Apeldoorn.

Chapter 4
Antwerp: The First Global Trade Capital (16th Century)

4.1 Introduction

On the morning of October 6, 1571, the sea was calm in the quaint bay of Lepanto, backed by hills dotted with lush green maquis. The town of Lepanto was situated on a gulf, the gateway to a long gulf between the Peloponnese peninsula and the Greek mainland, opening onto the Adriatic Sea. This city, known to Ottomans as Inebahti, was located on the northern shore of the gulf. The gulf narrowed down to Lepanto and then widened again after the town, continuing for hundreds of kilometers to become a natural harbor between the mainland and the Peloponnese peninsula, closed on the one side. In 1893, the Corinth Canal was to be built at the other end of this gulf, opening to the Aegean Sea, and the Adriatic and Aegean Seas were to be joined (Fig. 4.1). In those days, however, it was a closed bay and a natural refuge for ships. This area was Ottoman territory since 1499.

The Leponteans had some pretty special days. The Ottoman navy, which had become the strongest navy in the whole Mediterranean after winning victories in Preveza in 1538 and Jabre in 1560 and beating Spain and Venice, was in this bay for repairs and maintenance. The fleet had been on the move for months and had to deal with some very hard problems. There were ships of different colors in the sea, from the town's shore to the middle of the gulf. The seagulls screamed and flew around the ships because they could smell the food remaining on them. A lot was going on in the town. That morning, it was still warm, even though it was starting to feel like fall.

But the soldiers on the ships didn't care about the pleasant weather or the seagulls; they were really tense. The Ottoman navy had 278 ships and 65,000 soldiers and troops, and they were all on edge. A massive fight was going to place the next day. People already knew that the 212-strong Christian fleet of 67,000 soldiers and sailors, led by Don Juan, the illegitimate son of King Charles V of Spain, had come to the bay. The Ottomans took occupied Cyprus two months ago, and the Spanish and Venetian Duchies built this vast navy to get back at them. The commanders spent hours at

M. B. Karan, *A History of Stock Exchanges*, Contributions to Economics,
https://doi.org/10.1007/978-3-032-07788-2_4

Fig. 4.1 Map of Laponte. https://commons.wikimedia.org/wiki/File:Greece_location_map.svg

their headquarters, a chateau just outside the town walls, talking about strategies. In the meeting room were one vizier, four pashas, fifteen province governors, and the navy commander, Muezzinzade Ali Pasha. There were other famous sailors there, such Uluc Ali Pasha.

When it was his turn, Uluc Ali Pasha slowly stood up. A veteran of many battles, including the Malta and Cyprus campaigns, he commanded great respect. Earlier speakers had favored a naval battle outside the gulf, but Uluc Pasha respectfully disagreed. "*Our navy has been at war since spring, and our soldiers are tired. We need reinforcements, and our ships need maintenance. The enemy is fresh, their soldiers strong, and their ships better equipped. An open-sea battle is risky. We should fight defensively in the gulf*." After a brief silence, objections erupted, mostly from land commanders with no naval experience. They grumbled, eager to fight as the Sultan commanded. All eyes turned to the navy commander, Muezzinzade Ali Pasha. A former land commander, he took a deep breath and, after a pause, confidently declared his preference for an open-sea battle, envisioning a triumphant return to Istanbul.

The outcome of the war was a disaster for the Ottoman navy. 187 Turkish ships were sunk or captured by the enemy. Nearly 20,000 soldiers, including the commander of the navy, Muezzinzade Ali Pasha, lost their lives in this battle, and only 42 pieces of the Ottoman navy under the command of Uluc Ali Pasha were able to return to Istanbul. It was a massive blow to the Ottoman Empire, which had turned the Mediterranean into a Turkish lake for the last fifty years. Following this victory, the Ottoman threat in the Mediterranean largely disappeared, primarily for the benefit of the Spanish. They could now redirect their resources to Northwestern Europe to fight the Dutch rebel Protestants (Toledo, 1995). The victory was a relief for King Philip II of Spain, who had launched a holy crusade against the Ottomans. Apart from the Dutch war, he was interested in preserving Spanish influence in the Caribbean in the face of English and French rivalry, keeping France and England as weak as possible. Before 1570, he had made such a promise. These were all costly operations.

Above all, the King of Spain had to defend the Western Mediterranean against the Ottoman Sultan. For most of the 1570s, this was a significant challenge that involved many men, considerable financial resources, and substantial material resources. To defeat the Turkish fleet at Lepanto in 1571, capture Tunis in 1573, and defend Spain and Italy against Ottoman counterattacks, Philip II had to maintain a permanent fleet of 150 galleys in the Mediterranean. Several times between 1572 and 1576, the King's advisors had to decide whether to allocate resources to the Mediterranean or the Netherlands, and they prioritized the Mediterranean. Spain's commitment to the defense of the Mediterranean had certainly bankrupted it on numerous occasions. All these developments prevented Spain from achieving an early victory against the Dutch rebellion (Parker, 1976).

This defeat put the rebel reformist Dutch, who had been trying to gain independence in northern Europe since 1568 by fighting the fanatical Catholic Spaniards, in an even more difficult situation. Because Phillip II, now free from Ottoman pressure in the Mediterranean, could direct all his resources to the Protestant infidels in the Low Countries, his armies could easily fight the Dutch. Indeed, in November 1576, Antwerp was sacked in a raid dubbed the "Spanish Fury," and in 1585, the Spanish Army entered Antwerp and completely dimmed the light of Antwerp, which had been shining as a commercial and financial center for some time. After Leponte, Western Europe began to feel the pressure of Spain more strongly. The following year, the massacre of Saint Barthelemy in France, the elimination of the Catholic League's Calvinist rivals, the crushing of the Dutch rebels, and the growing threat of an invasion of England were no coincidence (Inalcık, 2008).

At the end of the sixteenth century, as the Ottomans entered a period of stagnation, the Reformation and Renaissance were on the rise in Europe. Western Europeans had gained new colonies by sailing the oceans. Western European economies were booming. However, there was significant discord among themselves. The Spanish, the Habsburgs, France, the Netherlands, and England were fighting a series of wars against each other. These conflicts involved religion, colonialism, dynastic strife, and, above all, trade. Antwerp was right in the middle of this turmoil. Had the Ottoman navy won this war, perhaps Antwerp would have been the rising city of the seventeenth century, not Amsterdam, becoming a city that would have had a very different historical trajectory.

Initially, Antwerp did not seem to be a top-rated trading center. Only in the first quarter of the fourteenth century did Antwerp fairs begin to develop. Together with the fairs in nearby Bergen op Zoom (North Netherlands), they accelerated Antwerp's medieval economic growth. By the fourteenth century, however, Antwerp's trade volume was significant enough to attract the attention of the Dutch Count Louis of Male. 1356 Count Louis annexed the city, making Antwerp part of the Dutch territory. For the next half-century, the people of Antwerp lived politically under Dutch rule while remaining economically dependent on Bruges. Only in the last quarter of the fourteenth century would Antwerp become more popular than Bruges (Van Roey & Sankovitch, n.d.).

4.2 Political Situation of the Region (15th–16th Centuries)

The Low Countries had 17 small city-states consisting of seventeen separate regions. In the fourteenth and fifteenth centuries, this region was ruled by the Duchy of Burgundy. However, from 1482 onward, they came under the tutelage of the Habsburgs, the powerful state of Central Europe. After the death of the last Valois-Burgonian ruler of this region, Maximilian I of Austria, in 1519, the Habsburg monarchy was suddenly left without a head. There were four candidates for the new Kingdom. Maximilian's grandsons were Charles V of Spain, Frederick III of Saxony, Francis I of France, and Henry VIII of England. After a shady election with huge bribes, the kingdom fell to Charles, whose electors had bought their votes with the support of essential financiers, such as the Fuggers. The fact that he had gold from the New World and the image of a strong ruler who would fight against the Muslim Ottomans played a significant role in his victory (Holborn, 1982). As a result of the election, Charles V became the ruler of both Spain and the Habsburgs. The new ruler, who declared himself the protector of the Catholic religion, would be in constant conflict with the French while fighting against the Ottomans in the Mediterranean and Vienna. Charles V (1500–1558) and his son Philip II (1522–1598) also began to clash with the Dutch and English in the north to prevent the conversion of the Low Countries to Protestantism. He often resorted to the Antwerp Stock Exchange to finance these wars, but repeatedly defaulted on his debts. The Low Countries were partially invaded by Spain in 1556 and became known as the Spanish Netherlands. In 1556, Charles V abdicated and divided the House of Habsburg into the Austro-German and Spanish dominions. His brother Ferdinand I became the ruler of Austria, Bohemia, and Hungary and the new Holy Roman Emperor. Ferdinand represented the Habsburg State. Charlemagne's son, King Philip II of Spain, inherited the Low Countries and Spain. He also included Southern Italy and the American territories (Karan, 2022).

In 1566, a Dutch revolt started the Eighty Years' War (1566–1648). In 1581, at one stage of the Dutch Revolt, the Seven United Provinces seceded from the rest of these territories to form the Dutch Republic. At the end of the rebellion, the 17 states were split into two, and two states emerged: the Netherlands and Belgium. The Netherlands retained its Protestant identity, while Belgium became Catholic. Antwerp, now part of Belgium, was mainly Protestant at the beginning of the rebellion.

4.3 The Antwerp Commodity Exchange

Events during the fourteenth and fifteenth centuries increased the city's importance (Hunt & Murray, 1999). As we have explained in the previous chapter, the political turmoil in Bruges and natural phenomena, as well as the rapidly developing land trade, increased the commercial importance of Antwerp. The city's moderate political administration was also becoming a center of attraction for merchants. However, above all, two different economic developments changed the fate of Antwerp and strengthened its position as an important trade center. The first was the pro-silver monetary policy of Burgundy, which diverted Central European silver to the Low Countries. The second was Dutch protectionism, which diverted British cloth exports away from Bruges and into the open arms of Antwerp (Adrian, 2006).

Between 1384 and 1482, the Burgundian Netherlands was established on the continental European side opposite the island of England and was part of the Low Countries, ruled by the Dukes of Burgundy (Fig. 4.2). Most of the fine cloth produced in England was exported unprocessed to Antwerp and elsewhere. Antwerp was the most crucial outlet for English cloth and the center of a vital filling, dyeing, and finishing industry whose raw material was English cloth. The shipment of fabric to Antwerp had the advantage of allowing the final fabric buyer to influence the final dyeing and finishing of the fabric to suit local preferences (Hunt & Murray, 1999). Thus, it had an intensive trade with its overseas neighbor, England. The successive readjustment of English and Burgundian coins in the 1460s was an essential event in Antwerp's development as a center of the European economy. Between 1464 and 1465, the economically troubled King Edward IV of England devalued the English silver coin by 20% and the gold coin by 25%. The devaluation of the currency weakened the English currency and made the price of England's exports to continental Europe cheaper. Thus, England's main export product, woolen cloth, became a threat to the Dutch cloth industry by having a lower price. In response, Philip the Good, Duke of Burgundy and ruler of a semi-centralized confederation of states in the Low Countries (Flanders and Brabant), devalued the Burgundian silver coin by 12.7% and the gold coin by 3.3% to neutralize England's currency manipulation and increase the competitiveness of Dutch cloth. However, this was insufficient, as silver had a higher value and more purchasing power in Burgundian territory than elsewhere in Europe (Nef, 1941). This disparity pushed merchants with silver toward the Low Countries, where Belgium and the Netherlands are located today. Fortunately, advances in mining technology in Central Europe, particularly the discovery of lead compounding in 1451 (which facilitated the separation of silver from copper ore), significantly increased the amount of silver extracted from the region. Merchants thus found it highly profitable to buy English cloth with silver in the Low Countries and sell it elsewhere. Hence, the high value of silver in the Burgundian Netherlands began to attract English cloth dealers and Continental European buyers. By the end of the fifteenth century, the overvaluation of silver had increased the volume of trade in the Low Countries and greatly benefited the Antwerp economy (Nef, 1941).

The wool cloth trade, an essential commodity then, was also affected. Faced with the threat of a massive increase in English wool imports after 1466, the Dutch cloth-making guilds, especially those strongly organized in Bruges, quickly reacted with protectionism. They imposed tariffs and embargoes to keep English woolen fabrics out of Flanders. They eventually banned Dutch citizens from wearing English clothing, confiscated garments, and imposed heavy fines. Instead of staying in Bruges, the dominant market in northwestern Europe, the British turned to Antwerp, where there was less state intervention. The British not only had a temporary presence in Antwerp during the Fairs but had already established a permanent base there.

Fig. 4.2 Political map of the low countries during the eighty years' war period and before (1656–1648). https://commons.wikimedia.org/wiki/File:The_Low_Countries.png

English cloth exporters, the "*Adventurous Merchants*," often London merchants, rented warehouses for their cloth throughout the year before 1474. Since most English cloth was exported unprocessed, a considerable cloth finishing industry, especially dyeing, naturally developed in and around Antwerp. Eventually, English fabrics began to be completed in Antwerp before being sold to northern and western Germany (Spufford, 2006).

Bruges' protectionism thus effectively cut it off from the intra-continental economy, just at the moment when Burgundian monetary policy was further boosting the volume of trade in the Low Countries. English woolens and Central European silver headed for Antwerp instead of Bruges. By 1492, Antwerp had replaced Bruges as the commodity exchange of the Low Countries. In addition to the silver and cloth trade, other commodities were also being shifted to this city: Baltic grain, French laurel salt, Italian silk, and Spanish leather were of considerable importance in the sixteenth century. As the historian Munro writes, Antwerp might even have been "*the decisive driving force of the European commercial economy*" at that time. However, despite its growing economic power, Antwerp was not a global center but merely a warehouse of Europe (Munro, 1973). By 1500, however, Antwerp had attracted increasingly dynamic sectors of Europe's economic expansion to its markets. In the words of historian Munro (1994), "*Antwerp's rise rested on a three-legged trestle of English woolen cloth, Portuguese-Asian spices, and South German copper and silver.*"

The history of the Antwerp Stock Exchange has much in common with that of Bruges. Before a stock exchange was built, merchants regularly met at a specific time and place. Naturally, such meeting places were located in neighborhoods with the highest concentration of established merchants. In Antwerp, this was the area near the central marketplace, known as the English ghetto ("*Engelse wijk*"). The location of the "Bourse" remains obscure throughout this period, and the name was probably given to several houses; a member of the Bruges family owned one such house on the "Zilversmidstraat" in 1411. The Old Exchange finally settled in 1515 in an open square surrounded on four sides by a covered gallery. Antwerp became the preferred exchange point for English cloth on the continent and Portuguese and South German trade, so the Bourse began overflowing with merchants from all corners of Europe. The Bourse became an accurate capital market when the future emperor Charles V turned to the Antwerp colonies of foreign merchants, primarily the Augsburg merchant-banker Fugger, to raise the money he needed to buy the imperial crown (Hunt & Murray, 1999).

After 1520, the Habsburgs regularly sold short-term government bonds on the Antwerp Stock Exchange. The actual growth of the Antwerp capital market came with the city's remarkable development and growth spurt after 1500. The growing bond market was driven by loans to support royal consumption and regional wars. The city's population tripled between 1480 and 1568, and the volume of business conducted in the old commercial quarter surrounding the Old Stock Exchange far exceeded the capacity of its commercial buildings and squares. Recognizing the growth challenges, in 1531, the rulers of Antwerp built the "*New Stock Exchange*," designed and built with the requirements of a stock exchange in mind and located in a planned neighborhood with wide, straight streets (Fig. 4.3). This revolution in architectural design marked another step in the evolution from the medieval to the modern stock exchange (Hunt & Murray, 1999).

Fig. 4.3 Historic Antwerp stock exchange building. https://commons.wikimedia.org/wiki/File:Maxime_Lalanne_B%C3%B6rse_von_Antwerpen.jpg

At the beginning of the sixteenth century, the Americas were discovered, and gold and silver from the New World began to flow to Europe via Spain. The intensification of international trade in precious metals was the most critical factor in Antwerp's transition from the axis of intra-European continental trade to a global, intercontinental trading center. It also offered a free environment compared to Bruges, which had stringent laws regarding foreign merchants (Allen, 2004).

Antwerp's relationship with the Portuguese and Spanish empires and its dominance of the European silver and copper markets enabled it to profit and become a truly global metropolis in the early period of globalization. In contrast, the Portuguese trading colonies on the African coast had made Lisbon a trading hub for commodities such as gold, ivory, slaves, sugar, and Guinea pepper. Antwerp was favored for three reasons by Portugal, which had the most prominent colonies and global trade network at the time (Fig. 4.4). First, Antwerp had well-developed trade networks. Second, the number of foreign merchants residing there made Antwerp a market for spice sellers. For example, pepper prices in Antwerp could be about 13% higher than in Lisbon. Third, and most importantly, Antwerp was already a clearing and financial center for copper and silver, two commodities essential for Portugal's trade with Africa and Asia (Adrian, 2006).

After 1451, Antwerp benefited greatly because Germany significantly increased its supply of precious metals by extracting silver and separating silver from copper ore. Thus, not only did the supply of silver increase, but so did the supply of copper. This technology turned Antwerp into a storehouse of both silver and copper. It was more valuable than gold in Portuguese exchanges with Africa and Asia. Thus, in 1499, King Manuel of Portugal granted Antwerp the privilege of being a monopoly port for all Portuguese spices.

Meanwhile, from the end of the fifteenth century, the Ottomans began to dominate and greatly influence the spice trade to Europe. Their strategic dominance over important trade routes enabled them to act as intermediaries between Asia and Europe and

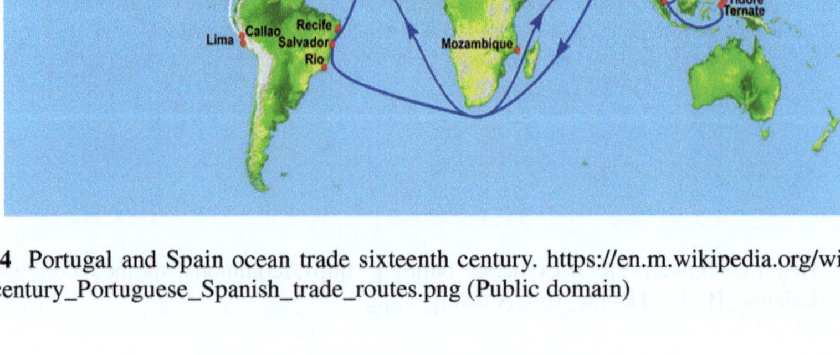

Fig. 4.4 Portugal and Spain ocean trade sixteenth century. https://en.m.wikipedia.org/wiki/File:16th_century_Portuguese_Spanish_trade_routes.png (Public domain)

to impose taxes and tariffs on goods, including spices. In 1503, the Portuguese started to bring spices from India to Portugal and from there to Antwerp. These spices were going to Venice, which until then had been supplying spices to the Red Sea, Alexandria, and thus to the whole Christian world. The Portuguese monopolized spices and sent their goods to Lisbon and Antwerp, the trade center. Therefore, the traditional Silk Road would change from India, the Middle East, and the Mediterranean to the oceans. While the conventional Silk Road was losing power, the Middle East had left its glittering years behind. Meanwhile, the Portuguese had become a threatening force in the Indian Ocean. They also halted trade on the Silk Road by blocking the traditional Silk Road, attacking caravans passing through the region, harming pilgrims, and monopolizing their trade. The shift of the Silk Route to the Atlantic Ocean reduced the income of the Ottoman Empire and other Islamic countries while enriching Western Europe (Inalcık, 2008).

The prices of pepper and spices were the primary speculative commodities on the Antwerp Stock Exchange. News affecting transportation, such as peace, war, or shipwrecks, caused their prices to fluctuate wildly. Market players were chasing any information that might come in. One of the events that probably influenced this betting was the conflict between the Ottomans and the Portuguese in the Red Sea. In 1517, with the defeat of the Mamluk Empire and the annexation of Egypt to the Ottoman Empire, the Ottoman Empire's sphere of influence expanded to the Persian Gulf. The Ottomans started to show their presence in the Red Sea and the Indian Ocean. The Ottoman Empire, which wanted to control the Silk Road and the status of Muslim pilgrims, entered into a struggle for dominance in the Indian Ocean with Portugal. The Portuguese conquered the island of Hormuz in the Persian Gulf in 1507 under the command of Afonso de Albuquerque. This conquest gave the Portuguese complete control of the trade between India and Europe through the Persian Gulf (d'Alòs-Moner, 2012). From 1538 to 1553, the Ottomans fought several wars with the Portuguese in the Persian Gulf. However, the Ottomans could not revitalize the Silk Road as they could not cope with the Portuguese navy, which was built more suitable for the oceans.

Meanwhile, the Portuguese had established a trade triangle in the Atlantic. They bought English cloth and various manufactured goods as barter goods for the African trade, sold them in Africa, bought slaves to work on cotton plantations in the New World, and sold American sugar, tobacco, and cotton in Europe. In 1560, Antwerp had 300 Spanish merchants, 150 Portuguese, 200 Italians, about 100 French and English merchants, and 250 Germans. Antwerp also had the most cosmopolitan and diverse produce market in Europe. Goods from all over Europe could be bought there, as well as exotic goods from Africa and Asia (Adrian, 2006). Antwerp thus consolidated the flow of international trade and hence enabled large-scale transactions. It became the most important center of Western European trade, surpassing Bruges and Venice (Puttevils, 2012).

Meanwhile, the industrial sector also grew. By 1550, no fewer than 19 sugar refineries were operating in Antwerp, making it the leading sugar supplier in Europe. The city entered its golden age, and the region's rapid development led to a rapid increase in population. At the beginning of the sixteenth century, Antwerp had a population of around 40,000. Half a century later, it had grown to almost 100,000, making Antwerp one of the largest cities in Europe. A stone above the city's main gate proclaimed that the town was "*for merchants of all nations*." Even citizens of a country with which it was at war were allowed to trade freely in Antwerp. By the mid-sixteenth century, Antwerp controlled more than 75% of international trade through the Low Countries (by sea and land) (Puttevils, 2012). The French historian Fernand Braudel wrote that Antwerp was an Atlantic capital like Seville or Lisbon. In the 1530s, Antwerp was much more than the capital of the Atlantic; it was the world's economic capital, given that it connected European markets with Africa, Asia, and America (Adrian, 2006).

4.4 The Public Order of Antwerp

The rise of guilds in the Middle Ages provided necessary privileges to their members and made trade more organized. However, as Ogilvie (2011) argues, guilds could exclude large segments of society from long-distance trade. According to Ogilvie, merchant guilds were inefficient economic institutions because they did not guarantee commercial security, enforce contracts, solve principal-agent problems, remedy information deficiencies, or stabilize prices while benefiting themselves. Indeed, merchant guilds created social capital and trust for their members within their ranks, but this was not beneficial for the pre-industrial economy. Thus, their presence in Antwerp in the early sixteenth century probably worked to the detriment of local merchants trying to gain a foothold in European markets. However, Antwerp solved this problem over time and succeeded considerably as a significant commercial center in the sixteenth century (Puttevils, 2012).

With the transition from the guild system to a public administration system where the state set the rules in the Low Countries, including Antwerp, urban and central governments engaged all actors in economic development, fostering more significant potential for growth through a merchant-dominated order. By the late sixteenth century, the administration became more inclusive, offering security and contract enforcement to all, regardless of identity or guild membership. As Acemoglu and Robinson (2019) emphasize, inclusive economic and political institutions are vital for long-term prosperity. Such institutions safeguarded property rights, the rule of law, fair economic competition, and broad political participation, encouraging innovation, entrepreneurship, and sustained growth. Gelderblom (2015) also noted the rise of open-access institutions in these regions, ensuring market access, financial systems, contract enforcement, and protection from violence. This uneven process led to a framework that no longer discriminated against traders, local or foreign, enabling emancipation and democratization (Puttevils, 2012).

Antwerp's municipal court, or Schepenbank, played a central role in administering justice for both civil and criminal matters. This court operated based on customary laws and was accessible to local and foreign merchants. Specialized courts, such as merchant courts, were established to handle trade disputes efficiently and accommodate Antwerp's growing status as a trading hub. These courts offered expedited processes to resolve disagreements swiftly, minimizing disruptions to commerce. Antwerp's authorities recognized the importance of attracting and retaining foreign merchants. To achieve this, the city provided legal protections and privileges, including freedom from arbitrary arrest and guarantees for fair treatment. Foreign trading communities, such as those from the Hanseatic League, often operated under their legal representatives or consuls. The legal system enforced strict regulations on markets and trade to uphold fairness and transparency. Authorities standardized weights and measures, monitored the quality of goods, and regulated prices to prevent fraud. Inspectors frequently checked compliance, ensuring that merchants adhered to these rules.

Contract enforcement was a cornerstone of Antwerp's legal system. Merchants relied on notaries to draft and authenticate contracts, bills of exchange, and other trade-related documents. These records served as evidence in court, ensuring that agreements were legally binding and enforceable. Dispute resolution often involved arbitration and mediation, which were preferred for speed and cost-effectiveness. Higher courts, including those associated with the Burgundian or later Habsburg rulers, were available for appeals.

The intense competition and rivalry between cities in the Low Countries did not result in legal or financial barriers aimed at controlling one another, unlike Northern Italy, nor did it lead to inter-city warfare. This was because commercial cities shared the financial and fiscal benefits of trade and prioritized preserving this value, avoiding costly conflicts and barriers. This structure persisted despite occasional destructive revolts or wars (Gelderblom, 2015). Cities like Antwerp heavily invested in commercial infrastructure and markets, enabling foreign merchants to trade transparently through intermediaries. City governments adopted commercial customs and rules, incorporated them into laws, set competitive tariffs and taxes, and opened markets to all economic actors, fearing revenue loss and the departure of merchants to rival cities. This inclusive regime persisted in sixteenth-century Antwerp and partly explains institutional changes. However, it was not solely maintained by statutes. A multilateral reputation mechanism or merchant coalition ensured fair dealings, with corruption leading to reputational damage and expulsion from networks. In Antwerp, personal relationships between merchants were vital for business transactions. In contrast, merchant diasporas, such as Sephardic Jews and Armenian Christian merchants from New Julfa, relied on extensive networks without state support (Puttevils, 2012).

In Antwerp, reputational mechanisms probably operated within small groups. More significant transactions, especially with foreigners, were conducted as formal transactions due to the high cost of enforcement. European merchants combined formal and informal sanctions and overcame the challenges of politically and legally fragmented long-distance trade in pre-modern Europe by relying on informal networks and formal institutions created by cities and states. Like all other merchants, Low Countries merchants relied on private solutions through networks of family, friends, and fellow citizens and public institutions that could enforce agreements made within these networks and transactions with foreigners.

4.5 The Business Environment of Antwerp

Antwerp's commercial success was mainly due to its educational system, which enabled merchants to increase their knowledge and skills before entering the trade. The high level of urbanization in the Low Countries led to the establishment of many schools in the cities. School numbers were relatively high, especially in a big city like Antwerp. The schools provided training in basic skills such as reading, writing, and counting and specialized and commercially valuable skills such as foreign languages, mathematics, and bookkeeping. Accounting teachers were active in the Dutch city; many had previously worked as professional traders and could integrate their commercial experience into their teaching. However, their numbers were small. The introduction of double-entry bookkeeping in many companies in the second half of the sixteenth century suggests that merchants using double-entry bookkeeping did not necessarily learn this skill from a teacher. School prices were also quite affordable. In 1529, the Antwerp school system was incorporated into the guild of schoolmasters, guaranteeing quality control. Many new merchants came from other Low Countries cities and were educated in their home towns, and since most of them came from artisanal circles, they had likely undergone craft guild-based apprenticeships. Many Antwerp and Low Countries merchants had apprenticed elsewhere in the Netherlands and abroad. In addition, merchants learned skills and knowledge by hiring people with specific skills and knowledge as their servants or partners. The demand for the services of Flemish cashiers in seventeenth-century Spain and Portugal is a good example of this and testifies to the high level of commercial education achieved in the Low Countries. Merchants could bring merchants with specific skills and intelligence into their families through marriage (Puttevils, 2012).

Since the registration of Antwerp companies was not compulsory, information on these contracts was limited. The known contracts were quite different, and there might be a need to register them if the company relationships are outside the family circle. The available documents show that Low Countries merchants could attract capital from outside their family circle and that such contracts were relatively flexible. In the Russian trade, a new trade line for Antwerp merchants, capital contracts were used to raise capital and information (Puttevils, 2012).

According to Antwerp law, profits had to be divided in proportion to the partners' investments or otherwise; the law recognized all partners as jointly and severally liable for the company's debts; however, they had to wait until the company creditors and other partners were paid, even though joint creditors had claims on the company assets. In time, limited liability was even established for passive investors. This shows that legal solid entity protection started early on in Antwerp. Thanks to this investor protection, merchants could raise additional capital from family and strangers; nevertheless, several well-known examples and evidence show that most of the equity capital came from partners or their family members (Postan, 1973). However, for the Baltic trade, partnerships with foreign capital were established. Thus, the rise of Antwerp merchants may have been influenced by the fact that trade was firmly grounded in Antwerp law, and it was relatively easy to obtain sufficient working capital and experiment with flexible contracts. In addition, equity contracts encouraged the subordination of partners to senior partners within the partnership. They also stipulated fiduciary duties and obligations that could be used to ensure that fraud and risky transactions were avoided (Puttevils, 2012).

In the sixteenth century, merchants had a range of borrowing instruments available to them. The choice of specific instruments depended on factors such as the purpose of the debt (investment, production, consumption, etc.), the type of collateral, the identity of the lender/borrower, and the duration of the debt (Willems, 2009). One of the earliest forms of debt financing was the annuity. In this arrangement, the borrower sold a right to receive periodic interest or remuneration to the lender in exchange for a principal sum. Unlike a traditional loan, an annuity was structured as a sale. It could be structured as an eternal annuity or one fixed for multiple annuity beneficiaries' lives. The annuity seller always had the right to redeem the debt, effectively canceling the annuity. Antwerp's annuity interest rates were 6.25% or lower in the sixteenth century. Most of these annuities were backed by real estate as collateral. Annuities had advantages and disadvantages. By mortgaging pieces of real estate, the annuity seller could obtain capital at a reasonable interest rate. He could also decide when to repay the capital. While higher (but more insecure) interest rates were possible for other types of debt, an annuity buyer could earn a low-risk and regular income from the annuity. In case of non-payment of interest, the movable and immovable property could be seized and sold to pay the annuity. In sixteenth-century Antwerp, municipal aldermen secured annuity-related property rights through compulsory registration. The main disadvantage for the annuity buyer was that the value of interest payments gradually decreased due to inflation and devaluation (Puttevils, 2012).

Given merchants' extensive use of annuities, their interest in real estate is understandable. Real estate offered them valuable collateral, a secure and regular income, and the possibility to speculate on real estate price increases. Antwerp merchants frequently bought and sold real estate, holding most of it in their investment portfolios. They acquired real estate within the city walls of Antwerp, but they also bought land and property in the countryside (Gelderblom, 2010). Commodities were also used as collateral in deferred payment transactions. Essential commodities were used as collateral in forward contracts. Bills of exchange were used to transfer money from one city to another in different currencies. Bills of exchange also had a credit function, as there was a time lag between the issuance of the bill and its final payment abroad. Which function was more important for merchants is a matter of debate: Brulez (1959) argues that sixteenth-century Low Countries merchants used bills mainly to transfer funds, while De Roover emphasizes speculation and arbitrage as the main functions of bills of exchange. The risk of such bills of exchange transactions was not only due to rapid changes in the exchange rate but could also arise from involvement in the transactions of insufficiently known persons. However, the merchants' financial acumen allowed them to control the risk by spreading the foreign exchange transactions across different bills and entrusting one bill to solvent traders (Puttevils, 2012). Another way to protect against risks was to insure.

Marine insurance was another way merchants could raise funds: insurers received insurance fees in exchange for promising to pay damages in case of disaster or insured risk. If the risk materialized, they paid out; if the risk did not, they recorded it as a profit for their company. By the sixteenth century, Antwerp had become a vital insurance market. Also, as in Bruges, although dowries were not technically loans, these funds could serve as working capital for merchants and be returned to the widow or family in case of a merchant's death (Puttevils & Deloof, 2017).

The promissory notes used in sixteenth-century Antwerp stemmed from the fair cycle that laid the foundations for Antwerp's extraordinary economic growth: these traditional promissory notes were written by buyers and sellers to be paid at the next fair in Antwerp or Bergen op Zoom (roughly every three months). Increasingly, these debt contracts were transferred by the creditor to others. While commercial growth was encouraged by this transferability of promissory notes, it could also be dangerous: the growing scale of the market, the permanent character it assumed, and the increasing population of merchants created a growing and potentially damaging anonymity. Necessary steps were taken in Antwerp, and international financial practices were changed (Puttevils, 2012).

4.6 The Antwerp Money Market

Throughout the sixteenth century, Antwerp occupied a privileged place in the financial network of Western Europe. Letters of exchange and bills of credit circulated between Antwerp and other financial centers such as Augsburg, Nuremberg, Cologne, and Hamburg in Germany, Milan, Venice, Florence, and Rome in Italy, Seville, Lisbon, Rouen, Paris, and London, and especially the fairs of Lyon, Besançon, Frankfurt, and Castile. Genoese bankers were the dominant group on the Antwerp exchange, but there were also bankers from Spain and Portugal. It was not only state finances that depended on the Antwerp money market. Even the trade of Italian, Spanish, Portuguese, and South Dutch merchants with the "rebellious" North Netherlands was financed in Antwerp (Spufford, 2006). Tawney (1925) describes the money markets of the sixteenth century as follows:

> In its economic organization, the machinery of international trade reached a state of efficiency not noticeably inferior to that of three centuries later. Before the most highly organized economic systems of the age were ruined by the struggle between Spain and the Netherlands and by the French wars of religion, there were perhaps ten to twelve commercial centers whose money markets were the financial power-houses of European trade and whose opinion and policy were decisive in determining financial conditions. In the Flemish, French, and Italian cities where it reached its zenith, and of which England was a pupil, the essence of financial organization of the sixteenth century was internationalism, freedom for every capitalist to undertake every transaction within his means, a unity which had as its symptom the movement of all the principal markets in sympathy with each other, and as its effect the mobilization of immense resources at the strategic points of international finance. Its center

> and symbol was the exchange at Antwerp, with its significant dedication, 'Ad mercatorum cujusque gentis ac linguae' where … every language under heaven could be heard, or the fairs at Lyon which formed, in the words of a Venetian, 'the foundations of the pecuniary transactions of the whole of Italy and a good part of Spain and the Netherlands.'

In need of money, princes, bankers, and merchants such as King Henry VIII of England, Manuel of Portugal, and even Cosimo de Medici turned to this market. On the other hand, large trading and financial companies tried to secure the necessary credit facilities for the ambitious political plans of the Habsburg (and Spanish) kings. They were able to obtain large loans from major international firms, including the Fuggers of Augsburg (Limberger, 2021). Antwerp was not just a hub of trade but also a strategic center of finance. The South Germans Welser and Herwart, the Spaniards de Vaille and de Moxica, and the Italians Gualterotti and Affaitadi were among the foremost financiers in the city. Their contributions, as well as those of numerous other merchants in Antwerp, were crucial. According to an English researcher, around 1564, thirty to forty Antwerp merchants could lend up to 300,000 guilders without damaging their business, a stark contrast to the mere two or three that existed thirty years earlier. The functioning of this market was so essential for the Spanish that they were prepared to make concessions to the city and its merchants. Charles V used as intermediaries respected figures of the time, such as Lazarus Tucher, Gaspard Ducci, or Erasmus Schets, to borrow money from the Antwerp bankers, highlighting the trust and reliance on the financial system. Meanwhile, European bankers' loans to Spain increased throughout the first half of the sixteenth century, reaching impressive proportions. Finally, in the 1550s, this financial relationship became a crisis (Limberger, 2021).

Meanwhile, the war between the French and Spain/Habsburg had been going on for a long time. Charles defeated the French army at Pavia in northern Italy 1525 and took the French king prisoner. The captive king was taken to Madrid and imprisoned. France inevitably saw its salvation in the great ruler of the East, Sultan Suleiman the Magnificent, and turned to him. Sultan Suleiman the Magnificent wrote a letter to King Francis I of France in response to a letter from the king's mother, reflecting the powerful position of the Ottomans in the sixteenth century. The letter begins with the words, "*I am the sultan of sultans, the padishah of kings, the shadow of God on earth who crowns rulers…*" and continuing with "*You, who are King Francis of the province of France…*" is still preserved in the French National Library (Afyoncu et al., 2011). A few years before this date, the Ottomans had gained control of the Mediterranean through the Ottoman-Venetian War. The Ottomans supported France and granted a series of capitulations. These were agreements between the Ottoman Empire and France, granting privileges such as extraterritoriality, trade rights, and legal autonomy to foreign merchants and communities within Ottoman territory. The French had various privileges, such as the right to organize in Ottoman cities, the jurisdiction of consulates in disputes between foreigners, freedom of travel, transportation, and sales in Ottoman territory, and the right to operate ships in the Ottoman seas (Inalcık, 2008).

In addition to Spain, France also borrowed money from the Antwerp and Lyon stock exchanges to finance the war and became the leading player in these exchanges.

In 1552, King Charles V of Spain and King Francis I of France were in another war. During these wars, these states resorted to the stock exchanges to borrow money, and under the pressure of these states, interest rates on the Antwerp Stock Exchange rose to double digits (Allen, 2004). Given that the interest rate on most government loans in Antwerp rose to around 12% per annum (sometimes exceeding 20%), lending became a popular side business among Antwerp's merchant class. Indeed, a growing number of Antwerp merchants abandoned commodity trading and devoted themselves entirely to financial pursuits. For the first time in history, the city became the center of a vast trade network that spanned the globe. Goods worldwide were unloaded in its harbor, and the money market financed European governments' and merchants' commercial ventures.

At this time, Christoffel Plantijn came from France and established the most prestigious printing house in Europe. His justification was as follows: "*No other city in the world can offer me more opportunities to carry on the trade I intend to start. Antwerp is easily accessible; the various nations meet in this marketplace; the raw materials necessary for the execution of the trade can be found here; craftsmen for all crafts can be easily found and trained in a short time.*" Plantijn's Antwerp had replaced Venice as the key printing center in Europe (Spufford, 2006). Antwerp's main innovation was the development of printing price lists on newly invented printing presses. Printed papers on exchange rates and commodity price flows had been available to Antwerp merchants since the 1530s, making Antwerp the "birthplace of the business press." Although it may seem like a small development, the public release of price data was revolutionary. It gave the trading community in Antwerp access to vital business information previously kept secret by traders and firms, making trading in the Antwerp market more efficient (McCusker, 2005).

The enormous size of Antwerp's printing industry facilitated the spread of a wide variety of printed merchant manuals that apprentices and established merchants could use to acquire knowledge and skills. Most of Antwerp's books were religious and cheap editions, such as pamphlets and news sheets. Among the printed books were merchants' manuals. They contained information about the different goods available in other markets, local trade practices and weights, measures, and currencies, as well as "*how-to*" information, such as how to make deals, how to write letters, contracts, and credit instruments, how to keep books, and how to behave. Handbooks on commercial arithmetic came second. Long before the printing industry gained a foothold in the Low Countries, manuals of commercial arithmetic circulated in manuscript form, such as the Bruges manual of calculation of 1463, which provided information on partnership calculations, swaps, profit and loss, foreign exchange arbitrage, etc. The increasing availability of bookkeeping information in printed form and its relatively low prices allowed Lowland merchants to learn bookkeeping methods without apprenticeship (Puttevils, 2012).

The flourishing trade in Antwerp and other northern markets was primarily conducted as an individual enterprise, which did not lend itself to complex control systems. However, in Antwerp in the sixteenth century, large southern German companies like Fugger had already started to adopt advanced Italian accounting concepts, including double-entry bookkeeping. It was not until the second half of the sixteenth century that Luca Paciolo's "*true*" double-entry accounting, written in 1494, gained widespread use (Hunt & Murray, 1999). Without the need for an apprenticeship or any related training, and with only a book as their guide, Low Country merchants could establish large businesses, thanks to Italian-style bookkeeping. This development became more pronounced in the second half of the sixteenth century, marking a significant shift in the economic landscape (Puttevils, 2012).

The years 1501–1557 were Antwerp's golden years. However, the conditions contributing to its development as a trade center began to reverse. In particular, regional wars waged by the Spanish were affecting Antwerp. Charles V and his son Philip II were constantly in debt to finance these wars, relying on gold and silver from the New World. Charles V fought against economic realities to keep the official bimetallic ratio between these two precious metals constant, even though the silver he brought to Europe from South America had caused its value to fall relative to gold. Through his proxies in the Netherlands, he tried to fix the value of gold to silver. Such decrees were issued in 1521, 1527, and twice in 1539. However, since the market value of gold in silver was always higher than the agreed price, merchants either stored it or sent it to France, where the price was higher. To stop the flow of gold bullion to France, Charles issued a decree in December 1541 requiring that two-thirds of all bills of exchange in the Low Countries be paid in gold coins. Despite this, merchants refused to do business in Antwerp. Gold continued to flow to France. As Europe drowned in New World silver, gold remained valuable. The famous English statesman and economist Sir Thomas Gresham operated in Antwerp on behalf of England at the time as the King's advisor and the representative of the British Crown in Antwerp. There, for more than twenty years, he was responsible for all the financial interests of his sovereign, both in terms of borrowing, the extension and repayment of debts, and the spending of revenues on war munitions, secret service, and other business. Based on his observation of this market, he made the statement, known as Gresham's law, that "*good money will be driven out by bad money.*" His experience from the Antwerp Stock Exchange led him to the principle known as Gresham's Law of Economics. Accordingly, he stated that when there are two types of commodity money with the same nominal values accepted as legal tender in circulation, the more valuable one will be hoarded. Gresham wrote on December 20, 1553: "*The strangest thing that has ever happened on the Antwerp Stock Exchange, which has no other payment than Spanish silver, is that there is no movement of gold on the exchange*" (Winjum, 1971).

One speculation in particular, made by Gresham, was so exciting and creative that it should be taught in textbooks. There was no investing public in Antwerp. The money was lent entirely by the big financiers, who saw the loans as speculation. The most extended term loan for the British Crown on the Antwerp market was twelve months, the majority six months. Every six months, representatives of the Crown came to the stock exchange for massive loan transfers between England and Antwerp. They aimed to take full advantage of the effect of their borrowing in Antwerp on the market rate while minimizing the opposite impact of repayments by various means (Buckley, 1924). Gresham understood that the glut of money in Antwerp was causing the stock market to rise. The first measure he took was to use the stock market prudently, choosing the times to send money and doing so cautiously, a little at a time. This allowed Britain to borrow at a favorable interest rate without creating too much demand in the stock market. He then proposed increasing the value of the pound sterling. With financial backing from the Crown, he began secretly collecting sterling on the Dutch market. Within two years, he raised the exchange rate in Antwerp and paid almost all of the Crown's debts (Stephen & Lee, 1890). Gresham's best service to England was the establishment of the Royal Exchange in London, which was initially called "*Bourse*" (1566).

In addition to trade with Lisbon, trade with Seville, financed by a mixture of Genoese, Burgundian, and Jewish capital, was growing. The Seville-Antwerp connection was much strengthened by the discovery of Potosi and later Zacatecas silver in the 1540s. This led to a considerable increase in demand for European goods from the New World. Most of the goods were supplied via Antwerp. Unlike their compatriots who had chosen exile to Portugal rather than baptism in 1492, a large group from the Seville Jewish community had moved to Antwerp as "New Christians," choosing both baptism and exile with their capital. They were initially unwelcome but played a significant role in trade with Portugal and Seville.

The South German trading houses in Augsburg and Nuremberg, through their contacts with Tuscan businessmen in Venice and Bruges, especially the Florentines, learned their trade and adopted their models of business finance. The Fuggers, in particular, were the most frequent lenders to Spain. By the beginning of the sixteenth century, the Fugger group of companies had surpassed in scale. It redefined the concept of a large company in Europe, outshining the famous Bardi of Florence in the early fourteenth century (Spufford, 2006).

By the late Middle Ages, a public financing system had been established in the Low Countries, paying the interest on debts, some for a few years, some for life, and many in perpetuity (indefinite maturity), through indirect taxes and annuities. This system, reminiscent of the "*Monte*" system previously practiced in the Italian city-states, profoundly impacted the financial landscape. The consolidation of public debt by the Italian state was a revolution in public finance because it facilitated the process of underwriting new debt issues. For example, in 1262, Venice consolidated all its outstanding debts in a structure called Monte. Accordingly, the original obligations were converted into shares, and investors could transfer ownership by assignment (Mueller, 2019).

German bankers lent Charles V an ever-increasing amount of money to be repaid from the subsequent revenues of the entire group of kingdoms. After the 1540s, for example, the imperial fifth of the silver mined in America was accepted as additional security for loans when it arrived or was expected to arrive in Seville. Genoese and Spanish financiers in the Seville-Antwerp trade joined their South German counterparts in lending silver bullion to governments. During this long commercial boom, Antwerp entrepreneurs lent large sums to the English, Portuguese, Spanish, and French governments (Spufford, 2006).

In the 1540s and 1550s, Antwerp was at its peak as a commercial metropolis of the West. The clearing system of the Antwerp Stock Exchange was also developed, and a third party could collect by signing (endorsing) the back of a bill of exchange. The discount on bills of exchange was also remarkable. On the other hand, the speculation on the price of black pepper, described in the commodity trading section, inspired today's derivatives trading.

4.7 The Clearing System

4.7.1 Endorsement of Promissory Notes

Although Antwerp was a trading center, its clearing system initially had serious problems. Antwerp essentially maintained a "*public*" market. Antwerp also had to rely on bankers to provide its payment system as a public market. Burgundian rulers banned deposit banks in the 1480s for various reasons. Antwerp had to rely on an alternative settlement method: debt assignment. With an assignment, the ownership of an asset is transferred with all its rights from the creditor to another person. This way, when the bill became due, the creditor could collect his money from the original issuer or the person who had endorsed and transferred it. Sometimes, instead of drawing up a promissory note, merchants would transfer a promissory note they had received from someone else in connection with a business transaction (Kohn, 1999). This transfer is a formal contract between the creditor and the third party who transfers the debt without the consent or knowledge of the debtor. Among Italian trading companies and merchant banks, the assignment of debt was recorded in the books of the parties involved. However, most merchants trading in Antwerp in the early sixteenth century were not Italian and often did not keep regular books. The usual way of recording a debt among these merchants was to issue a letter of credit (promissory note). This was a standard means of commercial credit, not only among Dutch merchants but also among all merchants trading in Antwerp. Therefore, such a letter or promissory note had to be given for exchange. Initially, only maturing promissory notes were assigned on the Stock Exchange, but increasingly, promissory notes were also assigned before maturity. To facilitate assignment, letters of credit (promissory notes) were often made "*payable to the bearer*" rather than payable to a specific party (Kohn, 1999).

While this seemed an attractive solution to the problem of barter, it faced a severe obstacle: There is an essential distinction in law between "*assignability*" and "*transferability*." Suppose that, for example, Andre owes Peter money and writes a letter (promissory note) in exchange for the debt. If Peter has the right to assign his right to collect the debt to a third party, Carl, before maturity without notice to Andre, this document is assignable. In addition, if Carl acquires all of Peter's rights, the instrument is transferable. This means that Carl, who becomes the owner of the promissory note, can sue Andre for non-payment if he fails to collect on the note. If he obtained the document from Peter in good faith, his rights are not impaired by defects in Peter's rights (for example, if Peter obtained the document fraudulently). Unlike a bond, which expresses a debt owed to a specific person, a transferable promissory note is not a personal financial instrument: it is evidence of a debt owed by the issuer to anyone who acquires it (the bearer). In this respect, it is like cash. The commercial courts of Bruges and later Antwerp recognized the complete transferability of bearer promissory notes. However, debtors refused to pay because they were unknown and untrusted merchants in the market and sought refuge in the civil courts, which did not recognize the transferability. This legal obstacle to the circulation of registered promissory notes was removed in 1507 when the law courts of Antwerp recognized transferability. However, while acknowledging this feature by the civil courts solved one problem, it would create another. The court treated the assignment of a transferable financial instrument as completely extinguishing the debt owed by the assignor, Peter, to the assignee, Carl: if the original debtor, Andre, failed to pay, Carl could sue Andre, who had initially signed the promissory note, but he had no recourse against Peter, who had assigned it to him. So, Peter had no obligation to pay (Karan et al., 2024).

This limited the circulation of registered promissory notes since, under these circumstances, no one would accept paper from someone with unknown or poor credit. The solution was found in applying the principle of negotiable instruments to debentures. Accordingly, Peter's debt to Carl would be extinguished only when Carl received the final payment (or a satisfactory equivalent). If Andre failed to pay, Carl had recourse against Andre and Peter (or, if there was a chain of assignment, against each assignee in turn).

The enforceability of bearer letters was recognized in Antwerp in 1536 and all the Low Countries in 1541. This principle was soon adopted in the Hanseatic (German) cities and England. While negotiability solved the credit problem, it also gave rise to a technical problem. Identifying the assigning debtors in a long chain of assignments, sometimes involving many people trading one after the other, was a problem. In the book credit, tracing the chain through the books of the parties involved was relatively easy. However, in the case of a financial instrument (a promissory note), it was necessary to create a record of the chain of assignment, either through a notary public or by attaching an additional formal document (a deed of assignment) to the instrument each time it changed hands. Both alternatives were cumbersome and costly. The ultimate solution was found in the practice of endorsement. Each assignee signed the back of the promissory note, as it does today, and this signature legally imposed on him the obligation to indemnify the assignee in the event of non-payment by the issuer and previous endorsers. This legal implication of endorsement, his signature indicated that he retained ultimate responsibility for his debt, was a significant development. The first examples of endorsements date from the 1570s, when the practice became widespread by the turn of the century (Kohn, 1999).

Initially, the financial instrument of choice for the northern merchants who dominated Antwerp was registered bills of exchange. Over the sixteenth century, northern merchants gradually substituted bills of exchange for registered promissory notes for remittances and loans, and by 1600, bills of exchange had become a standard financial instrument. As they became negotiable instruments, registered promissory notes and bills of exchange became a form of convertible money, similar in many ways to the deposits of deposit banks. Merchants in Antwerp used negotiable instruments as a means of payment. Instead of transferring the debt (deposits) of a depository bank onto the bank's books, they transferred the debt of non-banks in the form of negotiable instruments. Papers often changed hands ten or twenty times before maturity, sometimes even a hundred times. The paper with the best "name" circulated most freely, and the Fuggerbriefe, the paper of Fugger, the largest bank at the time, circulated almost like modern banknotes. In many cases, the circulating bill would revert to the original issuer, thus eliminating the debt and the need for clearing; this was a form of netting (Kohn, 1999).

4.7.2 Promissory Note Discount

Bills still outstanding at maturity had to be paid in cash. Letters of credit and Antwerp bonds were due in one of the quarters of the year (every four months), usually associated with fairs (on the tenth of February, May, August, and November), with the quarters of the year retaining their importance as settlement dates. On days that were quarters of the year, there was a netting process that minimized the need for cash settlement. Similar systems were established on the Lisbon and London stock exchanges. The usefulness of letters of credit and bills of exchange as credit instruments was further enhanced by discounting. While the assignment of commercial paper was acceptable as a means of payment, when money was tight, creditors offered discounts to pay in cash before maturity. Financiers with money could take advantage of this situation by offering to buy commercial paper at a discount for cash. Discounting a debt was not a new idea. Since the Middle Ages, it was typical for a creditor needing cash to demand early payment from a debtor in exchange for a discount. The interest charged in this way was invisible and did not violate the laws of the Church. In the fifteenth century, Florence had an active market for government debt, which was traded at a discount, like today's government bonds. What was new in Antwerp was the discounting of short-term commercial paper. Initially, due to the ambiguous legal status of assignment, moneylenders only discounted maturing promissory notes. However, after an imperial edict of 1541 recognized bills as negotiable instruments, they started discounting them before maturity. They began with registered promissory notes, but as bills of exchange became increasingly popular in Antwerp, they also discounted them. This practice was quite common in the 1550s (officially authorized in 1540 as long as the interest rate did not exceed 12%). In March 1560, for example, money changers immediately snapped up bills of exchange from Lyon and the neighboring city of Besançon, arriving in Antwerp to be paid at the next fair in May (Kohn, 1999).

Discounting significantly improved the commercial paper market by increasing liquidity. It also allowed bills of exchange to be used as a pure credit instrument; a merchant wishing to raise cash could write a promissory note and have it discounted by a foreign exchange dealer. Despite the lack of deposit banks and the initial lousy start, Antwerp eventually created a highly efficient payment system by assigning debt. Over time, tools and practices evolved to suit a market where anonymous trade between strangers is possible without knowing each other well enough. Moreover, discounting bills of exchange, a product of this evolutionary process, was a financial invention of enormous economic importance. Indeed, they would be widely used by Goldsmiths, who began accepting deposits in England in the sixteenth century and would be at the basis of modern commercial banking in the seventeenth and eighteenth centuries.

4.8 The Derivatives

In the second half of the sixteenth century, in Antwerp, contracts concluded not when the commodity arrived at the port but "*up to the arrival*" of the commodity provided sufficient liquidity to support trade development and contributed to the growth of this market. This was a derivative transaction known as a forward contract. Antwerp leather merchants are known to have entered into forward contracts with Russian leather dealers in Narva in the 1570s (Gelderblom, 2004). Various sources report that "*arrivals*" contracts, still at sea, were particularly active in speculative transactions in grain. At the same time, similar agreements were also important in the whale oil, herring, and salt trade. The role of speculation in these forward contracts is a fascinating aspect of their historical development.

It is not surprising that derivatives contracts began to be actively traded by speculators and, at the same time, were directly involved in trading the underlying physical commodity. Since maritime transportation was a risky business and information about cargoes arriving later could often be inadequate, the quality and quantity of physical commodities ready for delivery could not be known before the fleet arrived; forward sales of such cargoes were inherently speculative. Speculative liquidity on the Antwerp Stock Exchange was concentrated among significant merchants and large merchant houses that controlled financial activities or the trade in goods. The environment for such trading was closely tied to medieval gambling and insurance traditions, where betting on the safe return of ships, a primitive form of early insurance, was linked to the settlement of commercial transactions. An essential step in developing exchange-traded contracts came when "*until arrival*" contracts involved standardized transactions in fictitious goods for a future delivery, where trade was settled by payment of differences due to the new price when the goods reached the port. Buyers of such contracts would speculate on a price rise before the due date. If such a rise materialized, the contract could be sold, and the speculator would receive the price difference. This "*difference trading*" was also practiced by sellers of goods, who would sell for future delivery on the bet that prices would fall. The emergence of premium contracts for difference trading accompanied this practice. Accordingly: "*The buyer has entered into a contract for future delivery at a fixed price, but with the condition of reviewing it after two or three months: he may then withdraw from the contract on condition of paying a premium to the* seller." Little is known about the precise evolution of contracts used for speculative trading, but the existence of premium contracts for difference trading by speculators looks pretty logical.

The "*premium*" form of the futures contract was a staple of European securities trading until the twentieth century, for example German rämiengeschäfte (premium) contracts, which differ from options traded on modern markets. A Prämiengeschäft is a forward purchase or sale of securities with a right of cancellation for the buyer or seller. In a cancellation, the buyer or seller must pay a predetermined premium. In such contracts, a waiver was also possible. The buyer's risk in the future is limited because he can choose to pay a premium instead of fulfillment. The premium transaction resembles an option transaction (for a contracting party) because of its limited risk. Around 1908, on the Paris and Berlin stock exchanges, the premium payment at expiry was fixed by contract, and the "*price*" was determined by setting the strike price based on the initial stock or commodity price (Poitras, 2009). Thus, the system in which derivatives are traded today arrived step by step.

Meanwhile, Christopher Kurtz from Antwerp, who introduced himself as a market expert, had developed an interesting method of forecasting security prices. Kurtz claimed to have developed an astrology system that could predict the prices of spices and debt securities two weeks in advance. His reports, considered groundbreaking, were taken very seriously. The practice of betting on the stock market, as he proposed, was a unique concept: one bettor would wager that a certain exchange rate would rise or fall by three percent at a specified date in the future, while the other bettor would bet that the change in the exchange rate would be four percent. At the expiry date, the two bettors promised to pay each other the difference based on the outcome (Allen, 2004).

Access to the Antwerp Exchange was unrestricted, but those not connected to large-scale commodity trading and wanting to speculate needed a broker to create a position. These transactions, much like today, allowed the contract to be settled with a monetary payment without purchasing or selling a commodity. Brokers, who could also be commodity dealers, played a significant role in the exchange. The exchange was largely self-regulating, with brokers clearing derivatives transactions with other brokers. This can be considered the first implementation of over-the-counter exchanges. The rules of conduct for trading were primarily governed by the trader's agreement, with penalties for violations being loss of reputation and consequent inability to do business. The state officially recognized some "*sworn intermediaries*" (brokers) and established a civil court system for dispute resolution. Physical infrastructure and a legal and tax environment that was not too intimidating to investors were provided to encourage trade development. The use of premium contracts facilitated differential trading. Following the traditions developed in the bills of exchange market, brokers cleared positions in different contracts by coordinating with other intermediaries (Poitras, 2009).

4.9 The Fall of the Antwerp Market

Antwerp initially maintained a commodity market. The financial market developed based on financing commodity trade, and the city became a clearing and credit center. As the commodity exchange collapsed due to various problems, which we will explain below, its importance as a financial center declined because of the decline in trade in goods and because Spain repeatedly defaulted on its debts.

4.9.1 Decline in Commodity Trade

Antwerp's growth was essentially the result of the changing purchasing power of coins. This time, however, the situation was the opposite: the supply of Central European silver, which had stimulated Antwerp's economy, was declining rapidly after 1535. New World silver was flowing into Seville, Spain, to settle Spain's debts. This created a large class of lending merchants in Spain and reduced Spain's debts on the Antwerp money market. For example, between 1551 and 1555, Charles V's borrowing in Castile was four times greater than in Antwerp, reducing not only the amount of gold in circulation in Antwerp but also the amount of silver (Spufford, 2006).

The silver problem also negatively affected Antwerp's spice trade with Portugal. From the 1530s onward, Portuguese merchants could get the silver they needed for trade with Asia from neighboring Spain. Nevertheless, Antwerp remained a vital distribution center for spices. However, the Ottoman intervention in this struggle would significantly alter the commercial balance. The commercial concession granted by the Ottomans to France in 1536 included using Ottoman ports. Using this facility, French ships would return to Marseille via the Eastern Mediterranean with cinnamon, ginger, and other spices. This shipment interrupted the Portuguese trade via Antwerp and significantly shifted trade dynamics. 1580 Spain annexed Portugal, and the Portuguese were entirely out of Antwerp.

The first indication that the expansion of industry, trade, and finance in Antwerp would not continue indefinitely appeared in the late 1550s. At this time, the French, Spanish, and Portuguese monarchies had all declared that they could no longer repay the principal of the loans they had been granted. However, they were prepared to pay continuous interest on these debts at a low rate of 5%. At the same time, the British government had also eased its debts and moved away from Antwerp-based financing. Bankers struggled to collect their loans from governments, leaving the individuals and businesses that had created money for them as deposits in a problematic situation. In 1533–1560, Charles V was in financial distress and increased his debt to the Fuggers, a family of German bankers, from 147,000 florins to 2,160,000 florins. The Fuggers were not alone. Numerous South German firms also went bankrupt during these years. This also devastated the Spanish merchants, who were heavily involved in state finances. These developments undoubtedly affected the Antwerp commodity market. The government defaults (bankruptcies) of the 1550s were followed by a severe commercial and industrial decline (Spufford, 2006).

After 1563, a period of industrial contraction began. Due to high unemployment and grain prices, skilled artisans began to leave Antwerp and the surrounding area. In 1560, Elizabeth I revalued English silver and ended the favorable trading conditions that English cloth merchants had long enjoyed in Antwerp. Three years after the outbreak of the Anglo-French war, the Habsburg Governor of the Low Countries declared an embargo on English cloth, repeating Bruges' previous protectionist practices. English merchants had left Bruges years earlier and were soon on their way from Antwerp to Emden, a port further north. Although some would return to Antwerp briefly, the English cloth trade would never be the same. The pillar of the three-legged trestle, in other words, the goods on which Antwerp's success depended, had disappeared (Munro, 1994).

In 1566, calculations based on tolls on goods arriving by land in Brabant (Belgium) show that the number of merchants from Germany had halved. French shipping had also halved in 1568. Antwerp joined the provinces that rebelled against Philip II's oppressive policy. The famine of 1565–1566 created social conditions for the beginning of the Dutch Revolt. The brutal event known as the "*Spanish Fury*" of 1576, in which unpaid Spanish troops roamed the city and participated in looting, encouraged Antwerp residents to join the rebellion against Habsburg rule. During the Spanish Rampage, some 1000 buildings were set on fire, and some 17,000 men, women, and children were killed. However, the Spanish recapture of the city in 1585 ensured it remained under Spanish authority. After winning over the Ottomans at Loponte in 1571, they increased their pressure on this region. After the city's occupation, all Protestants and many Catholic merchants who saw more commercial opportunities in the independent Dutch provinces to the north were forced to leave. By 1589, the city's population had fallen to 42,000 from around 100,000 in 1560. Most of these immigrants fled to North Holland, and many to Amsterdam. The 1648 Treaty of Münster, which divided the country into the Netherlands and Belgium, was the final nail in the coffin. The northern provinces were united as a separate state, and today's Netherlands was born. The northerners' closure of the Scheldt River, which connected Antwerp to the ocean, did not stop the ships from coming to Antwerp, but significantly reduced the harbor. Antwerp would not re-emerge as a vibrant commercial port until the nineteenth century. After that, neither the Dutch linen industry nor industrial production in and around Hondschoote in southwest Flanders would recover. The Hanseatic League would leave Antwerp for good (Spufford, 2006). The international transit trade on which Antwerp's economic power was based was over. There would still be some growth in the industrial sector, but Antwerp would no longer be the global entrepot it had once been.

In 1577–1578, the Sephardic Jews had left Antwerp. Most of the Spanish businesses were also gone. In the quarter century from 1577 to 1610, small groups of Portuguese merchants, including some of Jewish descent, scattered across Europe. Despite the decline in commodity trade, Antwerp remained Europe's most important financial center for some time. Genoese bankers remained the dominant group, but there were also bankers from Burgos and Lisbon. Burgos' interest was in the wool, iron, and wine trade, while the Lisbon bankers were interested in financing Asian spices.

Antwerp's money market began to collapse in the 1600s. The Spanish state's third default in 1596 triggered a wave of bankruptcies across the Iberian Peninsula and Antwerp. Antwerp would not become a financial center until the first decades of the seventeenth century (Spufford, 2006).

4.9.2 Spanish Debt and the Antwerp Market

King Philip II's financial decisions profoundly impacted Antwerp, particularly his inability to pay his debts due to extensive spending on religious wars. When Charles V passed the reins to his son, Philip II, the country was teetering on the edge of bankruptcy. Between 1557 and 1666, the country declared bankruptcy nine times, a story of borrowing with significant local implications.

The borrowing took two forms. One was perpetual bonds, known as juros, with annual payments for life. The other was short-term loans (asientos). Between 1566 and 1600, the outstanding debt increased by 20.7 million ducats. In the same period, the king entered into short-term contracts for 83.2 million ducats. Both revenues and debts increased in parallel in the second half of the sixteenth century. Asientos were issued against the king's general credit, not against a specific tax stream. They usually met an urgent need for financing. In some cases, asientos were formalized by loan agreements made by field commanders. Long-term bonds (juros) constituted a large part of the royal debt. It was secured by regular taxes and approved by the Cortes (the representative assembly of Castilian cities). If the tax flow was insufficient, the juro owners suffered (Drelichman & Voth, 2011).

The borrowing took two forms. One was perpetual bonds, known as juros, with annual payments for life. The other was short-term loans (asientos). Between 1566 and 1600, the outstanding debt increased by 20.7 million ducats. In the same period, the king entered into short-term contracts for 83.2 million ducats. Both revenues and debts increased in parallel in the second half of the sixteenth century. Asientos were issued against the king's general credit, not against a specific tax stream. They usually met an urgent need for financing. In some cases, asientos were formalized by loan agreements made by field commanders. Long-term bonds (juros) constituted a large part of the royal debt. It was secured by regular taxes and approved by the Cortes (the representative assembly of Castilian cities). If the tax flow was insufficient, the juro owners suffered (Drelichman & Voth, 2011).

In 1557, when Spain and France went to war again, King Philip II of Spain could not pay the government bonds he had issued. To solve the cash shortage, he started to state that interest was forbidden in Christianity and aimed to eliminate a significant part of his debts in this way. In the negotiations that followed, he offered his creditors two options. Either they would stop collecting short-term bonds issued at 10–15% interest, or they would settle for five percent in the long term. The government bonds sold on the Antwerp and Lyon stock exchanges started to be sold at a fraction of their value. In response, the market borrowing rate rose to over 15%. As a result of these events, the credibility of government bonds was thoroughly diminished (Allen, 2004). The bankruptcy of 1557 ended the rise and the leading role of the bankers in Habsburg, South Germany. However, the Fuggers had also financed the Spanish from the Antwerp Stock Exchange. Some Genoese bankers provided loans to the Spanish kings through Milan, Piacenza, Besançon, and, to a lesser extent, Antwerp (Limberger, 2021).

Finally, in the first Spanish state bankruptcy, Philip II tied all Habsburg loans to a 5% annual interest rate. This was a terrible situation for the lenders in Antwerp. Moreover, the King's guarantee had previously been insufficient to obtain the sums needed. By issuing long-term bonds (juros), the managers of the King's estate (rentmeesters) stepped in to back the king's loan. In this case, the city's citizens had to give collateral to the bankers against the king's debt. As the most important commercial center of the kingdom, Antwerp had a solid credit; therefore, as a city, it was on the agenda to provide collateral. The interest rate the King had to pay for short-term loans was usually considerably higher than the interest rate that would have been paid if the city had borrowed directly. This was because the annual income generated by the city of Antwerp offered greater security of repayment than Charles' pledge. In short, Antwerp had more prestige than the King. This prompted the Emperor to ask Antwerp to borrow money, utilizing the city's credit. Antwerp's involvement lowered the interest rate to which the kingdom was subject. As early as the sixteenth century, Charles V had repeatedly asked the city to sell promissory notes on his behalf, which he would repay through the general tax collectors of Brabant, either on the land of the principality or by reducing taxes or other charges to the city. Thus, as long as the emperor repaid his debts on time, they would not incur any extra costs for the city. However, this process was quite risky for the city. If the debt was not repaid, the city was held liable, including the private wealth of the citizens. The inability of the Spaniards to pay their debts was followed first by the bankruptcy of the city, soon followed by the bankruptcy of local governments, and finally by the bankruptcy of firms and individuals. The extraordinary expenditures and access to credit that the city faced forced Antwerp to borrow more than other cities. Another bankruptcy under Philip II followed shortly after the first. Spain's revenues from New World silver were insufficient to cover its mounting debts, exacerbated by the costs of ongoing wars and administrative inefficiencies. Spain had broken down its relations with the Fuggers, its most prominent financier (Box 4.1). 1569 Antwerp had the highest urban debt in the southern Low Countries. Only in the late 1590s did the city's money market begin to collapse. Nevertheless, in 1595, King Philip II of Spain managed to secure a loan of four million euros from Antwerp, which was to be repaid in monthly installments, secured against its regular income. However, the third default of the Spanish state in 1596 would lead to a wave of bankruptcies in Spain itself and Antwerp (Limberger, 2021). Even after that, Antwerp did not wholly cease to be a financial center, but it was of much more limited importance (Spufford, 2006).

Box 4.1: Fuggers Banker Family and Spain Kings

On July 1, 1563, Fugger shareholders Georg, Raymund, and Christopher wrote to King Philip II of Spain, urgently seeking repayment of debts (Spain Defaults, n.d.):

> Your Majesty,
>
> We and our family have loyally served Your Majesty and Your Imperial Father for nearly fifty years, often at significant risk. Unlike others who supported your enemies, we used our credit and reputation to secure financing for the Habsburg cause.
>
> Now, we find ourselves at a disadvantage. Promises to us have been breached, and others are preferred. We have been unfairly treated and incurred the wrath of Eraso, who prioritizes personal gain over your benefit.
>
> We sincerely pray Your Majesty will honor our commitments. Otherwise, we will submit this dispute to arbiters under the Constitutio Commercialis Carolina.
>
> We remain, etc., Georg, Raymund, and Christopher Fugger.

Though polite, the letter ended with veiled threats—rare in those times. It invoked Charles V, whose loans had supported Philip's rise, but Philip denied the debt. While the claim went to court, the Fuggers eventually lost concessions and faced indirect punishment (Strieder, 2001).

The Fuggers started in textiles, later using mining operations as loan collateral. Jacob Fugger (1459–1525), the family's most successful financier, studied Venetian accounting before turning the family business into a banking powerhouse (Hunt & Murray, 1999). By 1495, they dominated Hungarian mining and metals. In 1519, they financed Charles V's ascent to the Habsburg throne.

The Fuggers became a major wholesaler and financier, connecting Antwerp to Venice and funding princes and businesses. Loyal Catholics financed the Church and, during the Italian Wars, recruited mercenaries for the Pope, earning a monopoly on Papal coin minting. Jacob Fugger pioneered sovereign debt by issuing bonds, influencing future financial systems. They were also significant players on the Antwerp stock exchange. Despite success, relations with the Crown soured. Emperor Charles and King Philip had poor credit records, with loans often carrying 12–14% interest. The Fuggers raised funds in Bavaria, where rates were lower, but repayment slowed, and Philip confiscated their mining leases and silver cargo. Spain's financial collapse, coupled with fraud and poor risk management, undermined the Fugger Company, leading to significant losses (Hunt & Murray, 1999; Strieder, 2001).

4.10 Concluding Remarks

In the late medieval period, Antwerp emerged as a central commercial hub in Europe, supported by a legal system to facilitate international trade and ensure market stability. The city's legal infrastructure blended local customs with specialized mechanisms to address the complexities of global commerce, fostering a dynamic and secure trading environment. From the late fifteenth century onward, Antwerp experienced a remarkable demographic and economic expansion, thus becoming the commercial metropolis par excellence in Western Europe. Merchants from other parts of Europe settled in Antwerp, giving the city a cosmopolitan character. The rapid economic growth had far-reaching consequences for the social and cultural life of the town. While a limited number of merchants in the city acquired considerable wealth, increasing prosperity created opportunities for a broad social middle group. Economic expansion greatly stimulated education and cultural and artistic activities. The book publishing industry also boomed, giving Antwerp a dominant position in the Low Countries. The city's cosmopolitan character, the availability of books, and the high level of education created an openness and critical attitude toward religious matters and contributed to the rise of Protestantism. Moreover, in 1566, Antwerp played a key role in the Dutch Revolt.

In the sixteenth century, Antwerp's success, as in other Low Countries, was driven by the transition from a guild system dominated by merchants to a public administration system in which the state set the rules. Thus, by establishing an inclusive structure, urban and central governments could involve all actors in their territories in economic development, creating a great potential for economic growth. Antwerp's governance fostered trade through a degree of civic autonomy. As part of the Duchy of Brabant, the city operated with a measure of self-rule through local councils and merchant guilds. This autonomy enabled the creation of policies to protect merchants and enforce contracts, ensuring a conducive environment for trade. The city also maintained a neutral and predictable legal framework, which attracted traders from various nations. While not politically democratic, Antwerp's inclusive economic policies were heavily influenced by the merchant class, which advocated for minimal trade restrictions and guidelines that encouraged commerce.

Antwerp's open-door trade policies and inclusive institutional structure welcomed merchants from across Europe and beyond, in contrast to the restrictive practices of other cities. This diversity created a dynamic and competitive marketplace, driving innovation and economic growth. Additionally, Antwerp's low tariffs and minimal trade barriers made it a preferred alternative to more restrictive markets, facilitating the flow of goods like spices, textiles, and precious metals.

The interplay between democratic governance principles and free trade had a transformative effect on Antwerp. The lack of monopolistic control over commerce promoted competition, with merchants, rather than state institutions, driving the economy. Antwerp's relatively inclusive trade practices allowed merchants from varied backgrounds to participate and prosper, contributing to its reputation as a leading trade and financial hub. Thus, the rising democratic environment and free trade played a pivotal but indirect role in shaping Antwerp's success and significance as a commercial hub. While Antwerp lacked a formal democratic system by modern standards, certain democratic principles, such as open access to trade and partial civic governance, merged with a free trade environment to bolster the city's prosperity. These factors collectively solidified Antwerp's significant economic and financial center position.

Antwerp's importance in the sixteenth century extended beyond trade. The city experienced significant economic growth driven by its governance and trade policies. It became a center for financial innovation, including developing exchange bills and letters of credit. Its ability to adapt to global economic shifts, such as the influx of silver from the Americas, highlighted the resilience of its open and inclusive policies.

In conclusion, Antwerp's partial embrace of democratic ideals and commitment to free trade were instrumental in its rise as "Europe's marketplace" during the sixteenth century. These principles fueled economic growth and innovation and connected European markets to the emerging global economy, cementing Antwerp's legacy as its era's pivotal commercial and financial center.

The heyday of Antwerp was between 1540 and 1556. The success of King Philip II of Spain in his struggle against the Ottomans in the Mediterranean and his victory in the Battle of Lepanto, which drove the Ottomans out of the Western Mediterranean, made things difficult for the Low Countries. Thus, the increasing pressure of the Spanish armies in the Low Countries was the beginning of the end for Antwerp. Things got even worse when the city joined the Dutch rebellion against Spain. Following the Spanish Fury in 1576, Spain occupied the town in 1585. Antwerp's economic activities slowed down, and it took a more modest place in history. Fleeing Antwerp, talented people, manufacturers, and merchants with a broader vision headed to Amsterdam.

However, Antwerp did not lose everything. The discovery of large quantities of rough diamonds in South Africa in 1866 was not difficult to absorb, as the city had already dominated the silver and copper trade for centuries. After the end of World War II, the vibrant Jewish community that had lived in the city for centuries dominated the diamond industry and made Antwerp the center of the world diamond trade. The mines of South Africa, Australia, Russia, and Canada ship diamonds directly to Antwerp.

An old text written in 1672 already describes Antwerp itself as a diamond in the following lines (Esser, 2014). "The Netherlands is the ring of the world, and Antwerp is the diamond on this ring." Today, diamonds symbolize love, wealth, and commitment, and adorn the fingers or dreams of millions of women. As expressed by the famous American actress Marilyn Monroe in the 1953 movie "Gentlemen Prefer Blondes," diamonds are a girl's best friend; they never lose shape and attractiveness.

Still, in the Diamond Quarter in the city center, skilled diamond artisans with international connections turn diamonds and other precious stones into expensive jewelry. Some 85% of the world's rough diamonds, 50% of polished diamonds, and 40% of industrial diamonds pass through the region. If Antwerp loses its chance to become a financial center, it may at least retain its glamorous jewelry stores, appeal to the ladies, and influence the diamond market for a long time.

References

Acemoglu, D., & Robinson, J. A. (2019). *The narrow corridor: How nations struggle for liberty.* Penguin UK.

Adrian, S. (2006). Burgundian/Habsburg mint policies and World bullion flows: A monetary interpretation of the rise and fall of Antwerp, 1400–1600. *The Hilltop Review, 2*(1), 3.

Afyoncu, E., Önal, A., & Demir, U. (2011). *Fransa'ya Osmanlı Tokadı.* Yeditepe Yayınevi.

Allen, L. (2004). *Global financial system 1750–2000.* Reaktion Books.

Brulez, W. (1959). *De Firma Della Faille En De Internationale Handel Van Vlaamse Firma's In De Zestiende Eeuw, Volume 35 of Klasse der Letteren.*

Buckley, H. (1924). Sir Thomas Gresham and the foreign exchanges. *The Economic Journal, 34*(136), 589–601.

d'Alòs-Moner, A. M. (2012). Conquistadores, mercenaries, and missionaries: The failed Portuguese dominion of the Red Sea. *Northeast African Studies, 12*(1), 1–28.

Drelichman, M., & Voth, H.-J. (2011). Lending to the borrower from hell: Debt and default in the age of Philip II. *The Economic Journal, 121*(557), 1205–1227. http://www.jstor.org/stable/41301355

Esser, R. (2014). The diamond of the Netherlands: Histories of Antwerp in the seventeenth century. *Netherlands Yearbook for History of Art/Nederlands Kunsthistorisch Jaarboek Online, 64*(1), 348–369.

Gelderblom, O. (2004). E. Wijnroks, Handel tussen Rusland en de Nederlanden 1560–1640. *TSEG—The Low Countries Journal of Social and Economic History, 1*(2), 156–157.

Gelderblom, O. (2010). *The golden age of the Dutch Republic. The invention of enterprise: Entrepreneurship from ancient Mesopotamia to modern times* (pp. 156–182). Princeton University Press.

Gelderblom, O. (2015). *Cities of commerce: The institutional foundations of international trade in the Low Countries, 1250–1650* (Vol. 45). Princeton University Press.

Holborn, H. (1982). *A history of modern Germany: The reformation* (p. 47). Princeton University Press. ISBN 978-0691007953. Retrieved 9 December 2021.

Hunt, E. S., & Murray, J. M. (1999). *A history of business in medieval Europe, 1200–1550.* Cambridge University Press.

Inalcık, H. (2008). *Devlet-i Aliyye* (Vol. 1). İş Bank Publication.

Karan, M. B. (2022). *Para Banka ve Finansın Sırları.* Scala Yayıncılık.

Karan, M. B., Westerman, W., & Wijngaard, J. (2024). *A history of banks.* Springer.

Kohn, M. (1999). *Bills of exchange and the money market to 1600* (Working Paper (99-04)). Department of Economics, Dartmouth College.

Limberger, M. (2021). 'The greatest marketplace in the world': The role of Antwerp in the economic and financial network of the Habsburg Empire. In *Les villes des Habsbourg du xve au xixe siècle: communication, art et pouvoir dans les réseaux urbains* (Vol. 2, pp. 45–62). Épure.

McCusker, J. J. (2005). The demise of distance: The business press and the origins of the information revolution in the early modern Atlantic world. *The American Historical Review, 110*(2), 295–321.

Mueller, R. C. (2019). *The Venetian money market: Banks, panics, and the public debt, 1200–1500.* JHU Press.

Munro, J. H. (1973). *Wool, cloth, and gold: The struggle for bullion in Anglo-Burgundian trade 1340–1478.* University of Toronto Press.

Munro, J. H. (1994). Patterns of trade, money, and credit. In *Handbook of European history 1400–1600: Late middle ages, renaissance and reformation* (pp. 147–195). Brill.

Nef, J. U. (1941). Industrial Europe at the time of the reformation (ca. 1515–ca. 1540). *Journal of Political Economy, 49*(1), 1–40.

Ogilvie, S. (2011). *Institutions and European trade: Merchant guilds, 1000–1800.* Cambridge University Press.

Parker, G. (1976). Why did the Dutch Revolt last eighty years? *Transactions of the Royal Historical Society, 26*, 53–72.

Poitras, G. (2009). The early history of option contracts. In *Vinzenz Bronzin's Option pricing models: Exposition and appraisal* (pp. 487–518). Springer.

Postan, M. M. (1973). *Medieval trade and finance*. Cambridge University Press.

Puttevils, J. (2012). *The ascent of merchants from the southern low countries: From Antwerp to Europe, 1480–1585* (Doctoral dissertation). University of Antwerp.

Puttevils, J., & Deloof, M. (2017). Marketing and pricing risk in marine insurance in sixteenth-century Antwerp. *The Journal of Economic History, 77*(3), 796–837.

Spain Defaults. (n.d.). https://www.uni-frankfurt.de/51529203/Case_Moot_2010-2011.pdf

Spufford, P. (2006). From Antwerp and Amsterdam to London: The decline of financial centres in Europe. *De Economist, 154*, 143–175.

Stephen, L., & Lee, S. (1890). *Dictionary of national biography* (Vol. 23). Smith, Elder & Co. https://archive.org/details/dictionaryofnati23stepuoft

Strieder, J. (2001). *Jacob Fugger the rich: Merchant and banker of Augsburg, 1459–1525*. Beard Books.

Tawney, R. (1925). 'Introduction' to *A discourse upon usury* by T. Wilson (1572); reprinted by London: Frank Cass (1962).

Toledo, P. (1995). İnebahtı: Dünya Egemenliği İçin Akdeniz'de Yapılan Son Deniz Savası. *Erdem, 6*(18), 861–876.

Van Roey, J. L. R., & Sankovitch, T. A. (n.d.). *Antwerp*. Encyclopedia Britannica, 8 June 2024. https://www.britannica.com/place/Antwerp-Belgium. Accessed 16 July 2024.

Willems, B. (2009). *Leven op de pof: krediet bij de Antwerpse middenstand in de achttiende eeuw* (Vol. 5). Amsterdam University Press.

Winjum, J. O. (1971). The Journal of Thomas Gresham. *The Accounting Review, 46*(1), 149–155.

Chapter 5
Amsterdam: The World's First Stock Exchange (17th Century)

5.1 Introduction

In 1555, when the Ottoman armies were sieging Vienna and taking Europe by storm, Ogier Gisleen van Busbeke (or in French, Ogier Ghiselin de Busbecq), a Dutchman, was sent to Istanbul as the envoy of Archduke Ferdinand of Austria (Fig. 5.1). His purpose was to represent the interests of the Habsburg State in a dispute over the control of Transylvania. He wrote about his appearance before Sultan Suleiman in his memoirs of the Ottoman Empire, "*Turkish Letters*": "*The Sultan was seated on a couch a foot above the floor, on which were spread many expensive embroidered covers and cushions. The hall was full of people. He had his bows and arrows with him. He sat smiling with a majestic sternness. A servant took our weapons. This practice had begun after a Croatian nobleman assassinated his grandfather, Sultan Murat. After pretending to kiss his hand, we walked back to the edge of the wall, not turning our backs to him. We listened to the reading of the message we had brought. The Archduke's message did not match the Sultan's expectations; it was honorable and full of information. So he did not respond except to say impatiently, Good, good, good. After that, we dispersed to our rooms*" (Clarendon, 1968).

As a result of this visit, Ogier Gisleen van Busbeke succeeded in concluding a six-month peace treaty between Austria and the Ottoman Empire. After returning to Vienna, Busbecq returned to Istanbul in 1556 as Ferdinand's permanent envoy, continued his mission until 1562, and left with vibrant memories. His work, which consists of four letters, contains valuable information and evaluations on all aspects of Ottoman socio-cultural life.

Ogier Gisleen van Busbeke was also interested in plants in Istanbul, and the tulip flower, unknown to Europeans in the sixteenth century, attracted his attention. He sent the bulbs of the tulip to his friend Charles de l'Ecluse, a professor of botany at Leiden University at the time. L'Ecluse developed the tulip and introduced it to the Dutch. The tulip attracted significant attention in the Netherlands and became a luxury plant for the gardens of the rich. It was considered a proof of bad taste

M. B. Karan, *A History of Stock Exchanges*, Contributions to Economics,
https://doi.org/10.1007/978-3-032-07788-2_5

Fig. 5.1 Ogier Ghiselin de Busbecq, a Dutch diplomat https://commons.wikimedia.org/wiki/File:Oghier_Busbeck_SIL14-B9-13a.jpg

for any man of wealth not to have a collection of tulips. The increased demand for the accidentally obtained mutated tulips, called "*Broken bulbs*," led to a vibrant and booming tulip market (Hayes, 2022).

In the first three decades of the seventeenth century, the passion for owning tulip bulbs was so great among the Dutch that even the lowest commoners began trading tulips. A single tulip bulb could be worth 4,000 or 5,500 florins (Dutch guilder). In a book published in 1841, Charles Mackay wrote: "*The price of 4 tons of beer is 32 florins. This is about 1,008 gallons of beer or 65 barrels of beer. A keg of Coors Light costs about $120, so 4 tons of beer is $7,800, and 1 florin is $244. This means that today's best tulips cost more than 1 million dollars. Nevertheless, many tulip bulbs are traded in the range of $50,000 to $150,000.*" By the 1630 s, the tulip trade had infected all sectors of Dutch society. Mackay claimed that "*from the richest merchants to the poorest, chimney sweeps jumped into the tulip market, buying bulbs at high prices and selling them at even higher prices.*" By 1636, the demand for the tulip trade was so great that regular markets for tulip sales were set up on the Amsterdam Stock Exchange in Rotterdam, Haarlem, and other cities (Fridson, 1995).

Investors thought the price could increase, and the passion for tulips would last forever. The tulip trade also extended to derivatives. They could already buy and sell tulip bulbs at a set price for future delivery. By 1637, buyers who had bid extremely high prices went bankrupt, selling the bulbs at low prices as prices fell. Confidence in the market had disappeared entirely. Investors lost a lot of money, and the Dutch economy was affected. Although this event, known as Tulip mania, is the first event that comes to mind when we think of the Amsterdam Stock Exchange today, the Amsterdam Stock Exchange was the first securities market where stocks of companies were traded publicly. The methods and strategies applied here inspired all the stock exchanges that followed.

During this period, the Low Countries experienced long, bloody wars and religious conflicts while new financial institutions emerged and economic development boomed. The first stock exchange in history, public companies, and the Bank of Amsterdam were established.

5.2 Historical and Economic Background

Sometime later in the sixteenth century, the territory of the Spanish Empire included Spain, Central Germany, Southern Italy, some French regions, and the Low Countries. When Charles V divided the empire in 1556 while still alive, his son Philip II inherited the Netherlands and Spain, while his brother, Archduke Ferdinand, became Holy Roman Emperor. Charles V died in 1558 (Karan, 2022).

During this period, the rulers of the 17 provinces of the Low Countries under Habsburg rule were not the nobility that other European countries recognized but a bourgeois class that had become rich from commercial activities, and assemblies governed these provinces with a moderate democracy composed of the wealthy urban population. In 1568, seventeen provinces united to rebel against Spanish rule, thus beginning the 80 Years' War. The Spanish also occupied Antwerp in 1585, changed the history of the city of Amsterdam, and increased its importance. The Dutch War of Independence lasted from 1568 to 1648 and lasted for a long time, and the country was divided into two, the Netherlands and Belgium. The war was relatively static, with few pitched battles where armies met on the field (Karan, 2022).

The Low Countries, with essential trading centers like Bruges and Antwerp, had already long been highly developed and prosperous through trade. Due to the war, from 1585 to 1620 onward, the (northern) Dutch introduced many innovations to establish a regular tax system, to increase their savings rapidly, and to ensure that their resources were successfully invested in the new financial instruments. These financial instruments included government debt securities issued by Dutch governments on a national, provincial, and municipal basis, acceptance loans and policies, maritime and other insurance investment instruments, and shares and derivatives of publicly traded companies such as the East and West India Company. The Netherlands owed its economic success in the Golden Period of 1581–1672 to the fact that, unlike the previous Italian and other European states, it was not limited to accessing markets but directly controlled raw material resources and markets with its naval fleets (Taylor, 2013). Until around the mid-1700s, the Dutch Republic's economic and financial system was the most advanced and best seen, and between 1600 and 1720, the Dutch had the highest per capita income in the world (Kaletsky, 2010). Behind this success was an innovative institutional structure based on the Bank of Amsterdam, the East and West India Companies, and the Amsterdam Stock Exchange (Karan et al., 2024).

Initially, Amsterdam was hard hit by Spanish oppression. During the Iconism of 1566, many Amsterdam merchants openly defended their Calvinist beliefs. When the Duke of Alba, acting on behalf of Spain, arrived in the Low Countries in 1567 to punish Protestants and restore order, dozens of merchants left Amsterdam to continue their business from the port of Emden and other ports in northern Germany (Pettegree, 1992). The city's commercial situation worsened in 1572 when the Catholic city council remained loyal to the Habsburg king and supported Spanish troops besieging Haarlem. In retaliation, a rebel Dutch organization called the Sea Beggars sank ships. It blocked the entrance to the Zuiderzee (now called Ijsselmeer because it no longer has direct access to the sea, in Dutch zee), an inland sea at the entrance to the harbor, to prevent boats from entering the port of Amsterdam. As Amsterdam could not participate in international shipping and trade for some time, many merchants decided to continue. Their business is elsewhere. However, a rebellion led by Prince William of Orange in February 1578 changed everything. In May 1578, Protestant rebels took over the city council and forced the Catholic rulers to leave, and the situation began to improve. Soon, most exiled merchants returned, and surprisingly, the city regained its leading role in merchant shipping and the Baltic. Trade. Although Amsterdam was not yet the commercial center it would become in later years, it proved a viable alternative for merchants leaving the Southern Netherlands (Gelderblom, 2003).

In the 1580 s, Amsterdam's appeal was based on textiles, transportation, and commodities. It was also a growing domestic market for foodstuffs. By 1590, Antwerp merchants accounted for at least a third of all merchants operating in the Dutch port. The supply of colonial goods was in the hands of Portuguese merchants in Antwerp and Hamburg (Gelderblom, 2003). The Dutch connections to the Far Eastern Market were already established before 1580, thanks to Portuguese sailors. Lisbon became a spice center, and the Dutch bought spices and Far Eastern goods. However, in 1580, after the mighty Spain conquered Portugal and united with it, the rebels provoked a trade embargo on the Netherlands, and the Dutch were motivated to enter the Far East trade directly (Fig. 5.2).

1589, when Philip II lifted the general embargo on trade between the Low Countries and the Iberian Peninsula, the Netherlands' international trade ties were reestablished. After 1590, merchants of the Dutch Republic had direct access to markets in Africa, America, and Asia. Between 1590 and 1609, the number of active merchants from the South Dutch territories increased to over 450. By 1609, the face of Amsterdam's merchant community had changed dramatically. Mass immigration would reduce the share of local merchants to around 40 percent (Gelderblom, 2003).

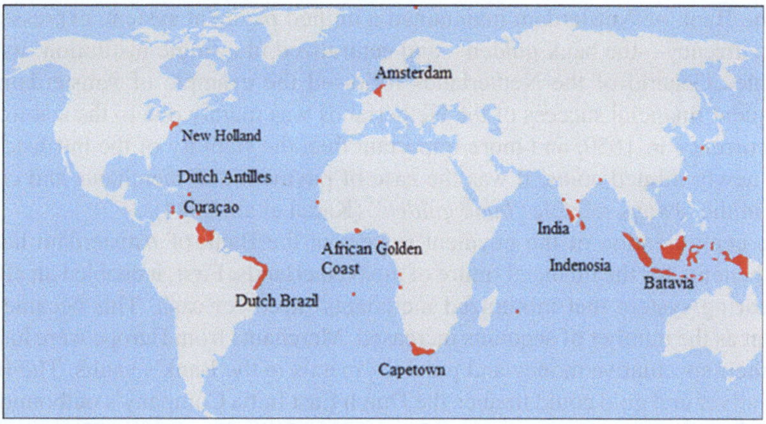

Fig. 5.2 Colonies and bases of the Dutch Republic (1650) https://en.wikipedia.org/wiki/File:Dutch-Empire-coloured.png (Public Domain)

Amsterdam's economic advantage was its role as an international storage center and its ability to link several regional economies. In addition, the city's communication and information-gathering capability was remarkable. Although earlier commercial centers, such as Venice, had similar characteristics, none achieved the reputation of seventeenth-century Amsterdam as a source of information. Amsterdam emerged as an information center after becoming a commercial center. The structure of computing in Amsterdam and its pioneering role in the modernization of capitalism led to the development of information exchange in Europe (Smith, 1984). At the beginning of the eighteenth century, Western European ports were connected by a transportation system of sailing ships, so-called packet ships. Couriers operated between major cities and ports. The ships carried newspapers, bringing news on everything from security prices to political and economic news and market conditions (Koudijs, 2015).

During Portugal's union with Spain (1580–1640), Dutch merchants expanded their trade to Asia, Africa, the Caribbean, and northern Brazil (Israel, 1989). However, the protracted war had taken its toll on their economy, and before the seventeenth century had even begun, the provinces together sought various solutions. The 14 mints in the Netherlands adopted a standard policy (Neal, 2000). Merchants from abroad also brought in large quantities of foreign coins. By 1610, it is estimated that the goldsmiths in Amsterdam had to keep track of around 1,000 different gold and silver coins (Carlos & Neal, 2011). They solved this problem with a clever app. Founded in 1609, the Amsterdamsche Wisselbank provided monetary stability. With the so-called bank money, merchants opened an account with their metal coins, and payments between merchants were made from account to account. The gold and silver deposited by the public were assayed and held against bank money. If the merchant wanted his gold, it was returned. Thus, coins with very different units and contents were standardized, and confusion about payment was eliminated. In this way, the Bank of Amsterdam maintained a unified payment system, expressed in a single currency—the bank gulden—and centralized in a single institution. In 1659, the States General of the Netherlands followed the example of Amsterdam. The subsequent financial success of the Netherlands was mainly due to the stabilization of its currency in 1659, and more important than the stability of the intrinsic value of the newly minted coins, it was the ease of payment that merchants and citizens found in the always reliable "*bank gulden*" (Karan et al., 2024).

The centralization of the payment system in the Bank of Amsterdam had two major benefits for the financial future of the Netherlands. First, it enabled an efficient net clearing system that minimized merchants' need for cash. This became more efficient as the number of accounts increased. Merchants from Europe were happy to leave their speculative money and precious metals in the Bank's vaults. The Bank's pile of silver and gold could finance the Dutch East India Company's outbound ships and the British, French, Austrian, and Danish East India Companies. The presence of real trade coins in the vaults of the Bank of Amsterdam meant that bills of exchange drawn in Amsterdam were both reliable and quick to pay. The second benefit was that the city became a financial center for Europe. The Dutch were thus able to take advantage of the benefits of a fixed exchange rate for international trade and financing, and they encouraged their own merchants as well as foreign merchants to use their financing facilities for long-distance trade and long-term funding, while at the same time enjoying the shock-absorbing benefits of a flexible exchange rate in times of crisis (Neal, 2000).

5.3 Formation of the Securities Market and Publicly Traded Companies

As part of other low countries, Amsterdam has similar inclusive institutions such as legal systems, litigation, and dispute resolution. One of the most innovative features of Amsterdam's legal system was its advanced notarial system. Notaries were critical in drafting and authenticating contracts, bills of exchange, and other commercial documents. These records were legally binding and provided a reliable basis for resolving disputes in court if necessary. This system offered merchants high security, essential for fostering trust in a rapidly expanding global trade network.

Dutch trade in the Far East was beginning to create a favorable environment for the formation of public companies. The Dutch had long since started to corporatize by pooling their capital and reducing the risk of commercial ventures with distant territories; they added clauses to existing partnership agreements that clearly defined the partners' purpose, duration, capital invested, and individual duties. The joint and several liability of the partners was strongly defined. Unique-purpose partnerships were usually designed for a short period, for example, for a specific operation or a shipping season, but could last several years if the partners wished. The shareholders, however, could continue and create a continuous enterprise in practice, if not in law. Between 1595 and 1601, at least seven cities sent voyages to Asia, totaling 65 ships. The fact that these voyages, called "*voorcompagnieën*" in Dutch, had at least a straightforward board governing the venture indicates the development of the unique purpose partnership (Gelderblom et al., 2013). In these boards, several merchants organized and managed the enterprise, each with a specific task, for which they received money or a percentage of the goods as remuneration (De Jong et al., 2013).

Two features of the Dutch commercial environment stood out. First, from the beginning of the Dutch Golden Age until the mid-nineteenth century, substantial sums of money could easily be raised without institutions such as large banking firms or specialized stock exchanges to structure the issuance and trading of financial instruments. Second, the legal framework is highly flexible, adapting to new business needs. Both characteristics stemmed from the peculiar conditions that shaped Dutch trade and finance. Markets were open to anyone and anything; anyone with something to sell or buy, goods, services, money, or securities could come and do business with anyone (Jonker & Sluyterman, 2001). The wealth accumulated during the Dutch Golden Age was widely dispersed, making it a period of economic opportunity for a large audience, ready to invest even modest sums in financial instruments ranging from shipping stocks to government bonds or more complex investment products such as mutual funds (De Jong et al., 2013).

Eventually, two large companies were formed. The East India Dutch Company (VOC) was the market's most important. Although the West India Dutch Company (WIC) was also traded on the market, it was never as crucial as the VOC and was never subject to intense stock trading. Apart from these two securities, many countries borrowed money from the Amsterdam Stock Exchange. With trade growth in the early eighteenth century, the shares of the British East India Company, the South Sea Company, and the Bank of England began to be traded on the Amsterdam Stock Exchange soon after their launch in London.

5.3.1 East India Company

In 1602, to prevent the fierce competition between Dutch companies that had entered the spice trade in the East Indies and caused spice prices to rise in Europe, the companies were merged by government decree into the United Dutch East India Company or Vereenigde Oost-Indische Compagnie (VOC). The VOC was granted a monopoly on all maritime trade with Asia via the Cape of Good Hope and the Strait of Magellan (Ota, 2021). It was a corporate company, with many companies formed to have an integrated organization under the VOC umbrella (Grenville, 2021). They were involved in shipbuilding, producing, and trading Asian spices, Indonesian coffee, and other goods. VOC was the first international and first publicly traded company in history. It issued bonds and shares to the public on the Amsterdam Stock Exchange (Stringham & Curott, 2015). With its corporate innovations and business practices, the company set an example for today's global corporations and capital markets (Steensgaard, 1982). In 1657, the British took the VOC as an example when establishing their East India Company (EIC) (Ferguson, 2002). The VOC was, in fact, more than a company; it was a kind of corporate state with military power. The Company acted like a state, negotiating treaties, issuing its currency, and establishing colonies (Ames, 2008). In 1619, the Company chose Batavia, now known as Jakarta, Indonesia, as its headquarters. The VOC had the upper hand over all its Western European rivals with its diplomatic solid, naval, and military power. Even the later British East India Company (EIC) operated as a client of the VOC for several decades. By 1647, the VOC had destroyed its Genoese rival (Bruijn & Gaastra, 1993).

At the peak of its existence, VOC had thirty-six thousand employees from different continents and origins. Although most of its shareholders were Dutch, about a quarter of them were investors from the region that today includes Germany, Belgium, and Luxembourg (De Vries & Van der Woude, 1997). VOC had two types of shareholders, as with Dutch companies at that time. Many did not have voting rights; around 60–70 investors had a say in the general management. One of the most critical aspects of the VOC was that its liability was limited to the paid-up capital. Therefore, the VOC was only liable for the capital invested, and investors wishing to sell their shares could only do so by transferring them to others on the Amsterdam Stock Exchange. After the 1730s, the company went through difficult times due to corruption, mismanagement, and unfavorable economic and business conditions, and ceased operations at the end of the century (Karan, 2022).

5.3.2 West India Company

The Dutch began trading with the west coast of the Atlantic in the late 1620 s to exploit commercial opportunities and undermine the interests of Spain and Portugal. In this context, the Dutch West India Company, or Geoctrooieerde Westindische Compagnie (GWC), was founded on June 3, 1621. According to its charter, the GWC monopolized shipping and trade in territories covering South Africa, America, the Cape of Good Hope, and the Pacific islands. It was authorized to establish colonies, sign treaties with local rulers, build forts, and wage war if necessary (Dutch West India Company, 2021).

The GWC, a publicly listed company, had a federal structure with five city chambers—Amsterdam, Zeeland, Rotterdam, West-Friesland, and Groningen. Each chamber had its directors, while a central board, Heeren XIX, set company policy and met twice or thrice a year. The GWC's primary goal was to build a commercial network in the Atlantic and defend its colonies. In 1623, the Central Board of Directors devised a "*grand design*" to undermine Spanish and Portuguese interests by planning attacks on enemy ships and building vessels suited for naval warfare (Dutch West India Company, 2021).

The company occupied northern Brazil between 1630 and 1654 and, noticing a demand for enslaved people in Brazil, turned to Angola. From 1637 to 1642, it captured Portuguese forts on the African Gold Coast and, between 1623 and 1674, shipped over 320,000 oz of gold and large quantities of ivory, wax, and tropical products to the Dutch Republic (Dutch West India Company, 2021). The GWC traded close to half a million enslaved Africans (Dutch Slavery Trade, n.d.). However, colonial wars drained its resources, and its financial situation deteriorated. Efforts to reform the company failed, leading to its dissolution in 1674 (Karan, 2022).

Ultimately, the GWC was less successful in the Atlantic than the VOC. Most Dutch ventures in the New World failed to establish colonies, mines, or plantations to produce goods for European markets. Lacking the ability to mobilize armed forces, control labor, or build social capital, Dutch investors could not scale their operations effectively. The GWC struggled to secure private capital, state support, and practical strategies, leading to its limited success and eventual collapse (Emmer, 1998; Goslinga, 2018).

5.4 Securities Trading in the Netherlands

In the seventeenth century, the Amsterdam Stock Exchange became the world's first proper stock exchange, mainly providing the three essential functions of modern securities markets: price discovery, liquidity provision, and easy access to market information. Amsterdam was not the only city in the seventeenth-century Dutch Republic where a secondary market for corporate shares had developed. The VOC's organizational structure of six semi-independent chambers led to six separate markets. Apart from Amsterdam were the chambers of Middelburg, Enkhuizen, Hoorn, Delft, and Rotterdam. Batavia was the seventh chamber. However, these peripheral markets developed differently due to their smaller capital stocks. In contrast, it was only in Amsterdam that the transition to a thriving securities market offering financial services to its participants occurred. The historical record of the VOC is excellent. Because each letter from Batavia was sent separately to all the other chambers, six copies of each letter provide sufficient evidence even if some archives are damaged. The States General of the Dutch Republic granted the VOC its charter in March 1602. The company's registers were to be open for sub-registrations in six different cities from April 1 to August 31. The chambers were independent in that each had its management and equipped its ships, which sailed in combined fleets (i.e., with the vessels of the other chambers) to the East Indies and back to the chamber that financed them. Thus, each chamber received its cargo and then organized its auction for the imported goods. However, the revenues of all the chambers were added together and then allocated back to the chambers according to their share of the total (Gelderblom & Jonker, 2004).

This somewhat complex company structure influenced the organization of the secondary market for VOC shares. Investors committed their capital to one of the chambers and received a share. Although these shares were essentially equal, they could not be traded. For example, a share in the Delft chamber was not transferable in the Amsterdam chamber's books. However, they could be transferred among themselves. Thus, there were six different company shares. Having agreed on a share transfer, the investors went to the headquarters of the East India Company. They asked their accountant to officially transfer the shares from the seller's account to the buyer's account in the company's capital books. The accountants would only carry out this transfer after the approval of two directors (Gelderblom & Jonker, 2004). Transfer and ledger books were kept in the company's six rooms. The transfer books were available four or five days a week, and the book entries of both the seller and the buyer, the amount of stock transferred, and the names of two witnesses and the clerk were recorded (Neal, 1990). A minimal transfer fee was charged per share. Dissatisfaction with the speed of transfers meant that much of the trading in VOC shares was done based on forward contracts. These were settled on regular rescontre (settlement day) dates set every three months. Repeatedly traded shares did not need to be formally transferred each time, so stockbrokers tracked their transactions with each other by establishing settlement days when all bargains could be adjusted or continued until the following agreement (Stringham, 2003). Before 1650, settlement procedures were less formal. An essential feature of the rescontre was the concentration of liquidity, which allowed, for example, more accessible settlements (Poitras, 2009). According to the 1602 concession rules, the last subscription installment indicating partnership was due in 1606. Market players started trading immediately after the subscription books closed. Thus, until then, investors were selling the right to invest rather than actual shares (Gelderblom & Jonker, 2004).

Trading VOC shares looked different from today's share trading. There was no standardized value for a "VOC share," so stock traders always had to indicate the nominal value of the share they were trading. Therefore, the market value of the shares was expressed as a percentage of the nominal value. Moreover, bearer shares of the VOC did not exist. The only proof that an investor owned share was a positive balance in an account in their name in VOC's capital books (Gelderblom & Jonker, 2004).

Initially, there was no stock exchange building where stocks were traded. Therefore, although the East India Company was one of the leading destinations for stock traders in the city, traders gathered at a few points in Amsterdam to trade. In the medieval period, exchanges occurred on the Warmoesstraat, the city's main street. However, this became problematic as economic activity increased, as traders blocked the street and shop entrances. The Nieuwe Brug, the bridge crossing the Damrak right next to the harbor of Amsterdam, was used for commercial transactions. These were where commodity traders gathered; the same traders also dominated the financial securities trade. Ships from overseas delivered international correspondence at Paelhuysgen, a small building on the west side of the bridge. Merchants on the bridge were thus quickly informed about the latest commercial information.

As trade in Amsterdam grew, the Nieuwe Brug was insufficient. In 1607, he ordered the construction of a stock exchange modeled on the Antwerp Stock Exchange. Each commodity traded on the exchange had a designated place next to one of the pillars holding up the roof of the passage. Trading in financial securities occurred near one of the pillars at the back of the Exchange. Five days before the opening of the Exchange, on July 26, the magistrate issued an ordinance on trade in the city. Trading was to occur exclusively at the stock exchange from 11 a.m. to noon

Fig. 5.3 Historic Amsterdam stock exchange building https://commons.wikimedia.org/wiki/File:Old_Bourse_of_Amsterdam.jpg (Clarity improved with deepimage, AI))

every day, except Sundays, and from 6.30 to 7.30 p.m. during the summer months (May–August) (Fig. 5.3). The city administration probably thought that concentrating trade in one place with limited opening hours could increase market liquidity. In 1613, the magistrate and the city administration further tightened regulations in 1619; brokers were no longer allowed to linger around the exchange or on the Dam Square in the city's center after market hours. Notaries specializing in commercial and financial transactions also moved their offices to the Dam Square area (Van Dillen, 1929).

5.4.1 Development of Derivative Transactions

The Amsterdam Stock Exchange was the first place where derivatives trading was systematized. In addition to forwards, there were options, repos, short selling, etc. As early as 1609, forward trading in VOC shares had appeared. The following year, the States General banned short selling and all other option derivative transactions. This ban would be repeated many times in the following years. However, speculation in the prices of VOC and other joint-stock company shares was illegal (Stringham, 2003). Published in 1688 as a primary source by the stockbroker and author Joseph Penso De la Vega, "*Confusion de Confusiones*" provides an exciting account of a highly developed financial market. De la Vega describes trading in stocks in the East and West India Companies and notes that short sales, futures contracts, option contracts, and other transactions existed. However, most were officially prohibited since they began appearing in that century (De la Vega, 1996). The Amsterdam Stock Exchange was initially not a formal exchange with defined rules. Therefore, futures should be defined as forwards and not futures. Chapter Three explains that futures on grain, pepper, and various food products have already been traded on the Antwerp exchange.

However, in the seventeenth century, the Amsterdam Stock Exchange created surprisingly sophisticated trading instruments when the state courts were unfamiliar with and unable to deal with derivative transactions, which today are considered everyday financial transactions. Many of the transactions that took place were prohibited by law, but the law was ineffective and not strictly enforced. However, the relative freedom of the market allowed traders to experiment and develop new trading instruments, even if they were officially prohibited. Government directives did not drive the development of instruments on the Amsterdam Stock Exchange, but rather the self-interest of traders who found engaging in new financial transactions profitable. Contrary to the view that financial markets are subject to government rules and regulations, the historical record shows that contracts are self-enforcing and market participants are self-monitoring. Without a legal system on which to rely, the Amsterdam stockbrokers conducted trade solely on the discipline of continuous agreement and reputation (Stringham, 2003).

5.4.2 Forward Contracts

Forward contracts appeared frequently in the Amsterdam notaries' records in 1607. Grain traders, mainly from Antwerp, often used forward contracts in the Amsterdam grain market from the mid-sixteenth century onward, and the market became familiar with these instruments (Van Tielhof, 1995). In the second half of the seventeenth century, the futures market became the most critical part of the VOC stock market. While it was initially obligatory to register their transactions with notaries, this requirement was lifted in the late seventeenth century. These court decisions paved the way for developing a market with meager transaction costs. When large amounts of money were lost in stock futures trading, and the problem of counterfeiting these contracts arose, the system was reorganized. Accordingly, once investors had agreed on all the contract details, they would fill in a standard printed form. Two standard forward contracts were printed on a single sheet of paper, and three fancy letters (A, B, and C) distinguished the two contracts. After the traders had filled out the contracts, they would cut out the letters and separate the forms, and each received a signed copy. When they completed their contracts, either through the transfer of shares and money to be paid or the payment of the price difference, if the letters did not match precisely when combined, the traders knew that one of the parties had cheated (Petram, 2011).

Here, however, a danger emerged. Some bankers could use forward transactions for usury. They would disguise their high-interest loans in a forged forward contract. Usury was prohibited in the Dutch Republic; moneylenders were allowed to charge 6% interest to ordinary people and 8% to traders, merchants, and shopkeepers. Some forwards were well above the usury limit. However, neither the courts nor merchants ever invoked usury regulations to invalidate a transaction (Gelderblom & Jonker, 2005).

In forward contracts, counterparty risk arises when the counterparty fails to fulfill its obligations. As we explained earlier, forward contract holders could agree to deliver a future commodity at a specific price without making an initial investment payment. Therefore, if there were excessive movements in stock prices during the contract term, the buyer or seller could withdraw from the contract instead of continuing to honor the contract. In this case, when making a contract, it was necessary to choose people whose financial status was sufficient and known, which caused the market to be limited to wealthy traders. If a trader decides to renounce the contract, the other party could sue to force the other party to honor the contract. However, this was a very costly procedure, and traders generally tried to avoid going to court. As a result of these features of the forward market, forward traders traded contracts only with well-known traders with high reputations. It would take until the second half of the century for the forward market to become accessible to lower-status participants (Barbour, 1950).

From around 1660 onward, the forward market saw a significant development with the emergence of trading clubs. These clubs provided a platform where traders could meet regularly to trade derivatives. Among the participants of these clubs, in addition to a reputation based on the trader's wealth or past reputation for many successful trades, they began to gravitate toward members of the same congregation, religion, or social group. This social aspect of trading added an interesting dimension to the market dynamics. For instance, Amsterdam stock market traders favored members of the same ethnic community, considering them to be more reputable (Stringham, 2003).

5.4.3 *Options*

Shortly after establishing the VOC, they started trading derivative instruments such as options. The underlying assets of such transactions were VOC shares. In this type of investment, the investor immediately invests a specific value of 10–20% of the total investment as a premium. In the event of favorable price changes, the gain is credited to his account. If future price expectations are unfavorable and a loss occurs, this is deducted from the initial investment expenditure, and, if necessary, an additional payment is made. For this reason, such investments are considered to be extremely risky (Stringham, 2003).

On the other hand, options allowed traders to manage the risk of their portfolios against price changes or to speculate on price changes at low cost. Option contract holders had the right to buy or sell a commodity. If they did not exercise this right, they lost their premium. If a trader entered into an option contract based on a commodity he already owned, he could protect himself against market risks. However, option contracts to sell VOC shares that they did not own were risky. To close their position, you had to buy this stock, which had reached an extreme price, from the market and give it to the other side to close your position. When used correctly, options are the most suitable derivative instruments for risk-taking and risk-reduction purposes. However, the stock traders of the early seventeenth century were not yet interested in these issues; in fact, option contracts at that time were, as Wilson (1941) put it, "*a gambler's business*." In contrast, forwards and repos were less risky derivatives for investors who wanted to participate in the East India trade and be entitled to dividends without tying up large sums of money in a stock. These derivatives were, therefore, already widely used in the first decades of the century (Petram, 2011). In Amsterdam, however, option contracts had an ambiguous legal status. Regulations only added to the confusion, as it was unclear how they would be applied. De la Vega (1996) wrote that experts' opinions differed widely on whether stock exchange regulations should apply to option contracts.

5.4.4 Repos

Another instrument used in the Amsterdam market was what we know today as a repurchase agreement. Repo is a borrowing transaction that refers to the sale of a security on a specific date with the promise to repurchase it at a specific rate. In this transaction, the borrower sells a security to the counterparty as collateral and is obliged to buy this security at a higher price (principal + interest) at maturity. The security subject to the transaction is collateral given for the money lent. The main advantage of repo over forwards is that the lender receives security collateral for the loan to the borrower. This significantly reduced counterparty risk because the lender could sell the collateral in the event of default and thus reduce its losses. Repos became accessible to a broader group of traders in the late 1610 s. However, they were unsuitable for speculative trading by stock traders, as a single repo involved the transfer of several shares and money, and thus higher transaction (trading) costs (Petram, 2011).

5.4.5 Short Selling

In Amsterdam, they allowed traders to short-sell shares. Short selling is a speculative transaction often practiced in today's stock markets. The market player could borrow and sell the VOC stock from someone else. If, as expected, the price fell, he could buy it from someone else at a lower price and return it to the borrower to repay the debt. Of course, if the price of the VOC stock rose, he would lose money. For example, when a forward short sale matured, there were two possibilities: either the spekülators would opt for money settlement, in which case they would be paid the difference in price between the forward price stipulated in the contract and the stock market price on the maturity date, or they would have to deliver the stock. In this case, the seller had to own or buy a share to transfer it to the buyer (Petram, 2011).

If the stock is expected to fall, it will allow the investor to make a profit on the fall in the price. In this case, the share price will be priced more efficiently. However, according to the historical documents of the Amsterdam stock market in 1609, short selling became a preferred trading method by traders who deliberately tried to lower the price. This forced the directors of the Amsterdam chamber to send a petition to the Dutch Provinces requesting a ban on short selling of VOC shares. The provinces would eventually accept this request (Murphy, 2009). In 1610, a decision was taken to prohibit trading in securities that were not owned. In addition, forward transactions were allowed for those who owned the stock. As crises arose, the short-selling ban was extended in 1621, 1630, and 1636.

5.4.6 Stock Market Manipulation

In 1621, the directors of the VOC petitioned the Dutch State, alleging that a group of stock traders had conspired to sell many forward contracts. They allegedly sold far more than the value of the shares recorded in the company's accounts in the capital books. When the agreed delivery date approached, the sellers began spreading nasty rumors about the company, driving down the share price. Later, this group sold a small number of shares at an even lower price, thus reinforcing the downward movement of the share price. The managers suspected that this action would damage the VOC and, thus, the intervention of the British East India Company, which was trying to weaken the Dutch company and, therefore, the Dutch Republic, which was fighting for independence (Murphy, 2009). However, behind the short-selling story was an attractive Dutch investor, Isaac Le Maire. In the Company and Investor Relations section, we will tell this story in detail later.

5.5 Dividend Policy of the East India Company

On the Amsterdam Stock Exchange, the way dividend distributions were to be made in forward contracts initially caused several controversies. Due to inexperience in stock futures trading, many futures contracts did not specify whether the dividend would be collected from the buyer or the seller. The fact that VOC's initial dividend distributions were commoditized further complicated matters and led to disputes between futures buyers and sellers on how the dividend should be valued (Petram, 2011).

Shareholders received their first dividend in April 1610, a payment made in spices. The spice mace they received was worth 75% of the nominal capital. In November of the same year, a 50% pepper dividend was paid to the shareholders, with 7.5% cash. This payment was exclusive to shareholders who had invested in spices. The following March, a 30% coconut dividend was to be distributed. Shareholders who received all dividends in commodities were to receive a total of 162.5% of the nominal value of their shares. However, the market value of spices was significantly lower, leading to a dispute. The sudden influx of spices in the market had driven prices down, leaving the average investor unsure of what to do with the spices. It was also unclear whether the company had enough spices in its warehouses to provide dividends to all shareholders (Petram, 2011).

Shareholders were now buying and selling shares of every conceivable value and with widely differing rights to dividends, leading to complex pricing negotiations. The VOC then decided in 1612 to distribute dividends in cash. Thus, after 1618, all shareholders received a 162.5% dividend on their shares.

5.6 Relationship Between the East India Company and Shareholders

Isaac Le Maire, the investor behind the aforementioned short-selling story, was originally from Belgium, one of the founders of the VOC in 1602, and served on its Board of Directors until February 22, 1605. However, Le Maire was implicated in fraud and faced allegations of embezzlement of VOC funds. Therefore, he was forced to resign from his position and was required to sign an agreement stating that he would not be involved in any company that traded between the Netherlands and the Cape of Good Hope or beyond the Strait of Magellan. These events caused Le Maire great bitterness and a desire for revenge. First, he approached the King of France to set up a rival company, and when that failed, Le Maire targeted the management of the VOC as an outsider. First, in 1609, Le Maire wrote a letter to Johan van Oldenbarnevelt, the director of the VOC and one of the most powerful men in the Dutch Republic, outlining his concerns about the VOC, including its management structure and governance. In particular, the Belgian merchant expressed concern that the VOC's Board of Directors was entirely composed of company employees and that shareholders had no say in how the company was run. Isaac Le Maire, who wanted transparency in governance, even threatened that a new company could replace the VOC if these changes were not implemented (Gelderblom et al., 2010).

This letter to Isaac Le Maire is history's first example of shareholder activism (Petram, 2011). Le Maire had three main criticisms (Van Dillen et al., 2006).

1. The company's increasing debt levels had reduced shareholders' profits to the point that dividends could not be paid.
2. The Board of Directors was not open to receiving advice or listening to investor demands and complaints.
3. The directors were "*enriching themselves at the expense of shareholders by trying to get the obligation to publish the accounts [financial statements] waived.*"

Le Maire was right to suggest that the management mistreated the VOC's shareholders. In 1610, the VOC board persuaded the authorities to waive the obligation to publish financial statements in April 1612. It was not in management's interest to provide information to shareholders. The board was concerned about the company's prospects and feared that "*disclosure would lead to a rapid withdrawal of capital.*"

Le Maire's demands were met with resistance by the VOC. The company's executives saw no need to give up their interests and change their business model. This refusal set the stage for history's first bear raid and short-selling campaign. In 1609, Le Maire founded the Groote Compagnie (the Great Company) in France because it was forbidden in the Netherlands to compete with the VOC. This company was an investors' syndicate focused entirely on overthrowing the VOC. Le Maire hoped investors would demand their money back in 1612 if VOC share prices fell below par value. This would necessitate the liquidation of the VOC and allow Le Maire to set up new trading companies. Le Maire and his friends put VOC shares up for sale for future delivery. This was a short sale, and the shares in question were shares they did not own. This action put downward pressure on VOC's share price. Isaac Le Maire had thus started short selling the most powerful company in the world at the time, and started the first bear market pressure. Le Maire and his syndicate also spread lousy news and false rumors about the company. For example, they spread rumors that VOC ships were sinking on their voyage home from the East Indies, driving down VOC share prices (Van Dillen et al., 2006).

Groote Compagnie's bear pressure was initially successful. VOC share prices fell from a high premium of 212% in 1607 to a low of 126% in 1609. VOC did not take long to identify who was behind this short-selling campaign and took counter moves. First, VOC paid its shareholders a long-overdue dividend. To appease shareholders and counter Le Maire's short selling, the company paid its first dividend, albeit in commodities, in 1610. The inadequacy of the dividends paid by the VOC was a significant criticism of Le Maire and other shareholders. Second, he petitioned government authorities to ban short sales. VOC executives argued that Le Maire's short-selling campaign was a "*dirty scheme*" that damaged the company's ability to compete with Dutch rivals. The VOC also sought to influence public opinion by emphasizing how Le Maire's bear raid negatively affected innocent investors in its shares, especially "*widows and orphans*"(Van Dillen et al., 2006).

The VOC's efforts paid off, and on February 27, 1610, the Dutch authorities announced an official ban on the sale of unclaimed shares. As expected, this government ban devastated Le Maire and his gang of short-selling speculators. By 1611, Isaac Le Maire was on the run from creditors and government authorities. Most of Le Maire's colleagues in the Groote Compagnie were unlucky, and several members were driven into bankruptcy by the failed bear raid. Nevertheless, Le Maire did not abandon his actions after fleeing from Amsterdam.

The relationship between the company and its shareholders was again debated in 1622 because the VOC contract ended that year. The shareholders expected the company's balance sheet to be published and to be informed about the company's financial situation. The VOC had not published a financial report from the beginning. However, the directors did not want to be held accountable and had other plans: they asked the General States to extend its charter for another fifty years. If the General Provinces granted this request, existing shareholders would receive no official information about the company in which they were shareholders for the rest of their lives. In response, the shareholders issued a series of declarations against continuing the privilege. The shareholders accused them of enriching themselves at the expense of the shareholders by chartering more ships than necessary and thus making an additional profit. Moreover, the shareholders suspected that the company directors were trying to profit by manipulating share prices. In 1623, shareholders wrote letters outlining their criticism of the VOC management. Known as the "*Dissenting Participants*," this group's complaints against the VOC directors were harsh (Petram, 2011):

> Dissident participants [shareholders] are not slaves, but free people in free countries. ....They only ask that they be allowed to appoint the managers to whom they entrust the management of their property. Does this not shame you, you shameless rulers? Or is there no red blood in your veins? However, neither law nor logic can force you to change your mind. Other countries are setting the standards, and you are stuck in your old ways. You do not follow any good example. It seems that greed has not blinded you but has made you insensitive and leprous.

Unlike Le Maire's attempt in 1609, the public opinion campaign of these new dissident participants against the VOC management worked, and their activism was successful. The 1623 Charter granted certain rights to large investors, including the right to nominate new candidates for appointment as directors. Charter 1623 also regulated insider trading by directors and encouraged directors to pay annual dividends to shareholders. In addition, a committee of nine shareholders was charged with overseeing VOC directors (Van Dillen et al., 2006).

This debate was about the principles of "*Corporate Governance*," a prevalent concept that advocates accountability and transparency in management. A series of letters published by shareholders expressed their dissatisfaction with corporate governance. Earlier, in 1613, a group of shareholders submitted an insinuatie (legal claim) to the directors of the Amsterdam chamber, claiming that the directors were mismanaging the company. According to them, the company was burdened with too many war responsibilities and could have been more profitable if it had reduced its war expenses and focused solely on trade. However, this legal claim did not impress the management. Because the company had just distributed dividends, its investors were not very unhappy. These protests resulted in the General Provinces granting another 21-year concession, and the VOC was to give the audit of its financial records to a special commission of shareholders. They would also change the rights and privileges of company directors to prevent personal enrichment. Despite these promises, shareholder activism in 1622 had little impact. Soon after the renewal of the charter, the chief participants had become deputy company directors rather than protectors of shareholders' interests. The new charter did not provide the company's regular shareholders with additional monitoring rights, nor were their interests adequately looked after by the chief participants (Petram, 2011).

5.7 Emergence of Intermediary Institutions

The rise of market activity during the 1630 s and 1640 s coincided with the growing importance of brokers' and market makers' intermediation services. The brokers' guild existed in Amsterdam long before the emergence of the secondary market for VOC shares, and by the early seventeenth century, several brokers specialized in stock transactions. Their service was to bring traders together; brokers were not allowed to take positions in the stock market. Brokers became more important later in the seventeenth century, but another group, the "*market makers*," began to play an essential role in the market. Market makers were constantly present in the markets, buyers for sellers and sellers for buyers. Their significant contribution facilitated investors' access to liquidity, as they were constantly in the market. They also made money by continuously buying and selling (Petram, 2011).

In the Amsterdam stock market, market-making was not an official profession; traders who started offering these services in the 1630 s realized they could only profit by providing liquidity. Between 1626 and 1642, the Raphoen brothers, Christoffel and Jan, were the first to become market makers. In their joint account at the VOC, they traded many stocks. Trading in shares of 3,000 florins had become very common on the Amsterdam market. Futures almost always involved shares of 3,000 florins or multiples of this amount. However, many people had "non-standard" capital that did not amount to 3,000 florins or integer multiples. These shares were less traded, i.e., less liquid, than the "standard" 3,000 florin shares. Thus, they provided liquidity to the market for unpopular stock transactions and contributed to the standardization of the market for VOC shares. Finally, the Raphoen brothers made the market more accessible to shareholders and inexperienced traders. Investors could always turn to them to buy or sell a share. They helped overcome the asynchronous timing of investor orders, a significant problem in many markets. The Raphoen brothers were the main link between a trader willing to sell and a trader willing to buy, who were not in the same place at the same time. The Raphoen brothers were not the only market makers operating on the stock exchange during the seventeenth century. However, no other brokerage house had the characteristics described above (Petram, 2011).

The market had become increasingly complex. It made it difficult to obtain all the information for investments. Hiring a brokerage firm specializing in gathering information also costs money. Almost all brokers became members of the brokers' guild in the 1640 s or later. According to the brokers' guild membership lists, the real surge in demand for brokerage services occurred in the 1640 s. When Portugal gained independence from Spain in 1640, Jewish account holders from Portugal more than doubled. During this period, Portuguese Jews were involved in trading VOC shares. It was also possible to see intensive commercial relations between Jewish and Christian stock traders. Capital ledgers provide evidence of frequent stock transfers between members of the two religious groups. Still, it is not possible to conclude from this that both groups of stock traders were fully integrated (Swetschinski, 1980).

In the late seventeenth century, the service of brokerage houses went beyond bringing together a group of traders who wanted to buy and sell shares. Traders usually learned who the counterparty was only after the deal was done. In other words, brokers handled all the negotiations, and traders were left only to sign the contract. Over time, brokers started to transform from intermediaries into business partners. Notarial data from 1672 shows that traders fully trusted the information provided by brokers unless the risk involved in the transaction was very high. In the case of forward contracts, where the demand for withdrawal within the contract period was much higher, they wanted to know their counterparties personally and, therefore, relied more on community ties (Petram, 2011).

In Amsterdam, where formal regulations were based on outright prohibitions rather than on supporting markets, for such informal relationships to function, there had to be some other mechanism to ensure that traders honored their contracts. Brokers use an informal network to mitigate a problem and to get information about the trustworthiness of others. Members of the Sephardic Jewish community that emerged on the Amsterdam Stock Exchange at the end of the seventeenth century could be an example of informal networks. Still, the stock exchange was not a homogeneous group, socially or religiously, so religious and social sanctions were not the most crucial factor. As Neal and Quinn (2001) have shown, kinship or religious ties were often insufficient to encompass the vast trading network that flourished at the time. Inevitably, mechanisms such as social ties or economic sanctions would be required, as with the Maghribi merchants (Clay, 1997). Although the Amsterdam brokers had no formal rules and could not exclude cheaters, they could share information about trustworthiness and were required to boycott the untrustworthy (Stringham, 2003). This reputation network created incentives for brokers to fulfill their contracts. De la Vega (1996) wrote: "*The stock market business is like a game. Some players behave like princes, combining power with compassion, kindness, and intelligence. Still, some participants lose their reputation, and others lack commitment to their work even before the game begins.*" De la Vega also spoke of the disreputable: "*Since the status of such people, their petty capital, low reputation, and limited credibility are well known, they do not dare to do any noteworthy work.*" Although notorious brokers were banned from most trades, the exchange was not a closed club. The exchange had brokers of various characters. De la Vega said, "*There are an infinite number of these freelance brokers. The brokerage profession is often an easy field to enter for poor businessmen and the best refuge for many ruined careers.*" While the exchange was open to newcomers, participants had to work to build their reputations before making significant trades.

Every broker had to work loyally and honestly on the Amsterdam Stock Exchange to get business. De la Vega (1996) wrote about the honesty of brokers: "*The loyalty of some brokers to their principals, whom they usually call their masters, is so great, and their industry, activity, diligence, and vigilance so great, that the clients get their money's worth.*" Brokers had to act virtuously if they wanted to be patronized. Therefore, it was in their interest to keep their promises and be true to their word. He also added the following:

> To be sure, there is widespread honesty and discovery in the Stock Exchange. For example, the stock business and the flurry of selling when unexpected news arrives is something to behold. No one changes their decisions in the heat of the moment, and their word is

sacred, even with a 50% price difference. Although traders do enormous business without the intermediation of brokers who can testify, there is no confusion and no fighting... Such honesty, cooperation, and integrity are admirable and astonishing.

Because of the discipline of continuous dealings, "such honesty, cooperation and integrity" is not surprising. In the 1600 s, the first century when stocks were traded, we saw considerable financial innovation. Regulation did not advance the market but restrained it, but it flourished despite the law. The state was unnecessary for financial innovation and contract performance (Stringham, 2003).

5.8 Trade Clubs and Standardization of Exchange Transactions

With the emergence of trading clubs in the second half of the seventeenth century, sub-markets with strong inter-trader ties were formed. A group of traders would meet at an inn or coffeehouse on specific dates to trade stocks. Trading in one of the sub-markets had several closely related benefits. First, all members traded frequently. Thus, they formed a community of very experienced active traders. Second, because they traded frequently, their reputation was essential to them. Moreover, the limited size of the community ensured that members kept track of each other; the pressure of the environment ensured that everyone followed the rules. These clubs were very different from the secondary market for VOC shares: membership was not compulsory, and there were no formal requirements even to enter the Exchange building. The word collegie implies that the meetings had a formal character and that some committees organized and managed the meetings. This committee is also supposed to have the power to settle disputes. Collegie also means a company of share traders, and the traders met in the evenings at the De Plaetse Royael Inn in Amsterdam's financial district. The Collegie was a predominantly Jewish place; the ledger's names are largely Sephardic. There was another meeting of stock traders, called the monthly rescontre meeting. Anyone who holds a futures contract due to expiration on the first day of the following month could attend the rescontre; traders met at the rescontre to mutually settle futures contracts. The rescontre was essentially a meeting to settle contracts, rather than a sub-market in its own right, like trading clubs (Petram, 2011).

In the Collegie, buyers had to pay a 2.5% "*wine money*" fee, with a maximum of three guilders per transaction. All contracts were with individual counterparties rather than with the Exchange. The Dutch referred to the derivative tulip contract trading as "windhandel" (wind trading) (Goldgar, 2007).

The activities of the Rescontre in colleges gradually led to the standardization of stock exchange transactions and contributed to the development of today's stock exchanges. The general meaning of the word rescontre is "meeting." Traders gave the word a more specific meaning, using it mainly to describe the meeting of two traders at the expiration of a contract to settle the contract, or more specifically, to cancel one transaction with another. Rescontre's settlement procedure had its roots in the

Champagne fairs. During the fairs, settlement meetings were organized for traders with bills of exchange. At that time, the rescontre was a quarterly event, similar to today's standard contract periods in futures trading. Merchants met quarterly, in February, May, August, and November. The system of fixed payment dates was very advantageous for late medieval trade because it facilitated international payments. Many merchants from all over Europe gathered in the same place, and all had payment orders due in the same month. Having a large number of contracts due on the same day was advantageous because it made it easy to close them by canceling different buy and sell contracts, which required only a relatively small payment of money, and to get a large number of contracts due, futures trading had to be standardized first. The oldest surviving printed forward contract dates from 1629. The standard forward transaction clauses appear to be pre-printed, stipulating, for example, that the seller can deduct any interim dividends from the forward price. There were spaces in the printed paper for contract holders to enter their names, the forward price, the possible dividend deduction interest rate, and the contract's maturity (Petram, 2011).

However, at least from 1683 onward, the payment date was always the first day of the month. Between 1683 and 1688, printed forward contracts set out the terms of delivery and payment of a share at the bottom to ensure that the rescontre proceeded smoothly. A date was always defined as 20 days after the original maturity date. This made it possible for traders to submit or transfer the share to the next rescontre meeting. Notarial deeds show that futures trading was standardized from the 1660 s onward, with the first day of the month almost without exception being the settlement date. Derivatives trading was hazardous, and it was therefore never possible for investors to use the derivatives market to its full potential without the legal framework and the unique enforcement mechanism of the trading clubs and rescontre (Poitras, 2009).

5.9 Access to Information

There has always been an information asymmetry in the market. Therefore, investors had to interpret the various decisions of company managers and utilize bits of information from different sources. Initially, investors took the risk of investing money in the VOC in 1602, even though shareholders had no say in the management. How they would use the funds collected through stock subscriptions was not determined. Four factors were essential for them to take this risk. First, investors have been waiting long for an organization like the VOC. The second factor was that the shareholders' investment expectations were mostly short-term, ten years. Third, investors were confident that they could trust the elite and highly reputable traders running the business. Finally, investors felt they were investing in a company and the Dutch cause (Poitras, 2009).

Seventeenth-century Amsterdam gained a reputation as an information center. The city became a crossroads for information flows, especially from the Dutch Revolt, and contributed to the development of capitalism through innovations in commercial information processing. How this information was used had not yet entered a legal status. It was also possible to make money by accessing information before anyone else or by insider trading (Koudijs, 2015). Although information came to Amsterdam from around the world through different channels, there was not a sufficient flow of information from the VOC (Neal, 1988). As the market grew in the 1630 s, shareholders became demanding information about the company's finances. The discussion on corporate governance did not yield any results. The chief participants in the company did not share the information they had access to with other shareholders and only acted in the interests of the directors.

The primary sources of market news were the communications between them. For example, investor Anthoine l'Empereur's correspondence with her nephew Jacques de Velaer Junior, who lived in Amsterdam, about the trading of VOC shares is instructive. De Velaer did not offer his services for free; he charged his uncle a commission of 1% of the nominal value of the shares bought and sold. According to one correspondence between the two men, reports of an approaching fleet in 1610 described how this information reached the Amsterdam Stock Exchange. Between May 25, when the first rumors circulated, and July 26, when De Velaer finally checked the accuracy of all the information, there were many different and sometimes contradictory rumors on the exchange. Interestingly, building a short-term speculative trading strategy was impossible based on the information going back and forth between these two people. The correspondence also shows that l'Empereur was not only after financial gain; his decision to invest in the VOC showed his desire to promote Dutch interests (Poitras, 2009).

The market also reacted rationally to information. With the first dividend announcement in March 1610, market participants revalued the share price. The correspondence between l'Empereur and De Velaer clearly shows that the company's decision to distribute spices forced investors to make a difficult choice. According to the correspondence, the market reacted positively to the dividend announcement. Shareholders probably saw this as an official confirmation of the news that shareholders had already received through information channels outside the company. From what they heard, things were going well in the East Indies. The VOC began to distribute dividends regularly from 1623 onward. The company's dividend policy change, 1623, responded to activist shareholders' demands for financial reports. That was a sign that the company's financial situation was improving. The absolute value of the dividend was of no particular importance to shareholders; what interested them was the size of the dividend compared to previous years and, thus, the information value of the dividend (Poitras, 2009).

In the first half of the seventeenth century, company directors determined the dividend amount immediately after the return fleet's arrival, usually in the fall. This policy changed in the second half of the century. Dividends were now announced at the end of Heeren XVII's annual meeting in the spring. The directors also prepared the annual report, allowing them to adjust the dividend size to the company's overall performance. The outcome of this meeting was significant for shareholders. Data from the VOC capital books show that stock trading intensified during the spring meetings in March. As soon as the first rumors about the dividend spread on the stock exchange, investors immediately began to speculate on the rumors' integrity and the dividend's impact on the share price. For example, in 1688, many traders expected 25% of the dividend to be paid in cash. However, the investor Velters heard a rumor that the distribution would be only 22.5% of the nominal value of the company's shares. He immediately liquidated his position and sold two forward contracts, anticipating that the price would fall. However, when the company made its payment on May 1, the price unexpectedly rose within a few days.

In another example, "*On the night of the meeting, Gerrit Loot, a broker, offered many shares for sale. However, no one dared to buy the shares as there was an expectation that the price would fall by 2%. This lasted until 8.30 pm and then reversed: the price rose to 566, and only buyers entered the market. Minutes earlier, the Heeren XVII meeting at East India House, less than 500 m from the Dam Square, had ended (Fig. 5.4). The company executives did not want to give any information about the size of the dividend. Still, after talking to some of the directors, shareholders felt it had been a pleasant meeting. They, therefore, concluded that the dividend would be higher than expected. The next day, many shareholders thought that the company would distribute 22.5% in cash and another 15% if the return fleet arrived safely*" (Poitras, 2009).

During the meeting, many shareholders were present at the Dam Square to react immediately to rumors about the dividend. Therefore, share price movements around the annual meeting are particularly informative about how shareholders interpreted

Fig. 5.4 Dam Square with the City Hall, the Waag, the New Church with tower and Damrak, copy of print by Jacobus van der Ulft.jpg, 1653 https://www.wikidata.org/wiki/Q17781747#/media/File:SA_9722-De_Dam-De_Dam_met_het_Stadhuis,_de_Waag,_de_Nieuwe_Kerk_met_toren_en_Damrak,_kopie_naar_prent_van_Jacobus_van_der_Ulft.jpg (Public Domain)

the signal hidden in the proposed dividend distribution. Political and military events are also known to impact share prices significantly. 1672 and 1688 witnessed large share price drops, leading to numerous rumors. Stock investors were interested in news about the situation in the East Indies, the sailing of ships, the size of dividend distributions, and the political and military situation in Europe. Speculators needed constant updates on all these different categories of information. Moreover, for their transactions to be profitable, they needed to be the first to receive news that could affect the share price (Poitras, 2009).

One of the sources of information for traders is the information networks of traders from different religions and communities. These networks also monitored each other. The Jewish diaspora had a unique information network. Christian merchants tried to take advantage of their knowledge networks. Portuguese Jews in Amsterdam sent their information by special couriers to their agent at the stock exchange. Their agents were the first to receive war news and could make profitable trades. English merchants also had reliable information from England. New news from England was also essential because the threats of a naval war significantly impacted the profitability of the VOC and, thus, share trading (Swetschinski, 1980). Although the regular sailings and package ship service with the UK were the most important source of information for Dutch investors, ships were not the only news source. Investors could set up private initiatives to receive information from London. For example, Dutch investors hired fishing vessels during the South Sea Bubble 1720 (Koudijs, 2015).

In the late seventeenth century, active traders established private information networks that informed them of the latest information. They could also make targeted short-term profits if they received new information earlier than their main competitors. Speculative trading became the domain of (semi-) professional traders who made great efforts to gather the latest information. Less active traders could not keep up with these (semi-) professionals, but they were lucky that, due to the high trading activity of speculators, the share price always reflected the latest news; they could trust that the share price reflected the actual market price. Although newspapers published information on share trading, the news always reached the market too late, and traders with private information networks had already made a profit. The printed news media did not contribute to the growing enthusiasm for stock trading after 1640.

The people with the best insider information were company executives and chief participants in the VOC. However, analyzing how much they took advantage of their position is impossible. Amsterdam's position as an important trading port in international trade made information from abroad quickly available on the stock exchange. To get news from the Dutch East Indies before the arrival of the VOC return fleet, merchants would send their informers' letters about the British fleets to Europe, hoping to gain early access to the news. The Portuguese Jews, who had established their information networks long before their involvement in stock trading, demonstrated remarkable foresight and would later reap significant benefits from these networks. These interconnected relationships and activities played a crucial role in Amsterdam's evolution into an information exchange and the modernization of finance (Swetschinski, 1980).

The financial development in the Netherlands had the most significant impact on England. The commercial cooperation between the two countries was quite extensive. Throughout the seventeenth century, the Dutch elite amassed vast amounts of wealth. Lacking investment opportunities and assets at home, they looked to England to diversify their portfolios. By the beginning of the eighteenth century, active markets for British securities had emerged in London and Amsterdam. They traded futures and options to hedge risks or speculate (Bowen, 1989). Securities transactions included both Dutch joint stocks and British funds. The emergence of publicly traded securities of British companies led to widespread speculation. By permitting gambling on foreign securities, the Amsterdam Stock Exchange became a stage for the most abstract and exciting international finance in the world at the time (Wilson, 1941). However, this close relationship allowed for unethical practices such as insider trading, in which even politicians were involved (Box 5.1).

An extensive system of intermediaries emerged in both countries to support the British securities market. Securities were in the form of entries in the books of companies or the government and had to be transferred in London; Amsterdam had no separate registers. When two traders agreed on a transaction, they would send an order to an agent in London to execute the transfer. A transaction was only officially executed after the traders received confirmation from London (usually within two weeks). Brokers also collected and remitted dividends, executed orders in the London market, and provided valuable information about market conditions and general events. One of them was the famous economist David Ricardo, who was sent to London by his father, an Amsterdam broker. Well-connected bankers and brokers traded on their accounts, engaged in arbitrage, and often acted as liquidity providers. Futures markets operated in much the same way on both sides of the North Sea. In future trading, payments had to be made within three weeks; otherwise, the person would be considered bankrupt. There was no central clearing party monitoring transactions between settlement periods, nor did contracts have collateral requirements. Enforcement of contracts was based on reputation. Courts approved futures contracts only when actual delivery of the underlying securities was intended—the lack of formal enforcement limited market access to well-connected, highly reputable traders. A default could trigger a chain of bankruptcies. In Amsterdam and London, the market scope was limited: everyone knew each other so that reputations could be built (Koudijs, 2015). However, the Amsterdam Stock Exchange was not only a stock exchange. It was also a commodity exchange with fish, cereals, and spices.

Box 5.1: Insider Trading at the Amsterdam Stock Exchange
In the fall of 1772, Thomas Walpole joined Amsterdam's Hope & Co., specializing in speculating on British East India Company (EIC) stocks. By the 1780s, Hope & Co. was the leading underwriter of government loans to Spain and Russia (Jackson, 2022). Walpole, a political insider and nephew of former British Prime Minister Robert

Walpole, sent a letter to Mr. Hope on December 18, 1772, "A report on the British East India Company suggests its stock will likely fall. Resume sales cautiously, targeting prices between 170 and 166. Avoid going lower, as speculation may drive a rise once relief plans are announced. If the price falls to around 154, settle positions and consider buying to benefit from the anticipated rebound."

Walpole's predictions proved accurate. On January 14, 1773, EIC executives secured a government loan and access to the American tea market, aligning with his forecasted price movements. This made it possible to speculate on the EIC shares traded in Amsterdam. EIC shares in Amsterdam dropped from 169.5 on December 30 to a low of 157.50 on January 4 before rebounding to 169.5 by January 29. He had to be careful not to trade too aggressively and not to disclose information to other market participants. Hope did this through intermediaries. His records show that all share transactions on the Amsterdam stock exchange were made by brokers such as David Pereira and Sons. Quarterly profit and loss statements show that Mr. Hope made a substantial profit (Koudijs, 2015).

In London and Amsterdam, insider trading was not illegal until the 1980s. Private information could earn influential organizations extraordinary sums of money. In January 1731, the Amsterdam broker Robert Hennebo wrote in a letter to one of his clients that EIC shares were being actively bought on the stock exchange and that these orders were probably coming from London from John Bance, one of the directors of the EIC. Evidence shows that EIC directors James Cockburn and George Colebrooke traded on the Amsterdam market in 1772 "to raise prices" (Sutherland, 1952). Besides EIC executives, British politicians were also involved in insider trading using political developments/(Koudijs, 2015).

In London and Amsterdam, insider trading was not illegal until the 1980s. Private information could earn influential organizations extraordinary sums of money. In January 1731, the Amsterdam broker Robert Hennebo wrote in a letter to one of his clients that EIC shares were being actively bought on the stock exchange and that these orders were probably coming from London from John Bance, one of the directors of the EIC. Evidence shows that EIC directors James Cockburn and George Colebrooke traded on the Amsterdam market in 1772 "to raise prices" (Sutherland, 1952). Besides EIC executives, British politicians were also involved in insider trading using political developments/(Koudijs, 2015).

The most interesting of these commodities was undoubtedly tulip bulbs. In 1636, tulip prices soared wildly, creating great fortunes and a terrible crisis, and henceforth, the Amsterdam Stock Exchange was known as Tulipmania.

5.10 Tulipmania

The Dutch floriculture industry, which is very important today, did not know tulips in the seventeenth century. A fascinating tulip craze began in the Netherlands sometime after the arrival of tulips from Istanbul. In the 1630 s, the tulip represented novelty, unpredictability, and excitement. The tulip reflected the exotic East, a collector's item for the curious and the wealthy, rather than a simple and unpretentious flower in a vase on the kitchen table. "*It may be said that he who is not attracted by the charms of this object is not humane*," wrote the English gardener John Parkinson about tulip clusters in 1629. The Dutch were even more enthusiastic in their praise of tulips. The preface to a 1636 watercolor tulip album depicting a tulip garden included "*Oh noble tulip sweet, Oh precious tulip.*" This passion created an eclipse of reason in the Netherlands (Goldar, 2019).

5.10.1 The Causes of the Tulipmania

The emergence of Tulipmania is actually due to a series of events. Foremost among them, however, was the accelerated trading of derivatives on the Amsterdam Stock Exchange. In the Tulipmania of 1636, the ban on derivatives trading was again extended and enforced. However, the authorities did not prosecute people for participating in prohibited futures contracts; they stopped the legal enforcement. Investors willing to take excessive risks could do so secretly (Garber, 2001).

The bubonic plague that swept the Netherlands at the time was the second development that encouraged this tulip mania. The plague ravaged the Netherlands from 1635 to 1637. Between August and November 1636, it killed 14 percent of the population of Haarlem, the center of tulip speculation. In Amsterdam, it killed one-tenth, eighth, and one-sixth of the population, respectively. The Dutch were anxious to get rich quickly, probably to forget the pain of this pestilence. The easiest way to do this was through the tulip trade. Between 1635 and 1637, the same period as the tulip speculation, the Dutch population faced the possibility of imminent death by plague or Spanish invasion. The idea that this excellent tulip gamble was a reaction to the threat of death has gained favor (Garber, 2001).

The third development was the emergence of a mutated species of tulip known as the broken tulip. The emergence of the broken tulip is related to the nature of the tulip plant. As a bulbous flower, the tulip can reproduce through seeds or buds that form on the mother bulb. Properly grown buds can directly propagate another bulb. Each bulb, once planted, eventually disappears during the growing season. At the end of the season, the original onion is replaced by a clone, the primary bud, which is now a functioning tuber, and several secondary buds. Asexual reproduction through buds, the primary propagation method, gives a maximum annual increase of 100 to 150 percent of bulbs over regular onions. While a bulb produced directly from seed requires seven to twelve years to flower, the flowers of tulips from bulbs appear in April or May and last about a week. The time needed for the secondary buds to bloom depends on the size of the bulb produced from the bud. The bulbs can be removed from their beds in June but must be replanted by September. Interestingly, tulips were infested with a mosaic virus during this period, called "*breakage,*" which creates remarkable patterns on the flower, some considered beautiful. The pattern applied to a particular flower could not be reproduced through seed propagation, as the seeds were unaffected by the virus. It was possible to produce a specific pattern by growing the buds into new bulbs. In this case, the mosaic virus sickened the bulbs and reduced the reproduction rate. This made it more challenging to obtain broken tulips. Today, there are still examples of these then-popular broken bulbs. The tulip craze, i.e., the high market prices for tulips, was mainly for the beautiful "*broken*" bulbs. Broken bulbs only fell out of fashion in the nineteenth century. Indeed, since breakage is unpredictable, some have characterized the tulip craze among growers as a gamble, with growers "*competing to produce better and more bizarre varieties and feathers*" (Garber, 2001).

5.10.2 The Tulip Market and Its Collapse

Market participants could deal in many types. Tulip bulbs could also be sold by weight, as larger bulbs were more productive. The weight standard was "*aas*," about one-twentieth of a gram. A purchase between September and June was necessarily a contract for future delivery. There were also markets for rarer bulbs. The bulbs could not be delivered immediately, as they had to reach a minimum size before being separated from the mother bulb to allow the new bulb to survive. Therefore, contracts for growing bulbs were also for future deliveries. Formal futures markets developed in 1636 and became the primary focus of trade before the collapse in February 1637; earlier agreements used written contracts made in the presence of a notary public. Trading became so widespread in the summer of 1636, at the height of the plague, that traders gathered in groups called "*Collegie*" in numerous taverns, as we have already described in the stock markets. Here, trading was regulated by a few rules governing the method of bidding and fees. In the tulip trade, it was possible to enter into contracts without collateral being required from either side. Hence, in the tuber market, market rules did not limit the size of an individual's position, and investors could quickly enter into such contracts. Moreover, traders could sell tubers they did not own. Neither party intended to deliver on the settlement date; only the difference between the contract and the settlement price was expected to be paid (Moore et al., 2017).

Contracts based on non-owned goods and money made the tulip market extremely risky. It is unclear which date was set as the settlement date for the "*collegie*" contracts. According to the agreements made in the new futures markets in 1636–1637 before the collapse, no onions were delivered because it was necessary to wait until June after the crisis to extract them. Beckmann (2020) notes that the settlement price was "*determined by the price at which the most bargains were made,*" probably when a particular contract expired. Serious and wealthy tulip enthusiasts who regularly traded in rare varieties did not participate in the new speculative markets. Even after the collapse of speculation, they continued to buy and sell rare bulbs "*in large quan*tities." For most of the period of tulip speculation, high prices and recorded trade were realized only for rare bulbs.

Posthumus (1929) told the sequence of events: "*By the end of 1634, new non-professional buyers were on the move. By the middle of 1635, prices were rising rapidly; people could buy without collateral and usually deliver a valuable product immediately; at the same time, selling by the AAS was introduced. "The trade-in unowned onions began; by November of the same year, the trade was extended to common varieties, and the thousand aas and pounds sold onions.*"

In 1635, several people were known to have invested a fortune of 100,000 florins to buy forty roots of tulips. Speculators were so eager to acquire broken tulips that one person offered the price of twelve acres of land for a Harlaem tulip. The Amsterdam tulip was bought for 4600 florins, a new carriage, two horses, and a complete harness (Fridson, 1995). Tulip speculation has also been the subject of many intriguing stories and rumors.

A sailor once informed a wealthy merchant with rare tulips of a precious shipment of goods from the Levant. He hosted the sailor in his warehouse, and to reward him for his news, he gave him a beautiful red herring for breakfast. The sailor had a great fondness for onions, and when he saw a lump on the generous merchant's counter that looked very much like an onion, he pocketed it to savor the herring. This onion was the valuable Semper Augustus tulip, worth three thousand florins, or about £280. He was distraught when the merchant sailor left and could not find his bulb. Finally, it occurred to him that the sailor might have it. The unhappy merchant rushed out into the street and ran to the ship. He was very disappointed to see the sailor chewing the last morsel of his "*bulb.*" The cost of this tulip bulb was large enough to entertain an entire ship's crew for twelve months. The merchant said the sailor had eaten a breakfast that "co*uld have sumptuously feasted the Prince of Orange and his entire court.*" Most unfortunately, he was imprisoned for only a few months on a charge brought against him by the merchant (Fridson, 1995).

The tulip market collapsed in the first week of February 1637. Before then, however, the more prudent began to see that the madness could not last forever. The rich no longer bought flowers to keep in their gardens but resold them at a hundred percent profit. Eventually, it became clear that someone had to pay for this madness. As word spread, prices fell and would never rise again. A great panic gripped the sellers. Every day and in every city in the Netherlands, there were announcements of defaulters. Hundreds of people who had described themselves as very wealthy a few months earlier suddenly found themselves the owners of vast quantities of onions that no one else would buy. The few who managed to get rich hid their fortunes from their friends, sent them to Britain, or invested in other funds. Many who had escaped from the humbler walks of life would return to their poorer days, even if only briefly. Necessary merchants were reduced almost to beggars. There were threats of lawsuits in all the country's courts for breach of contract, but the courts refused to hear the gambling transactions (Fridson, 1995).

On April 27, 1637, the Dutch Provinces suspended all contracts, giving the seller of existing bulbs the right to sell the contracted bulbs at market prices during the suspension. The contract buyer would be liable for the difference between the market price of the tulip and the price that the authorities finally set for the contract settlement. Posthumus (1929) notes that many cities followed Haarlem's example, and in May 1638, the city council passed an ordinance allowing buyers to terminate their contracts by paying 3.5 percent of the contract price. The status of forward legal contracts was still unclear before the collapse (Posthumus, 1929).

The tulip fashion then spread to London and Paris. These cities were decorated with tulips, and tulip bulbs were sold at high prices, although not as high as in the Netherlands (Fridson, 1995). The tulip fashion would not be limited to Europe; Istanbul rediscovered the tulip at the beginning of the eighteenth century, and the city would be adorned with tulips. After giving its name to an era in the Ottoman Empire, the tulip caused a bloody rebellion.

The Tulip Era (1718–1730) marked a period of peace and cultural flourishing in the Ottoman Empire following the defeat at the Second Siege of Vienna in 1683. Under the leadership of Grand Vizier Nevşehirli Damat İbrahim Pasha, significant reforms and cultural advancements took place. European influence grew as ambassadors were sent abroad for the first time, and diplomatic relations with European states deepened. The first Turkish printing house was established in 1727, ushering in intellectual and artistic development. Architecture, poetry, music, and translations of Eastern and European works flourished, making this era a "*Renaissance movement*" for the Ottoman Empire (Erimtan, 2008). For the first time, the state recognized the superiority of Europe. French experts in architecture and the military were invited. Eastern works, including Ibn Khaldun, were translated, and music, poetry, and fine arts flourished. This was a period of intellectual awakening (Inalcık, 2016).

Ibrahim Pasha encouraged the construction of ostentatious palaces and mansions in Istanbul and established tulip gardens in many parts of the city. While the palace and its environs participated in these entertainments, the financial difficulties caused by the protracted wars and the weight of taxes, which had previously been imposed for war expenses but had become permanent over time, put the productive class in a difficult situation. There was also unrest among the Janissaries, who had not received their salaries for long. The different lives of both ends of society prepared an environment where reaction could survive (Finkel, 2007).

On the morning of Thursday, September 28, 1730, a rebellion started under the leadership of a Janissary named Halil, nicknamed Patrona, claiming that Grand Vizier Nevşehirli Damat İbrahim Pasha was indulging in pleasure and debauchery and that he had apostatized from religion. The Sultan was obligated to kill Grand Vizier İbrahim Pasha. However, the rebellion grew even more, and Sultan Ahmet III was deposed. Although the new sultan, Mahmut I, ambushed and killed Patrona Halil, who terrorized the city and his friends a few months later, the Tulip Era was over (Finkel, 2007).

5.11 Concluding Remarks

In the seventeenth century, Amsterdam was a vital global trade hub driven by a robust and innovative legal system that supported market activity, commerce, and international finance. The city's legal framework was a cornerstone of its success during its "Golden Age," creating an environment of stability, inclusivity, and efficiency. The Amsterdam Stock Exchange emerged as a hub for securities trading, replacing the traditional goods and money markets during the seventeenth century. During the golden age of Amsterdam, it hosted the development of joint venture companies, common shares, bonds, and derivative instruments. Shares represented partial company ownership, while bonds allowed governments and businesses to raise capital through debt. Additionally, the era witnessed the emergence of derivatives, such as forward contracts and options, which offered tools for hedging and speculation. These instruments demonstrated a remarkable sophistication that would influence financial markets for centuries. Another hallmark of this era was the exchange's contribution to liquidity and market efficiency. Investors could trade shares with relative ease, enhancing the accessibility and fluidity of capital. Moreover, the stock exchange pioneered price discovery and transparency, ensuring fairer and more efficient markets that inspired trust and participation.

This period also underscored the symbiotic relationship between finance and global trade. The VOC and other trading companies utilized the stock exchange to raise capital for far-reaching expeditions, linking Europe with Asia, Africa, and the Americas. Amsterdam's role as a hub for global commerce was pivotal, as these ventures brought immense wealth and resources back to Europe, fueling economic growth and prosperity.

The democratization of investment in the Netherlands fueled the development of the market with inclusive institutions. Unlike earlier systems where investment opportunities were limited to the elite, the Amsterdam Stock Exchange allowed a broader segment of society, including merchants and ordinary citizens, to participate and benefit from economic growth. This inclusivity laid the groundwork for a more accessible and participatory financial system.

The practices and institutions developed during this period profoundly influenced modern capital markets. Concepts such as limited liability, joint-stock ownership, and corporate governance were introduced, creating a framework that underpins contemporary financial systems. Thinkers and writers like Joseph De la Vega documented these developments, offering insights into market behavior in works such as Confusion de Confusiones. Their analyses contributed to the early intellectual foundations of finance.

As a result, by the middle of the seventeenth century, the Netherlands had managed to maintain its political independence through the mercantilist system it had established and had built the power to capture and hold "extraordinary shares" of the economic gains from intra-European and intercontinental trade. Above all, in their long struggle against the Spanish, the Dutch established, maintained, and consolidated their Protestant identity. They competed aggressively against their Catholic enemies, rivals, and adversaries (O'Brien, 2000). Eventually, Spain collapsed with Louis XIV's accession to the throne in 1643.

However, the weight of long-standing tradition, vested interests, unresolvable conflicts of interest between sectors and industries, and groups of merchants, and a century or more of stability in the Netherlands led the system to inertia and conservatism. As explained in the next chapter, England made the Glorious Revolution

(1688–89), and conditions began to change to the detriment of the Netherlands. From the eighteenth century onward, London was the strongest player in the market. This would be one of the most famous examples of "institutional" change in world history and would create an environment conducive to making England the world's first industrialized country (Pincus & Robinson, 2011). At the end of the seventeenth century, investors who had gained extraordinary experience on the Amsterdam Stock Exchange turned to London and developed its dimension.

As a result of the ensuing War of Austrian Succession in the 1740s, Amsterdam and other Dutch cities' hegemonic position in providing shipping, mercantile services, financial intermediation, marine insurance, commodity brokerage, warehousing, and other functions as Europe's leading warehouse for international and intercontinental trade was eroded while the British economy was growing. London ended Amsterdam's dominance as a global stock exchange (O'Brien, 2000). The Dutch Republic survived at considerable cost in three wars against England in the seventeenth century and was invaded by the armies of Louis XIV between 1672 and 1674 (Jones, 1980). Meanwhile, after the great revolution of 1688, in London, it was realized that France was the most severe enemy in the competition for overseas trade and empire. The wars changed direction, but the Netherlands could not escape them. Between 1689 and 1815, the Second Hundred Years' War against Napoleonic France occurred in a series of wars. The results of the wars against England in alliance with France were devastating for the Dutch economy. With Napoleon's annexation of the Netherlands in the summer of 1810, the capital market collapsed, and the banks that tried to maintain their ties with the continent through Amsterdam were devastated. One was Hope & Co, which had to sell its London assets to Barings Bank (Jackson, 2022).

As the twentieth century began, the Amsterdam Stock Exchange continued to evolve, navigating economic shifts brought on by World War I (1914–1918). The war presented challenges, including market closures and disruptions in international trade. Despite these obstacles, the Netherlands' neutrality allowed Amsterdam to retain some of its position as a financial hub. After the war, the interwar period (1918–1939) saw fluctuations in economic activity. The 1920s brought a brief post-war boom, followed by the Great Depression of the 1930s, causing a sharp decline in stock prices and trading volumes. The exchange implemented regulations to protect investors, stabilize the market, and prevent excessive speculation.

After World War II, the Amsterdam Stock Exchange was vital to the Netherlands' economic reconstruction. The Marshall Plan and post-war recovery in Europe spurred renewed investment and industrial growth. The 1970s brought new challenges, particularly the 1973 oil crisis, which profoundly affected the Netherlands and its multinational corporations and led to instability. Despite these difficulties, Amsterdam remained a key player in the global financial system thanks to its established financial institutions and innovative practices.

The 1980s and 1990s brought modernization and globalization to the exchange. Electronic trading replaced traditional open-outcry systems in the 1980s. Amsterdam also became a hub for derivatives trading, further integrating the exchange into the global financial network. The turn of the century saw a significant transformation with the Euronext merger in 2000. Amsterdam, Paris, and Brussels exchanges combined to form Euronext, Europe's first cross-border stock exchange. This merger reflected globalization and technological advancements in financial markets.

The Amsterdam Stock Exchange has endured for 400 years and played a key role in financial success. As a result, it has defied crises and wars and attracted investors with its steady growth. This confirms the popular saying, "It is not about spending time in the market; it is about timing your moves well, which increases wealth."

References

Ames, G. J. (2008). The globe encompassed: The age of European discovery, 1500–1700. s. 102–103.

Barbour, V. (1950). Capitalism in Amsterdam in the seventeenth century. (No Title).

Beckmann, J. (2020). *A history of inventions, discoveries, and origins: Volume 2*. BoD–Books on Demand.

Bowen, H. V. (1989). Investment and empire in the later eighteenth century: East India stockholding, 1756–1791. *Economic History Review*, 186–206.

Bruijn, J. R., & Gaastra, F. S. (1993). Ships, sailors and spices: East India Companies and their shipping in the 16th, 17th and 18th centuries.

Carlos, A. M., & Neal, L. (2011). Amsterdam and London as financial centers in the eighteenth century1. *Financial History Review, 18*(1), 21–46.

Clarendon, P. (1968). *The Turkish letters of Ogier Ghiselin de Busbecq, imperial ambassador at Constantinople, 1554–1562* (E. S. Forster, Trans.). Clarendon Press.

Clay, K. (1997). Trade, institutions, and credit. *Explorations in Economic History, 34*, 495–521.

De Jong, A., Jonker, J., & Röell, A. (2013). Dutch corporate finance, 1602–1850. ERIM Report Series Reference No. ERS-2013-008-F&A.

De la Vega, J. P. (1996). *Confusion de confusiones* (M. Fridson, Trans.). Wiley.

De Vries, J., & Van der Woude, A. (1997). *The first modern economy: Success, failure, and perseverance of the Dutch economy, 1500–1815*. Cambridge University Press.

Dutch Slavery Trade. (n.d.) UNESCO.Slavery and remembrance. https://slaveryandremembrance.org/articles/article/?id=A0145

Dutch West India Company. (2021). https://www.encyclopedia.com/history/modern-europe/benelux-history/dutch-west-india-company

Emmer, P. (1998). *The Dutch in the Atlantic Economy, 1580–1880: Trade, slavery, and emancipation*. Routledge.

Erimtan, C. (2008). *Ottomans looking west? The origins of the tulip age and its development in modern Turkey*. Bloomsbury Publishing.

Ferguson, N. (2002). *Empire: The rise and demise of the British world order and the lessons for global power* (p. 15).

Finkel, C. (2007). *Osman's dream: The history of the Ottoman Empire*. Hachette UK.

Fridson, M. S. (Ed.). (1995). *Extraordinary popular delusions and the madness of crowds and confusion de confusiones*. Wiley.

Garber, P. M. (2001). *Famous first bubbles: The fundamentals of early manias*. MIT Press.

Gelderblom, O. C. (2003). *From Antwerp to Amsterdam: The contribution of Merchants from the Southern Netherlands to the commercial expansion of Amsterdam* (c. 1540–1609). Review (Fernand Braudel Center) (pp. 247–282).

Gelderblom, O., & Jonker, J. (2004). Completing a financial revolution: The finance of the Dutch East India trade and the rise of the Amsterdam capital market, 1595–1612. *The Journal of Economic History, 64*(3), 641–672.

Gelderblom, O., & Jonker, J. (2005). Amsterdam as the cradle of modern futures trading and options trading, 1550–1650. In *The origins of value: The financial innovations that created modern capital markets/Goetzmann*, William N.[edit.]; vd. (pp. 189–206).

Gelderblom, O., De Jong, A., & Jonker, J. (2010). An Admiralty for Asia: Isaac le Maire and conflicting conceptions about the corporate governance of the VOC.

Gelderblom, O., De Jong, A., & Jonker, J. (2013). The formative years of the modern corporation: The Dutch East India Company VOC, 1602–1623. *The Journal of Economic History, 73*(4), 1050–1076.

Goldgar, A. (2007). *Tulipmania: Money, honor, and knowledge in the Dutch Golden Age*. University of Chicago Press. ISBN 978-0-226-30125-9. Archived from the original on March 15, 2024, and retrieved September 17, 2017

Goslinga, C. C. (2018). *The Dutch in the Caribbean and on the Wild Coast 1580–1680*. University Press of Florida.

Grenville, S. (2021). *The first global supply chain*. Lowy Institute.

Hayes, A. (2022, November 22). *Tulipmania: About the Dutch tulip bulb market bubble*. Investopedia. Retrieved from https://www.investopedia.com/terms/d/dutch_tulip_bulb_market_bubble.asp

Inalcık, H. (2016). Devlet-i'Aliyye: Osmanlı İmparatorluğu Üzerine Araştırmalar-IV Ayanlar, Tanzimat, Meşrutiyet. Türkiye İş Bankası Kültür Yayınları.

Israel, J. I. (1989). *Dutch primacy in world trade, 1585–1740*. Clarendon Press.

Jackson, T. (2022). *Impunity and capitalism*. Cambridge University Press.

Jones, J. R. (1980). *Britain and the World 1649–1815*. Harvester Press.

Jonker, J., & Sluyterman, K. (2001). *At home on the world markets: Dutch international trading companies from the 16th century until the present*. McGill-Queen's Press-MQUP.

Kaletsky, A. (2010). *Capitalism 4.0: The Birth of a new economy in the aftermath of crisis*. Public Affairs. s. 109–10.

Karan M. B. (2022). *Secrets of money, banking and finance* (Para Banka ve Finansın Sırları)".Scala Publishing

Karan, M. B., Westerman, W., & Wijngaard, J. (2024). A history of banks. Contributions to economics.

Koudijs, P. (2015). Those who know most: Insider trading in eighteenth-century Amsterdam. *Journal of Political Economy, 123*(6), 1356–1409.

Moore, A., Artz, J., & Ehlen, C. R. (2017). Tulip Mania. *International Journal of the Academic Business World, 11*(2).

Murphy, A. L. (2009). *The origins of English financial markets*. Cambridge Books.

Neal, L. (1988). The rise of a financial press: London and Amsterdam, 1681–1810. *Business History, 30*(2), 163–178.

Neal, L. (1990). The Dutch and English East India companies. In J. Tracy (Ed.), *The rise of merchant empires* (pp. 195–223). Cambridge University Press.

Neal, L. (2000). How it all began: The monetary and financial architecture of Europe during the first global capital markets, 1648–1815. *Financial History Review, 7*(2), 117–140.

Neal, L., & Quinn, S. (2001). Networks of information, markets, and institutions in the rise of London as a financial center in the seventeenth century. *Financial History Review, 8*, 7–26.

O'Brien, P. (2000). Mercantilism and imperialism in the rise and decline of the Dutch and British economies 1585–1815. *De Economist, 148*, 469–501.

Ota, A. (10 Nisan 2021). *The Dutch East India Company and the Rise of Intra-Asian Commerce*. Nippon.com (Nippon Communications Foundation).

Petram, L. O. (2011). *The world's first stock exchange: How the Amsterdam market for Dutch East India Company shares became a modern securities market, 1602–1700* (Doctoral thesis, University of Amsterdam).

Pettegree, A. (1992). *Emden and the Dutch revolt*. Oxford University Press.

Pincus, S. C., & Robinson, J. A. (2011). *What really happened during the Glorious Revolution?* (No. w17206). National Bureau of Economic Research.

Poitras, G. (2009). The early history of option contracts. In *Vinzenz Bronzin's option pricing models: Exposition and appraisal* (pp. 487–518). Springer.
Posthumus, N. W. (1929). The tulip mania in Holland in the years 1636 and 1637. *Journal of Economic and Business History, 1*(3), 441–442.
Smith, W. D. (1984). The function of commercial centers in the modernization of European capitalism: Amsterdam as an information exchange in the seventeenth century. *The Journal of Economic History, 44*(4), 985–1005.
Steensgaard, N. (1982). The Dutch East India company as an institutional innovation. In M. Aymard (Ed.), *Dutch capitalism and world capitalism/Capitalisme hollandais et capitalisme mondial* [Studies in Modern Capitalism/Etudes sur le capitalisme moderne] (pp. 235–257).
Stringham, E. (2003). The extralegal development of securities trading in seventeenth-century Amsterdam. *The Quarterly Review of Economics and Finance, 43*(2), 321–344.
Stringham, E. P., & Curott, N. A. (2015). *On the origins of stock markets* (pp. 324–344). Oxford University Press. ISBN 978–0199811762).
Sutherland, L. (1952). *The East India company in eighteenth-century politics*. Oxford Univ. Press.
Swetschinski, D. M. (1980). *The Portuguese Jewish merchants of seventeenth-century Amsterdam: A social profile*. Brandeis University.
Taylor, B. (2013). *How 3 countries lost their position as the world's dominant financial power over the last 800 years*. Global Financial Data.
Van Dillen, J. G. (1929). *Bronnen tot de geschiedenis van het bedrijfsleven en het gildewezen van Amsterdam* (Sources to the history of business and the guild system of Amsterdam, Nyhoff Publishers.
Van Dillen, J. G., Poitras, G., & Majithia, A. (2006). Isaac Le Maire and the early trading in Dutch East India company shares. *Pioneers of Financial Economics, 1*, 45–63.
Van Tielhof, M. V. (1995). De Hollandse graanhandel, 1470–1570: Koren op de Amsterdamse molen.
Wilson, C. (1941). *Anglo-Dutch commerce and finance in the eighteenth century*. Reprinted in 1966 by Cambridge University Press.

Chapter 6
London: The First Truly Global Stock Exchange (18–19th Centuries)

6.1 Introduction

On a rainy London autumn day in 1722, Asley Barnhill walked through the door of Garraway's coffeehouse in Exchange Alley. Although he had an umbrella, his trousers were wet. He wiped the drops of water from his black bowler hat, straightened the sleeves of his jacket, and looked around; he was looking for the wily Jack. Jack was the most well-known stockbroker in this coffeehouse.

Asley Barnhill was one of London's young merchant bankers. He had a very ambitious personality. He was determined to get rich quickly and put some of his money into securities. Although government bonds provided a good return, he was not making as much profit as he would have liked. As a speculative investment, he bought East India stocks, which were fashionable then. Two large ships were expected to bring spices from India soon. When this expedition is completed, the share price will rise. However, one of his clients, who worked for the East India Company, had whispered this morning that he had heard that the ships had been caught in a big storm and that one had sunk. Barnhill had come here to cash in his stock even before the news had spread to London. If the news were confirmed, the value of the stock would plummet. He thought: "*I should sell my stock before the news runners bring it here.*" In London at that time, some people, known as news runners, would go around the coffeehouses and give the latest news. This type of trading, now banned as insider trading, was widespread.

In the corner sat the stockbrokers. He looked at them in disgust; they were talking loudly, their feet outstretched disrespectfully. They never swore, although they spoke in slang. He was not surprised because, according to the rules of the day, if someone swore, he had to forfeit twelve pence. If a fight broke out, the person who started it had to buy the offended party a cup of coffee. They were vulgar men, he muttered inwardly, but he needed them to sell his stocks. Jack, the wily broker, was among them. He politely approached him and asked him how the stocks were going. To his delight, he was told that many investors were showing interest in the stock of the East

M. B. Karan, *A History of Stock Exchanges*, Contributions to Economics,
https://doi.org/10.1007/978-3-032-07788-2_6

India Company. Soon, there would be an auction for the shares. After a while, when the café became crowded, a broker lit a small candle on the coffee shop counter. The bidding would continue until the candle went out. The last bid before the candle went out would set the value of the shares. Burnhill was very happy when he left the coffee shop in the evening. He had sold his shares for more than he had expected. The runners still had not arrived. He congratulated himself for putting up with these rude men. At the same time, he was still worried. "*I hope the news is accurate,*" he thought; otherwise, he might regret selling.

London coffeehouses played a pivotal role in the emergence of stock trading, providing a space for social interaction, exchanging financial ideas, and developing new investment practices. These helped lay the foundation for the establishment of the London Stock Exchange. London's first coffeehouse, founded by Pasqua Rosée in 1652, became a popular social spot. Coffee was believed to cure ailments and "*invigorate the spirit*" (Dawson, 1934). After the Ottomans left behind 500 sacks of coffee after the Vienna siege in 1683, Georg Franz Kolschitzky, a Polish-Ukrainian spy, opened Vienna's first coffee shop using them, sparking the spread of coffee across Europe, including London. By the eighteenth century, coffeehouses replaced pubs, awakening people and fostering serious conversations. These gatherings encouraged the development of financial trading and investing, as coffee's energizing effects kept people alert and focused on discussions of business and securities (Carabelli et al., 2020).

In the sixteenth century, Sir Thomas Gresham, who was stationed in Antwerp on behalf of England, was impressed by the stock exchange activities in Antwerp and offered to build a stock exchange in London at his own expense if a suitable plot of land could be secured (Fig. 6.1). Thus, in 1571, the first Royal Exchange was established as "*a fine exchange for the gathering of merchants*" and opened by Queen Elizabeth I. However, the new Exchange quickly became a hangout for idlers. On Sundays and holidays, many children and vagrants gathered there, shouting and screaming, so that honest citizens could not quietly go there to rest. In 1590, it was known that some women were sued for selling apples and oranges at the gate of the Borsa and "*amusing themselves by swearing to the great annoyance and distress of the inhabitants and passers-by.*" In 1592, a tavern-keeper with a shop under the Exchange was fined for allowing drinking and frying herring, anchovies, and bacon to the annoyance of the traders who came to the Exchange (Thornbury, 1881). Despite the existence of the Royal Exchange, the pricing of securities took place in coffeehouses.

After the siege of Vienna, Europe entered a new era. With the reforms initiated at the end of the seventeenth century, England would enter the twentieth century as the world's most significant power. England's success was based on an essential social pact that balanced society and the kingdom. A series of events that inspired Europe and even the world made London an international financial center.

In the last quarter of the seventeenth century, there were essential conflicts. France had invaded the Netherlands, whose Golden Age was over. Nevertheless, under the leadership of Prince William of Orange, the Dutch regained lost territories, and this success made him a leader in domestic politics. Finally, by the end of the century, the

Fig. 6.1 Sir Thomas Grasham (1519–1579) https://commons.wikimedia.org/wiki/File:Anthonis_Mor_-_Sir_Thomas_Gresham_-_WGA16185.jpg

wars had subsided a bit, and there was a renewed air of unity in Protestant Europe. While England was expected to join this union, James II (1633–1701), a Catholic, ascended the throne in February 1685. In England, which had abandoned the Catholic faith and turned to the Calvinist faith since the 1550 s, the accession of a Catholic to the throne caused a great deal of controversy. However, even though James was a Catholic, it was seen as positive that his daughter (Mary II), the heir to the throne, was Protestant. Mary had married William, Prince of Orange. William, a Protestant, had the title of "*stadtholder*" and was the most important ruler in the Netherlands. Meanwhile, the British had long envied the Netherlands for the financial institutions they had developed. Amsterdam was the financial center of Europe in the seventeenth century. However, King James II of England had a new son. The baby James Edward (1688–1766), baptized as a Catholic, succeeded his older sister Mary as heir apparent. James's increasingly pro-Roman Catholic stance, the suspension of the legal rights of dissenters, and the prospect of a Catholic heir to the throne brought discontent to a head (Karan et al., 2024). There was an anti-king mood in the country's parliament. Everything would change after a secret meeting one summer day in 1688.

The seven members of parliament who attended this meeting discussed it for some time and came up with an agreed-upon letter. The leading figure at this meeting was 35-year-old Edward Russell, a politician and fleet commander. They all signed the letter, but if things did not go as expected, they could be declared traitors and lose their lives. However, none of them hesitated; they would all sign the letter. The purpose of the meeting was to write a letter of invitation to Prince William of Orange of the Netherlands. With this letter, they were inviting the Prince to come to England and sit on the throne of England with his wife, Mary. This was a very audacious undertaking. None of the seven wrote their names on the invitation; instead, they identified themselves by a secret code, a two-digit number. Seven prominent British aristocrats would later become known as the Immortal Seven. Besides Edward Russell, the Earls of Danby, Shrewsbury, and Devonshire, Viscount Lumley, the Bishop of London, and Henry Sydney signed the letter. The letter read as follows (Vallance, 2013):

> "...the people, in general, are so dissatisfied with the present attitude of the government about their religion, liberty, and property (all of which have been largely invaded), and so great is the expectation that their prospects are daily growing worse, that Your Excellency may be assured that the people throughout the kingdom desire a change."

The letter concluded: "*Come to England, overthrow James, take the crown, rule in his place—we will support you.*"

The letter was duly delivered to the Netherlands by Arthur Herbert, Earl of Torrington, codenamed Mr H, requesting military and naval preparations for William of Orange's invasion of Britain. William came to England upon this invitation. King James II, who could not find enough support around him, had to flee the country. Prince William of Orange came to the throne with his wife to become King William III (1672–1702). His wife shared the throne as Mary II (1662–1694). This event, the Glorious Revolution, would lead to the creation of an English nation, limiting the king's power and providing protection for his subjects. In October 1689, England established a constitutional monarchy with the Bill of Rights. This ensured the independence of Parliament from the monarchy and protected certain rights, such as freedom of speech, the right to regular elections, and the right to petition the King. The 1689 Bill of Rights also guaranteed certain rights to all English subjects, including trial by jury and habeas corpus (the obligation of the authorities to bring an imprisoned person before a court to show cause for their imprisonment). In what some historians call the "*Bloodless Revo*lution," the King agreed that he could not suspend laws passed by Parliament, impose taxes without the consent of Parliament, violate the right of petition, raise a standing army in peacetime without the permission of Parliament, or deny Protestant subjects the right to bear arms. He also approved restrictions on his powers to interfere unduly in Parliamentary elections, to punish members of the Chamber of Deputies for their testimony during debates, and to inflict cruel and unusual punishments. In the years after the Glorious Revolution, while the influence of the monarchy declined, inclusive institutions were established. The power of Parliament in Britain continued to grow, and Britain became a model for democracy in the world at the time (Davies, 1999).

The economic and political aspects of the Great Revolution are essential. Decisions were no longer made by the king's advisors but by the "*Whig Party*," a political movement that opposed absolute monarchy and believed in constitutional monarchism. Inspired by the Dutch system, a series of economic and financial reforms were implemented, especially the institutional strengthening of the economic structure and the establishment of public finance on a legal basis. The first government bonds were also issued in 1693, while in the second phase of the reform, the Bank of England was established (1694), and soon after, English joint-stock companies were taken public. Scholarly studies underline a strong link between the Glorious Revolution, the Financial Revolution, and England's rise to world domination in the eighteenth century. In the country, Parliament's approval of royal borrowings guaranteed that the debt would be repaid and indirectly legitimized the interests of bondholders. This decision was particularly influential in the development of banking and capital markets. With such a "*credible commitment*" to public debt, Britain could borrow at lower interest rates than absolutist states such as France, where bondholders' voices were not represented in the government (Neal, 1994).

The most crucial difference between the examples from English and Dutch was the organization of trade. This was also due to differences in political institutions. In the Netherlands, granting trade monopolies was essential in generating revenue for the rulers. In England, on the other hand, since the power of kings was restricted, the Parliament blocked attempts to create such monopolies (Hill, 2018). One of these was the Royal African Company, which monopolized the slave trade. It was backed by the Duke of York, brother of King Charles II of England. It is estimated that this company sent more enslaved Africans to America than any other company during the Atlantic slave trade. After King William III of England, under pressure from the Parliament of England, revoked the company's monopoly in 1697, the company's activities were weakened (Robinson & Acemoglu, 2012). Despite this, England's decentralized trade system created more competition, driving economic innovation and efficiency. On the contrary, the Netherlands' reliance on monopolies initially brought stability but eventually made the economy less adaptable to changing global trade patterns. England's parliamentary restrictions on monopolies encouraged broader economic participation and growth, while the Netherlands' monopoly-based system ultimately hindered long-term financial flexibility. This difference was crucial in shaping the rise of Britain as the dominant economic power of the eighteenth century.

6.2 Formation of the London Stock Exchange (18th Century)

The Royal Exchange of London, which opened in 1571 under the leadership of Thomas Gresham, was created to support and facilitate international trade. Although it also played a significant role in domestic commerce, the Royal Exchange was a centralized hub where merchants, financiers, and traders could gather to conduct business, negotiate deals, and exchange information. The Royal Exchange was an innovative institution for its time, reflecting the expanding scope of English commerce during the Elizabethan era. It operated at the intersection of trade, finance, and networking, supporting the burgeoning global trading networks that characterized the sixteenth century. While it was not exclusively focused on international trade, its structure and purpose significantly contributed to London's role in the global economy. This building, built by Gresham, was destroyed in the Fire of London in 1666. A second building, opened in 1669, was destroyed by fire in 1838.

A securities market existed in London long before a formal stock exchange was established. There is evidence of shares being traded in the few joint-stock companies in the sixteenth century. However, the ownership of shares was concentrated in a tiny group of wealthy individuals. Therefore, there was no need for intermediaries and organized markets to bring buyers and sellers together. It is pretty clear that by the last decade of the seventeenth century, a continuous market for the exchange of securities existed, and a well-recognized class of brokers had formed, with a regular fee ranging from 1/2 shilling to 1/4 shilling per share (Smith, 1929). Before 1700, the basis of investment was land, and the primary purpose of finance was debt (credit), not equity capital. Inspired by the Dutch East India Company (VOC), the British established an East India Company (EIC) private company in 1600 for Atlantic trade. The EIC was the most influential company in history. It dominated global trade between Europe, South Asia, and the Far East, fought numerous wars using its army and navy, and conquered and colonized modern-day India, Pakistan, Bangladesh, and Burma. However, we know more about the VOC than the EIC because the VOC had seven chambers, with each letter sent to all, ensuring multiple copies. In contrast, the EIC had only one head office, resulting in fewer copies and a more challenging reconstruction of its history.

Before 1689, there were around 15 sizeable joint-stock companies in England with a total share capital of £0.9 million, most focused on overseas trade. In these, shares were transferable in the same way as in the VOC. From the seventeenth century onward, with the confidence generated by the Bank of England, Britain's systematic borrowing led to the proliferation of instruments such as treasury bills and bonds. By 1695, companies in England had a capital of £4.3 million and numbered around 150. Although foreign trade remained important, local banking and water supply projects were gaining prominence. This development was one of the achievements of the Glorious Revolution. The development of the formation of joint-stock companies put the securities market on a more permanent and critical basis than before, and the focal point of this market was London (Michie, 2001).

In London, the emergence of transferable (bearer) shares issued by companies, similar to the Dutch practice, created a volume of securities business. This development led to the emergence of professional brokerage and organized markets. During this period, the most important securities in the market were the so-called *consol* bonds issued by the Treasury, which had no maturity and provided indefinite annual interest. Treasury debt and interest were attractive to investors because the state guaranteed them. Still, only a certain number of investors could afford to buy this debt, which had an indefinite duration and no repayment (redemption) date. However, the fact that the bonds could change hands under a market mechanism (transferable bonds) facilitated this exchange. Thus, the government could borrow indefinitely with only a commitment to pay a fixed interest rate, while the bondholders could sell it to someone else at the prevailing market price. A similar situation existed with large-scale joint-stock companies, especially the British East India Company, established to pioneer long-distance trade between Western Europe and India. The companies guaranteed the shareholders a share of that year's profits through an annual dividend. Although the size of the capital required by joint-stock companies was small compared to the needs of the government, the volume of trading in their securities was often high, as every rumor about the arrival of ships and current prospects led to speculative trading (Michie, 2001).

6.3 Development of the Securities Market

In the early eighteenth century, new companies were being established—the number of securities to be traded and the number of interested investors increased, thus expanding the market. In the 1710s, in the run-up to the so-called South Sea Bubble and a series of speculative ventures, some 190 new joint-stock companies were founded. The South Sea Company was founded in 1711 to supply enslaved people to the Spanish colonies in South America. The company received huge loans from the Bank of England and was encouraged to invest by the British government. In exchange for a monopoly in the South American colonies, it also assumed the debt incurred by Britain during the war. However, speculation in the company's shares following the initial good news led to a new financial crisis known as the "*South Sea Bubble,*" following the "*Mississippi Crisis*" in France in 1720 (Garber, 1990).

By the 1720s, investors were attracted to the South Sea Company. South Sea shares traded at £130 in January 1720 and peaked at £1050 in June 1720. Everyone, from princes to farmers, from all levels of society, was on a buying spree. One of them was the famous scientist Isaac Newton. When asked about the South Sea stocks in the spring of 1720, Sir Isaac Newton said he could "*calculate the movements of the stars, but not the madness of men.*" The South Sea bubble burst in August 1720, and a significant crisis ensued. By 1722, share prices had fallen by two-thirds. Newton probably lost a fortune of 20 million dollars in today's money in the South Sea bubble (Odlyzko, 2019).

Before the crisis, the securities market was active, with shares changing hands at vastly inflated prices. The government passed the Bubble Act in 1720 to prevent entrepreneurs from lying and cheating when setting up companies, protect investors from being tricked into giving their money to fake companies, and ban joint-stock companies unless authorized by Parliament. Limiting the number of licenses also benefited existing companies by reducing competition in the capital markets, but the law was repealed in 1825 (Patterson & Reiffen, 1990).

Merchants invested their profits from banking or trade in government bonds. People holding government bonds with no maturity needed a market where they could sell them to liquidate the funds they had invested. Gradually, a solid demand for government securities began to emerge. In this market, a large and permanent mass of securities was based on a significant and regular volume of transactions. This created an infrastructure on which a newly organized and established securities market could develop.

Trading occurred on the streets or in coffeehouses such as Jonathan's or Garraway's, where buyers and sellers could meet and negotiate. Until the mid-seventeenth century, alcohol, especially beer, was widely consumed in England. As

Fig. 6.2 London Coffeehouses-17th Century https://commons.wikimedia.org/wiki/File:10_The_Coffee_House.JPG

we explained at the beginning of the chapter, the introduction of coffee in London kept people sober and thinking clearly. Interestingly, new investment pursuits and organizations began to emerge among the population. The creative ideas generated in the coffeehouses triggered the spectacular economic growth of the following decades (Fig. 6.2).

Garraway's Coffeehouse was famous for its candlelit auctions, which meant the last bidder would win the auction before the candle went out. It was a very old coffeehouse, and it claimed that in 1671, the Hudson's Bay Company held its first fur sale at Garraways. "In the 1720s, it was one of the main places where investors fell victim to the South Sea Bubble, which had bankrupted hundreds of people." In addition to goods, enslaved people were also traded in Garraway. The other famous coffeehouse was Jonathan's. John Castaing, a French Huguenot merchant, was a regular at Jonathan's in 1690, where he began to list stock prices, bullion prices, and exchange rates in a newspaper called "*The Course of Exchange and Other Things*." Published twice a week, the newspaper quickly gained a good reputation and was published for a century (Neal, 1988). Lloyd's Coffeehouse, frequented by merchants and sailors, was where deals in the shipping industry were conducted. It became the famous insurance company Lloyd's of London (Green, 2013).

6.4 Formation of Securities Intermediaries

In the 1690 s, the investment process went like this: "*The person wishing to invest goes to the brokers in the coffee house and asks how the stocks are doing and, on being informed, offers the broker to buy or sell if he can, such and such number of shares at such and such a price: the broker then tries what he can by bargaining among those who can buy or sell stocks*" (Cope, 1978). If one broker worked to buy, he would contact a second broker to sell (Dickson, 1967). The number and type of securities increased, and it was not easy for both buyers and sellers to access their counterparts in coffeehouses. For these reasons, auctions were held regularly in Garraways, where anyone interested could bid for securities. The 17th-century London market involved a bid-ask spread, but it was informed informally through broker negotiations rather than a transparent quoting system. While there are some similarities with modern stock exchange trading, the key differences lie in standardization, centralization, and speed.

Garraways was populated by people of all social classes, including lawyers, judges, and sailors. It did not matter whether a man was dressed in a tattered overcoat and found himself sitting between a pot-bellied count and a respected bishop; more than that, he could converse with them and know that he would be answered in a civilized manner. People also went here to trade stocks, ships, and enslaved people. Robert Hooke (1635–1703), known at the time for his astronomy and architecture and called the Leonardo (da Vinci) of England, was a regular at this coffeehouse (Ellis, 1956). For business to run smoothly, brokers who worked for customers who wanted to dispose of or buy securities were needed. People from various professions took on these tasks. The number of intermediaries began to increase rapidly in the 1690 s, and the government tried to limit the total number to 100 with a law passed in 1697. Still, the number continued to grow (Michie, 2001).

In those days, the stock market in London was in its infancy, prices were set in coffeehouses, and the brokerage function was left to some rude individuals. News agencies like Reuters and Bloomberg did not yet exist. News runners performed their roles. Transactions such as manipulation and insider trading, considered crimes today, could be done freely. The market volume was relatively low, and when investors did not show interest in the market for various reasons, trading in the market would fall.

A group of leading Dutch brokers also brought significant expertise to London. One of them was Abraham Ricardo. His father, a successful stockbroker in Amsterdam, sent him to London around 1759. His son, David Ricardo, became the most famous economist of his time (Kurz, 2016). David Ricardo made a fortune speculating on British government bonds during the Napoleonic Wars and became one of the most influential figures on the London Stock Exchange (Cathcart, 2015). Through his later writings, he shaped market movements and influenced economic thought.

Due to short-term trading, the profession of stockbroker became increasingly professionalized. Stockbrokers could only arrange sales or purchases on behalf of their clients if willing buyers or sellers could be found. The securities market became increasingly complex in the eighteenth century, with the practices of continental European bankers. Lastly, Dutch Jews and French Huguenots brought in their practices. Even before 1700, call/put options were used alongside futures. Option contracts had short maturities. The custom of making contracts for a month or longer had developed. In 1734, however, the government wanted to reduce speculation by banning options. In response, the option ban did not work well in practice, as in the Netherlands, and derivatives trading for speculation continued to flourish. There were various ways to speculate in the eighteenth century. Most of them had the characteristic of requiring only a small initial outlay of cash or even no cash at all. In most of them, significant losses could not be avoided when things went wrong. One way was to use put options and call options—another way to enter forward stock contracts. A third was short selling, i.e., selling borrowed securities and buying them later at a lower price. Of these, only the call option limited losses; if things went badly, the investor could burn the premium and stop trading. All forms of speculation, which probably dominated the securities markets for most of the eighteenth century, reflected the spirit of an age that tolerated gambling (Cope, 1978).

Isaac de Pinto, a Dutch banker of Jewish origin, wrote: "*Many people who borrowed stocks from others immediately sold them at a high price for speculation. Then, with the help of false news, they would alarm the public and sell some of the stocks lent to them for cash at five or even ten percent below the market price. A small amount sold for cash would dominate the market. As the excitement increased, they continued this game until finally, the people from whom they had borrowed the stocks were forced to sell them to them at the lowest price*" (De Pinto, 1771).

From 1700 onward, specialized dealers called "*jobbers*" emerged as market makers, buying and selling securities on their accounts. Their presence made the market more flexible and responsive to news. Using their funds, they aimed to profit from price fluctuations, including short selling. Between 1708 and 1755, 43 market makers operated in London, creating liquidity by acting as intermediaries. However, the constant buying and selling puzzled and even alarmed society, fueling anti-broker sentiment (Michie, 2001).

As early as 1716, an anonymous contemporary wrote a vicious attack on the general securities market and stockbrokers. "*From this corruption of the mercantile companies has sprung the vermin called stockbrokers, who prey upon, destroy, and discourage all Industry and honest gain; for as soon as any Mercantile Company is founded, or any bad project is formed to deceive the public, it is immediately divided into shares, and then bought and sold in the Stock Exchange Street, without knowing whether there is any real value in the project. If no such sound design has been made to promote Industry and Commerce, the stock trade will eventually damn it in its infancy.*" This author even went so far as to call for the prohibition of transferable securities, saying that "*the buying and selling of stocks, transfer or speculation, ruins everything and is a bane to all honesty and ind*ustry" (Michie, 2001).

The first detailed description of this market was published in 1761 in "*Every Man His Broker*" by Thomas Mortimer under the pseudonym "*Philanthropos.*" Mortimer was a prolific writer on political, economic, and business matters and had lost a considerable fortune in the stock markets (coffeehouses). He said of the term Bull, which today describes the rise of the stock market, that "*it is the name by which the gentlemen in the coffee-house had chosen to designate all persons who contract to buy any amount of government securities without the intention or ability to pay, and who are consequently compelled to sell them again at a profit or loss before the time comes when they contracted to buy them.*" According to him, market makers fell into three classes: foreigners working with foreign funds, those working with funds belonging to English gentlemen, and stockbrokers doing business on credit, called traders. Mortimer wrote that two-thirds of brokers were unlicensed, primarily buying and selling for themselves while sometimes acting as middlemen (Cope, 1978).

However, those who bought, held, or sold securities in the eighteenth century did so for various reasons, many of which were long-term investments for permanent income. Among investors in East India Company stock, for example, many were content to receive annual dividend payments without changing their holdings through sale or purchase. According to one estimate for January 1767, some 44 percent of East India Company Stockholders were of this type (Michie, 2001).

Throughout the eighteenth century, an inverse relationship developed between land investment and government debt. During wartime, high government borrowing led investors to favor bonds over land. In peacetime, lower borrowing revived interest in real estate. After wars, rising bond prices encouraged investors to sell and convert gains into land. Government debt's liquidity and safety made it an attractive alternative to land, especially for London insurance companies, which preferred easily cashable securities for large payouts. On the other hand, London insurance companies preferred securities to land and property because they could be easily converted into cash in an accident requiring a large, significant, and immediate payout to the policyholder (Michie, 2001).

Bank deposits also offered great flexibility but were not risk-free; many banks failed in this period. Investors mainly had a short-term view; it expanded the securities market, and the role of market-making increased. Throughout the eighteenth century, banks commonly invested their idle balances in short-term transferable securities, directly or indirectly. Moreover, contributed to the capital market (Pressnell, 1956).

In the eighteenth century, London's securities market became part of the money market but was never central to economic growth. Dutch investors dominated world trade, with Amsterdam as the leading financial center (Michie, 2001). The European economy began to move away from a system in which international payments were made only in gold and silver coins and in which goods had to be transported, i.e., taken to and from specific places, to be traded. Instead, multilateral payment systems based on securities and the use of credit became the norm. This inevitably required constant adjustment of balances between countries. Bankers with connections and activities in two or more countries sought to provide this service. The result was a market for claims and debts arising from international trade. By the middle of the eighteenth century, the securities market was part of it. In Amsterdam, as in London, there was a substantial market for securities issued by the British government. This was because the securities market was crucial in providing the finance to enable international trade, to manage risk, and to support infrastructure investment. The liquidity provided by the securities market expanded the scale of global trade while supporting the sustainable and safe conduct of trade. The synergy between these two structures was one of the cornerstones of the globalization process of the modern economy. As a result, debt and credit could be created in London or Amsterdam to meet the needs of traders in either country who wanted to make payments. The strong integration of London and Amsterdam's capital markets in the eighteenth century was a key development in European financial history, driving transnational finance and globalization. This connection facilitated trade and war financing, with domestic and Dutch conditions influencing stock prices. Until the French Revolution, interest rates in both cities converged, reflecting high monetary integration. Local banks, insurers, and bond brokers, acting for foreign clients, had to move quickly, requiring strong cooperation and trust to ensure payments and stock deliveries (Michie, 2001).

The Great Fire of London in 1666 destroyed the old stock exchange building and a third of the city, and a second building, designed by Edward Jerman in the Baroque style, opened in 1669. Traders and brokers operated there (Field, 2017). However, by 1688, many brokers had been expelled from the Royal Exchange for rude behavior. Brokers still operated in the streets and coffeehouses in the neighborhood, including Jonathan's Coffeehouse in Change Alley. However, there was not yet an organization in the market that everyone could trust.

6.5 The London Stock Market

The most significant risk for market players was that a default in the chain of transactions could jeopardize everyone's ability to make payments or deliveries, weakening the market itself. Indeed, the South Sea Bubble 1720 highlighted the dangers of default risk in 18th-century financial markets. Traders relied heavily on credit, and when one major player defaulted, it triggered a chain reaction of failures across Amsterdam, Hamburg, and London. Therefore, in the eighteenth century, the securities market also required a system of controls to guarantee that purchases and sales were honored when due. The Bernard Act of 1734 made futures trading illegal, considering it a form of gambling. Therefore, futures could not be traded. Consequently, it was left to market participants to establish a code of conduct that enforced the conditions necessary for trading (Neal, 1987).

Even without legal barriers, those actively participating in the market had to find a solution to their problems, independent of national laws and governments. For example, London bankers established the 31-member London Clearing House in 1773 to deal with interbank business, while marine insurers formed an organization called New Lloyds in 1774 to meet the specific needs of their business (Long, 2010). Essentially, what professionals wanted for speed and confidence was a reputable market in which everyone present was an active participant, ready to buy or sell when the opportunity arose, and trusted to fulfill their part of the bargain.

In 1772, a group of stockbrokers built a new building in Sweetings Alley called the Exchange next to Garraway's coffeehouse (Fig. 6.3). Intended as a private organization, the Exchange building seemed to have replaced Jonathan's as an essential

Fig. 6.3 Exchange Alley -17th Century https://en.wikipedia.org/wiki/Exchange_Alley#/media/File:Garraway's_Coffee_House.jpg (Public Domain)

center for securities trading. The way the market was organized and controlled was essentially unchanged. Professionals could pay daily entry fees to the exchange and conduct business with other professionals in the building. They could also frequent other buildings, especially the Bank of England, where they could deal directly with investors or with more ordinary intermediaries such as bankers or lawyers. Interest in joint-stock companies and their securities was also growing in the provinces. This interest focused on canal projects from the 1780s onward and would reach an investment frenzy in the early 1790s (Michie, 2001).

Most trades were speculative. Such transactions could be carried out "*on account*" without payment or delivery. This system allowed traders to go long or short without paying a premium upfront, effectively engaging in leveraged trading. This system functioned similarly to margin trading today, where an investor could control a prominent position with relatively little upfront capital. Thomas Mortimer's "*Every Man His Broker*" (1761) describes how speculators engaged in forward contracts, postponing payments while betting on price movements (Cope, 1978).

While speculators were major users of on-account transactions due to their profit-driven motives, other participants like hedgers, arbitrageurs, market makers, and businesses also benefit from these transactions' flexibility and efficiency. However, the existence of a settlement date required such transactions to result in some actual payment and bring order to the market. Speculators who bought when the price was rising or sold when it was falling and tried to close their trades before the settlement date helped smooth out market fluctuations. They stabilized markets by adding liquidity, correcting price overshoots, aiding price convergence, spreading risk, and shaping expectations. This encouraged investors to repurchase stocks. The fortnightly settlement system introduced in the stock market was a compromise between the convenience of deals of various durations and the need to curb speculative excesses by limiting the duration (Michie, 2001).

By the end of the century, the French Revolution of 1789 had shifted the balance. The French Revolution ushered in a period of instability and war until Napoleon's defeat at Waterloo in 1815. The Paris Stock Exchange was closed in 1793, and the leading Paris bankers moved their operations to London. Moreover, due to the French troops' occupation of Amsterdam in 1795, prominent bankers and brokers left Amsterdam to set up businesses in London (Ferguson, 1999). Meanwhile, the Frankfurt banker Mayer Rothschild had sent his son Nathan Rothschild to London. He would later send his other sons to Paris, Naples, and Vienna, laying the foundations of the Rothschild Empire in five major cities, including Frankfurt. By the end of the century, rival financial centers—Paris and Amsterdam—were simultaneously disappearing, while London was flooded with wealth and skilled traders (Ferguson, 1999).

By the end of the eighteenth century, the inadequate organization of the London securities market had become apparent as foreign investors became increasingly influential in the market. On January 7, 1801, the Committee of Proprietors, representing the owners of the Exchange building, proposed that the building be converted into a subscription-only system (Michie, 2001). Fraud was also widespread at this time, and users of the exchange room were required to pay a high fee to deter such transactions. They thought that a subscription-only system for the London Exchange building could prevent fraud by combining controlled access, accountability, high entry costs, peer regulation, and clear consequences for misconduct. This system could also create an environment where trust and professionalism are prioritized, discouraging fraudsters and enabling honest participants to trade more confidently. At a meeting of the subscribers on March 4, 1801, David Ricardo, one of the owners of the exchange, proposed that the powers of the owners of the new exchange be transferred to the Trustees and Managers and the powers of the subscribed members of the exchange be transferred to the General Purposes Committee. The powers of each were defined and separated from each other. Thus, while the London Stock Exchange (LSE) officially came to life, the governance structure it would maintain throughout the nineteenth century was also determined (Neal, 2006). In addition, a committee of full-time administrative staff was authorized to monitor these rules and regulations and to expel members from the market if necessary. In February 1802, 363 brokers and market makers were members of the Exchange (Michie, 2001).

6.6 Development of the London Stock Exchange in the Early 19th Century

6.6.1 The Organization of the Exchange

With the establishment of the Subscription Chamber in 1801, the exchange could now exclude undesirables and develop its own rules. Thus, it excluded people who were unreliable due to their past actions or current reputation or who posed a risk to other members due to their additional activities. Between February 17 and April 10, 1802, the first renewal date, 498 people were accepted for membership, while 17 were rejected. The Exchange moved to its new premises in Capel Court in 1802. In particular, applicants whose main occupation was not that of a stockbroker or market maker began to be rejected. By 1807, applicants were denied because they were "engaged in trade" or "engaged in other business." The ongoing development of the securities market changed with the establishment of the Stock Exchange. Henceforth, the securities market was no longer an open market where participants could enter at any time and act without paying a subscription fee. Instead, it encompassed business behavior and an institutional organization that separated members from non-members. From 1812 onward, all new members had to limit their business to buying and selling securities. The reason for this restriction was the fear that a significant loss incurred by a member outside the Exchange in trading or banking would spill over to other members who were in a position to make payments or deliveries, causing them to suffer significant losses as well and thus jeopardizing the stability of the entire market. For example, a six-month member, Thomas Manson, had outstanding commitments to other members totaling £134,000 when he went bankrupt on April 2, 1814, due to a sudden price drop. To pay these debts to other members, the exchange expected the member concerned to have all his assets available and not to be disputed with non-exchange creditors. As early as 1821, members recommending new applicants were required to guarantee losses of up to £250 due to recent failures. By 1832, this had been raised to £300. If multiple members recommended the same applicant, their combined guarantees might help, but it was still a tiny safety net compared to the potential losses a failing broker could cause. Groups such as London private bankers, merchants who were bankers, and discount or bond brokers were not allowed to become members of the exchange. These included well-known bankers such as Nathan Rothschild (Michie, 2001).

The exchange did not introduce minimum commission rates, which regulated the fees brokers charged their clients for trading. Since price competition was undesirable, a standard commission rate was used in practice. This rate was 1/8 of a pound for buying and selling for every £100 (Smith, 1929). Brokerage houses earned their income from trading commissions. On the other hand, dealers earned their income from bid-ask spreads or underwriting fees. In the absence of price competition in the stock market, brokerage houses sought to broaden their customer base by expanding their customer pools or increasing the variety of financial products they offered each customer. Market makers likewise sought to minimize market volatility by increasing trading volumes rather than bid-ask spreads because volatility increased their cost of equity (Neal, 2006).

The Bank of England and coffeehouses continued to be frequented by securities traders. Coffeehouses continued to be popular, especially among investors who were not stock exchange members. Investors and non-exchange brokers there were often uncouth, and the stock exchange would not have accepted vulgar people anyway. Members were not allowed to join another institution established as a securities market. A rival organization was not wanted. Securities trading under the Bank of England was closed in 1834. Although there were other alternative markets for securities in London, the supremacy of the Stock Exchange was now recognized.

The services provided by the Stock Exchange were still not respected enough. A satire in 1819 said: "*These are the crows that hunt the pigeons that flock around the house that Jack has built*"—the crows being the market makers, the pigeons the speculators, and the house the stock exchange. This metaphor draws from the traditional nursery rhyme "*This is the house that Jack built*," where Jack is a generic figure responsible for creating a structure or system. In this context, Jack likely refers to the owners of the exchange, the early financiers who established the stock exchange to facilitate trading and bring order to financial transactions. However, the satire implies skepticism or criticism of the institution's practices and its participants at the time, portraying it as a place rife with opportunism (crows) and naivety (pigeons). Other criticisms were much harsher. By the middle of the nineteenth century, however, it had come to be recognized that the job of the stock exchange was not only to bring order to transactions but also to bring assurance and transparency to the securities market. To achieve this, the emphasis was placed on all negotiations in the open market, usually, as far as possible, through brokers or market makers, and an official representative of the Exchange recorded prices. When a transaction was suspected, the Committee launched rigorous investigations. It was understood that it was in the best interest of the stock exchange to ensure that the investing public trusted the market (Michie, 2001).

The two groups of owners and members influenced the establishment of the exchange in 1801, but there were internal conflicts between them (Neal & Davis, 2005). The stock exchange owners were vital in managing the exchange, ensuring order, and setting rules for membership and trading. However, they were generally not as active in the ownership of stocks as the members or traders who bought and sold securities. Their importance lay in creating a reliable and regulated space for trading, from which they derived financial benefit through membership fees and their control over the exchange's operations. These debates included determining the fees charged, admitting new members, and setting the membership standard. The most serious dispute between owners and members occurred in 1821–1822. This concerned the question of whether derivatives trading should be banned. Many members had been concerned that extensive and long-term futures and options posed a real danger to the Exchange. If one or more members failed by owing significant amounts of securities or money to other members, this could lead to a cascading collapse to the detriment of all. In 1820, there was a call for the abolition of the option. Finally, in July 1821, it was decided that only futures options with a term of 14 days or less would be recognized as covered by Exchange regulations and, therefore, enforceable. In the end, the ban was significantly eased, if not repealed. By April 1815, the number of members had reached 541 (Michie, 2001).

In the eighteenth century, a period existed between sale or purchase and delivery or payment on the LSE. This time was necessary to cope with communication and transportation problems. In the early nineteenth century, settlement dates were known in advance every 19 or 20 days. The formal clearing systems were not as advanced as today, and settlements could involve physical paperwork and manual processes to transfer ownership of stocks or securities. This led to more flexible and sometimes more extended settlement periods than in modern times. The settlement system was more flexible and varied, with some transactions settling around 19–20 days, especially for government bonds. In contrast, other stock transactions could settle in a shorter period, typically no less than two to three weeks. Business could be conducted in cash, but it was standard practice to trade on account. The extended settlement date had other advantages. Much of the trading was of a technical or speculative nature, with operators buying what they could not afford or selling what they did not have in the expectation of turning the deal around at a profit. This could be done on the account without needing payment or delivery. However, the existence of a settlement date made it necessary for such transactions to result in some actual payment (Michie, 1986).

As a result, all the institutional structures that characterize an efficient stock market were in place at the beginning of the nineteenth century: rules for the transfer of ownership, professional arbitrageurs, freely available price information, and a wide range of potentially tradable instruments. No element of a modern market was missing. Moreover, by traditional criteria, the stock market was relatively efficient and could reflect incoming information in the price (Mirowski, 1981).

6.6.2 The Market After the Battle of Waterloo

During the Napoleonic Wars (1803–1815), most activity on the London Stock Exchange before the Battle of Waterloo was speculative, fueled by rumors and news about the war's progress. Brian Cathcart's book, The News from Waterloo, shows how news reporting shaped public perception and influenced financial markets. It highlights how rumors and facts about Waterloo impacted the prices of government bonds (Consols) on the Stock Exchange, driving market speculation.

News from continental Europe took 3–4 days to reach England. If there was a military success, it was expected that the war would end, and therefore, government borrowing would decrease, inflation would fall, interest rates would decline, and the stock market would rise. Conversely, defeat would prolong the conflict and its associated costs, pushing prices down. At this time, some speculators made huge profits through information manipulation (Box 6.1). The fact that the stockbroker Peter Templeman bought and sold £54,000 worth of government bonds on his account in May 1815 alone and emerged from the war a wealthy man as a result of these activities is an indication of the volume of business created in the war environment (Michie, 2001). There were also rumors of other stock manipulations involving the Rothschilds after the Battle of Waterloo (Cathcart, 2015; Karan et al., 2024).

Box 6.1: Stock Market Manipulation in 1814

In 1814, a group spread a false rumor claiming to be from France. In this case, a man in uniform, who identified himself as Colonel Du Bourg and claimed to be Lord Cathcart's aide, arrived at the Ship Inn in Dover, England, on the morning of Monday, February 21, 1814, with the news that King Napoleon I of France had been killed and Bourbon rule had been restored. He requested that the information be transmitted by telegraph to the Admiralty in London and then set off for London, stopping at inns to spread the news. Three men dressed in Bourbon uniforms, pretending to be French officers, were also seen celebrating. Rumors of Napoleon's defeat had circulated throughout the month. When the news began circulating among traders on the London Stock Exchange, the value of government bonds skyrocketed. However, with no official confirmation of the news, prices began to fall, only to rise again on news of the French officers' supposed celebrations. Later, when the whole affair became recognized as a manipulation, the stocks' prices immediately fell back to their previous levels. Suspecting stock manipulation, the Exchange Committee launched an investigation. It soon emerged that on that Monday, more than £1.1 million had been sold in two government-owned stocks, most of which had been bought the previous week. Lord Cochrane, an iconoclastic British politician and admiral who ranks among the most outstanding British seamen, was implicated in the scandal because his uncle, Andrew Cochrane-Johnstone, was a key organizer of the scheme. The central role in organizing the scheme was his alleged financial gains from inflated stock prices and a suspicious visit from one of the conspirators to his residence. Six others, including those involved in the purchase, were tried and sentenced to twelve months in prison; the most prominent were also sentenced to public pillory; fines were also imposed. Lord Cochrane was stripped of his naval rank and expelled from the Order of the Bath and the House of Commons. Andrew Cochrane-Johnstone fled the country after hearing the verdict. Despite his conviction for fraud, Lord Cochrane continued to claim his innocence. The public supported Cochrane; he was acquitted and re-elected unopposed to the House of Commons in Westminster. Lord Cochrane continued to petition the government for redress; in 1832, he was granted a free pardon, which included a return to the rank of Rear-Admiral. The Order of the Bath and other honors were restored in the following years (Cathcart, 2015; Pollard, 2010).

In the mid-1820s, attention turned to securities issued by other governments, especially those of neighboring Western European countries. Because of the high price of British securities, there was a significant public tendency to speculate on foreign securities. In 1822, at least five foreign government bonds with a nominal value of £8.9 million were issued in London, followed by two more in 1823 (£5 million), seven in 1824 (£14.7 million), and six in 1825 (£11.5 million), amounting to twenty bond issues with a nominal value of £40.1 million over four years (Michie, 2001). Due to the integrated nature of international capital markets, bonds issued in London were traded in other countries.

By the end of the Napoleonic wars, Spain's control over its South American colonies had weakened, and all South American countries had gained independence from Portugal and Spain. Most of these countries had mines producing gold and silver. In particular, newly independent Latin American countries such as Colombia, Chile, Peru, Mexico, and Brazil borrowed heavily in London during this period, realizing half the issue amount. Some European sovereign debt securities also attracted considerable interest in the London market. An active secondary market developed for these foreign government bonds. Most borrowing countries were unknown, and prices fluctuated wildly as rumors and expectations multiplied. During this period, foreign investment was continuing in London. When news from abroad was received, the fiscal prospects of various governments, and hence their ability to repay loans, were reassessed, significantly affecting the current price at which they were traded. By August 1822, foreign bond investments were risky but highly profitable for their investors. These included politically important bonds that supported the Greek revolt against the Ottomans (Harari, 2014).

While international bond investments were accelerating, regional stock markets were developing. British markets expanded beyond national borders at the end of the Napoleonic Wars. During the 1820–1850 period, London gradually turned toward becoming an international market.

6.6.3 *Foreign Investments and Other Market Developments Between 1820 and 1850*

Initially, trading in foreign bonds took place on the street, outside the Stock Exchange. However, after much debate, on January 1, 1823, a separate Foreign Funds market was opened on the Exchange. This market would accept existing members of the Exchange free of charge, but non-members would be charged an annual fee of 8 guineas. Thus, the membership structure of the Exchange would not change much. Rothschild was a member of the Foreign Funds market but was not eligible for admission to the Exchange. Investors and speculators were not satisfied with foreign government bonds for long and soon turned their attention to the issuance of newly established local and foreign joint-stock companies. Many of these were risky and were sold outside the stock market in coffeehouses. Foreign government bonds had relatively low returns and a growing risk of default; however, joint-stock companies were more dynamic and had profitable investment opportunities (Michie, 2001).

As South American bonds continue to attract attention, bonds from a fictional South American country called Poyais have appeared on the market. Nobody was looking to see if it was real or not. MacGregor, a Scottish adventurer who had fought for Venezuela in the war of independence against Spain, had created an entirely fictional state and convinced investors that the Central American principality of Poyais had enormous resources. MacGregor was so persuasive that he organized a significant bond issue for this country on the LSE in 1822 (Karan, 2022).

In 1817, Gregor McGregor served as a Colonel in the Venezuelan War of Independence under Simon Bolivar, fighting in Florida. In 1820, he returned to London and announced his appointment as Cacique (Prince) of the Principality of Poyais. The country was located in the Gulf of Honduras, and the land was granted to him by King Frederic Augustus I, the indigenous chief of the Mosquito Coast and Nation. In a book he published, Sketch of the Mosquito Shore, it was stated that British settlers had established St. Joseph as the capital in the 1730s and had untapped gold and silver mines, fertile soil, and other vast resources for the settlers to exploit. This was all a figment of the imagination. In reality, King Frederic Augustus had signed the document granting the land to McGregor in April 1820 after making him drink whiskey and run away. The estate had only four ramshackle buildings and was surrounded by a wild forest with no fertile soil, no gold or silver mines, and none of the other assets McGregor described in his book. The book was quite influential. On October 23, 1822, McGregor launched 2000 bonds for the wealthy at £100 each, resulting in sales of £200,000. The bonds were offered for sale at £80, and interest was payable at 3%. He offered land for sale for the poor at 3 shillings and 3 pence (later 4 shillings) per acre, which in 1822 was equivalent to about a day's wages. It, therefore, seemed a beautiful investment opportunity. Also, he sold positions in his army and the right to become a jeweler, teacher, clerk, or other artisan in the new country. He even issued his currency that settlers could use when they arrived in McGregor's El Dorado. The Poyaisian Embassy in England opened offices in London and land offices in Glasgow, Stirling, and Edinburgh to sell land to fellow Scots. By 1823, Gregor McGregor was a multi-millionaire in today's terms (Sinclair, 2003).

As surprising as it may seem, the Poyais Embassy had chartered two boats to take the settlers to Poyais. On September 10, 1822, the ship left London with 70 settlers, including doctors, lawyers, and bankers. Also, on January 22, 1823, the Kennersley Castle left the Port of Leith in Scotland with about 200 settlers. When the settlers arrived, they found an uninhabitable jungle with more tropical diseases than silver and gold. Of the first 240 settlers to reach Poyais, only 60 survived, and 50 returned to London on August 1 and arrived in London on October 12, 1823. Surprisingly, most of the settlers had defended Gregor McGregor. He then continued his activities in France, but without success. He was arrested for a time but acquitted in court (Sinclair, 2003). Gregor MacGregor's charismatic leadership, psychological defense mechanisms, colonial ideals of the period, and the shameful perception of being "*deceived*" in society caused the settlers to defend him. This incident is also one of the most interesting examples of "*the loyalty of the deceived to the deceiver*" in historical terms.

However, the speculative boom led to a crisis at the end 1825, and trading volume collapsed. Several banks that had lent heavily on the security of speculative stocks and shares went bankrupt. Only one-fifth of the joint-stock companies survived until the end of 1826; not only the Latin American republics but also Greece, Portugal, and Spain defaulted (Neal, 1998).

Trading in foreign securities continued to be seen by many members as a much riskier business than trading in UK sovereign debt. This was due to the poor record of foreign governments in securing their debts and the time it took for information from abroad to reach London. In the case of Latin America, it took months, and then the information was disseminated to the market through a wide variety of sources. As a result, trading in foreign securities was much more open to manipulation and rumors than in the British sovereign debt market, creating risks for the entire market. Those who subscribed to the Foreign Funds market either gave up their securities business or tried to join the Stock Exchange. After much debate, the Foreign Funds market and the Stock Exchange merged in February 1835 (Neal & Davis, 2006). However, the LSE had a separate market for foreign securities, often called the "Foreign Market" within the Exchange. This was a specialized section where trading in securities issued by foreign governments, municipalities, and companies took place. It developed in response to the growing internationalization of finance during the nineteenth century, driven by Britain's global economic influence and the increasing demand for foreign capital to fund infrastructure projects like railways and public works. The problem of false or incomplete information from abroad did not disappear until the development of international communication technology after 1851, when the international telegraph system began to transform the flow of messages around the world (Michie, 2001).

In the 1830s, regional stock exchanges in England gained importance due to the Industrial Revolution, which spurred growth in industries like textiles, coal, and steel. The railway boom increased investment demand, and local businesses sought capital outside London. Restrictions at LSE and the rise of regional banks encouraged local financial hubs. Wealthy provincial investors preferred trading closer to home, while improved transport and communication made regional exchanges more viable. By the mid-nineteenth century, cities like Manchester, Liverpool, and Glasgow had developed their financial markets, complementing but also competing with London (Michie, 2001).

The Joint Stock Companies Act of 1844 allowed companies in England to incorporate without a royal charter or private act, introducing official company registration and requiring basic transparency. By 1853, seventy-five percent of the securities traded on the LSE were still issued by governments, mainly the British. In contrast, corporate securities accounted for as little as a quarter of the total, with British railways being the largest at 16 percent. With the authorization of the establishment of joint-stock banks in England outside London in 1826 and the extension of this privilege to London in 1833, an increasingly large part of the country's banking was based in London. Banks were among the most active clients of the exchange member (Michie, 2001).

In eighteenth-century England, there was an industrial revolution in the North and a financial revolution in the South. The Industrial Revolution was based on introducing new technology and forms of industrial organization in the wool and worsted industries and later in the cotton, iron, and coal industries. The financial revolution was about the adoption of new financial instruments. This enabled London to challenge Amsterdam as the center of international capital while London continued to outpace all other European cities. London's financial markets were already weakly associated with real capital in the mid-eighteenth century and became strongly associated in the latter part of this century. Integrating the industry and financial sectors in

19th-century England was a symbiotic relationship. The financial industry provided the necessary capital, risk management, and credit infrastructure, while the real sector generated economic growth and returns for investors. This dynamic was central in establishing England as the world's leading industrial and financial power during the nineteenth century (Buchinsky & Polak, 1993).

By 1850, the British Stock Exchange had become a global hub, attracting foreign capitalists and bankers from every European capital city. The Limited Liability Act of 1856 enabled shareholders to limit their financial liability to the amount they invested, encouraging wider public investment and fueling industrial expansion. The growth of the stock exchange was remarkable, from 363 members in 1802 to 906 members in 1851. This expansion indicated London's establishment as the center of the world money market. Amsterdam was overshadowed. By the mid-nineteenth century, the LSE had firmly established itself as one of the city's most important institutions, a testament to the success of the financial revolution (Michie, 2001).

6.7 Expansion of the London Stock Exchange (1850–1914)

In general, London had a positive approach to quoting foreign government bonds. Paris, by contrast, heavily restricted the quotation of foreign government bonds and inevitably diverted much of the buying and selling of its citizens to London. Japanese loans, for example, were welcomed in London in the 1870s but not in Paris after 1900 (Michie, 2001). In 1850, the Stock Exchange was the largest and most important of its kind in the world, a reflection of the strength and vitality of the British economy. Its growth was increasingly underpinned by the international opportunities at its heart and by European investors moving in tandem with US investors. At the same time, the transformation of communications, beginning with the telegraph and culminating in the telephone, destroyed the viability of local markets and led to direct competition between distant exchanges for the first time. In 1850, financial assets such as shares, mortgages, bank deposits, commercial loans, and government and corporate debt represented an estimated 39 percent of all assets owned by the British public. By 1912/13, this proportion would reach 64 percent. The remaining were primarily real assets like land, property, industrial equipment, and natural resources. Within this rapid growth of financial assets, the fastest expanding group was transferable securities, which consisted of assets such as bonds and shares. In particular, the share of foreign assets rose from 8 to 28 percent between 1850 and 1913. In 1870, only 0.8 percent of the population could be classified as investors, while in 1913, this figure had risen to only 2.2 percent. While in the middle of the century, investors mainly focused on securities issued by governments or railroads, by 1900, they had shifted to stocks and bonds of industrial, commercial, mining, and other companies, domestic and overseas. Moreover, the average investor held seven to eight different securities by then. Joint-stock banks, insurance companies, and investment trusts were also crucial in financial investments. They were among the leading financial institutions that channeled an increasing share of collective savings into equities in 1850–1914 and did so increasingly professionally. London's financial ecosystem expanded beyond traditional banks, with insurance companies, pension funds, investment trusts, merchant banks, and other institutional players taking on increasingly diversified roles. These institutions professionalized investment management and mobilized British and global capital for industrial, infrastructure, and colonial projects, solidifying London's status as the world's financial hub (Michie, 2001).

6.7.1 The Stock Exchange Organization

In London, the dual control of owners and members continued to be a source of conflict within the Exchange, leading to repeated member conflicts between 1850 and 1914. The number of members was often at the root of this conflict. While the owners wanted to increase the number of members to generate more revenue, members complaining of stagnation did not want new competitors to come in. The divergence of interests and opinions among members and concern over exchange costs prevented any change in the dual control structure before 1914. Neal (2006) argues that the separation of ownership and operation of the LSE was a key factor explaining its success in becoming the world's leading stock exchange in the early period of global financial markets. The limited ownership of shares by shareholders of the company responsible for building and maintaining the physical facilities that housed the exchange meant that any changes in marketing strategy had to be agreed upon. The exchange owners were concerned that a rival exchange might emerge in London if they restricted membership or increased annual subscription fees, and their revenue-raising strategy depended on increasing the total number of subscribers. They, therefore, significantly restricted the ability to increase subscription fees. The large number of members competing for each source of revenue within the exchange and the increasing number of these members forced members to innovate constantly. Thus, brokerage houses maintained the stability of the structure by trying to expand their customer number and variety, either by expanding their customer pool or by increasing the variety of financial products they offered each customer.

After 1850, the LSE needed to diversify its list of stocks further to maintain its central position. To this end, during the years before World War I, the Exchange allowed its members to buy and sell securities that interested them. During the same period, the physical expansion of the floor allowed for listing opportunities for virtually any group of securities of sufficient interest. Investors also found the growing number of listed securities attractive. Once financial institutions realized that the securities had a market value, they could more easily finance activities for these securities (Taylor, & Tonks, 1989).

In the second half of the eighteenth century, brokerage firms began to use new financial instruments. Thus, capital market institutions reorganized and gained expertise in certain areas. As mentioned, the Barnard Act of 1734, which banned futures contracts, including options and forward contracts, was repealed in 1860 (Banner,

1998). A new type of financial institution called an investment trust was created—such institutions operated by issuing stocks and bonds, which were then listed on the stock exchange. The funds thus raised were used to purchase a portfolio of foreign and domestic assets, therefore providing investors with an income generated through an acceptable combination of risk and return. These assets could also serve as collateral for bank loans, which could be reinvested in equities (Michie, 2001).

Between 1850 and 1914, the Stock Exchange accepted a large number and variety of companies but rejected undercapitalized companies. Between 1853 and 1913, the number of different securities listed in London rose to over 5,000. It became impossible for the stock exchange to own all of them, and it became more selective. This was due to increased market complexity, concerns about financial stability, the growth of speculative trading, and the introduction of stricter regulations. By focusing on well-capitalized companies, the Exchange aimed to prevent market instability, protect its reputation, and ensure long-term investor trust. Many securities issues were minor in scale and narrow in scope, leading to an inactive market. Market makers could also not service so many shares (Michie, 2001).

Members had unlimited liability and could lose all their business and personal property in the event of failure, so all financial institutions whose business was risky continued to be restricted from membership in the exchange. In the 19th-century LSE, there were both firm and individual members. However, the structure and the roles of these members were highly regulated to ensure integrity and exclusivity in the operations of the Exchange. All partners of member firms had to be members of the Exchange simultaneously. The rule also prohibited members from sharing profits with non-members. If a firm had external partners who were not members of the Exchange, those partners could potentially benefit from the firm's trading activities without being subject to the Exchange's regulations. This was seen as a risk to market stability and fairness. Enforcing that all partners be members ensured that profits were shared only among those accountable to the Exchange's rules (Neal, 2006).

Before 1871, only two surety bonds (a promise to be liable for the debt, default, or failure of another) were required for a person to become a member of the exchange and a clerk, who could start service at the age of 16, had to serve for only two years to qualify for membership. From 1871 onward, clerics had to be 18 years old, three members had to sponsor a candidate, and each had to guarantee £750. Although no compulsory apprenticeship was required to serve, it gradually became routine to train as a clerk for some time before joining the Exchange. In 1886–1902, 70 percent of new members were clerks, rising to 80 percent in 1909. Thus, the stock exchange gradually became a more professional institution. Even those not serving as clerks often had other training, such as banking and accountancy (Neal & Davis, 2005).

Family connections were not formally required to pursue a career in the stock market or even to form partnerships, but there was some favoritism based on class, religion, and family. People who wanted to pursue a career in the stock market, had skills that could be utilized in the market, and could be trusted, were particularly sought after. In addition, well-established firms, in particular, looked for individuals who could advance the firm's interests through their connections, whether at home or abroad. Anyone with something extra to offer through expertise or connections could enter the stock market. In practice, however, family ties sometimes came to the fore. Family ties were particularly critical in building the trust needed (Wainwright, 1990). At the LSE, a career field was opened for the children of the aristocracy from the 1870s onward. Trust was paramount, as partners and their clerks had to work closely and rely on each other's actions and words. Experts came not only from Europe but from all over the world. The Exchange attracted talent from all over the world, and these members reciprocated by providing the connections necessary to make London a global center. However, it was not just connections that foreigners brought; they were also recruited for their language skills. In particular, the growing business in foreign securities and the techniques needed to trade between markets required individuals skilled in such transactions. The Exchange had a large pool of talented individuals who needed to generate business to survive. However, once received, these members had to operate within the rules and regulations imposed by the Exchange (Michie, 2001).

The stockbroking industry transitioned from sole proprietors to large firms, marking substantial growth and evolution. As various businesses expanded and contracted, the capacity to cater to them improved. However, brokers on the Exchange were bound by a strict rule—the ban on all forms of advertising. This regulation limited members' ability to attract new clients, advise on new issues, or propose potential sales and purchases. The underlying objective of this rule was to prevent members from engaging in competitive practices and to underscore the non-advertising nature of the Exchange, thereby distinguishing its members from non-members (Michie, 2001).

Increasing professionalism among members made them more respectable. During this period, stockbroking emerged as a respected profession in the eyes of the public, and very few members were recorded as defrauding customers. The profession was now well respected. This was also reflected in the novels of the time, which portrayed brokerage houses and investors as more respectable (Lannon, 2009). Brokerage house/customer relations were usually left to the member, except in cases where a customer complained. The Exchange then investigated this, and if unethical behavior was found, the member could be expelled, but usually, the punishment was left to the criminal courts. The mechanism for resolving disputes among members within the Exchange was by now well established, and the authority of the General Purposes Committee in this regard was largely unquestioned. The committee's members were appointed through a democratic process, based on elections held among the Exchange's full members.Candidates were selected for their experience, reputation, and proven ability to manage the Exchange's increasingly complex operations (Michie, 2001).

In the late nineteenth century, efficiency in trading increased, and the stock market began to demonstrate its adaptability as the gap between bid and ask prices narrowed. This adaptability was also evident in commission rates. However, a plan introduced in 1905 brought about a change—the number of members was limited. From then on, an applicant for membership had to purchase the candidacy of an existing member, in addition to paying an entrance fee and annual dues. The prohibition of dual capacity (acting both as brokers and representing clients, and as jobbers as market makers) in 1909, and the introduction of minimum commissions in 1912 disrupted the previously free and easy relationship with banks and other financial institutions. The combination of these two rule changes posed a serious threat. When a rule was introduced in 1909 that double capacity was prohibited and would be enforced, it technically cut off direct contact between market makers and non-members, such as traders and foreign banks. However, many intermediaries operated secretly, and the service was never terminated. The real challenge began in June 1912 with the introduction of minimum commission rates. The introduction of minimum commission rates disproportionately impacted smaller brokers and those serving retail investors. While the rates aimed to standardize fees, they favored large investors and well-capitalized firms, as the commissions were less significant for substantial trades. Smaller brokers, reliant on price-sensitive clients, struggled to compete, often resorting to informal fee reductions that undermined their profits and put them at regulatory risk. With higher operational costs and fewer resources than larger firms, many small brokers were forced to merge with larger entities or exit the market, accelerating the consolidation of the brokerage industry. However, the market found a solution. While a formal fee schedule was in place, a series of concessions and flexible application of rules ensured that established broker/client relationships continued past practices. These two changes had global implications for the securities market because the LSE served the UK and the world. Both regulations weakened the strengths of the LSE. They undermined its efficiency and competitiveness by increasing transaction costs, reducing market flexibility, and discouraging competition among brokers. These measures favored large firms and institutional investors while marginalizing minor participants, limiting accessibility and innovation within the market. Thus, in the five years preceding World War I, the LSE's role as an efficient and competitive market that attracted business nationally and internationally began to erode (Michie, 1986).

This practice continued until October 27, 1986. On this date, the "Big Bang" eliminated fixed commissions in securities trading. It allowed firms to operate in a dual capacity by representing investors in equities and government debt securities (broking) and buying and selling wholesale (dealing or jobbing). It also opened the LSE to foreign firms by making it a limited liability company and replaced trading in the exchange hall with a screen-based technological platform. These measures increased the volume and market capitalization of stocks on the LSE, strengthened London's role in interbank lending, bond, commodity, and foreign exchange markets, and facilitated 24-h trading worldwide (Barrett, 2024).

6.7.2 The Communication Revolution

After the 1850s, new means of communication, such as the telegraph and telephone, made it possible to communicate continuously between markets. Thus, information on securities was shared everywhere, and the efficiency of stock exchanges increased. At the same time, the need for local markets was diminishing. As local British exchanges began to close, securities trading was increasingly directed to a single national exchange, the LSE. A similar process was taking place internationally, creating significant new opportunities for the LSE (Fessenden, 2018).

From 1840 onward, London was connected by telegraph to all major cities in the UK; for example, Glasgow was reached in 1847. By 1850, a national communication system quickly put members of the LSE in touch with all centers where securities were traded. In 1851, the London-Paris telegraph connection was established. Then, the New York (1866) and Melbourne (1872) markets were connected by telegraph, and a member of the LSE now had access to prices on the New York Stock Exchange within only 20 min. Again, as technology improved, World War I would reduce this delay to 30 s. For the first time, describing a global securities market in which each exchange complemented and competed for business became possible. Expanded from the 1890s with telephone links to Paris and Brussels, the LSE members were now positioned to serve an international clientele (Campbell & Rogers, 2017). As London became the world's leading financial center and global trade and investment grew, it became increasingly important for banks and other financial institutions of different nationalities to have a presence in London. By 1910, there were 26 foreign bank branches in London, mainly from continental Europe. These banks were able to channel some of their business to London. The most active market for American securities, which were especially popular in Europe, was in London. During this period, brokerage houses from the United States and Canada were also increasingly represented in London. For example, Harris, Winthrop & Co., a New York Stock Exchange member, had an office in London in 1912, serving clients from all over Europe (Michie, 1986).

With the introduction of transatlantic telegraphic communication in 1866, the trading of American securities became more active and heavily influenced by conditions on the New York Stock Exchange. London was at its busiest during the hours when the New York Stock Exchange was open. New York's 10 A.M. opening took place at 3.00 P.M. UK time. During this time, the LSE closed at 4:00 PM. Trading hours were generally from 10:00 A.M. to 4:00 P.M. The most straightforward way for the two exchanges to trade simultaneously was to extend the Exchange's opening hours, but members initially refused. In their view, if the exchange were open, even if it were limited to American trades, there would be pressure to keep other businesses operating, forcing the rest of the members to do the same. For this reason, it was not until 1932 that London could ensure trading at a convenient time interval with the American market. The markets on the Exchange floor had to be reorganized to meet the need for access to telegraph offices. In 1884, the directors proposed relocating the foreign market as close as possible to the Post Office telegraph office (Campbell & Rogers, 2017).

With the introduction of the ticker tape machine in 1867, it became possible to transmit prices as they changed on the stock exchange to anyone who hired a receiver (Fig. 6.4). The ticker tape, a popular tool at the time, was the earliest electric private financial communication device that transmitted stock price information over telegraph lines and was used from approximately 1870 to the late 1960s. It consisted of a strip of paper passed through a ticker tape machine. It printed abbreviated company names as alphabetical symbols and recorded numerical stock trading price and volume information. The term "*ticker*" originates from the machine's sound when it is printing. This provided customers with instant access to market conditions, enabling them to trade at current prices. The ticker tape provided information but did not allow for a response. Investors had to contact their brokers to buy or sell if a price change aroused interest. Large clients made sure to be informed by their brokers in the hope that something would work out, and they ensured that a response, if necessary, would follow immediately after being informed. Therefore, in addition to the stock exchange bulletin, a continuous stream of prices was transmitted from the stock exchange by the membership system, and this information, including direct minute-by-minute price changes, was transmitted to the relevant investors and brokers (Handel, 2022).

In 1878, the telephone appeared. This allowed direct two-way communication between the parties involved. Through the telephone, bid and ask prices quoted on the exchange floor could be instantly matched with prices available elsewhere, creating the possibility that business could be diverted from the exchange. However, there was a danger that an inter-office market could be established through a broader telephone system between non-members who traded at Exchange prices. For this reason, the Exchange management opposed the introduction of telephony within the premises. However, under pressure from members, they agreed to install a telephone in February 1880, and by 1883, a telephone room was in use inside the Exchange. After that, the phone inevitably became an indispensable tool for business conduct (Michie, 2001).

Fig. 6.4 Ticker tape and female employees on the stock exchange -1867 https://en.wikipedia.org/wiki/Ticker_tape#/media/File:Women_in_Waldorf-Astoria.jpg (Public Domain)

The most important news source for the LSE was Reuters. The Reuters company, established alongside the development of mass media, gradually became the critical information intermediary of the British Empire. This organization started its activities in 1851 when German Paul Reuter moved to London and established a news-telegraph agency at the London Royal Exchange. Headquartered in London, Reuters initially focused on covering commercial news, serving banks, brokerage houses, and other commercial firms. Reuters could be the first to report financial news and stories of international importance. Reuters expanded to the Far East in 1872 and South America in 1874. Both expansions were made possible by developments in land telegraphs and submarine cables. Reuters had developed a specific imperial identity to gain respect and government support. By 1900, Reuters had established a network of approximately 260 offices and correspondents. Except in the most urgent cases, news from sources was compiled in offices in major regional centers such as Istanbul, Bombay, Cape Town, Melbourne, and Shanghai, and then telegraphed to the London headquarters. Reuters consolidated London's position as the news center of the Empire before World War I. Reuters became an international news agency that collaborated with other agencies to integrate the global economy with world news (Winder, 2010).

6.7.3 International Arbitrage

Telecommunications also paved the way for international arbitrage. This first happened with the London-Paris submarine cable in 1851. With this connection, traders were continuously informed of each other's activities throughout the trading day, and arbitrageurs were able to monitor the fluctuating prices of jointly traded securities in real time. When an opportunity for profit arose, they could buy or sell in both markets. The telegraph also gave way to a superior form of communication, the telephone, which connected Paris in 1891 and Brussels in 1903. Thanks to an open telephone line, it was now possible to have uninterrupted two-way communication between London and the Continent, thus eliminating even the minor delays of the telegraph. With arbitrage, a close correlation emerged between the yields on key US railroad bonds in London and New York from 1871 to 1913. As arbitrage became increasingly a matter of calculation and speed, it became the domain of a few specialists dedicated to its execution. Most were German Jews who had moved to London in response to diminishing opportunities and anti-Semitism in their home countries. From the early nineteenth century, many German states imposed legal restrictions on Jews, limiting their rights to own property, participate in certain professions, or reside in specific areas. These restrictions made it difficult for Jewish families to expand their businesses or fully participate in the local economy. The German Jewish banking families that settled in London transformed the city's financial markets and laid the foundations for modern global finance. Their ability to navigate international markets, innovate financial practices, and fund large-scale projects was critical to Britain's economic expansion and role as a global economic powerhouse during the nineteenth century. With their skills in securities arbitrage, they had become the elite of their profession in London before 1914 (Kurgan-van Hentenryk, 2016).

The price equilibrium between three popular financial assets traded on the London and New York stock exchanges was stabilized through arbitrage. These were the foundation bonds of the First and Second Banks of the United States, as well as the three-month government bonds of the United States. These three assets could be traded in New York and London, and their prices had to be the same on both exchanges. However, the fact that these securities sometimes differed in price between stock exchanges led investors to engage in arbitrage. The investor would profit by selling the more expensive asset and buying the cheaper one, and prices would inevitably level off. This movement in prices was the most critical test of international market equilibrium. The Rothschilds were the most crucial players in this market (Sylla et al., 2006).

6.7.4 The Link Between Money Markets and Capital Markets

The LSE in the nineteenth century effectively contained several markets, including the domestic, foreign, railway, mining, colonial, and money markets—domestic and foreign government bonds, railway and mining stocks, colonial securities, and short-term money market instruments. These specialized markets reflected the growing complexity and internationalization of the financial world during the Industrial Revolution. Important financial sector institutions, such as the Bank of England, the Royal Exchange, and the Globe Insurance Buildings, side by side, symbolize the center of London's financial and commercial power in the financial district at the end of the nineteenth century. This specialization contributed to London's dominance as the world's financial capital, offering a broad spectrum of investment opportunities and attracting domestic and international investors. The money market supported the liquidity needs of traders and facilitated short-term borrowing. Between 1850 and 1914, the scope and intensity of the LSE's engagement with money and capital markets underwent significant changes. London-based national and international banking groups were transferring funds to the London money market. Thus, they started to use the securities market more. Securities were also widely used as collateral. In 1914, approximately half of the loans extended by London banks on call and short notice consisted of loans to brokers and businesspeople against securities pledged as collateral. In general, approximately 80 percent of the purchases made on the Stock Exchange in 1894 were financed by credit, and this ratio increased to 90 percent by 1909. The promissory notes used as collateral for financial institutions could be easily and quickly traded in large quantities at a tiny discount. This reduced liquidity risk, allowing the London money market to operate more flexibly. Despite fluctuating economic conditions, they invested their cash efficiently in the securities market. They cashed out when needed, significantly reducing the need for banks and other financial institutions to hold large reserves (Michie, 2001).

It was essential for the financial stability of the banking system to be able to liquidate its long-term receivables instantly and to earn returns by investing its idle resources in money market instruments. In 1878, the City of Glasgow Bank collapsed due to excessive speculation. Then, in November 1890, Barings Bank faced bankruptcy due to excessive risk-taking in bad investments in Argentina. The Bank of England rescued Barings and an international association of companies, including the Rothschilds and most other London banks, which may have prevented the collapse of London's private banking system (Körnert, 2003).

Therefore, banks had to use the money market effectively. The role of the stock exchange mechanism was crucial as it provided this opportunity. The stock market became very liquid since funds could be used and released instantly. The extreme volatility of exchange rates in free market economies could be managed by continuous trading on the LSE and its foreign counterparts. The LSE's capital market, including stocks and bonds, became increasingly closely linked to the money market and a central and indispensable force behind market stability and flexibility. Even as crises persisted, money was easily channeled, and the relationship between securities and money markets provided a balance even in the worst-case scenario. This was crucial for the banking system, which operates with low equity capital. So, the LSE developed this role and dominated the emerging global market.

However, by 1914, the drums of World War I had begun to beat. During World War I, the LSE suffered, and its central role in the money market was virtually destroyed on all fronts. Public finance was taking its place. Banks were also in trouble. At the bank's general meeting on January 29, 1915, Edward Holden, Chairman of HSBC, outlined the sacrifices made by financial institutions as follows (HSBC, n.d.). "*We have sent 1,100 of our staff to join one or other of Her Majesty's Forces, which has been a great sacrifice. Those who stayed behind gladly and willingly sacrificed their vacations. I want to take this opportunity to express our gratitude for their loyalty.*"

6.8 The Great War and the London Stock Exchange

World War I had a profound impact on both the British economy and the LSE. The war necessitated massive government spending to finance military operations, resulting in increased borrowing and a rise in national debt. The national debt grew from £650 million in 1914 to over £7.4 billion in 1919. Inevitably, the priority during the war was to meet the government's sudden and massive demand for funds to finance purchases and payments at home and abroad. The government raised funds through war bonds and increased taxation. War spending led to inflation as the government printed money and borrowed heavily. To manage the crisis, the Bank of England raised its lending rate from 3 to 8% within days. As a result, although the United Kingdom was a global economic superpower at the turn of the century, the country inevitably became heavily indebted to the United States throughout the war. In 1917, the United States became the ultimate global credit supplier, marking the end of British hegemony (Ellison et al., 2019).

In anticipation of financial turmoil, the LSE closed in July 1914 for an extended period, marking the first time in its 117-year history that it had done so. It remained closed until the New Year. The closure was intended to prevent bank runs and stabilize the financial system. The outbreak of war led to a liquidity crisis as banks and investors scrambled to liquidate assets. Therefore, increasing the Stock Exchange's interest in foreign securities was impossible during the war, and no new issues were listed on the exchange. The stock of foreign securities available to finance the government's need for foreign currency, especially dollars, was significantly reduced. As a result, the international dimension of the LSE was drastically reduced, and the UK government's short-term debt was traded in its place. The conditions under which the LSE operated changed dramatically during the four years of war (Michie, 2001).

Historian Ferguson (2000) said Britain's entry into World War I was its greatest modern mistake. He argues that Britain should have stayed out, even if Germany won, as the war severely weakened the empire. By the end, Britain was burdened with enormous debt, limiting its military capacity, and had suffered significant manpower losses. Harvard historian Laurence A. Tisch compared World War I to the Napoleonic Wars, noting that Britain initially avoided direct involvement with Napoleon. He suggests that in 1914, Britain could have delayed intervention, leveraging its superior naval and financial power. Even if Germany had defeated France and Russia, governing a German-dominated Europe would have been an immense challenge, making it weaker than the British Empire (The Guardian, 2014).

6.9 Concluding Remarks

London's rise as a global financial center has been made possible by the country's democratization and the rise of inclusive institutions. The Glorious Revolution fostered a secure financial environment by reducing arbitrary government interference, strengthening property rights, and encouraging investment in England. These changes laid the groundwork for inclusive economic institutions, financial innovation, and, ultimately, the rise of the LSE as a significant financial center. Between the eighteenth and nineteenth centuries, the LSE became one of the world's leading financial centers. Its growth and challenges offer valuable lessons to other capital markets about market development, financial innovation, regulation, and the impact of globalization (Ferguson, 2001).

One of the most critical lessons from this period is the importance of institutional development in boosting investor confidence. Formalizing trading rules and establishing the LSE in 1801 helped create a stable and transparent financial environment. Membership requirements and trading regulations reduced fraudulent activity, increasing confidence in the system. Another important lesson is the role of financial innovation in market expansion. The introduction of joint-stock companies in the early nineteenth century led to broader public participation in investment. The development of new financial instruments, including government bonds, railway shares, and foreign securities, diversified investment opportunities and increased market liquidity. The South Sea Bubble of 1720 and the speculative railroad bubbles of the nineteenth century exposed the dangers of excessive market speculation and inadequate oversight. Effective regulation and the implementation of stricter regulatory measures, such as financial disclosure requirements and restrictions on fraudulent schemes, played a crucial role in restoring market confidence. Globalization and capital mobility also contributed to the success of the LSE. By the nineteenth century, the LSE had become the world's leading capital market, financing large-scale international projects, including railroads, mining, and colonial expansion. Moreover, the performance of the LSE during this period demonstrates the impact of economic and political stability on financial growth. Britain's strong legal system, industrial expansion, and political stability provided a solid foundation for financial development. This suggests that stable governance and inclusive institutions are key factors in sustaining the growth of financial markets.

Despite its success, the LSE has faced challenges due to market concentration and monopolistic tendencies. By the late nineteenth century, concerns about high commissions, restricted access, and the prohibition of dual capacity weakened its competitive position. Another challenge was the transition from domestic to international financing, which highlighted the opportunities and risks associated with diversification. While this diversification offered growth opportunities, it also introduced risks, including currency fluctuations, political instability, and sovereign defaults, particularly in Latin America.

For the United States, the situation was very different. Before the war, America was in a recession; the commercial environment provided by World War I would quickly end this. US exports increased from \$2.4 billion in 1913 to \$6.2 billion in 1917. Moreover, New York banks lent heavily to the British before the United States entered the war. At the beginning of the war, J.P. Morgan & Co. bank made an initial loan of \$12,000,000 to Russia; in 1915, it lent \$500,000,000 to France and the United Kingdom. Following the US' entry into the war in April 1917, the Treasury was to make long-term loans of \$10 billion to Britain, France, and other Allied nations, expecting repayment after the war. Some sources criticized the United States for financing British and French interests (Horn, 2000). If its allies lost the war, its economy would enter a major recession. Therefore, it could not remain indifferent to the loss of its allies. Financial reasons were likely a significant factor in the decision to join the war. The Great War marked an important shift in global power (Owen, 1971).

Before 1914, Britain believed that economic power and naval supremacy would be sufficient to maintain its dominance. However, World War I demonstrated that total war required full industrial mobilization. Britain had to convert its economy for wartime production, leading to food shortages, inflation, and labor strikes. The war revealed that economic strength alone was insufficient without industrial and logistical preparation for prolonged conflict. As a result, post-war Britain found itself in unexpected economic conditions. T.S. Eliot (1888–1965) depicted this best in his verse, reflecting themes of despair, emptiness, and existential uncertainty in post-World War I England (Eliot, 1964):

What shall we do tomorrow.
What shall we ever do?
We shall play a game of chess,
Pressing lidless eyes and waiting for a knock upon the door.

References

Banner, S. (1998). *Anglo-American securities regulation: Cultural and political roots, 1690–1860.* Cambridge University Press.

Barrett, E. (2024). The LSE. In *'Survival capitalism' and the Big Bang* (pp. 123–165). Manchester University Press.

Buchinsky, M., & Polak, B. (1993). The emergence of a national capital market in England, 1710–1880. *The Journal of Economic History, 53*(1), 1–24.

Campbell, G., & Rogers, M. (2017). Integration between the London and New York stock exchanges, 1825–1925. *The Economic History Review, 70*(4), 1185–1218.

Carabelli, G., Jovanović, M., Kirbis, A., & Walton, J. F. (Eds.). (2020). *Sharpening the Haze: Visual essays on imperial history and memory.* Ubiquity Press.

Cathcart, B. (2015). *The news from Waterloo: The race to tell Britain of Wellington's victory.* Faber & Faber.

Cope, S. R. (1978). The stock exchange revisited: A new look at the market in securities in London in the eighteenth century. *Economica, 45*(177), 1–21.

Davies, N. (1999). *The Isles: A history.* Oxford University Press. ISBN 0-19-513442-7

Dawson, W. R. (1934). The London Coffee-houses and the beginnings of Lloyd's. *Journal of the British Archaeological Association, 40*(1), 104–134. https://doi.org/10.1080/00681288.1934.11894253

De Pinto, I. (1771). *Traite de la circulation et du credit.* Marc Michael Rey. -- (1774). An Essay on Circulation and Credit. T. Ridley.

Dickson, P. G. M. (1967). *The financial revolution in England: A study in the development of public credit, 1688–1756.* Macmillan.

Eliot, T. S. (1964). The Waste Land 1922. Grolier Club.

Ellis, A. (1956). *The penny universities; A history of the coffee-houses.* Decker & War-burg.

Ellison, M., Sargent, T. J., & Scott, A. (2019). Funding the Great War and the beginning of the end for British hegemony. *Debt and Entanglements Between the Wars*, 59.

Ferguson, N. (1999). The house of Rothschild: Volume 1: Money's prophets: 1798–1848 (Vol. 1). Penguin.

Ferguson, N. (2000). the pity of war: Explaining world war I (Revised edition). Basic Books.

Ferguson, N. (2001). *The cash nexus: Money and power in the modern world, 1700–2000.* Penguin Books.

Fessenden, H. (2018). The great telegraph breakthrough of 1866. *Econ Focus, 2Q*, 28–30.

Field, J. F. (2017). *London, Londoners and the great fire of 1666: Disaster and recovery.* Routledge.

Garber, P. M. (1990). Famous first bubbles. *Journal of Economic Perspectives, 4*(2), 35–54.

Green, M. (2013). *The lost world of the London coffeehouse.* The Public Domain Review. https://publicdomainreview.org/essay/the-lost-world-of-the-london-coffeehouse/

Handel, J. (2022). The material politics of finance: The ticker tape and the LSE, 1860s–1890s. *Enterprise & Society, 23*(3), 857–887.

Harari, Y. N. (2014). *Sapiens: A brief history of humankind.* Random House.

Hill, C. (2018). *Reformation to industrial revolution: 1530–1780.* Verso Books.

Horn, M. (2000). A private bank at war: JP Morgan & Co. and France, 1914–1918. *Business History Review, 74*(1), 85–112.

HSBC. (n.d.). A bank at war. https://history.hsbc.com/exhibitions/a-bank-at-war10 July 2024.
Karan. M. B. (2022). Para, Banka ve Finansın Sırları, Scala Yayıncılık.
Karan, M. B., Westerman, W., & Wijngaard, J. (2024). A history of banks. *Contributions to Economics*.
Körnert, J. (2003). The Barings crises of 1890 and 1995: Causes, courses, consequences, and the danger of domino effects. *Journal of International Financial Markets, Institutions and Money, 13*(3), 187–209.
Kurgan-van Hentenryk, G. (2016). Jewish private banks. In *The world of private banking* (pp. 239–256). Routledge.
Kurz, H. D. (2016). David Ricardo (1772–1823). In *Handbook on the history of economic analysis* (Vol. I.) Edward Elgar Publishing.
Lannon, C. (2009). *Gambling and/or the exchange: The Victorian novel and the legitimization of the stock market* (Doctoral dissertation, Boston College).
Long, H. P. (2010). *Lloyd's of London: Information and influence in the nineteenth century*. University of Central Oklahoma.
Michie, R. (2001). *The LSE: A history*. OUP Oxford.
Michie, R. C. (1986). The London and New York stock exchanges, 1850–1914. *The Journal of Economic History, 46*(1), 171–187.
Mirowski, P. (1981). The rise (and retreat) of a market: English joint stock shares in the eighteenth century. *The Journal of Economic History, 41*(3), 559–577.
Neal, L. (1987). The integration and efficiency of the London and Amsterdam stock markets in the eighteenth century. *The Journal of Economic History, 47*(1), 97–115.
Neal, L. (1988). The rise of a financial press: London and Amsterdam, 1681–1810. *Business History, 30*(2), 163–178.
Neal, L. (1998). The financial crisis of 1825 and the restructuring of the British financial system. *Review-Federal Reserve Bank of Saint Louis, 80*, 53–76.
Neal, L. (2006). The LSE in the 19th Century: ownership structures, growth and performance (No. 115). Working Paper.
Neal, L., & Davis, L. (2005). The evolution of the rules and regulations of the first emerging markets: The London, New York, and Paris stock exchanges, 1792–1914. *The Quarterly Review of Economics and Finance, 45*(2–3), 296–311.
Neal, L., & Davis, L. (2006). The evolution of the structure and performance of the LSE in the first global financial market, 1812–1914. *European Review of Economic History, 10*(3), 279–300.
Neal, L. (1994). The economic history of Britain since 1700. Editors: Roderick Floud, Gresham College. N. McCloskey. University of Iowa.
Odlyzko, A. (2019). Newton's financial misadventures in the South Sea Bubble. *Notes and Records: The Royal Society Journal of the History of Science, 73*(1), 29–59.
Owen, G. L. (1971). 5. American financing of world war I. By Charles Gilbert. In *'Contributions in economics and economic history, No. 1*. Greenwood Publishing Corp., 1970. *The Historical Journal, 14*(4), 862–863.
Patterson, M., & Reiffen, D. (1990). The effect of the Bubble Act on the market for joint stock shares. *The Journal of Economic History, 50*(1), 163–171.
Pollard, J. (2010). *Secret Britain: The Hidden bits of our history*. Hachette UK.
Pressnell, L. S. (1956). Country banking in the Industrial Revolution. (No Title).
Robinson, J. A., & Acemoglu, D. (2012). *Why nations fail: The origins of power, prosperity, and poverty*. Profile.
Sinclair, D. (2003). *Sir Gregor MacGregor and the land that never was: The extraordinary story of the most audacious fraud in history*. Headline.
Smith, C. F. (1929). The early history of the London stock exchange. *The American Economic Review*, 206–216.
Sylla, R., Wilson. J. W., & Wright. R. E. (2006). Integration of trans-Atlantic capital markets. 1790–1845. *Review of Finance, 10*(4), 613–644.

Taylor, M. P., & Tonks, I. (1989). The internationalisation of stock markets and the abolition of UK exchange control. *The Review of Economics and Statistics*, 332–336.

The Guardian. (2014). Britain's entering the First World War was 'the most significant error in modern history'. https://www.theguardian.com/world/2014/jan/30/britain-first-world-war-biggest-error-niall-ferguson

Thornbury, G. W. (1881). *Old and new London: A narrative of its history, people and places*, by W. Thornbury (E. Walford) (Vol. 2).

Vallance, E. (2013). *The glorious revolution: 1688-Britain's fight for liberty*. Hachette UK.

Wainwright, D. (1990). *Government Broker: The story of an office and Mullens & Co*. Matham.

Winder, G. M. (2010). London's global reach? Reuters news and network, 1865, 1881, and 1914. *Journal of World History*, 271–296.

Chapter 7
Paris Bourse: The Financial Center of Continental Europe (18th–19th Centuries)

7.1 Introduction

Napoleon's angry voice rang out from a high-ceilinged, high-arched-windowed hall in the Tuileries Palace in June 1801. He denounced the agents of change: "*These men are without rank, without fortune, and no patriots.*" Count Mollien, the chief finance adviser of Napoleon, was sitting on a low chair in the hall used for official receptions, diplomatic meetings, and military briefings, and he looked ahead of him in silence. The hall had a formal, disciplined, and impressive atmosphere, with walls decorated with marble pilasters, gilded moldings, and neoclassical paintings depicting Roman victories, military achievements, or allegorical figures representing power and justice, reinforcing Napoleon's authority. Napoleon and the other Councilors, Cambaceres and Lebrun, were seated in raised armchairs. As Napoleon continued his speech, listing one negative opinion after another about them, other councils were listening carefully. He thought some exchange agents were doing illegal things, were greedy, and were distorting the market. Napoleon thought it was absurd that anyone could get into this business (agents of change) by paying a certain amount of tax. He felt it was necessary to restore the institutional discipline to which the agents of change had been subject before the revolution. He said there should be a financing fee instead of an annual tax. Before being admitted to the profession, a jury of leading change agents should evaluate candidates' moral character and capacity to serve (Mollien, 1845).

Count Mollien did not know what to say for a moment; he knew Napoleon was not gentle but was not a tyrant toward his staff (Fig. 7.1). He was demanding and often impatient. Summoning all his courage, he cleverly said, "*I agree with you that we should limit entry into this profession.*" However, he respectfully disagreed with the general that the agents of change were dishonest. He said to Napoleon, "*General, it is no easier for you to increase the number of honest men in business than to increase*

M. B. Karan, *A History of Stock Exchanges*, Contributions to Economics,
https://doi.org/10.1007/978-3-032-07788-2_7

Fig. 7.1 Count Nicolas François Mollien (1758–1850). https://commons.wikimedia.org/wiki/File:Comte_Mollien_%281758-1850%29.jpg

the number of brave men in the French army." Napoleon knew him and trusted the financial expertise of this clever man, so he let him speak (Mollien, 1845).

Mollien proposed a deposit of 100,000 francs as an entry fee, limiting the number of representatives to sixty. After Napoleon compared the Paris Bourse to the Amsterdam and London stock exchanges, Mollien pointed out that these exchanges were much larger markets. He argued that government bonds in Paris are more volatile because the Paris market is shallower. Small speculators were willing to trade in wide swings. Napoleon was impressed by Mollien's answers, but although he valued intelligence, he sometimes rejected advice if it went against his instincts. However, with his usual stubbornness, he still stood by the idea that change agents distorted the financial market. Then he questioned the motives of the agents of change in making futures trades, blaming those who engaged in this business and asking, "*If a man offers to sell a rente (government bond) for 38 francs in a month when the current price is 50 francs, is he not declaring his distrust of the government?*" Mollien said this transaction was not related to the government's actions but only reflected its expectations. Moreover, if the seller were wrong, the market would punish him. Napoleon still stubbornly insisted on his opinion and reminded him that futures trading had been banned before the revolution. In response, Mollien carefully explained that futures markets were standard for all commodities, and there was no reason to exclude them from the stock market. He argued that bills of exchange should not be abolished because some traders were abusing them. If contracts were being abused, taking the case to court would be better than banning them altogether. By the end of the meeting, Napoleon was convinced. So, he determined the structure of the stock market under the Empire. The Ventase IX law and the Code de Commerce gave stockbrokers a monopoly on trading government bonds and other securities "*eligible*" for listing. Securities not on the official list were traded on the coulisse, the sidewalk exchange, and the listing of foreign securities was prohibited until 1823 (Riva & White, 2011).

Napoleon transformed the Paris Bourse from a chaotic speculative market into a well-regulated financial institution. His reforms ensured stability, increased investor confidence, and made the Paris Bourse a model for future European financial markets. His policies also helped finance his military campaigns while laying the foundation for modern stock exchange regulations. However, to tell the story of the Paris Bourse, it is necessary to understand the developments that began in the last years of Louise XIV's reign and the turbulent periods before and after the Revolution.

7.2 France's Financial Situation in the 17th Century and the John Law Period

During King Louis XIV's final years, war devastated France's finances, necessitating extensive borrowing. Indirect taxes and tax farming complicate revenue collection, and bonds are traded at deep discounts in the secondary debt market. Efforts to establish financial institutions failed due to poor tax collection and declining confidence. Unlike England, France lacked a universal financial system, with exemptions and fragmented jurisdictions. The absence of joint-stock companies hindered capital markets. Major bankers financed the Crown, but financial instability led to crises, notably in 1704 and 1709. The collapse of financiers like Samuel Bernard disrupted European credit markets, highlighting systemic risk (Karan et al., 2024).

Frequent currency alterations between 1689 and 1715 caused instability. Mints issued interest-bearing "*Mint Bills*" as short-term credit instruments, but by 1704, rising war costs led to deflation and a financial crisis. The collapse of financiers like the Hogguer brothers worsened the 1709 crisis, compounded by severe winter and famine. Controller General Desmaretz devalued coins and used Mint Bills to ease debt burdens. Though Bernard recovered by 1712, the crisis shifted France's financial center from Lyon to Paris. The monarchy was bankrupt by the war's end, and the fragmented financial system failed to service its debt (Bouvier, 1970).

The instability set the stage for John Law's monetary experiments after 1716. John Law, a Scottish gambler and economist, fled England after killing a rival in a duel. With the support of his friend, the Duke of Orleans, he founded the Banque Générale in 1716 to address France's financial crisis. In 1717, he established the Mississippi Company, which monopolized trade in Louisiana. In 1719, as part of his broader economic reforms, Law merged the French East India Company with several other trading enterprises, including the Company of the West (Mississippi Company), the China Company, and the African Company. This newly unified enterprise was called the Compagnie des Indes, and it was granted a monopoly over France's entire overseas trade, including Asia, Africa, and the Americas (Buchan, 2018).

Under Law's system, the Compagnie des Indes became central to his vision of linking commerce, finance, and public debt. He allowed the company to issue shares bought using banknotes from his Banque Royale. The share prices soared due to rampant speculation, drawing investors eager to profit from the expanding colonial trade. By 1719, the company controlled tax collection, coin minting, and various industries, driving a speculative frenzy in its shares. John Law mandated banknotes for public payments, but as inflation soared and confidence plummeted, people hoarded coins and fled with their wealth (Karan et al., 2024).

By May 1720, paper money circulation had doubled, and foreign investors withdrew. The collapse of England's South Sea bubble worsened the crisis. By September, high-denomination banknotes were demonetized, triggering a panic known as the Mississippi crisis. Law, disgraced and blamed for the financial disaster, fled France, leaving chaos behind. Then, the Crown took over the Compagnie des Indes to stabilize the economy.

The Compagnie des Indes continued operating under government supervision after the crisis, engaging in profitable trade with India and China while competing with the British East India Company. However, it faced constant military and commercial challenges, and in 1769, King Louis XV revoked the company's monopoly due to inefficiency, British dominance, and internal corruption. It was officially dissolved, and its trade was opened to private merchants, marking the end of centralized French colonial commerce.

After John Law, the word "*banque*" (bank) aroused great antipathy in France. For this reason, the French did not dare to reestablish a public bank, or even an institution that used the word bank, for a long time. However, in 1763, Isaac Panchaud, a London-born banker who had moved to Paris in 1763, proposed a central bank modeled on the Bank of England, which received the support of the French Finance Minister Jacques Turgot. The new bank was called the Caisse d'Escompte. Marion (1934) explained this situation as follows: "*The disaster of the John Law system had made the term 'bank' so unpopular that it was necessary to wait a long time before trying again something that bore the slightest resemblance to a bank. Only in 1776, 56 years after the system's collapse, Turgot believed he could equip France with an institution for discounting bills of exchange...*"

7.3 The Paris Bourse

7.3.1 Early Years

While Lyon was still the financial center of France, in Paris, court officials and brokers traded in commodities and financial instruments. Over time, the growth of financial markets encouraged the specialization of activities, and the "*courtiers de change (agents of change),*" who dealt in barter, were first officially recognized by the royal proclamation in 1572. Although the Crown fixed the number of money changers in 1595, creating a monopoly, it changed the number over time to reflect the fluctuating demand for securities. From eight intermediaries for Paris in 1595, the number gradually increased to thirty in 1638. The following year, they were referred to as "*agents de Banque et de change.*" In 1684, securities brokers were differentiated from commodity brokers by prohibiting them from dealing in commercial goods. The Crown aimed to use bankers as a source of credit. The Crown established forty new offices in 1708. Their finance—a security deposit or forced loan to the Crown—was set at 20,000 livres, paying a gage of 10% interest. In addition, they were required to pledge an additional 1000 livres, earning a gage of 5%. Later, these requirements were reduced or increased depending on the context (White et al., 2003).

Agents of change houses were established as companies by royal decree in 1638. The companies were managed by a syndic (trustee) elected annually by the members and supported by a deputy. The syndic served as the official public representative of the company and presided over monthly company meetings. Trading occurred mainly in the open air, without a formal quotation registration system. There was little interest in establishing a stock exchange until the market was revived under John Law. He made a series of contradictory decisions regarding the players in the money market. Trading volume soared under the Law's System, stimulating interest in government debt and creating new securities offering extraordinary capital gains. Along Quincampoix Street in Paris, the financial center of the era, property owners leased all available space to speculators (Faure, 1977).

In the aftermath of the Mississippi crisis, establishing a regulated stock exchange was seen as a way to create rules that could rebuild transparency, oversight, and credibility. Financial activity before and during the crisis was highly chaotic. Much of the trading occurred in informal markets, especially in Rue Quincampoix, where prices fluctuated wildly due to speculation. John Law tried to prevent this by closing the unofficial agents, but France had no centralized authority to oversee financial transactions after his fall. An official exchange would help control speculation and stabilize securities trading. On the other hand, John Law's system relied on paper money, government bonds, and corporate shares to finance government spending, leaving France deeply in debt. With the collapse of the Law's system, the government needed a structured market to issue and manage public debt efficiently. A stock exchange would provide better control over government bonds and create a space where public debt could be bought and sold orderly. During the chaotic years, France lagged behind financial centers like Amsterdam and London, which had well-established stock exchanges facilitating trade, investment, and public finance. Amsterdam's and London's stock exchanges offered models of how a well-regulated market could promote economic stability. French authorities realized that an organized stock market could help attract capital, facilitate trade, and modernize the French economy (White et al., 2003).

A royal decree established the stock exchange on September 24, 1724, and the number of agents of change was set at sixty. Unlike the stock exchanges in London and New York, the government, not private interests, founded the Paris Bourse in 1724. The exchange was located on the Rue Vivienne. It was open from ten in the morning until one in the afternoon every day except Sundays and holidays. In Paris, all secondary transactions involving a broker in the money and capital markets, including stocks, debt, and bills of exchange, had to occur on the exchange floor. Individual investors could trade among themselves and register the transaction with a notary, but could not use an intermediary. Trading in contracts for the delivery of goods was permitted on the floor of the exchange, but was also allowed to take place off-exchange at fairs and marketplaces. The exchange was open to brokers, merchants, bankers, and other prominent persons living in Paris, but other French and foreigners could be issued certificates for access. Initially, the stock exchange could not prevent the frequent speculative fluctuations in the prices of the Compagnie des Indes, and the new organization was detrimental to trade and credit rather than beneficial for business (White et al., 2003).

During this period, broker dynasties dominated the stock market, passing offices through families and accumulating experience. Leading financiers influenced politics and the economy. In 1724, the Crown granted agents of change a securities trading monopoly, but weak demand led to its suspension in 1726. It was reinstated in 1733, with the number of offices reduced to 40 (White et al., 2003).

Each authorized person was given a "marque" identifying them and granting entry. In case of fraudulent entry, the violator was immediately deported and, if caught again, was subject to imprisonment and a fine of 1,000 livres. Guards patrolled the streets to protect and ensure the peaceful functioning of the exchange. Participants were allowed to trade bills of exchange and debentures, but securities were the exclusive business of exchange agents. In 1776, the newly created Caisse d'Escompte, which was mentioned in the introduction, was established with Minister Jacques Turgot's support and traded on the exchange. Its purpose was economic (stimulating commerce through credit) and political (helping the monarchy finance its expenditures without provoking immediate resistance through taxation). It served as a prototype for central banking in France.

While one agent was sufficient to mediate between buyer and seller for any bill of exchange, bond, or commodity, it required two agents for each party to be adequately represented by their respective agents and for the transaction to be completed. To keep the specialized activities of the exchange agents separate from the rest of the market, the Crown decided in 1774 to build a three-foot-high wooden parquet that only the exchange agents and the police could enter. Each agent was required to keep an audited ledger in which he recorded every securities transaction. From then on, the organized stock exchange in Paris would be called the parquet. In contrast, the sidewalk market was called the coulisse. This dual system had long existed in the Paris capital market. Although these markets often cooperated, competition between them continued. Agents were intended to be brokers only and prohibited from trading on their behalf. The commission for the purchase or sale of any security was set at 0.25% for every 1000 livres, equalizing the buyer's and seller's commissions. Thus, the commissions of both the buyer and the seller were equalized to 0.5% for the total purchase and sale. These basic rules established the Paris Exchange as an agency/auction market, in which market professionals on the exchange floor acted solely as brokers or commission agents for their clients (Schwartz, 1988). Agent de change had a legal monopoly as an intermediary in the buying and selling of exchange-traded securities; however, they could not act as market makers to stabilize prices, as they were prohibited from trading on their accounts. This rule was probably motivated by the concern that agents would not act in the best interests of their clients and prevent them from benefiting from any superior information (Martin, 1790).

Any person wishing to buy or sell on the exchange had to deliver their securities or money to their agent at least one hour before the session. This rule, which had the effect of consolidating order flow, would help to partially overcome a problem that arose in thin markets where price discovery was difficult due to the fragmentation of orders. Consolidating orders helped improve market liquidity by increasing the probability of matching orders and compensating for market makers' absence. However, the consolidation rule limited traders' flexibility regarding when they could enter the market. When an investor decides to enter the market, he usually authorizes his agent to modify limit orders for the maximum acceptable price for the purchase or the minimum acceptable price for the sale of securities, and he can also delegate to his broker the authority to negotiate. In the stock market, when agents discovered that they had mutually acceptable buy and sell orders, they would negotiate a price and execute the transaction, recording it in their logs (White et al., 2003).

Once a transaction was completed, the agent had to deliver the change securities and money on the same day. Initially, it was strictly forbidden to announce the price of securities aloud or to indicate the agreed price in any way for fear that brokers might try to manipulate prices. For such an infraction, brokers were threatened with expulsion and a fine of 6000 livres. After the end of the market, agents retired to a room and recorded market transactions on the official quotation sheet (White et al., 2003).

The official notes contain only partial information about the volume of trading on the Paris Exchange, where each transaction that caused the price to change is recorded. The announcement of prices during trading allowed individuals in the coulisse or sidewalk market to trade legally without the help of an intermediary.

7.3.2 The Period Before the Revolution

1783–1784, a wave of speculation between state funds and private shares swept the stock market. The American War of Independence had not yet begun, and the French provided material and military support to the beleaguered American Army between

1778 and 1782 (Balch, 1891). Following a series of public loans demanded by the American War of Independence, this wave brought an influx of foreign capital to Paris, mainly from the Netherlands, Switzerland, Genoa, and Spain. The market was also stimulated by the creation of the Caisse de Compte, which was a deposit institution, and the emergence of various joint-stock companies, such as the Compagnie des Eaux de Paris and the Banque de Saint-Charles de Madrid. Then, a group of speculators entered the market and turned it into a wild arena of manipulation and speculation. Speculators were called agiotors in France, and as in London, they had a bad reputation. Futures and options markets were the primary weapon of the financial wars. Although derivatives were banned several times during the reign of Louis XIV, they came to dominate the market with the issuance of shares in new companies. Agioteurs profited from fluctuations in securities, often through insider trading, speculation on government bonds, and currency arbitrage. The French monarchy had been borrowing heavily, and agiotors speculated on these debts, buying and selling them at fluctuating prices. Besides, the Caisse d'Escompte, founded in 1776, issued banknotes, but there was skepticism about their value. Agioteurs benefited by manipulating the market by hoarding metal currency and creating artificial shortages, driving speculation. Paris did not have a formal stock exchange like London or Amsterdam during that time, which worsened the situation. Still, unofficial trade in securities and bills of exchange occurred in coffeehouses and financial districts. Agioteurs played a role in fueling speculative bubbles, which worsened economic instability. London had more stability due to stronger institutions, but speculation remained in government bonds and company shares. Meanwhile, the Dutch Republic suffered an economic downturn due to losses from the Fourth Anglo-Dutch War (1780–1784). Investors panicked, causing bank runs and stock market instability. The banking sector, including the powerful Wisselbank (Bank of Amsterdam), struggled to maintain liquidity.

Almost all the managers of the financial houses established between France and all the other nations of Europe were foreigners. Swiss, Dutch, and Genoese bankers dominated finance, handling public debt and international trade. Although the profession was highly lucrative and the source of considerable fortunes, it did not enjoy any prestige in society as it did in England until the mid-seventeenth century. Under Louis XVI, speculation underwent a significant change, and the reputation of financiers began to grow, as frequent recourse to borrowing encouraged many owners of capital of all kinds to engage in stock market transactions. Martin (1790) perfectly summarized this enormous shift in mentality: "*Finance is the object of universal interest. (This) fashion of financial speculation must have the unique privilege of longevity; it has deep roots; for there are now speculators at every level of society, which was not the case in the past...*" In fact, until then, financiers who had been pushed and left on the margins of society, unsure of any return, just greedily chased opportunities; they took loans and invested in risky areas. Speculation at that time was concentrated exclusively on the shares of various private companies such as the Caisse de Compte, the Compagnie des Eaux de Paris, the Compagnie des Indes, and the Banque de

Saint-Charles. Initially, the government did not oppose this orientation but instead supported it. Charles Alexandre de Calonne, Louise XVI's Controller General of Finance, was undoubtedly the first to see the benefits that the state could derive from stock market movements. He believed that the speculation that animated the market would be favorable for public credit and that the price of royal bonds, now traded on the stock exchange, would rise in line with private bonds and stocks. Initially, the agiotors did not hesitate to intervene directly in the stock market to encourage it to act according to their wishes. The reorganization of the Caisse d'escompte in November 1783 revived confidence. The Caisse d'escompte issued new shares worth 3 million livres. Its price first fell and then rose rapidly (Thiveaud, 1998). Meanwhile, as in the Netherlands, two groups emerged: the first group was the "*bulls*," led by Beaumarchais (1732–1799), who had significant business and social connections and had made a considerable fortune through his activity as a diplomat and spy. In the second group were the "*bears*," led by the banker Panchaud (1737–1789), a slave trader, and Etienne Clavière. They predicted that the price rise could not continue indefinitely and that the share price would fall, with disastrous consequences for the company. During this period, the first great speculation occurred, and then the crisis of the Paris Bourse occurred (Thiveaud, 1998).

By the early 1780s, the financial needs of the state were increasing on the one hand, and economic practices were becoming increasingly complex on the other. Moreover, France faced the heavy burden of the American War of Independence. The John Law affair was still fresh in the memory, and the public was quite distant from banking operations. France's heavy debts were rapidly dragging the country into a crisis. The General Controller of Finance, Jacques Necker's minutes (Compte rendu) were published in 1781, revealing France's financial situation and sparking a primary debate. This was a novelty for an absolute monarchy where the economic crisis was always kept secret (de Staël-Holstein, 2009).

On the Paris Bourse, bankers sometimes acted as another layer of intermediaries, connecting clients with brokers on the Exchange. This activity had an essential market-making function. Since only brokers could legally trade on the Paris Bourse and most brokers operated solely on a person-to-person basis, many clients could place orders with a single banker, who could transfer them all to a single broker. Bankers both provided short-term credit and traded in short-term credit instruments offered by other bankers in their network. They also provided crucial marketing services and placed sovereign loans (Jackson, 2022).

Paris also became one of the leading centers of European finance. Parisian bankers often acted for provincial and foreign correspondents. In this context, they negotiated loans with bankers and investors in Lyon, Amsterdam, Geneva, Genoa, and other cities, increasing their volume and, thus, their profits (Taylor, 1962).

Private banks and their clients created an active secondary market, despite the legal monopoly of agents of change, who were forbidden to trade on their account on the Paris Bourse and had to execute deals on the day they were agreed (Taylor, 1962). Since markets were very shallow and too much capital was directed toward too few investments, having specialized knowledge provided essential advantages. Speculators or investors sought market information, sometimes through communication with brokers and bankers, sometimes by standing on the "*coulisse market*" on the sidewalk outside the Stock Exchange and listening to people shouting about prices (Marion, 1934). Using the price information they obtained, customers could pass on their orders to their bankers, gradually shifting some of the actual trading to the bankers, while brokers had to approve deals after the fact (White et al., 2003).

The number of exchange offices varied depending on the market interest. As the market developed, sixty bureaus were active on March 19, 1786. Over time, the Crown introduced some minimum qualifications for agents of change. By the end of the old regime, agents of change had to be twenty-five years old, French, Catholic, and of good reputation. They were forbidden to accept anyone from the lower class into their business and were subject to imprisonment and a fine of 6,000 livres. In 1781, the government stipulated that those wishing to become an exchange agent must have worked for five years in a bank, mercantile house, or a notary public. Family dynasties gave continuity to the change agent profession (White et al., 2003).

During the reign of Louis XVI (1774–1792), Western European financial markets reflected the era's broader political and economic transformations. While Britain maintained relative stability and economic growth, France faced increasing financial distress, culminating in a revolution. The Dutch Republic, once the financial powerhouse of Europe, experienced a decline due to war and internal instability. These factors set the stage for the financial upheavals of the French Revolutionary and Napoleonic Wars in the following decades. Government loans and the trading of anonymous shares took on the frenetic character of a boom. Several companies were founded during this period. One of them is the third version of the Compagnie des Indes. It was created in 1785 under Louis XVI with a capital of 20 million livres in 1787, and a further 17 million livres of shares were issued. This version aimed to revitalize French overseas trade, especially in India, China, and the Indian Ocean, and to compete with the British East India Company. However, in the early 1790s, the company would find it difficult to maintain its activities as revolutionary policies led to confiscations, economic isolation, and growing hostility toward monopolies. 1793, it was formally dissolved during the French Revolution, ending its monopoly. Also, the Compagnie générale des eaux (Paris Water Company) was established in 1777 with a capital of 12 million livres. The Compagnie d'assurances contre l'incendie (Fire Insurance Company) was founded in 1786 with 8 million livres and the Compagnie d'assurances sur la vie (Life Insurance Company) in 1788, also with 8 million livres. The issuance of new stocks stimulated a continuous increase in the prices of existing shares, and the Paris Bourse experienced a frenzied speculative boom from 1783 to 1789 (White et al., 2003).

Groups of speculators struggled to manipulate stocks through propaganda; like twentieth-century traders, they borrowed money to buy shares, sold them short, and invested in insurance and utility companies that functioned as investment trusts. Rival groups fought for control of the companies and demanded decrees that released them from unprofitable contracts or raised prices advantageously (Taylor, 1962).

These public and private securities could be traded on the stock exchange for cash, immediate delivery, or forward. Even though it was forbidden, speculators traded forwards and developed several sophisticated strategies, often making deals before owning the stock. Speculators effortlessly combined forward sales and purchases with call-and-put options, speculating that the price of a security would rise or fall by a certain amount. Economic historian Eugene White shows evidence of speculator Greffulhe selling a call option at a high strike price and then buying another call option on the same security at a lower strike price but with the same expiration date—in modern parlance, a "*bullish vertical call spread*" (Jackson, 2022). The weakness of the market and the presence of cash and forwards provided opportunities for market manipulation. Manipulators could put short sellers in a difficult position in futures markets. The Crown intervened from time to time to cancel contracts and disrupt the smooth functioning of the markets. Difficulties in transferring ownership of securities occasionally disrupted the functioning of the market.

The London Stock Exchange was no different in terms of manipulation. Wealthy investors and syndicates would accumulate large amounts of stock to artificially raise prices before disposing of shares at inflated prices. Wealthy investors and politicians could profit from early access to financial and political news before the public reacted. In the late nineteenth century, the LSE was a highly speculative and loosely regulated market where manipulation was standard. Gold and mineral booms, foreign bonds, and rapid industrial expansion fueled fraudulent schemes and speculation (Taylor, 2021a).

7.3.3 The Speculation of 1787 and Étienne Clavière

Around this time, stock manipulations on the Paris Bourse by a group of speculators (agiotors) led by Étienne Clavière led to a new crisis on the eve of the 1789 revolution. Étienne Clavière (1735–1793) was one of the fascinating figures of the French Revolution. He was a financier and politician of the late eighteenth century (Fig. 7.2). He is mainly known for his role in the French Revolution and was one of the key figures associated with financial reforms in France at the time.

Born in Geneva in 1735, Étienne Clavière was a brilliant but complex figure. Raised in a devout Protestant family that valued honesty in business, Clavière became a wealthy speculator but despised capitalism, which he saw as corrupt. He opposed the slave trade and nationalism and advocated global citizenship. His opposition to establishing a democratic constitution in Geneva and his disdain for the revolution led him to flee when the French army invaded his homeland. He tried to create a utopian city in Waterford, Ireland, but the project failed, so he moved to Paris (Luckett, 1992).

Fig. 7.2 Étienne Clavière (1735–1793). https://en.wikipedia.org/wiki/%C3%89tienne_Clavi%C3%A8re#/media/File:Etienne_Claviere.jpg (Public Domain)

By the time Clavière arrived in Paris, the Dutch Patriot Revolt and its financial crisis had weakened European credit markets. Clavière believed that a similar scenario would play out in France, allowing him to profit from the government bonds that had fallen into his hands. Clavière's letters make clear that he saw traders and speculators as two different groups. For traders, the aim was to limit risk as much as possible. For speculators, however, they tended to take risks and speculate by inventing justifications that reassured their bankers and, more importantly, themselves (Taylor, 1962).

During this period, relatively large pools of mobile capital in regions such as the Netherlands, London, Paris, and Geneva were constantly seeking safe investments and speculating (Taylor, 2021a). The owners of this capital were continually in search of safe investments. A limited number of companies traded in London, Amsterdam, and Paris, such as Royal Dutch Shell, De Beers, Société Générale, Compagnie des Wagons-Lits, Siemens & Halske, and Union des Mines, were investing in sovereign debt, ranging from funding short-term French government debt to consolidated British debt. They also engaged in commercial activities such as overseas trade or bills of exchange (Jackson, 2022). The Caisse d'Escompte played an essential role in the speculative bubbles of the period, while the Compagnie des Indes was the target of similar financial manipulations. Since there were no formal banks in eighteenth-century France, all large merchant houses had to act as banks, as they were responsible for granting loans, exchanging money, holding savings, and facilitating domestic and foreign payments to a considerable extent (Luckett, 1992).

Clavière worked closely with the journalist and politician Brissot. He was a French journalist, abolitionist, and revolutionary, leading the faction of Girondins (initially called Brissotins) at the National Convention in Paris. Clavière and Brissot combined political advocacy and financial speculation. Their aim was not only personal gain but also to undermine the monarchy's credibility and press for political reform toward a more democratic system. Clavière saw his speculations as part of a larger political mission to expose the monarchy's financial incompetence. He believed that financial markets could serve as a vehicle for political change and help hasten the fall of the ancien regime. Over time, however, he became a key figure in the financial system he loathed, speculating on fraudulent companies and contributing to the revolution by exacerbating France's economic crisis (Jackson, 2022).

Deeply critical of the capitalist financial system, Clavière mainly targeted institutions such as the Caisse d'Escompte. He saw these institutions as the epitome of the corrupt, speculative practices he despised. In 1887, Clavière's participation in speculation and public criticisms reflected his contempt for these systems, which he believed encouraged reckless trading, financial instability, and the exploitation of the public to benefit a few wealthy speculators (Jackson, 2022).

The speculative activities that artificially inflate their value and make profits at the expense of the masses surrounding the Compagnie des Indes and the Caisse d'Escompte also contributed to France's economic instability and influenced the French Revolution. Concerned with the system's moral flaws, Clavière believed that these speculative bubbles and manipulations were symptoms of a financial system that had become unsustainable. Clavière's involvement in such speculation illustrated the complex relationship between idealism and financial reality. While he opposed the system, his direct or indirect participation in these speculative activities contributed to the financial instability he sought to avoid (Luckett, 1992).

Speculators like Clavière and the authors they supported published pamphlets and newspaper articles to influence the market. Their aim at the time was to drive down the stock price of the Caisse d'escompte, and they succeeded. The Caisse d'Escompte was one of the financial institutions involved in speculative practices that artificially inflated stock prices. Speculators were engaging in risky behavior that made the stock prices of institutions like the Caisse d'Escompte unsustainable. Clavière advocated responsible economic reform and believed that this speculative bubble was dangerous for the economy as a whole. Clavière sought to curb this excessive speculative activity and prevent further destabilization of the financial system by aiming to lower stock prices. In 1782, they reduced the price of the Bank of St. Charles shares in Madrid from 800 livres to around 320. Finally, in 1785, they attacked the Paris Water Company, reducing its share price by 44% by the end of the year. Although the speculation of Clavière's decline caused general turmoil in the market, the public was getting used to long-standing accusations of financial malfeasance (Jackson, 2022). Clavière's attack on the Caisse de Compte provoked a political uproar, and some directors were forced to resign (Luckett, 1992). The

Caisse had lost public confidence in 1787 when it was moved to lend money to the King in exchange for a thirty-year extension of its concession. The bank's reserves would soon plummet, and the conversion of its banknotes into gold was suspended; it was liquidated in 1788, a year before the French Revolution (Kindleberger, 2015). The financial controller, Colanne, entrusted the Parisian bankers Girardot, Haller, and Company and the London bankers Bourdieu and Chollet with the task of issuing and marketing the new shares of the New Indies Company (Nussbaum, 1933).

The New Indies Company was embroiled in political controversy from the very beginning due to its commercial concessions. Merchants did not oppose the granting of concessions in the abstract. Still, they considered the actions of this company, which had a commercial monopoly and state backing, despotic and arrogant. However, the first link in the chain of events that led to the speculation began in September 1786. The Company administrators, strapped for cash, opted to market all of the new shares en bloc, a policy that backfired drastically almost as soon as it was implemented. Under the September 21 decision terms, shareholders could purchase a share of the new issue for every old share they owned, which effectively made the new shares available at discounted prices. This created an immediate incentive for shareholders to unload part of their old holdings to raise the cash that would enable them to pick up the newer stocks at face value. A mass exit from the market threatened to place downward pressure on prices generally, causing other investors to unload their holdings and thereby spread the crisis (Ghachem, 2008). Perhaps the existing shareholders feared dilution of ownership and thought that increasing the number of shares would undoubtedly lower the price. Whatever the case, a wave of selling began in the market, and the price of New Indies shares plummeted, triggering a general stock crash and a debilitating blow to the royal finances. Desperate, Calonne decided that he needed to prop up the price of New Indies shares. To do so, he entrusted 11.5 million livres worth of state funds to a syndicate of speculators composed of Baroud, Comte de Seneffe, and Pyron de Chaboulon (Jackson, 2022), who in turn worked with the Abbé d'Espagnac, one of the largest existing shareholders of New Indies shares. The Abbé d'Espagnac was a former student of Volter and a close friend of Calonne. First, Seneffe and Pyron immediately decided to take the New Indies stock market privately. They contracted to buy 42,000 Indies shares on both the spot market and the futures market, most for future delivery, and intended to be in a position to set monopoly prices when the contracts matured. However, the bear speculators they had bought soon realized what was happening and individually moved to take new positions to get out of their contracts. When Seneffe and Pyron realized their plan would not work, they transferred all their contracts to Abbé d'Espagnac. Meanwhile, Espagnac was buying forward contracts with a similar plan.

On March 18, 1787, Mirabeau signed a pamphlet by Claviere, exposing the conspiracy of Espagnac and Baroud. Mirabeau was a prominent figure in the early stages of the French Revolution. This news exploded like a bomb in Paris as Calonne persuaded the Assembly to accept his financial reforms. Although it was a collective conspiracy, it was identified with d'Espagnac's name (Taylor, 1962). To prove that he had nothing to do with it, the embattled Calonne promised all parties that he would implement a rescue package using government funds if they suffered losses. In the context of the day, Calonne's rescue of his fellow travelers from their own failed plans was a political disaster. As Robert Darnton (1974) notes, "*The message was clear: the controller general was diverting millions from the treasury to create an artificial bull market, while at the same time urging parliament to approve heavy new taxes on the pretext that the treasury was running dry*." Calonne then appointed two bankers, Emmanuel Haller and Barthélemy-Jean-Louis Le Couteulx de Noraye, to lead the forensic investigation into the affair and preside over the liquidation of outstanding forward contracts (Jackson, 2022).

The accusations were relentless, and the public impression that all state-sponsored financiers who played on the Stock Exchange were liars and thieves was strengthened. Haller and La Noraye were soon reimbursed 2 million livres for their Espagnac contract, but the controversy continued, and a series of denunciations were made. Calonne then fell out of favor and was exiled. His successors, Brienne and Necker, politically repudiated the policy, denied that Haller and La Noraye acted with royal authority, and launched a new investigation. In the end, the Abbé d'Espagnac was paid a compensation of around 4 million livres, and Haller and La Noraye were subsequently guillotined along with the Dantonists in 1794; the government lost a fortune of 25 million livres, or 5% of the gross national product. Indeed, Haller and La Noraye were executed not because of any specific crime but because they represented the financial aristocracy and were perceived as symbols of the corrupt financial system of the ancien régime. Their executions were part of the broader purge during the Reign of Terror, which aimed to eliminate perceived enemies of the Revolution (Tackett, 2015).

Meanwhile, news came that the five royal accountants who had opened this department had gone bankrupt. Furthermore, it was revealed that during 1786, a financial syndicate had forged and circulated at least 1.4 million livres in bills of exchange drawn on the Caisse de Compte. This discovery caused every bill drawn on Parisian businessmen to be viewed with suspicion and briefly paralyzed the French payment system. Indeed, by the 1780s, on the eve of the French Revolution, bankers and financiers could raise such vast amounts of capital from their continent-wide networks that they could collapse the Paris Bourse, destroy joint-stock companies, and ultimately paralyze the French money market. However, the crisis of 1787, while politically disastrous, did not stop the flow of capital to France. According to Fernand Braudel, the total market capitalization of all French joint-stock companies in 1789 was twice the French GNP (Jackson, 2022).

In retrospect, these speculators of the Paris Bourse seem far ahead of their time. In spirit and technique, they belonged to nineteenth-century finance capitalism. In other words, the boom of the 1780s was built on the aristocratic and monarchical institutions of the old order rather than on the nineteenth century's unborn industrial and financial system. It was an example not of the Industrial Revolution but of the courtly capitalism of early modern Europe (Taylor, 1962).

7.4 The 1789 French Revolution and the Financial Markets

The 1789 French Revolution decided to convene an assembly called the National Convention to draft a new constitution that would not upset the Paris market. This institution, the first French assembly elected by equal votes without class distinction, targeted speculation, and speculation became a crime during the revolution. The Paris Bourse was closed in 1791, and its joint-stock companies were indicted. Revolutionaries interrogated business people and stockbrokers outside Paris and elsewhere. However, even this repression did not stop the speculators. Although most merchants and provincial bankers have stepped aside, plenty of opportunists could invest in the occasional securities issues. They were shrewd, politically connected, and willing bankers who could always raise funds by pledging their assets as collateral for loans (Taylor, 1962).

The French Revolution of 1789, with its redefinition of the place of property in the constitutional order, reshaped the world of financial capitalism through banks, money, and debt. The revolutionaries abolished all exceptions to the tax system. The excise taxes and the church tax of Old Regime France, which were rules of exceptional law, were abandoned. Soon, tax revenues collapsed, and conditions were ripe for a default, but the revolutionaries were as determined to protect property rights as they were to end exceptional jurisdictions. They explicitly pledged to repay the debt in full, forbidding any debate on default in the National Assembly.

Finally, Charles Maurice de Talleyrand (1754–1838), Bishop of Autun and later a diplomat and politician, proposed expropriating church property. Étienne Clavière was one of the originators of this proposal (Jackson, 2022). This land, estimated to be worth 2–3 billion livres, had the potential to pay off the country's debt. Thus, in December 1789, the National Assembly issued "*assignats*," 5% interest bonds with the confiscated church lands pledged as collateral to pay off urgent debts. Assignats are paper money (fiat currency), used from 1789 to 1796, and had no equivalent in gold or silver. In September 1790, the Assembly converted assignats into paper money, and the circulation increased from 400,000,000 livres to 1,200,000,000 livres. Paper money's initial impact was beneficial because it stimulated economic growth and eliminated currency shortages. However, the public's deep mistrust of paper money and the fear that it would be worthless if the Revolutionary regime collapsed soon led to a devaluation of the paper money (Encyclopaedia Britannica, n.d.).

Constitutional monarchists such as Maury, Cazalès, Bergasse, and d'Eprémesnil initiated a political debate, opposing the assignation, seeing it as based on an illegitimate usurpation of property. In contrast, some eighteenth-century advocates of "*land banks*" argued that land was a more stable source of value than gold or silver. With this money, the state's creditors would be paid first. Creditors could buy national lands with it; for this purpose, assignats took precedence over other forms of money. If the creditor did not want to purchase land, it was thought that he could obtain their face value from those who wished to sell land. Assignats returned to the state as purchase money would be canceled, and it was argued that all assignats would disappear as national lands were distributed (Aftalion, 1990).

Mirabeau called this approach a "*monetary constitution.*" In his "*Conjuration contre les finances*" of 1792, Clavière pointed to a conspiracy of foreigners, bankers, agioteurs, and aristocrats to undermine public confidence in the assignats. By early 1793, the conditions of national unity had changed to the detriment of Clavière's technical solutions. The Girondin group's policies, especially the assignats' apparent failure, had weakened their popular legitimacy. The National Convention mandated an equal exchange of banknotes and coins, but this law was never implemented. Instead, the assignats continued to lose value. Rising prices and food shortages exacerbated public unrest in September. Laws such as the Maximum Price Act (1793) aimed to remedy this situation. On November 8, 1793, Lamarche, the production manager of Assignat, was executed. Then, on December 2, Clavière was arrested, tried, and sentenced to death along with his friends (Spang, 2015). He was targeted because of his close ties to the Girondins, a moderate political faction opposed by the radical Jacobins. After the Jacobins seized power, they launched a purge against the Girondins, accusing Clavière of financial mismanagement, corruption, and counter-revolutionary activities. His controversial role as Minister of Finance, particularly his support of the assignat paper currency, made him a scapegoat for France's worsening economic crisis. Additionally, the revolutionary government's distrust of bankers and financiers intensified the charges against him. Rather than facing trial and likely execution, Clavière took his own life in La Force Prison (Box 7.1).

7.5 The Napoleonic Era (1799–1815)

Napoleon seized political power in a coup d'état in 1799 and declared himself Emperor in 1804. Napoleon Bonaparte was undoubtedly the most important historical figure in creating the modern French State and its financial system. When he became First Consul, he made sweeping changes that completed the fiscal organization's reorganization. He did not hesitate to recreate many of the institutions of the old regime to restore France's economic power and maintain order. Tax revenues increased, and the budget gradually came into balance. To this end, he created a sinking fund in 1799, the Banque de France in 1800, and the country returned to the bimetallic standard in 1803 (White et al., 2003). The Bank of France was founded on January 18, 1800, as a private company and a "*public bank*," whose task was to issue bearer notes payable on demand in exchange for discounting commercial paper. In 1803, it obtained the privilege of emission for Paris, and later, in 1848, received the monopoly to print banknotes for the whole of France. The Banque de France actively stabilized the currency, provided liquidity, and supported economic activities. He also set up a sinking fund, whereby surplus funds from government revenues were set aside for the payment of both principal and interest, thus gradually eliminating the national debt. In this way, Napoleon balanced the budget until 1802, but the country would pay a heavy price in wars (UA University archives, n.d.). France left the livre and adopted the franc as its official currency in 1795 during the French Revolution. The French franc was introduced as a decimal currency, replacing the livre. In 1795, one franc was defined as 4.5 g of silver. Under Napoleon in 1803, the German franc was standardized as part of the monetary system. It was backed by a bimetallic standard (both silver and gold). The livre had been used for centuries, but by the late eighteenth century, it suffered from severe depreciation and inflation, leading to its replacement. The franc then became a more stable and modern currency.

Box 7.1: The Dramatic Death of Etienne Clavière

Born in 1735 in Geneva to a devout Protestant family, Etienne Clavière lay in his cell in the Conciergerie prison, west of the Île de la Cité, a small island in the Seine that bisects Paris, around midnight on December 7, 1793. His cell was dark, damp, and cold, but Clavière felt nothing. He had become accustomed to the screams of other prisoners rising from the adjoining wards. Although it was built as part of the Palais de la Cité, the former royal palace, it was used as a prison during the French Revolution of 1789. More than two thousand prisoners, including Queen Marie Antoinette, had previously been imprisoned, tried, convicted, and then guillotined at the Conciergerie. Clavière would meet the same fate the next day. He was not afraid of death; he just wanted to prevent the confiscation of his property and possessions so that he could leave them to his beloved wife. He had long believed that the world was coming to an end. A new dark age was coming. Tyrants were rising and would probably take over the free states. When the trading nations of Western Europe went bankrupt, invaders would come from the east. By morning he had made up his mind; he slit his throat with an ivory dagger hidden in the lining of his dress. He was in great pain, but if he made a sound, the guards at the gate who would take him to the gallows might wake up and save him. The next day, his wife, who learned the news in a letter, would commit suicide by throwing herself into the Seine (Engelsberg Ideas, 2021).

His faith taught that trade and the production of wealth served God, but at the same time, everything they did had to be open, honest, and moral. Clavière had a mind like a diamond in the rough; his ideas were sharp and elegant. He was good with numbers and eventually became one of the wealthiest speculators on the national stock exchanges. However, Clavière hated capitalism. He spent much of his life seeking an alternative to the corrupt capitalist system of commerce, which allowed merchants and bankers to buy politicians to make laws for their benefit rather than the common good. He was also committed to ending the slave trade. Describing himself as a citizen of the world, Clavière argued that nationalism and xenophobia were corrosive poisons in any society. With the 1789 French Revolution, Clavière was recognized as a brilliant economic theorist by key players in the French Revolution. With his newspaper and magazine, he found himself again at the center of events. In the fall of 1789, his former employee Mirabeau was now the revolution leader and was writing his speeches. Clavière was so respected as a political economist that he became the last chancellor of Louis XIV and then, in 1792, the first finance minister of the First French Republic. Nevertheless, when Robespierre and the Jacobins seized power through the Committee of Public Safety, Clavière's ministry was terminated. The post-revolutionary reign of terror was brutal, and Clavière was arrested and imprisoned, ending his life behind thick walls (Engelsberg Ideas, 2021).

Talented and skillful experts surrounded Napoleon. He favored a merit-based system of governance (Bertaud, 2017). One of them was his chief financial advisor, Nicolas-François, Count Mollien, who was also his nephew. He was a highly experienced statesman who had served in the administration of tax farms and the general control office before the revolution. Napoleon made Mollien director general of the sinking fund, which he established in November 1799. Mollien was minister of the public treasury during the imperial period from January 1806 to April 1814, and during the Hundred Days in 1815, he reorganized the treasury management (Mollien, 1845).

As explained in the introduction, one of Napoleon's first financial reforms was to reestablish and regulate the Paris Bourse in 1801. Under his leadership, the law of 28 Ventôse, Year IX (March 19, 1801) formally recognized the Paris Bourse as an essential financial institution, ensuring it operated under government supervision. This law was a critical step in organizing financial markets and preventing fraud and speculation, which had been rampant during the Revolutionary period.

A significant element of this reform was the official recognition of agents of change. Previously, brokers operated with minimal oversight, leading to instability. Under Napoleon's regulations, these brokers were now required to obtain government licenses and adhere to strict professional standards. This ensured that only qualified and trustworthy individuals could operate. Napoleon also gave brokers the right to trade bills of exchange and other commercial instruments in the Code de Commerce. They also gained the right to engage in speculative transactions with commodity brokers. Agents of change were to be submitted to the Emperor, who had the power to appoint eighty of them, subject to the scrutiny of local committees and the Minister of the Interior. They had the right to act as intermediaries, verify quotations, and testify before the courts on quotation questions. They had to be paid a fixed commission and were prohibited by law from trading on their behalf. The market was to be characterized as an agency/auction market where orders were consolidated, as in the past, by requiring clients to submit orders to their brokers before the markets opened. The Agent of Change would need to keep a journal of their transactions. Quotations were published after the markets closed. The exchange continued to operate in the former Petits-Peres Church until 1809, when it moved to the Palais-Royal. Except on holidays, the exchange was open daily from two to three in the afternoon for trading in securities and from ten to four for commercial transactions. According to the Napoleonic code, brokerage houses "*must not be allowed to expose themselves to the danger of jeopardizing the interests of their clients by compromising their fortunes in a risky or ill-fated venture*" (White et al., 2003).

After all, Napoleon Bonaparte did not like government policy being priced in the market, so he reorganized the stock market (Hautcoeur & Riva, 2012). The laws of the Napoleonic Exchange drastically reduced the number of stock brokers. The Almanach National de France reported that 106 stock brokers traded in 1799–1800. While the new law allowed Napoleon to select eighty brokers, on July 20, 1801, Napoleon found and appointed only seventy-one honest agents of change, and raised the margin of entering the business to 100,000 francs. He later increased the number of offices to 100, but by 1814, the number of agents had fallen to forty-one. The new law required brokers to carry securities for sellers and money for buyers when they went to trade. The design of this decree was intended to control transactions made by brokers for future delivery (White et al., 2003). Brokers were organized in 1807 under the name of the "*Compagnie des agents de Change (CAC)*," which became a syndicate that set detailed rules governing activities on the parquet and became a self-regulating organization, as in the case of London and New York. The members elected this Board of Directors, led by a union president. The Code de Commerce prohibited brokers from trading on their accounts. Commissions were fixed and set by the Chambre syndicale (CS). The decree entrusted brokers with establishing "*internal discipline rules*" (Neal & Davis, 2005).

In 1808, when the debate resumed, the president of the chamber, Jean-Baptiste-Joseph Boscary de Villeplaine, pointed out that the Emperor's belief that the Code de Commerce's rule on futures trading on assets in possession applied to all markets was incorrect. This rule only applies to the real estate market. Moreover, the futures market did not increase the short-term funds available for speculation. He explicitly told Napoleon that the spot market was small, that banks handled all domestic commercial paper, and that international financial transactions were almost nonexistent. The Chamber did not object to regulating futures and limiting them to two months. However, it warned that trying to ensure immediate possession for delivery would cause the securities markets to fall apart. The CAC president's bold words probably impressed the Emperor. Under Napoleon, the diversity of assets traded on the exchange gradually increased. Gold and silver in bullion, bars, and coins were also rising. In contrast to the rapid pre-revolutionary growth, the private debt market was almost stagnant in the first decade of the nineteenth century (White et al., 2003). Although the Banque de France was not directly linked to the Paris Bourse, its creation profoundly impacted financial markets. By ensuring a stable banking system, the Banque de France provided a reliable source of credit to businesses and investors. This, in turn, strengthened the financial markets and facilitated long-term economic growth.

Napoleon also played a crucial role in promoting the trading of government bonds on the Paris Bourse. These bonds were a secure investment option, offering investors stability while helping the French government finance its expenditures, including military campaigns. The introduction of rentes strengthened the connection between the state and the financial markets, as investors now had a direct stake in the economic health of the French government. By encouraging the purchase of government-backed securities, Napoleon ensured that France's financial markets remained stable and liquid. This policy also helped him fund his wars efficiently, as the government could raise money without excessive taxation or inflation.

The revolution devastated Parisian financial institutions intimately involved in functioning securities markets and market-making. Under the security of the Napoleonic regime, bankers returned to their former role in the financial markets. The restructuring of the banking sector was a slow process. Some bankers who had gone abroad, joining the general flight of capital to London, did not return as the war with Britain continued. Instead, new bankers came from Switzerland and Belgium (Bergeron, 2020).

Napoleon's financial reforms transformed the Paris Bourse into one of Europe's most structured financial markets. The strict regulations on brokers, the creation of financial institutions, and the promotion of secure investment options helped establish an efficient, transparent, and investor-friendly financial system. As Napoleon expanded his empire, many financial policies influenced other European nations. Countries under French rule or influence began adopting similar regulatory frameworks, making the Paris Bourse a model for modern stock exchanges across Europe. Even after Napoleon's fall, many of his financial reforms remained in place, shaping the development of European financial markets for decades (White et al., 2003).

From the exchange's founding until the end of the Napoleonic era, the rules of the Paris Bourse evolved in line with government orders, and political stability created a microstructure that provided liquidity to the system. On the eve of the revolution, trading issues of modest size on the highly regulated stock exchange had evolved to a point where trading costs to the public were relatively low. Although the Napoleonic government intervened in the market from time to time, it was not a daily intervention as a market maker but rather to counter excessive movements and provide more liquidity (White et al., 2003).

7.6 The Bourbon Restoration and the Second Empire Period

Following Napoleon's fall, the Bourbon Restoration (1814–1830) witnessed the monarchy's return. Louis XVIII ruled as a constitutional monarch, balancing tradition with revolutionary reforms. His 1814 Charter guaranteed civil rights and limited royal power. After he died in 1824, Charles X's conservative policies and press censorship sparked unrest. The July Revolution of 1830 overthrew him, ending the Bourbon Restoration and ushering in the July Monarchy under Louis-Philippe.

While the Bourbon Restoration retained much of Napoleon's legal and economic structure, including the stock exchange structure, in 1816, royal officials, including the agent de change, were given the right to elect a successor. Agents were also granted office ownership to sell freely if they met the minimum qualifications. The number of brokers was fixed at 60, while agents of change companies were reorganized. A Chambre Syndicale of six brokers assisted the syndic in its tasks. The Chambre Syndicale became responsible for the liquidity balance (Hautcoeur & Riva, 2012). The 1818 Paris financial crisis was a significant event in the Bourbon Period. It was triggered by speculative activities and government debt restructuring following the Napoleonic Wars. It highlighted the vulnerabilities of the newly restored Bourbon monarchy and the Paris financial markets and foreshadowed the future. The construction of the modern stock exchange building, which began in 1808 on Napoleon Bonaparte's orders, was finally completed in 1826 and opened as the "Palais Brongniart." (Fig. 7.3).

Fig. 7.3 An auction of agents de change at Palais Brongniart. https://fr.wikipedia.org/wiki/Palais_Brongniart#/media/Fichier:Die_Gartenlaube_(1854)_b_051.jpg (Public Domain)

Throughout the nineteenth century, the formal stock exchange structure did not change significantly. The innovations that mimicked foreign examples in London and New York came mainly from the coulisse, the informal market of traders, promoters, and sidewalks that developed just outside the official exchange. New issues were first issued on the coulisse, and once the government recognized their usefulness, it allowed them to be listed and traded on the parquet. Foreign government bonds and securities of foreign private companies were banned from trading on the parquet until 1859. When this exclusion created gaps in the market, these gaps were filled by coulisse (Neal & Davis, 2005).

The Napoleonic Code of 1807 classified futures contracts as speculative and akin to gambling, which meant they were not legally enforceable in court. The concern was that such contracts encouraged excessive speculation and could lead to market manipulation and instability. Although there was an active cash market for securities (marché au comptant), most of the activity was concentrated in the futures market (marché à terme). Forward contracts did not generally hinder the functioning of the market. However, stockbrokers described this as a "Sword of Damocles," as they could be accused of breaking the law (Hautcoeur & Riva, 2012). The futures market was estimated to be fifty times the size of the cash market (Vincens, 1821). In 1832, courts of law began to make forward contracts enforceable, recognizing their validity even if forward buyers deposited no money. Forward transactions increased for new railway shares and bond issues (Lagneau-Ymonet & Riva, 2018). In the futures market, buyers and sellers agree to exchange a quantity of shares at a fixed price on settlement dates (liquidation), the fifteenth or last day of the month. Bull traders had bought contracts in the futures market to resell them at a higher price on the settlement date, while bears sold contracts, hoping that prices would fall. There were no regulations governing the margin, which the broker set according to the underlying securities and the client's situation (Proudhon, 1869). On settlement day, traders in the futures market would decide whether they wanted to liquidate their positions. If the current cash price was below the contract price, a buyer could not buy the securities and instead replenish his position through a report. If he had contracted to buy at the end of the month, he would buy on that date at the contract price and sell the securities immediately at the settlement price (cours de compensation). On the next settlement date, he would enter a new forward contract to buy back the securities and borrow against this transaction. The syndicates set the settlement price. Usually, the average cash price is quoted on the settlement day. Given the delay between the contract and the delivery date, brokers were exposed to the risk of default by their clients when unexpected changes in their wealth altered their ability to fulfill their contractual obligations. The broker traded the securities if a client could not close their account. If collateral were insufficient, the broker would bear the loss. However, brokers were also exposed to the default risk of their counterparties (Riva & White, 2011).

The CAC had no absolute control over the agents. Partly due to political uncertainty and partly due to a lack of organization, there were considerable fluctuations in the market. The difference between parquet agents and coulissiers was negligible in this first phase. Both groups cooperated daily to create more or less a single market. Although the coulisses dominated the futures market, no registered rent transfer was possible without agents' intermediation. Parquet's month-end settlement, created in 1805, served the entire market. Moreover, the coulissiers also acted as dealers. Agents of change needed to be able to execute a significant portion of orders that could not be filled in a market that was still relatively tight. The high volume of agent transactions made them as risky as coulissiers. From 1801 to 1814, 115 agents were appointed, 65 left the profession before 1815, and 46 left due to bankruptcy. While the Coulissiers traded securities in the over-the-counter market, they carried out transactions prohibited by the Exchange rules. Coulissiers also competed in futures trading in significant bond issues, which was the core activity of agents of change (Hautcoeur & Riva, 2012). This competition strengthened the institutionalization of the Exchange through a process of differentiation from the OTC market and led to a beneficial complementarity (Lagneau-Ymonet & Riva, 2018). Since the Coulissiers dealt with each other and the agent de changes bilaterally and often acted in collaboration, their activities were neither public nor transparent. Still, they allowed for greater flexibility and transaction speed. On the contrary, Parquet's transparency and pure brokerage represented a reputational investment for investors and the public and political sphere (Hautcoeur & Riva, 2012).

Parquet and coulisse began to diverge over time. Given the pre-revolutionary situation, French investors wanted more security than the high returns. In this context, clearing and settlement were essential. Once this was in place, it gave the customer confidence. The monthly bilateral and decentralized clearing (liquidation générale) was reorganized in 1808 after the Bank of France threatened to close brokers' accounts due to disorganized transfers and a lack of control. The Chamber then introduced centralized clearing. Accordingly, each agent had to clear its clients' accounts, and then, on a fixed date, all agents had to net their remaining balances bilaterally. In 1836, the Banque de France agreed to combine the calendar of its monthly transactions with the central clearing and settlement of agents. By the 1840s, intermediaries were confident enough in their accounting and the group they formed to adopt multilateral clearing. The Exchange's clearing and settlement would help convince judges that futures trading was not gambling (Lagneau-Ymonet & Riva, 2018).

A sinking fund was established in the 1818 crisis; "Caisse d'Ámortissement" was used for the first time to rescue several agencies from bankruptcy under the sole authority of the Chambre Syndicale. This fund was financed by a stamp duty levied on the transactions of all agents. In 1822, the CAC made this fund permanent under the Caisse Commune (Common Fund). The Common Fund also covered the Chambre Syndicale's expenses and leveraged the Chambre Syndicale in institutional development. In addition to the Chambre Syndicale's fees and the payment to the Common Fund, the Common Fund paid an equal dividend to all members. The Common Fund then provided loans to agents with short-term liquidity and solvency problems, allowing them to manage counterparty risk (Hautcoeur & Riva, 2012).

In 1830, Paris was the center of a significant political upheaval known as the July Revolution or the Three Glorious Days (July 27–29). This event resulted in the overthrow of King Charles X, France's last Bourbon monarch, and the establishment of the July Monarchy (1830–1848) under Louis-Philippe, Duke of Orléans. Louis-Philippe I brought stability, and gradually, the period witnessed rapid growth driven by industrialization and government-backed infrastructure projects. The Common Fund was first used during the crisis of 1830–1831.

The cooperation and competition between Parquet and Coulisse became increasingly hostile toward the end of the 1850s. The crisis resulting from a series of revolutions across Europe in 1847–1848 had no impact on Parquet. On the contrary, some coulissiers had defaulted. Therefore, the coulisse was reorganized in a more formal structure and flourished simultaneously. In 1859, Parquet agreed with the government on reorganizing and strengthening the monopoly and took over Coulisse's staff and business without formally acquiring Coulisse's firms (Vidal, 1910). Immediately after adopting new internal rules that allowed Parquet's expansion, the Chambre Syndicale took an extremely harsh decision against Coulisse's leading, most respected members. However, this merger move was to fail. There are four main reasons for this. First, the brokerage houses could not adapt to this hierarchical organization. The Coulisses continued to run their operations off-exchange and took risks that an agent de change did not want to guarantee. Second, Parqueler could not provide all the services the market needed. Third, Parquet failed to give the international arbitrage required by international cross-listed securities. Finally, Coulisse, the large issuances on the French market had exceeded the market's absorptive capacity. Parquet's quotation policy for French securities was also unsatisfactory for many issuers. Moreover, Parquet's rigid treatment of futures made it less flexible than Coulisse's (Lagneau-Ymonet & Riva, 2018).

The July Monarchy under Louis-Philippe I brought stability. This period gradually witnessed rapid growth, driven by industrialization and government-backed infrastructure projects. However, it was also marked by speculative bubbles and financial crises that foreshadowed the political upheaval of 1848. In February 1848, public protests over political corruption and lack of suffrage erupted. Louis-Philippe abdicated and fled to England, marking the end of the July Monarchy and the beginning of the Second French Republic.

The Paris Bourse initially faced significant instability due to political upheaval and economic uncertainty after the Revolution of 1848. Stock prices collapsed as investors panicked and fled the market. Industrial and railway stocks suffered particularly severe declines, and credit tightened. The government's social programs, such as the National Workshops, worsened investor confidence due to concerns over public spending. After the June Days Uprising, stability began to return, but the market remained weak until Louis-Napoléon Bonaparte's rise to power. His election in 1848 and subsequent consolidation of power in 1851 reassured investors, leading to a gradual recovery and renewed confidence in the financial markets by 1852. The Paris Bourse experienced significant growth, reflecting France's industrial expansion and the stability of the Second Empire (1852–1870) under Napoleon III, followed by the early years of the Third Republic.

Modernization, speculative booms, and financial crises marked this period. The 1856 reform sought to adapt the Paris Bourse to the increasing number of industrial enterprises and the growing complexity of financial markets. It transformed the exchange into a central financing hub for industrial growth. The reform allowed more industrial companies to be listed on the exchange, particularly in the railway and banking sectors. This move expanded market participation and provided crucial capital for France's developing industries. Additionally, modernized trading practices reduced transaction delays and errors, further enhancing market efficiency and attracting more investors.

However, in 1857 and 1866, over-speculation negatively affected financial institutions. The Crédit Mobilier failed in 1867 due to over-speculation, mismanagement, and political corruption. The bank, led by the Péreire brothers, rapidly expanded by investing heavily in risky railway projects across Europe. Poor financial oversight and a lack of discipline made it vulnerable to market downturns. Political scandals and bribery further damaged its reputation, while conflicts with traditional institutions like the Banque de France isolated it from potential support. A financial crisis in the mid-1860s caused a market panic, exposing its over-leveraged investments and triggering its collapse. This failure marked a turning point for France's financial markets, promoting stricter regulation and more cautious banking practices (Kindleberger et al., 1996).

Following the crisis, the 1867 Company Law in France was accepted. Thus, corporate governance modernized and promoted economic growth by simplifying the formation of joint-stock companies. It removed the need for government approval to establish companies, introduced limited liability for shareholders, and required annual financial statements and shareholder meetings. The law mandated Board of Directors for companies and set clear guidelines for capital requirements and share issuance to prevent fraud. It boosted the Paris Bourse, expanded industries like railways and banking, attracted foreign investment, and increased investor confidence, making it a cornerstone of modern corporate capitalism in France (Rawlings, 1975).

In this context, the capital of brokerage firms was also strengthened. A broker's capital consisted of a "cautionnement" or compulsory security bond, the office's purchase price, and personal reserves. In 1818, the cautionnement was initially set at 125,000 francs and was raised according to need. From the reign of Napoleon III, this collateral in the Treasury was supplemented by a mandatory reserve to be used by agents of change to assist members in crises. The broker's personal reserve fund was primarily used to cover losses in cases where clients went bankrupt. In 1898, the number of brokers increased from 60 to 70, and the number of authorized commissioners rose from four to six (Neal & Davis, 2005).

7.7 The Crisis of 1882 and the Collapse of the Paris Bourse

After Napoleon III was deposed in 1870 following the Franco-Prussian War, France transitioned to the Third Republic. The immediate aftermath included the Siege of Paris (1870–1871) by Prussian forces and the Paris Commune uprising, which was violently suppressed. France lost Alsace-Lorraine to Germany and paid a large war indemnity. Despite early political instability, the Third Republic gradually stabilized, with economic recovery fueled by industrial growth. The Paris Bourse became more regulated and attracted foreign investment, laying the groundwork for a more resilient financial market.

However, political turmoil in the Balkans during this period deteriorated France's financial stability. The chain of events developed after the 1877–78 war between the Ottomans and the Russians, when France and Austria took a new position due to increased Russian influence in the Balkans (Cavus, 2016). In this context, the first reaction was led by Paul-Eugène Bontoux, once an employee of the Rothschild Railroad Company. Bontoux had taken over the management of the troubled General Union, founded in Lyon in 1875 by a group of Catholic and monarchist bankers. The General Union was then officially founded on June 3, 1878. The bank attracted great interest in Catholic and Legitimist circles and the support of the Count of Chambord, a pretender to the French throne. Bontoux established a new financial network to channel French capital to Central and Southern Europe. His plans also had a robust political agenda that appealed to French conservatives, especially the legitimist nobility and clergy, who were disillusioned with the success of the Third Republic. Using Jewish capital and anti-Rothschild rhetoric, Lyon-based Bontoux encouraged conservative Catholic investors in France to buy shares and invest their savings in his bank (Bouvier, 1970). The bank increased by multiplying risky investments, especially in Central and Danube Europe. While speculating on the stock market, it also financed operations in North Africa and Egypt with a group of banks.

Bontoux supported his ventures through a series of interlocking financial institutions. The capital raised by the General Union and its affiliated organizations was estimated at one billion francs (Vidal, 1910). In 1881, Bontoux founded the Österreichische Landesbank in Austria, where the General Union held a controlling stake. The government in Vienna granted this new institution all the privileges of the Bank of France, except for issuing banknotes. These institutions became the instruments of the Austrian imperial government, which aimed to increase its power in the Balkans and channel it into railroads that would enable it to dominate the region (White, 2007).

Bontoux's initiatives were central to the government's plans, and the Hungarians supported this policy. Following Bontoux's success, excitement about new investment opportunities in the Balkans spread. Other new banks were also established in Lyon. Banque de Lyon et de la Loire was one of them. Established banks also joined the boom. General Union, which had a share price of 500 francs in 1879, had risen to over 3000 francs. Speculators borrowed on credit and renewed their futures contracts from one deal to the next, hoping that prices would keep rising. Banks and new intermediaries provided funds for reports (White, 2007).

Banque de Lyon et de la Loire was very active in this market, investing heavily. Brokers found this market extremely profitable. The stock market was overwhelmed on clearing days, with increasingly long nights and long delays in clearing transactions, alarming the CAC, which claimed in its 1882 annual report that it was appalled by the increase in speculation and advised caution. The French Treasury issued one billion francs of 3% bonds in July 1881 in this favorable market. It tried to market the issue directly to the public by allowing installment payments, which allowed it to speculate by borrowing (Say, 1886). Seeing the market boom, investors got involved. Speculators also printed counterfeit money; they renewed futures contracts, hoping prices would continue rising (White, 2007).

The collapse began when the Austrian government refused to grant the Banque de Lyon et de la Loire a concession to establish the Banque Maritime de Trieste (Bouvier, 1970). The bank's shares fell from 1400 francs on January 4, 1882, to 540 francs on January 13. Investors in the futures market who had bought shares at 1800 francs in mid-January faced huge losses. At the same time, the share price of the Suez Company, a leading issuer, fell from 3440 francs on January 7 to 2900 francs on January 14. In this storm, General Union's price began to decline rapidly. Meanwhile, it was revealed that the bank had committed financial irregularities and falsified its quarterly report of September 1881, showing a fictitious profit of 34 million francs. When General Union collapsed at the end of January 1882, about a quarter of the stockbrokers were on the verge of bankruptcy. The closure of the stock exchange was averted by a loan from the Bank of France to agents of change. The collapse in 1882 led to a recession that lasted until the end of the 1880s. Immediately after the collapse, the bank's founder, Paul Eugène Bontoux, attributed the bank's collapse to conspiracies of "Jewish finance" and its ally "government freemasonry," whose aim was to destroy banks that supported conservative and Catholic political programs. At the time of the collapse, 14 of the 60 agents of change were in imminent difficulty, and seven were utterly insolvent (La Bris, 2010). Although this crisis was felt in other developed stock markets, none had experienced such devastation. Bontoux was arrested and imprisoned for several months. Later, he was sentenced to five years in prison and fled to Spain. He died in Cannes in 1904. According to White (2007), there are five possible contributing factors: (1) the lack of legal basis for forward contracts, (2) the size of forward markets, (3) the size of the crash, (4) the concentration of trading among brokers, and (5) the moral hazard arising from the operation of the common fund.

Forward contracts were discussed in the aftermath of the crisis. It was clear that forwards (or futures) were crucial for liquidity and, therefore, for market development. Once the legal status of futures was established, many investors could trade without legal risk. It was no longer possible to leave their obligations solely on the shoulders of intermediaries. In 1885, a new law legalized futures and options contracts, thus shifting the risk inherent in futures trading from brokers to their customers.

The 1885 reform took these changes further, focusing on professionalization and greater public access to financial markets. By this time, there was a growing demand for broader participation in the financial sector and increased protection for small investors. The 1885 reform introduced measures to make the market more inclusive and to prevent fraudulent activity by companies seeking to be listed. The publication of more comprehensive financial information became mandatory, increasing transparency and promoting informed investment decisions. This reform helped democratize financial markets, reducing the dominance of economic elites and encouraging middle-class participation.

In 1890, the government passed a decree on securities trading, and two years later, it approved a revised rulebook for agents. This institutional environment allowed for further regulatory changes, culminating in the reform of French financial markets in 1898 (Lagneau-Ymonet & Riva, 2018). The 1898 reform of the Paris Bourse was a vital step in modernizing French financial markets. It was introduced in response to growing concerns about excessive speculation, market manipulation, and investor protection.

One key aspect of the reform was strengthening oversight and regulation of agents of change. These brokers were subjected to stricter supervision and higher capital requirements to ensure their financial stability and reduce the risk of insolvency. Additionally, the reform introduced a modern centralized clearinghouse, which minimized counterparty risk and enhanced the reliability of securities trading by facilitating the settlement of transactions. The reform established new disclosure requirements for listed companies to protect investors further, ensuring that accurate and timely information was made available to the public. This increased transparency played a crucial role in restoring market confidence. The reform also formalized trading practices for futures and options, reducing opportunities for manipulation and creating a more structured market for derivatives. The 1898 regulatory reform was pivotal in developing France's contemporary and reliable financial system and Bourse (Fig. 7.4). It reinforced investor confidence, reduced speculative abuses, and laid the foundation for the continued growth and internationalization of the Paris Bourse in the twentieth century (Kindleberger, 2015).

Fig. 7.4 Paris Bourse-1900. https://commons.wikimedia.org/wiki/File:La_Bourse_-_Paris_ann%C3%A9e_1900.jpg

By the late nineteenth century, a large part of the securities market was out of the control of the agents of change and into the hands of traders on the coulisse, which was largely unregulated. Government efforts to tax securities transactions exacerbated the hostility between the two rivals (Neal & Davis, 2005). Even frequent lawsuits against coulissiers could not prevent the growth of this market. Although the stock market was heavily regulated, it was still relatively resilient. The markets and legal structures were still flexible enough to accommodate the expansion that resulted from the relocation of activities from the parquet to the coulisse. However, overall transaction costs were undoubtedly higher, and the system could have been more precise and efficient. London took the lead in the race to become the world's leading financial center at the beginning of the nineteenth century. Still, the Paris Bourse's architecture helped Paris remain in an international position alongside London for the rest of the century. Although it was as large as the New York Stock Exchange, it had a more global character (Hautcoeur et al., 2023).

The costs that market microstructure imposed on French securities markets were, to some extent, hidden by the markets' rapid growth. However, by the end of the nineteenth century, France, which had managed to emerge from the crisis, would become the world's second-largest exporter of capital after Britain. As a financial center, Paris was slightly superior to Berlin despite a much larger German economy on the eve of World War I (Rajan & Zingales, 2003).

Some ideas developed during this period formed the basis of modern financial theories. Jules Augustin Frédéric Regnault (1834–1894, Paris) was a French stockbroker who first proposed a modern theory of stock price changes using a random walk model in his Calcul des Chances et Philosophie de la Bourse (1863). A phrase he wrote in his book inspired later scholars working in this field: *"l'écart des cours est en raison directe de la racine carrée des temps (The price differential is a direct result of the square root of the times)."* He was also one of the first authors to try to create a "*science of the stock market*" based on statistical and probabilistic analysis. Inspired by his work, Louis Jean-Baptiste Alphonse Bachelier (1870–1946) is credited with being the first to model the stochastic process, now called Brownian motion, as part of his doctoral thesis Théorie de la spéculation, which he defended in 1900. Bachelier's arguments in his thesis inspired Eugene Fama's efficient market hypothesis in the 1960s. According to this hypothesis, stock prices are random. His work in finance is recognized as one of the foundations of the Black-Scholes model, which was used in futures markets in the 1970s (Bachelier, 2011).

Entering the twentieth century, France lived in the Belle Époque (1870–1914). Like Britain, its economy was doing well. During this period, it achieved the most significant power of European civilization in global politics and exerted maximum influence on people outside Europe (Kramer et al., 2020). However, as in London, everything would be turned upside down after World War I.

7.8 Concluding Remarks

The political environment of France was much more complex in the eighteenth and nineteenth centuries than in England. The stock market underwent the Crown, the Revolution, Napoleon, the Bourbon Restoration, and the Second Empire Period. The various ideologies of each period had a significant impact on the stock market. The government strictly regulates the stock exchange. As in London, market players could not play a decisive role in its establishment. The London system was much more liberal. What is unique about the Paris Bourse is the relationship between the various intermediaries, which was one of cooperation and competition, allowing each group to specialize significantly. Therefore, the constant interaction between the agents of change and their competitors, the bankers and coulisses, also had a significant role in its development. Coulisse reached large transaction volumes, especially in the late 19th and early twentieth centuries. Although the state tried to ban the Coulisse over time, it could not eliminate it. Consolidation began between the two markets from the 1930s onwards. In 1986, Coulisse was closed entirely, and all transactions started to be conducted through the official market. This historical competition is considered the forerunner of today's alternative trading platforms (OTC, fintech), while showing the balance between state intervention and market freedom and, as a result, becoming an early example of financial inclusion discussions.

Its efficient clearing and compensation procedures decreased transaction costs, and its collective guarantee procedures, which considered moral hazard and adverse selection issues, made it a structured structure that maximized transaction security. However, transaction costs were undoubtedly higher, and the system could have been more precise and efficient. There were other differences between the markets. Even in 1765, observers were astonished by the simplicity of the British ownership transfer system. The market was very shallow. There were, at most, a few trades each day. The movement of stock prices was expected since the intermediaries were not allowed to act as market makers but only as order takers. Bankers likely took on the role of market makers. Paris banks often held substantial portfolios of securities and served on the Board of Directors of companies. Given these positions, they could quickly smooth out fluctuations to ensure a continuous market for their clients. Banks were heavily involved in the market (White et al., 2003). However, its restrictive practices did not hinder the development of the securities market. London pulled ahead in the race to become the world's leading financial center at the turn of the nineteenth century. Still, the Paris Bourse's architecture helped Paris remain in an international position alongside London for the rest of the century. Although it was as large as the New York Stock Exchange, it had a more global character (Neal & Davis, 2005).

Several inclusive institutions established during the nineteenth century played a key role in developing the capital market in Paris. Legal reforms such as the Commercial Code of 1807 strengthened investor confidence by reducing uncertainty and protecting contracts and property, while the Companies Act of 1867 simplified the creation of joint-stock companies, increasing the number of listed companies and attracting foreign investment. The Banque de France stabilized financial markets by providing liquidity and issuing reliable currency during crises. The Paris Bourse was modernized through reforms in 1826, 1856, 1885, and 1898, ensuring transparency, reducing speculation, and increasing middle-class participation. Above all, France gradually became a democracy. These institutions made France's financial system more accessible and secure, making the Paris Bourse a major center for capital and innovation (Michie, 2006).

The Paris Bourse significantly influenced the organization and development of continental exchanges during the nineteenth century. The French capital, one of Europe's key financial hubs, set essential precedents in stock market practices, regulatory frameworks, and financial innovations, which were observed and adopted by other European exchanges. The Paris Bourse was a model for forming stock markets in other European cities; Brussels, Vienna, Madrid, and Istanbul were among them. Many different practices that became standard across Europe, such as trading hours, public listings, and corporate transparency, were first pioneered in Paris. The Paris Bourse (Stock Exchange) was instrumental in spreading the joint-stock company model across Europe, especially with the enactment of the 1867 Company Law. The law made it easier for companies to be listed on the stock exchange and raise capital through public investments. This became a critical model for corporate governance across continental exchanges, including those in Germany, Belgium, and Italy. Paris's efforts to regulate the stock exchange through legal reforms helped establish that exchanges should operate with transparency, corporate accountability, and legal protections for investors. These ideas were adopted by other exchanges in Europe as they sought to modernize their practices and provide investors with safer trading environments (Hautcoeur & Riva, 2012).

Innovations such as bonds, government securities, and investment funds were also pioneered in Paris and spread to other continental exchanges. These innovations provided new ways for companies to raise capital, contributing to the broader development of European financial markets. The Paris Bourse's emphasis on investor protection and reliable financial reporting had a long-lasting impact on how other exchanges structured their regulations. As one of the first exchanges to adopt practices like corporate disclosures, it set the stage for similar reforms in London, Amsterdam, and Berlin. Paris played an essential role in integrating continental markets. With its size, influence, and position as a global financial center, Paris attracted international investors, encouraging the development of cross-border financial interactions among European exchanges. This integration allowed for better liquidity and deeper markets across the continent (Hautcoeur & Riva, 2012).

The historical heritage has significantly contributed to the Paris Bourse today. For example, we understand that the most crucial contribution of Louis XIV to Paris was the proud court society of Versailles and the powerful consumer model and luxury goods industry that attracted all of Europe. Following this ancient tradition, the Paris Bourse has become a stock exchange where luxury goods companies such as LVMH, Kering, and Hermès, which are recognized worldwide, are listed. This makes Paris a global hub for luxury consumption, offering a sectorally differentiated investment space for investors. As Bernard Arnault, founder, chairman, and CEO of LVMH, the world's largest luxury goods company, says, "*Luxury goods are the only area in which it is possible to make luxury margins*" (Taylor, 2021b).

References

Aftalion, F. (1990). *The French revolution: An economic interpretation.* Cambridge University Press.

Bachelier, L. (2011). *Louis Bachelier's theory of speculation: The origins of modern finance.* Princeton University Press.

Balch, T. (1891). *The French in America during the war of independence of the United States, 1777–1783* (Vol. 1). Porter & Coates.

Bergeron, L. (2020). *Banquiers, négociants et manufacturiers parisiens du Directoire à l'Empire* (Vol. 51). Walter de Gruyter GmbH & Co KG.

Bertaud, J. P. (2017). Napoleon's officers. In *Warfare in Europe 1792–1815* (pp. 121–141). Routledge.

Bouvier, J. (1970). Vers le capitalisme bancaire: l'expansion du crédit après Law. *Histoire Économique Et Sociale De La France, 2*, 1660–1789.

Buchan, J. (2018). *John law: A Scottish adventurer of the eighteenth century.* Maclehose Press.

Cavus, R. (2016). İngiliz Basınında Plevne Savunması (19.07. 1877-10.12. 1877). *Vakanüvis-Uluslararası Tarih Araştırmaları Dergisi, 1*(1), 165–179.

Darnton, R. (1974). The high enlightenment and the low-life of literature in pre-revolutionary France. *Studies in Eighteenth-Century Culture, 3*(1), 83–124.

de Staël-Holstein, A. L. G. (2009). Œuvres complètes: Oeuvres historiques. Champion.

Engelsberg Ideas. (2021, April 21). Étienne Clavière – the revolutionary who hated revolution. *Engelsberg Ideas.* https://engelsbergideas.com/portraits/etienne-claviere-the-revolutionary-who-hated-revolution/

Encyclopaedia Britannica. (n.d.). Assignat. In *Encyclopaedia Britannica.* Retrieved February 6, 2025 from https://www.britannica.com

Faure, E. (1977). *La banqueroute de Law: 17 Juillet 1720.* Gallimard.

Ghachem, M. W. (2008). At the origins of public credit: A story of stock-jobbing and financial crisis in prerevolutionary France. *The Financial Crisis of*, 151–199.

Hautcoeur, P. C., & Riva, A. (2012). The Paris financial market in the nineteenth century: Complementarities and competition in microstructures 1. *The Economic History Review, 65*(4), 1326–1353.

Hautcoeur, P. C., Rezaee, A., & Riva, A. (2023). Competition between securities markets: Stock exchange industry regulation in the Paris financial center at the turn of the twentieth century. *Cliometrica, 17*(2), 261–299.

Jackson, T. (2022). *Impunity and capitalism.* Cambridge University Press.

Karan, M. B., Westerman, W., & Wijngaard, J. (2024). *A history of banks.* Contributions to Economics.

Kindleberger, C. P. (2015). *A financial history of Western Europe.* Routledge.

Kindleberger, C. P., Manias, P., & Crashes, A. (1996). *History of financial crises.* Macmillan.

Kramer, L. S., Palmer, R. R., & Colton, J. (2020). *A history of Europe in the modern world: To 1815.* McGraw-Hill.

Lagneau-Ymonet, P., & Riva, A. (2018). Trading forward: The Paris Bourse in the nineteenth century. *Business History, 60*(2), 257–280.

Le Bris, D. (2010). Les krachs boursiers en France depuis 1854. *Revue Économique, 61*(3), 421–430.

Luckett, T. M. (1992). *Credit and commercial society in France, 1740–1789.* Princeton University.

Marion, M. (1934). La Fondation de la Banque de France et ses premières années (1800–14). *History of the Principal Public Banks*, 301–318.

Martin, M. (1790). *Étrennes financières; ou, Recueil des matières les plus importantes en finance, banque, commerce.* [s.n.].

Michie, R. C. (2006). *The global securities market: A history.* Oxford University Press.

Mollien, F. (1845). *Memoires d'un Ministre du Tresor Public.* Guillaumin.

Neal, L., & Davis, L. (2005). The evolution of the rules and regulations of the first emerging markets: The London, New York, and Paris Bourses, 1792–1914. *The Quarterly Review of Economics and Finance, 45*(2–3), 296–311.

Nussbaum, F. L. (1933). The formation of the New East India Company of Calonne. *The American Historical Review, 38*(3), 475–497.

Proudhon, P. J. (1869). *Manuel du spéculateur à la Bourse* (Vol. 11). Librairie internationale.

Rajan, R. G., & Zingales, L. (2003). The great reversals: The politics of financial development in the twentieth century. *Journal of Financial Economics, 69*(1), 5–50.

Rawlings, B. M. (1975). The French company law: Choice of corporate form available to the foreign investor. *The Business Lawyer*, 1251–1271.

Riva, A., & White, E. N. (2011). Danger on the exchange: How counterparty risk was managed on the Paris exchange in the nineteenth century. *Explorations in Economic History, 48*(4), 478–493.

Say, L. (1886). Les interventions du Tre´sor a' la bourse depuis 100 ans. Annales de l'E´ cole libres des.

Schwartz, R. A. (1988). *Equity markets: Structure, trading and performance.* Harper and Row.

Spang, R. L. (2015). *Stuff and money in the time of the French revolution.* Harvard University Press.

Tackett, T. (2015). *The coming of the terror in the French revolution.* Harvard UP.

Taylor, G. V. (1962). The Paris Bourse on the Eve of the Revolution, 1781–1789. *The American Historical Review, 67*(4), 951–977.

Taylor, J. (2021a). Inside and outside the London Stock Exchange: Stockbrokers and speculation in late Victorian Britain. *Enterprise & Society, 22*(3), 842–877.

Taylor, I. (2021b). M2. https://m2now.com/bernard-arnault-the-unassuming-billionaire/

Thiveaud, J. M. (1998). Le mercantilisme au xvii ème siècle Les banques et les billets de monnaie sous la régence. *Revue d'économie financière*, 29–53.

UA University archives. (n.d.). https://www.universityarchives.com/auction-lot/napoleon-signed-sinking-fund-letter-our-present_EC143D7816

Vidal, E. (1910). *The history and methods of the Paris Bourse* (No. 573). US Government Printing Office.

Vincens, É. (1821). *Exposition raisonnée de la législation commerciale et examen critique du code de commerce* (Vol. 3).
White, E. N. (2007). The crash of 1882 and the bailout of the Paris Bourse. *Cliometrica, 1*(2), 115–144.
White, E. N., Engerman, S. L., Hoffman, P. T., Rosenthal, J. L., & Sokoloff, K. L. (2003). The Paris Bourse, 1724–1814: Experiments in microstructure. *Finance, Intermediaries, and Economic Development, 34*, 1–36.

Chapter 8
The Istanbul Bourse: The First Stock Exchange of the East (19th Century)

8.1 Introduction

On the morning of May 29, 1453, the janissaries (Ottoman elite troops) broke through the walls of Constantinopolis / Constantinople and entered the city. As smoke rose over the city, screams and cannons were heard. Soldiers were collecting booty and captives, and the people of Byzantium were taking refuge in the church of Hagia Sophia and praying. Mehmet the Conqueror would enter the city on his white horse in the afternoon. There was great confusion all over what would become Istanbul later. Meanwhile, in Galata, on the opposite shore of the Golden Horn, the Genoese, who had been watching the fall of Constantinople, were terrified and tried to get on ships and leave the city. The chain blocking the Golden Horn was also broken. The Genoese were about to lose this base, which they had held for nearly two centuries under the treaty of Ninfeo, which they had signed with Byzantium in 1261.

Zağanos Pasha, the famous commander of Mehmet the Conqueror, had taken the hills behind Galata with his troops. This panic did not escape him. Pasha's loud voice echoed on the Galata coast. He was shouting to the Genoese who were trying to escape by boarding their ships, "*Do not flee, I swear to you, 'do not be afraid; you are friends of the Sultan, and you will hold your city without being harmed by anyone; you will also benefit from the treaties you have made with the Emperor until now and from others (new treaties to be made with us). Therefore, do not bother about anything else; do not anger the Sultan.*" Zağanos thus tried to prevent the Genoese from leaving. The Genoese merchants and soldiers panicked after Constantinople's conquest, fearing their fate. Those who found an opportunity escaped and left on Genoese ships just before the Ottoman soldiers entered Galata, as described by the historian Doukas (Margoulias, 1975). In a letter to his brother, Angelo Giovanni Lomellino, the Podesta (city administrator) of Galata, describes this event as follows: "*Since I was sure that we would reach an agreement with the Sultan, I sent word to the captains that, for God's sake and mercy, they needed to stay until the next day. However, they ignored this and set sail at midnight. In the morning, the sultan,*

M. B. Karan, *A History of Stock Exchanges*, Contributions to Economics,
https://doi.org/10.1007/978-3-032-07788-2_8

hearing that the ships were gone, told our envoy to open the city to him and that we could hardly keep our lives and property safe" (Şakiroğlu, 1981). Indeed, a significant number of Genoese were still in the city. Those who had left were gone; those who remained would now wait for the Sultan's decision.

For centuries, the Genoese lived in Galata (Pera), across the Golden Horn, establishing a colony in 1267. Settling behind fortified walls, they traded across the Black Sea and Mediterranean. The Galata Tower, built in 1348, stood on the northeast hill. The region's name may derive from "*galaktos*" (milk) or "*calata*" (stairway) due to nearby stables, while "*Pera*" (meaning "other land") reflected Byzantine locals' separation from foreign merchants (Fig. 8.1). Another theory links the name to Galatia, a Central Anatolia region once inhabited by Gallic warriors from 278 BC (Kömürciyan, 1988; Ortaylı, 1996).

As the Ottomans gradually gained power in Anatolia after the 1350 s, the Genoese pursued a flexible and manipulative policy toward them. They wanted to preserve their economic privileges from Byzantium and, at the same time, maintain good relations with the Turks. The Genoese colony of Galata was always attentive to maintaining the balance between the powers in their interests and taking their positions according

Fig. 8.1 Galata Tower, 1840. https://commons.wikimedia.org/wiki/File:Galata_Tower_%28Francois_Lemaitre,_1840%29.jpg

to the political developments of the time, even if they were in confrontation with the Ottomans. During the conquest of Constantinople, they did not directly fight the Ottomans but took a neutral position. Sultan Mehmet, the Conqueror, who shifted his ships from the hills of the Golden Horn and launched them in front of Galata, told the Genoese that they would continue to live in this region if they supported him.

As described above, on the day of the conquest, Zağanos Pasha himself reminded them of Sultan Mehmet's promise. The Ottomans thought they would benefit from the activities of the Genoese merchants. Istanbul had to remain a trade center. The Genoese were already enemies with Venice, and in this way, they could divide their enemies. According to the case historian Doukas (1400–1462), the Galata colony was expected to maintain its semi-autonomous status in a walled area with its own administrative and judicial bodies, as in Byzantine times. Sultan Mehmet the Conqueror granted the Genoese the autonomy of Galata on June 1, 1453. With this proclamation, the people of Galata were given religious, commercial, and administrative freedom. However, the new situation was to be somewhat different. The Ottomans soon had the fortifications on the land side of Galata demolished, ended the rule of the Genoese Podesta, and appointed a governor and a person in charge of security and taxation, respectively, to the city. Galata was thus incorporated into the Ottoman administrative system (Kastritsis, 2017).

The Sultan also addressed the Jews living in Istanbul. He promised to grant them freedom of religion and conscience if they cooperated with the Ottomans to repair old synagogues and allow the conversion of houses into places of worship, since establishing new places of worship was forbidden. In addition, Mehmet the Conqueror sent letters to the Jewish communities in Anatolia and invited them to Istanbul to increase the Jewish population in the city. When the Jews were expelled from Spain in the 1590 s during the reign of Sultan Beyazıt II, the Ottomans welcomed them and admitted many Jews to Istanbul. Some settled in Galata in the following centuries (Rozen, 2010). The number of Jews in this area increased significantly after the seventeenth century. Even in the nineteenth century, the population of Istanbul reached approximately 900 thousand, of which 630 thousand were Muslims, 50 thousand Jews, 120 thousand Greeks, and nearly 100 thousand Armenians (Kara, 2010). The Galata district was increasingly favored by non-Muslims, with Jews and Greeks living there the most.

Galata had always been a lively commercial center, but its heyday came in the second half of the nineteenth century. When the Ottomans started to adopt Westernization reforms, the rights of minorities also improved. With the 1839 Tanzimat Edict, foreigners and minorities were granted new privileges, became increasingly powerful, and grew more affluent and significant in Galata, extending to today's Beyoğlu. With the 1856 Reform Edict, they were granted the same rights as Turks and (other) Muslims. The Port of Galata had always been one of the busiest ports in Europe and was the center of international trade, especially in the nineteenth century. Galata was more cosmopolitan than any other city in Europe. Italians, Germans, French, English, Armenians, Greeks, Jews, Hungarians, and Russians had their communities. Not only according to denomination but also according to ethnicity, each group had its own place of worship. This is why many churches and synagogues belonged to different groups side by side.

Wealthy non-Muslim merchants in the region, known as Galata Bankers, thrived through ties with Europe, engaging in money exchanges and interest-based loans. With Muslims avoiding interest charges, they had a broad field of action. Some Italian and French traders, who had been active in Mediterranean trade since Byzantine times, intermarried with locals, forming the Levantine class. In Türkiye, Levantines—mainly of European descent—settled in Izmir and Istanbul, creating a distinct culture between local minorities and Westerners. Over time, they became part of the Galata neighborhood (Çakıcıoğlu, 2007).

The Galata Bankers, the leading actors of our story in this chapter, made an economic contribution to the last period of the declining Ottoman Empire by establishing the Istanbul Bourse, especially in the second half of the nineteenth century. Introducing financial markets to an Empire built on conquest and war, they created the first emerging stock exchange in the East, the Istanbul Bourse (1873), before the Bombay (1875), and Tokyo (1878) stock exchanges.

8.2 Historical and Economic Developments in the Ottoman Empire in the 19th Century

8.2.1 Wars and Economic Situation

Throughout the 19th and early twentieth centuries, the Ottoman Empire faced significant political and economic problems. The Ottoman Empire, which had been a spectator to the developments in the West for a long time, realized its weaknesses after the eighteenth century when it entered an arduous struggle with its powerful neighbor to the north, the Russian Empire. It fought a series of wars with the Russians, who wanted to reach the warm seas but were defeated in most of them. On the other hand, Russia had become a powerful country in the eighteenth century after the reforms of Peter the Great.

From the eighteenth century onward, the Janissaries became increasingly corrupt. Sultan Mahmut II, who ascended the throne after an internal rebellion of the Janissaries (reign 1808–1839), finally, on June 16, 1826, destroyed the Janissary Corps and had many of them executed. However, these events disrupted the economy and weakened the newly established army (Pamuk, 2004). Sultan Mahmut was a reformist sultan, and the westernization of the country began with him. Innovative practices such as European-style dress, architecture, legislation, institutional organization, modern schools, and land reform immediately affected the Empire's social and legal aspects of life. However, these reforms failed to revive the economy immediately and provoked a strong reaction from reactionary sectors.

At the beginning of the nineteenth century, the Ottoman monetary system was based on gold and silver coins. During the reign of Mahmut II, the financing problem of the treasury was deepening considerably. The most common method used during this period was to reduce the silver or gold content of the money. This practice led to a decline in confidence in cash and a deterioration in social stability. As the Ottomans weakened after the French Revolution, nationalist movements rose. Then, two other significant developments were the Greek independence movement against the Ottomans and the revolt of the Egyptian governor Kavalalı Mehmet Ali Pasha. The army of Mehmet Ali Pasha successfully suppressed the Greek rebellion in the first stage. Then, when Britain, which supported the Greek independence movement with loans, and France and Russia, acting in concert with it, destroyed the Ottoman-Egyptian navy at the Battle of Navarin in October 1827, the balance of power shifted in favor of the Greek rebels. Finally, under pressure from Russia, which declared war on the Ottoman Empire, the Treaty of Edirne was signed in September 1829, and Greece gained independence in 1931 (Karan et al., 2024).

The rebellion of the Governor of Egypt, Mehmet Ali Pasha, who was promised some privileges in return for suppressing the Greek movement but could not obtain them, also disturbed the Ottomans until 1841. After a series of wars with Egypt, with the Ottomans supported by the Russian army, Egypt became an autonomous state (province) under the Ottomans. Initially indifferent to this event, Britain considered the development of Ottoman relations with Russia as an essential threat to its interests. In the meantime, when the Ottomans sought help from Britain to stabilize their foreign ties, Britain demanded a trade agreement (the Treaty of Balta Port, 1838), granting great commercial privileges in return for this help. In the meantime, Sultan Mahmut II died, and Sultan Abdülmecid ascended the throne.

In the early nineteenth century, the world entered a period of globalization led by England. England had economic interests stemming from the Industrial Revolution, which created a demand for raw materials and a market for English goods. English policymakers believed that free trade would increase prosperity and pressured the Ottomans to adopt free trade. This was difficult for the Ottomans to avoid, given their financial weakness and need for Western currencies. The traditional economy was closed to international competition, and industry was weak and primitive. However, this agreement strengthened the friendship with Britain, and thus, from the signing of the deal in 1838, it became British state policy to protect the Ottoman Empire for about 50 years. This agreement exempted British merchants from domestic customs. Inevitably, with the Treaty of Balta Port, the Ottoman Empire was turned into an open market, and the process of economic dependence of the state on European states had begun. The Ottoman economy, weakened by the influence of European capital, had no choice but to reform and adapt to modern understanding. Mustafa Reşit Pasha, the Ottoman ambassador to London at the time, had established excellent relations with the West and managed to convince Sultan Abdülmecid, who had just ascended the throne on July 1, 1839, of the need for a comprehensive reform program. This reform aimed to equalize the legal status of all citizens in the country. However, implementing this reform was not easy. For centuries, non-Muslims had been seen as second-class citizens. Granting them equal citizenship rights was not something that the Muslim population of the state would readily accept. There could have been a great reaction. As the first step and legal basis for this, the sultan was tasked with promulgating the Tanzimat Edict on November 3, 1839.

8.2.2 The Tanzimat Edict

3 November 1839 was a typical autumn day in Istanbul. The rains that had been falling for some time had given way to clear and warm weather. Although the yellowing leaves of the trees had fallen, the flowers in various city gardens were still alive. Istanbulites woke up with the morning call to prayer. In the twilight, many people were on their way to the mosque for morning prayers. Some Istanbulites preferred to perform their morning prayers at home, as usual. One of them was Mustafa Reşit Pasha, the Grand Vizier of the Ottoman Empire, who had spent the night sleepless (Fig. 8.2). After the prayer, he hugged his wife and children. He bade them farewell. He was unsure that he would make it home safely that evening. On that day, one of the 500-year-old Ottoman Empire's most important decisions was to be announced in Gülhane Park, and he was worried that this decision would provoke people in the country (Karal, 1964).

Fig. 8.2 Mustafa Reşit Paşa (1800–1858). https://commons.wikimedia.org/wiki/File:Resid_pasha.jpg

Mustafa Reşit Pasha (1800–1858) appeared in the Gülhane garden in front of the ministers, religious leaders, other state leaders, representatives of guilds and tradesmen, and ambassadors of foreign countries and read the proclamation. Everyone was in great excitement. A new era was beginning. All citizens in the country were declared to have equal rights. Then, sacrifices were slaughtered, and cannons were fired. The next day, state leaders, especially the sultan, swore an oath on the Koran that they would abide by the provisions of the edict. This proclamation was a constitutional document declared to make the reforms permanent, to prevent the deterioration of the state order, and to save the state from the adverse effects of the spreading nationalist movements. It was an essential stage in the transition of the Ottoman Empire to constitutionalism. Beyond being the first concrete step toward Westernization in Turkish history, the "Tanzimat Edict" paved the way for radical and lasting changes in the Turkish thought system with reforms in the military, legal, and civil administration fields. The principle that people of all religions would be equal in applying the law represented the most radical departure from the Islamic tradition up to that time. Although this edict was not much welcomed within the country, it received tremendous support from the Western states. The freedom to own property in the Ottoman Empire was now open to everyone, including minorities (Karal, 1964).

The proclamation of the Tanzimat Edict all over the Empire had vast repercussions among the people. As Reşit Pasha had feared, each region and caste began to interpret the reforms differently. Muslims generally did not like the rights granted to non-Muslims. It had a tremendous impact, especially in the Balkans. C. Hamlin, a US missionary in Istanbul at the time who closely followed these events, describes the developments as follows (İnalcık, 1964): "*The Gulhane Line was met with shock in the country. Conservative Muslims condemned it, claiming it violated Shari'a by equating Muslims with non-Muslims. In contrast, Christians saw it as a new era. A triumph of British politics, its real impact lay in spreading principles of equality and legal rights across the empire. It was the first official declaration of the government's goals, encouraging people to fight for their rights and reducing the Ulema's (religious staff) authority in civil matters. In Plovdiv, news of slavery's abolition sparked excitement, though landowners resisted. It also fueled Bulgarian nationalism in Bulgaria and Macedonia.*"

Against the discontent that led to the Egyptian rebellion and the Serbian and Greek uprisings in the Balkans, the edict aimed to repair the Ottoman social fabric with a new understanding of justice and equality and to emphasize "*Ottoman*" citizenship (Afyoncu, 2007). One of the Tanzimat Edict articles was "*To realize a reform of the financial and monetary system, and for the creation of capital to be used to increase the sources of material gain in the sultan's estate, steps will be taken to open banks and similar institutions*" (Lewis, 1961). This was quite a fundamental issue and would be desperately pursued throughout the century.

Two important laws were enacted in the period following the Tanziman edict. The Ottoman Commercial Code of 1850, inspired by the French Commercial Code, was a vital reform to modernize trade and integrate the Ottoman economy into global markets. It created a more predictable business environment by introducing straightforward trade, contracts, partnerships, and bankruptcy rules. It encouraged private enterprise and joint-stock companies, reduced the power of traditional guilds, and established secular commercial courts to handle disputes. The Ottoman Land Code of 1858 was a critical reform to modernize and centralize land administration in the Ottoman Empire. The right to private property in the modern sense was established with the Tanzimat Edict of 1839. However, it introduced private land ownership and established a land registry system to improve tax collection and control. These legislations played an essential role in harmonizing the Ottoman economy with European standards and laid the foundation for future commercial laws in Türkiye and the Middle East.

The Tanzimat Edict was a concrete document of the Ottoman intention of Westernization and consisted of three rules. The first was to ensure the security of every subject's life. Secondly, it proposed an orderly system for assessing and collecting taxes, as well as the length of service for soldiers. Finally, the third part dealt with reforms in human rights and the justice system. The country entered a new era after the Tanzimat, but economic problems persisted. The Ottoman rulers were in a predicament and inevitably had to fully adopt free trade practices from 1839 to 1878. As free trade led to the closure of small businesses, accelerated financial collapse, plunged the country into debt, and increased unemployment, it was impossible to develop the economy in the old ways (Karan et al., 2024).

8.2.3 The Crimean War and Financial Problems

In the 1840s, to overcome the money bottleneck experienced during the accession of Sultan Abdülmecit to the throne, the first paper money, "kaime," inspired by the French, was issued. In today's language, this banknote, a "Money Substitute Paper," was a debt note rather than money. The first kaime had an 8-year maturity and an annual interest yield of 12.531 percent. The kaime was a semi-paper currency issued by the Ottoman Treasury, unbacked by reserves. Kaime was issued mainly to cover the government's short-term debts to the Galata Bankers. They were never widely used outside Istanbul (Toprak, 2016). Moreover, the kaime was only intended for use in the domestic market, while foreign payments were made using coin policies. The Ottoman Empire issued kaime in various forms and quantities until 1862 (Erdem, 2006). However, as the value of the kaime declined and counterfeits flooded the market, coins were first burnt in 1852 after an intensive collection campaign to restore confidence in the monetary system. Later, however, the government would be forced to reissue the kaime in the face of future difficulties. By 1844, with the monetary reform known as "Tahsis-i Sikke," the Ottoman Empire adopted "Bimetallism," a system based on gold and silver as practiced by the French. After this date, the Ottoman Lira, Mecidiye, and Kuruş became the main currencies in the country (Tekeli & İlkin, 1997).

The Crimean War (1853–1856) was one of the most significant events of the nineteenth century for the Ottoman Empire. The Russian Empire, based on expansionist policies and looking for an excuse to reach the Mediterranean, had started to use the issue of the holy places in Jerusalem to weaken the Ottoman Empire. As a result of escalating events, this war broke out. The Russians were defeated in the Crimean War, with Britain and France on the Ottoman side. However, after the Crimean War, the Ottoman Empire was financially weakened due to military expenses and economic deterioration, and it began its first Period of foreign borrowing. The debts, which would continue until the end of the century, pulled the state into a debt trap. These debts were costly and not rationally utilized. The first loan was £200,000 from the British government. Between 1854 and 1875, millions of liras were borrowed, accompanied by 15 additional contracts. By 1880, the total debt had reached 252 million Ottoman liras (Kopar & Yolun, 2012). A significant portion of these borrowings was made through the foreign-led Ottoman Bank, established in 1856 and later becoming the state bank of the Ottoman Empire (Karan et al., 2024).

On February 18, 1856, the Edict of Reform was declared to achieve gains in the Treaty of Paris that would end the Crimean War. In this way, the support of European states was secured, and the rights of non-Muslims living in the Ottoman Empire were expanded, making them entirely equal to the Muslim population (İnalcık, 2016). The new constitution partially prevented the great powers from exploiting the events. 1861 Abdülmecid died, and his brother Abdülaziz (reigned 1861–1876) ascended the throne. The country's financial situation was deteriorating, and minority revolts were on the rise. Intellectuals' demands for constitutionalism were growing.

In 1876, reformists, including Mithat Pasha, deposed Abdulaziz in a palace coup 1876 and installed Abdulhamid II, who promised to proclaim a constitutional monarchy. Sultan Abdülhamid II (reigned 1876–1908) proclaimed the 1st Constitutional Monarchy. However, the 1877 war with Russia had damaged the state financially and politically. The Russo-Turkish War financially bankrupted the Ottoman Empire, which had signed 16 foreign debt agreements up to that point (Yıldız, 2011). Using this defeat as an excuse, Sultan Abdülhamid II ended the Constitutional Monarchy in 1878 and established a thirty-year autocratic regime. Britain's termination of its policy of protecting the Ottoman Empire after 1875 and its occupation of Cyprus (1878) also played an essential role in the end of the Constitutional Monarchy (İnalcık, 2016).

As the Ottoman Empire entered the twentieth century exhausted and weak, the "Young Turk" revolution movement began, supported by young officers and students who wanted to solve the country's problems. In the first months of 1908, unrest broke out in Macedonia, considered the Ottoman homeland, due to ethnic issues. The events culminated in the establishment of the 2nd Constitutional Monarchy in 1908 and the subsequent deposition of Sultan Abdülhamid. The new Sultan, Mehmet Reşat, was no longer in power, and the party behind the revolution, the Committee of Union and Progress (CUP), ruled the country.

After a brief period of brotherhood among different ethnic groups following the establishment of the Second Constitutional Monarchy, the Ottoman-Italian War broke out in 1911 with the Italian invasion of Tripolitania (Libya). The Balkan War broke out in 1913, and the Ottoman Empire lost most of its territory in the Balkans. Meanwhile, the rivalry between Germany and other European great powers dragged the European continent into a new war. The Ottoman Empire, which could not get much attention from England and France, improved its relations with Germany (İnalcık & Quataert, 1994).

World War I, which finally broke out in 1914, led to the collapse of the Ottoman Empire, which had sided with Germany. With the Treaty of Sèvres (1920), the Turks were left with some territory in central Anatolia. With the support of the British, the Greeks occupied Izmir and advanced into Central Anatolia. However, under the leadership of Mustafa Kemal Atatürk, the Turks defeated the Greeks and won the "War of Liberation" (1922). Türkiye's independence was ensured by the Treaty of Lausanne (1923).

8.3 Formation of the Stock Exchange

In the nineteenth century, when the Ottoman Empire was looking for a solution to its financial problems, similar to the examples in Western Europe, the stock exchange was first established informally on the streets and in coffeehouses. Later, on the initiative of bankers in Galata, the Galata Stock Exchange was established. It was a private exchange like the London Stock Exchange. In 1873, when the state regulated the capital market, the Galata Stock Exchange (Bourse) was transformed into a state stock exchange. The institutional structure of the Istanbul Bourse (Dersaadet Bourse) was formed. The Galata Stock Exchange was over then, and the Istanbul Bourse became the only market. We must go back to the late eighteenth century to understand this process.

8.3.1 Galata Bankers Before the 19th Century

Until the mid-nineteenth century, banking activities in the Ottoman Empire were mainly in the hands of Galata Bankers. However, they were not organized; for centuries, various families had been involved in treasury and financial affairs in the empire. Their role in the national economy was limited. Galata bankers provided financial services to the Ottoman population, such as money exchange and lending. In the bazaar districts of major cities and even towns of the Empire, they formed part of a group of tradesmen called "*corner jewelers (Sarraf),*" whose business was to exchange coins. In addition to buying and selling various coins. From the beginning of the eighteenth century onward, they traded in interest-bearing and time-bearing paper, usually certifying the state's debts to merchants. Nevertheless, they were part of a widespread financial network in the Ottoman Empire until the formation of the stock exchange, where bonds, stocks, and the papers documenting them belonging to state and private institutions were traded, and their daily values were determined (Kazgan,

1995). Until the seventeenth century, Jews were in the majority, but later, Armenians and Greeks, who had extensive trade and shipping agreements with Europe, played a significant role as bankers.

In time, the jewelers, who became indispensable financiers of the Ottoman finances, were organized around a guild in the late seventeenth century. Later, the introduction of the state borrowing system in the last quarter of the eighteenth century and the prolonged wars led to further consolidation of the importance of non-Muslim jewelers. In the mid-nineteenth century, although banks gradually replaced them and continued to exist even until the Empire's collapse, they were playing a dominant role as financiers and intermediaries in the relations between the Ottoman rulers, courtiers, local power centers in the provinces, and other members of society as needed.

The duties related to the treasury and the mint that Galata bankers held in the palace were quite risky. If they were successful, they received great rewards, but if they were involved in any corruption, they could be executed with a mandate, even if they were Muslims. For example, Bedros or Petraki, as he was known, worked at the Mint during the reigns of Mustafa III (reigned 1757–1774) and Abdülhamid I (reigned 1774–1789). It is guessed that his origin was Greek. Bedros was appointed to this position by using his relations, and while he was initially appreciated, he was executed on the grounds of corruption at the Mint, and his vast fortune was confiscated (Ünlü, 2018). In the second half of the eighteenth century, Galatians of Armenian descent were in charge of finance and treasury affairs. The Armenian-origin Düzoğlu family and Kazaz Artin had a special place among them. Kirkor, who took office in 1812 after Mihail and Hovannes of the Düzoğlu family, was involved in a mint corruption case. For this reason, he was executed together with Abdurrahman Feyzi Bey, the mint director of the time, and his brother Sarkis. On December 4, 1819, Kazaz Artin, appointed as the mint's goldsmith, was very successful. As Mahmut II's financial and personal advisor and close friend, Artin Amira solved the country's financial problems by finding efficient solutions throughout his tenure (Dadyan, 2021).

Moreover, the services of Galata bankers as intermediaries in monetary transactions were vital, as they guaranteed the weights and purity standards of Ottoman money; coins minted by the state often did not match their face value. The Galata Bankers provided three services: money exchange, granting loans, and discounting salaries paid in promissory notes. In dealings with the Palace or the Government, collateral was usually tax receipts, which were expected in cash or kind. Thus, the banker eventually became a tax collector. Bankers were also indispensable for the transfer of funds. Most of the revenues collected by the collectors were transferred in bills of exchange or debit notes, usually to be paid upon presentation to the bank. Merchants also tended to settle their debts and claim this way (Toprak, 1995).

8.3.2 The Galata Stock Exchange

As the nineteenth century progressed, the role of Galata bankers changed from money changers serving the Palace to essential players in the money market. From the 1820s onward, the increase in the Ottoman State's foreign trade and the stabilization of foreign exchange became the main issue for the Galata Bankers. The large war indemnity paid by the Ottomans to the Russians at the war's end in 1839 disrupted this stability. Under these conditions, Galata Bankers became more organized with the effect of a free trade economy that started to be implemented in the nineteenth century. Although documents indicate that merchants gathered in a coffeehouse in Istanbul's Perşembe Pazarı area in 1834 to establish a stock exchange, it is believed to have been inaugurated in 1844. This stock exchange was not an official structure but a private initiative of the Galata Bankers. Antonie Cucci was the first manager of the stock exchange, which spent its first years in coffeehouses. The exchange moved to a new building in 1852 (Al & Akar, 2013a).

Both domestic borrowing and kaime, used as a substitute for money, also mobilized the Galata Stock Exchange. The fact that later kaime was issued in bearer form and had a fixed maturity made it easier for them to be used as money and made it possible for them to be endowed in this way. The fact that kaime yielded interest and was used as a means of payment in trade made it a more accessible instrument. These papers could be discounted by Galata bankers and converted into cash. Since the issuance of kaime was uncontrolled, its prices fluctuated and could lead to speculation. In 1844, Galata had a well-functioning money and foreign exchange market with 146 members (Al & Akar, 2013a).

When a war broke out, the discount rate of the kaime rose sharply to 30%, and the government had to intervene. After the Crimean War, the Stock Exchange moved to its new building. The government issued a new domestic debt security called "*Esham-ı mümtaze*" to meet the war's financing needs in 1854. These bonds were issued in bearer form with a 10% interest rate and a three-year maturity. The fact that the auctions for the first issuance of these bonds were held on the stock exchange increased the importance of the stock exchange. Ottoman bonds were usually sold below their nominal value, providing an additional return to the buyers in the initial public offering.

After the Crimean War, the allocation of a line from the Galata telegraph office significantly increased the stock exchange's interaction with international markets. However, within the framework of the hot political relations of that period, the telegraphic news made the Galata Stock Exchange highly speculative. With an announcement published at the beginning of 1859, the stock exchange committee announced that the quotations on bond prices, exchange rates, discount rates, and commodity prices would be announced via telegrams received from London on Mondays and Marseille on Saturdays (Al & Akar, 2013a). In early 1860, elections were held, and a new stock exchange committee was formed. All members of this committee were non-Muslims (Zarifi, 2002).

The growing commercial integration of the Ottoman Empire with Europe and the adoption of new commercial laws allowed foreign investors to establish joint-stock companies in the Ottoman Empire quickly. This process was particularly strengthened by adopting a commercial code in 1861, based on France's, which authorized the establishment of joint-stock companies. This development undoubtedly contributed significantly to the activities of the Galata Stock Exchange. Most of the new companies were based on commercial concessions granted by the Ottoman authorities. Until the Crimean War, foreign investment was limited to small-scale enterprises, such as import-export houses, silk-processing workshops, and shipping facilities. Between the Crimean War and the turn of the century, numerous companies were established in railroads, banking, insurance, and industry. However, these businesses were still the domain of non-Muslims. In 1849, the Bosphorus Navigation Company, or Şirket-i Hayriye, was granted a concession to operate ferries on the Bosphorus. Finally, in 1866, the Golden Horn Navigation Company was established to operate on the Golden Horn. In 1867, a law was passed allowing non-Ottoman citizens to acquire property, which led to increased foreign investment and the development of several companies (Toprak, 1995).

During this period, trade, commerce, and foreign investment flourished partly due to increased commodity prices during the American Civil War (1861–65). Rising imports and budget deficits led the Ottoman State to borrow continuously. As the value of the kaime fluctuated against the coins, the street-based money changers were increasingly creating turmoil in the market despite the prohibition. There was a shortage of small coins, and some money changers started introducing coins banned in European countries into the market in Istanbul. Copper coins were in vogue. After several unsuccessful borrowing projects, the Government could not pay its debts. Therefore, in 1861, bankers and businessmen involved in the Levant trade, which extended to Marseille and London, went bankrupt. With the outbreak of the crisis, the money market was in turmoil. When the Government lost hope of borrowing from the foreign market, it reissued kaime. Speculation increased in the Galata market, which was already troubled due to the commercial bankruptcies. Meanwhile, it was rumored that the Government would pay to mature domestic debt securities with kaime instead of cash. This led to a sharp decline in the prices of domestic debt securities. People even started to fight for food in the streets, and shopkeepers took up arms to protect themselves. In addition to the Galata Stock Exchange, which the government saw as the source of mischief, the Havyar Building, where street brokers traded extensively, would be closed for a while. It resorted to this method in every future crisis (Al & Akar, 2013b).

After the war, the Ottoman State's domestic borrowing bonds were traded on the Galata Stock Exchange. At the same time, Pera (Galata) newspapers began to publish the trading prices of the bonds regularly. The most famous place of this period was the Havyar Building mentioned above. It was a place where street transactions took place, like in London coffeehouses. An old Greek source describes the Havyar Building as follows (Türker, 2000):

> The Havyar (Caviar) Building, true to its name, is the center of the caviar trade, but despite the newly constructed stock exchange building opposite, it is still the center of the stock exchange. The most valuable bonds are traded here, and the fate of the largest trading houses is decided here. In this place where the value of money is determined, the financial power of the Ottoman Empire is also shaped. Because of this important position, even one square meter of space on either side of the ten-foot-long corridor of the Havyar Building can be rented for thousands of liras. It is difficult for someone passing through these corridors for the first time to see the statue of the God of Trade standing there. Nevertheless, a glance at the crowds, the brokers, and the moneylenders reveals the seriousness of the matter. These people constantly whisper in each other's ears as they hurry back and forth. The excitement here is like the excitement at the gambling tables. However, there is a constant movement where people sit at the gambling table.

In 1861, the stock exchange moved to another building known as the Municipal Building. In 1861, when the crisis affected European economies due to the US Civil War, the Government closed the Caviar Building again, citing market turmoil as an excuse. However, trade continued on the street. Thereupon, the government took action to reorganize stock market activities. For this purpose, in 1864, the Government issued the "*Regulation on the Corner Jewelers*" to distinguish the corner jewelers (Sarraf) accused of causing the crisis from the banks, bankers, and prominent sarrafs engaged in money trading. Also, it adopted the "*Murabaha Regulation,*" which regulated interest-bearing money lending transactions.

During this period, speculative transactions such as options and futures, known as air games, were also carried out. The word "*air games*" comes from the nickname of the derivative trade in Amsterdam, "*windhandel.*" People from all parts of society were among those who played air games. Civil servants, merchants, and even the ladies of the Palace played air games (Köse, 2020). Since it caused big money to be won or lost with little investment, it increased the appetite of gamblers. The tense political and economic environment in the nineteenth century probably encouraged people to gamble and play games of chance. The lack of regulation initially resulted in huge fortunes being lost.

Proposals to regulate the stock market could not be implemented due to the political and economic problems of the time. The main reason was that the new regulations did not suit the interests of merchants subject to foreign states, which put pressure on the government through their ambassadors (Kazgan, 1991).

After the 1861 crisis, the Havyar Building and similar venues, which had closed down, resumed stock exchange operations. Havyar Building continued to be popular. In a review of the Galata Stock Exchange by the Levantine Banker Biagiotti, it is described that the Greeks and their cronies at the Havyar Building speculated on government domestic debt securities and even began to manipulate the prices of Ottoman bonds traded on the London and Paris stock exchanges. One of the reasons for the increase in speculation was not so much the exploitation of loopholes in the legal infrastructure but the active use of the new telegraph facilities by opportunistic bankers. The French Havas News Agency was the first to open an office in Istanbul, followed by Reuters, Bullier, Bordeano, Pangolo, and Fournier news agencies in 1869 (Al & Akar, 2013a).

In 1870, the stock exchange moved to the Commission Building and had a more proper infrastructure. This building was also called the Consolidated Building. In 1866, all Ottoman bonds were consolidated; different government bonds issued on various dates were combined under the label "*consolidated.*" Since these consolidated securities were essential stock exchange instruments, this is how the building was popularly referred to. According to the decision, an entrance fee of two Ottoman Liras was to be charged to the stock exchange brokers. The bond market at the Havyar Building was moved to the Commission Building soon after. However, stock market transactions at the Havyar Building continued. It is understood that the legal regulations introduced to prohibit air games were not very effective. On September 30, 1869, Ceride-i Havadis, one of the most critical newspapers in Istanbul, reported that the stock market was under the influence of a small number of traders (Al & Akar, 2013a).

Between 1870 and 1872, the government again turned its attention to reorganizing the stock exchange. There were two main reasons behind the Ottoman government's efforts to regulate and register the Galata Stock Exchange. The first was to prevent investor victimization caused by the arbitrariness of the stock market traders due to the lack of regulation, and the second, and perhaps more importantly for the period, was to collect taxes from the stock market, where huge profits were generated. At a time when the Ottoman State was only able to balance its budget by borrowing more each year, it was unable to tax a sector such as the stock market, where large profits could be generated. On the other hand, stock brokers, who conducted their transactions in a club-like atmosphere and resolved their disputes without resorting to the judiciary, always opposed government intervention (Yılmaz, 2014). However, everything changed with the 1873 crisis. Following the over-expansion of the European economy after the Franco-Prussian War, widespread market manipulation, and the impact of the global new gold standard, the Vienna Stock Exchange collapsed on May 9, 1873. Vienna's banks went bankrupt, and the money available for commercial loans became scarce (Karan et al., 2024).

It broke the resistance of the Galata Bankers, who were now resisting attempts at regulation. They began to demand that the Government regulate the stock market, hoping that coming under government control would increase confidence in the stock market and prevent its decline. The Government was also worried that weakening the stock market would disrupt financial stability. The loss of power in the stock market would mean that the Government, which was in constant need of borrowing and rolling over its existing debts, would find it more challenging to borrow (Yılmaz, 2014).

Meanwhile, the Galata Bankers, short of money after the "*Long Depression*" that began with the crisis of 1873, increased their stock market speculation with false news and fake telegrams. The news about brokers fleeing the country and people committing suicide after losing all their money in the stock market began to appear frequently in the press. The bonds of the Rumelia Railroads, which were being established with loans provided by the state from abroad, and the shares of newly established banks and companies were the subject of speculation. Stock market players were divided into groups like at other stock exchanges: the "*bears*" and the "*bulls.*" As the problems deepened, resignations began in the stock exchange committee of the Commission Building. At the Government's behest, the executives of the significant banks came together and reported that regulation was necessary. Finally, in 1873, the "*Istanbul Bourse Regulation*" was adopted. The Galata Stock Exchange was believed to accelerate the integration of the Ottoman economy with Europe by creating a new capital market, the Istanbul Bourse (Dersaadet Tahvilat Borsası), which expanded existing financing instruments and centralized the Ottoman financial markets (Al & Akar, 2013b).

The Istanbul Bourse replaced the Galata Stock Exchange after the onset of the 1873 financial crisis, when all major stock exchanges worldwide were in decline and faced intense political and economic difficulties. Legalizing the Ottoman Stock Exchange effectively mitigated the adverse effects of the stock market crisis that had spread to the Ottoman Empire. In this way, it sent a positive message to the Galata market, which was feared to collapse, by providing it with state regulation and supervision (Yılmaz, 2014).

8.3.3 The Istanbul (Dersaadet) Bourse

The establishment of the new stock exchange was inspired by the Paris Bourse and provided a high level of government oversight. Although there was a Bourse Committee, the Ministry of Finance had oversight authority, as it did not trust the stock exchange to regulate itself. A Commissioner was appointed to ensure that trading complied with the newly established regulations. The commissioner of the Istanbul (Dersaadet) Bourse exchange (Dersaadet Tahvilat Borsası) was Abidin Pasha. The word "*Dersaadet*" in the name of the stock exchange means "*Gate of Happiness.*" During the Ottoman period, this word was used to mean Istanbul. Pasha's published book became a fundamental source for understanding this Exchange (Paşa, 2018).

8.4 Organization of the Bourse

In addition to the exchange commissioner, a council of 20 people elected from the exchange members was formed. They were elected by secret ballot from among the brokers and were responsible for administering the exchange. All of them were prestigious; there were also citizens of a foreign country. They did not receive any salary, and in the event of a dispute, the provisions of the bylaws were applied first. If there were no such provisions, they resolved it according to tradition and, if necessary, by reasoning. In Dersaadet Tahvilat Borsası, lawsuits regarding air games could not be brought before the regular courts. The Stock Exchange Council acted as a court in this matter, and those who did not comply with its decision were expelled from the stock exchange. Since these players paid "deposits" to the stock exchange administration in advance, their debts were collected from there (Paşa, 2018).

Bond and stock prices were announced after the approval of the bourse committee. Trading was restricted to the exchange floor, and violators were fined and expelled. Trading took place in a large hall on the upper floor of the building through auctions between middlemen (mubayaacı), brokers (Dellal), and market makers (Cober). Mubayacı acted as intermediaries in transactions. They facilitated trade by connecting buyers and sellers, often handling negotiations and ensuring that deals were completed. Their role was primarily focused on the logistics of trade rather than on market influence. They could not trade on their behalf and accounts; they could only trade on customer accounts and not engage in commercial business other than stock exchange transactions. Dellals were more formalized agents who specialized in executing trades on behalf of clients, typically for a commission. They had a deeper understanding of market conditions and advised their clients, playing a crucial role in price discovery and liquidity by matching orders. They traded on their behalf and for their clients, while cobers traded on their behalf. Cobers were responsible for providing liquidity by being ready to buy and sell securities at any time. They ensured that there was always a market for a given security, helping to stabilize prices and manage volatility. Their role was essential in maintaining an orderly market. Exchange members would have to pay a specific fee every year. Those who failed to pay the dues would have their membership canceled; since Abidin Pasha's examples in his book are always based on 1000 bonds, it is estimated that there were 1000 bonds in a lot in the Istanbul Stock Exchange, i.e., trades were made on one lot or 1000 bonds. Therefore, when the price of a bond changed by one kurus, the income or expenses of the buyer or seller would change by 1000 kurus.

The leading securities traded on the stock exchange were Ottoman government bonds with an interest rate of 5% and other Ottoman company bonds. In addition, banks were to be established by the Sultan's decree, and shares of industrial and commercial companies were to be traded. Transactions were to be made in Ottoman Lira and Kuruş. At least 25% of the established companies' capital had to be paid in cash. It was forbidden to trade outside the stock exchange or outside the hours when it was closed. The accounts of Ottoman bonds were to be closed every 15 days on Mondays, while the accounts of other bonds and stocks were to be closed once a month on the first Friday of each month. Apart from these, the provisions also regulated the reflections of the transactions in other exchanges. The prices of British and French bonds, bonds belonging to the Ottoman State, and other bonds on the London and Paris stock exchanges and the discount rate prevailing in these markets were to be learned and announced before the stock exchange's opening (Al & Akar, 2013b).

The Istanbul Bourse building in the Commission Han was directly opposite the Havyar Building in Galata. It was a three-story building with an entrance. The front of this building, the most crucial place in the Istanbul market, was always very noisy. Visitors would probably think people had gone mad when they heard this noise. In the work "Allote Ke Turka" by I.N. Karavias, quoted by Orhan Türker, this place was mentioned as follows (Türker, 2000):

All the great moneylenders of Galata played on their behalf or on behalf of others. All the liveliness would cease with the Building closing in the evening. Most of the vaults of the stockbrokers and moneylenders in Galata were located in the Galata Building and guarded by many guards at night. The entire area between the stock exchange and the Havyar Building opposite it was covered with the stalls of the moneylenders. Almost all of the moneylenders were rich people. Most of them were bankers. Makris, Çiliyanis, Andrias, Altıparmaklı Antipas, Zanetos, Kaloyeras, Pulusis, Yakovidis, Alevrolulos, and Mavromatis were among them. Jewelers (Sarraf) were exchanging gold, which the poor people of Istanbul and even the provinces resorted to in times of distress. People in distress could borrow money in return for the gold or jewelry they gave to the jewelers. Sarrafs always had a red wooden box in front of them to put the money from various countries. During money exchange, they would earn two kurus from 1 British lira and one from 20 francs. They would convert gold liras into paper money and paper money into coins, which were very scarce at that time, again with a slight difference.

8.5 The Instruments of Bourse

The most traded instruments on the markets, which operated successively as the Galata Stock Exchange and the Istanbul Stock Exchange, were the bonds issued by the Ottoman Empire under various names. In 1866, these bonds were combined (consolidated) into a standardized bond.

8.5.1 *Kaime*

The interest-bearing kaime, which began to be issued after the proclamation of the Tanzimat Edict, is a more advanced form of borrowing instrument. We do not have any information about whether they were officially traded on the Galata Stock Exchange. However, Galata Bankers were very influential in the exchange of kaime. While the first kaime issue was done for 8 years, the maturity was extended to 10 years in later issues (Al & Akar, 2013a).

8.5.2 *Ottoman Government Bonds*

The government issued different bonds under different names. Since each bond was unsuccessful after a while, they were reissued under various names to restore confidence in borrowing. The first domestic borrowing bond issued in 1854 to finance the Crimean War (1853–56) was "*Esham-ı mümtâze*" (1854–1863). These bonds were issued with an interest rate of 10% and a maturity of 3 years. In 1857, the government also issued a new domestic borrowing bond called the"*Treasury bond*" (1857–1861) with an interest rate of 6%, a maturity of 3 years, and a price in Ottoman Lira. The Ottoman government failed to repay the treasury bonds, which matured in early December 1860, *due to high military expenses, court spending, and fiscal mismanagement, which drained state finances. Nevertheless, a different method was followed, and a new domestic borrowing instrument, "Tahvilât*-ı mümtâze" (1861–1865), was issued for the redemption of treasury bonds. The bonds were traded on the Galata Stock Exchange. In 1865, they were fully consolidated and converted into a standard domestic debt instrument named "*Esham-ı umûmiyye*" (Al & Akar, 2013a). Thus, domestic borrowing bonds with different names, maturities, and interest rates were taken out of circulation and converted into standardized bonds, thus ending the domestic borrowing structure that increased transaction costs for public finance (Demir, 2018).

The Rumelia railway bonds (1870–1881) traded on the Istanbul Bourse were issued for railway construction, just like railway projects in Europe. In addition, bonds named "esham-ı cedîde" were issued in 1872 for the construction costs of the İzmit-Eskişehir Railway. The annual interest rate was 10 percent. Some of the Rumeli bonds were bonus bonds. Those who bought bonus bonds could earn additional returns through drawings held at specific intervals (Al & Akar, 2013a).

In 1877, the government borrowed money for war expenses under "istikraz-ı mecburî." This borrowing, in which all subjects were obliged to participate according to their wealth, was targeted to collect 6 million Ottoman Liras. The annual interest rate was 10 percent (Al & Akar, 2013a).

8.5.3 Equities

Many joint-stock companies were established in the 19th and early twentieth centuries. At that time, there were criticisms that the government did not seriously supervise joint-stock companies and that some fraudsters deceived the public. There is no consensus in the literature on the number of companies established. According to a German catalog, 60 companies were established by 1906. Twelve were railway companies, 8 were banks, 7 were mining companies, 5 were mining companies, and 5 were joint-stock companies. Seven were on mining, five on harbors, eight on water, electricity, and gas, three on tramways, four on maritime affairs, and 13 on other sector companies. The number of shares traded on the Galata Stock Exchange was around 10. During the initial public offering of stocks, newspaper announcements were published to fulfill today's prospectuses and circulars (Yılmaz, 2013).

8.5.4 Foreign Bonds

Until 1869, the foreign debt bonds issued by the Ottoman Empire had not been offered to the public in Istanbul. In 1869, foreign borrowings were sold simultaneously in Istanbul, Paris, and London stock exchanges for the first time. This practice was also applied to the foreign borrowings of 1872, 1873, and 1874, and the bonds of

1863 and 1865 started to be traded on the Istanbul Bourse in 1870. However, the trading volume of these bonds remained low. Bonds of neighboring countries were also traded on the Istanbul Stock Exchange. In this context, Greek government bonds were also listed. In addition, some of the bonds from the United States and France were offered to the public in the Istanbul Bourse (Al & Akar, 2013a).

8.6 Stock Market Operations

According to the notes of Abidin Pasha, there were two ways of buying and selling government domestic borrowings at the Dersaadet Bond Exchange. The first method was the cash transactions of these securities. The second method was derivative transactions like options and repos.

8.6.1 Cash Transactions

At the Dersaadet Tahvilat Borsası, buying any bond or stock with cash was possible. In initial public offerings, bonds were usually sold below their nominal value, and coupon interest was charged twice a year. For example, if a bond's nominal value was 50 kurus, it could be sold at a discount in an initial public offering for, say, 45 kurus. If the buyer needed money before maturity, he could sell the bond at the market price (Paşa, 2018).

To buy in the secondary market, an investor could purchase securities from a middleman (mubayaacı). According to Abidin Pasha's advice, asking the middlemen and a few trusted people for their prices would first be necessary. The only thing to be considered was that the coupons showing the interest to be paid each year on the bonds should not be torn. These coupons were placed on the underside of the bond document, and the state official would cut out the coupon he had paid. Generally, the prices of the different Ottoman government bonds were less volatile than the prices of the banks' stocks. Direct purchases of bonds were always cheaper than purchases under option contracts. For example, if the bonds subject to options were 50 kurus, this amount could fall to 49.7 kurus in direct purchases. Abidin Pasha describes this in 19th-century terms in his book as follows:

> When the price of a government bond is 50 piastres today, one investor thinks its price will rise, and another says it will fall and enters into an agreement. Suppose a man shouts on the stock exchange to sell 10,000 liras of government paper at 50 piasters a barrel. He may not have any paper in his hand. Another investor says he will buy them all. He has only 80-100 liras in cash. He aims to express that he can purchase air (option) for 10 thousand liras of government paper for 100 liras. Then, when the government paper is 50 kurus, ten coins (1 kurus = 40 coins), the investor who says he will buy 10 thousand TL worth of paper wins. With a difference of 20 piastres, the buyer gets a difference of 5,000 piastres, and the seller loses 5,000 piastres. The opposite happens if the government paper falls to 49 kurus 20 coins: the seller wins, and the buyer loses.

8.6.2 *Options and Repos (Air Games)*

The most critical transactions on the Istanbul Bourse were options, a derivative transaction called "*air games*" in local terms. These transactions were quite risky, but by the end of the nineteenth century, they had spread like a gambling disease in some parts of Istanbul. Many people went bankrupt, their families were ruined, and they committed suicide at times. Abidin Pasha (Paşa, 2018) states, "*There is no more destructive tool in this world than the air game, which will destroy one's money, home, mind, and body... How many hearths have burnt down, how many dynasties have collapsed, how many wealthy people have executed themselves out of grief and left their children orphaned.*" He observed that 98% of those investing options, except for some big players, were losing. The 2% who won were doing so temporarily and were destined to fail.

Regarding call options, an investor goes to the stock exchange to buy a call option on 1000 bonds. He goes to the mübayacı (the middleman) and buys, for example, a call option on a thousand bonds at a deal price of 50. The middleman, in turn, executes this order on the stock exchange. If, after a few days, the value of the bond falls below 50 kurus, the investor loses the premium. If, on the other hand, it rises to 51 kurus, the middleman pays the money. In a put option, an investor buys a bond. He then goes to the middleman and sells an option on a thousand bonds at, for example, 50 kuruş. He pays the middleman the premium for this. If the bond price rises above 50 cents, he sacrifices his premium as the transaction will not be profitable. The middleman executes this order on the stock exchange. If, after a few days, the value of the bond falls to 49 cents, the counterparty is contractually obliged to buy it at 50 cents.

According to Abidin Pasha's book, repos and reverse repos were traded alongside options transactions on the Istanbul Stock Exchange. Some brokers also engaged in arbitrage. Repos practices at that time were different from today's. Suppose someone has 1,000 call options with a contract price of 50 cents that have not yet expired. In the meantime, if he needs money, he can go to the option seller and say, "I *have a call option that I hope will rise in price after 15 days, but since I do not have 50,000 kurus to buy it, let you keep my option, pay me 50,000 kurus, and I will pay you whatever the interest is.*" If the counterparty agrees to receive interest, the repo transaction is made by paying the money immediately. If the bond price rises at the end of the maturity, the buyer will receive more money, and their profit will increase. However, if the price falls, he may lose money. The interest rate of this practice, which is similar to "*repos*" today, was sometimes very high, depending on the supply and demand in the repos market at that time. A reverse repo is a transaction made when options contracts are scarce in the market, but cash is abundant. At the bourse, settlement transactions were carried out every 15 days, making it possible to implement this transaction. An investor who buys an option on a bond at an agreement price of 50 kurus before the liquidation every 15 days expects to buy 1000 bonds from the counterparty at 50,000 kurus in the first liquidation. The option seller realizes that there are not enough bonds in the market and that they are expensive. Therefore, if the buyer says, "*I will not give you the bonds immediately, but in the next liquidation (15 days later), I will give you the bonds physically; I will pay you an additional payment due to this delay,*" and the other party accepts, this is called reverse repo. In other words, it is the money to be paid to extend the liquidation day to 15 days.

Abidin Pasha noted that successful arbitrage depended on three factors: timely receipt and writing of special telegrams, having a reliable partner in London or Paris, and sufficient capital. Sometimes, this required physically transporting bonds from Europe to Istanbul. However, arbitrage carries risks; if bonds are cheap in Europe and expensive in Istanbul, a trusted European may buy in Europe, but rapid market changes could lead to potential losses for buyers in Istanbul.

According to Abidin Pasha, brokers act quickly and perform standard transactions in derivative transactions involving bonds. Transactions in this market are conducted as follows: a broker goes to the stock exchange and shouts, for example, "*Who wants to buy 1,000 bonds for 50 kuruş?*" A voice from the other side responds, "*I will take it.*" At this point, the purchase contract is finalized. Both brokers record this transaction in their ledgers. If 4–5 brokers shout "*I will take* it" simultaneously while the broker shouts "*I will buy the option,*" he can purchase it from any of the buyers. However, if it is discovered during an investigation that one of them had already shouted earlier, the transaction is conducted with that person. A commission was charged for each transaction at the Istanbul Stock Exchange. While these commissions were generally subject to negotiation, it is understood that the commission was approximately 25 kuruş in the 1880s. The brokers themselves meticulously carried out settlement transactions.

8.7 Volume of the Market and Other Developments

The Galata Stock Exchange, like the stock exchanges in Europe at the time, was predominantly a bond exchange. Estimating the total market value of the bonds and stocks traded on the Galata Stock Exchange is difficult. The market values of the traded securities, and even the types of capital market instruments traded, are not precisely determined. As reflected in a British report, "*No one but God knows the total amount of Ottoman debt.*" The same applies to the instruments initially traded on the Galata Stock Exchange (Yılmaz, 2014).

The nominal value of bonds and the total nominal or market value of shares traded on the Galata Stock Exchange in the early 1870s was about 25 million liras, approximately 180 tonnes of gold by the monetary standard of the time. The number and depth of stocks traded were much smaller. Calculations show that stocks comprised less than 10% of the market, with a total value of under one million liras. These figures represent the capitalization of spot-tradable instruments. However, most Galata transactions were financial derivatives—the market capitalization of assets in derivative transactions served as the underlying asset for options in the market. Today, derivatives markets have a trading volume five times larger than spot markets. While no exact data exists for the 1870s, indicators suggest that this multiple was higher at the

Galata Stock Exchange. Assuming modern coefficients apply, the volume of Galata's derivative transactions likely exceeded 150 million Ottoman liras (Yılmaz, 2014).

The 1870s were a difficult period in Ottoman financial history. In 1874, the drought that started in Anatolia reduced tax revenues. On October 6, 1875, the government of Grand Vizier Mahmut Nedim Pasha announced that, without agreeing with creditors, the Ottoman Empire had decided that half of the payments of Ottoman bond coupons would be made in cash and the other half in the form of 5% interest bonds for five years. This decision led to panic selling of Ottoman bonds both within the country and in London and Paris. This announcement, which amounted to a moratorium, created a fait accompli and destroyed the creditworthiness and credibility of the State. Since the Ottomans were politically and financially obliged to get on good terms with their creditors, it was a scandal that the decision was taken without consulting them. Therefore, there were two views on this decision. According to a claim, Nedim Pasha made this decision at the suggestion of Galata Bankers. In 1874, some Galata Bankers, who had become state creditors with an interest rate of up to 25%, had persuaded Nedim Pasha to receive their receivables. Following this decision, they increased the payments allocated to them. However, the second allegation, which was the most favored, was based on the influence of the Russian ambassador, General Ignatyev, a close friend of Mahmut Nedim Pasha at the time. Nedim Pasha was influenced by Ignatyev and was known for his pro-Russian policies. For this reason, people even nicknamed him "*Nedimov*" (Kazgan, 1991).

With this decision, the Ottoman Empire's honor and political prestige in Europe were significantly damaged and wholly excluded from the European financial markets. Perhaps the Ignatyev move, cheating Nedim Psha, had dragged the Ottomans, who were trying to cope with the uprisings in the Balkans, into a position where they could not get loans.

As the rebellions in the Balkans became widespread, the Ottoman Empire was once again confronted with the Russians. During the Ottoman-Russian War (1876–78), the Government was in such great financial distress that it resorted to issuing "kaime" again. The Ottomans would not resist the Russians in the 1877 war due to the lack of financial support from the West (Blaisdell, 1929). At the war's end, the Ottoman government found itself with a debt of £200 million and a large war indemnity to the Russians. Not only could these debts not be repaid, but in 1879, the state even borrowed from the Ottoman Bank and Galata Bankers a defense loan of £9 million. Meanwhile, the disorganization of the money market created new opportunities for stock market speculators. Galata Bankers were speculating on copper coins and options on kaime. Although the state tried to stop such speculation through police measures, it was unsuccessful (Al & Akar, 2013b). Five weeks after this announcement, his opponents removed Nedim Pasha from power due to the financial crisis he had initiated. Although Grand Vizier Mahmut Nedim Pasha was well versed in economic and monetary affairs, he had been implicated in much corruption for personal gain. In this case, it was alleged that Mahmud Nedim Pasha, Ignatyev, and some Ottoman pashas secretly speculated by taking positions in the stock market. On the other hand, the Galata Bankers, famous for being informed about government decisions before they were announced, were not allowed to access this news.

The fact that the Galata Bankers were not informed about the news was an event that undermined their reputation in Europe (Kazgan, 1991). Air games on the kaime were banned in March 1878. However, when these games could not be prevented, it was decided that as of December 9, 1880, air games would be held in a room allocated for this purpose in the Borsa Building and banned outside of it.

8.8 Rusum-u Sitte (Six Indirect Taxes) and Ottoman Public Debt Administrations

During the Ottoman-Russian War of 1877–1878, after the state announced that it would not pay its debts to the Ottoman Bank and the Galata Bankers, an agreement known as the Decree of 1879 (November 22, 1879) was concluded between the Government, the Ottoman Bank, and the Galata Bankers. This agreement was a plan with favorable terms for the bankers and guaranteed payment. The government had consolidated the short-term debts it had previously taken from the Ottoman Bank and the Galata Bankers, which amounted to 9 million gold liras, and agreed to pay them in equal installments over ten years by showing some state revenues in return. The administration established by the Ottoman Bank and Galata Bankers to collect and manage the receivables above and to pay the domestic debts specified in the decree was called the "*Rüsum-u Sitte (Six Indirect Taxes)*" administration (Buluttekin, 2016).

The Rüsum-u Sitte administration, operating under the Ministry of Finance, was tasked with collecting allocated taxes on behalf of the state and distributing them to creditors. Its unique aspect was that the state's debt to the Ottoman Bank and Galata Bankers was based on a specific source, paving the way for the future Public Debt Administration (Duyun-u Umumiye). Hamilton Lang, a Scotsman and Ottoman Bank director, was appointed president. Lang, well known to Ottoman officials and European financial circles, painted an optimistic picture in his report published in major European journals. He praised Ottoman officials as skillful, receiving regular salaries, and argued that the Empire's inability to pay its debts was due to mismanagement, not poverty. His assessment proved accurate—the administration's first-year revenues exceeded expectations, and Ottoman bonds appreciated in Istanbul and European markets. This success attracted creditor interest, and by October 3, 1880, the Government (Porte) invited European creditors for negotiations (Varol, 2007). 1881 the Ottomans issued the Muharrem Decree, linking part of tax revenues to the newly established Public Debt Administration (Duyun-u Umumiye). Although it resolved a significant financial crisis, it marked the first primary intervention of Britain and France in Ottoman finances.

With the Muharram Decree, the management of the state's economic activities was given to the control of foreigners to pay the debts. With this, the influence of European capital increased. Thus, not only some state revenues but also the assessment and collection of these revenues and all legal and administrative dispositions related to them were left to representatives of the creditors; in other words, some fundamental sovereign rights of the state were transferred to foreigners.

On the other hand, the state's foreign and domestic debts to the Ottoman Bank and Galata Bankers began to be repaid, and the state was allowed to borrow from foreign markets again. Moreover, a significant reduction in the foreign debts of the state was accepted, and the debt consisting of principal and interest, estimated at 253 million British pounds, was reduced to 107 million British pounds (117 million Ottoman Liras) (Toprak, 1995). The most significant contribution of the Public Debt Administration to the Ottoman Empire was the reduction of borrowing costs and the introduction of modern accounting practices (Karan et al., 2024).

8.9 Other Events and the End of the Road

After the Muharram Decree, many new companies emerged, but the stock market declined steadily after 1883. Significant events on the Turkish and global agenda affected the market, causing several key companies to go bankrupt. The Balkans were in turmoil, and war with Greece began. By 1888–1889, the political atmosphere eased, stabilizing the market. Although the early 1890s saw fluctuations, 1895 was a terrible year due to speculation led by Sir Edgar Vincent, General Manager of the Ottoman Bank. He spread false claims about a significant gold discovery in the Transvaal (South Africa), urging friends to form a Gold Company with foreign partners. Share prices soared, creating a public frenzy. When prices collapsed, panic followed, and the public rushed to the Ottoman Bank to sell shares. Vincent's involvement in the speculation severely damaged the bank's credibility. By year's end, depositors lined up to withdraw their funds. The Ottoman Empire intervened to prevent the bank's collapse, which would have endangered its finances and reputation. The stock market crashed, ruining many investors and brokers. In response, the Stock Exchange Committee shut the market for four months. A government-backed decree suspended the Bank's payments until new gold reserves arrived from London. The collapse's effects lingered until 1898 (Toprak, 1995).

At the beginning of the twentieth century, the Istanbul Bourse showed an up-and-down trend, according to the news from the world stock markets. In 1906, the government, responding to the need for a more tightly controlled stock exchange, changed the name of the exchange after it moved to a new building. The new name of the exchange was determined as the "*Stock and Bond Exchange (Esham ve Tahvilat Borsası).*" The latest exchange was managed by government personnel from the Ministry of Treasury, and the old advisory board of twenty members was transformed into a more petite body of seven members known as the Exchange Assembly (Al & Akar, 2013b).

1908 Abdulhamid II was dethroned, and the second constitutional monarchy was declared. Although the stock market was affected by uncertainty for a while, it recovered quickly. The period between 1911 and 1918 was a difficult time for the Ottomans. There would be a series of wars that would accelerate the collapse of the state. During the Balkan War of 1912–13, the state lost almost all its European territories. Then, World War I of 1914–1918 began. When the war broke out, the government temporarily closed the stock exchange on July 30, 1914. The stock exchange was only reopened on May 14, 1917. Subsequently, the stock exchange of the war-defeated Ottoman Empire would witness a major currency crisis. In 1919, Greece occupied Izmir. From 1919 to 1923, under the leadership of M. Kemal Atatürk, a War of Liberation was fought, and the Republic of Türkiye was established. As a result of the rumor that some Greek bankers had speculated in favor of Greece during the war, opposition against non-Muslim bankers spread after the Republic, and non-Muslim bankers trading on the stock exchange left Türkiye. The great crisis of 1929 put an end to the activities of the stock exchange. Since the young Turkish Republic did not follow a liberal policy, the Galata Stock Exchange was no longer needed.

8.9.1 Concluding Remarks

The nineteenth century marked the beginning of the Ottoman Empire's gradual collapse. The free trade regime upheaved its outdated economic structure. Its military structure had weakened, and the empire was falling apart with rising nationalist movements. It had to continue its existence under the protection of England for a long time. Therefore, the Ottoman Empire had to introduce several inclusive institutions to promote development after 1839. The Tanzimat Edicts (1839 and 1856) guaranteed equality, property rights, and civil liberties for all citizens, improving legal protection and attracting investment. The Ottoman Bank (1856) stabilized the economy and supported the growth of the capital market. New secular schools and universities trained skilled professionals while expanding media fostered public awareness and literacy. Investments in railways, ports, and urban modernization enhanced trade and facilitated connections between rural areas and markets. The Commercial Code (1850) and Land Code (1858) encouraged entrepreneurship and formalized property rights. The Galata Stock Exchange, later reorganized under the name of the Istanbul Bourse, emerged in this environment, which played a significant role in the Ottoman Empire's economy and the early development of capital markets in the region. The Istanbul Bourse thrived due to the presence of inclusive institutions and legal reforms, which fostered equal rights, robust financial regulations, and robust investor protections. These changes attracted domestic and foreign capital, making the bourse a key player in Ottoman economic modernization. Despite these efforts, challenges such as weak enforcement, political instability, and unequal access limited the full impact of these reforms. However, they laid the groundwork for modernization and economic integration. Although the Ottomans were too late to transition to the new order of the changing world, their reforms prepared the base for establishing the new Republic of Türkiye under the leadership of M. Kemal Atatürk in the twentieth century. Therefore, Turks are grateful to him for transforming their nation from a poor and helpless empire into a secular and fully independent republic in the twentieth century.

The Istanbul Bourse, one of the earliest stock exchanges in a developing economy, set an example for others. It helped fund key projects, such as railways and banks, aiding Ottoman modernization. Foreign investors, primarily from Britain and France, actively traded Ottoman bonds, illustrating how emerging markets attract international investment while managing associated risks. The bourse introduced financial regulations and investment tools, guiding other developing nations in establishing stock exchanges. It influenced markets in Egypt (1883), Greece (1876), and former Ottoman territories, which shared a reliance on government bonds, foreign investors, and trade finance, thereby shaping the financial systems in the region.

The Istanbul Bourse had a formal institutional structure modeled on the Paris Stock Exchange. As in Paris, market dynamics initially developed in the stock market and were subsequently regulated by the government. The market players were also modeled after Western European examples. The Istanbul Stock Exchange, like the Paris Stock Exchange, was primarily based on government bonds and derivative instruments. The Istanbul Bourse is the oldest known thriving Eastern stock exchange in the modern sense. Despite numerous shady transactions, including manipulation and insider trading, it maintained a significant trading volume. It has maintained strong relations with international exchanges, including London, Paris, and Vienna. It was effective in solving many financial problems of the Ottoman State. However, it disappeared from the historical stage after the Empire's collapse after World War I. However, the liberalization policies that began in the 1980s would revive the markets in Istanbul.

On June 23, 1982, Turkish headlines reported that Cevher Özden—known as "Banker Kastelli"—had fled the country, triggering massive financial losses. During the inflationary 1970s, when annual inflation ranged between 50 and 100%, independent bankers like Kastelli offered 10% monthly returns. Few questioned how such rates—equivalent to over 200% annually—could be sustained. In reality, it was a classic Ponzi scheme.

The roots lay in the 1970s oil crisis, which destabilized Türkiye's economy. In response, Prime Minister Süleyman Demirel introduced neoliberal reforms on January 24, 1980, abandoning import substitution. Interest rates were liberalized by July, enabling bankers to offer far higher returns than traditional banks—through deposit certificates and promissory notes.

After the military coup on September 12, 1980, Turgut Özal was put in charge of economic policy. Though high interest rates initially curbed inflation, regulation lagged. A 1981 capital markets law failed to oversee banking activities. When the finance minister issued a warning, panic withdrawals ensued. By spring 1982, even major players like Kastelli had collapsed.

These events fueled calls for the establishment of a stock exchange. Following the 1981 creation of the Capital Markets Board—Türkiye's version of the US SEC—the Istanbul Bourse was established in 1986. However, the lack of experienced brokerage houses remained a problem. By the early twentieth century, with the collapse of the Ottoman Empire, Galata Bankers, such as Kamondos, Jacques Alléon, the Baltazzis, and Yorgo Zarifi, had either moved abroad or left the profession.

For example, the Kamondo family, known as the Rothschilds of the East, fled from the Inquisition in Spain in the sixteenth century, first to Venice and then to Istanbul. The most important member of the family, Abraham Salomon Kamondo, was one of the founders of modern banking and a pioneer in the modernization of Istanbul's domestic life. When Salomon died, he was buried in a mausoleum with a grand state ceremony attended by the Sultan. The family settled in Paris in the 1870s, and later members were tragically exterminated in Nazi concentration camps during World War II (Malino & Sorkin, 1990).

Finding it challenging to find brokerage houses with sufficient savings, the Capital Markets Board of Türkiye compulsorily allowed brokers who had previously worked with the Street bankers to join the system by establishing brokerage houses. However, while they were excluded from the system over time, new institutional players and banks became the most critical players in the capital market. In 1996, similar to the Glass-Steagall Act in the United States, banks' equity activities were restricted. Banks were required to establish their brokerage houses as separate legal entities. Over the past decades, Borsa Istanbul has risen to a strong position among emerging stock exchanges.

Throughout Ottoman history, approximately 58% of Istanbul's population identified as Muslim, while 42% identified as Christian and Jewish. Today, the Galata neighborhood is far removed from the multicultural and multi-religious cosmopolitan structure of the Ottoman period (Fig. 8.3). Due to various political events, non-Muslims in the Galata district, where dozens of churches and synagogues are located, have left the country, and their numbers have dwindled considerably.

In 21st-century Türkiye, the Istanbul Stock Exchange, known as "Borsa Istanbul" since 2013, is located on the Istinye ridges on the European side of the city. In contrast, the Commission and Havyar Buildings, formerly Borsa Istanbul buildings, were demolished in 1958 as part of a development plan. The Galata district, the center of attention for both local and foreign travelers, with its historical buildings dating back to the Genoese era, bears the traces of its colorful past. The impressive Galata Tower, the symbol of the district, resists time, being "very tired and a little stagnant," as described in a poem.

Fig. 8.3 A 1901 postcard depicting Galata, showing signage in Ottoman Turkish, French, Greek, and Armenian. https://en.wikipedia.org/wiki/Galata#/media/File:Galatapostcard.jpg (Public Domain)

References

Afyoncu, E. (2007). *On Soruda: Tanzimat Düşüncesinin Gelişimi*. Dünya Publications.

Al, H., & ve Akar, Ş. K. (2013a). *Osmanlı'dan Günümüze Borsa: Galata Borsası, 1830–1873*. Borsa İstanbul Publications.

Al, H., & ve Akar, Ş. K. (2013b). *Osmanlı'dan Günümüze Borsa: Galata Borsası, 1874–1828*. Borsa İstanbul Publications.

Blaisdell, D. C. (1929). *European financial control in the Ottoman Empire: A study of the establishment, activities, and significance of the administration of the Ottoman public debt*. Columbia University Press.

Buluttekin, M. B. (2016). The Fırst Domıno Faıled: The foreign borrowing process of the Ottoman Empire starting with the Crımean War (1854–1914). *International Journal of Arts & Sciences, 9*(3), 273.

Çakıcıoğlu, R. O. (2007). Levanten kavramı ve Levantenler üzerine bir inceleme. *Selçuk Üniversitesi Türkiyat Araştırmaları Journal*, (22), 337–356.

Dadyan, S. (2021, 6 Nisan). *Kazaz Artin Amira Bezciyan.* https://www.academia.edu/8185584/Kazaz_Artin_Amira_Bezciyan
Demir, K. (2018). External Borrowing Issue in the Ottoman Empire (1854–1876 Term). In *Global approaches in financial economics, banking, and finance* (pp. 91–110).
Erdem, E. (2006). Osmanlı Para Sistemi ve Tağşiş Politikası: Dönemsel Bir Analiz. Bankacılar Journal. Sayı 56.
İnalcık, H. (1964). Tanzimat'ın Uygulanması ve Sosyal Tepkileri. *Belleten, 28*(112), 623–690.
İnalcık, H. (2016). *Devlet-i 'Aliyye: Osmanlı İmparatorluğu üzerine araştırmalar* (Vol. 4). İşbank Publications.
İnalcık, H., & Quataert, D. (Eds.). (1994). *An economic and social history of the Ottoman Empire, 1300–1914.* Cambridge University Press.
Kara, M. (2010). Bisav Bülteni. E.Z. Enver Ziya (2017). Gülhane Hatt-I Hümayunu'nda Batının Etkisi. Tanzimat, Editör Halil İnalcık ve Mehmet Seditdanlıoğlu, T. İşbankası Kültür Publications.
Karal, E. Z. (1964). Gülhane Hatt-ı Hümayununda Batının Etkisi. *Belleten, 28*(112), 581–602.
Karan, M. B., Westerman, W., & Wijngaard, J. (2024). *A history of banks: From the knights templar to the present era.* Contributions to Economics. Springer Nature.
Kastritsis, D. (2017). Legend and historical experience in fifteenth-century Ottoman narratives of the past. How the Past was Used.
Kazgan, H. (1991). Galata Bankerleri. TEB Publications.
Kazgan, H. (1995) Tarih Boyunca İstanbul Borsası. İstanbul. Istanbul Securities Exchange Pub.
Kopar, M., & Yolun, M. (2012). 18. ve 19. yüzyıllarda Osmanlı borçlar tarihine bir bakış. *History Studies International Journal of History, 4*, 335–358.
Kömürciyan, E. Ç. (1988). İstanbul Tarihi XVII. Asırda. İstanbul, 2.
Köse, M. (2020). Osmanlıda Borsa Ve Galata Bankerlerinin Devletin Mali Yapısındaki Yeri. *Atatürk Üniversitesi Türkiyat Araştırmaları Enstitüsü Journal, 8*(18).
Lewis, B. (1961). *The emergence of modern Turkey.* Oxford University Press.
Malino, F., & Sorkin, D. (1990). *From East and West: Jews in a Changing Europe, 1750–1870.* Blackwell.
Margoulias, H. J. (1975). *Decline and fall of Byzantium to the Ottoman Turks, by Doukas. An annotated translation of "Historia Turco-Bysantina" 1341–1462.* Wayne State University Press.
Ortaylı, İ. (1996). "Galata," İslam Ansiklopedisi, İstanbul: Türk Diyanet Vakfı Yay, Cilt 13,303.
Pamuk, Ş. (2004). Osmanlı İmparatorluğunun Ekonomik ve Sosyal Tarihi 1600–1914. Ed.: İnalcik, H., ve Quatert, D. Eren Yayıncılık.
Paşa, A. (2018). *Borsa risalesi: Hava oyunları.* Vakıf Bank Kültür Publications.
Rozen, M. (2010). *A history of the Jewish community in Istanbul: The formative years, 1453–1566* (Vol. 26). Brill.
Şakiroğlu, M. H. (1981). AGOSTINO PERTUSI, La Caduta di Constantinopoli. 2 cilt: I-Le Testimonianze dei Contemporanei. 2-L'Eco net Mondo, Milano 1976, XCI+ 467. Fondazione Lorenzo Valla Arnoldo Mondadori Editore.
Tekeli, & İlkin, S. (1997). *Para ve Kredi Sisteminin Oluşumunda Bir Aşama Türkiye Cumhuriyet Merkez Bankası.* T.C.Merkez Bankası.
Toprak, Z. (2016). The financial structure of the stock exchange in the late Ottoman Empire. In *East meets west-banking, commerce and investment in the Ottoman empire* (pp. 163–180). Routledge.
Toprak, Z. (1995). From imperial debt to global offerings: The history of the Istanbul stock exchange. In *From imperial debt to global offerings - The rise of the Istanbul stock exchange* (pp. 14–15). Mepa.
Türker, O. (2000). Galata'dan Karaköy'e: Bir Liman Hikayesi (Vol. 118). Sel Yayıncılık.
Ünlü, E. (2018). 18. Yüzyılda Osmanlı eliti bir darphane sarrafının muhallefatı: Bedros nam-ı diğer Petraki. *OTAM Ankara Üniversitesi Osmanlı Tarihi Araştırma Ve Uygulama Merkezi Journal, 43*, 281–318.
Varol, Ö. (2007), II. Abdülhamit Dönemi'nde Düyun-u Umumiye İdaresi, Kuruluşu ve İşleyişi. Yüksek Lisans Tezi, Ankara Üniversitesi Sosyal Bilimler Enstitüsü.

Yıldız, A. (2011). Osmanlı Devletinin Borçlanmasında Osmanlı Bankası'nın Rolü Ve Önemi (The Role and Importance of the Ottoman Bank in the Borrowing of the Ottoman Empire). *Elektronik Sosyal Bilimler Journal, 10*(36), 318–330.
Yılmaz, C. (2013). Osmanlı Anonim Şirketleri. Scala Yayıncılık.
Yılmaz, C. (2014). Osmanlı Borsasının İşlem Hacmi Ne Kadardı? *Muhasebe ve Finans Tarihi Araştırmaları Journal*, (7), 49–60.
Zarifi, Y. L. (2002). *Hatıralarım: Kaybolan bir Dünya. Istanbul 1800–1920*. Literatür.

Chapter 9
The New York Stock Exchange: The Birth of Wall Street and the Stock Barons (18th–19th Centuries)

9.1 Introduction

On a hot and humid August day in New York City in 1866, it was just beginning to get dark, and workers were making their way home. The streets were crowded, and the businessmen and stockbrokers of Wall Street were gathered in their clubs as usual, discussing the day's developments and trying to stay informed about the market news. Since the stock market was active during those days, many people came to the club. Although the windows were open, some members had removed their jackets due to the hot weather, while others tried to cool off by drinking beer. The topic of conversation for some time was the stocks of railroad companies. In particular, they were discussing the stock of the popular Erie Railroad of the time. The company was known as the "Scarlett of Wall Street"; investors had their eyes on it, and many stock brokers were waiting for its price to rise further. In walked Daniel Drew, a member of the Erie Railroad's Board of Directors since 1857 (Fig. 9.1). Known for his pious and cantankerous personality, Drew was one of the most renowned railroad speculators before and after the American Civil War (1861–1865). Daniel Drew had amassed a fortune through his frequent short selling, and by middle age, his speculation and tactics had become legendary. Club members immediately surrounded him. They were asking questions and trying to get a word in edgewise about the company. In a very calm and confident tone, Drew said the company's business was generally doing well. He even said he expected the stock price to increase slightly, but the members were wary, given Drew's reputation for dishonesty. He could have fooled them. Meanwhile, Daniel Drew took a handkerchief from his pocket to wipe the sweat from his forehead. A piece of paper with the handkerchief slipped out of his pocket and fell under the table. Drew pretended not to notice it. When Drew left the club, someone picked it up off the floor. It contained statements that supported a substantial increase in Erie's share price. One had probably gotten some vital and confidential information from Daniel Drew. The following day, when the news spread to the New York Stock Exchange (NYSE) brokerage houses through the grapevine, Erie's stock

M. B. Karan, *A History of Stock Exchanges*, Contributions to Economics,
https://doi.org/10.1007/978-3-032-07788-2_9

Fig. 9.1 Daniel Drew (1797–1879). https://commons.wikimedia.org/wiki/File:Daniel_Drew_1872.jpg

soared. What they did not know was that Drew had deliberately dropped the paper. He knew that greedy investors would jump on the news. The Company was not doing well. Its railcars were unreliable, and its tracks were deplorable, causing numerous accidents. Drew immediately took a position to short-sell when the stock price went up and a position to sell short when the stock went down. Within a few days, when the company's condition was revealed and prices fell well below their previous level, Drew made a fortune. Later, Daniel Drew's handkerchief trick became very famous. These kinds of tricks were trendy. However, he died a poor man in 1879, having lost all his wealth. One of the best-known Wall Street sayings at the time was (Browder, 2014; Geisst, 2018):

> When Uncle Daniel says, 'Up,' Erie goes up. When Uncle Daniel says "Down," Erie goes down; when Uncle Daniel says, "Swing, swing," Erie swings from side to side.

Daniel Drew, the protagonist of the above story dramatized according to actual events, was a typical nineteenth-century stock market speculator. During this period, the theory of evolution, developed by Charles Darwin, was the prevailing market understanding. They believed in natural selection and survival of the fittest. The stock markets were the personal battlegrounds of the American capitalist class, the robber barons of the time. The American market differed significantly from the London Stock Exchange (LSE). England had developed a stock exchange as a financial structure, characterized by strong government bonds and banks. The country had strong traditions, institutions, and a robust business ethic. The market economy was at the forefront in the United States. As in Europe, the state did not play a leading role in investments. All kinds of investments were made through companies. The stock market was where robber barons rode the rails for a long time. In the first half of the nineteenth century, business, in general, was developing much faster than the government. The government was too preoccupied with ideological issues, such as states' rights and slavery, to devote full attention to business practices until the late nineteenth century. Wild capitalism was on the rise in the marketplace. The development of capital markets in the United States would be significantly different from that in Europe. As in Europe, inclusive institutions would emerge not despite the state's power but with wild capitalism (Geisst, 2018; Thoreau, 1964).

In Great Britain, the system was powered by banking. Historically, the Lombard Street Bankers, the Chartered Bankers of London, and the Bank of England played a significant role in developing the London Stock Exchange. In contrast, the market economy was much more critical in the United States, where the functions of the state were limited. The country did not have a strong banking tradition or a central bank until the early twentieth century. A financial market that had been poorly regulated for a long time was beginning to emerge.

9.2 The 1780–1840 Period

9.2.1 The Origins of Wall Street

At the beginning of the eighteenth century, the United States was a land of unparalleled opportunities for people. Trade centered on essential commodities, including furs, natural resources, and tobacco. Land speculation was another area that attracted attention. The primary motivation of the people living in this country was the desire to own property. James Madison (1751–1836), the fourth president and one of America's founding fathers, said: "*Government is established to protect property of all kinds*" (Ball, 2017). However, doing business in the United States at that time was not an easy matter. Each colony had its own currency and jealously guarded its economic position, even after the federal government was established following independence. After 1789, the Constitution prohibited the states from issuing their own money. Since large companies and banks had not yet been established in the country, trade could not develop quickly or effectively in the new country without an organized stock exchange; such an exchange was needed. After the Revolutionary War, the first Congress met in New York in 1789 and 1790, and the new government assumed all the war debts of the former colonies. Out of necessity, the US government issued federal bonds in New York and borrowed $ 80 million (Geisst, 2018). Thus, the American capital markets were born, albeit modestly. In the eighteenth century, economic activity in the United States developed between New England and New York in northeastern America (Bowden, 1989).

New York, Boston, and Philadelphia were the places where nascent American capitalism began. Philadelphia had the distinction of hosting the first actual stock exchange. Boston continued to be a shipping and banking center, while New York rapidly developed into a hub for financial services, including insurance and banking. Although government bonds were sold in all three places and other major cities such as Baltimore and Charleston, New York had developed the first active market for bonds and shares of emerging companies. Local merchants and traders had gathered in various parts of lower Manhattan around Wall Street, along a barricade built in 1653 to protect the first Dutch settlers from Indians. Later, they began to gather here to buy and sell stocks and debt securities. As the securities business developed, two classes of traders emerged. These were auctioneers and dealers. After the auctioneers set the initial price, the market makers traded among themselves. This form of trading set a precedent that would become ingrained in American market practices for the next two hundred years (Geisst, 2018).

In March 1792, the excessive risk-taking of a local New York trader named William Duer, combined with the collapse of many of his speculative positions, served as a wake-up call for market players to get their affairs in order. The organized market in New York began on May 17, 1792, when twenty-four New York stockbrokers and traders signed the Buttonwood Agreement under a Buttonwood tree off Wall Street (Box 9.1). They aimed to strengthen their position against the auctioneers who dominated the market. Their agreement was written as follows (Sobel, 2000):

> We, the subscribers, brokers for the purchase and sale of public stocks, do hereby solemnly promise and pledge ourselves to each other that we will not buy or sell from the date, for any person whatsoever, any kind of public stocks at a less than one-quarter of one cent commission on the specie value, and that we will give preference to each other in our negotiations.

Although this oath was similar to the banking oath of today's European Union, there were essential differences between them. The EU Banking Oath focuses on individual ethics in banking, while the Buttonwood Agreement created structural rules for a securities market. The EU Banking Oath is a regulatory measure, whereas the Buttonwood Agreement was a private contract that later influenced the development of financial infrastructure.

Box 9.1: William Duer and America's First Financial Scandal

On April 19, 1792, a crowd of angry rioters surrounded the jail near City Hall in New York City, chanting, "*We'll get Mr. Duer; he's got our money*!" William Duer, a former member of the Continental Congress and once Alexander Hamilton's right-hand man in the US Treasury, had been imprisoned there for playing a key role in the 1792 crisis. The sheriff dispersed the crowd, but the city was in a panic. Duer had tried to corner the market for government bonds and shares of existing banks by borrowing as much as he could from everyone. Before the panic, credit was readily available. Still, when the largest lender, the Bank of the United States, began to call in its loans, Duer's creditors began demanding their money back. Panic set in when it became clear that he had no money to pay them, and the resulting collapse shook the city. In response, the New York State Legislature passed a law prohibiting public trading, which led to the creation 1792 of a private association of merchants that would eventually evolve into the New York Stock Exchange. Duer eventually died in debtors' prison, one of the principal actors in America's first financial scandal, a fiasco involving corruption, outright fraud, and greed on a grand scale (Brooks, 1995).

Thus, the New York Securities and Exchange Board was established. Initially, five securities were traded on the exchange, with the Bank of New York as the first listed company. Others included the First Bank of the United States and the Bank of North America. The 24 brokers who signed the agreement thus became the first members of the exchange. Securities could be bought and sold in gold, silver, or cash, typically in New York dollars issued by banks (Cowen, 2010).

The First Bank of the United States was America's first central bank. In 1791, it was chartered by the United States Congress for a period of twenty years. It was part of the tripartite expansion of federal fiscal and monetary power, along with the federal mint and excise taxes advocated by Alexander Hamilton, the first Secretary of the Treasury. Hamilton believed that a national bank was necessary to stabilize and improve the nation's credit and to better manage the financial affairs of the US government under the newly enacted Constitution. However, once established, it did not fulfill the functions of a modern central bank, as it neither set monetary policy nor controlled private banks. It did not hold excess reserves or act as an authority of last resort. The bank was national insofar as it was allowed to have branches in more than one state and to lend to the US government. The other banks in the United States were chartered by only one state and allowed to open branches in those states (FED History, n.d.).

By the time the central bank was dissolved in 1811, after its charter had expired, more than 120 state banks had already been incorporated. Many of them had started having bond issues. The main reason for the central bank's closure was the authority of other banks to print banknotes, which many new banks and their owners did not want to surrender to a powerful central bank (Wilkins, 1989).

Between 1790 and 1817, no permanent central location for the NYSE existed. Dealers operated over the counter, buying and selling among themselves without formally meeting to set a price for a security. Government bonds gained popularity, accounting for approximately one-third of all securities traded during this period. In 1812, the Franklin Bank, City Bank, Phoenix Bank, and Bank of America were established. New York City also entered the market with a new bond issue. Stocks related to canal investments became a favorite of investors, and Erie Canal stocks were the most common in New York (Geisst, 2018).

9.2.2 New York Stock and Exchange Board

In 1817, traders established the New York Stock and Exchange Board, the first organized stock exchange in the United States. During this period, competition between New York and Philadelphia was fierce, with each wanting the same thing and claiming leadership for the entire nation. The stock auctions had been held at the Tontine Coffeehouse, located at 82 Wall Street, on the northwest corner of Water Street in New York, since 1793. Some Wall Streeters felt that the inefficiency of the small Tontine auction was one reason why their Philadelphia counterparts received most of the business in Europe. They had to admit that the Philadelphia auctions were better organized, more carefully supervised, and less speculative than the frenetic Tontine sessions. It was, therefore, decided to create a new organization similar to the one in Philadelphia. In 1817, they sent one of their own to Philadelphia to learn more about the operations there. The New York agents then met "*to draft a new cons*titution," almost an exact copy of the Philadelphia charter. A new Board of Brokers was formed, consisting of twenty-eight members from seven firms, and an admission fee of $25 was set. This group of brokers marked the beginning of the renamed New York Stock Exchange (Sobel, 2000).

The first stock exchange operations took place in the boardroom of Tontine's Coffeehouse. Trading was restricted to members only (Fig. 9.2). Tontine's Coffeehouse served a dual function as both a club and a meeting hall, while also hosting auctions, banquets, and balls. The coffeehouse also provided a place for the registration of shiploads and the slave trade. Fights often broke out in this place where people of all classes came. The English traveler John Lambert wrote the following in 1807 (Tontine Coffee House, n.d.):

> The Tontine Coffee House was filled with underwriters, brokers, merchants, traders, and politicians; selling, purchasing, trafficking, or insuring; some reading, others eagerly inquiring the news […] The steps and balcony of the coffee house were crowded with people bidding or listening to the several auctioneers, who had elevated themselves upon a hogshead of sugar, a puncheon of rum, or a bale of cotton, and with Stentorian voices were exclaiming, 'Once, twice. Once, twice.' '"Another cent.' 'Thank ye, gentlemen.' [...] The coffee-house slip, and the corners of Wall and Pearl-streets, were jammed up with carts, drays, and wheelbarrows [...] Everything was in motion; all was life, bustle, and activity...

The new exchange then rented a room at 40 Wall Street, where brokers met twice a day to trade a list of 30 stocks and bonds. The chairman called out the name of each security in turn from the dais while the brokers shouted their bids from their

Fig. 9.2 Tontine Coffee House, New York, 1872. https://commons.wikimedia.org/wiki/File:New_York_Tontine_Coffee_House_1797.jpg

assigned seats. This originated the term "*seat*," which has since come to refer to NYSE membership. The new organization elected a president and secretary among senior members of "Buttonwood." The new management set minimum commissions. This quickly established the tradition that brokerage firms on the exchange enjoyed a privileged position over those that traded only with or for the public. Although the prices of securities were recorded daily, they were not always available to the press. Prices were not uniformly available in New York; different prices were offered in other places, which could be learned through intermediaries (Sobel, 2000).

In 1818, the stock exchange listed a few securities, including US government and New York State bonds, shares in ten banks, and thirteen insurance companies. Speculation and manipulation were common. The "*members only*" rule and a $25 membership fee restricted participation. Non-member brokers traded on Wall Street sidewalks, dealing in unlisted stocks, which led to the establishment of the New York Curb Market, the forerunner of the American Stock Exchange (Eames, 1894). The curb brokers were driven out of the Mills Building in 1907 and given a "*small paved area*" fenced off by police on Broad Street between Exchange Place and Beaver Street. Orders to buy and sell securities were shouted down from the windows of nearby brokerage houses (NYSE American, n.d.). The curb market's decentralized nature also foreshadowed the development of the over-the-counter market. Despite improvements, the exchange's image remained poor, and people believed that wealth was valued mainly when converted into real estate (Geisst, 2018).

The Second Bank of the United States, founded in 1816 to aid the economy's recovery from the Napoleonic Wars, had a 20-year charter set to expire in 1836. Seen as favoring wealthy elites over small farmers and businesses, it faced opposition from state banks, which resented its restrictions on the issuance of paper money. Public distrust of central banking and a preference for gold and silver led to its downfall, similar to the First Bank (Dangerfield, 1965). After much debate, a dual banking system emerged, allowing both state and national banks, a structure still in place today. In the dual banking system, banks are chartered and supervised at either the state or federal level, sometimes both (Scott, 1977).

By the early nineteenth century, transportation companies gained strength in the stock market, and the capital market specialized in bank stocks, insurance companies, and government bonds. The United States, a debtor nation, relied on foreign investment. As New York became the banking hub, its banks held large deposit balances from across the country, fluctuating with the agricultural cycle. Farmers' money accumulated in New York banks in the fall was then withdrawn for wages and purchases in the spring. Surplus bank loans fueled stock speculation, but banks called in loans when balances fell, forcing borrowers to sell securities. This cycle drove capital flows and influenced the stock market and the economy (Banner, 1998).

Stock markets were insignificant in the early nineteenth century, and traders viewed securities trading as a lazy or foolish endeavor. Speculative booms occurred, but they were viewed more as a form of gambling than as a legitimate investment. Only after the post-Napoleonic era, when foreign capital began to flow into American businesses, did stock markets gain importance (Sobel, 2000). While stock prices were not regularly reported, news about new companies was widely covered. Manipulators often publish laudatory or defamatory articles to sway public opinion, which can sometimes cause investors to withdraw (Geisst, 2018).

One dubious practice was "*Forward delivery,*" an early form of futures trading. Traders bought stocks at a fixed price for future delivery, delaying payment and hoping for a price increase to sell at a profit. If the trade was short term, no cash payment was needed. These transactions were familiar but not legally binding. If a trader defaulted, there was no legal recourse. Instead, deals relied on honor among gentlemen. However, insider manipulation was rampant (Geisst, 2018). It was a customized, private agreement with high default risk and required physical delivery. It was not a standardized deal and did not allow cash settlements like futures.

The NYSE moved to its new location in the Merchants' Exchange Building, at the corner of Wall Street and William Street, in 1827. Meanwhile, Investors were divided into bulls (expecting price increases) and bears (short selling). The stocks that both were most interested in were so-called *fancy stocks*. These offer great opportunities for stock gambling since they have no actual value, and the fluctuations in their price are artificial (Murray, 1958). In other words, they were "*bubble*" companies whose value would soon erode. In an era of slow information dissemination, speculating on these stocks became a game. Although numerous regulations have been made on this issue, such market manipulations still occur frequently today. One of the more subtle methods of price manipulation was the "*wash sale.*" An investor sells a security at a loss and then buys the same or substantially similar security within a very short period, then deducts the loss from the tax. Thus, less tax is paid by deducting the taxable income. The Revenue Act of 1921 was later designed to prevent capital losses, such as tax deductions. In the early years of the stock market, it meant the same thing, but there was no income tax. If two traders wanted to drive down the stock price to accumulate, they would conspire to buy each other's stocks at a lower price than the current price and then sell them. The net result would be no gain or loss for either side. However, those who witnessed the selling on the stock market would think the stock was weakening and would sell in anticipation of further price declines (Grinblatt & Keloharju, 2004).

The 1837 economic panic led to mass bank failures, business closures, deflation, and unemployment. However, railroads expanded, industry grew, coal dominated, and agriculture advanced. The population surged in the 1840s, gold was found in 1848, and investors began demanding corporate financial transparency (Timberlake, 1997).

Meanwhile, the change in economic activities led to the restructuring of the financial sector. While financial capitalism, which started in England in the eighteenth century, had long been dominated by merchants, financiers, and landowners who profited from trade, speculation, and rent-seeking activities, in the late eighteenth century and throughout the nineteenth century, industrial capitalism introduced a new system in which economic power was increasingly concentrated in manufacturing, technological innovation, and mass production. This period is called industrial capitalism. This transition reshaped industries and financial institutions and profoundly impacted labor, urbanization, and global markets. The expansion of financial institutions played a crucial role in this transition. Banks, stock markets, and joint-stock companies developed mechanisms to pool and distribute capital for large-scale industrial projects. Early financiers and merchant banks, which had primarily focused on trade and colonial investments, adapted to the new industrial landscape by financing railroads, steel mills, and other large-scale enterprises.

9.3 The 1840–1890 Period

The Mexican War of 1846–1848 and the Civil War (1861–1865) played important roles in American financing and helped develop financial markets. They spurred US financial market expansion through government bond issuance, the introduction of greenbacks, and increased stock market speculation in war-related industries. The National Banking Acts (1863–1864) standardized currency and strengthened federal oversight, while heavy railroad investment fueled market growth. These changes modernized the financial system and set the stage for post-war industrial expansion. The New York Stock and Exchange Board only traded those of interest to New York or had a broader business. The name was officially changed in 1863 to the New York Stock Exchange (NYSE). During this period, a competitor to the stock exchange emerged. The Open Board of Stock Brokers was founded in 1864 as a competitor to the NYSE. While the Open Board of Stock Brokers rivaled the NYSE, which had 354 members, it had 533 members: "*It used a more modern, continuous trading system than the NYSE's twice-daily call sessions*" (NYSE, n.d.). The Open Board of Stock Brokers would merge with the NYSE in 1869. Robert Wright of Bloomberg wrote that the merger increased the NYSE's membership and trading volume (NYSE, n.d.).

9.3.1 Investment Banks

By the 1830s, new investment houses emerged, facilitating stock and currency trading while raising capital. Merchants collaborated with bankers, linking commercial and investment banking. Businessmen, brokers, and other financiers who turned to banking, especially by channeling depositors' funds into securities issued for the first time, established strong links between what is now known as commercial banking (accepting deposits and making loans) and investment banking (brokering securities). Most of these were based in New York. They became increasingly influential in the economy. Private merchant bankers, who used their capital to finance their activities, were not required to have a contract with the state deposit banks. They did not have to disclose their finances to the public. Because successful private bankers were not accountable to anyone but their customers, they could become a significant financial force without outside oversight. Their independence kept them from states' rights debates and the money printing issue (Frydman & Hilt, 2017).

The nature of private banking attracted foreign firms eager to do business in the United States. In 1774, the great British bank Barings had begun operating in North America. In 1796, the bank helped finance the purchase of nearly 1 million acres (4000 km^2) from the Commonwealth of Massachusetts. The land became part of the US state of Maine. In the 1830s, under the leadership of new American partner Joshua Bates, the bank believed there were more significant opportunities in the United States. In 1843, Barings became a special representative of the US government. In particular, Barings helped finance America's arms purchases (Tamaki, 1974). The other central British bank, Rothschild, had established "*August Belmont and Company*" in New York in the late 1830s through its agent, August Belmont. Belmont was a very talented investor. He was a pioneer on Wall Street, rapidly shifting money and commodities in complex international credit spirals that New York had never seen before. He was also recognized as a skilled arbitrageur, nicknamed "*King of the money changers.*" He was only twenty-six when he became one of the US's three most critical private bankers (Black, 1981). Belmont was involved in Rothschild's investments in American railroads, government bonds, and international trade. The Rothschild family relied on Belmont to navigate the American financial world and avoid direct involvement in risky ventures. Later, Belmont became one of America's most powerful financiers, advising corporations and politicians. The Rothschild-Belmont partnership was a strategic move that allowed the Rothschilds to expand their influence in the growing American economy without directly operating a bank in the United States. However, the waning entrepreneurial spirit and ambition of the new generations of Rothschilds and the failure to establish a central bank similar to the Bank of England in the United States limited their interest in the United States.

Banks, many of them founded by German Jewish merchants, quickly became a significant force in the financial sector. Marcus Goldman, a Bavarian Jew, founded Goldman Sachs and Company in 1869. In 1896, the firm was listed on the NYSE. By 1897, Goldman Sachs had established relationships with financial firms in major European capitals, providing services such as foreign exchange, letters of credit, gold shipments, and arbitrage. In the early 1900s, as clients required increasingly large amounts of long-term capital, the firm began to build its investment banking business and has remained a significant force in the commercial paper market ever since (Goldman Sachs, n.d.).

In the United States, communication was slow, and town merchants did not know enough about many businessmen seeking loans. After the 1837 crisis, New York merchants established a system to share customer reports. Lewis Tappan (1788–1873), founder of the Journal of Commerce (1828), turned to this area in 1841 when he founded the Mercantile Agency, the first of its kind, which would later become the Dun & Bradstreet Corporation. In 1962, Dun & Bradstreet acquired another rating company, Moody's. Moody's was founded in 1909 by John Moody to produce statistical guides on stocks, bonds, and bond ratings. In the 1850s, Samuel C. Thompson launched an agency publishing the Bank Note Detector, helping bankers identify counterfeit notes. The history of Standard and Poor's, one of the two other major rating companies known today, dates back to 1860 when Henry Poor (1860) published his book "*History of Railroads and Canals*" in the United States, which compiled comprehensive information on the financial and operational condition of US railroad companies. In 1941, it merged with Standard Statistics to become Standard & Poor's Corp. The other major rating company, Fitch, was founded in 1914. Investors now understood that manipulations can be prevented by sharing financial information (Poon, 2012).

9.3.2 Prominent Speculators of the Stock Market

In the mid-nineteenth century, Jacob Little (1794–1865), then known as the "*Big Bear of Wall S*treet," was one of the first and greatest speculators in stock market history (Fig. 9.3). A market pessimist, Little made his fortune by cornering the markets, sometimes by short selling various companies and sometimes by profiting from other short sellers. The concept of cornering the market, which gained control over a particular asset, commodity, or security to manipulate its price and limit competition, became popular in the nineteenth century when speculators tried to control markets by hoarding stocks or commodities. This often involved buying up a large portion of the available supply, creating artificial scarcity and increasing prices. Jacob Little was nicknamed the "*Bear*" because he profited from falling markets (Geisst, 2018). Little was positioning long and short. Long positions were for situations where he expected stock prices to rise, while short positions were for profiting from falling stock prices. He was shorting stocks he thought were overpriced, trying to corner short sellers, or going long during a bull market. Little could remember every trade he made, and paid attention to every detail of his trades. He would even personally deliver the shares he sold to ensure no mistake. Until Jacob Little arrived, most speculators used inside (non-public) information to make fortunes. But Little relied on predicting the future direction of stocks and manipulating stocks to make his fortune. Little was an incorrigible gambler who wanted the cards to be stacked in his favor. Jacob Little's spirit was summarized in the quote, "*I don't care what happens as long as I'm in it.*" Thanks to his great financial foresight, Little amassed an enormous fortune, becoming one of the wealthiest men in America and a leading Wall Street financier in the 1830s and 1840s. However, his fortunes later turned sour, and he was penniless on his deathbed in 1865 (Maccaro, 2004).

1835 a fire destroyed the Merchants' Exchange Building, forcing the NYSE to relocate temporarily. But, by 1865, the NYSE moved again to 10–12 Broad Street, and later, in 1903, it settled in its current building at 18 Broad Street. The exchange used to occupy the largest hall in the building and, until this time, held two sessions a day, one in the morning and one in the afternoon. To limit membership to a more affluent class of traders, the entrance fee was raised to $400 (Geisst, 2018).

Another highly influential speculator on Wall Street in the 1860s was Jay Cooke (1821–1905) (Fig. 9.4). He was known for financing the Union effort in the American Civil War by selling government bonds. After the war, he helped fund the construction of several major railroads. Cooke became heavily involved in financing and constructing the North Pacific Railroad, the first transcontinental line to the Pacific

Fig. 9.3 Jacob Little (1794–1865). https://commons.wikimedia.org/wiki/File:Jacob_Little.png

Northwest. In this way, he entered the Wall Street arena and realized that the government's attempt to complete a second transcontinental railroad could raise serious money through land donations. After a financial panic that year, he over-financed the project and was forced into bankruptcy in 1873. Cooke could escape poverty by investing a small sum of money in a silver mine in Utah. This investment would later enable Cooke to retire as a small millionaire (Larson, 1936).

9.3.3 The Long Depression, Railway Wars, and Stock Exchange Barons

Various scams and speculations in the market had motivated Wall Street to make multiple reforms over time. Stock indicators were first used in 1867 with the advent of the telegraph. Initially, seats on the stock exchange were held for life and could not be transferred, but after 1868, with a new regulation, members could sell their seats to others. Members also had to pay their annual dues and participate in exchange activities to keep the seats active. The return on a seat was relatively high for early members who were still active. In 1868, the price of a seat ranged from seven to eight

Fig. 9.4 Jay Cooke (1821–1905). https://en.wikipedia.org/wiki/Jay_Cooke_%26_Company#/media/File:JayCooke-BW.JPG (Public Domain)

thousand dollars. However, the NYSE was a hotbed for railroad and bank speculators. More shares of industrial companies were traded on the Boston Stock Exchange than in New York. The Boston Stock Exchange (BSE) focused heavily on railroads, banks, insurance companies, and industrial firms. Boston was a significant financial center, especially for New England's railroads, textile mills, and banking institutions. Traders in Boston were considered a safer place, even though they practiced the same methods as those on the NYSE. New York would nonetheless remain the best-known stock exchange and home to many of the legendary speculators of the era (Geisst, 2018).

Most Wall Street firms had become multi-partner corporations in the early nineteenth century. As the number of partners increased, the power of the partners diminished. This began what became known as the era of "managerial capitalism." In this new approach, shareholders were separated from the management of companies, and management was left to professional managers. This system emerged in the late 19th and early twentieth centuries as businesses expanded beyond the capacity of individual owners to manage effectively. Professional managers brought expertise and long-term vision, helping companies to grow and adapt to changing market conditions. However, a potential disadvantage was that managers without direct ownership may prioritize personal benefits, such as high salaries and job security, over shareholder value. With this new trend, the emerging managerial class would also give rise to an adequate social status in the future, and company chief operating executives (CEOs) would become an essential force of the modern era.

However, the panic of 1873 was a financial crisis that triggered an economic depression from 1873 to 1877 in Europe and North America, known as the Long Depression. The panic had several causes. These included American inflation, widespread speculative investment, the monetization of silver in Germany and the United States, the economic shocks in Europe caused by the Franco-Prussian War (1870–1871), and the massive property losses in the Great Chicago Fire (1871) and the Great Boston Fire (1872). In addition, bank reserves in New York, which fell from $50 million to $17 million between September and October 1873, put tremendous pressure on the economy (Musson, 1959). When Europeans started selling railroad bonds, the railroads could no longer find anyone to lend them money, and many railroads went bankrupt. When people saw that big banks had failed, they ran to their banks and demanded all their money back. At least 100 banks failed nationwide. The NYSE was also closed for 10 days (Newbold, 1932). Interestingly, the fall in the prices of so many banks and businesses and the distress of so many businesses increased the popularity of publicly traded companies by preventing the bankruptcy of investors in stock companies, where shareholder liability was limited. Many saw this period as an opportunity for corner-cutting operations, while others seized opportunities to attack troubled companies to build more giant corporations to dominate the market. The robber barons and their bankers significantly changed US institutions by merging many small companies into large industrial groups.

Daniel Drew, whom we mentioned in the introduction, had been a cattle trader, tavern owner, pawnbroker, steamship owner, and finally, a broker with a bad reputation for everything he did. Finally, on Wall Street, Drew joined Robinson and Company as a partner. He had previously been a cattle trader, transporting long distances across upstate New York by rail without watering them. When they neared the destination where their buyers were waiting, he would allow the cattle to drink water to make them heavier. It was an interesting coincidence that Drew's most tremendous success in the stock market involved a financial version of the diluted stock. As we will explain below, most railroads in the 1860s were financed with bonds, and bondholders assumed all the risks of the projects; if the projects went bankrupt, they suffered losses. Shareholders, often including the company's executives, held on to the stock at a price well above its actual value by advertising it favorably in the press and advertisements. However, if a short-selling raid occurred, the stock was highly vulnerable. Drew recognized the opportunity of the situation. That is why he lent money to the Erie Railroad Company in 1857 and became a partner at a later date. His goal was to make big money by short selling the company he owned. The partnership gave him a steady supply of shares to sell short. Despite its terrible reputation in the market, the railroad's assets were worth ten times the price at which he became a partner. After first driving up prices with the handkerchief trick we described at the beginning of the chapter, he began to short-sell his shares, even putting more on the market than before. Typically, such an exercise should have resulted in a write-down as the position could not be closed. But he had a stock reserve that the rest of the market didn't know about. Drew bought convertible bonds and used them to cover his shorts, diluting the market by increasing the number of stocks like watering cattle. While he made a fortune in the process, he became a phenomenon that diluted both the cattle and the stock market (Chandler, 1954).

This crisis empowered stock market speculators and bankers. A new era was beginning. The period from the late 1870s to the early 1900s is called the Gilded Age. Mark Twain and Charles Dudley Warner coined it in their book The Gilded Age (Twain & Warner, 1890). It was about the vulgar and uncouth rich of the age. It was a period of rapid industrialization, economic growth, and prosperity for the rich. It was also a period of exploitation and extreme poverty for the working class. This period's most important stock market players (barons) were Sage, Gould, Vanderbilt, Carnegie, Morgan, and Rockefeller.

9.3.3.1 Russell Sage, the Vanderbilts, and Jason Gould

Described by one contemporary as "*gloomy, shrewd, reclusive*," Russell Sage (1816–1906) was one of the most ruthless stock market operators of the Gilded Age, which lasted from after the Civil War until the early twentieth century (Fig. 9.5). He was dubbed the "*Money King*" by the newspapers of the time. He became one of Wall Street's most successful investors by cornering its most cunning players (Remsen, 1938). In 1852, at 36, Sage was elected to the US House of Representatives. He said: "*Any man can make a dollar, but it takes a wise man to keep it.*" Another principle he relied on was, "B*uy straw hats in the winter when no one wants them and sell them in the summer when everyone needs them.*" Sage was willing to take smaller profits that were guaranteed, or at least close to it, rather than taking big risks to make a significant return on his investments. He explained it this way: "*If you watch the pennies, the dollars will care for themselves*" (Geisst, 2018). Throughout his life, good fortune seemed to follow him on just about every business venture he embarked. This incredible luck became known as "Sage luck" by those familiar with his accomplishments.

Sage pioneered using options, especially in setting up complex strategies, which are popular now. He short-sold only when he had inside information (non-public information on companies) or manipulated the stock without covering his bet with a call option. Nowadays, financial authorities enforce strict regulations to ensure that markets remain transparent, competitive, and accessible to all investors. Because lending money to other exchange operators was a significant source of profit for Sage, he developed a novel way to get around New York state usury laws. He charged for long-term loans, and 40–80% for short-term loans. But, instead of allowing customers to borrow cash to buy stock, Sage would buy the stock in his name and sell the customer a call option at an inflated price. This transaction allowed the customer to use Sage's capital to take advantage of the price increase. However, the customer paid a premium for the option instead of paying interest, which is subject to state usury laws. If the stock price fell below the call option's strike price, the customer

Fig. 9.5 Russell Sage (1816–1906). https://commons.wikimedia.org/wiki/Category:Russell_Sage#/media/File:Portrait_of_Russell_Sage.jpg

would not exercise it, leaving Sage with a depreciating asset, so he would also buy a put option to protect himself. This cost was passed on to the person who bought the call option. If he could not predict the direction of prices in the market, Sage would purchase combinations of puts and calls, known as "*straddles.*" This way, the speculator would profit whether the stock price rose or fell and only lose money if the stock price remained stagnant (Sobel, 2000). He was also called "*Father of Puts and Calls or Old Straddle.*"

Russell Sage was linked to two Wall Street speculators, Cornelius Vanderbilt and Jason Gould. Surprisingly, even when Vanderbilt and Gould were in violent conflict with each other, he maintained a lucrative relationship with both. Cornelius Vanderbilt, one of America's wealthiest businessmen, had made his fortune in shipping. In the early 1860s, he believed that the future of the United States lay in the railroad business. Because of his shipping background, he was nicknamed "*Comador,*" which means commanding officer in the business world. He was a plain man of few words and had a legendary reputation for stinginess. The Vanderbilts began their railroad empire in 1862 by buying the New York and Harlem Railroad, whose stock was cheap due to competition from two other railroads (Alef, 2009). The purchase of the Harlem stock was a particularly complicated affair. The share price rose from $25 to over $150 during an acquisition. It was then subjected to a speculative attack by Daniel Drew. Drew spread rumors that some members of parliament were reconsidering the acquisition, and with the help of rumors, he proceeded to devalue the stock.

In the process, he launched a bear raid, short selling the stock to ruin Comador. This takeover turned into a typical stock market raid and counter-raid, a struggle between the most notorious manipulators of the era—Drew, the excellent bear raider, and Vanderbilt, the master of the cornering operation. When the stock reached $285, the Vanderbilts would emerge victorious, wiping out most of their rivals (Geisst, 2018).

Later, the Vanderbilts expanded their railroad investments and consolidated them under the New York Central Railroad. They also acquired the Lake Shore and Michigan Southern Railroad in 1873, bringing the New York Central under a corporate structure. Thus, they created a railroad system extending from New York to Chicago. In the 1870s, they also took control of the Canadian Southern Railway and the Michigan Central Railroad, as well as smaller lines, coal mines, and other assets adjacent to the railroads. The Vanderbilts turned to Russell Sage to arrange the complex Wall Street transactions necessary to acquire controlling blocks of stocks and bonds of these companies. Despite being perhaps the wealthiest man of his time, Cornelius Vanderbilt had cash flow problems and occasionally relied on Sage for short-term credit. Not only did Sage profit from them by serving as their securities broker, but he also served as their banker and charged them high interest rates. He also used insider information to trade on his account and made extraordinary profits (Geisst, 2018).

When Cornelius Vanderbilt died in 1877, his son William Henry Vanderbilt took over the business. In 1879, William Henry Vanderbilt reduced his stake in the company to a minority stake to avoid harsh scrutiny from the press and the state legislature for owning most of the New York Central Railroad stock. Still, he maintained control behind the scenes while reducing his stake in the New York Central to a minority stake.

It was noteworthy that Russell Sage, while maintaining his relationship with the Vanderbilts, chose to ally himself with their great enemy, Jay (Jason) Gould. Widely known as the "*Mephistopheles (Demon) of Wall Street,*" Gould was arguably the most uninhibited and ruthless of the Wall Street manipulators of the era. Joseph Pulitzer, a famous US journalist who knew Gould personally, described him as "*one of the most sinister figures to fly like a bat in the eyes of the American peo*ple." Others have argued that Jay Gould, though ruthless like many great speculators, was more creative than most (American Heritage, 1989). In 1867, Gould was pitted against the Vanderbilts for control of the Erie Railroad. Gould had established relationships with notoriously corrupt politicians, bribing legislators and courts. He also used Sage's services to manipulate stocks while bribing journalists for favorable press coverage (Geisst, 2018).

Eventually, the Vanderbilts found a way to acquire most of Erie's shares and took legal action to remove Gould from the company's management. Gould and Fisk, already in control of Erie, used a legal loophole to issue thousands of new shares (known as "*watered* stock"). They represent ownership of overvalued assets, the stock of a corporation whose total worth is less than its invested capital. As Vanderbilt kept buying, they flooded the market with new shares, diluting his holdings and making his investments worthless. Gould and Fisk bribed New York legislators and judges, securing legal protection. When Vanderbilt sued, the courts (which Gould had influenced) ruled in favor of Gould and Fisk. Realizing he had been tricked and lost millions, Vanderbilt negotiated a settlement. He agreed to stop the fight in exchange for a payout of around $1 million and favorable business terms elsewhere.

In early 1869, Jay Gould hatched a plan to take over the gold market, perhaps the most audacious target in the American financial system. At the time, gold was still the official currency of international trade, but the United States had gone off the gold standard during the Civil War to finance the war. Located near Wall Street, the Gold Room operated separately from the NYSE. It was one of America's first commodity markets, influencing future gold and currency exchanges. Since there was only about $20 million in gold in circulation at the time, Gould realized that a sufficiently wealthy speculator could corner the market by buying a certain amount of the precious metal. They could then drive up the price and sell at astronomical profits. But for this plan to work, the Treasury would have to allow it. Because if a speculator tried to corner the market, President Grant could order the Treasury to sell large quantities of gold and drive the price down. For Gould's gold plan to work, President Grant must refrain from selling gold (Klein & Calandro, 2016).

Therefore, Gould tried to influence the President by bribing Abel Corbin, who was married to Ulysses Grant's sister, Jennie. By bribing and using his influence, Corbin began to gain knowledge of the government's gold sales. Corbin also used his family connections to bring Grant together with Gould (Klein & Calandro, 2016).

Jay Gould and several other friends had been secretly stockpiling gold since August. Gould sought to manipulate the gold market by cornering it—buying up large amounts of gold to create artificial scarcity and drive up prices. He aimed to make a substantial profit by selling gold at inflated prices once the market was manipulated, and he believed that he could use this strategy to control the market. Gould had also enlisted the help of his wealthy friend Jim Fisk. As Gould bought with Fisk, the value of the gold would climb to dizzying heights. In August, a $100 piece of gold sold for about $132 in dollar terms, and just a few weeks later, the price had soared to $141. Gould's shopping spree continued unabated until September 22, when he learned from Abel Corbin that the President was on their trail. Corbin had written a letter to Grant seeking assurances that he was steadfast in his non-interventionist gold stance, a note that eventually raised suspicions that the President's brother-in-law might be involved in a gold scheme. Furious at being manipulated, the President began selling gold. On September 24, 1869, the stock market crashed, and the date was dubbed Black Friday. But Gould predicted before anyone else that his efforts would be fruitless. Before the news spread, he had shorted gold, among other assets, using Russell Sage as his broker, and made a fortune on Black Friday. Interestingly, Gould did not share these expectations with his chief conspirator and seemingly closest friend, Jim Fisk. This event highlighted the risks and ethical concerns of market manipulation, leaving a lasting impact on financial regulation (Andrews, 2014).

Sage also worked with Gould to manipulate the stock of the Union Pacific Railroad, where he was a board member. Another target was Western Union, which Gould had taken control of from the Vanderbilts with Sage's help. Sage and Gould repeatedly shorted and drove down the company's price by spreading rumors of impending disaster. After making huge profits, they went long and made even more money as the stock price recovered (Andrews, 2014).

In 1881, Sage and Gould spread rumors that the commuter line was going bankrupt while accumulating stock in the Manhattan Elevated Railroad in New York. Once in control, they revealed that the company was profitable and financially secure. In summary, they first manipulated the price down and made a good profit by manipulating the price back up (Andrews, 2014).

In 1884, Gould had attempted a hostile takeover of Vanderbilt's Lake Shore and Michigan Southern Railroad. Sage was part of the deal because Gould needed to borrow money, and his services as a master stock manipulator were required. This time, however, William Henry Vanderbilt made a counter-move by retaining control of the Lake Shore and Michigan Southern Railroad. Meanwhile, Gould had incurred excessive debt and experienced a sharp drop in stock prices. All these events triggered a Wall Street crisis in May 1884. Everyone wondered whether he could fulfill his option contracts for this venture and get away with it. However, he surprised Wall Street by fulfilling all contracts. According to some reports, Sage lost as much as seven million dollars, but there were rumors that he recouped his losses by short-selling shares (Geisst, 2018).

By 1885, Jay Gould's health had deteriorated, and he was also under increasing financial pressure. By then, he had become synonymous with everything wrong with Wall Street. Sage felt that working with Gould was no longer in his best interest, and he reduced his ties with the evil god of Wall Street. But in 1890, with Sage's help, Gould would regain control of the Union Pacific Railroad. Gould was a very frail man, only 120 cm tall, and he had struggled with illness and indigestion for most of his life. Tuberculosis killed him in 1892 when he was only fifty-six years old (American Heritage, 1989). The Union Pacific Railroad declared bankruptcy the following year. William Henry Vanderbilt died in 1884 and the new generation of Vanderbilts was more interested in collecting dividends and socializing than in financial struggle. The Vanderbilt fortune was so large and solid that they didn't need Sage (Gordon, 1988).

9.3.3.2 J.P. Morgan, Andrew Carnegie, and John Rockefeller

The crisis of 1884 brought J.P. (John Pierpont) Morgan to the fore. A natural leader, J.P. Morgan had founded his own company in 1860. While working with the Vanderbilt family, he thought he could make large profits from the railroad investments he was interested in. At that time, railroad investments were in a complete mess. The lack of government supervision left the market to dishonest players, and railroads became the plaything of uninformed investors and unscrupulous manipulators like Gould, Sage, and Vanderbilt. While sectors such as iron, steel, and oil had fallen into the hands of the great barons, railroads had not yet established a monopoly. When J.P. Morgan entered the industry in 1869, he had a plan and thought he would be successful as an investor by taking an active role in company management. Since the law allowed it, he began to place himself or one of his men on the Board of Directors of the companies he financed. In this way, he not only directed the company's management but also had access to all information about the company and increased his power in the sector. Later, this practice would be called "Morganization" and become widespread in all his investments. Pierpont not only developed and financed a railroad empire of more than twenty companies through restructuring and mergers all over the United States but also attracted the attention of European investors to this sector and raised significant funds (Karan et al., 2024).

As a banker, J.P. Morgan successfully sold a large part of Vanderbilt's New York Central holdings in 1883, and by 1885, his own company was operating the New York Central-Buffalo Railroad line. He reorganized the Philadelphia Reading in 1886 and the Chesapeake and Ohio Lines in 1888. He was also involved in civil society activities in the railroad industry. He showed himself to be an indispensable player in the business world by organizing conferences that brought together railroad executives to pass new rules and monitor existing practices. In addition, J.P. Morgan's banks financed many railroads between 1869 and 1899, especially the street railroads in New York (Carosso & Carosso, 1987).

In the 1880s, J.P. Morgan restructured struggling railroads, brokering a merger in 1885 to end a destructive price war. By the 1890s, he faced rival businessmen James J. Hill and E.H. Harriman, leading to a fierce battle over the Northern Pacific Railroad in 1901, causing a market frenzy (Chernow, 2001). After this battle, Morgan created the Northern Securities Company to consolidate railroad control. Still, President Theodore Roosevelt and the Justice Department challenged the company's legality, citing the Sherman Antitrust Act. In 1903, the Supreme Court dissolved it under the Sherman Antitrust Act, damaging Morgan's political reputation despite no financial loss (Carosso & Carosso, 1987).

Andrew Carnegie was a significant figure in shaping the American business world, particularly in the steel industry. Starting with iron and steel bridges, he later built railroads. Carnegie focused on manufacturing and discouraged market speculation, owning only one stock—the Pennsylvania Railroad. His steel company, Carnegie Steel, merged in 1892. While he was considered a friend to workers, his reputation was marred by the violent Homestead Strike in 1892, where workers protesting wage cuts clashed with armed guards. After a bloody conflict, the strike ended in the union's defeat. In 1901, Carnegie sold his company to J.P. Morgan, facilitated by his loyal employee, Charles Schwab (Vivian, 2020).

John D. Rockefeller, another crucial businessman, entered the oil business in 1859 when oil was discovered in Titusville, Pennsylvania. Recognizing the industry's instability due to overproduction, he sought to replace competition with cooperation, eventually forming the Standard Oil Company in 1870. By 1881, Rockefeller created the first significant trust in the United States, consolidating control of oil refineries and achieving a near monopoly in the industry by 1882 (Harr & Johnson, 1988). Standard Oil's aggressive competitive practices, seen by many as ruthless, and growing public hostility to monopolies, including Standard, led some industrialized nations to pass anti-monopoly laws. Rockefeller was forced to dissolve the trust. In 1914, an incident in Ludlow, Colorado, involving Pinkerton's men against striking workers discredited

John D. Rockefeller, the most powerful man in the world at the time, and his public reputation plummeted. The Ludlow Massacre intensified debates on labor rights and the monopoly power of Rockefeller (Karan, 2022).

9.3.4 The Communication Revolution

The communication revolution in stock exchanges started with the invention of Morse code. Samuel Morse (1791–1872) developed the telegraph, which revolutionized the field of communication and made stock exchanges work more efficiently, primarily by ensuring that capital markets had access to all kinds of news. The telegraph and the subsequent use of new technologies in communications dramatically increased the speed of information on Wall Street and in financial markets, as well as the speed and efficiency of financial markets by enabling traders to react in real time. The telegraph helped integrate different regional financial markets and led to globalized markets. It attracted international investors to Wall Street. Financial services expanded. The telegraph led to the creation of new financial services such as "*ticker tap*e," which transmitted stock prices in near real time directly to brokerage houses. This, in turn, led to a market for speculators thanks to faster access to information. Later, telephone communication took this revolution to a higher level. This has made Wall Street more dynamic and prone to panic and speculative bubbles. As a result, it increased the speed, connectivity, efficiency, and complexity of financial markets, making Wall Street a global financial center. Using the telegraph allowed for cross-border communication, helping the markets of New York, London, and Paris become more interconnected. Information on stock prices, commodity values, and foreign exchanges could be sent across the Atlantic in minutes, facilitating international investments and cross-border trading. The speed of communication allowed for more speculation, as traders could quickly react to market movements. This led to greater volatility and increased opportunities for profit through arbitrage—buying an asset in one market and selling it in another to take advantage of price differences. The telegraph also enabled more market manipulation. Information could be spread more quickly to influence stock prices, as speculators could now create rumors or quickly respond to financial news in ways that shifted public sentiment and stock prices (Sobel, 2000).

London had the initial advantage because it was already the world's financial center before the technology arrived. The London Stock Exchange was the first to adopt new communication technologies, benefiting from Britain's early telegraph network and the Reuters news agency (1851). London's Influence remained dominant in the nineteenth century due to its established infrastructure, connections to colonies, and international banking systems. However, New York's financial sector began to grow rapidly due to technological advancements, industrialization, and the increased flow of international capital facilitated by new communication technologies like the telegraph. The NYSE followed, introducing the stock ticker in 1867 and widely using the telephone in the 1870s. The Paris Bourse was slower to adapt due to its centralized structure and reliance on banks, integrating the telegraph in the 1850s and the telephone in the 1880s (Sobel, 2000).

9.4 The 1890–1914 Period

Meanwhile, a new competitor to the NYSE had emerged. This was the Consolidated Exchange. When it was officially established in 1885, 400 of its 2403 members were members of the NYSE. The main reason why 400 members of the NYSE left the NYSE to form the Consolidated Stock Exchange was the NYSE's refusal to sell sub-lot (less than one lot) shares. From its inception, Consolidated used the most advanced clearinghouse methods at the time, effectively preventing fraud and reneging on bargains (Geisst, 2018). The ability to trade sub-lot shares (less than one whole lot) was crucial for traders because it provided greater flexibility, accessibility, and liquidity in the stock market. Many investors, especially small traders, could not afford expensive stocks. Allowing sub-lots meant stocks could trade at more precise price levels, reducing inefficiencies. Charles A. Stoneham, known as "*Odd-lot Charley,*" was a famous New York stock trader and financier in the late 19th and early twentieth centuries. He earned this nickname because of his expertise in handling odd-lot trading—transactions involving less than 100 shares, which were generally ignored or disfavored by the NYSE. His success in this niche made him well known in Wall Street circles.

During its nearly 40-year existence, the Consolidated Exchange accounted for an average of 23% of NYSE volume, significantly impacting the stock market. Economists note that "NYSE bid-ask spreads fell by more than 10% when Consolidated began trading NYSE stocks and widened when Consolidated ceased operations." This reduction in bid-ask spreads, a direct result of the Consolidated Exchange's operations, had practical benefits for the market. A declining spread suggested better price discovery, meaning stock prices reflected their true value more accurately. Increasing liquidity reduced transaction costs, thus improving price efficiency and making the exchange more accessible and efficient. Despite the NYSE's fierce opposition and its prohibition of its members from trading with Consolidated members, the Consolidated Exchange made a significant mark on the stock market before ceasing operations in 1926 due to corruption and legal problems (Brown et al., 2008).

The post-1880 period in the United States was marked by the formation of cartels, which gradually gained control over all sectors of the American economy. This consolidation of power led to a reduction in competition and efficiency. The influence of the stock market barons during this period led to the concentration of economic power in the United States. This concentration of power gave rise to large trusts, which had the potential to disrupt many markets.

9.4.1 Trusts

In the United States in the nineteenth century, the term trust was defined as a substantial monopolistic organization controlling the market for specific products. A trust was an arrangement in which shareholders in various companies transferred their shares to a single board of trustees. In return, the shareholders received a trust certificate entitling them to a share of the consolidated earnings of the jointly managed companies. All members of a pool of acquired companies would surrender their shares in exchange for certificates issued by a trust. Standard Oil, as a symbol of trust, converted its joint-stock company status into a trust, which gave the owners the right to receive a portion of the earnings and to vote for the trustees who administered the trust. Each shareholder received 20 trust certificates for each share of Standard Oil stock. All profits of the component companies were sent to the nine-member board of trustees, which determined the dividends. The nine trustees elected the directors and officers of all the component companies. This allowed Standard Oil to function as a monopoly, as nine trustees managed all the component companies (National Archives, n.d.). The trust was a predominantly American phenomenon, shaped by the US's industrial landscape, legal framework, and economic philosophy during the late nineteenth century. While other parts of the world had forms of business consolidation, American trusts were a key feature of the country's economic transformation, particularly during the Gilded Age and Progressive Era. The rise of trusts in the United States led to significant debates on competition and the regulation of monopolies, influencing future global business practices.

Trusts in the late nineteenth century grew without issuing new stock, primarily by using holding companies, interlocking directorates, and pooling agreements to consolidate power across multiple companies. The trusts' ability allowed them to grow efficiently, leveraging existing capital and resources to dominate sectors like oil, steel, and railroads. The market did not need to absorb additional stock or adjust to new financial instruments, making the process smoother for the companies involved. This allowed businesses to control large sectors of the economy without public stock offerings, avoiding market dilution and regulatory scrutiny. Their success in dominating industries was driven by their ability to use private financing and coordination strategies, which allowed them to grow in size and influence while maintaining tight control over the market. Trust certificates replaced ordinary shares in these enterprises and were traded on stock exchanges. Since trusts relied on their funds and the funds of the companies they acquired, investment bankers were usually excluded (Geisst, 2018).

However, the passage of the Sherman Antitrust Act in 1890 seriously affected the influence of trusts. This was a landmark US law aimed at promoting competition and preventing monopolies. It was the first federal legislation to prohibit anti-competitive business practices and had a lasting impact on American business life. This law banned trusts or business organizations that "restrained" trade. Any organization in violation could be sued for treble damages, and anyone found to have created such structures could be imprisoned for one year. Although a valuable source for defining monopoly, the Sherman Antitrust Act was not strong enough (Montague, 1909). The Sherman Antitrust Act's vague wording, weak enforcement, and misuse of labor unions made it ineffective in its early years. It was not until the early twentieth century, with stronger laws and court rulings, that accurate antitrust enforcement took shape.

Nevertheless, the first target of the Law was the Standard Oil of the Rockefeller Company. One of the Law's main provisions prohibited all corporate models restricting trade between states or foreign nations. This prohibition applied to formal cartels and any agreement to fix prices, limit industrial production, share markets, or exclude competition. A second key provision made illegal any attempt to monopolize any part of commerce in the United States. These two provisions, which formed the heart of the Sherman Act, could be enforced by the US Department of Justice through litigation in federal courts. The courts and injunctions could dissolve firms that violated the law and be issued to prohibit illegal practices (Britannica, 2024).

In 1892, the Ohio Supreme Court ruled that the Standard Oil Trust was a monopoly violating an Ohio law prohibiting monopolies. While Rockefeller escaped the ruling by dissolving the trust and transferring its properties to companies in other states, the same nine men had to control the activities of affiliated companies. These companies were reunited in 1899 into a holding company called Standard Oil Company (New Jersey). This structure existed until 1911 when the US Supreme Court declared it violated the Sherman Antitrust Act and, therefore, was illegal (Geisst, 2018).

The first robust implementation of the Sherman Act took place during the administration of US President Theodore Roosevelt (1901–1909). He played a crucial role in preventing and breaking up cartels and monopolies through his trust-busting policies. He believed that large corporations (trusts) should not be dismantled simply for being big but should be regulated to ensure they operated in the public interest. His actions against monopolistic business practices set a precedent for government intervention in the economy. In 1914, Congress passed two legislative measures in support of the Sherman Act. One was the Clayton Antitrust Act, which elaborated the general provisions of the Sherman Act and identified many illegal practices that contributed to or resulted from monopolization. The other measure was the establishment of the Federal Trade Commission. This agency authorized the government to investigate possible antitrust legislation violations and issue orders prohibiting unfair competitive practices. In 1920, however, the US Supreme Court applied the so-called rule of reason interpretation of the Sherman Act, according to which not every contract or combination in restraint of trade is illegal. Only "unreasonable" restraint of trade through acquisitions, mergers, exclusionary tactics, and predatory pricing violated the Sherman Act (Tanenbaum, 1993). The decision was in keeping with the business-friendly climate of the 1920s and significantly strengthened corporate power. It was a significant defeat in the fight against big business and would not be the last.

In 1889, when Charles Dow and Eddie Jones founded the Wall Street Journal, the quality of financial newspapers changed for the better. Financial Information was distributed among all investors. The front page was devoted to market news, and the paper promised to provide its readers with facts, not opinions, about the market. In

1896, these two men founded the first stock market index, the Dow Jones Industrial Average (DJIA 30 index). This index included the 30 largest US industrial corporations. It was significant because it provided a standardized measure of stock market performance, increased market transparency, and offered vital tools for investors. Later, Charles Dow became the founder of the technical analysis method with his graphical analysis in the Wall Street Journal from 1900 to 1902, and his approach became known as the "*Dow Theory*" (Sechel, 2014).

9.4.2 The Panic of 1907 and the Founding of the Fed

The American economy could continue its economic activities without a central bank. The markets were destabilized after the 1906 San Francisco earthquake, leading to a massive flow of money from New York to San Francisco for construction investments. In the summer of 1907, money was scarcer in New York, and interest rates were high. In the first nine months of 1907, stock prices fell by 24.4% (Tallman & Moen, 1990). Economic events made the market highly volatile during the summer months.

The trigger of the 1907 panic was a failure by F. Augustus Heinze. Augustus, with the help of his brother Otto, thought he controlled the majority of United Copper stocks. The brothers' strategy involved buying up most of the stocks to gain control over United Copper's available shares, thereby "cornering" the market, which was short-selling United Copper stocks. In this case, Augustus and his brother Otto were acting on the assumption that speculators were shorting a significant portion of United Copper's shares in anticipation of falling prices. They thought that if they raised United Copper's share price, the speculators, who had to close their positions, would be forced to buy these shares regardless of their price and thus make easy money. According to their plan, on Monday, October 14, the two brothers began aggressively collecting shares. One day, they raised United Copper's stock price from $39 to $52. On Tuesday, October 15, when the stock price had risen to about $60, they called on short sellers to return the borrowed stock, but no one bought stock from them because speculators could find plenty of United Copper stock from sources other than the Heinze brothers. When the brothers could find no one to sell the stocks they had bought on credit, the value of the shares they had bought for $39 dropped to $10 within a few days (Bruner & Carr, 2007).

The scheme's failure left the two brothers unable to fulfill their obligations, and the brokerage firm Gross & Kleeberg went bankrupt. On Thursday, October 17, the NYSE suspended Otto Heinze's trading privileges. United Copper collapsed, and the Montana State Savings Bank, owned by F. Augustus Heinze, also declared bankruptcy. The depression became widespread, leading to the collapse of several central banks directly and indirectly involved in the operation. As word spread, other banks and trust companies became reluctant to lend to investors. Soon, loan interest rates soared to 70%, and stock prices fell to a low not seen since December 1900, as brokerage houses could not collect. Panic quickly spread to two other large trusts, the

Trust Company of America and the Lincoln Trust Company. By Thursday, October 24, more than ten trusts could not move (Bruner & Carr, 2023).

Realizing that the market was approaching a crisis, J.P. Morgan met with the trusts and Treasury Department officials, halting the public rush to the banks. Despite the influx of cash, New York banks were reluctant to make the short-term loans they usually made to facilitate daily stock trading. Stock prices were constantly falling. Moore & Schley, one of the exchange's largest brokerage firms, was heavily indebted and in danger of bankruptcy. The firm had borrowed a large sum of money using the stock of the Tennessee Coal, Iron, and Railroad Company (TC&I) as collateral. If TC&I's position were not strengthened by Monday, the crisis would spread exponentially, and many trusts and banks would fail. To this end, Pierpont called a meeting of over a hundred financial institutions at the Morgan Library. On the table was TC&I, which had been offered to him, and if he bought this company and strengthened its financial position, it would be possible to solve the crisis. However, other financial institutions had to provide loans of 25 million dollars. Under Morgan's pressure, the deal went through in the early morning, but there was a chance the transaction would run afoul of antitrust laws. JP Morgan and his friends then went to Washington to request President Theodore Roosevelt's approval. After a brief hesitation, President Roosevelt approved the deal. When the news reached New York, market confidence soared. Newspaper headlines heralded that the crisis was over, and it was already being said that JP Morgan was the most profitable party (Chernow, 2001).

Afterward, J.P. Morgan's growing power drew a rising reaction from the public. Arsène Pujo, a member of the House of Representatives and Chairman of the House Committee on Banking and Currency, had convened a special committee in 1912 to investigate the "money trust," the de facto monopoly of Morgan and other influential New York bankers. The Pujo Committee issued a scathing report on the banking industry, finding that some financial leaders had abused public trust to consolidate control over many industries. The report found that the J.P. Morgan banking group had grown to gigantic proportions, sitting on the boards of 112 institutions, including its own companies and those it lent to (Chernow, 2001). A central bank had to be established. Key necessities of establishing a central bank were the inelastic money supply, lack of a lender of last resort, inefficient banking operations, and the rising dominance of large banks like J.P. Morgan. International competition and political considerations also played a role. In May 1908, Congress began to search for a solution by passing a law establishing the National Monetary Commission to investigate the panic and regulate banking (Miron, 1986).

At the beginning of the twentieth century, although almost every free country had a central bank, the United States did not. While European states could maintain a balance in the economy by increasing the money supply when necessary, the US economy's lack of a central bank made the economy fragile. Woodrow Wilson, elected President in 1912, vehemently opposed "*any plan to concentrate control in the hands of the banks*" (Fed, 2021). Instead of recommending the creation of a single central bank, the new commission called for establishing twenty or more regional reserve banks that would hold a portion of the reserves of member banks and could issue currency in exchange for gold and perform other central banking functions.

Wilson endorsed the idea but insisted on creating a central board to control and coordinate the work of the regional reserve banks (Fed, 2021). Later, with some modifications, a Federal Reserve Bank (Fed), operating under a supervisory board in Washington, DC, was authorized, and after approval by Congress, President Wilson signed the law. The law allowed the Fed to establish a flexible currency, to provide funds to the banking system by rediscounting commercial paper held by banks if necessary, and to supervise the country's banking system more effectively. It would also designate a minimum of eight and a maximum of twelve cities as Federal Reserve cities. As a result, New York became the most important Federal Reserve city in the system (FED, 2021).

9.5 The Comparison of London, Paris, and NYSE Exchanges

Despite their origins in coffeehouses, the development processes and organizational structures of the London Stock Exchange (LSE), the Paris Bourse, and the NYSE differed significantly. The LSE emerged in 1773 as a response to the need to organize the sidewalk trading of government debt, and it did not become a formal entity until 1801. By contrast, the NYSE was informally founded in 1792 and became a formal entity in 1817. By the time the NYSE was founded, the LSE had already established itself as the most prominent exchange in the world. However, from its inception, London's financial market was dominated by banks, while the US market was characterized by a strong presence of corporations, reflecting its market economy. The Paris Bourse was established in 1724, and its financial markets were influenced by banking institutions similar to those in London. Each stock exchange developed following its country's economic, political, and social structures. While influenced by external factors, each is designed according to its unique internal dynamics.

There were significant differences in market discipline and stock market organization; each exchange developed differently. The state had a limited role in market discipline and organization in the early US stock market. It primarily focused on providing legal frameworks and infrastructure support (e.g., railroad funding) rather than direct oversight of stock trading. In Victorian England, by contrast, the market was a constructed, not a natural phenomenon, and was repeatedly reshaped throughout the nineteenth century. The British capital market struggled between free market ideals and the evolving New Liberal interventionism, which refers to a shift in British political and economic thought, where classical liberalism evolved to accommodate a more active role for the state in economic and social affairs. It restricted market freedom to increase the majority's welfare. To some extent, this involved bargaining and compromise between different interest groups (Johnson, 2005). In contrast to the London and New York markets, the government tightly regulated the Paris Stock Exchange. Despite the efforts of various reformers, the architecture of the market reflected its history rather than any rational design (Neal & Davis, 2005). In short,

European markets were not wholly free markets, unlike the United States. This is also reflected in their market organization. In the United States, even though the free market economy led to significant scandals and corruption, historical circumstances helped them to have a dynamic and growing economy, making them the largest market in the world.

The different attitudes toward membership in London, Paris, and New York were also important differences between the exchanges. The owners of the LSE derived their income from the entrance and subscription fees paid by members. As they did not want to discourage members or encourage the establishment of a competing exchange with lower costs, the owners kept their fees at reasonable levels, which increased their loyalty. Regarding the Paris Bourse, the government restricted the number of agents of change, and they had to pay a deposit to conduct their business operations. At the NYSE, members recognized the advantages of membership and were wary of destroying them. In 1868, it was decided to make memberships available for sale so that retiring members could realize their investments, while entry was restricted. In 1868, the NYSE restricted membership sales to preserve its exclusivity. As securities trading surged post-Civil War, the Open Board emerged (1864) but merged with the NYSE in 1869. A new rival, the Consolidated Exchange (1885), created fierce competition until World War I, leading the NYSE to ban dual membership (Banner, 1998). To avoid the wrath of the NYSE, many other brokers remained unorganized, homeless, and unregulated and conducted their business in groups on the street, in the "*sidewalk*" market. Unlike London, the NYSE covered only part of the New York market and prevented the rest from operating as efficiently as possible (Michie, 1986).

Another critical difference between the exchanges was the trading system adopted by each. On the LSE in the early nineteenth century, settlement dates were known in advance every 19 and 20 days. Paris had a month-end settlement created in 1805. In contrast, delivery and next-day payment were the standard trading patterns in New York. It was possible to extend the settlement period, but this extension required the interest payment to the broker holding the stock. This system was adequate for New York's local investment market in the early nineteenth century. However, it created many problems, such as scandals, as trading volumes increased and trading became more speculative (Michie, 1986). Therefore, trading in New York was repeatedly interrupted by the need to deliver securities or to finance cash payments, disrupting the smooth functioning of the market by discouraging technical and speculative trading. Brokerage firms in New York needed constant access to funds to finance their assets. In Paris and London, most brokerage transactions occurred within the accounting period and were not subject to any financing costs. Particularly in London, there was considerable alignment between the securities and money markets. In New York, the daily settlement system tended to exaggerate crises. The short time before payment was due made it difficult for bankers or brokers to take measures to avoid a crisis. Since almost all borrowing was done for day money, any contraction in the money available in the call loan market had an immediate and all-encompassing effect. If stocks could not be cashed in immediately, or if prices fell so low that they no longer covered the loans, brokers could not repay the banks (Michie, 1986). In Paris, the money market (short-term financing) and capital market (long-term investment) were closely linked but highly centralized and dominated by banks.

Regarding commission rates, Paris had the most rigid system, with government-imposed fixed rates benefiting official brokers but limiting market competition. London had the most flexible system, where commissions were market driven and negotiable. New York had a hybrid system with official fixed commissions, but traders found ways to offer lower rates through informal markets (Michie, 1986).

One area where there was a clear distinction between the exchanges was the role of market players. In LSE, there was a division between market makers and brokers. The Paris Bourse also had a clear broker-dealer separation, with Agents de Change acting as brokers and Coulissiers functioning as dealers. This system, unique to France, was heavily regulated and favored stability over market flexibility. On the NYSE, market makers made a market via auctions in securities, always ready to quote prices and trade accordingly, while brokers traded on behalf of clients on commission. The system was designed to ensure fair and accurate pricing by forcing the broker to trade through a market maker rather than offering its price to the customer. At the NYSE, brokers specialized in specific tasks as the volume and diversity of business increased. By 1865, a class of intermediaries called stockjobbers, who traded on their accounts, had emerged. They grew in number and sophistication; some specialized in making a market in a particular stock or stocks at a single trading post, while others roamed the market to trade in a specific group of securities. Under the New York system, to ensure that the broker's client received the market price, the broker had to publicly announce his bids on the market where the stock was traded. In London and Paris, trading occurred in more controlled, reserved environments, where brokers negotiated privately and often relied on personal relationships to execute trades. Thus, unlike the silent bargaining in London, the "*open market*" emerged in New York (Michie, 1986).

As a final difference, exchanges diverged in their listed securities. While New York focused on American stocks and bonds, London increasingly traded global securities. Paris shared some traits with London but lacked its international dominance. The NYSE was more selective, requiring companies to be five times larger than London's criteria. Many city or state bonds were too small for NYSE listing. Despite its strict policies, NYSE balanced regulation with flexibility, expanding through national brokerage firms while curb markets provided liquidity. This adaptability helped it surpass London and Paris. However, reliance on day trading and restrictions on listings deepened financial crises and fueled mergers (Michie, 1986).

This difference affected technology adoption. In New York, founders and members were the same, avoiding conflicts. In London, divided control led to friction, delaying innovations like tape and telephones. The NYSE swiftly embraced new technologies, gaining a communication edge, while London took a decade to provide telephone access despite its more extensive market. By the late nineteenth century, technology helped the NYSE become the world's most advanced exchange (Geisst, 2018). The Paris Bourse cautiously adopted the telegraph and telephone, maintaining strict regulation and centralization. This slower adaptation reflected France's preference for stability over market-driven flexibility. This slower adaptation reflected France's preference for stability over market-driven flexibility.

When the telegraph emerged, NYSE members quickly leveraged it to surpass rivals, notably the Philadelphia Stock Exchange, which lost prominence. Wall Street soon connected to major US cities, setting nationwide prices. By July 27, 1866, a transatlantic cable linked Britain and America, enabling New York and London brokers to trade securities and conduct arbitrage. In 1867, Edward A. Callahan invented the first stock tape ticker, "*a mechanical device capable of printing on a paper tape the prices of stocks sent to it by telegraph from the floor of the exchange*." Wall Street quickly adopted the new machine. The famous speculator Daniel Drew used this machine in 1868 for his enormous speculations. Later in the century, Henry Clews, a prominent Wall Street banker, astonishingly summarized the close relationship between the Stock Exchange and technological innovation: "*Wherever the electric wire has gone, the Wall Street broker has followed*" (Van der Yeught, 2006).

LSE operated under self-regulation, where brokers and dealers set the rules. Transactions occurred through open outcry, with prices negotiated face to face. Membership was limited to approved brokers and dealers, ensuring exclusivity. Formal listing rules did not emerge until the late nineteenth century, though companies needed sufficient capital. Insider trading and market manipulation were loosely regulated, relying on members to govern themselves. The Paris Bourse operated under informal government regulation. Companies needed government approval to list, often relying on influential financial figures. Speculation, particularly in railroads and colonial ventures, drove volatility. Financial transparency was weak, and market manipulation was common. The government played a more active role than in London, approving listings and influencing trading. The NYSE formalized membership by requiring brokers to purchase seats, creating exclusivity. Listing requirements emerged mid-century, though they were less strict than in later years. The regulation was informal, enforced by the board of governors rather than an independent body. Insider trading was also widespread.

In the nineteenth century, all three exchanges—London, Paris, and New York—co-shaped global financial markets but differed in regulation and market conduct. The LSE and NYSE were largely self-regulatory organizations, while Paris had more government influence. Transparency was limited across all three, with stricter regulations emerging due to market abuses in the twentieth century.

9.6 Concluding Remarks

The stock market emergence in the United States was different from that in Europe. A weak federal government and a strong market characterized the early nineteenth-century structure. The common understanding of market mechanisms was primarily shaped by laissez-faire capitalism, emphasizing minimal government intervention, free competition, and self-regulation. Until the early twentieth century, the United

States was characterized by wild capitalism. American business agreed with the poet and philosopher H. D. Thoreau (1817–1862) that "*government that governs least is best*." The state's neglect to regulate the market led to speculators and barons dominating the market. The US economy was based entirely on the free market and invested through corporations. Cartels, significant players, and unregulated financial institutions in the marketplace, rather than the state's power, were the biggest obstacles to reasonably functioning commerce during this period. The nation's decentralized banking led to a fragmented financial system. Due to the prevailing mentality at the time, the First and Second Banks of the United States were dissolved in the first half of the nineteenth century, eliminating federal oversight, and economic regulation was left primarily to the states, leading to frequent financial crises due to speculation, lack of regulatory control, and unstable banks. They did not have an official monetary policy until 1913 because they did not have a central bank. As the railways, industrialization, and westward expansion fueled the need for capital, financial markets were designed to meet these demands, and capital markets grew along with economic development. Interestingly, corporate bonds, preferred stocks, and investment banking rose during this period, and early venture capital-like financing for railroads and infrastructure projects helped new financial instruments to support economic progress. The nineteenth century saw significant crises in 1837 and 1873, with excessive leverage and lack of financial oversight contributing to these collapses. However, the post-Civil War period from the 1860s onward led to the National Banking Acts (1863, 1864), strengthening federal authority and creating a more unified financial system. This was the initial step toward establishing inclusive institutions in the economy.

Although the state intervention partly stabilized financial markets, it was not enough to prevent significant crises (e.g., the Panic of 1873 and the Panic of 1893). By the late nineteenth century, corporate finance was increasingly dominated by investment banks like J.P. Morgan's, signaling a shift toward financial centralization. Without a central bank, the US financial market oscillated from very little regulation to financial oligarchy with the dominance of large financial institutions during the nineteenth century.

Nonetheless, the NYSE became dominant, proving that well-organized exchanges increase investor confidence. Railroad stocks became the first "*blue-chip*" investments, demonstrating the importance of liquidity and transparency. Fraud and market manipulation were so widespread that the public realized they needed to fight for rules against insider trading and manipulation. A significant effort was made to ensure this and to increase market transparency.

During the nineteenth century, England had more inclusive institutions than the United States and France due to its strong legal protections, open markets, and financial infrastructure that supported broader economic participation. New York was catching up and becoming more inclusive over time, while Paris remained relatively centralized and elite dominated throughout the nineteenth century. Despite this, New York provided the best credit access for small businesses, thanks to its decentralized banking system, regional banks, and pro-entrepreneurship culture. State banks helped local development; railroads and canals were financed by private investors, governments, and sometimes foreign capital, creating decentralized and competitive markets. However, the lack of centralized oversight often leads to financial instability, such as bank failures and currency depreciation. As London focused on big businesses and trade finance, the banks of Paris were highly centralized and catered mainly to elites and government-backed industries.

In the late nineteenth century, Wall Street barons controlled most of the financial system. Large investment banks and trusts had excessive influence over capital allocation, making the system less inclusive. The rise of monopolies and banking cartels made financial markets exclusive and favored the elite at the expense of small businesses. The "*Gold Room*" market manipulation of 1869 presented clearly how financial elites could distort markets for personal gain. Insider trading was common and unchallenged until 1906, when Union Pacific Railroad executives were accused of delaying a dividend announcement to buy stock before a price surge (Perino, 2019).

The public backlash against financial elites led to progressive reforms like the Sherman Antitrust Act of 1890 and, eventually, the FED's creation in 1913 to prevent crises and make financial markets more inclusive. Building inclusive institutions between weak state capacity and a powerful oligarchy that favored the elite required significant effort. The lessons from this period shaped future reforms and gradually moved the United States toward more inclusive financial institutions in the twentieth century. A more balanced system leading to the modern regulatory framework would only emerge after the creation of the Fed in 1913.

However, World War I was a significant turning point in the history of global finance. The LSE suspended trade for five months to prevent capital flight and financial collapse, causing uncertainty in international markets. European governments diverted their financial resources to finance the war effort, accumulating massive debt. This economic pressure weakened London's financial supremacy and created an opportunity for New York to rise as a financial center (Sobel, 2000).

Before the war, the United States was a net debtor and relied on European capital to support industrial growth. However, as European countries borrowed heavily from American banks to finance war spending, the United States became a creditor nation. The significant accumulation of gold in American reserves further strengthened the country's financial position, providing the necessary stability for international investment and currency support. On the other hand, the war also undermined the credibility of the British pound as the world's reserve currency. Inflation and debt undermined confidence in sterling, forcing investors and governments to seek a more stable alternative. This transition marked the beginning of US dominance in global finance. During World War I, the NYSE benefited by financing the war through bond sales, supporting industrial growth, and attracting foreign investment. The war boosted US industry, strengthened the dollar, and shifted global financial power from London to New York. Despite initial disruptions, the NYSE emerged stronger, helping fuel post-war economic expansion and the Roaring Twenties.

The "G*ilded* Age" ended because its extreme inequality, financial instability, and corporate monopolies created unsustainable economic conditions at the beginning of the twentieth century. President Theodore Roosevelt actively challenged some of these excesses. He took the first step for a clear transition from the Gilded Age to the Progressive Era, but the financial markets were still compelling. However, another Roosevelt (Franklin D.) would open a new age by saying, "*The liberty of a democracy is not safe if the people tolerate the growth of private power to a point where it becomes stronger than their democratic state itself (1938)*." This would inevitably motivate government intervention, leading to antitrust laws, financial regulations, and labor protections, shaping the modern regulated economy of the twentieth century.

References

Alef, D. (2009). *Cornelius Vanderbilt: The Colossus of Roads*. Titans of Fortune Publishing.

American Heritage. (1989). The business of America. Mephistopheles of wall street. https://www.americanheritage.com/mephistopheles-wall-street

Andrews, E. (2014).The 'Black Friday' gold scandal. *History*. https://www.history.com/news/the-black-friday-gold-scandal-145-years-ago

Ball, T. (Ed.). (2017). *James Madison*. Routledge.

Banner, S. (1998). The origin of the NYSE, 1791–1860. *The Journal of Legal Studies, 27*(1), 113–140.

Black, D. (1981). *The king of fifth avenue: The fortunes of august Belmont*. Dial Press. ISBN 9780385271943

Bowden, E. V. (1989). *Money, banking, and the financial system*. West Pub. Co.

Britannica. (2024, April 19). The editors of Encyclopedia. "Sherman Antitrust Act". Encyclopedia Britannica. https://www.britannica.com/event/Sherman-Antitrust-Act. Accessed 17 July 2024.

Brooks, C. (1995). 'The King of the Alley': William Duer. Politician, entrepreneur and speculator, 1768–1799. *The English Historical Review, 110*(439), 1285–1287.

Browder, C. (2014). *The money game in old New York: Daniel Drew and his times*. University Press of Kentucky.

Brown, W. O., Jr., Mulherin, J. H., & Weidenmier, M. D. (2008). Competing with the NYSE. *The Quarterly Journal of Economics, 123*(4), 1679–1719.

Bruner, R. F., & Carr, S. D. (2023). *The panic of 1907: Heralding a new era of finance, capitalism, and democracy*. Wiley.

Carosso, V. P., & Carosso, R. C. (1987). *The Morgans: Private international bankers, 1854–1913* (No. 38). Harvard University Press.

Chandler, A. D. (1954). Patterns of American railroad finance, 1830–50. *Business History Review, 28*(3), 248–263.

Chernow, R. (2001). *The house of morgan: An American Banking dynasty and the rise of modern finance*. Grove Press.

Cowen, D. J. (2010). William Duer and America's first financial scandal. *Financial History, 97*.

Dangerfield, G. (1965). *The awakening of American Nationalism: 1815–1828*. Harper & Row. ISBN 978-0-88133-823-2

Eames, F. L. (1894). *The NYSE*. TG Hall.

FED History. (n.d.). The First Bank of the United States | Federal Reserve History. www.federalreservehistory.org. Archived from the original on July 1, 2021, and Retrieved on January 7, 2023.

Fed. (2021). *The founding of the fed*. https://www.newyorkfed.org/aboutthefed/history_article.html

Frydman, C., & Hilt, E. (2017). Investment banks as corporate monitors in the early twentieth-century United States. *American Economic Review, 107*(7), 1938–1970.

Geisst, C. R. (2018). *Wall street: A history*. Oxford University Press.

Goldman Sachs. (n.d.). *A brief history of Goldman Sachs*. https://www.goldmansachs.com/our-firm/history/a-brief-history-of-gs.pdf

Gordon, J. S. (1988). *The Scarlet Woman of wall street: Jay Gould. Jim Fisk, Cornelius.*
Grinblatt, M., & Keloharju, M. (2004). Tax-loss trading and wash sales. *Journal of Financial Economics, 71*(1), 51–76.
Harr, J., & Johnson, P. J. (1988). *The Rockefeller Century*. Scribner.
Johnson, P. (2005). Market disciplines in Victorian Britain. Working papers on the nature of evidence: How well do 'facts' travel? (Vol. 6, pp. 1–32).
Karan, M. B., Westerman, W., & Wijngaard, J. (2024). A history of banks. Contributions to economics.
Karan, M. B. (2022). Para Banka ve Finansın Sırları. (Secrets of Money, Banking and Finance): Scala Yayıncılık.
Klein, M., & Calandro, J., Jr. (2016). Jay Gould, the Union Pacific railroad, and value creation. *Financial History, 119*, 24.
Larson, H. M. (1936). *Jay Cooke*. Harvard University Press.
Maccaro J. (2004). Jacob Little, Wall Street's First Tycoon, Mercantile agencies (n.d.). Wikipedia. https://en.wikipedia.org/wiki/Mercantile_agencies
Michie, R. C. (1986). The London and NYSEs, 1850–1914. *The Journal of Economic History, 46*(1), 171–187.
Miron, J. A. (1986). Financial panics: The seasonality of the nominal interest rate, and the founding of the fed (PDF). *American Economic Review, 76*(1), 125–40.
Montague, G. H. (1909). The defects of the Sherman Antitrust Law. *The Yale Law Journal, 19*(2), 88–109.
Murray, R. F. (1958). Institutional influences on the stock market. *Financial Analysts Journal, 14*(2), 15–16.
Musson, A. E. (1959). The great depression in Britain, 1873–1896: A reappraisal. *Journal of Economic History, 19*(2), 199–228. https://doi.org/10.1017/S0022050700109994
National Archives. (n.d.). *Sherman Antitrust Act (1890).* https://www.archives.gov/milestone-documents/sherman-anti-trust-act
Neal, L., & Davis, L. (2005). The evolution of the rules and regulations of the first emerging markets: The London, New York, and Paris stock exchanges, 1792–1914. *The Quarterly Review of Economics and Finance, 45*(2–3), 296–311.
Newbold, J. W. (1932). The beginnings of the world crisis, 1873–96. *Economic History, 2*(7), 425–441.
NYSE. (n.d.). Wikipedia. https://en.wikipedia.org/wiki/New_York_Stock_Exchange. 10 July, 2024.
NYSE American. (n.d.). Wikipedia. https://en.wikipedia.org/wiki/NYSE_American
Poon, M. (2012). Rating agencies. *The Oxford handbook of the sociology of finance* (pp. 272–292).
Perino, M. A. (2019). The lost history of insider trading. *The University of Illinois Law Review, 951.*
Poor, H. V. (1860). History of the railroads and canals of the United States (Vol. 1). JH Schultz & Company.
Remsen, J. (1938). Russell Sage: Yankee. *The New England Quarterly, 11.1*, 4–28.
Scott, K. (1977). The dual banking system: A model of competition in regulation. *Stanford Law Review, 30*(1), 1–50. https://doi.org/10.2307/1228174
Sechel, I. C. (2014). From the history of stock market indexes. Managerial challenges of the contemporary society. *Proceedings, 7*(2), 113.
Sobel, R. (2000). *The big board: A history of the New York stock market*. Beard Books.
Tallman, E. W., & Moen, J. (1990). Lessons from the Panic of 1907" (PDF). *Federal Reserve Bank of Atlanta Economic Review., 75*, 2–13.
Tamaki, N. (1974). The merchant bankers in the early 1830s. *Keio Business Review, 13*, 59–70.
Tanenbaum, M. (1993). The historical evolution of US telecommunications. *Technology in Society, 15*(3), 263–272.
Thoreau, H. D. (1964). *Essay on civil disobedience*. Pyramid Books.

Timberlake, R. H. Jr. (1997). "Panic of 1837". In D. Glasner, & T. F. Cooley (Eds.), *Business cycles and depressions: An encyclopedia* (pp. 514–156). Garland Publishing. ISBN 978-0-8240-0944-1

Tontine Coffee House. (n.d.). Wikipedia. https://en.wikipedia.org/wiki/Tontine_Coffee_House

Twain, M., & Warner, C. D. (1890). *The gilded age: A tale of to-day* (Vol. 19). American Publishing Company.

Van der Y. M. (2006). The NYSE: A conservative or innovative market?. Revue LISA/LISA e-journal. *Littératures, Histoire des Idées, Images, Sociétés du Monde Anglophone–Literature, History of Ideas, Images and Societies of the English-speaking World, 4*(1), 327–338.

Vivian, C. (2020). *Henry Clay Frick and the golden age of coal and coke, 1870–1920.* McFarland.

Wilkins, M. (1989). *The history of foreign investment in the United States to 1914.* Harvard University Press.

Chapter 10
The Roaring Years, the Great Depression, and the New Deal (Early 20th Centuries)

10.1 Introduction

October 24, 1929, at noon, Charles E. Mitchell (Fig. 10.1) walked briskly up the stairs of the Morgan House, a modern fortress-like, flat, thick-walled, members-only club across from the New York Stock Exchange. It was one of the worst days in Wall Street history. Stocks had fallen so fast that the stock market's system could not keep up with the madness. The news was particularly horrifying for Mitchell, the chairman of the National City Company. He fueled the bull market of the 1920s, but now that market was in danger. At the House of Morgan, Mitchell and Jack J.P. Morgan, Thomas Lamont, and Albert Wiggin were waiting for him inside. They were all worried. They went into Morgan's room and talked in detail for some time while smoking and drinking. About two hours later, before leaving the club, they embarked on a stock-buying spree to instill confidence in investors. Jack Morgan, the leader of this group, like his father, Pierpont, had to act as a leader. He knew that all eyes would be on him. The news of their massive stock buying spread through the stock market, and miraculously, the market stabilized quickly. A few days later, Mitchell convinced that the worst was over, told reporters, "I *still do not see anything to worry abo*ut." However, the previous day was Black Thursday; Black Monday and Tuesday followed the following week. The indicators suggested the onset of a significant crisis; the market was now in a terrible state (Huertas & Silverman, 1986).

A few weeks later, when the smoke had cleared enough to assess the damage, bankers and politicians began to blame Mitchell. Publisher Carter Glass, a Virginia Senator, later said: "*If 50 people caused this stock crash, Mitchell is the first one*" (Dent, 2023).

Charles E. Mitchell never forgot his father's advice, "*If you want a pony, you must be its groom.*" He was one of the most disciplined businessmen on Wall Street. Despite being one of the wealthiest men in New York, he worked 12-h days and walked five miles from his Fifth Avenue mansion to the financial district. In 1916, National City Bank, now known as Citibank since 1974, appointed Mitchell to head its new

M. B. Karan, *A History of Stock Exchanges*, Contributions to Economics,
https://doi.org/10.1007/978-3-032-07788-2_10

Fig. 10.1 Charles E. Mitchell (1877–1955). https://commons.wikimedia.org/wiki/File:Charles_E._Mitchell_%28Men_of_Mark_in_Connecticut%29_61.jpg

investment banking subsidiary, the National City Company. City Bank specialized in commercial banking, mainly for the wealthy, but later diversified into securities sales (Geisst, 2018).

After the Great War, Americans invested more, and the Dow Jones quadrupled between 1920 and 1929. Mitchell, the City's president since 1921, helped open 69 branches in 58 cities and launched an intensive ad campaign. One reporter noted Mitchell transformed banks from "*scary places*" into "*department stor*es." The city's strategy combined commercial and investment banking. Local branch employees persuaded customers to move money from savings or conservative bonds into exotic securities or City stocks, vouching for safety. In the 1920s, the bank sold $20 billion in securities, the highest in the country (Geisst, 2018).

Mitchell became wealthy, living in an Italian Renaissance-style mansion near Central Park with his family and 16 staff members. The soaring stock market relied on shady strategies by City Bank and others, including aggressive speculation, selling risky bonds as safe, and insider trading. Banks promoted stock purchases on credit, lending to investors who paid just 10% upfront. Like pump-and-dump schemes, they organized private equity offerings with low participation, selling shares at inflated prices for quick profits. Until 1929, these stocks generated high returns, allowing margin investors to repay loans and keep investing as values rose (Dent, 2023).

"There is nothing to worry about with the financial situation in the US," Mitchell told the New York Times on October 1 as he prepared to leave for a four-week European vacation. However, there was too much speculation and over-leveraging (using too much debt compared to the investors' account balance in the market). When stocks fell, brokerage firms would unexpectedly sell off the market when they demanded more equity contributions (margin) from indebted investors. On Black Tuesday, Mitchell would lose about $14 billion. *"Every day in the newspaper*s," a 1920s brokerage executive later said, "I would see Charlie Mitchell writing something about how well J.P. Morgan was doing," and I thought, "They know a lot more about this market than I do." After the collapse. City Bank had struggled, but it had not failed. Mitchell seemed to have gotten away with it" (Dent, 2023).

Nevertheless, Mitchell would find himself subpoenaed on February 21, 1933, to appear before the Senate Subcommittee on Banking and Currency, chaired by Ferdinand Pecora, in the Senate office building on Capitol Hill. Pecora was a cigar-smoking, fedora-wearing New York prosecutor who liked to refer to bank executives as "banksters" because he viewed them as financial gangsters. Pecora found that the City Bank had not adequately vetted many of the securities he had sold to his clients as safe investments. In addition, Mitchell had admitted to selling National City Bank shares to his wife in 1929 to avoid a massive tax penalty. President Franklin Roosevelt then authorized the banker's arrest for tax evasion. However, nothing came of these investigations into the elites, and Mitchell was exonerated. By contrast, ordinary Americans who had trusted City Bank were not so lucky. During the Senate hearings, one aggrieved investor took the stand and made his case very clear (Huertas & Silverman, 1986).

According to his story, Edgar Brown, who had $100,000, became a City Bank customer after seeing its magazine advertisement. His goal was financial security rather than quick profits. Still, an employee of the City's investment subsidiary convinced him to borrow money and sold him securities and stocks, such as those from Anaconda Copper and City Bank. On October 4, 1929, Brown realized that the market was falling and went to a local branch to unload his entire portfolio. However, according to Brown's testimony, he was *"suddenly surrounded by all the dealers th*ere" and was virtually forced to hold on to his securities. Pecora asked Brown if he had received anything from the money he had entrusted to the City. Brown answered that thousands of people who did business with City Bank and Mitchell could understand: *"Not a dime*" (Huertas & Silverman, 1986).

The story, which is dramatized in the opening lines, presents the most important figure of the Great Depression of 1929. Nevertheless, to understand all the developments, we must return to the story's beginning, the 1920s, and the roaring 1920s.

10.2 The Roaring Twenties (1920–1929)

Everything changed in 1914 when World War I broke out, initially shocking Wall Street. To prevent mass foreign sell-offs, the NYSE closed in July and reopened in December. The war raised the importance of bankers and financiers. They had among the best diplomatic skills in the country and were among the most successful ambassadors and experts of their time. Bankers and skilled diplomats used this opportunity to strengthen ties with the government and, later, the Federal Reserve, gaining influence. Skepticism toward bankers faded, and the 1920s saw unprecedented tolerance of their actions as they learned to act discreetly and shape public opinion (Geisst, 2018). Before the war, one-third of global securities were traded in London. However, by the mid-1920s, the US dollar had overtaken the British pound in bond markets, increasing the appeal of financial markets (Chitu et al., 2014).

While US markets soared with this appeal, Italian-born speculator Charles Ponzi (1882–1949) practiced a financial method in Boston that made his name synonymous with fraud. Ponzi planned to profit from international reply coupons (IRCs) by exploiting exchange rate differences. Purchased at local postage rates, IRCs could be exchanged for stamps in another country, creating a potential profit. Post-World War I inflation reduced Italy's postage costs in US dollars, allowing cheap Italian IRCs to be swapped for higher-value US stamps and resold. Ponzi saw a 400% net profit opportunity and raised money at an interest rate of 50%. The plan was impractical despite its promise, and Ponzi never used the stamps. Instead, he paid earlier investors with new investments, requiring a constant inflow of funds. His scheme, later termed "*Ponzi Finance*" by Hyman Minsky in his Financial Instability Hypothesis (FIH), described a situation where debtors pay interest with new debt rather than income (Minsky, 1992). Even after his downfall, the "*Ponzi scheme*" remained a lasting synonym for financial fraud (Matulich & Currie, 2017).

10.2.1 Silent Cal

The Roaring Twenties began under the Presidency of Warren Harding (1921–1923). When Harding died suddenly on August 2, 1923, in San Francisco, Vice President Calvin Coolidge assumed office. Born in Vermont in 1872, Coolidge had served as the governor of Massachusetts before becoming vice president in 1920. Known as "*Silent Cal*," he was often ridiculed for his naps, but he was far from lazy. Unlike his predecessors, he avoided sweeping reforms, preferring to delegate tasks and leave most issues to the states (Greenberg, 2006).

Coolidge prioritized maintaining economic prosperity. He balanced the budget, cut taxes, and reduced national debt, believing lower taxes would spur investment and boost revenues. His policies inspired Ronald Reagan in the 1980s, and he even posed with his portrait (Calvin Coolidge, n.d.). However, tax cuts worsened income inequality and fueled stock market speculation. Weak antitrust enforcement, deregulation, and margin trading expanded market risks, while banks encouraged speculation with loans. Though these policies led to strong growth, rising wages, and a booming stock market (Coolidge Prosperity), they also deepened rural economic struggles, particularly for farmers (Greenberg, 2006).

10.2.2 Excessive Speculation and Credit Crunch

Liberty bonds, sold in the United States to support the Allies in World War I, were very popular after the war (Kimble, 2006). Bond investment became a symbol of patriotic duty in the United States, and the public became familiar with securities. These bonds helped some sidewalk firms gain a stronger foothold in the market. Salomon Brothers, by then a tiny money broker, seized the opportunity to make a name for itself by joining the sales effort and eventually entered the government bond market full-time. Solomon Brothers would become a major corporation after the 1970s (Sobel, 1986).

Before World War II, bankers directed most of their sales to large investors, leaving retail sales to small-scale intermediaries and bucket shops. In a sense, bucket shops were a kind of small gamble. Brokers ran a betting shop with their clients' money, allowing their clients to buy a stock position with small amounts of money dropped into buckets. If the stock went up, they won; if it went down, they lost money. However, those who put money in the bucket never owned the stock. The broker takes a stock position in his name by borrowing the client's money upfront (margin trading). If his investment earned a return, he paid him back. Dishonest brokers could take the money and run. At the time, some of Wall Street's best-known speculators started in bucket shops (Lefevre, 2004).

It was very popular to avoid taxes by hiding profits made through speculation from the Internal Revenue Service. The most common methods were wash selling, which was explained in Chap. 9, creating dummy companies, reporting fake losses on investments to offset real profits, and transferring stocks or assets to family members in lower tax brackets. Commercial and trust banks were heavily involved in market speculation and lent large sums to intermediaries. When the brokers lent the same funds to all kinds of investors, the financial system became a pyramid of speculation built on borrowed money.

In 1916, the National City Bank of New York established the National City Company in New York to gain a foothold in the corporate securities business and serve the emerging middle class. To do so, they invented the first financial marketing term of the century: the department store of finance. The main thrust of the new idea was to sell corporate bonds to the public. Before 1927, NYSE sales were primarily dominated by corporate and government bonds, with the bond department being the most significant part of the financial store (Geisst, 2018).

In the 1920s, many municipalities borrowed, using the market to meet the growing demand for municipal services. Some foreign governments and companies also entered the market. Borrowers came from both Eastern and Western Europe, as well as Latin America. Since investors bought such bonds by paying in dollars, they were called "*Yankee B*onds" (Coles, 1981).

After the war, the British economy sought to return to the gold standard, which had been suspended at the war's end, in an effort to address its problems, as explained in part four later. As a result, the Bank of England and the Fed worked out a deal to protect Britain's post-war markets from capital outflows. This deal was very beneficial for Wall Street. They would keep London's stock and money markets closed to foreigners and direct investors and companies to New York. That is why US interest rates were kept lower than in the UK, so companies and countries needing money could raise dollars instead of pounds. The deal worked well, with New York's markets soaring while London's was protected. Most importantly, the United States went from being a debtor after a century of being a creditor. However, there were risks in lending to other countries (Eichengreen & Flandreau, 2012).

Initially, curb brokers on the Street avoided formal organization to prevent restrictions from other exchanges. However, in 1908, they formed the New York Curb Market Agency, followed by the informal Curb Association in 1910, which set trading rules. The curb market clashed with the NYSE for years, which dismissed it as a hub for low-quality stocks. In 1911, brokers drafted a charter and founded the New York Curb Market Association. In 1921, the New York Stock Exchange (NYSE) opened a modern building at 86 Trinity Place. Meanwhile, a street market for smaller, undercapitalized companies thrived, occasionally trading more extensive stocks and remaining competitive. This loosely organized curb market on Broad Street in Manhattan, led by sidewalk dealers, evolved into the Curb Exchange, now known as the American Stock Exchange (AMEX) (NYSE American, n.d.).

The American Stock Exchange was officially renamed in 1953. It later merged with NASDAQ, the world's first electronic stock exchange, established in 1971 by the National Association of Securities Dealers. In 1998, they restructured to form the "Nasdaq-Amex Market Group" (Sobel, 2000). This merger was temporary, as the exchanges later separated again. Mergers and separations among United States exchanges continued in subsequent years.

One of the most significant figures of the 1920s was William Crapo Durant, a co-founder of General Motors (Fig. 10.2). After leaving his responsibilities at GM, Durant immediately began speculating in the market and became a legend for his successful speculation. He formed a syndicate of wealthy friends and associates. The syndicate was a pool of investors' funds and became a common way of investing during the bull market. In the months before the crash of 1929, Durant made $50 million in three months speculating. Some newspapers described him as the most successful market operator of all time. However, during the 1929 crisis, Durant secretly borrowed money to buy stocks. Six months later, his $90 million was gone. He would be bailed out if he resigned from GM altogether. His image in the market had changed from "*a genius to a stupid speculator*." Durant was 59 years old and unemployed (The Rise of Durant, n.d.).

Another vital investor of this period was Ivar Kreuger (1880–1932). He built a global match and finance empire through risky investments and innovative financial

Fig. 10.2 William C. Durant (1861–1947). https://commons.wikimedia.org/wiki/File:William_C._Durant_-_Account_of_Flint.png

instruments. Interestingly, Kreuger had a deal with the Hitler regime in 1933 that, for fifty years, he was the only person who was allowed to sell matches in Germany. This monopoly ended in 1983. Kreuger's financial empire would later be described as a Ponzi scheme (Churchill, 1957). Although Kreuger did this to some extent by paying dividends to early investors in Ponzi schemes from his own or subsequent investors' money, he also controlled many legitimate and often very profitable businesses. Although Mr Kreuger had a money shortage, he sometimes paid his creditors twice without asking for the money back, pretending he had no cash issue. Many companies have survived to this day. He was nicknamed "*the genius and the swindler*" (Shaplen, 1960). He was called "*the Leonardo da Vinci of thieves.*" This quote is often attributed to J. K. Galbraith, the renowned economist and historian. A Price Waterhouse report on his financial empire said: "*The manipulations were so childish that anyone with a rudimentary knowledge of bookkeeping could see that the books had been falsified.*" In March 1932, he was found dead in the bedroom of his Paris apartment. The police concluded that he had committed suicide (Ivar Kreuger, n.d.).

10.2.3 Reduction in Tax Rates

In 1919, a powerful anti-prohibition movement had started in the United States. This movement was led by the Association Against the Prohibition Amendment

(AAPA). They wanted not only to repeal prohibition but also to abolish income taxes. In the 1920s, wealthy individuals who owned dividend-paying stocks also paid income tax, after corporations had already paid their taxes. For the rich who owned companies, this meant a double tax burden. These rates were considered excessive by the rich (Geisst, 2018). Meanwhile, thanks to prohibition, gangsters like Al Capone became the barons of their time, selling moonshine across the country. Meanwhile, businesspeople started to develop new methods to avoid taxes. Primarily, the wash sale rule was applied. One person would sell a stock to another at an artificially low price and claim the loss as a tax deduction. He would then buy another stock from the same person at a gain, allowing one party to cover for the other (Scott, 2023).

One of the most blatant abuses of the tax system was perpetrated by Albert Wiggin, president of the Chase National Bank in New York and one of a handful of senior New York bankers who formed the 1920s incarnation of the money trust. Wiggin was known at the time as "*the most colorful and influential figure in commercial banking*" (Klebaner, 2000). He would continue to trade using insider information even after the collapse, making almost eleven million dollars when his status was revealed in congressional hearings in 1933. Executives often sold in collaboration with members of their families, usually their spouses, to avoid taxes. In his history of the collapse, Professor Galbraith noted that "*tax avoidance brought the most respected men into extraordinary financial relationships with their wives*" (Galbraith, 1975).

As a result of these efforts, tax rates were sharply reduced. The combined top marginal normal and surtax rate fell from 73 to 58% in 1922 and 50% in 1923 for income over $200,000. In 1924, the top tax rate was reduced to 46% for incomes exceeding $500,000. From 1925 to 1928, the top rate was reduced to 25% for incomes exceeding $100,000 and then to 24% in 1929. Secretary Mellon argued that higher tax rates narrowed the tax base and that lower rates would boost economic growth. Ronald Reagan would make a similar argument in the 1980s. In 1924, Mellon stated, "*The history of taxation shows that taxes that are 'excessive in nature' are not paid. High rates inevitably put pressure on taxpayers to withdraw their capital from productive work*" (Smiley, 1996).

Stock prices doubled between 1925 and 1928, but many thought the rally was unsustainable. The warnings were not heeded. Before the stock market crash of 1929, economist Roger Babson (1875–1967) predicted a "*potentially dire*" downturn. Still, Lawrence of Princeton and Kemmerer of Yale refuted him, arguing that Wall Street had a bright future (Sobel, 1999). When President Coolidge left office in 1928, prices peaked, but he still declared the market "*a good time to buy.*" Low interest rates attracted banks and corporations, who saw a profit opportunity. With the Fed's interest rate at 3.5%, stock speculators could lend at 12% or more (on margin). Brokerage firms received funds from banks and corporations that lent to them. Banks sometimes formally lent to their subsidiaries because they owned the brokerage firms. Everyone profited as long as stocks were considered good collateral (Geisst, 2018).

Throughout the 1920s, most stock underwriting and trading were still the purview of investment banks. Commercial banks remained tied to bonds of all kinds, as they were prohibited from engaging in equity underwriting if not strictly supervised. However, things began to change dramatically in 1927, when banks were allowed to underwrite stocks (Preston, 1927). After doing so, new stock issuance increased eightfold between 1926 and 1928, while new bond issuance remained virtually unchanged.

In March 1929, the skyrocketing stock market began to fall. The stock market's fall triggered a dispute between the Federal Reserve Board and the Federal Reserve Bank of New York. The Fed wanted the regional banks to raise the interest rates they charged their member commercial banks, thereby reducing lending by member banks to the money market. The New York regional bank, on the other hand, was in favor of a general increase in the discount rate by the Fed to reduce speculation. This disagreement highlighted the lack of coordination within the Federal Reserve System. When the market began to decline in March 1929, Charles E. Mitchell authorized National City to add up to $25 million to the funds used to purchase shares on credit, aiming to stabilize the stock market. The result was positive: the money market stabilized, and the stock market stopped falling. Mitchell had played the role of J.P. Morgan during the 1907 crisis, and a major crisis was averted. His ingenious maneuver earned Mitchell bonuses of over 1 million dollars a year for three years (Wheelock, 1990).

10.2.4 Investment Syndicates, Pools, and Investment Trusts

Three new methods used during this period contributed to the increase in stock prices. This gave less wealthy individuals access to the stock market, and a structural increase in demand led to higher stock prices. The first one was IPO syndicates. As IPOs increased, syndicates expanded, and investment bankers used them more strategically. JP Morgan, National City, and First Nation had a long-standing agreement where the lead underwriter provided the others with a 2.5% stake on favorable terms. When a company or government decides to sell securities, the investment banker leading the deal forms a syndicate of other banks, buys the securities from the issuer, distributes them to the syndicate, and then sells the new issue to the investing public. A second method was through mutual funds. The 1920s saw a boom in investment pools, precursors to mutual funds. Speculators targeted stocks for manipulation, often using debt-funded trades. While technically legal, many loans went unrepaid after the crash. At the Bank of the United States in New York, speculation with depositors' money was so blatant that the institution's investment strategy relied entirely on it. The two best-known pooling operations of the 1920s were organized for Anaconda Copper and Radio Corporation of America. Anaconda had strong Morgan Bank backing. Some of National City's directors, including Mitchell, were also directors of Anaconda. When the shares were first floated, there was skepticism about the worldwide price of copper, Anaconda's main product. In Chile, where the company conducts most of its business, prices were reported to be falling; however, this did not deter National City from launching. Initially, the price rose due to the stock's support, but it soon fell. The consensus was that National City executives were aware of Chile's weak raw materials prices when they launched this issue (Geisst, 2018).

In the 1920s, Sarnoff ran Radio Corp, famous for being the first reporter to report the sinking of the Titanic over the radio. Investors believed the stock price was undervalued and formed a pool to raise the price. In total, the pool would raise just over $ 12 million. After a series of pre-planned glowing newspaper articles, the stock and price rose from $81 to $92. The pool earned almost $5 million for its short-term efforts, while some investors who shorted Radio at lower prices also suffered losses. In this case, the spouses' names were used to avoid any rumors or accusations by investors (Geisst, 2018).

The third type of initiative employed was through investment trusts. These pools of money were similar to what we know today as investment funds or investment companies. Most early US investment trusts in the 1890s were closed-end funds, meaning they issued a fixed number of shares. New share issues or buybacks were rare and unrestricted. The first open-end funds, i.e., funds that did not limit the number of shares, were introduced in 1924 by the Massachusetts Investors Trust in Boston (Rouwenhorst, 2004). Trusts gained popularity during the significant investment frenzy that followed the end of World War I. Managers of trusts used investors' funds to purchase stocks in targeted companies, opening up a world of opportunities for small investors. For a relatively small amount, the investor could invest not in a single stock but in a wide range of stocks. Investment trusts ranged from highly reputable to extremely risky. However, many of them failed at that time.

J.P. Morgan and Company, along with Goldman Sachs, provided financing and organized some of the best-known trusts, which operated as investment trusts. One of the main attractions of trusts was their ability to offer stocks to the public that were rapidly becoming unavailable through other means. Due to the high prices required for many stocks, small investors could not afford to buy a share in some companies, but through the trust, they could still invest in a piece of the action. This way, the 1920s marked the beginning of a consolidation trend in the market. Large conglomerates, especially after 1927, turned to stock offerings to swallow smaller companies. Much of this consolidation occurred in the electric utility sector. The trusts then bought the shares of the holding companies. When a general shortage of stock occurred due to merger activity, existing prices continued to rise. This time, the big bankers brought the trusts together and set an issue price that was always lower than the publicly announced offering price. Many investors also accepted stocks as payment for trust shares instead of cash. Setting the issue price lower than the public offering price and accepting shares instead of money was part of a broader strategy to benefit insiders and create artificial market demand. Issuing shares to insiders at a lower price made an immediate paper profit when the public bought at the higher offer price—this established form of profit-making transferred wealth from ordinary investors to the financial elite. Additionally, bankers generated excitement by setting the issue price low and making the trust appear like a significant investment. Many investors accepted stock instead of cash when selling their companies to trusts because it gave them a stake in the growing trust and made them feel part of a great success. It also allowed trust organizers to avoid large cash payments and retain capital within the trust for future expansion. The investor did not realize that, in most cases, they were indirectly investing in highly leveraged stocks. The stock market, therefore, continued to rise. Investors could divert profitable companies to other investments without selling their shares. The fundamental problem with this type of financing was that it created artificial demand, manipulated stock prices, and transferred wealth from small investors to insiders, contributing to financial instability and ultimately leading to the 1929 stock market crash. Even the famous economist Irving Fisher believed in a strong market based on low interest rates. He did not expect stock prices to fall. Many, including Harvard professors, also failed to predict the crisis (Friedman, 2013). While outright fraud and trust manipulations from the 1920s have been curbed, loopholes and modern versions of stock market exploitation still exist. The financial elite continues to benefit from privileged access, asymmetric information, and market influence, often at the expense of small investors (Friedman, 2013).

10.3 The Great Depression (1929)

In August 1929, the Federal Reserve Bank of New York raised its interest rate by one percentage point to 6%. The market temporarily declined for a weekend and then began to rise again. By early 1929, many prudent brokerage houses, including those of Joseph P. Kennedy, who would later become the first President of the Securities and Exchange Commission (SEC), had begun liquidating their positions. However, trading volume was still high in the winter and spring (Nasaw, 2013).

10.3.1 The Black Thursday

On October 24, Black Thursday, while the Federal Reserve Board was meeting in Washington, bankers gathered at the Morgan House in New York, as in the story we told in the introduction. Led by George Mitchell and Jack Morgan, they pledged $240 million to support stock prices, hoping to restore confidence. While this temporarily slowed the crash, it failed to prevent further declines on October 28 and 29 (Black Monday and Tuesday). The press reported that the amount was more than adequate, recalling Morgan's bailout of 1907. The move partially stabilized the market, which remained flat for two days. Hoover made his famous statement that the nation's affairs were on a sound footing. Within days, however, the decline resumed (Geisst, 2018).

Some bankers tried to make money by taking advantage of the crisis. Chase's Albert Wiggin started short selling during the intervention and continued to do so the month after the collapse. Tuesday, October 29, was an even bigger disaster for the market than the previous days. Whispers of investor suicides were rife. However, this was not entirely true. "*The wave of suicides that followed the stock market crash in the US is part of the myth of 1929*," Professor Galbraith (1975) claimed in his book The Great Crash of 1929. "*Nothing of the sort happened*," he wrote.

The Fed has yet to lack the leadership to impose its will. Many in the financial district looked to the bankers for help, but even they lacked the knowledge and economic power to prevent prices from falling. The crisis exposed the limitations of private banking intervention and underscored the need for more robust government regulation and monetary policies.

The Fed's intervention was debated later due to its limitations. Regional governors set local policies, but some decisions needed approval from Washington, DC. The Board lacked authority and tools for independent action, making coordination difficult. Governors often disagreed, as experts disagreed on the best policy or framework (Wheelock, 1992).

Anaconda Copper was one of those that went bankrupt in the crisis. The market had gained a few points after October 29, and there was a feeling that the worst was behind us. The Fed and the Bank of England subsequently lowered the discount rate to prevent funds from fleeing their countries. Several companies also announced extraordinary dividends at the end of the week to attract investors back into the stock market. However, the reassuring moves were short-lived. In the first week of November, prices were hit hard again by a wave of selling. At the worst collapse, the Dow Jones Industrial Index lost nearly 50% of its value, falling from 381 in September to 198 in mid-November before rebounding to 248. However, the damage had been done. Many Wall Street firms had collapsed, and the country struggled (Geisst, 2018).

Surprisingly, the brokerage community did not suffer as much as it had in the past, but brokerage firms' clients were much worse off. The simple reason was that brokers liquidated their stocks using inside information before selling stocks for their clients, and took priority on sell orders wherever possible. They put their interests ahead of those of their clients. Despite stricter regulations, insider trading still occurs. Advanced technology and sophisticated surveillance systems have reduced its prevalence, but loopholes and innovative ways of exploiting non-public information continue to emerge. In the United States, the Securities Exchange Act of 1933 and 1934 would be the first regulations in this area. Over time, laws such as the Insider Trading Sanctions Act (1984) and the Insider Trading and Securities Fraud Enforcement Act (1988) would increase penalties, and the Dodd-Frank Act (2010) would further strengthen the legal status.

President Hoover, inaugurated in 1929, predicted a short-lived crisis. After Black Tuesday, he urged business and labor leaders to avoid wage cuts and work stoppages. Lowering the Fed's interest rate aimed to prevent deflation and stimulate the economy. However, most politicians and economists, including Hoover, prioritized a balanced budget. He sharply increased taxes on the rich to avoid deficits, raising the top bracket from 25 to 63%. He also doubled the estate tax, raised corporate taxes by nearly 15%, and enacted a two-cent check tax, later seen as a key factor in the severe monetary contraction (Kennedy, 1999).

10.3.2 Causes of the Crisis

There were also more profound reasons for the crisis. By the 1920s, nations had recovered from World War I, with factories and farms back in production. However, economies had changed, with ordinary consumers increasingly buying durable goods like appliances and cars on credit. Borrowing surged, making the United States a consumer society. While this fueled business wealth, it also heightened vulnerability to shifts in consumer confidence. Meanwhile, competition among exporting nations intensified, and war weakened the cooperation needed for a stable international financial system (Richardson, 2013).

Another key factor was rampant speculation. The 1920s boom fueled the belief that quick riches were possible with the right investment. This environment enabled fraudsters like Ponzi and encouraged risky Wall Street bets. Investors bought stocks on margin, putting down just 10% and borrowing the rest. Stock prices soared, brokers profited, and speculation ran wild. By 1932, listed companies had lost 89% of their value, leaving investors ruined and businesses struggling to survive (Richardson, 2013).

The Fed made critical mistakes. Established in 1913, it not only failed to stop the Depression but may have caused it to widen. Between 1921 and 1929, the money supply grew by 67%, lowering interest rates, encouraging borrowing, and fueling a speculative bubble. Typically, overinvestment raises interest rates, preventing bubbles, but the Fed failed as a lender of last resort, mismanaging the money supply and interest rates. Internal disagreements also hindered its response, leading to a 30% decline in the money supply from 1930 to 1933. Deflation followed, increasing debt burdens and triggering bankruptcies. The Fed could have prevented deflation by stabilizing banks or expanding the monetary base, but it failed (Wheelock, 1992). It was an important lesson for the economists. Unlike in 1929, modern policymakers have learned to use monetary and fiscal tools, financial regulation, and other tools to manage crises more effectively, as seen in 2008 and COVID-19.

Another factor was the gold standard. In 1929, the US dollar was pegged to gold, and after the crash, investors rushed to exchange dollars for gold. As the US economy contracted, foreign gold flowed into the United States, prompting central banks worldwide to raise interest rates to counteract trade imbalances. This led to a global monetary contraction, mirroring the US decline, making the crisis universal (Romer & Pells, 2024).

Finally, trade protectionists in Congress enacted the Smoot-Hawley Act in early 1929, when the economy still seemed strong. Only after the Wall Street Crash weakened the economy would President Hoover sign it into law in 1930. The law raised US tariffs by an average of 16% to protect American factories from competition from lower-priced foreign goods. However, the move backfired when other countries imposed tariffs on US exports, and the reciprocal imposition of tariffs by other countries weakened the entire world economy (Richardson, 2013).

10.4 London and Paris Markets Before the Great Depression

While the United States was experiencing the roaring years leading up to the Great Depression, the European markets, which had emerged from World War I with considerable wear and tear, had a different agenda. Between 1920 and 1935, Britain and France had a significant dispute over the gold standard, while the LSE and Paris Bourses underwent a series of reforms to capture a larger share of the booming capital market.

10.4.1 The End of the Gold Standard

Before World War I, Britain and France, along with the most advanced economies, adhered to the classical gold standard, which provided fixed exchange rates based on gold reserves. London was the most important financial center during this period, and the pound sterling was the world's reserve currency. However, both countries suffered heavily during the war, and Britain and France suspended the gold standard in 1914 to finance the war effort through deficit spending and inflation. In 1925, Britain rejoined the gold standard with the support of the Fed, as explained in part 2.2, at the pre-war exchange rate of £1 = $4.86, despite significant inflation and economic decline. However, the overvaluation of the Pound hurt British exports and led to economic stagnation and high unemployment. Unlike Britain, France delayed returning to the gold standard, fearing economic instability. By 1928, after stabilizing the franc, France re-entered the gold standard at a much lower exchange rate than Britain. France accumulated large amounts of gold by taking advantage of its trade surplus and investor confidence in its monetary policies (Johnson, 1997).

Under Prime Minister Raymond Poincaré, France fixed the franc at a devalued rate (1/5 of its pre-war value) before reverting to the gold standard in 1928. This policy made French exports more competitive and allowed France to accumulate gold reserves, strengthening its economy. Emile Moreau, president of the Bank of France, marked the 1920s. President of the Bank of France from 1926 to 1930, Emile Moreau, put France's national interests ahead of international cooperation. Moreau also advocated the accumulation of gold reserves and the creation of a stabilization fund (fonds de stabilization) in the years leading up to the Great Depression. He wanted to make the Bank of France a leading bank in Europe. In doing so, he pursued an insidious policy. When the gold standard was returned in 1928, Moreau launched a covert operation to increase France's gold reserves and made large purchases of gold. However, he tried to keep these gold purchases as secret as possible from the UK and the United States, as he was concerned that these countries might take measures to prevent gold outflows. There were even rumors that Moreau was trying to weaken the gold reserves of the Bank of England by buying gold from the Bank of England. Moreau's strategy was successful, and by the early 1930s, France had one of the largest gold reserves in the world. While these secret gold purchases helped France maintain its economic stability, they caused international financial tensions (Eichengreen, 1992). While Moreau was concerned with ensuring France's monetary stability in the 1920s and 1930s, he considered the Paris Bourse important in the financial system. Still, his main priority was to preserve France's monetary stability and ensure that the country remained strong, especially in the face of international financial competition. For this reason, he took a conservative approach toward the Paris Bourse. The Great Depression of 1929 and the subsequent unstable monetary and economic policy diminished the importance of the Paris Bourse until World War II (Quennouëlle & Cassis, 2011).

In 1931, France held about 30% of the world's gold reserves. In the same year, Britain suspended the gold standard and lost a large part of its reserves, and its gold reserves declined significantly. Britain's overvalued pound sterling made its exports expensive and its imports cheap, leading to a trade deficit. Losing the investor confidence in September 1931, Britain abandoned the gold standard, devaluing the pound and adopting a floating exchange rate. The exit from the gold standard proved beneficial for the UK, and from 1933 onward, a recovery from government spending and low interest rates helped stimulate market activity. After the UK's exit, France led a group of European countries (Belgium, Switzerland, Italy, and the Netherlands) to form the "*Gold Bloc*," strictly adhering to the gold standard (Johnson, 1997).

During this period, France accused Britain of fiscal irresponsibility and feared that devaluations would lead to inflation and economic chaos. In 1933, the United States under Franklin D. Roosevelt abandoned the gold standard, further isolating France. As global trade declined, France and its allies suffered severe economic setbacks. Finally, in 1936, France followed the UK and the United States in devaluing the franc and abandoning the gold standard.

10.4.2 Developments on the LSE and Paris Bourses Between the Two Great Wars

The period between 1914 and 1938 was characterized by World War I, post-war recovery, legislative changes, and economic fluctuations that forced the LSE and the Paris Bourse to adapt to new conditions.

On July 31, 1914, just before Britain entered World War I, the LSE was closed to prevent panic selling and capital outflows. The closure lasted about five months, partially reopening for limited trading in December 1914 and entirely in January 1915. Following the war's end in November 1918, the LSE experienced a brief post-war boom (1919–1920) amid optimism and increased investment in industrial companies. Still, inflation and economic instability soon led to a recession in 1921, dampening market confidence. During this period, the LSE introduced new listing rules to attract domestic and international companies. Stricter disclosure requirements for listed companies were introduced to boost investor confidence. This period saw increased investment trusts, allowing small investors to participate in the stock market through diversified portfolios (Michie, 2001).

Before the Great Depression, the LSE remained one of the world's leading financial centers but faced increasing challenges from Wall Street and economic uncertainties that would shape future market developments. However, while the crisis did not affect the LSE as adversely as the NYSE, it weakened investor confidence and reduced trading volumes. Nonetheless, the LSE continued to self-regulate, and only the crisis of the early 1930s led to increased scrutiny. The Macmillan Committee, officially known as the Committee on Finance and Industry of 1931–1932, was initiated after the Great Depression and the 1931 financial crisis. The British government sought to evaluate the role of the LSE in the financial system, particularly in terms of market stability, speculative practices, and investor protection. The committee criticized the LSE's focus on short-term speculation rather than long-term industrial financing. This added to broader discussions about the role of capital markets in supporting economic growth (Stamp, 1931). The inquiry laid the groundwork for future financial regulations, including stricter listing requirements and corporate disclosure rules. Although the LSE remained largely self-regulated, the government increased its monitoring of financial markets. The recommendations helped restore some confidence in the LSE during financial uncertainty. The Companies Act of 1929 (which came into effect in 1930) was a significant legislation in England and Wales aimed at improving corporate governance, financial transparency, and investor protection. It was enacted in response to financial scandals, economic uncertainty, and increasing public concern over inadequate business regulations in the 1920s. The Act revised and consolidated previous company laws, particularly the Companies Act of 1908 and 1913, by strengthening disclosure requirements, shareholder rights, and financial reporting standards (Cheffins & Reddy, 2023). By 1945, the London market had undergone a significant transformation. Brokers had withdrawn mainly from financing their clients' speculations. None of this happened because a regulator had decided that this was the case, but because the outcome better reflected the preferences of investors and dealers. Before 1914, the Exchange had provided a place for people to speculate on share prices, and its members had also been willing to help by financing their clients' speculations. It was an exclusive club where dealers could hope to make a profit by selling their shares. Now, the Exchange no longer saw itself as an exclusive club but instead recognized its responsibility to the broader community (Swinson, 2016).

The two world wars represent two major turning points in twentieth-century French history. The human and economic toll of World War I was disastrous: a population reduced by almost 7%, a quadrupling of the public debt in nominal terms, a real GDP in 1918 representing only 66% of its value in 1913, and double-digit inflation. Following World War I, which had a substantial economic toll, 10 years of unstable exchange rates affected France. However, the 1920s were the golden age, especially on the Paris Bourse: trading volume increased tenfold, and the index increased 4.4 times between the end of 1921 and the end of 1928. However, the role of the Coulisse was greatly diminished during the two conflicts because it was mainly run by foreign, naturalized, or Jewish intermediaries, most of whom were forced to flee in 1914 and

1939, and because it could no longer negotiate on foreign securities, which had nevertheless traditionally been at the heart of its activity. Furthermore, during World War II, the Coulisse would close for many months from May 1940 with reduced activity. In many respects, the situation in the 1930s was very similar to the period before World War I. After a brief upturn in the 1920s, regional stock exchanges, like the Paris Bourse, suffered financial setbacks in the early 1930s after the great depression. France experienced several high-profile financial scandals after World War I. Also, the regional markets lost some of their autonomy and increasingly acted as branches of the Paris Bourse, sending it most of the orders they received (Ducros, 2018).

10.5 The New Deal and Franklin D. Roosevelt

The 1929 crisis left a lasting impact on the US Bankers lost public trust, capital markets stagnated, unemployment surged, and bank failures soared. It appeared that many banks had speculated with deposits, and executives looted widely. The tension between Washington and Wall Street, which had been brewing since the late 1930s, escalated as politicians blamed Wall Street for the downturn (Geisst, 2018).

One of the most damaged figures was President Hoover. By 1931, his reputation was in ruins. A major mistake was signing the Smoot-Hawley Act in June 1930, which was intended to protect American jobs but was widely opposed by economists. Hoover could have vetoed it, but feared political fallout within his party (Eckes, 1998). While this law has recently been compared to Trump's planned 2025 tariff on China, Canada, and some other countries, Trump's approach was more strategic, selective, and negotiable.

On December 10, 1930, a crowd stormed the Southern Boulevard branch of the Bank of the United States in the Bronx to withdraw their money. According to The New York Times, the panic stemmed from a rumor that a small local merchant who owned bank stock had spread. The bankruptcy became one of the biggest fiascos in US banking history. The bank's Jewish directors, Marcus and Singer, catered to New York's immigrants. They used deposits to buy their stock earlier, profiting from inflated prices. When stock values collapsed, their shares and self-issued loans became worthless. Fearing a bank run, the directors closed it. When New York State Superintendent Joseph Broderick asked to take over the bank's assets, the NYSE reacted negatively. The stock peaked at $91.50 that year and plunged from $11.50 to $3.00. Broderick sought a merger with three banks, but Wall Street banks refused aid, possibly due to anti-Semitism. Antisemitism in the United States during the 1930s was widespread, manifesting in social discrimination, political rhetoric, and organized hate groups. Unable to obtain the $30 million loan, the bank went bankrupt. Governor Franklin Roosevelt ordered its closure, revealing that 400,000 depositors had lost over $300 million. The failure shocked the banking industry, which had not seen a significant and prominent New York bank collapse since 1929. Marcus and Singer were imprisoned, and Broderick faced scrutiny for not acting sooner.

The event deepened public distrust, triggering nationwide bank withdrawals and widespread hoarding of money (Gray, 1991).

Scientific studies of the stock market began gaining traction after the crisis, with Cowles (1891–1984) making the most significant contribution. Few researchers have been as thorough and creative in aiding others. In 1932, he founded the Cowles Commission, funding it himself. Eleven economists from this organization later won the Nobel Prize (Bernstein, 2009). Meanwhile, value investing emerged in the 1920s, introduced by Graham (1894–1976) and Dodd (1885–1988), both finance professors. They argued that a stock's true worth could be determined through research. Their value investing method focused on identifying and purchasing securities priced well below their intrinsic value. Graham and Dodd's approach to securities analysis provided a rational investment framework, emphasizing intrinsic value over price predictions, as market and inherent values tend to converge over time (Graham et al., 1934).

John Burr Williams then revealed how to calculate the intrinsic value of stocks (1900–1989). Contrary to popular belief at the time, the essence of Williams' theory was that a company's intrinsic value was equal to the present value of its future dividends, not its earnings. "*Earnings are merely a means to an end,*" Williams argued, "*and means should not be confused with ends. Therefore, we should say that a stock derives its value from its dividends, not its earnings.*" Just as Benjamin Graham is considered the father of value investing, John B. Williams is recognized as the forefather of dividend investing (Williams, 1938).

10.5.1 From Collapse to Reform

Congress created the Reconstruction Finance Corporation (RFC) in December 1932 to help fix the economy. As an independent federal agency, the RFC was a lender of last resort, providing financial support to state and local governments, strengthening banks' capital, and making loans to railroads, mortgage associations, and large businesses (Sprinkel, 1952). Initially allocated $500 million, the program aimed to assist banks and financial institutions; however, most loans went to large money-center banks. Ironically, many RFC loans were used to repay bankers' debts, deviating from their intended purpose (Geisst, 2018).

The economic turmoil of the 1930s had global consequences, fueling political unrest and unexpectedly leading to the rise of dictatorial regimes like Adolf Hitler's Nazi party. Germany, heavily dependent on American loans, suffered immensely after the Wall Street Crash. By 1932, unemployment had soared to 30%, businesses collapsed, and millions faced economic despair. The Weimar government's response was inefficient. The Nazis that promised strong leadership exploited this crisis, blaming Jews, Communists, and Weimar politicians for Germany's suffering (Roselli, 2021).

Secretary of the Treasury Mills and Fed Chairman Meyer proposed using open market operations to stimulate banks and markets. The Fed planned to inject cash into the financial system by buying government bonds, enabling banks to issue more loans. Hoover supported the plan but failed initially due to weak business activity and low credit demand. He suspected Wall Street was part of an international conspiracy to discredit his administration.

In February 1932, Hoover urged Congress to investigate the stock market, leading to Senate hearings that began on April 11. Over nearly two years, Wall Street's elite testified, including Morgan, Wiggin, Mitchell, Dillon, Kahn, Meehan, and Smith. The first witness, NYSE Chairman Whitney, defended speculation as essential to capitalism and dismissed Hoover's concerns about short selling, arguing it eventually boosted buying power. Short selling meant sellers would eventually have to buy back the stocks they sold, thus providing purchase power to the stock market. In later sessions, Kahn, a partner at the investment bank Kuhn Loeb, took a much more pessimistic view of short selling. Kahn was a prominent figure, appearing on the cover of Time magazine and sometimes referred to in the media as the "*King of New York.*" "*The looting of the stock market, the violent pulling up and down of other people's property, I think, is a social evil,*" he told the committee bluntly. Many politicians and some other bankers shared Kahn's view (Geisst, 2018).

The investigation then turned to pools and investment trusts, notably Goldman Sachs Trading Corporation, accused of exploiting investors. Interestingly, the commission income and interest on margin accounts earned by brokerage houses between 1928 and 1933 were not illegal under existing laws at the time. The financial sector operated with minimal regulations, and practices such as high commissions, margin lending, and speculative trading were common. Despite outrage, outrage grew over brokerage firms' earnings—$1.6 billion in commissions and $325 million in margin interest between 1928 and 1933, suggesting they profited from the crash. In addition, specialists who controlled order flow were found to trade over a third of some stocks, manipulating prices. The public could not accept the market in which brokerage firms made profits at the expense of small investors through insider trading and manipulation (Geisst, 2018).

Brokerage houses and banks were found to have caused significant losses through fraud or deceit. Congress finally passed the Trust Indenture Act (TIA) in 1939, a little-known but still valid law that regulated bankers' behavior regarding collateral for borrowing. Closely linked to the Securities Act of 1933, the TIA protected certain rights of security holders, imposed minimum obligations on broker-dealer managers and borrowers, and gave broker-dealer managers the authority and resources needed to fulfill their commitments to investors (Hayes, 2024).

In the 1932 election, the Republicans lost their majority in the House of Representatives. The new president was Franklin Delano Roosevelt, and a new policy had to be implemented. In the interim period between the elections and Roosevelt's inauguration in March 1933, Ferdinand Pecora, an assistant district attorney in New York in the 1920s, gained public notoriety for successfully prosecuting many crooked stock dealers and corrupt politicians (Fig. 10.3). His exposé of the National City Bank (now Citibank) made headlines and forced the bank's president to resign.

Fig. 10.3 Ferdinand Pecora (1992–1971). https://en.wikipedia.org/wiki/Ferdinand_Pecora (Public Domain)

10.5.2 The Pecora Investigations

The new president, Roosevelt, had asked Pecora to continue the investigation as soon as he took office. The Pecora Inquiry uncovered many abusive practices by banks and bank subsidiaries. The hearings generated broad public support for adopting new banking and securities laws. As a result of the Pecora Commission's findings, the US Congress passed the Glass-Steagall Banking Act of 1933 to separate commercial and investment banking, the Securities Act of 1933 to penalize providing false information about stock offerings, and the Securities Exchange Act of 1934, which created the SEC to regulate stock exchanges (Benston, 1990).

One of Pecora's first tasks was investigating Samuel Insull's Chicago-based utility empire. A former assistant to Thomas Edison, Insull monopolized Chicago's utilities and built an empire across two dozen states, profiting about $170 million pre-crisis through various manipulations. Fearing retribution, he fled the country in 1932 before the inquiry began but later returned and was acquitted. These investigations led to the Public Utility Holding Company Act of 1935 (PUHCA), granting the SEC authority to regulate and break up electric utility holding companies. It would also break up holding companies with more than two tiers, forcing the divestiture of each to become a single integrated system serving a limited geographic area. Another goal of PUHCA was to prevent utility holding companies engaged in regulated business from engaging in unregulated business (Holding, 2005).

In May, Jack Morgan appeared before the subcommittee. Pecora discovered that 20 of the bank's shareholders did not publicly disclose their accounts and that Morgan held absolute control over his partners. Further investigation revealed that Morgan's authority extended into other areas (Pecora, 2014).

Public discontent with investment bankers inevitably affected securities legislation. The main objectives of the Securities Act 1933 were to provide greater transparency in financial statements so investors could make informed investment decisions and to create safeguards against misrepresentation and fraudulent activity in the securities markets. Congress did not allow investment bankers to issue bonds for foreign entities indiscriminately. Roosevelt said in March 1933 (Geisst, 2018):

> The Federal Government.... cannot and should not take any action which could be construed as endorsing or guaranteeing that newly issued securities are sound in that their value will be preserved or that the property they represent will be profitable. However, we must insist that any issuance sold in interstate commerce be accompanied by full publicity and disclosure.

Roosevelt's support for the Pecora Commission upset Wall Street circles and sparked some whispers and rumors of a coup in the public sphere. The matter became even more serious, and in November 1934, retired Marine General Smedley Butler revealed that some businessmen had offered him support to establish an authoritarian regime. This plan aimed to halt New Deal policies and establish a "shadow leader" system that would render Roosevelt ineffective. However, Butler thwarted the attempt by revealing it to the public, and the McCormack-Dickstein Committee investigated the incident. Known as the "Business Plot," this coup attempt had been planned in the summer of 1933. It was linked to some Wall Street companies, including JP Morgan, National City Bank, and DuPont. However, no direct legal action was taken against these individuals. The coup plan was taken seriously, but criminal investigations were not initiated due to political, legal, and economic reasons. Authorities chose to close the case without widely publicizing it, and the incident has been historically referred to as the "covered-up conspiracy" (Archer, 2007).

10.5.3 The Glass-Steagall Law

In late spring, a new bill was introduced in Parliament. It was known as the Glass-Steagall Act of 1933, also referred to as the Banking Act. The New York Times wrote that it was necessary "*if we are to remove from this country the charge of having the worst banking system in the world.*" The most important provision of the Glass-Steagall Act was the separation of commercial and investment banking activities. Banks were given one year to decide whether to engage in commercial or investment banking. Commercial banks were also prohibited from trading securities other than government bonds, which were considered low-risk investments. Investment banks were not required to perform the functions of commercial banks, which would put depositors' funds at risk. The law also established the Federal Deposit Insurance Corporation (FDIC) to insure bank deposits. The FDIC was authorized to insure banks within the Federal Reserve System and to act as a regulator of banks authorized by state governments but not within the Federal Reserve System. At its inception in 1933, the FDIC insured deposits up to $2,500, and this limit was increased to $5,000 when the institution became permanent in 1935. The limit would grow over the years to $250,000 by 2019. When a bank was declared insolvent, the FDIC could assume the role of a receiver and would be tasked with protecting depositors' funds and recovering debts owed to creditors (Alper, 2014).

The distinction between the two types of banking was the real revolution. However, Europe generally favored a universal banking system, and regulatory measures in some countries (especially the UK) will impose a degree of separation later. The need for long-term industrial financing, historical banking traditions, and a preference for a bank-based financial system over market-based models drove Europe's preference for universal banking. However, large banks still engage in commercial and investment banking under the same corporate umbrella, with varying degrees of internal separation. Banks in the United States were not very happy with this distinction.

Jack Morgan opposed the decision, arguing that losing the right to accept deposits would force his firm to downsize, reducing its ability to finance the country's development. While Morgan chose banking, most private banking institutions on Wall Street preferred the securities business. Morgan then set up the securities business as a separate company. That company was Morgan Stanley, which absorbed Morgan's bond and equity business. Chase also divested the American Express Company and its subsidiaries (Geisst, 2018). The battle between Wall Street and the New Deal would intensify as news spread that the Roosevelt administration sought new legislation to regulate the stock markets (Schlesinger, 2003).

Under the 1934 Securities Exchange Act, stock exchanges had to register with the Securities and Exchange Commission. Exchange practices, including short selling, were now regulated. Collateral requirements became uniform and subject to Fed control. "*Regulation U*" was introduced to limit collateral to reduce excessive leverage and potential losses for borrowers and lenders (Fortune, 2002).

In the 1930s, four types of traders operated on stock exchanges. The largest group was "*floor traders,*" who traded on their accounts. "*Specialists*" focused on specific stocks and made markets using their expertise. "*Broker-dealers*" traded for their accounts and acted as market makers. Most traders were "*commission brokers*" who executed trades for clients.

10.5.4 Establishment of the SEC and Joseph Kennedy

The newly established SEC (1934) was an independent regulator of securities markets, overseeing public companies, brokerage houses, exchanges, and over-the-counter markets and registering the securities traded there. It could investigate exchange members and securities issuers, requiring statements from directors, officers, and major shareholders. Companies had to submit financial data, including annual reports, which was unprecedented and unpopular earlier among market players. Firms now had to disclose information whenever selling public securities or acting as investment bankers. With control over investment banking and brokerage, the SEC's leadership became crucial.

President Roosevelt chose Joseph Kennedy (1888–1969) for the presidency on June 30, 1934 (Fig. 10.4). Kennedy was the only member of the SEC with securities market experience. The others were all lawyers with different backgrounds. Kennedy had a background as a stock market player operating in a bear market (Geisst, 2018). Kennedy had established regional offices in New York, Boston, Atlanta, Chicago, Fort Worth, Denver, San Francisco, and Seattle, and by the end of his tenure, the agency had 692 employees. Kennedy adopted a cautious approach to enforcement and began to look into suspicious-looking "*curb exchanges*." As a result, several curb exchanges were merged with other exchanges, and some were shut down (Dallek, 2013).

The SEC also established a national commission to gather information on securities violators. On April 16, 1935, the SEC issued sixteen rules for traders. Some of these included that exchange members would not be allowed to engage in "*excessive*" trading for their accounts, prohibiting the sale of the same stock at successively higher or lower prices to create the appearance of activity, and limiting short selling (Durr & Kinnane, 2005).

Fig. 10.4 Joseph Kennedy (1888–1969). https://en.m.wikipedia.org/wiki/File:Joseph_P._Kennedy,_Sr._1938.jpg (Public Domain)

Richard Whitney, the President of the New York Stock Exchange, believed that the NYSE was perfect and considered any interference a personal threat. Nevertheless, the SEC began by issuing thirteen regulations for registering exchanges in August 1934, including the submission of statistical data on operations, the provision of a constitution and bylaws, and a commitment to discipline members who failed to comply with the Securities Exchange Act. Twenty-five exchanges were approved as "n*ational securities exchanges*" within a month. According to the SEC report, the exchange was dominated by a few floor traders and specialists. The SEC issued eleven recommendations to increase brokerage firms' influence and make the stock market more responsive to the public. None of these rules were mandatory, but Kennedy laid out the principles of the SEC (Durr & Kinnane, 2005).

The most challenging issue for Joseph Kennedy was the Public Utility Holding Company Act. The Utilities Act was intended to ensure that financial structures such as Samuel Insull's utility empire would never be allowed to exist again. PUHCA gave him this power (Durr & Kinnane, 2005).

Joseph Kennedy's priority as president was to restore the health and vitality of the capital markets. The SEC mandated "*fair and full disclosure of material facts concerning securities offered for sale*." In August 1934, the SEC issued interim rules for registering existing securities, which required disclosure from those holding more than 10% of a company's stock, returned insider trading profits to the company, and used only current data. An explanatory footnote was needed for complex transactions. Kennedy also established the "*independent public or certified public accountant*" profession to certify the accuracy of financial statements (Durr & Kinnane, 2005). His short tenure left the impression that he scrutinized Wall Street fraud in great detail (Vise & Coll, 1991).

Joseph Kennedy resigned in 1935 after 431 days in office, and James Landis (1935–1937) became the SEC chairman. As chairman, Landis, who felt that the NYSE was dragging its feet on further reform, pushed hard for sweeping stock market measures that would remove the entrenched power of some of its former members. During this period, it was discovered that NYSE chairman Richard Whitney had begun embezzling to recover money lost on his speculative trades. Whitney became the first NYSE chairman to serve time in the infamous Sing Sing prison for fraud (O'Brien, 2014).

William Douglas (1937–1939) succeeded him after James Landis. Douglas was much more distant from Wall Street. As a member of the SEC, he formerly gave a speech at the University of Chicago expressing his views on contemporary finance and financiers. His words caused Wall Street some concern (Douglas & Allen, 1940):

> The world of finance and industry is infested with termites as insidious and destructive as insect termites. Instead of feeding on wood, they feed and grow on other people's money. These financial termites are predators or practitioners of the art of high finance. They destroy the legitimate function of finance and become the common enemy of investors and businesses. One of the hallmarks of this type of finance is its inhumanity and disregard for social and human values. During his tenure as SEC chairman, Douglas continued to push for financial reforms.

The new chairman, Douglas, wanted the NYSE to have a new salaried chairman rather than a volunteer from the stock exchange community so that floor traders would not influence final decision-making. In the end, 31-year-old William McChesney Martin became chairman of the New York Stock Exchange, with newspapers describing him as "*Wall Street's wonder boy.*" Under Martin's leadership, the NYSE focused on cooperation with the SEC to increase exchange regulation.

Roosevelt's 1936 election victory strengthened his position. Meanwhile, the US over-the-counter market, operating independently of any stock exchange, was largely unregulated. While the most prominent companies were traded on the New York Stock Exchange (NYSE), many smaller or unlisted stocks were traded on regional exchanges or informal markets like the New York Curb Exchange (later AMEX), often referred to as the "*sidewalk exchange.*" The SEC moved to control this, leading to the 1937 Maloney Act. This law created the National Association of Securities Dealers (NASD) to oversee and regulate the over-the-counter market. Nearly all brokerage houses and market makers joined. In 1971, NASD led to the establishment of NASDAQ, now the largest over-the-counter exchange. Douglas also addressed brokerage firms holding securities in escrow for clients. Stocks held in escrow could be lent to short sellers. According to Douglas, this new depository would reduce the number of operations involved in the securities business and create significant economies for brokerage firms (Geisst, 2018).

The New Deal also regulated the residential mortgage market in the 1930s. In 1938, Congress created Fannie Mae (Federal National Mortgage Association) to stabilize the economy during the Great Depression. As a government-sponsored enterprise, it buys mortgages from lenders, ensuring liquidity in the housing market and enabling more home loans. Fannie Mae expanded the mortgage market by securitizing loans and reducing reliance on local savings and loan associations. In 1968, it became a quasi-government corporation owned by shareholders, allowing it to purchase any mortgage, including NYSE-listed ones. In 1970, Freddie Mac was established. With its sister organization, Fannie Mae, Freddie Mac purchased mortgages, pooled them, and sold them as mortgage-backed securities (MBS) to private investors on the open market. The secondary mortgage market thus increases the money supply available for mortgage lending (Federal Housing Finance Agency, n.d.).

Despite banking and securities regulations, J.P. Morgan remained active in investment banking. After 1934, U.S. Steel, many NYSE companies, and utilities worked with Morgan Companies. Democrats saw financial monopolies as still powerful and sought to regulate them. In June 1938, Congress and the President created the Temporary National Economic Committee (TNEC), which included senators who were skeptical of big business. Unlike previous hearings, Douglas assured there would be no "*witch burnings*" (Geisst, 2018).

The government argued that monopolistic behavior reduced production, inflated prices, prolonged the 1929 crisis, and triggered the 1937–1938 recessions. Indeed, six New York firms dominated institutional equity underwriting: Morgan Stanley, First Boston, Kuhn Loeb, Dillon Read, Smith Barney, and Blyth & Co., handling

57% of IPOs between 1934 and 1939. Fourteen other New York firms contributed 21%, while upstate firms managed only 12% (Geisst, 2018).

Even among the top six firms, Morgan's influence remained dominant. Charles Mitchell, who had left National City to lead Blyth & Co., believed the best way to access Morgan Stanley was to open an account with J. P. Morgan and secretly work through J.P. Morgan & Co. Morgan executives owned 50% of Morgan Stanley's preferred stock. Under mounting pressure, Morgan Stanley repurchased all its preferred shares in December 1941, officially severing ties with the bank (Geisst, 2018).

In 1941, the SEC mandated competitive bidding for IPO firms. It also enforced Regulation U, introduced in 1936, to regulate credit transactions. The U-50 rule capped loans at 50% of the collateral securities' market value.

The TNEC held hearings from December 1938 to March 1941, focusing on regulatory scope. A key testimony in the spring of 1939 came from Harvard economist Hansen, a proponent of countervailing deficit spending. British economist Keynes advocated compensatory deficit spending, arguing that full employment required time and government intervention. By then, Keynesian ideas had gained traction, and more economists and New Deal officials supported Keynesian policy. The economy's improvement following the 1938 public spending decision highlighted the potential of such policies to drive recovery (Temporary National Economic Committee, n.d.).

With the outbreak of World War II, the Fed became active in money and bond markets to keep interest rates low and stable, making borrowing cheaper. Between 1941 and 1945, the Treasury issued seven war bonds. During this time, stock market trading shifted from large industrial firms to smaller companies, attracting investor interest (Geisst, 2018).

In July 1944, the victorious Allied nations met in Bretton Woods, New Hampshire, to establish a new monetary system. The gold standard had failed due to war-driven inflation and economic instability, leading countries to abandon it—Britain in 1931, the United States in 1933, and most of Europe by 1936 (Allen, 2004). Moreover, all countries except the United States were devastated and exhausted after the war and had no gold reserves left. At the 1944 meeting, the US dollar became the international reserve currency under the weight of the war victor and the United States, with the most substantial gold reserves. An ounce of gold was pegged at 35 US dollars. Henceforth, the US dollar would be pegged to gold, and the currencies of all the world's countries would be pegged to the dollar. On the other hand, the IMF was defined as an institution that supports economic growth through international trade and financial stability. The meeting also decided to establish the World Bank. The first task of the Bank was to provide loans to the states that emerged from the war, which was devastating and exhausting (Kapur et al., 2011). However, there were still some problems. By 1947, European countries suffered from chronic balance of payments deficits, which led to the rapid depletion of dollar and gold reserves—this hurt world trade. Therefore, in 1948, the United States provided Europe with 13 billion dollars in financing through the Marshall Plan (Bossuat, 2008).

After the post-war period finally ended around 1954, the markets slowly rose. In the late 1940s, the Fed abolished collateral requirements for stock market loans.

Borrowing margins on stock purchases were reduced from 50 to 25% in 1945 and abolished entirely in late 1946.

10.6 The Post-War US Markets (1954–70)

The early 1950s saw a post-war boom unprecedented in American history. Investment soared, and the average American household was financially better off. Demand for consumer goods was booming, and industrial stocks were soaring. The NYSE extended its trading hours starting in 1952. The housing boom that began after the war continued into the 1950s. As the number of investment bankers increased, the price of a seat on the NYSE rose dramatically. Radio stock advertisements also began, and the public started buying more stocks. The Fed would intervene in the post-war money market only to influence short-term interest rates and let bond yields move as they pleased. As a result, bond interest rates naturally began to rise as inflation pushed interest rates higher in the 1950s. Most of the activity in the stock market came from institutional investors and professionals (Geisst, 2018).

However, from even before the 1950s onward, the "*Cold War*" with Russia had begun. With government support, it turned to high technology to develop weapons systems. From now on, the most powerful firms on Wall Street would be defense-oriented arms manufacturing companies. The finance sector was increasingly interested in the defense industry. The defense industry, which had grown under the conditions of World War II, was constantly exploring new conflicts to expand its market after the war. When Dwight Eisenhower, having completed his term as President, said his political farewell to the American people in a speech of fewer than 10 min on national television on January 17, 1961, he issued strong warnings about the dangers of the "*military-industrial complex.*" Although he did not say so explicitly, his position as a military leader underscored that he would find it difficult to resist the pressures of this new and powerful interest group. The war industry could search for new conflicts (National Archives, n.d.):

> This conjunction of an immense military establishment and a large arms industry is new in the American experience. . . .However, we must not fail to comprehend its grave implications. . . . In government councils, we must guard against the military-industrial complex's acquisition of unwarranted influence, whether sought or unsought. The potential for the disastrous rise of misplaced power exists and will persist.

Indeed, the US defense industry has played a crucial role in global conflicts, particularly during the Cold War and wars like Vietnam, Iraq, Afghanistan, and Ukraine. Its influence probably extends beyond supplying arms to shaping military strategy, geopolitics, and the global economy. While wars bring destruction and instability, the US weapons industry thrives financially and strategically. It outperforms the market indices and benefits from the continuous conflict, ensuring long-term profits and political influence (Capelle-Blancard & Couderc, 2008). This raises ethical concerns about whether wars are prolonged or initiated due to industry interests rather than national security needs. Authors such as Chomsky and Perkins criticized the US wars in Vietnam, Iraq, and Afghanistan because they served the interests of the defense industry. It has even been argued that the United States has supported wars and coups worldwide for its economic and military interests and that big defense companies and the government collaborate to promote crises and wars (Chomsky & Herman, 2002; Perkins, 2016).

The booming securities market attracted more and more new investors every year. By 1959, the number of retail investors buying securities had doubled. Retail investors accounted for about 55% of turnover at the NYSE, while institutions accounted for 25%. Floor members traded the remaining 20%. Half of all investors came from New York. Ostracized a generation earlier, by the end of the 1950s, stock market specialists had entered the highest-status group of professionals (Geisst, 2018).

10.6.1 Conglomerates and Mergers

In the late 1950s, investment diversification became important on Wall Street. This was done mainly to protect companies' operations against economic downturns. Scientific work in this area also gained momentum. Investment analysis uses methods from statistics, econometrics, and operational research. Harry Markowitz (1952) started a new trend on Wall Street when he wrote a paper on portfolio selection. He introduced a method of increasing returns while reducing risk through diversification and optimization. Mathematical and econometric methods were now being used in stock market analysis. Markowitz and the scientists who followed him, such as Sharpe and Miller, received the Nobel Prize in 1990 (Bernstein, 2009).

Conglomerates were the products of merger and diversification activities. This trend began in the mid-1950s and would continue into the 1960s. The theory behind a conglomerate was simple. To boost the parent company's profits, an acquiring company would bring other companies under its umbrella, sometimes in entirely different lines of business. If the core business was terrible, the others helped offset losses. The company was protected against business cycles. If business was awful in one sector, gains in the other offset their profits, and investment bankers enjoyed healthy incomes. Some mergers were friendly, others were hostile. They were often arranged by investment bankers who received a fee based on the size of the deal. Because dissimilar companies merged under a single umbrella, antitrust laws generally did not cover them. Powerful companies took over companies whose prices had fallen too low. Sometimes, these companies were broken up and sold in parts (Phillips & Hall, 1961).

Some conglomerates had organizations with significant influence overseas. ITT, the world's tenth-largest conglomerate with sales of around $7 billion in the late 1960s, was very prominent. ITT would make headlines in the early 1970s when it meddled in domestic politics, plotting to overthrow the newly elected Marxist government of Salvador Allende in Chile. Servan-Schreiber (2014), the American Challenge, first published in Paris in 1967, argued that US overseas investment was one of the world's great powers. He suggested that Europe unite economically, welcome any investment from anywhere, and start emulating American innovation and management. In the end, however, the Conglomerates proved not to be very successful for their shareholders in the long run. Many were found to be profitable only after the merger, using accounting methods that tended to overstate the parent company's earnings, creating a consolidated earnings statement. Nevertheless, Wall Street was optimistic during this period.

One of the most significant growth sectors in the securities industry in the 1950s and 1960s was mutual funds. They had not been so popular since the 1920s. Because they were easy to invest in, their growth increased in the 1950s as more investors decided to enter the stock market. However, some of them caused significant scandals.

10.6.2 The Mutual Fund Scandals and New Regulations

In the 1960s, some funds caused a series of scandals. One of them, Investors Overseas Services Limited (IOS), was founded by Bernard Cornfeld, an American businessman. While marketing mutual funds worldwide, including Luxembourg, IOS opened a bank, Investors Bank, in 1963. He set up a complex accounting system and a complex structure of dozens of subsidiaries, banks, insurance companies, and investment funds in various tax havens. In effect, it was a gigantic Ponzi scheme. Regarding the company's workings, the economist Galbraith (1994) said: "*IOS was primarily a gigantic vending machine in which securities dealers recruited other dealers, who in turn recruited other salespeople who recruited other salespeople, who received commissions on their sales. The recruits, in turn, recruited other salespeople who received commissions. In Germany, the pyramid was finally six-fold, and only a fraction of the actual investments were allocated to the securities they still had to buy. All the rest went on commissions. It would be hard to imagine a less financially viable company for investors.*" Bernie Cornfeld saw that the SEC had no oversight overseas, where large sums of dollars flowed around. So he began marketing Investors Overseas Services (IOS) funds to Americans abroad and foreigners looking for a piece of the bull market action. It was claimed to advocate for "*people's capitalism*," a movement that would make everyone better off, no matter how small their investments were. Germans were most interested in this fund. The increase in value was not the only attraction of Cornfeld's funds. The following statement was on the front page of one of his funds: "*The names and addresses of all investors are kept strictly confidential at all times.*" This suggested to domestic investors that investing in an offshore vehicle would allow them to avoid taxes. However, Cornfeld's mutual fund empire would be shattered when a minor market crisis hit in the late 1960s. On the horizon was a white knight who bid for IOS and bought it. This was Robert Vesco, a dishonest financier. With dubious loan deals, people like Cornfeld and Vesco would become synonymous with deceit (Aliber, 1988).

The other scandal involved Equity Funding Corporation, founded in 1960 and based in Century City in Los Angeles. It was a combination of life insurance and mutual funds. The sellers sold the package to investors as life insurance, the premiums for which would be paid with dividends from the mutual fund. As the market rose, the increased dividends would pay for the insurance, and soon, the insurance would be paid in full, ahead of schedule. This idea was used in England but never tried in the United States. Equity Funding Corporation initially made very high profits, and sales soared. Many of the policies it wrote were sold to reinsurance companies. The company was thus able to raise cash to write more policies and spread its risk. Investors were particularly impressed by the number of clients fascinated by the new method. Within five years, the stock had risen from six dollars to over ninety dollars and had become a market favorite. However, the market's deterioration, the stock market's fall, and some underhanded practices would leave the company in financial trouble as the 1970s began (Hancox, 1997).

The situation at Equity Funding Corporation unraveled when Ray Dirks, a financial analyst unhappy with his Christmas bonus, exposed the company's massive fraud by creating fake insurance policies and selling them to reinsurers. The investigation indicated that the company had fooled everyone, including its auditors. Investor losses exceeded $300 million, while the NYSE fell 3% when the fraud was revealed in 1973. Interestingly, Dirks faced harsh punishment for expecting a reward when he publicized the information that sank the company. While the NYSE threatened to bar him from working at any member firm for disclosing confidential information and violating its internal rules, Equity Funding's shareholders sued him for $100 million (Hancox, 1997).

The collapse of mutual funds had significant consequences. First, it led to the creation of Cedel—the future Clearstream—a clearing and settlement company that placed all securities under centralized custody and replaced the then-norm of physical delivery of securities with electronic transfers. At that time, in the event of a purchase or sale, securities had to be physically delivered from the seller to the buyer, including overseas, and payment was usually made through separate channels after delivery of the securities. The second consequence was increased oversight of the mutual fund industry. The third result was the development of accounting and insurance industry standards and significant reforms. In this context, it prompted the SEC to strengthen its oversight of insurance companies and increase financial reporting requirements. Moreover, the scandal emphasized the importance of transparency and accountability in the insurance industry, leading to changes in corporate governance and risk management practices. These events would also result in an important legal precedent on insider trading. This case established the legal principle that persons who trade in material non-public information can be held liable for insider trading, even if they are not themselves insiders, establishing a new legal precedent on insider trading (Geisst, 2018).

By the late 1960s, all market indices had quadrupled in value, the price of a seat on the NYSE had quadrupled, and the number of individual investors was estimated at just over 20 million. One of the significant concerns about securities investments was that market investments were not insured, despite offering higher interest and capital gains. For all its shortcomings, savings deposits in banks were uninsured. Congress addressed this problem in 1971 by establishing the Securities Investor

Protection Corporation, commonly referred to as SIPC. This was the equivalent of FDIC insurance for the securities industry. Brokerage accounts were now insured against fraud or misuse. No matter what happened to the brokerage firms, the accounts were guaranteed to be kept in a safe place (Fons, 1987).

10.7 The Developments on the LSE and Paris Bourses After World War II

The development in the United States had a mixed effect on European markets—while it stabilized financial markets and influenced economic policies, it also maintained protectionist trade barriers that slowed Europe's recovery. The legacy of the New Deal shaped post-war economic policies as European nations embraced state-driven economic models.

The period between 1946 and 1970 was crucial for the development of the LSE and the Paris Bourse. Both financial institutions underwent significant reforms to modernize their trading systems, expand market access, and increase regulatory oversight. By the late 1940s, the London Stock Exchange had not regained much of its pre-war role in the stock market. Moreover, its position at that time had been weakened by either government controls and intervention or competition from non-members. Nevertheless, in 1967, there were more than twice as many companies listed on the London Stock Exchange (3,574) as in 2017 (1,740). The Companies Act 1948 gave shareholders the legal right to vote by proxy and to remove directors mid-term. They would be supplemented by the Companies Act 1967, which significantly expanded the information companies must disclose to the public. In particular, the 1967 legislation also tightened the regulation of related-party transactions, on which company insiders could rely to obtain the private benefits of control. State intervention had now increased; the Labour Party, which had been the party's main advocate in the 1945–1951 campaign for nationalizing industry, had begun to weaken the stock exchange. Nationalisation thus "removed from the London Stock Exchange all categories of securities traded," including the railways, which had been a fixture on the exchange for over a century, and reduced the size of the exchange by a third. According to a new regulation from 1946 to 1958, a company had to obtain permission from the Treasury to raise more than £10,000 of equity capital in a calendar year. In addition, dividend controls, which prevented companies from significantly increasing their payouts to shareholders, were in place for most years from the mid-1960s to the late 1970s. In addition, in 1965, the government imposed a capital gains tax on profits from the sale of shares at a level (30%) higher than in other countries. There was widespread awareness that government policies after World War II were unfriendly to stock market investment. In 1962, the chairman of the London Stock Exchange suggested that the government focus on removing "restrictions and obstacles" rather than "conceiving new schemes which will restrict and hinder a business." The proportion of public company shares in the UK directly owned by individuals fell from 65.8% in 1957 to 28.2% in 1981. The effects of post-World War II government policies on the stock market would have been genuinely dire if domestic institutional investors had not come to the rescue by replacing individual investors as buyers of shares (Cheffins & Reddy, 2023).

After World War II, tape and telephone trading became more widespread on the LSE, enabling faster dissemination of stock prices and market information. This technological change facilitated the participation of institutional investors and increased market liquidity. The unit trust market in England started in 1931 with the launch of the first unit trust, the M&G First British Fixed Trust. This market provided a pool of money from multiple investors to invest in a diversified portfolio of assets by a fund manager. Equity investing became more accessible to the general public by giving small investors access to diversified portfolios. The old building was inadequate when the stock exchange business developed. On 8 November 1972, the building was inaugurated; with 23,000 m^2 of trading floor space, it became the city's new landmark.

The Paris Bourse also underwent significant changes during this period, driven by the need to modernize trading practices and improve market surveillance. The period 1945–1960 witnessed the disappearance of local markets. After establishing the Comité des Bourses de Valeurs (CBV) in 1967, which coordinated and regulated France's regional stock exchanges, standardized trading practices, ensured market stability, and advised on financial reforms. In 1988, it merged into the Société des Bourses Françaises (SBF), which later became Euronext Paris in 2000. First, the action of the CBV, which decided on the listing of securities and allocated them to the nearest exchange, made competition over issuers impossible. These reforms were part of broader efforts to revitalize the French economy and attract foreign investment. The reform, which introduced a single listing system, made competition on volumes impossible: each security is now listed on only one organized exchange. Finally, the creation of the Compagnie Nationale des Agents de Change (CNAC) in 1967, which united all the Compagnie des Agents de Change (CACs) except Toulouse, strengthened the position of the Paris Bourse, putting an end to any possibility of competition between financial centers in France (Ducros, 2018). In 1968, the Paris Bourse began using electronic price indicators to replace traditional blackboards. Telephone trading also became widespread, reducing reliance on the open market system and making market operations more efficient.

10.8 The Nixon Shock and the Markets

On the weekend of August 13–15, 1971, the markets were about to face an unexpected event. On that date, US President Richard Nixon (1913–1994) summoned several of his advisors and the chair of the Fed to Camp David, known as the Presidential Retreat. Federal Reserve Chairman Arthur Burns, Secretary of the Treasury John Connally, and top Treasury officials Paul Volcker and George Shultz were present. Moreover, the only expert from the private sector was Peter Peterson, the coordinator of international economic policy. At Camp David, they were to decide on creating a new global trading and world monetary system. This crucial meeting was destined to be very difficult with Nixon's presence. Nixon was a man who trusted his intelligence more than the intelligence of others. He had a remarkable capacity to read and understand technical papers. He was a gifted president, able to weigh the pros and cons of a problem after retiring to a room alone and writing down the gist of important speeches at length on a yellow legal pad. In Arthur Burns' view, he was a brilliant man who "*held down a chair in political science of law in any of our major universities*" (Wicker, n.d.). Nixon clung to the idea of being "*tough*" and thought this was the quality that brought him to the brink of greatness (Greene, 2011).

At the end of World War II, without a functioning global economy in the true sense of the word, the Bretton Woods monetary system, adopted in 1944, was necessarily pegged at less than $35 an ounce. Other central banks could exchange their dollars for gold. In this sense, the dollar was as good a currency as gold. However, when the Nixon administration took office in 1969, the world economy was booming. Demand for dollars was high, so the Federal Reserve printed too many dollars. As a result, four times as many dollars were in circulation as the amount of gold in the reserves. The dollar-gold exchange rate was still stable at the same level, but by 1971, the dollar was overvalued. This meant that imports were too cheap and exports too expensive. In addition, inflation soared. The Nixon administration was afraid that other countries would ask the United States for gold, and the United States would not accept it. This would have been a considerable inconvenience and would have meant breaking their commitment to exchange gold for dollars. The United States wanted a way to devalue the dollar, but the administration could not do that because it was pegged to gold (Garten, 2021).

Most of the participants at the meeting were respected technocrats. Secretary of the Treasury John Connally was Lyndon Johnson's right-hand man and had served three terms as governor of Texas, so he was an experienced politician. Connally did not hesitate to break the link between the dollar and gold, showing excellent leadership. Paul Volcker, Connally's undersecretary of the treasury, was a technocrat familiar with the international monetary system. George Shultz, who was to become one of the great statesmen of the twentieth century, also joined. He was then head of the Office of Management and Budget. He was a supporter of Milton Friedman's free market view. Shultz did not want a devaluation of the dollar but a free market system like the one we have today, where every currency floats against every other. Peter Peterson believed the United States needed more labor and high-technology investment. On the other hand, Fed Chairman Arthur Burns knew the importance of the Fed's independence, but because he had known Nixon for so long, he tried to ensure it by being close to the President. Nixon was worried that global markets would go crazy if Burns questioned his decisions, so he took Burns with him. While this was a good political move for Nixon, it was not good for the Fed's reputation (Garten, 2021).

At the meetings, Burns and Volcker were concerned about how foreign countries would react to closing the gold market. Connolly argued that doing so would help force surplus countries to revalue their currencies. Shultz favored floating exchange

Fig. 10.5 President Richard Nixon (1913–1994) addressing the nation from Camp David. https://commons.wikimedia.org/wiki/File:President_Richard_Nixon_delivers_his_Labor_Day_radio_address_from_the_Presidential_retreat_Camp_David.jpg

rates that would make the whole issue moot, while Nixon cared less about foreign central bankers and was only concerned about the American public's reaction. After much deliberation, immediately after the meeting, on Sunday night, Nixon went on television and announced that, among other actions, the dollar would no longer be backed by gold (Fig. 10.5). There would be a wage freeze in the United States for 90 days to reduce inflation. The President had imposed a 10% tariff on all imports, which would be lifted only after a new international monetary agreement had been concluded. This decision meant threatening all other countries. It was a show of power (Garten, 2021).

The so-called *Nixon Shock* was met with tremendous approval at home, and the NYSE reacted by rising. The NYSE recorded a record trading day. The Dow Jones index climbed 32 points to close at 889. It had the effect Nixon wanted. Rising inflation and a growing trade imbalance were brought under control. The wage-price freeze had never been done in peacetime. He knew 90 days would not be enough, but it was a way of saying that the United States was ready to take drastic steps to control inflation. However, markets abroad were initially thrown into chaos as the news spread. The United States would send Paul Volcker and John Connally to all the key countries for negotiations to calm their counterparts and international markets (Garten, 2021). Global markets stabilized in a couple of weeks, but the door to a new period, neoliberalism, was opening. Market players would face more volatile and deregulated markets in the new era.

10.9 Concluding Remarks

Between 1920 and 1970, the evolution of inclusive institutions in US and Western European capital markets was shaped by crises, regulatory responses, and technological advancements. The introduction of regulatory agencies, legal frameworks, and financial instruments has enabled greater fairness, transparency, and accessibility in stock markets. By the end of this period, capital markets had transitioned from being dominated by a small elite to becoming more open, structured, and participatory. These developments laid the groundwork for modern, efficient, and inclusive financial systems, ensuring broader economic benefits and financial stability for decades. The New Deal reforms played a crucial role in shaping inclusive capital market institutions by enforcing stricter regulations, improving investor confidence, and broadening market participation. The policies of this era laid the groundwork for a more resilient and fair financial system by limiting speculative excesses and ensuring greater government oversight. Before the 1929 Crash, stock ownership was concentrated among wealthier Americans. Following New Deal regulations, stock ownership gradually expanded; however, the real boom occurred after World War II. By the 1950s and 1960s, institutional investors, pension funds, and middle-class Americans increasingly entered the stock market. According to Piketty (2020), the twentieth century witnessed significant changes in income distribution, particularly regarding fixed income (wages, salaries, pensions) versus capital income (returns from investments, rents, dividends, etc.). He argues that the shocks of the two world wars, the Great Depression, and the New Deal helped reduce income inequality.

However, regulated financial markets also had significant shortcomings. The New Deal was inadequate in fully curbing the power of market elites. Financial elites were finding new ways to circumvent restrictions despite the regulatory framework through lobbying, financial innovation, and offshore banking. On the other hand, many countries heavily controlled financial institutions, often leading to politically motivated lending and inefficiencies. Public sector dominance in the banking sector led to a lack of innovation and competition, while capital controls limited foreign investment and hindered economic integration. Moreover, fiscal policies that relied on public sector borrowing and expenditure sometimes resulted in inflationary spirals. The rigid exchange rate systems that prevailed under the Bretton Woods framework were also seen as untenable, particularly after their collapse in the early 1970s, which highlighted the limitations of state-controlled financial systems.

Meanwhile, influential thinkers such as Milton Friedman and Friedrich Hayek, from the Chicago School of Economics, argued that free markets, rather than government regulation, were the most efficient means of promoting growth and prosperity. The Nixon Shock after 1971, when the monetary system's dependence on gold was removed entirely, created a plethora of money, and ideas on freer markets gained increasing support. This opened the way to neoliberalism.

Since the 1973 Nixon shock, the creation of bank money has increased uncontrollably, increasing financial market volatility. This opened the door to arbitrageurs, short sellers, and other players seeking to make money through speculation. With a solid track record of trading on behalf of their clients with small fees, financial institutions and banks were ready to move in to capture and control a large part of a nearly booming market. A different world appeared in the last quarter of the twentieth and early twenty-first centuries. It was a world where institutional investors were going to be powerful. The financial markets would change from one dominated by corporate managers to one in which money managers would take center stage. From now on, professional money managers would start to decide which instruments to invest in, and investors would insatiably pursue short-term methods that would increase the value of stocks instead of long-term investments. In other words, managerial capitalism, prominent in the twentieth century, would be replaced by investor capitalism in the twenty-first century (Useem, 2015).

Briefly, the phrase "*Greed is good*," popularized by the character Gordon Gekko played by Michael Douglas in the 1987 film Wall Street, would come to embody the excesses and materialism of the era, capturing the aggressive, profit-driven attitude that defined much of the new financial world.

References

Aliber, R. Z. (1988). The rise of the house of Cornfeld—And the fall. In *The international money game* (pp. 272–285). Palgrave Macmillan.

Allen, L. (2004). *Global financial system 1750–2000*. Reaktion books.

Alper, C. E. (2014). Banking act of 1933 (Glass-Steagall bill). *St. John's Law Review, 8*(1), 38.

Archer, J. (2007). *The Plot to Seize the White House: The shocking true story of the conspiracy to overthrow FDR*. Skyhorse Publishing Inc.

Benston, G. J. (1990). *The separation of commercial and investment banking: The glass-Steagall act revisited and reconsidered*. Oxford University Press. ISBN 9781349112807

Bernstein, P. L. (2009). *Capital ideas are evolving*. Wiley.

Bossuat, G. (2008). The Marshall Plan: History and legacy. The Marshall Plan: Lessons learnt for the 21st century (pp. 13–28).

Calvin Coolidge. (n.d.). https://coolidgefoundation.org/blog/president-reagan-extols-president-coolidge/

Capelle-Blancard, G., & Couderc, N. (2008). What drives the market value of firms in the defense industry? *Review of Financial Economics, 17*(1), 14–32.

Cheffins, B. R., & Reddy, B. V. (2023). Law and stock market development in the UK over time: An uneasy match. *Oxford Journal of Legal Studies, 43*(4), 725–752.

Chitu, L., Eichengreen, B., & Mehl, A. (2014). When did the dollar overtake sterling as the leading international currency? Evidence from the bond markets. *Journal of Development Economics, 111*, 225–245.

Chomsky, N., & Herman, E. (2002). *Manufacturing consent: The political economy of the mass media*. 1988. Pantheon.

Churchill, A. (1957). *The incredible Ivar Kreuger*. Weidenfeld, Rinehart & Co.

Coles, M. H. (1981). Foreign companies raising capital in the US. *Journal of Comparative Corporate Law and Securities Regulation, 3*, 300.

Dallek, M. (2013). *The Patriarch: The remarkable life and turbulent times of Joseph P. Kennedy*.

Dent, M. (2023). The banker who caused the 1929 stock crash. *The Hustle*. https://thehustle.co/the-banker-who-caused-the-1929-stock-crash

Douglas, W. O., & Allen, J. (1940). Democracy and finance: The addresses and public statements of William O. Douglas as member and chairman of the Securities and Exchange Commission. (No Title).

Ducros, J. (2018). Rôle des marchés financiers régionaux et concurrence entre bourses: grandeur et décadence de la Bourse de Lyon, 1800–1945 (Doctoral dissertation, Université Paris sciences et lettres).

Durr, K., & Kinnane, A. (2005). 431 Days: Joseph P. Kennedy and the Creation of the SEC (1934-35). SEC. https://www.sechistorical.org/museum/galleries/kennedy/index.php

Eckes, A. E. (1998). Smoot-Hawley and the stock market crash, 1929–1930. *The International Trade Journal, 12*(1), 65–82.

Eichengreen, B. (1992). *Golden fetters: The gold standard and the Great Depression, 1919–1939.* Oxford University Press.

Eichengreen, B., & Flandreau, M. (2012). The Federal Reserve, the Bank of England, and the dollar's rise as an international currency, 1914–1939. *Open Economies Review, 23*(1), 57–87.

Federal Housing Finance Agency. (n.d.). About Fannie Mae & Freddie Mac. https://www.fhfa.gov/about-fannie-mae-freddie-mac

Fons, J. (1987, July 7). A critical look at SIPC. *Economic Commentary, 3.*

Fortune, P. (2002). Security loans at banks and nonbanks: Regulation U. *New England Economic Review, 3*, 3.

Friedman, W. A. (2013). *Fortune tellers: The story of America's first economic forecasters.* Princeton University Press.

Galbraith, J. K. (1975). *The great crash 1929.* Penguin.

Galbraith, J. K. (1994). *A short history of financial Euphoria.* Penguin.

Garten, J. E. (2021). *Three days at Camp David: How a secret meeting in 1971 transformed the global economy.* Amberley Publishing Limited.

Geisst, C. R. (2018). *Wall street: A history.* Oxford University Press.

Graham, B., Dodd, D. L. F., & Cottle, S. (1934). *Security analysis* (Vol. 452). McGraw-Hill.

Gray, C. (1991, August 18), Streetscapes: The Bank of the US in the Bronx; The first domino in the depression. *The New York Times.*

Greenberg, D. (2006). *Calvin Coolidge: The American Presidents series: The 30th President, 1923–1929.* Macmillan.

Greene, J. R. (2011). *Nixon and Ford. A Companion to Richard M. Nixon* (pp. 499–518).

Hancox, D. R. (1997). Could the equity funding scandal happen again? Auditors need to guard against the scenario that led to one of auditing's darkest hours. *Internal Auditor, 54*(5), 28–33.

Hayes, A. (2024). Trust Indenture Act (TIA) of 1939: History and Requirements. Investopedia. https://www.investopedia.com/terms/t/trustindentureactof1933.asp

Holding, P. U. (2005). *Public utility holding company act of 1935.*

Huertas, T. F., & Silverman, J. L. (1986). Charles E. Mitchell: Scapegoat of the crash? *Business History Review, 60*(1), 81–103.

Ivar Kreuger (n.d.). Wikipedia. https://en.wikipedia.org/wiki/Ivar_Kreuger

Johnson, H. C. (1997). *Gold, France, and the great depression, 1919–1932.* Yale University Press.

Kapur, D., Lewis, J. P., & Webb, R. C. (2011). *The World Bank: Its first half century* (Vol. 1). Brookings Institution Press.

Kennedy, D. M. (1999). *Freedom from fear: The American people in depression and war, 1929–1945.* Oxford University Press. ISBN 978-0195038347

Kimble, J. J. (2006). *Mobilizing the home front: War bonds and domestic propaganda* (Vol. 15). Texas A&M University Press.

Klebaner, B. J. (2000). Wiggin, Albert Henry (1868–1951), banker. *American national biography.* Retrieved January 18, 2023, from https://doi.org/10.1093/anb/9780198606697.article.1001751

Lefevre, E. (2004). *Reminiscences of a stock operator* (Vol. 175). Wiley.

Matulich, S., & Currie, D. M. (2017). Charles Ponzi. In *The handbook of frauds, scams, and swindles.* Routledge.

Markowitz, H. (1952). Portfolio selection. *Journal of Finance, 7*, 77–91.

Minsky, H. P. (1992). The financial instability hypothesis (No. 74). Working paper.
Michie, R. (2001). *The LSE: A history*. Oxford University Press.
Nasaw, D. (2013). *The Patriarch: The remarkable life and turbulent times of Joseph P*. Penguin.
National Archives. (n.d.). *President Dwight D. Eisenhower's Farewell Address (1961)*. https://www.archives.gov/milestone-documents/president-dwight-d-eisenhowers-farewell-address
NYSE American. (n.d.). Wikipedia. https://en.wikipedia.org/wiki/NYSE_American
O'Brien, J. (2014). *The triumph, tragedy, and lost legacy of James M Landis: A life on fire*. Bloomsbury Publishing.
Pecora, F. (2014). *Wall street under oath: The story of our modern money changers*. Graymalkin Media.
Perkins, J. (2016). *Confessions of an economic hit man*. Berrett-Koehler Publishers.
Phillips, C. F., Jr., & Hall, G. R. (1961). Merger litigation, 1951–1960. *Antitrust Bulletin, 6*, 19.
Piketty, T. (2020). *Capital and ideology*. Harvard University Press.
Preston, H. H. (1927). The McFadden banking act. *The American Economic Review, 17*(2), 201–218.
Quennouëlle-Corre, L., & Cassis, Y. (Eds.). (2011). *Financial centres and international capital flows in the nineteenth and twentieth centuries*. Oxford University Press.
Richardson, G. (2013). Banking crisis and the Federal Reserve as a lender of last resort during the great depression. *NBER Reporter, 3*, 7–10.
Romer, C. D., & Pells, R. H. (2024, July 02). *Great depression*. Encyclopedia Britannica. https://www.britannica.com/event/Great-Depression. Accessed 18 July 2024.
Roselli, A. (2021). Hyperinflation, depression, and the rise of Adolf Hitler. *Economic Affairs, 41*(2), 300–308.
Rouwenhorst, K. G. (2004). *The origins of mutual funds*. Available at SSRN 636146.
Schlesinger, A. M. (2003). *The coming of the new deal: The age of Roosevelt, 1933–1935* (Vol. 2). Houghton Mifflin Harcourt.
Scott, G. (2023). Investopedia. https://www.investopedia.com/terms/w/washsale.asp
Servan-Schreiber, J. J. (2014). *The American challenge*. Versilio.
Shaplen, R. (1960). *Kreuger, genius and swindler*. Alfred A. Knopf Inc.
Smiley, G. (1996). Cutting marginal tax rates: Evidence from the 1920s. *Freeman-New York-Foundation for Economic Education, 46*, 674–677.
Sobel, R. (1986). *Salomon Brothers, 1910–1985: Advancing to leadership*. Salomon Brothers.
Sobel, R. (1999). *Panic on wall street: A history of America's financial disasters*. Beard Books.
Sobel, R. (2000). *AMEX: A history of the American stock exchange*. Beard Books.
Sprinkel, B. W. (1952). Economic consequences of the operations of the reconstruction finance corporation. *The Journal of Business of the University of Chicago, 25*(4), 211–224.
Stamp, J. C. (1931). The report of the Macmillan Committee. *The Economic Journal, 41*(163), 424–435.
Swinson, C. (2016). Share Trading and the LSE 1914–1945: The Dawn of Regulation (Doctoral dissertation, Durham University).
Temporary National Economic Committee. (n.d.). Encyclopedia of the Great Depression. Encyclopedia.com. 12 July 2024. https://www.encyclopedia.com
The Rise of Durant. (n.d.). GM. https://www.gm.com/heritage/durant
Useem, M. (2015). Investor capitalism. *Wiley encyclopedia of management*, 1–2.
Vise, D. A., & Coll, S. (1991). *Eagle on the street: Based on the Pulitzer Prize-winning Account of the SEC's battle with wall street*. Collier books.
Wheelock, D. C. (1990). Member bank borrowing and the Fed's contractionary monetary policy during the great depression. *Journal of Money, Credit and Banking, 22*(4), 409–426.
Wheelock, D. C. (1992). Monetary policy in the Great Depression: What the Fed did, and why. *Federal Reserve Bank of St. Louis Review, 74*(2), 3–28.
Wicker, T. (n.d.). RICHARD M. NIXON. Essays. https://www.pbs.org/newshour/spc/character/essays/nixon.html
Williams, J. B. (1938). *The theory of investment value*. Harvard University Press.

Chapter 11
The Post-bretton Woods Era and Financial Scandals (20th–21st Centuries)

11.1 Introduction

The trial of former Enron Chairman and CEO Kenneth Lay and Jeffrey Skilling began on January 30, 2006. In the eleventh week of the trial, Jeffrey Skilling, who took the stand as the defendant, showed no trace of the arrogance and bullying behavior he had exhibited when he ran Enron (Fig. 11.1). Skilling, who once believed the world existed for him, was extremely humble. He even told the jury that he had been admitted to Harvard Business School "*was a big mistake*." Later, speaking like a business professor, he delivered a mini-seminar on Enron's business and the gas and electricity markets to the jurors. "*I am innocent*," he said at his previous trial. He said he had resigned abruptly a few months before Enron collapsed because he needed time for his neglected family. It certainly was not because he knew a catastrophe was coming. Daniel Petrocelli's lawyer inquired whether there were any indications that Enron would collapse in a scandal less than four months later. "*Not in my wildest dreams, no. What happened is now almost inconceivable*," the former CEO said. "Would you have left if you thought the company would experience the events that later unfolded?" Petrocelli asked. "*No*," Skilling replied firmly (Linder, n.d.).

The trial of Enron's founder, Kenneth Lay, and some of its top executives was at the top of the US agenda. The defendants were accused of fraudulent accounting practices and repeatedly lying to investors and employees about Enron's financial health. They allegedly transferred Enron's loss-making projects to more than a thousand subsidiaries. They were suspicious about establishing an accounting system that only recognized profitable transactions in Enron's books, boosting its stock price. Among the accusers was Andrew Fastow, the company's former Chief Financial Officer, who struck a deal with prosecutors. In December 2001, Enron, once the most admired and prominent company in the US natural gas market, announced unprecedented losses and initiated bankruptcy proceedings six weeks after intense scrutiny by regulators revealed a massive reduction in equity (Thomas, 2002).

M. B. Karan, *A History of Stock Exchanges*, Contributions to Economics,
https://doi.org/10.1007/978-3-032-07788-2_11

Fig. 11.1 Enron CEO, Jeff Skilling. https://en.wikipedia.org/wiki/Jeffrey_Skilling#/media/File:Jeffrey_Skilling_mug_shot.jpg (Public Domain)

Skilling and Lay blamed former Enron CFO Andrew Fastow and said there was no fraud apart from some corruption by a few individuals. That bad publicity and a loss of market confidence had doomed the company to failure. "I know of no reason why Enron would resort to fraud," Skilling said (Thomas, 2002).

When it was revealed that its advice had deepened the scandal, Andersen, which had served as an advisor and auditor to Enron and was one of the five largest consulting firms in the world, could no longer continue its operations. At the time, Enron, one of the most important companies on Wall Street, was the biggest bankruptcy in US history and its most significant audit failure. As a result, many Enron executives were indicted on various charges and sentenced to prison. Skilling was initially sentenced to more than 24 years in jail, but would ultimately serve only 12 years. Kenneth Lay died of a heart attack before he was convicted (Thomas, 2002).

The most important question was why such an important company had systematically manipulated its financial statements, how executives could receive high salaries when things were going badly, and why its value had suddenly almost disappeared. Enron was not alone in this. It was followed by companies like Worldcom, Adelphia, Xerox, and Tyco. In the 1970s, the exit from the gold system after the Nixon Shock and a series of developments that followed made markets much more volatile and changed both regulations and the expectations of the securities market. In 2001, the financial scandals that erupted in the United States were to change the usual patterns of the capital market and the stock market. With this event, the stock market rules would change, and a new wave of regulation would come.

11.2 The Post-Bretton Woods Era

By late 1972, world money markets were in a very unsettled state following an exit from the Bretton Woods monetary system of stable foreign exchange rates. In particular, the state of the dollar had triggered the most severe wave of inflation since World War II, followed by a major crisis in the British banking system as the pound depreciated. Meanwhile, when the Organization of the Petroleum Exporting Countries (OPEC) suddenly raised oil prices by 300% in early 1973, the crisis deepened and shocked the world's economies. Industrial democracies, accustomed to uninterrupted supplies of cheap, imported oil, were soon in serious economic trouble. As the stock market plunged into recession, companies borrowed by issuing bonds, adding to the unfolding debt explosion. As interest rates rose, the debt explosion was compounded by an inflationary spiral. This combination created a new set of problems on Wall Street, which faced significant structural changes in its business.

The corporate debt explosion had a scientific basis. In 1958, US professors Franco Modigliani and Merton Miller (M&M) developed a theory that sparked decades of debate on firms' capital structure. Their main idea was that, without taxes, a company's capital structure does not affect its value, even if entirely financed by debt. This view fueled the 1970s borrowing frenzy. Modigliani and Miller later won the Nobel Prize for this and other work. Their second hypothesis was that borrowing increases the firm's value in a world with taxes. This theory eroded equity's importance and boosted debt financing (Modigliani & Miller, 1963). Firms asked, "*If equity is not crucial, why not raise debt and shareholder returns*?" Other economists later legitimized corporate borrowing, seeing debt as a tool for discipline and economic dynamism (Jensen & Meckling, 2019). Since the 1970s, US corporations and the country became debtors, and by 1986, the United States was the world's second most indebted nation after Brazil (Zysman, 1987).

The debate over NYSE broker commissions, which began in the 1960s, continued into the 1970s. Advocates of competitive rates pushed for freely negotiated commissions, while most NYSE members favored fixed rates. Eventually, the NASD launched NASDAQ, an automated quotation system that allowed market makers to post prices nationwide, creating a virtual quoted market for unlisted securities. NASDAQ's flexible commissions impacted the NYSE, leading to the May 1, 1975, shift from fixed to negotiated commissions, fostering a more competitive environment (Geisst, 2018). This spurred stock ownership growth, mutual fund expansion, and frequent trading. Rising brokerage volumes enabled low-cost and zero-commission online trading. Index funds emerged in the 1970s, later joined by zero-commission Exchange-traded Funds (ETFs) (Duca, 2005).

Meanwhile, derivatives markets also expanded, adapting to the volatile market conditions of the post-Bretton era. Futures contracts had long been traded by specialized firms, with the Chicago Board of Trade (CBOT) leading in agricultural and metal contracts. In 1971, the Chicago Mercantile Exchange (CME) International Monetary Market (IMM) introduced currency futures, pioneering financial futures. In 1973, CBOT launched a stock options market, prompting Amex to follow suit. By 1975, IMM added Treasury bill futures, giving rise to interest rate futures. Initially used for hedging, derivatives soon became tools for speculation. Chicago dominated the derivatives market, but in 1980, the NYSE launched the New York Futures Exchange (NYFE), which struggled against the Chicago exchanges. Amex became the second-largest options exchange after the CBOE. As markets evolved, the risk increased (Geisst, 2018; Weber, 2009).

The post-Bretton Woods era also impacted European economies. In 1979, the EEC created the European Monetary System (EMS) to stabilize exchange rates and enhance monetary cooperation. Concerned about currency instability, Giscard d'Estaing, the president of France, and Helmut Schmidt, the chancellor of West Germany, led the formation. The euro bond market emerged in England, and European economies adapted to floating exchange rates, inflation, and deregulation. This period accelerated monetary integration in Europe.

11.3 Post-Bretton Woods Era in London and Paris Markets

11.3.1 Emergence of the Euro Bond Market and LSE

In the 1960s, it was tough for foreigners to hold dollar accounts in the United States, mainly because of tax regulations. There were calls for an offshore market for dollars. While the United States was having these discussions, the London market, which had been losing power against the United States since World War I, wanted to take advantage of this situation as an opportunity. The UK government was open to establishing such a market if the dollar was created as an offshore market outside the British banking system. The UK recognized this potential and opened its offshore dollar market by lifting currency exchange restrictions. Markets were turning to strategies suitable for the volatile foreign exchange market.

In 1956, the Soviet Union's intervention in Hungary led to an unexpected financial shift. Fearing US confiscation of their dollars, the Russians moved funds to European banks, with a French bank accepting deposits, marking the birth of the Eurodollar market. By 1963, a British merchant bank, S.G. Warburg, launched the first Eurobond syndication in London for Autostrade, Italy's highway authority. This offshore market, soon called Eurobonds, attracted international investors, offering a regulation-free alternative to Yankee bonds, which required SEC registration. Initially dollar-based, the market expanded to Marks, Yen, Pounds, and Euros, reducing the US Yankee bond market. In 1981, the SEC responded by creating the International Banking Facility (IBF) to retain some offshore capital (O'Malley, 2015).

Investment banks quickly recognized the Eurobond market's potential. In the 1970s, Morgan Stanley and Lehman Brothers opened London offices, followed by Salomon Brothers, Goldman Sachs, and Merrill Lynch. Unlike the United States, Europe allowed universal banking, enabling banks to engage in capital markets without restrictions like Glass-Steagall. While US investment banks handled Eurobond IPOs, they faced competition from capital-rich European banks like Deutsche Bank and Credit Suisse, which had broader international client networks. US banks, envious of this advantage, pushed for Glass-Steagall's repeal. In response, the Fed began loosening its interpretation of the law, marking a turning point on Wall Street (Geisst, 2018).

In the early 1970s, beyond the minimum capital requirements, the LSE remained conservative, setting extensive and rigorous rules on how members could conduct their business and refusing to admit women as exchange members. However, the admission of women to the LSE was an essential milestone in finance and gender equality. This restriction finally ended in the early 1970s, reflecting broader social and legal changes in the UK. This change inspired more women to pursue stockbroking, investment banking, and asset management careers (Michie, 2001).

By the mid-1970s, however, momentum was building to challenge the LSE's right to be the sole authority for the securities market. As a result, the Council of the Securities Industry (CSI) was established in 1978 to take over responsibility from the Exchange. The Stock exchange and other components of the securities market would come under the control of this regulatory body, the Council, and the whole organization would be supervised by the Bank of England. However, its role was changed when the Securities and Investments Board (SIB) was established in 1986 as part of broader regulatory changes resulting from the Big Bang reforms (see the next section). The shift to centralized regulation aimed to keep the UK's financial markets competitive and secure amid globalization. The SIB was the forerunner of the Financial Services Authority (FSA), which was established in 1997 to oversee all financial services in the UK, further consolidating the regulatory framework for financial markets (Briault, 1999).

The City Takeover Panel (formerly the Panel on Takeovers and Mergers) was established in 1968 to regulate mergers and acquisitions (M&A) in the UK, bypassing the LSE. Its key role is to prevent insider trading by ensuring transparency, requiring investors who buy 3% or more of shares to disclose holdings, and mandating public announcements for takeover bids. The Panel remains crucial to the UK's financial regulatory framework, adapting to globalization and reforms like the 1997 Financial Services and Markets Act. Despite changes in the broader regulatory landscape, its role is to enforce the Takeover Code, ensure fair M&A processes, and maintain trust in corporate governance (Johnston, 2007).

In the years since the end of World War II, the London Stock Exchange has lost markets it once dominated, such as South African mining securities and American equities. However, in the mid-1970s, the LSE gained complete administrative control over all stockbrokers and street dealers in the British Isles for the first time. This was mainly due to the 1973 merger between the London Stock Exchange and the United Kingdom and Ireland regional exchanges. Given the increasing integration in the British securities market, creating a single stock exchange was long overdue. This reform improved the efficiency of the market. Then, the LSE introduced the first computer-based information system that allowed investors to access stock prices and market data electronically rather than relying on manual price boards (Michie, 2001).

Another development in the 1970s was options, which grew in popularity during monetary instability following the collapse of the Bretton Woods system of managed currencies. Initially, the Bank of England was responsible for limiting options in London because it considered them speculative and destabilizing instruments. By 1973, however, the Bank had realized how options could limit risk rather than increasing it, as was the case with foreign securities transactions during fluctuating exchange rates. As a result, it relaxed its rules, making it easier for persons in the City of London with transactions sensitive to changes in the value of currencies and interest rates to insure against adverse trends through an option contract. The

LSE established LTOM in 1978 to provide a regulated platform for equity options trading. Initially, options were introduced on five UK equities, adding more over time (Michie, 2001).

Resisting fixed commission and double capacity, the LSE no longer offered a cheap alternative to the commercial banks in realizing minor new issues; instead, it focused on retailing issues made by the commercial banks and provided the secondary market. By the 1970s, stockbrokers had ceased to be dynamic elements of the primary capital market and began exploiting the niche that the established commercial banks had ignored. The stock market was now entirely at the mercy of the large financial institutions that provided the bulk of the business. The stock market had recovered from the challenging conditions of the 1970s, but its position at the end of the decade was as precarious as it had been in the late 1940s. It was now inevitable that reforms would be made in the LSE and the country.

11.3.2 Tracherism and the Big Bang

The oil crisis initiated by OPEC in the mid-1970s and rising inflation affected all world economies. The UK faced economic challenges such as rising inflation, stagnant growth, and labor unrest. The previous Labour government, led by James Callaghan, sometimes clashed with the LSE and struggled to manage the country's growing inflation and economic problems. The Conservative Party presented itself as a solution to these problems and contrasted sharply with existing financial policies, and Margaret Thatcher became Prime Minister in 1979.

Thatcher's economic philosophy was deeply influenced by monetarism, a theory advocated by economist Milton Friedman, who argued that controlling the money supply was the key to reducing inflation. Her economic policy is called Tracherizm, which is described as an ideology that advocates a free market economy, limiting state intervention, privatization, and traditional social values. Thatcher's approach also reflected the broader global trend toward neoliberalism, as seen in Ronald Reagan's policies in the United States. After taking office, Thatcher introduced a series of radical economic reforms that characterized her tenure as Prime Minister. These reforms aimed to reduce the state's influence on the economy and move toward a more market-oriented approach. Thatcher introduced a series of reforms to reduce trade unions' power with the Employment Act of 1980. The Thatcher government also introduced significant tax cuts for both individuals and businesses. So, it encouraged investment, entrepreneurship, and economic growth. One of the most striking aspects of Thatcher's economic reforms was privatizing state-owned industries. British companies, including British Telecom, British Gas, British Airways, and British Steel, were sold to private investors. Privatizing big monopolies was crucial in expanding and modernizing the London Stock Exchange. It increased market capitalization, trading volumes, and liquidity, attracted millions of new investors, and strengthened the LSE's global position. Additionally, it influenced broader financial reforms and contributed to the growth of institutional investment. The success of these privatizations helped shape the modern UK financial system and set a precedent for similar programs worldwide (Michie, 2001).

Thatcher's most transformative reforms were in financial deregulation. In 1986, the government implemented a reform program called the Big Bang, a series of sweeping changes that modernized the LSE and opened it to global financial markets. The reforms had a profound and lasting impact on the financial sector and transformed the LSE into one of the world's leading financial centers.

The Big Bang made them more competitive by allowing stockbrokers to set commission rates. Another significant reform was the end of the single capacity system, which previously forced firms to choose between acting as brokers or jobbers. Under the new regulations, firms were allowed to operate in both capacities, leading to the rise of integrated investment banks. Then, the intermediaries could increase their ability to facilitate trades, quote prices, and manage market liquidity. This flexibility allowed financial institutions to offer a broader range of services, making them more competitive globally. The Big Bang also introduced electronic trading, which replaced brokers' traditional floor trading system. The transition to computer-based trading was crucial in modernizing the market, making transactions faster, more transparent, efficient, and accessible to a broader range of investors. This change not only streamlined the trading process but also enabled the LSE to keep pace with advances in global financial technology. Another significant reform was the removal of restrictions on foreign ownership of financial companies in the UK. Before 1986, only UK-based firms could own stockbrokers and investment banks, limiting international capital flow. The Big Bang significantly increased the participation of international banks in the UK market by allowing foreign financial institutions to acquire UK firms. This opened the door for Central American and European banks to enter the London market, further strengthening the city's status as a global financial center (Michie, 2001).

The London International Financial Futures Exchange (LIFFE) was established in 1982 to adapt London to international financial developments. It expanded beyond equity options to include financial futures and index options, becoming a major European derivatives trading center. In 1993, LTOM was merged with the London International Financial Futures and Options Exchange (LIFFE). LIFFE then moved to fully electronic trading and was eventually acquired by Euronext in 2001.

The Big Bang also signaled a shift in the ownership structure of financial firms. Before 1986, UK stockbrokers were largely privately owned partnerships. After the reforms, various organizations, including banks, corporations, and foreign investors, could own firms. This change allowed firms to raise capital more efficiently, enabling them to expand their activities and compete with the most important international financial institutions. The result was the growth of larger, more sophisticated firms able to offer a broader range of services, from investment banking to asset management and trading (Michie, 2001).

The removal of exchange controls in the UK in the late 1970s played a critical role in the expansion and success of the Eurobond market. This deregulation and other Thatcher-era reforms helped the UK participate thoroughly in the rapidly expanding global economic system. However, the reforms also had some unintended consequences. The newfound ability to trade more quickly and competitively contributed to market volatility and the increased use of speculative financial practices. While these changes made the market more dynamic, they left it vulnerable to subsequent financial crises. Indeed, the LSE fell by more than 10% on October 19, 1987, and fell by around 47% from its pre-crisis peak to its lowest point during the 2008 crisis. The Big Bang made them more competitive by allowing stockbrokers to set commission rates. Another significant reform was the end of the single capacity system, which previously forced firms to choose between acting as brokers or jobbers. Under the new regulations, firms were permitted to operate in both capacities, resulting in the emergence of integrated investment banks. Then, the intermediaries could increase their ability to facilitate trades, quote prices, and manage market liquidity. This flexibility allowed financial institutions to offer a broader range of services, making them more competitive globally. The Big Bang also introduced electronic trading, which replaced brokers' traditional floor trading system. The transition to computer-based trading was crucial in modernizing the market, making transactions faster, more transparent, efficient, and accessible to a broader range of investors. This change not only streamlined the trading process but also enabled the LSE to keep pace with advances in global financial technology. Another significant reform was the removal of restrictions on foreign ownership of financial companies in the UK. Before 1986, only UK-based firms could own stockbrokers and investment banks, limiting international capital flow. The Big Bang significantly increased the participation of international banks in the UK market by allowing foreign financial institutions to acquire UK firms. This opened the door for Central American and European banks to enter the London market, further strengthening the city's status as a global financial center (Michie, 2001).

Before the 1980s, financial regulation in the UK was largely self-regulated, with different financial institutions operating under separate regulatory frameworks. The UK government passed the Financial Services Act 1986 and established the Securities and Investments Board (SIB). It was key in transitioning the UK from self-regulation to a modern financial oversight system. However, its reliance on multiple self-regulatory bodies led to enforcement issues, ultimately prompting the creation of the Financial Services Authority (FSA) in 2001. In the aftermath of the financial crisis of 2008, government officials decided to revise the regulatory structure of the financial markets in the U.K., passing the Financial Services Act 2012 and dissolving the FSA beginning in April 2013. Two new agencies were created to continue with the financial regulation needs: the Financial Conduct Authority and the Prudential Regulation Authority of the Bank of England.

11.3.3 *France's Economic Policy After the War and the Paris Bourse*

After World War II, the French government developed a highly administrative monetary and credit policy system to promote economic modernization and growth. Key instruments in this system included administered interest rates, capital, and credit control systems. By the early 1980s, however, these instruments were not working anymore in the new global finance system. Interestingly, the neoliberal policies that began in the United Kingdom and the United States were initiated by left-wing President François Mitterrand, whose turn toward neoliberalism in the mid-1980s was influenced by both domestic economic pressures and international influences, including the global rise of neoliberal ideas. The early socialist agenda led to market-oriented reforms, including privatization, austerity measures, and increased European integration. While these reforms contributed to France's economic recovery and global competitiveness, they also had social costs, particularly for the working class and the public sector. Mitterrand's change is an essential example of how neoliberalism began to take hold in Europe in the 1980s, even in countries with a strong tradition of social welfare and state intervention in the economy (Goodman, 1992).

Under President Mitterrand, the French government nationalized many sectors, including banks and large corporations, in the early 1980s. However, in the mid-1980s, following the neoliberal trend, the Mitterrand government reversed this course. It began privatizing key sectors: in this context, many prominent French companies such as Air France, France Télécom, and Renault were privatized. The Paris Bourse played a crucial role in these privatizations by acting as a platform for publicly selling shares in these companies. This helped to widen the pool of investors and increase market activity, further modernizing and globalizing the exchange. The privatization wave also increased the number of IPOs on the Paris Bourse, providing new opportunities for investors and helping deepen the market. The reforms continued under the right-wing Chirac Government (Goodman, 1992).

One of the most significant changes during this period was the liberalization of financial markets. Before the 1980s, France had relatively tight controls on financial transactions, including stock trading. However, under the influence of neoliberal ideas, France reduced restrictions on foreign investment and allowed greater freedom for domestic and international investors to participate in the stock market. Reforms introduced since 1983 fall into six major categories: authorization of new financial instruments and decompartmentalization of various capital markets; extension of the negotiability of commissions; tightening of regulatory supervision; privatization; modifying the role of the agents de change; and attempts to start a process of internationalization. The Paris Bourse underwent significant changes during neoliberal reforms in the 1980s, reflecting broader trends in financial deregulation, globalization, and the shift toward market-oriented economic policies that characterized the period. These changes were part of efforts by France and other Western countries to become more integrated into the global financial system. The most essential structural breakthrough was the 1986 opening of the Pan's financial futures market—M.A.T.I.F.

(Cerny, 1989). It is a private corporation that is both a futures exchange and a clearing house in France. It was absorbed in the merger of the Paris Bourse with Euronext NV to form Euronext Paris.

In the 1980s, an end to the agents de change monopoly seemed inevitable. Since 1986, a series of reforms have placed three main groups overseeing France's financial markets, and the CAC's (Compagnie des Agents de Change) powers have been abolished. The Commission des Operations de Bourse (COB), the Conseil des Bourses de Valeurs (CBV), and the Société des Bourses Françaises (SBF). The COB, the government agency primarily responsible for regulating French securities markets, was established in 1967. Before the reforms of the late 1980s, the COB's enforcement powers were minimal. The agency had jurisdiction only over companies offering shares to the public on an organized stock exchange or through an initial public offering. It could only investigate irregularities in information disclosed by these companies. In 1988, the French government passed a law strengthening the COB's role in ensuring the accuracy of information disseminated to the public. This law broadened the COB's oversight responsibilities by making the Commission responsible for the proper functioning of the Stock Exchange. The 1988 law also gave the COB greater authority to investigate documents necessary for investigations and investigations of illegal activities and impose sanctions on parties that do not cooperate with ongoing investigations. The CBV is specifically responsible for regulating and disciplining the "*Societes de Bourse*" and drafting the rules for the exchange operation. The SBF derives its power from the CBV. The CBV delegates to the SBF the authority to supervise and control the market's management, security, development, and promotion. The SBF also acts as a clearing house for transactions between stockbrokers. The French securities regulator, the Autorité des Marchés Financiers (AMF), was established on November 24, 2003, under the Financial Security Act of August 1, 2003. It was created by the merger of three regulatory authorities: the Commission des Opérations de Bourse (COB), the Conseil des Marchés Financiers (CMF), and the Conseil de Discipline de la Gestion Financière. Today, the AMF is an independent public authority that regulates and supervises France's financial markets to protect savings and investments (Saxena, 2013).

In the late 1980s and early 1990s, the Paris Bourse was also influenced by the broader European integration process, particularly by creating a unified European market under the European Single Act of 1986, which aimed to develop a more integrated European economy. In 2000, several European exchanges, including the Paris Stock Exchange, merged to form Euronext, a pan-European exchange that would further integrate European financial markets and create a more competitive environment. Euronext introduced Xetra, a fully electronic trading platform, to handle trades across multiple European exchanges, including Paris. Euronext was formed in 2000 by combining the Paris, Amsterdam, and Brussels Stock Exchanges to create a unified European exchange. It expanded by acquiring the Lisbon Stock Exchange in 2002 and merged with the New York Stock Exchange (NYSE) in 2007 to become NYSE Euronext. With this merger, the NYSE became a truly global exchange, reaching European derivatives markets through LIFFE. In 2014, Euronext regained its independence and went public again. It grew by acquiring the Oslo, Dublin, and Milan stock exchanges. Today, Euronext operates across several European countries and is a major player in global financial markets. Although Euronext was established after the 1980s, the foundation for this integration was laid in the 1980s, mainly through the modernization and deregulation of the Paris Stock Exchange.

11.4 Junk Bonds and Michael Milken

By 1982, high-tech stocks had emerged as market leaders. Apple Computer and other affordable personal computers entered IBM's market and even wiped it out. The desktop began to challenge the mainframe and change the work habits of millions forever. Steve Jobs and Bill Gates were replacing industrial empires with their personal computers. Biotech companies were taking off. Software entrepreneurs were building their businesses in garages with almost no capital, borrowing money, and making millions of dollars quickly, at least on paper (Townsend, 2001). The hi-tech companies and others have turned to the bond market.

The SEC became concerned about the excessive borrowing of companies and, in particular, their tendency to engage in takeover operations by lending. The market was becoming increasingly risky. On June 7, 1984, SEC chairman John S.R. Shad gave a speech titled "*Borrowing America*" at the New York Financial Writers' meeting. He said, "*In today's corporate world, Darwin's principle of survival of the fittest has become: Either you take over, or they take you over .... There will be as many bankruptcies tomorrow as acquisitions and takeovers today*," he said. He warned the market that the whole country would be at risk in the long run. One of the targets of this conversation was Michael Milken. Milken was funding corporate takeover operations by issuing junk bonds to companies (Vise & Coll, 1991).

In the 1970s, the SEC's Rule 415 created a stir. It is also known as Shelf Registration; with this rule, the very slow process of going public became relatively fast. As simple as Rule 415 sounds, it significantly harmed traditional IPO groups. There was no longer time to put together a syndicate through a series of negotiations and bargaining. Underwriters seeking authorization from companies had to step forward, agree to organize the entire issuance, and, once committed, form a syndicate. Investment banks recognized the opportunity here and opened a window of opportunity for new, ambitious firms that trusted their expertise. Michael Milken, the Drexel architect of the "*Junk Bonds*" project, first became the most critical investment banker on the stock exchange with his business model. Junk bonds, rated BB or B, were speculative and risky but offered high returns, unlike investment-grade bonds (AAA-BBB) (Kashyap, 2019).

Milken created both a supply and a demand for originally issued speculative-grade bonds (Fig. 11.2). To do so, he turned to industrial firms financed by bank loans and said, "*Instead of using costly bank credits, you can use the capital markets to finance yourself. With bond debt, you can expand your business, territory, and product range.*" he said, encouraging them to enter this market. Another source of speculative-grade issuance was LBOs (Leveraged Buyouts), so-called acquisitions

Fig. 11.2 Michael Milken (1946) King of Junk Bonds. https://commons.wikimedia.org/wiki/File:Mike_Milken.jpg

of companies financed entirely with debt (leveraged) by the investor. Milken's strong support and Drexel's ability to sell a company's debt allowed financial and strategic buyers to make friendly or hostile takeovers of targeted companies using much higher-than-normal leverage levels (Geisst, 2018).

Milken was quite convincing that the higher return on debt offset the risk. He created and controlled both sides of the market. Milken's position within Drexel was influential, as reflected in his profit-sharing agreement with his company. His compensation exceeded $1 billion over four years in the 1980s. Milken's project also broke the preexisting monopoly of commercial banks on speculative-grade corporate finance (Stories Finance, n.d.).

The Wall Street Journal immediately dubbed Milken "*the king of junk bonds.*" In 1982, President Reagan announced a proposal to liberalize existing banking laws. The Depository Institutions Act, better known as the Garn-St... The Germain Act allowed banks, savings, and loan associations to purchase corporate bonds. This was most useful to Milken. In addition to the commercial banks to which he could sell junk bonds, he now had new players to target, such as the Savings and Loan Association (S&L), the socially motivated mortgage lenders. Every year, Drexel organized events and balls where dozens of academics and politicians with financial connections spoke about the virtues of the market. Milken was estimated to have amassed a personal fortune of over $3 billion from the junk bond craze before Drexel closed its doors in 1991 (Stories Finance, n.d.).

In the aftermath of the October 1987 securities crisis, the cause of which is still poorly understood, investors became risk-averse, re-evaluated the performance of junk bonds, and moved away from the junk bond market. Meanwhile, S&Ls had gone bankrupt. The post-1970 high inflation hit them hard, and they invested heavily in junk bonds, which had fallen in value in recent years. As S&L went bankrupt, the funds that would have come to Milken disappeared.

However, it would all end for Milken in 1986, when Ivan Boesky, manager of an investment arbitrage fund called the Hudson Fund, turned himself in to federal authorities on insider trading charges. "*Today is a very honorable day for the SEC,*" said Gary Lynch, a lawyer at the SEC that day. "*At a press conference downstairs at 4:30 p.m., the commission will announce that Ivan Boesky has agreed to provide information and pay a $100 million fine for insider trading.*" Dennis Levine, an investment banker at Drexel, had admitted to authorities that he had given Boesky inside information about acquisitions and that Boesky had traded the stock for his gain (Vise & Coll, 1991).

Boesky was a Russian-born stockbroker who had established a prominent position on Wall Street in the 1970s. After pleading guilty, Boesky was sentenced to three and a half years in prison. One of the people he turned in in a plea bargain with the prosecutor was Michael Milken. The good times were over for Milken, and his empire at Drexel was abruptly destroyed when he was convicted under federal fraud laws. Milken's sentence was 10 years in prison and $1 billion in restitution, $200 million of which was withheld during the execution of his sentence. He would later serve three years in jail under the law. One of Wall Street's most spectacular success stories came nearly two decades after Milken started at Drexel, a success story that ended in a stunning collapse (Truell, 1997).

11.5 Proxy Wars

After the 1970s, shareholder value became a priority, financial markets grew, and large investors (e.g., funds) began to orient company management toward shorter-term profitability. In the process, CEO salaries also became based on financial targets. Thus, in the second half of the twentieth centuries, the transition from managerial capitalism to investor capitalism began with the growth of financial markets, globalization, and the spread of neoliberal policies. Meanwhile, mergers and acquisitions surged on Wall Street as firms targeted struggling companies. To gain control, acquirers sought minor shareholders' proxies, leading to intense proxy fights after 1980 (Cappucci, 2019).

By 1987, the annual value of merger activity had reached almost 300 billion dollars. Hostile takeovers were particularly prevalent. The hostile company would start by buying significant shares in the target company. The hostile investor would then write a "*green mail*" offering to sell the shares back to them at a premium. He threatened to launch a hostile takeover bid if the company did not accept. The company has two options: either buy back the shares at a premium price or risk losing control of the company to the investor. If the company agreed to buy back the shares at a premium price, this could significantly reduce the company's resources. This could affect the company's ability to invest in growth opportunities, research and development, and other strategic initiatives. In addition, greenmail could result in a loss of shareholder value, as the company would have to pay a premium price for the shares. In contrast, "*poison p*ills" were measures taken by companies to deter hostile takeovers. These measures were designed to make it more difficult for a hostile bidder to acquire a significant stake in the company. In Delaware, the Court of Chancery was particularly flexible (Cox, 1989). Therefore, companies under such pressure could transfer their headquarters to this state. Poison pills can give new shares to existing shareholders and make takeovers more complex, such as adopting anti-takeover provisions in the corporate bylaws (Bhagat et al., 1985). However, the poison pill can sometimes cause significant problems for the company. With their help, the target company could survive the takeover bid but emerge from the battle very weak because of its accumulated extra dividends and interest. The companies involved were left in a difficult situation after the smoke cleared. One of the takeovers that marked the 1980s was the acquisition of cosmetics giant Revlon by Ronald Perelman.

This hostile takeover, which was fiercely contested, took place in 1985 for 2.3 billion dollars. The acquisition, made with the help of Michael Milken using junk bonds, left Revlon with a massive debt burden of $2.9 billion, which remained an albatross around the company's neck for years. The chain of events began when Pantry Pride (CEO of Ronald Perelman) offered to buy any or all of Revlon's 38.2 million outstanding shares for $47.5 per share when the market price was $45. When Pantry Pride's offer was initially rejected, he repeatedly raised the price until it reached $53 per share. Meanwhile, another company, Forstmann Little & Company, bid at $56 per share, followed by a brief bidding war (Stevenson, 1985).

In response, Pantry Pride raised its bid to $58 per share and went to the very liberal Delaware Court to accuse the Revlon Board of Directors. It argued that they breached their fiduciary duties by pushing shareholders away from the Pantry Pride sale and toward a sale that offered Revlon less financial return. The Court of Chancery's decision was that in certain circumstances, i.e., if the sale or dissolution of a company is inevitable, the Board of Directors must have a specific fiduciary duty, and that is to sell the company's shares at as high a price as possible so that shareholders can receive as much money as possible for their shares. This case had essential consequences, and the Delaware court changed corporate law and the business world. After this landmark case, the term "*in Revlon mode*" became widely known in the corporate world as a company for sale that would auction or sell its shares to the highest bidder (Coffee, 2012).

This case has had significant repercussions in the US business community. Accordingly, every Board of Directors must act conscientiously. They must act in good faith and genuinely believe all actions are in the company's best interests. According to the Court's ruling, as long as the board consistently acts in the best interests of the company's shareholders, it allows Board of Directors to manage their companies with flexibility within a solid margin of action. According to the court ruling, the board must be fully independent and enter into negotiations in good faith. The board should focus on the outcomes that provide the highest value for shareholders (Coffee, 2012).

Delaware's corporate law structure allows entrepreneurs to create different types of business entities, and these alternative entities provide business owners with flexibility not typically found in other states. It has had a significant impact on the business world as more than 65% of the Fortune 500 companies are incorporated in Delaware and are therefore affected by the decisions of the Delaware Court. Today, many states have started to follow their choices closely (Coffee, 2012).

11.6 The 1987 Crisis and the End of the Glass-Steagall Act

The stock market unexpectedly plunged about 30% on October 19, 1987. Worldwide losses were estimated at US$1.71 trillion. Possible reasons for the initial fall in stock prices included significant overvaluation of equities, persistent US trade and budget deficits, and rising interest rates. Another explanation for the decline was the fall of the dollar and subsequent distrust of government efforts to stop the crisis (Bates, 1991). NYSE chairman John Phelan described the performance as "*the worst market I have ever seen, the closest to a financial meltdown I would ever want to see*" (Geisst, 2018).

The Fed, more experienced than in previous crises, urgently announced that it would provide emergency reserves to all banks that needed them. The crisis did not deepen this time, and normalcy was quickly restored. Much of the suspicion about the crisis centered on newly developed sophisticated computer-driven trading software that allowed arbitrage between stocks, options, and financial futures. The software was designed to automatically send buy and sell signals when one market looked cheap or expensive relative to another, potentially triggering a market crash. Despite debates, computer-driven trades were seen as a contributing factor, not the leading cause of the crash. The Reagan administration swiftly formed a presidential committee to investigate. The chairman of this committee, Nicholas Brady, recommended installing a "*circuit breaker*" that would automatically stop trading if prices fell too fast. The idea was to allow backrooms to catch lagging orders and give floor traders some breathing space if prices started moving quickly. The idea came from commodity exchanges and the Japanese market, where breakers were used for some time.

The banks were now lobbying intensively to repeal the Glass-Steagall Act. The Fed and J.P. Morgan & Co. relationship was still as strong as it had been since the 1920s. There were frequent personnel transfers between the two institutions. Many Fed employees were former Morgan employees. The famous Fed chairman Alan Greenspan (1987–2006) had been a Morgan executive before becoming Fed chairman, replacing the previous chairman Paul Volcker. In 1984, before Greenspan became Fed chairman, Morgan published an article titled "*Rethinking Glass Steagall,*" advocating repealing the fifty-year-old law. The article backed Alan Greenspan's thesis that if banks could engage in investment strategies, they could diversify their business, avoid risk, and increase returns for banking customers (Morgan, 1984). The article also used the scandals in the securities industry as an excuse, and all the crises of the 1980s provided an even more substantial justification for repealing the Glass-Steagall Act. Morgan argued that the securities industry was still in a relatively weak position while the industry's demands for financing were increasing. During this period, US banks took advantage of the pervasive role of lobbying in the political system. They sought to influence the views of legislators and regulators on these and other issues. Eventually, by the last quarter of the twentieth centuries, they persuaded politicians and regulators to back down and lift various restrictions. Greenspan's policies at the Fed indirectly benefited the banks by allowing them to expand, take on more risk, and dominate the financial sector. In turn, J.P. Morgan and other big investment banks leveraged Greenspan's regulatory stance to develop and market complex financial products, some of which contributed to economic instability. Their relationship is an example of how central banking policy and Wall Street influence reinforce each other in a system of corporatocracy, in which corporations wield significant power and influence over government policies, economic decisions, and social structures. The International Monetary Fund (IMF) warned that banks would likely capture regulators (Hardy, 2006). The concept of "*regulatory capture*" was coined by the Nobel Prize-winning economist George Stigler. In his view, if regulators are captured, the dominance of regulators can be dominated by the industries or interests they are supposed to regulate. Thus, an agency charged with acting in the public interest has to work in a way that benefits the incumbent firms in the banks it is supposed to regulate (Stigler, 2021).

Before long, some banks could circumvent the limits set by the Glass-Steagall Act through loopholes in the law. For example, according to the law, as long as a bank was not "*principally engaged*" in securities activities, it could become a shareholder in a company engaged in such activities. However, banks could be indirectly affected if there were a market crash. Naturally, this thinned the dividing line between Wall Street and commercial banks. In the fall of 1996, banks were allowed to underwrite securities and sell insurance to their customers if they did so through subsidiaries. Nevertheless, despite Congress's refusal to remove Glass-Steagall altogether, the Fed and the Comptroller of the Currency, the agency charged with regulating and supervising all national banks and financial institutions, began to erode it out of the public eye. The pressure was mounting. Later in the year, the Fed strengthened its hand by increasing the investment banking fees allowed to banks from 10 to 25 percent. Although Alice Rivlin, the Fed's vice chairwoman, said, "*We hope the next step will be up to Congress,*" the Fed was not shy about helping banks expand their limits on investment banking. As a result, in 1999, Congress would partially repeal the Glass-Steagall Act. In the 1990s, two walls came down at once. One was the Berlin Wall that divided East and West Germany, and the other was the Glass-Steagall Wall. The fall of both walls would have serious economic consequences (Geisst, 2018).

11.7 Electronic Markets and the Rise of Internet Technology

In the 1990s, the NASDAQ-NYSE rivalry intensified. NASDAQ saw itself as the future market and presented itself as the natural successor to the NYSE. It is argued that in the future, all markets will be fully computerized and that this will be the norm of the twenty-first centuries. On the other hand, market developments were not going in the same direction, and the NYSE successfully listed many new companies, but the NASDAQ lost listings. Many new technology companies preferred the NYSE over the NASDAQ for listing. Seeking to strengthen its exchange and eclipse the NYSE, NASDAQ acquired Amex, a former US exchange, in 1998, in a merger that NASDAQ Chairman Frank Zarb called "*the market of markets.*" Amex had recently become a place where innovation abounded. Unfortunately, this marriage would not last long, and NASDAQ would start looking for a buyer a few years later (Egginton et al., 2012). The NASD sold Amex to a private investor group in 2004, and in 2008, that group sold Amex to NYSE Euronext.

In 2006, the NYSE merged with Archipelago, adopting a hybrid system that combined floor trading with electronic trading and expanded into options, ETFs, and derivatives. Today, it is operated by the Intercontinental Exchange (ICE), founded in 2000 in Atlanta, a global leader in exchanges, clearing, and financial data. ICE began in energy trading and, through acquisitions, has become one of the most influential players in global finance, regulated by the SEC under principles of transparency and fair access.

In the late 1990s, interest rates had fallen. Internet companies, which emerged as a new trend, benefited the most from this opportunity. Many saw the Internet as a tool to make business operations more efficient, and the Internet sector's future looked very bright. When companies traded business to business over the Internet, they could often avoid the costs of traditional intermediaries and reduce costs. These privately owned firms invested hundreds of millions of dollars in New Economy (Internet) companies. These companies quickly went public without a good track record and tangible evidence of success. Venture capitalists could earn 20% or more returns in less than a year (Geisst, 2018).

Since the 1971 Nixon shock that pre-empted the 1973 crisis, bank money creation grew uncontrollably. By the 1990s, sizeable offshore hedge funds had become popular among institutional and wealthy individual investors. These funds, which first emerged in the 1970s, aimed to do precisely what their name implied: hedge risk. Simultaneously taking long and short positions in securities or currencies, these funds hoped to benefit from a narrowing spread between positions over time. Over the years, however, hedge funds moved away from their original concept, becoming excessive risk-takers. The returns were relatively high, but the fund took precarious positions, and investors who wanted to withdraw their money from the fund had to wait for close to a year. Like mutual funds, hedge funds manage pooled money, but their managers have greater flexibility in investment strategies. This allows for higher risks in pursuit of higher returns. Many operate globally, managing billion-dollar portfolios. Participation requires a significant initial investment, usually over $1 million, limiting access to high-net-worth investors. Many were initially offshore, with some achieving extraordinary success. During this period, two funds left their mark in the 1990s: Long-Term Capital Management (LTCM), based in Connecticut, and the Quantum Fund, founded by George Soros (Crockett, 2007).

11.8 Hedge Funds and the Asian Crisis of 1997

John Meriwether, a former bond trader at Salomon Brothers, founded the LTCM. The firm took long and short positions in bonds with similar characteristics but different yields, thinking there was an arbitrage opportunity. When the market saw this similarity, the price of the bonds would converge, and they would make a profit. Together with David W. Mullins, a former member of the Federal Reserve, they assembled a star-studded team of investment professionals (Fig. 11.3). They recruited Myron Scholes and Robert Merton, who had made a name for themselves with their work on option pricing. These two scientists later won the Nobel Prize for discovering a new option pricing formula called Black-Merton-Scholes for determining the value of an option. Unlike other hedge funds, this group seemed to be the best of the best and planned to mitigate that risk, a persistent concern among investors because hedge funds are notoriously secretive and do not disclose their positions to investors, would be eliminated by this super team. Investors had to put at least $10 million into the fund. LTCM's client list was as impressive as its partners, and the program quickly became very successful (Allington et al., 2012).

LTCM was a relatively small organization. Within a few years, its capitalization grew to $5 billion. Many other funds and investment firms tried to imitate LTCM and make arbitrage profits in the bond markets. When too many firms entered the market, arbitrage opportunities disappeared. Inevitably, the fund started investing outside its core expertise and trading derivatives of equity investments called equity swaps. LTCM did not know as much about the companies involved in equity swaps as it did about bonds. By 1997, the derivatives portfolio had doubled compared to the previous year. Such extraordinary figures made the fund a bank-like financial institution, not just a mutual fund. Large banks typically accumulated swaps of this value as off-balance sheet liabilities. Still, their economic structures were more substantial; with an individual capitalization of more than $5 billion, they had more muscular capital structures against market risks that could arise. However, LTCM was not a bank and performed no traditional banking functions. All it did was borrow money and make

Fig. 11.3 Myron Scholes (1941) (left) and Robert C. Merton (1944). https://en.wikipedia.org/wiki/Long-Term_Capital_Management#/media/File:Myron_Scholes_2008_in_Lindau.png (Public Domain). https://en.wikipedia.org/wiki/Long-Term_Capital_Management#/media/File:Robert_C._Merton.jpg (Public D)

money by taking advantage of yield spreads and arbitrage opportunities in exotic investment vehicles in equities. This left it vulnerable to market risk (Allington et al., 2012).

At the end of 1997, LTCM returned its profits and all the money invested after 1994 to its investors ($2.7 billion). Investors nonetheless had a return of over 80 percent. The same year, Merton and Scholes were awarded the Nobel Prize in Economics for their academic work, which once again boosted the fund's public relations and morale. However, LTCM had underestimated the fundamental behavior of bond markets. When market conditions become uncertain, investors sell their risky investments quickly and buy US Treasuries as a haven. While such events were relatively rare, they were to be expected in a crisis (Geisst, 2018).

Real estate prices had soared in the Far East, which developed into an attractive market in the 1990s. This development, which followed months of speculative pressures that largely depleted Thailand's official foreign exchange reserves, marked the beginning of a deep financial crisis in much of East Asia in 1997. Soros's fund was at the center of the events and attracted the attention of the press. On July 2, 1997, Thailand was forced to devalue its currency against the US dollar. In the following months, Thailand's currency, stock, and real estate markets weakened further, and its difficulties turned into a balance of payments and banking crisis. Malaysia, the Philippines, and Indonesia also allowed their currencies to weaken significantly in the face of market pressures, with Indonesia increasingly embroiled in a multifaceted financial and political crisis. Meanwhile, Hong Kong faced several large but unsuccessful speculative attacks on its currency peg to the dollar, the first of which triggered a worldwide short-term stock market sell-off. In South Korea, severe balance of payments pressures pushed the country to default. Thus, across East Asia, capital inflows slowed or reversed course, and the growth rate began to fall sharply. Banks came under significant pressure, and some Asian countries went into deep recessions, infecting their trading partners worldwide with their risks (Carson & Clark, 2013). Moreover, this crisis began to spill over to other countries. Investors started withdrawing their money from South American countries with similar problems, and then from Russia. Russia's declaration of a moratorium on sovereign debt effectively triggered a default. However, the issue was not limited to investments with Russia. Investors were buyers of high-yielding Russian government bonds, which suddenly became unable to pay interest, and the currency deteriorated. And then the most feared situation suddenly arose. LTCM was exposed to market risk from Russian bonds and suffered as a result (Sutela, 2000).

These developments increased the fund's risk because the fund had bought Russian government bonds while short-selling US Treasuries of similar maturities. The fund's value evaporated overnight as Russian obligations plummeted and investors switched to US Treasuries. The fund was on the wrong side of the trade on both sides. The value of the Russian bonds it had invested in was falling, while the prices of the US bonds it had shorted on the assumption that their prices would fall were rising. It worsened when market players realized LTCM was in dire financial straits. Commercial banks, mainly, had lent so much to the fund that losses without regulation could have jeopardized their capital. Nevertheless, the solution to the problem was somewhat unusual according to Wall Street practices and was treated as controversial. Despite being a private investment fund, LTCM was rescued by a consortium of 50 banks and investment banks in a deal organized by Alan Greenspan at the Fed (Geisst, 2018).

Merriwether's former partner, former Salomon Brothers partner Henry Kaufman, later commented: "*LTCM got into big trouble, however. Surprisingly, the firm's analytical wizards failed to consider some financial market fundamentals. They failed to appreciate that large positions in individual securities could not always be liquidated quickly, especially when the liabilities were of poorer credit quality. Moreover, they misread the complexities of arbitrage trading*" (Koehn, 2002).

The crisis did not stop there. Russia's default on its sovereign debt triggered widespread panic, particularly in emerging markets, and a sharp decline in asset prices, including Russian government bonds and other securities tied to Russian and emerging market risk. This event led to a flight to quality as investors moved their assets into safer investments such as US Treasuries. This event, linked to LTCM and the Russian default, is known as "*the 1998 options crisis*" and was caused by market disruptions resulting from increased volatility and a breakdown in the pricing relationships between options and their underlying assets. It also highlighted the risks associated with financial innovation and the reliance on mathematical models without adequate consideration of real-world market complexities.

George Soros became popular in the 1990s and was born in Budapest to a Jewish family (Fig. 11.4). He studied at the London School of Economics and earned a master's. Soros began his career working for British and American commercial banks, and in 1969, he founded his first hedge fund, Double Eagle. Profits from this fund provided the initial capital for his second hedge fund, Soros Fund Management, in 1970. Double Eagle was later renamed Quantum Fund (Osnos, 2022). Considered one of the most influential investors of all time, George Soros is best known for his position against the British pound in 1992. Soros was skeptical of the UK's decision to join the European Exchange Rate Mechanism (ERM), which pegged exchange rates to the German mark due to its economic woes. Together with other speculators, he had built up a sizeable short position in the preceding months, which would become highly profitable if the British currency fell below the lower band of the ERM. On September 16, 1992, known as Black Wednesday, the British government, under pressure from speculators, decided to withdraw the pound from the ERM, and chaos ensued. Soros's short position involved borrowing pounds, selling them, and repurchasing them at a lower price when the pound fell. As expected, the pound depreciated rapidly, earning Soros and his Quantum Fund an estimated $1 billion profit. While this action alone did not trigger a currency collapse, it made a significant contribution (Budd, 2005). Another legendary transaction of Soros was his bet against the Thai Baht in 1997. Soros predicted that the currency was overvalued and vulnerable to a crisis and started short selling the baht. His actions played a role in triggering a broader financial crisis in Asia. Soros is believed to have earned around $750 million from this operation. The Prime Minister of Malaysia, Mahathir Mohammed, denounced Soros, saying, "*Currency trading is unnecessary and immoral... Currency traders have become very rich by impoverishing others.*" In a televised speech the next day, Soros harshly said that the idea of banning currency trading was too frivolous to be taken seriously and

Fig. 11.4 George Soros. https://commons.wikimedia.org/wiki/File:George_Soros_-_World_Economic_Forum_Annual_Meeting_2011.jpg

that "*Dr. Mahathir is harming his own country*." As a result of these harsh words, which only added to already shaky market conditions, Malaysian stocks plunged further (Henderson, 2000).

11.9 September 11 and Financial Scandals

In the early 2000s, two events made Wall Street headlines: the September 11 attacks and financial scandals involving Enron.

As the center of capitalism, Wall Street was constantly under attack. For the first time, in 1916, a bomb exploded at a government ammunition dump across the Hudson River in Jersey City, shattering windows along Wall Street. In another attack at the corner of Broad and Wall Streets in 1920, a car bomb exploded outside the offices of a Wall Street company, killing dozens of people. In 1975, a bomb exploded on Lower Broad Street, killing several people who were having lunch. Islamic terrorist organizations targeted the World Trade Center as a symbol of capitalism. On February 26, 1993, a terrorist attack was carried out by detonating a van bomb under the North Tower of the World Trade Center complex in New York City, which was intended to bring down the North Tower on top of the South Tower, destroying both skyscrapers and killing tens of thousands of people. Although it failed to do so, it killed six people and injured more than a thousand (Murphy, 2002).

However, the impact of September 11, 2001, was much more serious. Many Wall Street firms operating in the building suffered huge losses. The NYSE and Amex closed their doors for several days after the attacks, their most extended closures since the bank shutdowns of the 1930s. As a result, the exchanges and many financial firms in the immediate vicinity were forced to make plans to diversify their operations by moving employees away from the area to protect themselves against future problems. Even securities firms that had relocated from Lower Manhattan to other parts of the city decided to fragment their operations so that similar events would not leave them stranded. After the attacks, stocks naturally lost significant value along with the market. The Dow Jones 30 was down 7 percent when it reopened a few days later (Chen & Siems, 2007).

The roots of the Enron incident date back to the 1980s. In the 1980s, US President Ronald Reagan abandoned Keynesian policies in favor of taxes and government expenditures, as well as deregulation during the period of stagflation. This escalated the arms race and ended the détente with the Soviet Union. He stabilized the economy by implementing "*Reaganomics*."

Over time, the Fed's commitment to low inflation gained credibility, unemployment fell, and the economy entered a sustained growth and stabilization period. Reagan received the most incredible support from British Prime Minister Margaret Thatcher. The most important part of the Energy Policy Act 1992 privatized utility companies and allowed free energy trade. Meanwhile, the Act liberalized rules on mergers between holding companies. As a result of the law, mergers between energy companies and utilities also began. The sector entered a new competitive environment. Many states wanted to allow consumers to choose their suppliers freely. In this environment, mergers seemed a viable way to achieve economies of scale and produce cheaper prices. Wall Street was happy to let energy prices be free and volatile. For them, volatility was an opportunity for return. One company that wanted to take advantage of these opportunities was the Enron Company (McLean & Elkind, 2013).

In the 1990s, Houston-based Enron was initially a natural gas distribution company. In 1997, it expanded into electric utilities by acquiring the electric utility Portland General Corporation. The company's Chairman and CEO, Kenneth Lay, was an energy economist with an academic background. The company was proliferating through the merger and was eagerly implementing its more aggressive business model. Soon, Enron became more of an energy trading company than a traditional supplier. Jeff Skilling, who came from the McKinsey consulting firm, became CEO. Jeff Skilling thought that Enron could make money by capitalizing on price volatility in the industry. As soon as Skilling took over, he instituted a system whereby employees were graded on a scale of 1–10. Every year, he fired those in the bottom 10%. This competitive system was very popular with investors, and the company's value rose rapidly. It also began to act as an intermediary in the gas market, making deals that could secure fixed prices in the future. Enron controlled 24% of the gas market and brought many energy-related commodities into the industry. Enron now had 90% of its revenue from energy trading (McLean & Elkind, 2013).

Enron had excellent relations with both Republicans and Democrats. The share price had quadrupled in the last five years, and when it started to serve customers via the Internet, the share price reached over 90 dollars in 2001. Things were not as good as they seemed. Enron had begun to overstate its profits, using complicated accounting techniques and tricks to keep its shareholders from worrying. In this way, it maintained the image of a successful company. Indeed, Enron had committed accounting fraud by utilizing the accounts of nearly a thousand independent subsidiaries following Andersen's advice. Interestingly, Andersen was also an auditor of Enron. These companies had very low equity capital and were 90% financed by debt. Enron systematically transferred the losses that appeared in its books to them. As the value of the parent company, Enron, skyrocketed, the loss-making subsidiaries could quickly obtain loans from banks because they used Enron's stock as collateral.

On August 14, 2001, Jeff Skilling resigned as CEO, citing personal reasons, which sparked controversy. Kenneth Lay became CEO again. This was a big shock for investors, and by the end of the week, the share price had fallen another $4. The departure of Clifford Baxter, another Enron executive who resigned in May and then shot himself, also showed that something was not going well. The magnitude of Enron's problems worried the auditing firm Andersen (McLean & Elkind, 2013). Because Enron had hedged thousands of subsidiary companies against risks by pledging its stock as collateral, neither Enron nor the subsidiary companies could save themselves when the stock price fell. On October 12, Arthur Anderson's Houston office employees began destroying Enron-related documents after an Arthur Anderson lawyer said the firm did not have to retain documents it did not need when contracting with one of Enron's principal subsidiaries. Enron, once the seventh-largest company in the country (measured by assets), and its accounting firm, Anderson, would not survive the scandal. Andrew Fastow, Enron's former chief financial officer, testified against Skilling and Lay, saying that Skilling and Lay also told investors that Enron was profitable and healthy when they all knew that was false. On June 15, 2002, Andersen was found guilty of destroying evidence and lost its license to practice public accounting (Thomas, 2002).

Almost 70 years after adopting stricter securities legislation, questions have been raised about how a publicly traded company could commit such a massive fraud. Enron was not the only one, as WorldCom's telecom company would later be implicated in an even bigger scandal with extensive accounting fraud. Adelphia and several other essential companies followed. The crisis in the US stock markets, later called the dot.com bubble, had begun (Petra & Spieler, 2020).

The crisis began on Friday, April 14, 2000, when the Nasdaq Composite index fell 9% after reaching its peak, ending a week in which it lost 25%. On November 9, 2000, Pets.com, backed by Amazon.com, went bankrupt just nine months after completing its IPO. The September 11 attacks accelerated the stock market's decline. Investor confidence was further eroded by several accounting scandals and resulting bankruptcies, including the Enron scandal in October 2001, the WorldCom scandal in June 2002, and the Adelphia Corporation scandal in July 2002. On October 9, 2002, the lowest point was reached; the NASDAQ-100 fell 78% from its peak to 1,114, and stocks lost $5 trillion in market value since the peak (Geisst, 2018).

The Enron scandal reinforced the importance of corporate governance in ensuring accountability, protecting investors, and maintaining trust in financial markets. New regulations and legislation designed to increase publicly traded companies' financial reporting accuracy have been developed in this context. The most important of these measures was the Sarbanes–Oxley Act (2002), which imposed severe penalties for destroying, altering, or fabricating financial records. The law also prohibited audit firms from simultaneously performing consulting and auditing work for the same clients. In addition, the company's financial statements would henceforth have to be disclosed as consolidated financial statements, i.e., including subsidiary companies. The law introduced new requirements for corporate governance and financial reporting, including creating an independent audit committee, requiring CEOs and CFOs to certify the accuracy of their companies' financial statements, and increasing penalties for corporate fraud. However, the scandal revealed how corporations, regulators, and politicians collaborate in a system of new elitist capitalism. While some high-level executives were punished, the underlying corporate favoritism and regulatory capture system remained intact. The case served as a warning that, without structural changes, big corporations would continue to manipulate markets with political backing until the next major crisis.

Another considerable outrage was the NYSE Specialists Scandal (2003–2004), which occurred just after Enron. It exposed how firms responsible for ensuring fair and orderly trading manipulated the market for personal gain. These intermediaries engaged in illegal practices such as front-running client orders, interposition, and delaying trades to maximize profits at the expense of investors. After the scandal, the NYSE lifted the traditional specialist system but replaced it with a Designated Market Maker (DMM) system. While floor brokers operating in physical locations continue to exist, their roles are more limited and have shifted to handling large and complex transactions (Christie & Thompson, 2006).

At the time, the New York Stock Exchange (NYSE) used a specialist system where certain firms were appointed market makers for specific stocks. Each stock on the NYSE had a specialist firm responsible for handling orders and ensuring a fair market price. Specialists were supposed to match buyers and sellers reasonably and step in to provide liquidity when needed. Instead of fulfilling their duties somewhat, specialist firms engaged in illegal trading practices. They could see sizeable pending buy or sell orders before they were executed. They used this information to trade ahead of these orders, guaranteeing profits. For instance, if a specialist saw a large buy order at \$50, they would buy shares at \$49.90 and then sell at \$50, making a risk-free profit. Instead of directly matching a buyer with a seller, specialists inserted their trades in between. This resulted in worse prices for investors while specialists pocketed. The investor unknowingly pays more than necessary. Sometimes, specialists hold back trades to take advantage of price movements, executing transactions only when they benefit them. This slowed down the market and harmed investors, especially during fast-moving conditions. Five major specialist firms—LaBranche & Co., Bear Wagner Specialists, and Spear, Leeds & Kellogg—were caught manipulating over 2 million trades, generating illegal gains of at least \$157 million. Despite these violations, the penalties were minimal. The firms collectively paid \$240 million in fines, significantly less than their profits, and no top executives faced criminal charges (Christie & Thompson, 2006).

While the new system DMMs still oversee trading for specific stocks, their influence has been reduced due to electronic trading and stricter oversight. Unlike specialists, DMMs cannot engage in front-running, and multiple liquidity providers ensure greater market competition. Although DMMs still help maintain orderly trading, most market activity is now handled by automated systems.

11.9.1 The 2008–2009 Crisis

The US economy entered a period of growth after these scandals and attacks. This period's boom was based on Chinese production and US consumption. At the beginning of the twenty-first centuries, China, which had managed to build a large economy, invested in US Treasury bonds, and capital inflows to the United States were increasing. Meanwhile, anticipating a mild recession beginning in 2001, the Fed cut interest rates 11 times between May 2000 and December 2001, from 6.5 percent to 1.75 percent. Consumers took advantage of the cheap credit they could get from banks to buy consumer goods such as appliances and automobiles, and especially real estate such as houses. By the early 2000s, a "*housing bubble*" was forming (Duignan, n.d.).

Moreover, thanks to changes in banking laws in the 1980s, banks could offer mortgage loans to subprime customers on favorable terms. In the US system, a house remained in the bank's ownership until it was paid off. However, banks immediately transferred their securities and rights to investment banks. Investment banks needed continuous mortgage securities for the securitization method they applied. As long as house prices continued to rise, subprime borrowers could protect themselves against high mortgage payments by refinancing, borrowing on the increased value of their homes, or selling their homes at a profit and paying off their mortgages. In the event of default, banks could repossess the property and sell it for more than the original loan amount. Subprime loans were, therefore, a lucrative investment for many banks. Accordingly, many banks aggressively marketed subprime loans to low-income or less affluent customers, knowing their customers could not repay the loans and often misleading them about the risks involved. However, the general assumption in this trade was that the price of houses would keep rising. No one knew what to do if there was a housing crisis and banks had to repossess thousands of homes. As a result, the share of subprime mortgages in all housing loans rose from about 2.5 percent to about 15 percent per year from the late 1990s to 2004–07 (Duignan, n.d.).

Investment banks bundled thousands of subprime mortgages and other less risky forms of consumer debt and marketed them (or parts of them) in the capital markets. It was a common securitization practice to sell them as short-term debt securities called Asset-Backed Securities (ABS) to other banks and investors (including hedge funds and pension funds). Thus, banks could collect funds in one year, which they could collect in 20–30 years. Because investment banks were overly eager to buy mortgage securities, they probably did not do the kind of rigorous credit risk analysis that the banking system is supposed to do when lending.

The process worked like this: investment banks pooled the mortgage securities they received from commercial banks and insured them against the risk of non-payment with American International Group (AIG). They then issued short-term ABS based on the collateral of the insured mortgage securities pool and received ratings such as AAA from rating agencies. Competing with each other, the rating agencies gave these securities generous ratings. While selling subprime mortgages was a good way for commercial banks to increase their liquidity and reduce their exposure to risky loans, buying ABS was an excellent way for investment banks and investors to diversify their portfolios and make money. Few considered the risk that the housing market might fall. As housing prices continued to skyrocket in the early 2000s, ABS became widely popular, and their prices in the capital markets increased accordingly.

In 1999, the Depression-era Glass-Steagall Act (1933) was partially repealed, allowing banks, securities firms, and insurance companies to enter each other's markets and merge, creating "*too big to fail*" banks. In addition, in 2004, the Securities and Exchange Commission (SEC) passed resolutions encouraging banks to invest even more money in ABS. Riding the wave of globalization, banks claimed that they had entered a different era and underestimated the risks that might arise. Thus, they continued their reckless lending, borrowing, and securitization practices.

By 2007, house price growth had stalled, and subprime borrowers began to default on their payments. The sharp decline in the value of ABS caused enormous losses for many banks, hedge funds, and mortgage lenders, forcing even some large and prominent firms to liquidate hedge funds that had invested in ABS, apply to the government for loans, seek mergers with healthier companies, or declare bankruptcy. Credit rating agencies then downgraded ABS and became "*toxic*" (essentially worthless) assets. In April 2007, New Centuries Financial Corp, one of the largest subprime lenders, filed for bankruptcy, and shortly after that, many other subprime lenders ceased operations. In August, France's largest bank, BNP Paribas, announced billions of dollars in losses, and another major US firm, American Home Mortgage Investment Corp., declared bankruptcy (Acemoglu, 2009).

It was the end of the road. The size of ABS and subprime debt was difficult to determine. ABS were typically sold in pieces, mixed with other debt, and resold as new securities in the capital markets, a process that could go on indefinitely. As a result, banks began to doubt each other's solvency, leading to a pause in the Fed funds market with potentially unintended consequences. Northern Rock, the UK's fifth-largest mortgage lender, ran out of liquid assets and asked the Bank of England for a loan. News of the bailout caused panic among depositors, leading to the first bank failure in the UK in 150 years. Northern Rock was nationalized by the British government in February 2008 (Acemoglu, 2009).

In the United States, in March, Bear Stearns, Wall Street's highly reputable investment firm, was acquired by JPMorgan Chase, which had exhausted its liquid assets and suffered billions of dollars in losses. Fearing that Bear Stearns' bankruptcy would threaten the other big banks it had borrowed from, the Fed facilitated the sale by assuming $30 billion of the firm's high-risk assets. Meanwhile, the Fed cut the federal funds rate from 4.25 percent in early January to 0 percent in December. By the summer of 2008, Fannie Mae and Freddie Mac, the federally chartered companies that dominated the secondary mortgage market, were in serious trouble. To prevent their collapse, the US Treasury Department was forced to nationalize both companies in September, replace their executives, and cover their debt of $1.6 trillion (Wallison, 2011).

Later that month, Lehmann Brothers, a 168-year-old investment bank with $639 billion in assets, suffered the largest bankruptcy in US history. A day later, however, the Fed agreed to lend $85 billion to AIG, the country's largest insurance company, to cover losses related to the sale of credit default swaps (CDSs) that protect holders of various debt instruments in the event of default. Unlike Lehmann, AIG was deemed "*too big to fail.*" If AIG had collapsed, it would have caused the collapse of many banks that had bought CDS. Less than two weeks after Lehmann's collapse, Washington Mutual, the nation's most significant savings and loan, was seized by federal regulators and sold the next day to JPMorgan Chase (Wallison, 2011).

The Fed then undertook a variety of extraordinary quantitative easing (QE) measures to prevent a complete collapse of the financial system and lasting damage to the US economy. It is named programs designed to use money created by the Fed to inject liquidity into capital markets and thus stimulate economic growth. The mistakes of the 1929 crisis were not repeated. Central banks had undertaken similar interventions in other countries. The Fed's measures included the purchase of long-term US Treasuries and agency market-backed securities, Mortgage-backed securities for primary mortgage lending, credit facilities for holders of subprime securities, and the purchase of ABS and other debt held by Fannie Mae and Freddie Mac. By the time the QE programs officially ended in 2014, the Fed had pumped more than $4 trillion into the US economy (Chen et al., 2016).

In the process, millions of families lost their homes, businesses, or savings; millions of workers lost their jobs and faced long-term unemployment; millions of people fell into poverty. Their situation was in marked contrast to the bankers who helped create the crisis. Some of these managers lost their jobs when the extent of their mismanagement became clear to shareholders and the public, but those who resigned usually did so with generous bonuses. Moreover, in stark contrast to earlier financial scandals, such as the savings and loan crisis in the 1980s and the Enron collapse in 2001, no American CEO or other top executive has gone to jail or been charged with criminal offenses. Overall, key leaders of financial firms and other wealthy Americans did not lose proportionately as much as members of the lower and middle classes. While they largely recovered their losses by 2010, the crisis-struck public never recovered. These developments would lead to the emergence of the "*Corporatocracy and Crony Capitalism*" concept, which will be discussed in the last chapter (Rex & Headworth, 2021).

This glaring inequality generated great public resentment, which came together in 2011 in the "*Occupy Wall Street*" movement. This movement targeted economic elites and a political and economic system that seemed to be designed to serve the interests of the very rich—the "*1 percent*" as opposed to the "*99 percent.*" At the very least, it raised awareness of economic inequality in the United States. This decisive issue soon became a theme of Democratic political discourse at both the federal and state levels. However, partly because the movement had no organized leadership or concrete goals, it did not result in any specific reforms, let alone a complete transformation of "*the system,*" as some of its members had hoped (Calhoun, 2013).

However, this crisis brought a new corruption to the surface. One of these was the Madoff crisis. Madoff, the son of European Jewish immigrants, founded his brokerage firm in 1960, which evolved into Bernard L. Madoff Investment Securities, which he headed until his arrest by the US Federal Bureau of Investigation (FBI) in December 2008. Madoff also served as NASDAQ chairman in the early 1990s, and Madoff Investment Securities was, for a time, the exchange's most prominent market maker. However, he continued to collect money from his clients for a very long time by presenting himself as a successful brokerage firm. He paid off old clients with the money he collected from new clients (Heydenburg, 2015). They would give account statements based on unreal stock purchases to satisfy their clients. Madoff had created a new example of Ponzi finance.

In 2009, the Financial Times described Madoff's method: "*After deciding, for example, that all his clients' accounts would increase by 1 percent in November 2008, he would work backward to work out which stocks he would need to trade to gain 1 percent and prepare his report accord*ingly" (Banker, 2021). Eventually, Madoff's Ponzi scheme unraveled when the global financial crisis prompted clients to attempt to withdraw nearly $7 billion from his funds. In November 2008, with so little new money flowing in due to the crisis, Madoff could not keep up with the volume of withdrawal requests. As bank loans dried up, it became impossible for Madoff to obtain the funds necessary to meet the mountain of repayment demands. When his sons, learning of the matter, reported him to the authorities on December 10, the case was exposed. Investigators found that Madoff had not made a single trade for many years. Instead of implementing a portfolio management strategy, as he marketed to his clients, he deposited investors' funds into a bank account. He paid other clients who wanted to withdraw those funds. He also provided his clients with falsified account statements showing fictitious scenarios of achieving investment returns. Madoff was sentenced to 150 years in prison and died in prison sometime later (Geisst, 2018).

11.9.2 The Post-Global Crisis Era: Ethical Issues and Speculation

In 2009, in response to the global financial crisis, the Fed bought Treasuries and ABSs. On May 21, 2013, Fed Chairman Ben Bernanke signaled tapering, stating that asset purchases might slow if improvements continued. In December 2013, the Fed reduced purchases from $85 billion to $75 billion monthly, cutting another $10 billion at each meeting. As the economy normalized, the program ended in October 2014, and the Fed began shrinking its balance sheet in October 2017 (Milstein et al., 2021).

As the causes of the global crisis were being investigated, the importance of ethics and values such as social responsibility began to come to the fore. In addition to the self-interested behavior of investment banks and speculators that disregarded these values, the focus of the discussions was on the fact that rating agencies assigned ratings based on their self-interest and without due diligence to earn more. However, it was not easy to prevent such behavior on Wall Street. As communication technology developed, new methods began to emerge.

In this context, significant crises and scandals emerged between 2015 and 2020. One of them was the short-lived market crash that occurred on May 6, 2010. During this crash, major US stock indices, including the Dow Jones Industrial Average, the S&P 500, and the Nasdaq Composite Index, fell by more than 10% in less than an hour and partially recovered. Behind the event was high volatility in trading all types of securities, including stocks, futures, options, and Exchange-Traded Funds (ETFs). Although market indices partially recovered on the same day, the sudden collapse caused a loss of almost $1 trillion in market capitalization. As with the 1987 crisis, the cause of this collapse was initially poorly understood. However, the SEC investigation cleared the fog a bit. According to the SEC report, a single sell order of a considerable quantity of "*E-Mini*" S&P contracts, followed by aggressive sell orders executed by high-frequency algorithms, triggered a massive drop in market prices, which had already increased exponentially due to the negative market trends prevailing. High-frequency traders were blamed for the collapse. According to the investigation report, aggressive trading of large volumes of securities had led to enormous price volatility in financial markets. Indeed, such trading continued, and in another incident in 2015, London-based trader Navinder Singh Sarao was arrested following allegations of market manipulation that resulted in a Flash Crash. According to the accusations, Sarao's trading algorithm executed a series of large sell orders to drive down the prices of E-Mini S&P contracts, which ultimately triggered the market crash. It was evident that high-frequency trading posed a significant problem (Kirilenko et al., 2017). Regulations could not cope with high-tech. While high-frequency trading and algorithmic strategies created massive volatility, large financial institutions were often shielded from risks while retail investors bore the brunt of market fluctuations. This period laid the groundwork for widening wealth inequality and financial instability, issues that continue to define market structures today.

Another scandal that rocked the 2015s originated in London but involved several Wall Street banks. This scandal of flagrant breaches of ethics was revealed in a Financial Times article on July 27, 2012, with the confession of a former trader. The trader stated that Libor manipulation has been widespread since 1991. Investigations that began in 2012 and lasted until 2016 revealed that Deutsche Bank (DB), Barclays (BCS), Citigroup (C), JPMorgan Chase (JPM), and the Royal Bank of Scotland (RBS) had manipulated Libor, the London interbank market's market interest rate, which has the power to influence the price of $350 trillion in assets. Libor's influence on derivatives meant the manipulation was massive. Banks adjusted rates to benefit themselves, impacting trillions in global transactions. They falsely inflated or deflated rates to profit or appear more creditworthy (Huan et al., 2023). As I will detail in the last chapter, the Libor scandal exposed the corrupt relationship between big banks, regulators, and governments in shaping financial markets. Instead of allowing fair competition, these institutions colluded to manipulate one of the most important financial benchmarks in the world, knowing they would face fines, not jail time (Joint Economic Committee, 2012).

These ethics scandals were followed by the Martin Shkreli Drug Price Scandal in 2015. As CEO of Turing Pharmaceuticals, Shkreli raised the price of a life-saving drug from $13.50 to $750 overnight, sparking public outrage. He was later arrested for securities fraud and sentenced in 2017, igniting a debate on drug pricing and corporate responsibility (Zu, 2022). In another 2015 scandal, Volkswagen paid huge fines after it was revealed the company had manipulated US diesel vehicle emissions tests using special software (Jung & Sharon, 2019). Goldman Sachs also faced an ethics scandal involving Malaysia's 1MDB fund, where $6.5 billion in bonds were misused. Former Malaysian Prime Minister Najib Razak and officials embezzled funds, leading Goldman Sachs to pay billions in fines (Jones, 2020).

These scandals have led to a reexamination of the regulatory gaps on Wall Street and the ethical behavior of financial institutions, making the need for transparency, accountability, and regulation of the economic system even more evident. In the first decade of the 2000s, the United Nations and OECD established international standards on environmental, social, and governance (ESG) factors. The 2010 Dodd-Frank Wall Street Reform and Consumer Protection Act introduced stricter rules after the financial crisis. Additionally, after 2015, capital markets and banking commissions continued implementing regulations restricting market rules. In addition, significant changes were made in consumer protection and risk management. During this period, corporatocracy and crony capitalism were often argued, which refers to an economic system in which business success depends on close relationships with government officials rather than market competition. Although there have been instances where governments or public pressure have led to punitive actions against them, major players were often shielded from the consequences of their unethical actions, which will be discussed in the next chapter; they typically paid minor fines.

11.9.3 Concluding Remarks

The Nixon Shock (1971) profoundly impacted financial markets from a macroeconomic and microstructural perspective and had significant sociological and political consequences. From a macroeconomic perspective, the Nixon Shock increased currency volatility, which in turn affected commodity and stock markets. The floating exchange rate system encouraged financial liberalization, as governments no longer had to manage exchange rates directly. Then a chain reaction started, causing the deregulation of banking and financial markets with fewer restrictions on capital flows. Greater competition spurred the derivatives market as firms hedged currency risks and encouraged speculative trading on exchange rate fluctuations. Removing the gold standard expanded liquidity and risk-taking. Rising oil prices and inflation in the 1970s led central banks to hike rates, peaking in the early 1980s. This heightened market risk and investment uncertainty. Floating exchange rates enabled more unrestricted capital flows, spurring the Eurodollar market, offshore banking, and multinational hedging strategies. In conclusion, the financial sector has become more dominant relative to the real economy, with an increased use of leverage and speculative instruments, resulting in the financialization of the global economy.

At the micro level, the liberalization of financial markets after 1980 led to a profound transformation in the structure and functioning of global financial markets. As governments removed restrictions on capital flows, trading practices, and financial instruments, exchanges became more interconnected, technologically advanced, and dominated by institutional investors. While these changes increased market efficiency and liquidity, they also increased systemic risks and volatility. One of the most essential effects of deregulation has been the globalization of capital markets. The United States, European, and Asian markets have become increasingly interconnected, allowing investors to trade across time zones and regions. Developing countries have also opened their stock markets to foreign investors, increasing liquidity and exposing them to sudden capital outflows and financial instability.

The rise of the Nasdaq in the 1970s and the adoption of electronic trading platforms in the 1990s revolutionized global stock markets. Electronic trading increased the speed and efficiency of transactions, making markets more accessible to investors worldwide. However, it also led to the rise of high-frequency trading (HFT) and algorithmic trading, where computers execute trades in milliseconds. Deregulation spurred financial innovation, expanding asset classes and derivatives trading. Exchanges introduced futures, options, ETFs, and credit derivatives, making global hubs like CME and LIFFE key markets. While aiding risk management, these instruments increased complexity, borrowing, and speculation, contributing to crises like 2008, especially those who took overly leveraged positions and suffered a lot. As Warren Buffett said, investors stayed naked when the tide went out.

Liberalization sparked mergers among global stock exchanges, transforming them into for-profit entities. Major mergers like NYSE Euronext, Nasdaq OMX, and the London Stock Exchange Group created powerful institutions. While enhancing efficiency and investment options, these mergers reduced competition and concentrated power in a few dominant exchanges.

Investment funds gained power in the capital market, promoting short-term investment strategies. Fund managers' focus on short-term gains led to practices that manipulated stock prices, contributing to scandals like Enron and the 2008 crisis. These events sparked corruption cases, including Madoff and Libor, and a public backlash against Wall Street. As Glass-Steagall regulations faded, inclusive institutions were useless. However, technological advances allowed small investors, as seen in the GameStop case, to influence the market to a limited extent. Corporate governance and ethical and social responsibility concerns grew, prompting regulators like the SEC to introduce Dodd-Frank and Basel III reforms. Public discontent with hedge funds and speculators, amplified by social media and movements like Occupy Wall Street, highlighted these issues. However, regulations and protests failed to curb the financial lobby's power.

Corporate lobbying grew in the late 20th and early twenty-first centuries, pushing policies that favored the wealthy. Former financial executives of big banks like Morgan and Goldman Sachs took key positions in regulatory bodies, and corporate influence grew. Lobbying secured deregulations, tax breaks for the rich, weakened oversight, and cut social programs. Increasing money in politics made MPs more responsive to donors, eroding inclusive institutions and democratic representation, and disturbing income distribution. The inequality of income distribution has become a significant problem for all countries, including the United States, at the end of the 2000s. On a global scale, the Nixon Shock made developing countries more vulnerable to currency crises and debt burdens. The IMF and World Bank imposed austerity measures and privatization, further widening inequality in many nations.

As a result, corporatocracy and crony capitalism have deepened economic inequality, weakened democratic institutions, and intensified environmental problems at the beginning of the twenty-first centuries. While corporations wield enormous influence and are protected and under-punished in financial scandals, growing public awareness, regulatory efforts, and grassroots movements are pushing back against unchecked corporate power.

Following the 2008 financial crisis, US Senator Dick Durbin revealed the House of Representatives' weakness toward big business by saying, "*Frankly, this place belongs to them.*" With these words, he implied how Wall Street used its influence in Congress to block meaningful financial reforms in 2009 and revealed his concerns about the future (Grim, 2009).

References

Acemoglu, D. (2009). The crisis of 2008: structural lessons for and from economics. Globalization and Growth, 37.

Allington, N. F., McCombie, J. S., & Pike, M. (2012). Lessons not learned: From the collapse of Long-Term Capital Management to the subprime crisis. *Journal of Post Keynesian Economics, 34*(4), 555–582.

Banker (2021). Bernie Madoff's Ponzi scheme. https://internationalbanker.com/history-of-financial-crises/bernie-madoffs-ponzi-scheme-2008/

Bates, D. S. (1991). The crash of '87: Was it expected? The evidence from options markets. *The Journal of Finance., 46*(3), 1009–1044. https://doi.org/10.1111/j.1540-6261.1991.tb03775.x

Bhagat, S., Marr, M. W., & Thompson, G. R. (1985). The Rule 415 experiment: Equity markets. *The Journal of Finance, 40*(5), 1385–1401.

Budd, A. (2005). Black Wednesday: A re-examination of Britain's experience in the exchange rate mechanism. IEA Occasional Paper, (135).

Briault, C. (1999). The rationale for a single national financial services regulator. *World Bank*, 211.

Calhoun, C. (2013). Occupy wall street in perspective. *British Journal of Sociology, 64*(1), 26–38.

Cappucci, M. (2019). The proxy war against proxy advisors. *NYUJL & Bus., 16*, 579.

Carson, M., & Clark, J. (2013). Asian financial crisis. *Federal Reserve History*. https://www.federalreservehistory.org/essays/asian-financial-crisis

Cerny, P. G. (1989). The 'little big bang ' in Paris: Financial market deregulation in a dirigiste system. *European Journal of Political Research, 17*(2), 169–192.

Chen, A. H., & Siems, T. F. (2007). The effects of terrorism on global capital markets. In *The economic analysis of terrorism* (pp. 99–122). Routledge.

Chen, Q., Filardo, A., He, D., & Zhu, F. (2016). Financial crisis, US unconventional monetary policy, and international spillovers. *Journal of International Money and Finance, 67*, 62–81.

Christie, W. G., & Thompson, R. B. (2006). Wall street scandals: The curative effects of law and finance. *Washington University Law Review, 84*, 1567.

Coffee Jr, J. C. (2012). Delaware court of chancery: Change, continuity, and competition. *Columbia Business Law Review*, 387.

Cox, L. L. (1989). Poison pills: Recent developments in Delaware law. *University of Cincinnati Law Review, 58*, 611.

Crockett, A. (2007). The evolution and regulation of hedge funds. *Financial Stability Review-Special Issue on Hedge Funds, 10*, 19–28.

Duca, J. V. (2005). Why have U.S. Households increasingly relied on mutual funds to own equity? *Review of Income and Wealth, 51*(3), 375–396.

Duignan, B. (n.d.). Key events of the crisis, Britannica. https://www.britannica.com/money/financial-crisis-of-2007-2008/Key-events-of-the-crisis

Egginton, J. F., Van Ness, B. F., & Van Ness, R. A. (2012). Exchange entrances, mergers, and the evolution of trading of NASDAQ-listed securities, 1993–2010. *Journal of Accounting and Finance, 12*(4), 66–85.

Geisst, C. R. (2018). Wall Street: A history. Oxford University Press.

Goodman, J. B. (1992). Monetary policy and financial deregulation in France. *French Politics and Society*, 31–40.

Grim, R. (2009). Dick Durbin: Banks "Frankly Own The Place". *HuffPost*. https://www.huffpost.com/entry/dick-durbin-banks-frankly_n_193010

Hardy, D., Regulatory Capture in Banking (January 2006). IMF Working Paper No. 06/34, Available at SSRN: https://ssrn.com/abstract=892925

Henderson, C. (2000). Asya Krizi ve Sonrası Asya'nın Çöküşü. Birinci Baskı, Çev., Meral Günenç, Alfa Yayınları, İstanbul.

Heydenburg, M. R. (2015). The Ponzi scheme as a deception operation: The Bernie Madoff case study. *American Intelligence Journal, 32*(2), 27–34.

Huan, X., Previts, G. J., & Parbonetti, A. (2023). Understanding the LIBOR scandal: The historical, the ethical, and the technological. *Journal of Banking Regulation, 24*(4), 403–419.

Jensen, M. C., & Meckling, W. H. (2019). Theory of the firm: Managerial behavior, agency costs and ownership structure. In Corporate governance (pp. 77–132). Gower.

Jones, D. S. (2020). 1MDB corruption scandal in Malaysia: A study of control and accountability failure. *Public Administration and Policy, 23*(1), 59–72.

Johnston, A. (2007). Takeover regulation: Historical and theoretical perspectives on the City Code. *The Cambridge Law Journal, 66*(2), 422–460.

Joint Economic Committee. (2012). https://www.jec.senate.gov/public/_cache/files/5906a359-6ecd-4aba-ba23-ae71706575a6/libor-scandal-final.pdf

Jung, J. C., & Sharon, E. (2019). The Volkswagen emissions scandal and its aftermath. *Global Business and Organizational Excellence, 38*(4), 6–15.

Kashyap, R. (2019). Michael Milken. *The Journal of Private Equity, 23*(1), 39–54.

Koehn, D. (2002). John Meriwether and the Promethean hero: A cautionary tale in financial ethics. *Teaching Business Ethics, 6*, 27–43.

Kirilenko, A., Kyle, A. S., Samadi, M., & Tuzun, T. (2017). The flash crash: High-frequency trading in an electronic market. *The Journal of Finance, 72*(3), 967–998.

Linder, D. O. (n.d.). Famous trials. https://famous-trials.com/enron/1787-home

Michie, R. (2001). *The LSE: A history*. OUP Oxford

Milstein, E., Powell, T., & Wessel, D. (2021). *What does the federal reserve mean when it talks about tapering?* Brookings. https://www.brookings.edu/articles/what-does-the-federal-reserve-mean-when-it-talks-about-tapering/#:~:text=In%20December%202013%2C%20the%20Fed,took%20over%20as%20Fed%20Chair

McLean, B., & Elkind, P. (2013). The smartest guys in the room: Enron's amazing rise and scandalous fall. Penguin.

Modigliani, F., & Miller, M. (1963). Corporate income taxes and the cost of capital: a correction. *American Economic Review, 53*(3), 433–443. JSTOR 1809167.

Morgan, J. P. (1984). *Rethinking Glass-Steagall*. J. P. Morgan & Co. Incorporated. https://www.sechistorical.org/collection/papers/1980/1984_1231_RethinkingGlass.pdf

Murphy, S. D. (2002). Terrorist attacks on the world trade center and the Pentagon. *American Journal of International Law, 96*(1), 237–254.

O'Malley, C. (2015). *Bonds without borders: A history of the Eurobond market*. John Wiley & Sons.
Osnos, P. L. (Ed.). (2022). *George Soros: A life in full*. Harvard Business Press.
Rex, J., & Headworth, S. (2021). *The global financial crisis and white-collar crime*. Oxford University Press.
Petra, S., & Spieler, A. C. (2020). Accounting scandals: Enron, Worldcom, and Global Crossing. In *Corporate fraud exposed: A comprehensive and holistic approach* (pp. 343–360). Emerald Publishing Limited.
Saxena, S. (2013). Regulation of Stock Markets in France. Available at SSRN 2223580.
Stevenson, R. (1985-11-05). *Pantry pride control of Revlon board seen near* (p. D5). New York Times.
Stigler, G. J. (2021). The theory of economic regulation. In *The political economy: Readings in the politics and economics of American public policy* (pp. 67–81). Routledge. https://www.taylorfrancis.com/chapters/edit/10.4324/9781315495811-8/theory-economic-regulation-george-stigler
Stories. Finance (n.d.). Meeting Michael Milken. https://www.stories.finance/stories/watson
Sutela, P. (2000). The financial crisis in Russia. *Global financial crises: Lessons from recent events* (pp. 63–73). Springer, US.
Thomas, C. W. (2002). The rise and fall of Enron. *Journal of Accountancy-New York, 193*(4), 41–52.
Townsend, A. M. (2001). The Internet and the rise of the new network cities, 1969–1999. *Environment and Planning b: Planning and Design, 28*(1), 39–58.
Truell, P. (1997). *Market place: Lessons of Boesky and Milken Go unheeded in fraud case*. The New York Times.
Vise, D. A., & Coll, S. (1991). *Eagle on the street: Based on the Pulitzer Prize-winning Account of the SEC's Battle with Wall Street*. Collier Books.
Wallison, P. (2011). The true story of the financial crisis. *The American Spectator, 13*, 2011.
Weber, E. J. (2009). A short history of derivative security markets. In *Vinzenz Bronzin's option pricing models: Exposition and appraisal* (pp. 431–466). Springer.
Zu, L. (2022). The crisis of leadership: Failure of business ethics. *Responsible and Sustainable Business: The Taoism's perspective* (pp. 57–62). Springer International Publishing.
Zysman, J. (1987). Debt and US Decline. *Stanford Journal of International Law, 23*, 131.

Chapter 12
Conclusion: Inclusive Institutions and the Future of Stock Markets

12.1 Introduction

At the peak of the COVID-19 pandemic in 2020, which forced billions to stay home worldwide, Keith Gill was working online in his rented home in Brockton, Massachusetts, next to the air conditioner on a sweltering July evening. Newly married with a child and barely scraping by, he spent his days as a financial analyst at MassMutual. In the evenings, he opened r/WallStreetBets on his computer, ignoring mockery from some who called him "*nerdy garbage.*" Wearing a Ninja Headband, he was making himself look like a warrior. This platform was a popular Reddit community focused on high-risk, high-reward stock and options trading. He supported his family by sharing his views on the site through YouTube live streams (real-time video broadcasts) under Roaring Kitty. He also searched for meme stocks that gained viral popularity due to social media hype rather than fundamental value. The popularity of meme stocks was often based on highly speculative and volatile Internet memes shared among traders on these and similar platforms, such as Reddit. The investors it appealed to were usually young and inexperienced traders. He had noticed for some time that GameStop's (GME) stock would be too low. GME's technology was outdated, but according to his calculations, its stock was undervalued. When Keith advertised the stock on the platform, he did not hesitate to put his entire savings of $53,000 into it.

It quickly gained popularity on social media forums, such as the Reddit chatroom r/wallstreetbets, which had 4.8 million members. Most of the members of r/WallStreetBets were also users of the Robinhood marketplace platform. Since March 2015, Robinhood Market platforms have used the Payment for Order Flow (PFOF) system, which offers commission-free trading in stocks and exchange-traded funds. With this system, Robinhood routed incoming orders to large market makers, such as Citadel Securities, instead of sending them directly to the exchange. The market maker, in turn, would get a slight price advantage when executing these orders and would pay Robinhood in return. It was a relatively simple mobile app that appealed

M. B. Karan, *A History of Stock Exchanges*, Contributions to Economics,
https://doi.org/10.1007/978-3-032-07788-2_12

to a younger population. It attracted users with fun tools that made trading more engaging, such as the firm's name and digital confetti displays on specific customer actions. Robinhood thus made stock trading cheap and accessible to the lay public in the United States and other countries. The Bulgarian-American Vlad Tenev was the co-founder and later sole CEO of Robinhood.

During the pandemic, the FED encouraged borrowing with quantitative easing (QE—buying debt securities) while lowering interest rates to zero to prevent the economy from entering a recession. This environment also made it easier for speculators to enter short positions and sell forward. Speculators and hedge funds were engaging in bearish operations on the stocks of companies performing poorly. This time, their target was GME, which was rooted in presumed outdated technology. In response to the company's dire financial situation, some speculators, notably Melvin Capital, of which Gabriel Plotkin (a top-earning, brilliant top university graduate) was the CEO, had been shorting the company's stock for some time (Li et al., 2021).

Encouraged by social media platforms to engage in this trade, GME shares rose from \$4.99 on January 13, 2021, to \$86.88 on January 27 (Table 12.1). This instantly changed the agenda of the financial press and media. Keith Gill and his followers were ecstatic. The rise in GME's price put Melvin Capital in a problematic position (Mackenzie & Fletcher, 2021). On January 2, Elon Musk tweeted, "*Gamestonk*!!!" on Reddit, along with a link to the r/wallstreetbets chat room. Musk's Twitter profile, which had 48 million followers, further fueled the explosive rise in GME's share price, and consequently, Melvin Capital's value decreased by 30% in one month. By the end of January, the company had lost 53% of its investments (Mackenzie & Fletcher, 2021).

Then the SEC (Securities and Exchange Commission) stepped in amid speculation that they "*may also have been the target of blatant social media attempts to inflate stock prices artificially*." Everything changed when r/WallStreetBets was temporarily

Table 12.1 GameSpot common stock price chart 2020–2021. *Data Source* Yahoo Finance

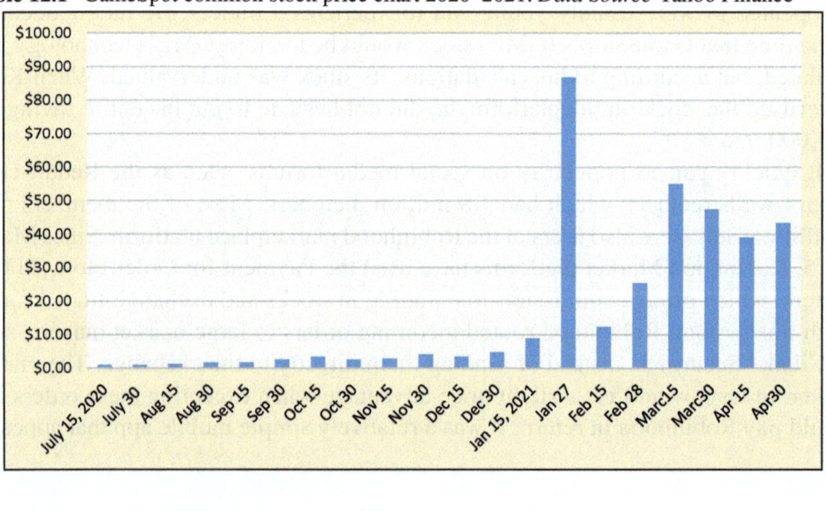

shut down on January 28, 2021, due to "*inflammatory and vulgar content*," causing a massive wave of panic selling in GME shares. As GME shares became highly volatile, the NSCC (National Securities Clearing Corporation) required additional large-margin deposits from brokers, significantly contributing to the site's closure. These were pretexts; there was a greater concern for market security or institutional repression. Although the NSCC's request was technically directed at Robinhood, individual investors bore the cost. In response, many angry individual investors filed numerous lawsuits against Robinhood, reacting to the fact that institutions were not subject to similar bans and trading restrictions.

One of the key players in this case was Citadel Securities, where the CEO, a wealthy mid-life US citizen, was Ken Griffin. Much of Robinhood's revenue came from routing orders to Citadel Securities, the market maker. On the other hand, when Melvin Capital, which had engaged in excessive short selling of GME, suffered huge losses, Citadel Securities and its business partner, Point72 Asset Management, provided it with financial support of $2.75 billion. This support led some investors to believe Citadel was intervening in the market. However, Keith Gill's YouTube rebroadcast, which showed that he still held a large amount of GME stock and remained optimistic, reignited excitement in the r/WallStreetBets community and boosted interest in GME. On March 1, GME rose 10.1% and continued to increase thereafter.

The US House Financial Services Committee launched investigations into Vlad Tenev (Robinhood), Ken Griffin (Citadel), Gabriel Plotkin (Melvin Capital), and Keith Gill (Citadel)—the first three for their roles in the fiasco and the last for alleged public deception and self-enrichment. While investors defended their actions, Gill firmly denied wrongdoing, stating that he acted as any investor would.

As a result, Plotkin was forced to close Melvin Capital due to heavy losses, and no illegal involvement by Citadel was found. Robinhood faced multiple lawsuits and paid a $70 million fine. Tenev's reputation suffered, but he remained CEO of Robinhood. Keith Gill retired from YouTube in late April to escape the spotlight. Meanwhile, the PFOF model became increasingly controversial, with growing criticism that small investors were unprotected.

Although the SEC's goal was to prevent broader market contagion, break the momentum of retail-driven squeezes, and ultimately help restore institutional control over pricing and volatility, Robinhood's trading restrictions on January 28, 2021, magnified losses for retail traders. Robinhood's structure meant retail investors had little access to shorting, reinforcing the unequal playing field. The decision was widely seen as protecting institutional investors, as hedge funds were forced to close short positions on GME at a loss. The SEC did not classify this as "*market man*ipulation" or "*illegal tr*ading" and chose to monitor the situation rather than intervening. However, the public perception was that the SEC favored corporate interests over the rights of retail investors.

Citadel's investment in Melvin Capital, keeping it afloat longer, was viewed as another example of the SEC protecting large institutions. Meanwhile, small investors suffered due to Robinhood's trading restrictions and stock market volatility. The SEC did not directly address their losses but focused on institutional influence in market regulation. As a result, the SEC does act against unusual price surges. Still, this case exposed how definitions of "*market manipulation*" may vary depending on who is winning and who is losing.

The GME event had two key consequences. First, it highlighted the financial system's institutional transformation since the 1980s and the weakness of inclusive institutions that aim to establish predictable rules, provide equal opportunities for all actors, remove artificial barriers to market entry, ensure transparency in decision-making, and institutionalize accountability, as later Nobel Prize winners Acemoğlu and Robinson (2012) noted. Partially excessive financial liberalization widened inequality, fueled crises, and strengthened large financial institutions, notably. The repeal of the 1933 Glass-Steagall Act, which had previously prohibited investment banks and hedge funds from engaging in riskier transactions, enabled them to do so, thereby increasing the dominance of large investors. Despite SEC and congressional scrutiny of Robinhood and Citadel, no significant regulations have followed. When considered alongside past scandals—such as the "NYSE Specialist Case" (2003–2004), the "High- Frequency Trading" misconduct (2012), and the Libor interest rate manipulations—these events have reinforced a troubling public perception that market manipulation persists and continues to favor large institutional players. In contrast, small investors' access to information, influence over price formation, and ability to trade on fair terms have been significantly weakened. In this context, the limited interventions of regulatory bodies such as the SEC in response to both historical market abuses and key actors involved in the GME episode have revealed the dysfunctionality of what was once intended to be an inclusive institutional structure.

Second, the GME event marked a shift where social media and digital communication gained influence in financial markets. This inefficiency of market regulations has been filled through digital collective action. Thus, the GME case can be considered a financial event and a digital response to institutional exclusion. Social media platforms such as Reddit, Twitter, and Discord provided an alternative space for individual investors to organize their voices in the market. Unlike the traditional system, GME showed that individual investors could organize via Reddit, Twitter, and Discord to challenge Wall Street hedge funds. Even Elon Musk, the later owner of X (formerly Twitter), fueled investor momentum with a tweet. The financial world began recognizing social media as a market force, with concerns that dominant platforms could directly impact market efficiency.

This development highlights structural issues that necessitate reevaluation of the legitimacy and inclusiveness of the financial system. The GME case has demonstrated that even in a country with historically strong institutions such as the United States, the functions of inclusive economic institutions can be weakened and historical gains can be reversed. This has profound implications not only for market efficiency but also for democratic legitimacy and institutional trust.

These developments reflect the evolution of the stock market over the past 500 years and suggest that its future may change in unforeseen ways. What started as disordered coffeehouse exchanges has become a highly regulated virtual space where millions trade online. Nevertheless, advancing technology pushes trading beyond regulators' oversight, making it harder to predict how markets will evolve in a world shaped by innovation and shifting ideologies.

Stock markets have long been driven more by perception and narrative than pure data, serving as hubs for risk-takers who weave stories from fragments of information. Harari (2024) notes that investors are strangers united by shared stories. They constantly seek news and invest based on perception. While regulation has helped guide them toward accurate information, it has not always succeeded. Over time, regulations and inclusive institutions have evolved inconsistently—rules have loosened at times, empowering major market players. Social media now provides instant news access, but has not made markets more efficient. Platforms like Twitter, Instagram, and Facebook have instead amplified noise, speculation, and emotional trading.

The GME case reminds us of how inclusive institutions have evolved across different stages of capitalism and how corporate management styles and information flows have influenced trade over time. As Andrew Lo (2004) emphasizes in his Adaptive Markets Hypothesis, we need to explain the history of financial markets not through fixed rules, but through environmental change, human behavior, and institutional evolution. In this context, it is worth examining how the logic of ownership and value has evolved and how institutions have developed over time, from the inception of capitalism to the present day (Fig. 12.1). Undoubtedly, it is also necessary to reveal how inclusive institutions increase information effectiveness during this transition.

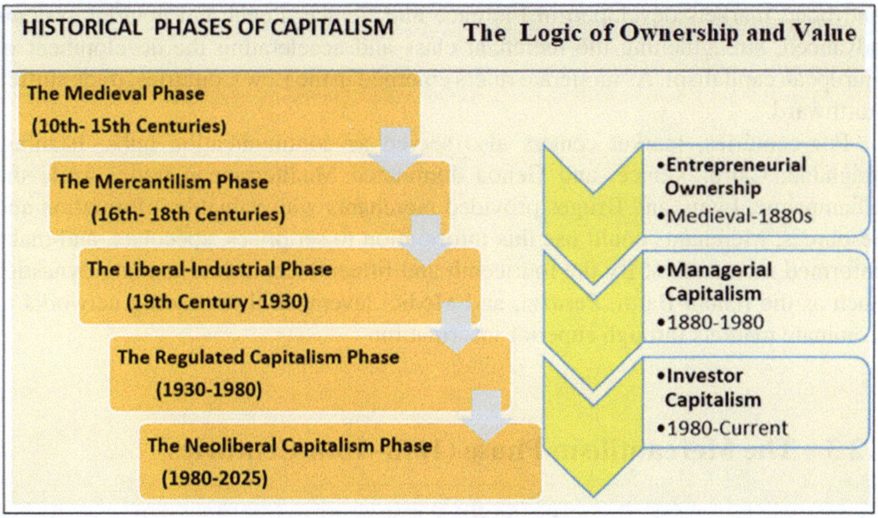

Fig. 12.1 Historical phases of capitalism and understanding of ownership and value. It is drawn by the author

12.2 The Medieval Phase

During the so-called feudal or medieval era, economic activity was primarily based on agriculture, and these economies were closed. The commercial activities following the Black Death era enabled the expansion of economic activity, the accumulation of capital, and the emergence of innovative financial practices. Inclusive institutions in the Middle East and Europe during this period were often legal, financial, and commercial, supporting trade growth.

Between the eighth and fourteenth centuries, the Islamic world was a hub of commercial innovation. Islamic law protects contracts and property rights, fostering investor confidence. As commodity markets grew, firms specializing in deposits, remittances, and credit emerged. However, religious constraints prevented Islamic law from adapting to broader commercial ventures, and autocratic rulers stifled the emergence of new economic dynamics. Still, cities like Baghdad, Cairo, Damascus, and Bukhara became key financial centers, influencing European merchant states such as Genoa and Venice.

In Europe, trade expanded as feudalism weakened and city-states rose. Merchant guilds cooperated with city-states to protect members, accumulate capital, and promote international trade through fairs. Trade organizations safeguarded merchants from pirates and unfair taxation. By the thirteenth century, Italian banking families laid the groundwork for modern finance. The Champagne and Lyon became trade hubs, and the Bruges trade inspired the first stock exchanges. Usury laws were eased, and bond markets developed in Florence and Venice. Legal and notarial systems advanced, strengthening the merchant class and accelerating the development of European capitalism. As moderate rulers emerged in the Low Countries, trade shifted northward.

For centuries, market centers also served as communication hubs. Istanbul, Baghdad, Cairo, Venice, and Genoa dominated Mediterranean trade, while the Champagne, Lyon, and Bruges provided merchants with valuable information and resources. Merchants could use this information to set prices, speculate, and make informed investments. By the fourteenth and fifteenth centuries, banking dynasties such as the Italian Bardi, Peruzzi, and Medici leveraged their trading networks to dominate markets through superior information.

12.3 The Mercantilism Phase (16th–18th Centuries)

Mercantilism, the early stage of capitalist transformation, is an economic policy based on the state's power to direct economic activities, which was particularly effective in Europe from the sixteenth century to the eighteenth century. Its primary purpose is to increase the country's wealth, primarily through gold and silver stocks, by generating a trade surplus with foreign governments. Over time, this policy understanding has also transformed into a protectionist, competitive, and colonialist trade system in international relations. The early development of mercantilism in the Low Countries was due primarily to the region's strong maritime trade, early capitalist relations of production, well-developed financial institutions, and the process of political independence.

In the sixteenth century, Antwerp emerged as a significant financial and commercial hub, thriving during a period of transition from a guild-based to a state-led administration. By fostering inclusive institutions, central and urban governments involved all stakeholders in economic growth, strengthening trade and financial markets. The Antwerp, one of Europe's first modern money and bond exchanges, played a pivotal role in the development of finance. It was the first organized market in a fixed location, established in the sixteenth century, where goods and financial instruments were regularly bought and sold. A sophisticated banking system, supported by Italian and German bankers, facilitated international money transfers and short-term loans, thereby ensuring safer trade and commerce. Legal protections, including commercial law and specialized courts, gave merchants a sense of security and confidence. Guilds and trade associations, notably the Hanseatic League, significantly enhanced Antwerp's commercial expansion by protecting the interests of merchants. However, the Spanish occupation had destroyed the luster of its institutions.

In the seventeenth century, Amsterdam emerged as a global center for trade and finance. Investment democratization and the development of inclusive institutions broadened economic participation, enabling elites, merchants, and citizens to share in the growth. Founded in 1602, the Amsterdam Stock Exchange enabled trading in the world's first publicly listed company. With the establishment of the East India Company and the West India Company, Amsterdam became a central hub for trade.

The banking system was crucial; the Amsterdamsche Wisselbank, established in 1609, facilitated secure international money transfers and capital flows. Amsterdam was strategically positioned as a significant port in trade between Europe and Asia, as explained in Chapter 5. Commercial law evolved to protect contracts and business practices. Special courts and regulations resolved disputes, providing legal security to merchants and investors and further boosting trade. The decline of the Amsterdam financial market in the eighteenth century was driven by political instability, the loss of Dutch maritime dominance, and the rise of London as a more dynamic financial center.

The Glorious Revolution of 1688 introduced institutional reforms that helped transform London into a leading financial center. Limiting royal power, securing property rights, and preventing state interference boosted market confidence and capital accumulation. English commercial law provided an exceptionally stable, flexible, and enforceable legal framework for trade and finance, thanks to the common law tradition and institutional support for contracts, credit, and commercial innovation. Founded in 1694, the Bank of England was responsible for managing government borrowing and regulating the money supply. London became a hub for international trade and financial innovation, supported by strong commercial law. In the eighteenth century, the London Stock Exchange (LSE) gained prominence, particularly with large firms like the British East India Company going public. The LSE facilitated capital raising, trade growth, and financial liquidity.

Paris also became a significant financial center in the seventeenth and eighteenth centuries. The Paris Bourse played a key role in trading government bonds, company shares, and other financial instruments. By the eighteenth century, it held a crucial position in international markets. Napoleon's reforms strengthened the Bourse, supporting capital raising and economic growth. The Bank of France, established in 1800, managed monetary policy and stabilized the financial system, albeit only briefly. Then, it briefly surpassed the Bank of England in terms of centralized control, nationwide note issuance, and integration with state fiscal policy.

During the mercantilist era, economic institutions such as exclusive trading companies, state-sponsored monopolies, and limited property rights were largely exclusionary. However, in countries such as the Netherlands and England, the initial steps toward inclusive institutions were taken during this period, mainly due to the rise of the mercantile bourgeoisie and the subsequent development of parliamentary structures.

12.3.1 The Importance of Information in the Mercantilism Phase

Bruges, Antwerp, Amsterdam, and London, where money and securities markets originated, had strategic coastal locations that provided them with access to news from Europe, the New World, and the Far East. In Antwerp (sixteenth century) and Amsterdam (seventeenth century), easy access to information fostered the growth of plain securities and derivatives markets. Transparent information flow enabled investors to anticipate market movements, making derivatives popular for hedging against price fluctuations. Speculation and arbitrage enabled profits from price differences, while derivative operations helped reduce business risks.

However, until the twentieth century, there was no regulation, and market information was often biased, leading to manipulation and insider trading. Commercial and financial information circulated among traders, bankers, and officials, usually excluding ordinary investors. Executives at the East India Company and government officials exploited early information, while traders had access to non-public data on cargoes and trade routes. The Rothschilds were rumored to have profited from insider trading during the Napoleonic wars, and many politicians were involved in such practices. The speculation of Parisian revolutionary Etienne Clavière highlighted one of the early crises of the Paris Bourse. During the Napoleonic wars, false news spread to influence prices. Stock market barons dominated in the United States, and manipulation and insider trading were widespread until the early twentieth century.

12.4 The Liberal-Industrial Phase (19th–Early 20th Centuries)

By the early nineteenth century, Western Europe and the United States had entered the industrial era. The interaction between industrialization and finance capitalism accelerated market development through free competition, despite the presence of speculation and financial crises. The Industrial Revolution increased capital demand, boosting the importance of stock exchanges and banks. London became the global financial hub. In the nineteenth century, London banks financed significant industrial investments. Central banking evolved, while private and investment banks provided large-scale loans. The LSE expanded, with regulations improving investor confidence through anti-fraud laws, transparent transactions, and standardized trading rules. The London Stock Exchange reinforced investor confidence in the nineteenth century with regulations such as the Joint Stock Companies Act (1844) and the Limited Liability Act (1856). Legalizing joint-stock companies enabled broader participation in capital markets, deepened financial markets, and supported industrial investment. London's financial model inspired markets in the U.K., the United States, and beyond, while international bond markets also emerged in London.

In 19th-century Paris, the development of the capital market was driven by inclusive institutions, legal reforms, and financial stability. State intervention proved pivotal, enhancing economic power and financial appeal while supporting trade and industrial policies, most notably in the railroad sector. Strict commercial and company laws were implemented to ensure secure trading, guarantee the validity of contracts, and establish courts to resolve disputes. These measures contributed to the establishment of a stable environment for traders and investors. A highly structured financial market was developed, anchored in state oversight, legal codification, and public trust in institutions such as the Bourse and Crédit Mobilier. While London relied on decentralized, private-market mechanisms under common law, Paris exemplified a more centralized and codified path to capital market maturity—one in which state coordination played a defining role, particularly in infrastructure finance. The decline of the Paris Stock Exchange in the nineteenth century was due to political turmoil, restrictive regulations that undermined inclusive institutions under the auspices of state-controlled finance, and the increasing dominance of the more liberal and internationally connected London market.

The Ottomans faced significant economic and political challenges, but they introduced key financial reforms. The Tanzimat Reform (1839) and the Islahat Edict (1856) liberalized the economy, easing the application of Islamic law and allowing foreign merchants and minorities to participate. These changes enabled the creation of the Ottoman Bank and the Istanbul Stock Exchange, shaping Istanbul's financial infrastructure. However, excessive borrowing and political instability ultimately led to economic decline, although the reforms had a significant impact on emerging stock exchanges in the Middle East and the Balkans.

Industrial capitalism expanded rapidly in the United States during the late nineteenth century. Following the Civil War, industrial production surged, railroads expanded, and large corporations emerged. The NYSE played a crucial role in financing this growth as companies went public to raise capital, and stocks became more widely available. NYSE financed key sectors, including railroads, steel, and oil, which drove economic expansion. During this period, the lack of regulations on the stock market caused the market to fall into the hands of robber stock barons. Financial fluctuations, such as the Panic of 1873 and the 1907 Banking Crisis, demonstrated that the stock market was susceptible to speculation. Large concentrations of capital led to the formation of monopolies, and it was only after the Civil War that regulations, such as the Sherman Antitrust Act of 1890, were introduced to address this issue. At the beginning of the twentieth century, the NYSE became one of the centers of financial markets. Fraud was rampant in Europe and the United States during this period; however, by the end of the nineteenth century, public awareness of insider trading and market manipulation had increased.

12.4.1 Rising Awareness of Fair Trading in the Liberal-Industrial Phase

In the early 1900s, the government did not plan to regulate insider trading, and market players did not demand it. The lack of market transparency contributed heavily to the early tolerance of insider trading. Nevertheless, this was reinforced by legal norms, ideological commitments to laissez-faire principles, and a narrow investor base. Stock market manipulation and fraud were treated separately, with legal, cultural, and public perspectives evolving gradually over time. Before the Great Depression and the creation of the SEC, insider trading was not explicitly prohibited. Instead, the focus was on securities fraud and market manipulation, though regulations remained inadequate. Tactics such as spreading fake news, wash trading, and speculative price manipulation were commonplace. Those with insider information often profited without legal consequences. As Manne (1966) argues, "Before 1910, no one had publicly questioned the morality of corporate officers, directors, and employees buying and selling company stock….there is no evidence that either the business community or the public had a general revulsion against insider trading in the 'good old days,' and there is no indication that the public 'lost confidence in the stock market because of the existence of insider trading." By 1910, some legal scholars, economists, and financial journalists had begun to question insider trading more broadly, particularly after Union Pacific Railroad executives were accused in 1906 of delaying a dividend announcement to buy stock before the price surged (Perino, 2019).

As a result, the inclusive institutions established during this period ensured that financial markets became stable and reliable. The rule of law, economic regulation, and the protection of investor rights supported the development of stock markets. Stock market investors and traders understood that access to accurate news immediately provided them with significant gains. However, although there was an awareness of manipulation and insider trading, there was no regulation in financial markets. Before the twentieth century, financial markets relied on self-regulation through exchange rules and reputational discipline. While this created a degree of order among insiders, it proved insufficient to protect outside investors or prevent market abuse. The macroeconomic developments during this period affected firm management. Large listed companies altered their management approach by adapting to the prevailing conditions of the period, and the distinction between professional managers and shareholders became more pronounced. Thus, managerial capitalism emerged. This arose from the need for technical management of large-scale companies that were created by the Industrial Revolution, preceding the Great Depression. This management approach continued until the last quarter of the century.

12.4.2 The Rise of Managerial Capitalism

The era of managerial capitalism emerged with the separation of management from ownership as industrial enterprises developed into large corporations between the late nineteenth century and the 1980s. In this process, corporate managers dominated business decision-making, developing inclusive institutions that shaped financial markets. The era of managerial capitalism gave rise to a complex web of institutions—from stock exchanges and investment banks to business schools, accounting standards, and regulatory bodies—that embedded the authority of corporate managers at the center of financial capitalism. These institutions structured capital allocation, shaped investor expectations, and professionalized corporate governance, reinforcing the dominance of large-scale enterprise from the early twentieth century through the 1980s. Berle and Means (1968), in their 1932 edition of the book "T*he Modern Corporation and Private Property,*" inspired this movement by arguing for the separation of ownership and management in large joint-stock companies, suggesting that professional managers should run the companies. In addition, Max Weber, in The Protestant Ethic and the Spirit of Capitalism (1905), John Kenneth Galbraith's The New Industrial State (1967), and Milton Friedman's Capitalism and Freedom (1962) contributed to the view that managers would and should primarily serve the interests of shareholders.

Managerial capitalism understanding continued in the market for about a century, and financial regulations of the New Deal, banking systems, and capital markets evolved to support long-term industrial investment, creating a stable economic environment that fostered corporate expansion. Gradually, corporate management developed into a specialized profession, and MBA programs became increasingly widespread. The Board of Directors and CEOs became the leading actors in the company's strategic decisions. With companies opening to the broader public, small shareholders, in particular, were excluded entirely from company management. This process had many significant consequences. Large companies became more efficient due to effective corporate governance and expanded into international markets.

Financial markets grew, and investors became increasingly dependent on the decisions of professional managers. As a result, managerial capitalism enabled the efficient management of large companies and supported economic growth. However, over time, the excessive power of managers has led to problems such as financialization and income inequality, resulting in criticism of the system. CEOs of large corporations, such as Jack Morgan, Charles E. Mitchell, and Albert Wiggin, became the most critical players in capital markets.

12.5 The Regulated Capitalism Phase (1930–1973)

After the 1929 crash, public outrage over unregulated markets led to financial reforms aimed at stability and inclusivity. Following the free market approach, regulations were introduced to ensure economic stability and create more inclusive institutions. The financial world opposed this at every stage, but bowed to social pressure. The goals of state intervention were to protect national industries from overseas competition and to encourage the growth of national companies through social welfare programs and state investment in infrastructure. This new approach to managing the economy was known as "*state capitalism or Keynesianism.*" The New Deal reforms in the United States and similar state interventions in Europe ensured the safety of financial markets. The New Deal included regulations separating commercial and investment banking, most notably the Glass-Steagall Act of 1933, and increased tax rates on wealthy individuals and corporate profits. Transparency in financial markets increased during this period. Financial reporting standards for companies became mandatory, and institutions such as the Securities and Exchange Commission (SEC) introduced regulations to reinforce investor confidence. Similar reforms in Europe stabilized financial markets. Governments issued bonds to finance public spending, ensuring liquidity and market stability.

The Bretton Woods Agreement, established in 1944, facilitated the development of international trade and investment by stabilizing the exchange rate system. It stabilized global markets and spread the effects of regulated (state) capitalism. The (neo-) Keynesian model adopted in the United States, combined with the production boom generated by World War II, fostered economic growth and accumulation for United States corporations, propelling the United States to become a global economic power during this period of capitalism. In conclusion, regulated capitalism has increased state intervention, strengthened financial transparency, and limited excessive corporate profits while fostering innovation in the financial market.

12.5.1 The Road to Efficiency: Insider Trading, Market Regulation, and the Rise of EMH

The Securities Exchange Act of 1934 established the SEC and the first regulations on market manipulation and insider trading. Initially, the SEC focused on preventing fraud and market manipulation rather than insider trading. Although increasingly viewed as unethical in the United States, insider trading did not remain illegal until the 1960s, when public concern began to grow (Perino, 2019).

Financial markets initially relied on self-regulation and ethical norms at the LSE and the Paris Stock Exchange. The UK's Companies Act of 1929 introduced rules but did not explicitly prohibit insider trading. It was not until the Companies Act 1948 that directors and key shareholders were required to disclose their trades, marking an early attempt to improve market fairness. Despite these efforts, insider trading remained legal in the U.K. for several more decades. In France, insider trading was not formally addressed until 1967. Although enforcement remained weak, the September 28, 1967, law authorized the Commission des Opérations de Bourse (COB—Exchange Transactions Commission) to investigate irregularities in information disclosed by companies offering shares to the public through initial public offerings.

In the 1960s, the SEC took significant enforcement actions on insider trading, notably the Texas Gulf Sulphur (TGS) case in 1966. In 1964, TGS, a mining company, discovered substantial deposits of copper and other minerals in Canada. The company's directors and employees, aware of the highly favorable mineral discovery, purchased company stock before its public announcement. In response, the SEC investigated TGS executives and others for insider trading, charging them with trading company stock based on material, non-public information about the mineral discovery. The SEC's actions were based on the presumption that those possessing confidential material information about a company's prospects had a fiduciary duty to refrain from trading on that information. Ultimately, the court established important principles regarding insider trading, including the notion that "*a duty to refrain from trading or to make disclosures arises when an individual possesses material, non-public information.*" This case helped clarify what constitutes insider trading and solidified the SEC's role in enforcing the relevant securities laws (Bromberg, 1968).

A crucial development in the early 1970s was the theoretical demonstration of how information can improve the efficiency of stock markets. This information was not only about insider trading but also included the company's past price movements and publicly disclosed information. Eugene F. Fama, the 2013 Nobel laureate in economics, is often referred to as the "*father of modern finance*" (Fig. 12.2). In particular, his name is synonymous with his research on the Efficient Markets Hypothesis (EMH).

In 1970, Eugene Fama defined the concept of efficient markets. According to this definition, an informationally efficient market is a market in which the value of stocks is determined impartially based on all publicly available information. In an efficient market, competition among a large number of informed participants leads

Fig. 12.2 Eugene Fama (Nobel Laureates 2013). https://commons.wikimedia.org/wiki/File:Eugene_F._Fama_%2850372828402%29.jpg

to a situation in which, at any point in time, the actual prices of individual securities reflect the effects of unbiased information based both on events that have already occurred and on events that the market currently expects to happen in the future. In other words, in an efficient market, the actual price of a security at any point in time is a reasonable estimate of its intrinsic value (Fama, 1970).

According to Fama, as markets become more efficient, they will become more efficient, with everyone receiving all kinds of information simultaneously and perfectly fulfilling the price-setting function, which is the primary purpose of stock exchanges. Since the establishment of stock exchanges, regulations have aimed to make the prices of goods and services on these exchanges more efficient. Even if the efficiency of exchanges is a theoretical assumption, the frequency and quality of information entering the markets increase market efficiency. In this case, no one can systematically earn returns higher than the market average using any method. Fama recognized that the market was not wholly efficient. Like all perfectly competitive supply–demand economics, efficiency is an ideal that only fundamental world markets can approach.

Fama categorized market efficiency into three levels: weak, semi-strong, and strong. In "*weakly efficient markets,*" past price movements cannot be used to consistently achieve returns above the norm; however, public information, manipulation, and insider trading can still provide an advantage. In "s*emi-strong efficiency*," even public information cannot be used to achieve returns above the norm. In "*strong efficient*" markets, neither insider information nor manipulation can outperform the market; only luck can explain above-normal returns (Fama, 1970).

This provided a theoretical framework for the practices that have for centuries supported efforts to achieve better price formation in stock markets, i.e., a roadmap for achieving efficiency. The more participants in a market, the more efficient it will become as more people compete and bring more and different types of information to bear on price. As markets become more active and liquid, arbitrageurs will emerge, and the market will reach equilibrium as they profit from correcting small inefficiencies that may arise and quickly restore efficiency. According to the Efficient Market Hypothesis (EMH), higher returns are only possible through riskier investments due to the linear relationship between risk and expected return.

12.6 The Neoliberal Capitalism Phase (1980–2025)

The Regulated Capitalism Phase ended with the Nixon Shock in the early 1970s, and neoliberal capitalism became dominant after the 1980s. Unlike classical capitalism, neo-capitalism views the state as an active participant in maintaining economic balance, enhancing social welfare, and addressing market failures. This period emphasized the importance of free markets, deregulation, privatization, and individual entrepreneurship. Many countries loosened restrictions on banks and financial institutions, allowing riskier activities. In 1999, the United States repealed the Glass-Steagall Act, which had previously separated commercial and investment banking.

Following the 1980s, the reduction of trade barriers and liberalization of capital flows across borders created an increasingly interconnected global market. This globalization of markets, combined with financialization—the increasing dominance of financial markets—shifted the focus of economies from industrial production to speculative financial activities. At the firm level, managerial capitalism was replaced by investor capitalism, which was characterized by excessive speculation. Investors and companies started to organize according to this business model. This period was characterized by excessive speculation and a widespread vision of short-term investment.

Although inclusive institutions were generally weakened, some laws and regulations were enacted to protect investors and consumers during this period. Despite financial deregulation after 1980, inclusive institutions emerged to enhance market accessibility, transparency, and stability, balancing liberalization with investor and consumer protections. Key developments included the strengthening of roles for securities commissions in the United States and Europe, the Sarbanes–Oxley Act (2002)—enacted in response to scandals like Enron to protect investors—and the Dodd-Frank Act (2010), which addressed systemic risks, consumer protections, and the derivatives market in response to the 2008 financial crisis.

Institutional investors were also encouraged to consider environmental, social, and governance (ESG) factors following the adoption of the 2006 UN Principles for Responsible Investment. The OECD Principles of Corporate Governance (1999) promoted best practices to protect shareholders and support long-term value. The Sustainable Stock Exchanges Initiative (2009) further advanced ESG transparency across global markets.

12.6.1 *Excessive Speculation and Bad Finance in Neoliberalism*

The financialization of the economy after the 1970s accelerated excessive speculation and more risky financial practices. The collapse of the Bretton Woods system, following the Nixon shock of 1971 and the adoption of financial liberalization policies, led to the financial sector becoming increasingly important. During this period, instruments such as bank loans, securitization, and derivatives expanded, while investment growth in the real economy decreased. Financialization inevitably created a system that encouraged excessive speculation and a return to the pre-1930 period, but with a much larger economy and broader investor base. As financial markets increasingly focused on short-term gains, the negative impact on the real economy intensified, leading to more frequent crises and long-term instability.

Minsky (1989) distinguished two forms of capitalism in post-World War II United States: the first was "*paternalistic, managerial, and welfare state capitalism,*" where the state supported aggregate demand through fiscal policy and monetary management. Financing activities in this context were sound financial practices, encouraging entrepreneurship. The second form of capitalism emerged after the Nixon Shock when Wall Street began to move beyond the limits of sound finance and into worse finance. Minsky (1986) used the term "*bad finance*" to describe the characteristics of an economic system in which the financial system is dominated by actors whose ultimate goal is not to promote entrepreneurship but to maximize short-term profits for shareholders through (even speculative) trading activities. This paradigm eliminated the distinction between company and financial stakeholder value.

The proliferation of a paradigm that neglected the distinction between good and bad finance provided a theoretical justification for the deregulation of financial markets and the liberalization of capital movements, which led to the preference for "*speculation*" over "*enterprise*" by professional intermediaries who became powerful enough to dominate the markets (Bertocco & Kalajzic, 2018). Minsky called it "*money manager capitalism.*" It provided the theoretical justification for a political program based on the deregulation of markets, mainly labor and financial markets, as well as the liberalization of goods and capital movement, resulting in a clear break with the rules introduced after the Great Crash of 1929 (Karan et al., 2024).

According to Minsky (1993), good finance promotes economic stability. It encourages investments that support productive activities, such as infrastructure, businesses, and long-term projects, which create sustainable growth. In Minsky's model, good finance contributes to a stable and healthy economic system by maintaining confidence in financial institutions. Bad finance occurs when financial behavior becomes excessively speculative, risky, or driven by short-term gains, contributing to economic instability.

Minsky argued that the relationship between good and bad finance is cyclical. Initially, when the economy is stable, there is more good finance, as cautious lending and investing dominate. However, over time, as confidence grows and investors see increasing returns, they tend to take on more risk, which can lead to poorer financial decisions. This transition can cause financial instability. As speculative behavior (bad financial decision-making) grows, it can inflate asset prices and lead to an economic boom; however, this also creates the conditions for a crisis. Eventually, the financial system becomes overly leveraged, and when confidence wavers, the bubble bursts, leading to a financial crisis or collapse. This crisis then forces a return to more cautious behavior as institutions and individuals reassess risks. Thus, the shift from good to bad finance and back again is a fundamental aspect of Minsky's theory of financial instability.

Financial crises, including the 1987 stock market crash, the 1997 Asian financial crisis, and the 2008 global financial meltdown, exposed the dangers of excessive leverage and risky financial instruments. However, instead of addressing these structural weaknesses, policymakers and central banks reinforced the role of financial markets by implementing bailouts and quantitative easing strategies that prioritized asset prices. This environment enabled institutional investors, including pension funds, mutual funds, and sovereign wealth funds, to gain unprecedented influence over corporate decision-making. As a result, companies shifted from managerial capitalism, where professional managers prioritized long-term stability and growth, to investor capitalism, where firms are primarily accountable to shareholders and other financial market participants.

12.6.2 Emergence of Investor Capitalism

Financial market liberalization increased speculative trading, and corporate financialization has shifted economic priorities from productive investment to short-term profit maximization, albeit to varying degrees. This transformation has altered corporate governance, heightened financial instability, and exacerbated wealth inequality (Stiglitz, 2000).

From the 1970s onward, the shares of publicly traded companies, particularly in the United States. Moreover, other major developed countries began to be included in the portfolios of institutional investors, rather than those of individual investors. While individuals decided which instruments to invest in, as Minsky emphasized, professional money managers began determining their approach from this period onward. In this way, by concentrating significant assets in a few funds, institutional investment brought corporate managers into direct contact with money managers. Since these institutional owners were more demanding and less patient than individual owners, they focused on the short term while seeking greater company competitiveness. Against this backdrop, professional investors were given unprecedented influence over the firm. The corporate world has shifted from one dominated by corporate managers to a universe in which money managers are increasingly central. In other words, managerial capitalism gave way in the twenty-first century to investor capitalism, as it was called (Khurana, 2010).

Shareholder primacy, the idea that a company's primary responsibility is to maximize shareholder value, was popularized in the 1970s by economist Milton Friedman. He argued that managers should work for the owners (shareholders) and that a company's primary social responsibility is to increase its value, provided it engages in open competition without deception or cheating (Asness et al., 2021). Then Jensen and Meckling (1976) developed the Agency Theory, explaining the conflicts of interest between shareholders and managers in companies. They argued that managers do not always act in the interests of shareholders, which leads to agency costs. Therefore, they suggested compensation policies that would align the interests of managers and partners. By then, publicly traded companies in the United States, the UK, and other developed countries had restructured to focus on increasing shareholder returns, establishing personalized relationships with major shareholders, and aligning executive compensation with investors through bonuses and stock options. Stock options gave executives the right to buy or sell company stock at an agreed price. As stock prices rose, executives could profit by buying at the lower price and selling at the market price. This alignment of interests encouraged executives to prioritize stock price growth, sometimes leading to unethical behavior, such as in the case of Enron (2001). The pursuit of shareholder value has contributed to actions such as environmental harm, employee exploitation, and corruption. Starting in the 1960s, 5-year distance salary levels among CEOs increased steadily, peaking in 2020. Through 2007, just before the worldwide economic crisis, the average salary was around $4 million. Considering other forms of compensation and stock gains, the total compensation level amounted to approximately $17 million. The share of fringe benefits and incentives, such as stock options, was relatively high (McCarthy, 2013).

This led to a fundamental shift in financial education. Whereas students were previously taught that the purpose of business was to make a profit or survive in the market, textbooks now define a firm's goal as enriching its shareholders (Salter, 2019). Methods of speculation began to be glorified in teaching how to make money from extreme market volatility. With the development of derivative instruments, strategies to address market volatility have gained strength. Highly paid specialists with this skill, known as financial engineers, emerged. With the understanding that when stock prices rise, shareholders will also become more affluent, (short-term) share value maximization became the primary goal, overshadowing companies' (long-term) health, and future finance managers began to be trained with this perspective.

On the other hand, in the new economy, many companies are leveraging their capabilities, such as with software, tapping into the Internet, or entering into artificial intelligence, and investing in virtual assets, including patents and goodwill, rather than traditional real estate, like land and factory buildings, next to conventional servicing. Virtual assets are also easily affected by technological changes, technical issues, speculative attacks, or systemic risks, making their value significantly more volatile than fixed or human assets.

Today, corporate managers must master new skills to lead in an environment defined by fewer and fewer large investors. Above all, they must communicate a persuasive strategy to increase share value and ultimately deliver that intended value to money managers who are likely to invest in them. The institutional transformation of the stock market was followed by the accelerated globalization and internationalization of corporate shareholding in the 1990s. Privatizing state-owned enterprises facilitated this process, including the liberalization of domestic equity markets and cross-listing stocks on foreign exchanges. Moreover, governments that have demonstrated a commitment to working with the international investment community have gained a competitive advantage in attracting global capital investment (Useem, 2015). As institutional investors increasingly compare investment opportunities worldwide, they raise the bar for success. Instead of comparing companies and their managers with local companies in their own countries, companies and their managers have started to be compared with the best companies and their managers worldwide. They have come to expect more performance from the managers of these companies, impatiently and in the short term, as the corporate world has evolved into international investor capitalism. Consequently, increasing firm value in the short term precedes long-term strategies, as seen in the Enron case. However, prioritizing short-term returns and a "do-anything-to-win" attitude encouraged large companies to lobby and influence regulatory bodies. It was no coincidence that so many Morgan employees worked at the Fed. At the end of this road, there was a risk of the corporatocracy, a system in which corporations control or heavily influence the government, or crony capitalism. As a result, crony capitalism began to spread alongside the globalization of business-government relations in developing countries and the deregulation of markets in developed countries, thereby increasing economic inequalities and granting small groups undue control over significant powers.

12.6.3 Insider Trading: Legal Evolution and Modern Challenges

The most significant legal framework for regulating insider trading in the United States was established by the Chiarella v. United States (1980) case. The defendant, Vincent Chiarella, was employed by a printing company that prepared documents for mergers and acquisitions. During his activities, he obtained confidential information and used this information to generate high pre-merger stock market returns on the shares of these companies. The primary legal issue in the case was whether Chiarella had violated insider trading laws despite not being an officer, director, or other insider of the companies involved. The Supreme Court ruled in Chiarella's favor, overturning his earlier conviction. The key reasoning was that Chiarella had no duty to disclose or refrain from trading because he was neither an insider nor a fiduciary of the companies involved. This decision narrowed the scope of insider trading laws by requiring a fiduciary duty to shareholders to establish liability.

In contrast, United States v. O'Hagan (1997) introduced the misappropriation theory, extending liability to anyone who misappropriates confidential information for trading when they have a duty to the source of that information. Finally, the 2009 Dorozhko Case in the United States significantly expanded the scope of insider trading laws. The Court clarifies who can be held liable for insider trading. It holds that misuse of information (even if it does not originate from an insider or a fiduciary relationship) can still lead to insider trading charges. The United States has adopted an increasingly aggressive approach to insider trading enforcement since the early 2000s, marked by high-profile cases and rigorous investigations by the Securities and Exchange Commission (SEC). The Galleon Group case (2009) was one such case in which several hedge fund managers were convicted of insider trading offenses.

Following the passage of the Sarbanes–Oxley Act of 2002, which mandated greater financial transparency for publicly traded companies in the United States, stock market volatility decreased after companies released their quarterly reports. Financial statements became more credible, making the information more reliable and increasing confidence in security prices. Zolotoy's (2007) findings supported the Efficient Markets Hypothesis, which suggests that improving financial statement quality reduces transaction costs. A study by Frost et al. (2006) found a strong link between information transfer to market players and market development across 50 member stock exchanges of the World Federation of Exchanges.

While various European countries gradually followed the United States in banning insider trading, it was not until 1989 that the European Union (EU) instructed all Member States to restrict such activities. The 1989 EU Directive on Market Manipulation and Insider Trading served as a model for US law. While lacking an inclusive reference to fiduciary relationships underpinning US law, the EU categories largely covered manipulation, the same type of insider trading, and parties misusing information that the US prohibition also addressed. In 2003, the EU issued a new directive, the Market Abuse Directive (MAD). The Market Abuse Regulation (MAR) replaced the MAD in 2014. One of the main differences between MAR and MAD is the enforcement mechanisms: a regulation (MAR) under EU law is a directly binding law, while a directive (MAD) is an instruction to EU member states on what their national laws should contain (Gevurtz, 2018). This move also aligned the EU's regulatory approach with global standards (Ventoruzzo, 2015).

There is a slight difference in approach between the United States and the EU regarding insider trading. In the United States, violations are defined through fiduciary duty, which means insiders owe a duty to shareholders, and breaching this duty leads to sanctions. The EU, however, focuses more on ensuring equal access to information, which is easier to implement across various markets and transactions. The US regulatory system is complex, with multiple regulations covering different market participants shaped by the SEC's guidelines. In contrast, the EU system is more straightforward, emphasizing equal access to information and facilitating prosecution even without a traditional fiduciary duty. However, enforcement in the EU is more fragmented due to varying effectiveness among Member State regulators. The US system targets individuals with precise rules and harsh penalties, while Europe adopts a more flexible, principle-based approach, holding companies accountable. Although both regions aim for fair and transparent markets, the US approach is stricter, with harsher punishments, while Europe employs more flexible and comprehensive regulations (Ventoruzzo, 2015).

However, despite all these regulations, the scandals that emerged in the first quarter of the twenty-first century are striking. According to a report by Price Waterhouse, 47% of companies reported experiencing fraud in 2018–2020, the second-highest reported level in 20 years (PWC, 2020). Technological advancements and the consolidation of the social media sector have significantly increased the risks of market manipulation and insider trading. In this context, it increases the capacity of large technology companies to disseminate and manipulate information rapidly, creating an unfair environment for small investors. Moreover, with algorithms and fast trading, confidential information is more easily disseminated, which can be used to manipulate market movements. The Bank for International Settlements has reported that the global foreign exchange trading volume has reached $7.5 trillion daily. This figure significantly exceeds the volume of foreign exchange transactions required for international trade or direct and portfolio investment activities. The annual value of US equities turnover has amounted to $85 trillion, or 370% of GDP. An estimated 60–75% of this has been executed by algorithmic and high-frequency trading, buying and selling securities in seconds (Hunt, 2023). On the other hand, it was observed that large and powerful corporations began to regain power through lobbying, establishing business relationships with politicians, or capturing regulators. Some researchers have referred to this period as a corporatocracy (Stiglitz, 2012).

12.6.4 Beyond Corporatocracy: The Growing Influence of Big Business

While the rising power of corporations in the United States is being debated, Citizens United, a conservative nonprofit organization, produced a documentary called "*Hillary- The M*ovie" that criticized Hillary Clinton during the 2008 Democratic primary elections. However, the McCain-Feingold Act (Bipartisan Campaign Reform Act (BCRA) of 2002) prohibited corporations and unions from running independent political ads during the election. Citizens United sued, arguing that this ban was unconstitutional. The US Supreme Court ruled 5–4 that restricting political spending by corporations and unions did not violate free speech rights. The decision sparked a significant debate in the country and substantially increased political spending by outside groups, amplifying the influence of ultra-wealthy donors, corporations, and special interests. Analysts initially focused on the Court's framing of corporate election spending as a form of free speech. Still, its most lasting impact was the rise of super Political Action Committees (PACs) and dark money—anonymous political contributions made through nonprofit bodies. Technically known as independent expenditure-only committees, super PACs may raise unlimited sums of money from corporations, unions, associations, and individuals, then spend unlimited sums to advocate for or against political candidates overtly. These trends reached their peak in the 2024 elections. Billionaire-backed super PACs heavily funded the winning candidate, while a group funded by Elon Musk handled voter outreach. Dark money donations exceeded $1 billion, with at least $182 million funneled through groups linked to the congressional campaigns of both major parties.

A corporatocracy is a term used to describe an economic and political system in which corporations or corporate interests hold significant influence. Sachs (2011) already described the United States as a corporatocracy. He argued that this was due to four trends: weak national parties and strong regional political representation, the large US military establishment following World War II, big corporate money financing election campaigns, economic globalization, and the offshoring of manufacturing, all of which tipped the balance away from workers. The term is also defined by Perkins (2023) as a collective of corporations, banks, and governments. Power elites in key positions within corporatocracies pull the strings behind the curtain and control the process of determining society's economic and political policies. Moreover, this concept has been used to explain grievances such as bank bailouts, exorbitant CEO bonuses, and exploiting national treasures, people, and natural resources.

Nobel laureate Joseph E. Stiglitz (2019) has frequently criticized the corporatocracy in the United States, arguing that corporations wield significant political power, allowing them to shape policies in their favor. Stiglitz (2012) highlights how powerful corporations use their influence to secure tax breaks, subsidies, and deregulations that benefit the wealthiest individuals and firms, further widening inequality. Public resources are diverted to corporate elites rather than benefiting the public. Stiglitz also points to regulatory capture, where corporations strengthen their ties with the government by recruiting former policymakers, such as Goldman Sachs hiring Henry Paulson, who protected the corporation's interests as Treasury Secretary during the 2008 crisis. He argues that the financial system, dominated by large banks, allows the well-connected to enjoy privileges such as bailouts and tax breaks.

Despite this, Timothy Geithner (2015), former US Treasury Secretary, defends the controversial decisions made during the 2008 financial crisis—especially the government's protection and support of major financial institutions. He maintains that letting big firms fail would have caused far more significant economic damage and that the government's role was not to punish but to stabilize. His stance reflects a pragmatic, crisis-management view: prioritize restoring confidence and functionality in the system, even if that means bailing out institutions seen as partially responsible for the crisis. At the same time, ordinary citizens bear the consequences of financial instability. Citigroup and JPMorgan Chase have used similar tactics to influence policy, while Boeing's politically connected board was linked to the 2018–2019 737 MAX plane crashes, which exposed a lack of safety standards (Brown, 2022).

During the 2008 crisis, corporatocracy was evident in insider trading by political and financial elites. Before the Troubled Asset Relief Program (TARP) was announced, rumors of bailouts raised suspicions of insider trading. Proving these cases was complex due to the difficulty of tracing leaks. The $700 billion TARP bailout primarily benefited large banks, such as Goldman Sachs and Citigroup. At the same time, smaller institutions and homeowners received limited aid, which inflated stock prices and reassured investors that politically connected firms would be rescued (Katz, 2010).

The SPAC (Special Purpose Acquisition Company), created in 1993, allowed companies to go public faster, with less cost and uncertainty, while providing a predetermined valuation and additional capital support. However, it became popular after 2019, and the boom exemplified corporatocracy, allowing politically connected firms to bypass traditional IPO scrutiny. In 2021, Trump Media & Technology Group merged with Digital World Acquisition Corp. (DWAC) with minimal oversight, which was later investigated by the SEC. Similarly, Facebook's 2012 IPO benefited from SEC ties despite technical issues. Bernie Madoff's Ponzi scheme persisted for decades due to his powerful connections, delaying accountability (Tadić & Elbasani, 2020). During the COVID-19 pandemic, the US government supported companies under the $2 trillion CARES Act. Major airline companies, such as American Airlines, United Airlines, and Delta, received billions due to effective political lobbying (Salter, 2014), while small businesses struggled to secure sufficient support (Ritter & Tennant, 2021).

There is a danger that the "*Power Elite*" will drive US public policy and turn it one step ahead into crony capitalism. While corporatocracy refers to a system where corporations control or heavily influence government, crony capitalism is a specific form where businesses gain uneven advantages through political connections. Both systems lead to the concentration of wealth and power, adversely affecting market competition, democratic governance, and economic equality.

Crony capitalism involves rent-seeking, regulatory capture, political entrepreneurship, and interest group politics, where political power benefits some at the expense of others. The term was coined by George M. Taber while studying the Philippines in the 1980s. It was initially used to describe the economy under Ferdinand Marcos. It is often linked to economies such as Russia, India, Malaysia, and Turkey, where weak institutions hinder property protection and an impartial judiciary (Aligica & Tarko, 2015). Crony capitalism thrives when governments regulate, tax, and provide subsidies while businesses profit by securing favorable regulations and financial support (Holcombe, 2013).

In economies with crony capitalism, where business success relies on government connections rather than competition, stock markets are often distorted, particularly in emerging markets. Since 2014, The Economist's Crony Capitalism Index has ranked countries based on the share of billionaire wealth in rent-seeking sectors, including banking, construction, real estate, and natural resources. A higher percentage indicates a more significant impact of crony capitalism. Russia, the Czech Republic, and Singapore top the list (Economist, 2023).

From 2014 to 2023, the United States and Western European countries consistently ranked low in crony capitalism, as most billionaire wealth originates from competitive sectors such as technology, finance, and manufacturing rather than crony sectors like natural resources, real estate, or construction. However, concerns persist about corporate lobbying and government influence in finance and defense. Over the last century, the United States has seen a rise in billionaire wealth from crony industries, contributing to global crony capitalism. According to The Economist (2023), the wealth of crony sector billionaires accounts for approximately 2% of US GDP, rising to 6% if tech is included (Economist, 2023).

Rising income inequality, migration, and new social dynamics have revealed that neoliberalism has failed to offer real solutions to these problems. Donald Trump skillfully read the social unrest and anti-system sentiment, indirectly fueled by growing corporatocracy and crony capitalism, and turned it to his advantage. He positioned himself as a figure "*against the system*," which resonated especially with economically struggling voters. As a result, he gained strong support and won the presidency in the 2024 elections. This began a new era for the United States and the global economic order (Time Magazine, 2024).

12.7 Lessons from History: The Red Queen Dynamic

Acemoğlu and Robinson (2019) use the "Red Queen" concept to show that the narrow corridor created by inclusive institutions is not static. The Red Queen said the famous sentence to Alice in Through the Looking Glass (written in 1871): "You have to run as fast as you can just to stay here, in the same place" (Carroll, 2025).

Acemoglu and Robinson used this metaphor to show that inclusive institutions are not static goals; they require constant effort to sustain. Checks on state power, civil society's vigilance, and the protection of freedoms are continually under threat. To stand still is to regress. The central thesis of the Narrow Corridor is that freedom depends on both a strong state and a strong society. The state must be strong enough to maintain order without becoming tyrannical, while society must be organized to restrain the state without causing chaos. This balance is not a fixed equilibrium, but rather a "balanced imbalance" that requires constant renewal. The Red Queen Dynamic captures this need for ongoing restructuring. Inclusive institutions do not arise by chance—they are upheld through persistent effort. Each advance invites new threats and crises often cause systems to stall. When institutions stagnate, progress turns to regression. Today, this dynamic is threatened by state power and corporatocracy, as growing corporate control over the system undermines it.

The "Golden Age" of the Islamic world, spanning from the 8th to the thirteenth century, was a product of inclusive institutions, scientific freedom, and multiculturalism. Over time, however, the static nature of Islamic law and limits on intellectual debate halted institutional vitality. Society did not demand more. When Muslims stopped running, it fell behind its European rivals. This decline was the direct result of stagnating institutions.

With the rise of guilds in Europe, money markets developed, helping to strengthen mercantilism. After the fifteenth century, as guilds declined, legal systems emerged that offered merchants greater certainty and more inclusive opportunities in the Low Countries. However, later, Bruges declined due to local unrest and political tensions with the Burgundians. Antwerp fell after the Dutch Revolt, the 1576 Sack, and the 1585 Spanish takeover, which severed its trade routes. In both cases, political instability and conflict undermined their positions as leading commercial hubs and weakened their inclusiveness.

In this pioneer of modern capitalism, companies like the VOC and the Amsterdam Stock Exchange became global trade hubs through institutional innovations in the early seventeenth century. Over time, however, the VOC fell victim to its success: internal corruption, unaccountability, and self-interest grew. Its closeness to the state made it an unchecked force—an early example of today's "corporatocracy." By the late seventeenth century, the wars with England, followed by the French invasion in 1795, had severely damaged its financial system. Political instability shook investor confidence, weakening inclusive institutions and undermining the rule of law. These conditions led to institutional stagnation in Amsterdam, clearing the way for a new actor: Britain.

In the eighteenth and nineteenth centuries, the Glorious Revolution and Industrial Revolution made London the world's financial center. The Bank of England's stabilizing role and the rise of the LSE positioned the UK as a global economic leader. Over time, however, financial and political power increasingly concentrated in the aristocracy and major capital owners, who began shaping laws to serve their interests. Big banks, such as Rothschild, drove London's financial ascent, but this success also fostered a concentration of power that threatened institutional balance and market inclusiveness. The London financial market alternated between rapid growth and stagnation due to its monopolistic structure. Foreign capital inflows declined after World War I, weakening London's dominance. Institutions lost their inclusiveness, and progress gave way to inequality and regression.

The decline of the Paris Stock Exchange after the nineteenth century was primarily attributed to France's political and economic struggles, slow industrialization, wars, and increasing global competition. Its weaker ties with banks and rigid structure hindered adaptation to innovation and change, reducing its competitiveness against other financial centers.

The Istanbul Stock Exchange emerged in the mid-nineteenth century as the Ottoman Empire faced internal and external pressures, resulting in the loss of financial independence. Its collapse during World War I showed that inclusive institutions cannot be imposed externally or sustained without internal social balance and participation.

In the twentieth century, the United States stood out as an example of a victorious Red Queen run. The New Deal reforms introduced after the Great Depression of the 1930s emphasized the state as a regulatory power. Institutions like the SEC increased market supervision, and banking reforms provided stability. Since the 1980s, however, financial liberalization and the growing influence of corporations in the political sphere have given rise to a new threat: institutions that stabilize the state have been replaced by corporations that influence the state.

Today, corporatocracy is a significant threat to inclusive institutions in the United States and globally. The 2008 financial crisis clearly illustrated this danger: the risky, unregulated actions of large corporations led to a systemic collapse. Nevertheless, many of these firms were bailed out with public funds while their executives escaped accountability. Corporate inclusiveness suffered as the state prioritized rescuing companies over citizens. The crisis served as a modern warning of the Red Queen dynamic: systems must continuously adapt and uphold checks and balances to prevent excessive concentration of economic power.

In conclusion, history shows us that institutional success cannot be achieved by a momentary setup, but rather through constant struggle and multifaceted balancing. This struggle must be waged against state arbitrariness and the domination of significant capital. In today's world, the Red Queen's metaphor applies not only to the state but also to corporations: the biggest lesson from the history of financial markets is that markets cannot stand still; systems that fail to improve themselves weaken inclusive institutions and will collapse.

12.8 The Future of Financial Markets

President Trump's 2025 economic policy focused on protectionist trade measures and tax reforms aimed at revitalizing domestic industries and increasing workers' incomes. However, these policies have led to significant market fluctuations, causing the most severe market drop in April 2025, and raised concerns about potential long-term economic impacts, including increased federal deficits and strained international trade relations. Trump's 2025 economic doctrine is not just post-neoliberal—it is counter-neoliberal. It revives mercantilist logic, national industrial policy, protectionist tariffs, and populist redistribution (targeted tax cuts). It does not seem to replace neoliberalism with a coherent new paradigm yet—more like a disruptive transition phase, echoing early 20th-century "beggar-thy-neighbor" policies. This was usually achieved by encouraging the consumption of domestic goods over imports through protectionist policies, such as import tariffs or quotas, which limited the amount of imports. It is too early to see this as a phase in capitalism; it seems just a post-liberal experiment. It would have to solve the current rising wealth inequality to be a permanent policy. However, the question of whether neoliberalism, which is supported by globalization, is nearing its end has started to be asked. New searches might start after this experiment.

The centuries-long journey of financial markets has shown us that market players are not particularly grateful to the inclusive institutions that give them and firms a widening corridor. They did not hesitate to weaken them when they felt strong enough. Philippon (2019) argues that financial market players have actively resisted and undermined inclusive institutions over the past century in pursuit of greater autonomy and profits. This strategy is self-defeating as weakening regulatory frameworks lead to financial instability, reduced investor confidence, and recurrent economic crises. He underlined that short-term gains may be tempting, but history has shown that a well-regulated market benefits all stakeholders, including those pushing for deregulation.

This can be likened to the story of a scorpion riding on the back of a frog to cross a river. Although the frog must not be harmed to survive when it reaches the center of the river, the scorpion stings it. As the frog slowly sinks under the effect of the poison, it asks with its last effort: "Why did you do that?" "Now we are both going to die!" The scorpion replies helplessly, "What can I do? It is my nature!" With his concept of "animal spirits," Keynes posited that market participants act based on psychological factors that exist in their nature rather than rationality, and speculation is inherently difficult to control. Today, technological development makes it much easier for market players to enter the market, and combined with humans' insatiable ambition, it is ushering in a new era.

12.8.1 Capitalism and Digital Shifts

The rise of social media platforms has enabled individuals and groups to disseminate rumors, misinformation, or coordinated campaigns that can artificially inflate or depress stock prices, as seen in the case of GameStop. While big data analytics and artificial intelligence can provide significant advantages to institutional investors, they can also widen the gap between professional and retail investors. Those without access to such technology may find it challenging to compete in the market, potentially leading to the concentration of wealth in the hands of a few. With a growing reliance on digital platforms for trading, the stock market is becoming increasingly vulnerable to cyberattacks. Data breaches, hacking, or system failures can erode confidence in financial markets and result in substantial economic losses.

Meanwhile, the US social media market has evolved into an oligopolistic structure dominated by Large Technology companies. As of the first quarter of the twenty-first century, a few major players dominate the market, including Facebook (now Meta), Google (via YouTube), Twitter (now X), TikTok, and Snapchat. Oligopolistic structures in social media concentrate power in a few major tech firms, limiting competition and innovation.

Research has shown that fraudulent news disseminated on social media has a direct impact on retail trade and prices (Kogan et al., 2023). A study by Ante (2023) reveals that the social media activities of influential individuals can have a significant impact on cryptocurrencies. Indeed, Elon Musk's tweet in 2021, "Tesla suspends car purchases using Bitcoin," caused the price of Bitcoin to drop 10% within hours. His Dogecoin-related tweets "Doge to the Moon!" led to a 5,000% increase in the value of Dogecoin before it crashed (Li et al., 2024).

In another case, in 2013, the Associated Press Twitter account was hacked, and a fake tweet claiming "Breaking news: Two explosions at the White House and Barack Obama injured" caused a massive uproar in the market. The Dow Jones Industrial Average dropped 140 points within minutes, and $136 billion was wiped off the market value before it recovered (Ferrara, 2015). In addition, organized groups on Telegram and Discord have repeatedly manipulated small cryptocurrencies. In 2017, a false rumor spread on Twitter that Vitalik Buterin, the founder of the cryptocurrency Ethereum, had died, causing Ethereum's price to drop sharply before recovering. Social media has shown to be a powerful tool for market manipulation, affecting everything from stocks to cryptocurrencies to commodities, thereby democratizing markets while increasing their volatility, susceptibility to misinformation, and vulnerability to mass psychological manipulation (Shin, 2022).

12.8.2 Sustainability and Democracy

In recent years, the damages caused by short-term investor capitalism, combined with growing awareness of climate, ESG, and sustainability issues, have prompted businesses to shift toward "Stakeholder Capitalism" rather than traditional investor capitalism. Stakeholder capitalism is a system in which companies prioritize serving the interests of all stakeholders, including shareholders, employees, suppliers, and customers. Essential stakeholders include customers, suppliers, employees, shareholders, and local communities. In this system, the goal of a company is to create long-term value rather than maximizing profits and increasing shareholder value at the expense of other stakeholder groups. Rather than maximizing profits and increasing shareholder value, proponents of stakeholder capitalism believe that serving the interests of all stakeholders, not just shareholders, is essential to the long-term success of any business. Reflecting this shift in thinking, the Business Roundtable—a prominent association of US CEOs—issued a groundbreaking statement in 2019, redefining the purpose of a corporation to promote an economy that serves all Americans, signaling a clear move away from shareholder primacy (Business Roundtable, 2019). Such a system would likely benefit society significantly. However, it is likely to be a long time before this idea becomes widely accepted.

Despite all the developments, after nearly a thousand years, financial markets are again recognizing the importance of the East. In the first half of the twenty-first century, we will likely witness the rise of Chinese and Far Eastern stock markets. Organizations such as the International Monetary Fund (IMF) and the World Bank predict that Asia, particularly China, will increase its share in the global economy. The market capitalization value of the three independently operating stock exchanges in Mainland China is just behind that of the New York Stock Exchange (NYSE) and the Nasdaq exchange, a technology firm. The Shanghai Stock Exchange is also the most prominent Chinese exchange in Asia. However, unlike the other major stock exchanges in this region, the Shanghai Stock Exchange remains partially closed to foreign investors, unlike the Hong Kong Stock Exchange. Central government decisions often affect it due to capital account controls imposed by the Chinese authorities. Although some inclusive institutions exist in China's capital market, improvements are needed in areas such as corporate governance, regulatory framework, investor protection, and the diversity of financial institutions. Addressing these deficiencies will help make the market more inclusive and sustainable. Geopolitical risks, regulatory policies, and relations with the West will undoubtedly influence this process (Bencivelli et al., 2020).

Donald Trump's authoritarian leadership opened a corridor to legitimize authoritarian governments in various countries. It now appears that the assumption that markets will semi-automatically evolve into an increasingly democratic and global structure is not realistic enough. A trend in authorization is apparent, and inclusive institutions are being weakened.

12.8.3 *Navigating Between Progressive Capitalism and Emerging Paradigms*

In a digitalized, AI-driven world, political and economic systems will inevitably shape financial and equity markets. The question is whether the future of financial markets will be determined by corporations (thus by digital technology) or democratic institutions. Various theories predict the market structure that may emerge by predicting the dominant political system of the future. While some scholars predict a strengthening of participatory democracy and propose models with stronger inclusive institutions, many others expect a shift away from classical liberal democracy to hybrid political systems that are more technologically advanced, controlled, yet also responsive to public reactions. The most democratic of these is progressive capitalism, an economic framework proposed by Stiglitz (2019), which aims to recalibrate the roles of the market, the state, and civil society to enhance social welfare. This approach advocates for a new social contract that utilizes market forces and entrepreneurship to address problems such as market dominance, inequality, and the consequences of globalization. Progressive capitalism emphasizes the need for state investment in technology, education, healthcare, and green infrastructure, as well as implementing public options for basic services.

This model does not advocate for a complete abandonment of the free market economy, but rather for a more equitable, sustainable, and inclusive one. The stock and capital markets are reformed within this framework to preserve market efficiency. According to Stiglitz (2019), financial markets are primarily based on speculation and short-term gains under neoliberal capitalism. In the new model, the stock and capital markets should be directed toward real economic growth and innovation. In this context, long-term sustainable investments should be prioritized over short-term speculation and high-frequency trading. In the traditional system, corporations' primary goal has been to maximize shareholder profits. Progressive Capitalism, however, advocates that companies create value for all stakeholders, including employees, consumers, and society, rather than just shareholders. Publicly traded companies should pay more attention to their social and environmental responsibilities.

Stiglitz (2019) criticizes the lax supervisory policies that led to the 2008 Global Financial Crisis and argues that financial regulation should be strengthened. He emphasizes that stricter rules should be introduced to prevent systemic risks, and the hazardous investments of large financial institutions should be better supervised. In this context, financial markets should operate in the best interest of society by reducing income inequality. Stiglitz also emphasizes the importance of green finance and sustainable investments. Capital markets should be shaped according to environmental, social, and governance (ESG) criteria, with green finance projects prioritized over carbon-based investments. In this way, the financial system should play an active role in combating climate change and achieving the Sustainable Development Goals. In conclusion, Stiglitz's "Progressive Capitalism" model seeks to transform the stock market and capital markets into a structure that better serves the real economy and encourages productive investment rather than speculation. Tighter regulation, sustainable investment, and policies that reduce inequality are key to making the financial system work for the wider society.

Other alternative scenarios have a variety of hybrid structures with relatively limited power of democratic institutions. The first of these is called the Technocratic-Neoliberal Continuity thesis. It envisages a structure in which neoliberalism has not formally ended, but is more deeply sustained through technological means (artificial intelligence, big data, algorithmic regulation). While market mechanisms remain decisive, public control is increasingly replaced by technocratic decision-making processes and intra-market control tools (Brown, 2015; Davies, 2014; Mirowski, 2013). The Chinese model serves as the basis for the second thesis. In this thesis, where state capitalism is strengthened, the state utilizes the stock market for strategic objectives, integrating capital markets with development and industrial policy. In this model, public–private boundaries blur and geopolitical orientations emerge (Bremmer, 2010; Huang, 2008; Wu, 2016). Another thesis can be called Digital-Decentralized Capitalism. In this thesis, where blockchain-based systems replace traditional financial institutions, DAOs and DeFi applications offer an alternative to centralized actors in capital allocation. While crypto assets assume the role of financial intermediaries, regulation and security issues carry significant risks (Ammous, 2018; Dixon, 2025). Finally, in the Ecosocialist/Green Transformation scenario, where financial markets serve environmental sustainability goals, ESG criteria, carbon markets, and natural capital accounting take center stage. Finance is oriented toward economic and ecological value creation (Carney, 2021; Raworth, 2018; Tirole, 2017).

As the twenty-first century unfolds, markets shift rapidly between globalization and protectionism, democracy and authoritarianism. Despite the above theories, the future remains uncertain. A completely different system may emerge, driven by overlooked factors that could significantly shape political systems and financial markets. Nassim Nicholas Taleb (2007) proposed this issue with his "Black Swan" theory. This theory emphasizes the impact of rare, unpredictable, and high-impact events that deviate from regular expectations.

Perhaps we must trust Adam Smith's notion of the "invisible hand," believing that markets will ultimately self-regulate. Alternatively, we can assume Andrew Lo's (2004) Adaptive Market Hypothesis, which suggests that markets evolve through ongoing adaptation—participants constantly learn from dynamic environments rather than relying on fixed notions of efficiency.

This tension between control and adaptability is captured in the 2010 film Black Swan, which shares its name with Taleb's concept. In one memorable scene, the ballet director (played by Vincent Cassel) tells the protagonist, "*Perfection is not just about control. It is also about letting go.*" This paradox encapsulates the challenge of our time: institutions must strike a delicate balance between vigilance and flexibility, constantly running, like the Red Queen, to remain resilient in an unpredictable world.

References

Acemoglu, D., & Robinson, J. A. (2019). The narrow corridor: States, societies, and the fate of liberty: Winners of the 2024 Nobel prize in economics. Penguin UK.

Acemoglu, D., & Robinson, J. A. (2012). *Why Nations Fail: The Origins of Power, Prosperity, and Poverty* (pp. 45–47). London: Profile.

Aligica, P. D., & Tarko, V. (2015). Crony capitalism. CESifo DICE Report, 13(3), 27–32.

Ammous, S. (2018). *The bitcoin standard: the decentralized alternative to central banking.* John Wiley & Sons.

Ante, L. (2023). How Elon Musk's Twitter activity moves cryptocurrency markets. *Technological Forecasting and Social Change, 186*, Article 122112.

Asness, C., Hubbard, G., Lipton, M., & Strain, M. R. (2021). American enterprise institute roundtable: Was Milton Friedman right about shareholder capitalism? *Journal of Applied Corporate Finance, 33*(1), 36–47.

Bencivelli, L., Tonelli, F., Bencivelli, L., & Tonelli, F. (2020). China in the Global economy. *China's International Projection in the Xi Jinping Era: An Economic Perspective*, 9–35.

Berle, A. A., & Means, G. (1968). The modern corporation and private property. Harcourt, Brace & World, Inc.

Bertocco, G., & Kalajzic, A. (2018). How much does finance benefit society? *PSL Quarterly Review, 71*(287), 419–437.

Bremmer, I. (2010). *The end of the free market: Who wins the war between states and corporations?* New York: Portfolio.

Bromberg, A. R. (1968). Corporate information: Texas Gulf Sulphur and its implications. *Southwestern Law Review, 22*, 731.

Brown, R. S. (2022). Cronyism as strategy: How firms co-opt government and privatize rents. *Journal of Managerial Issues, 34*(4), 334–353.

Brown, W. (2015). *Undoing the demos: Neoliberalism's stealth revolution.* New York: Zone Books.

Business Roundtable. (2019). *Business Roundtable redefines the purpose of a corporation to promote 'an economy that serves all Americans'*. Business Roundtable. https://www.businessroundtable.org/business-roundtable-redefines-the-purpose-of-a-corporation-to-promote-an-economy-that-serves-all-americans

Carney, M. (2021). *Value(s): Building a better world for all.* New York: PublicAffairs.

Carroll, L. (2025). *Through the looking-glass: Classic edition republished by North Publishers.* North Publishers.

Davies, W. (2014). *The limits of neoliberalism: Authority, sovereignty and the logic of competition.* London: SAGE Publications.

Dixon, C. (2025). *Read write own: Building the next era of the Internet.* Random House.

Economist (2023). The 2023 crony-capitalism index. https://www.economist.com/international/2023/05/02/the-2023-crony-capitalism-index

Fama, E. F. (1970). Efficient capital markets. *Journal of Finance, 25*(2), 383–417.

Ferrara, E. (2015). Manipulation and abuse on social media by Emilio Ferrara, with Ching-man Au Yeung as coordinator. *ACM SIGWEB Newsletter, 2015*(Spring), 1–9.

Fletcher, L., Ortenca, A., & Kruppa, M. (2021). US hedge funds Melvin Capital and Light Street suffer further losses; Asset management. *The Financial Times*, 13–13.

Frost, C. A., Gordon, E. A., & Hayes, A. F. (2006). Stock exchange disclosure and market development: An analysis of 50 international exchanges. *Journal of Accounting Research, 44*(3), 437–483.

Geithner, T. F. (2015). *Stress test: Reflections on financial crises.* Crown.

Gevurtz, F. A. (2018). The road not taken: a comparison of the EU and US insider trading prohibitions. *Washington University Journal of Law and Policy, 56*, 31.

Harari, Y. N. (2024). *Nexus: A brief history of information networks from the Stone Age to AI.* Signal.

Holcombe, R. G. (2013). Crony capitalism: By-product of big government. *The Independent Review, 17*(4), 541–559.

Huang, Y. (2008). *Capitalism with Chinese characteristics: Entrepreneurship and the State*. Cambridge: Cambridge University Press.

Hunt T. (2023). Atlantic Council. Financialization has increased economic fragility. https://www.atlanticcouncil.org/blogs/econographics/financialization-has-increased-economic-fragility/?utm_source=chatgpt.com

Jensen, N. C., & Meckling, W. H. (1976). Theory of the firm: Managerial behavior, agency costs, and ownership structure. *Journal of Financial Economics, Elsevier, 3*(4), 305–360.

Karan, M. B., Westerman, W., & Wijngaard, J. (2024). *A history of banks*. Contributions to Economics.

Katz, J. G. (2010). Who benefited from the bailout? *Minnesota Law Review, 95*, 1568.

Khurana, R. (2010). *From higher aims to hired hands: The social transformation of American business schools and the unfulfilled promise of management as a profession*. Princeton University Press.

Kogan, S., Moskowitz, T. J., & Niessner, M. (2023). Social media and financial news manipulation. *Review of Finance, 27*(4), 1229–1268.

Li, W., Bao, L., Chen, J., Grundy, J., Xia, X., & Yang, X. (2024). Market manipulation of cryptocurrencies: Evidence from social media and transaction data. *ACM Transactions on Internet Technology, 24*(2), 1–26.

Lo, A. W. (2004). The adaptive markets hypothesis: Market efficiency from an evolutionary perspective. *The Journal of Portfolio Management, 30*, 15–29.

Mackenzie, M, & Fletcher, L. (2021). Melvin Capital, GameStop and the road to disaster. *Financial Times*. February 11, 2021.

Manne, H. G. (1966). *Insider Trading And The Stockmarket*. New York: The Free Press.

McCarthy, N. (2013). *Two decades of CEO Pay in the United States*. Statista. https://www.statista.com/chart/1168/two-decades-of-ceo-pay-in-the-united-states/

Minsky, H. (1986). Money and crisis in Schumpeter and Keynes. In H. J. Wagener, & J. W. Drukker (Eds.), *The Economic Law of Motion of Modern Society: A Marx-Keynes-Schumpeter Centennial* (pp. 112–122). Cambridge University Press.

Minsky, H. (1993). Schumpeter and Finance. In S. Biasco, A. Roncaglia, & M. Salvati (Eds.), *Markets and Institutions in Economic Development: Essays in Honour of Paolo Sylos Labini* (pp. 103–115). Macmillan.

Minsky, H. P. (1989). Financial crises and the evolution of capitalism: The crash of '87—What does it mean? In M. Gottdiener & N. Komninos (Eds.), *Capitalist development and crisis theory: Accumulation, regulation, and spatial restructuring* (pp. 391–403). New York: St. Martin's Press.

Mirowski, P. (2013). *Never let a serious crisis go to waste: How Neoliberalism survived the Financial Meltdown*. London: Verso Books.

Perino, M. A. (2019). The lost history of insider trading. *University of Illinois Law Review*, 951.

Perkins, J. (2023). *Confessions of an economic Hitman*. Berrett-Koehler Publishers.

Philippon, T. (2019). *The great reversal: How America gave up on free markets*. Harvard University Press.

PWC (2020). Global economic crime rates remain high as customer fraud continues to rise. https://www.pwc.com/sk/en/current-press-releases/global-economic-crime-rates-remain-high.html?utm_source=chatgpt.com

Raworth, K. (2018). *Doughnut economics: Seven ways to think like a 21st-century economist*. Chelsea Green Publishing.

Ritter, D., & Tennant, R. (2021). Ethical issues related to Covid-19. *Southern Journal of Business and Ethics, 13*, 70–81.

Sachs, J. (2011). *The price of civilization: Economics and ethics after the fall*. Random House.

Salter, M. S. (2014). Crony capitalism, American style: what are we talking about here? *Harvard Business School Research Paper Series, 15–025*, 15–025.

Salter, M. S. (2019). Rehabilitating corporate purpose. Harvard Business School NOM Unit Working Paper, (19–104).

Shin, L. (2022). *The cryptopians: Idealism, greed, lies, and the making of the first big cryptocurrency craze*. Hachette UK.

Stiglitz, J. E. (2000). Capital market liberalization, economic growth, and instability. *World development, 28*(6), 1075–1086.

Stiglitz, J. E. (2012). *The price of inequality: How today's divided society endangers our future*. WW Norton & Company.

Stiglitz, J. E. (2019). *People, power, and profits: Progressive capitalism for an age of discontent*. Penguin UK.

Tadić, K., & Elbasani, A. (2020). State-building and patronage networks: how political parties embezzled the bureaucracy in post-war Kosovo. In *International-Led statebuilding and local resistance* (pp. 37–54). Routledge.

Taleb, N. N. (2007). Black swans and the domains of statistics. *The American Statistician, 61*(3), 198–200.

Time Magazine. (2024, November 6). Trump supporters knew exactly who they were voting for. *Time*. https://time.com/7175545/trump-election-authoritarian-democrats-loss/

Tirole, J. (2017). *Economics for the common good*. Princeton: Princeton University Press.

Useem, M. (2015). Investor capitalism. In *Wiley Encyclopedia of Management* (pp. 1–2).

Ventoruzzo, M. (2015). Comparing insider trading in the United States and the European Union: History and recent developments. *European Company and Financial Law Review, 11*(4), 554–593.

Wu, M. (2016). The 'China, Inc'. Challenge to global trade governance. *Harvard International Law Journal, 57*(2), 261–324.

Zolotoy, L. (2007). The Sarbanes-Oxley Act of 2002: Implications for market efficiency and analysts' performance. Available at SSRN 964210.

MIX
Papier aus verantwortungsvollen Quellen
Paper from responsible sources
FSC® C105338

If you have any concerns about our products,
you can contact us on
ProductSafety@springernature.com

In case Publisher is established outside the EU,
the EU authorized representative is:
Springer Nature Customer Service Center GmbH
Europaplatz 3, 69115 Heidelberg, Germany

Printed by Libri Plureos GmbH
in Hamburg, Germany